Ethiopia at Constitutional Crossroads

Ethiopia at Constitutional Crossroads

In Search of a Fair and Durable Settlement

Edited by:
Adeno Addis, Kebadu Mekonnen Gebremariam,
Adem Kassie Abebe, and Abduletif Kedir Idris.

TSEHAI
Publishers & Distributors

TSEHAI
Publishers & Distributors

Ethiopia at Constitutional Crossroads: In Search of a Fair and Durable Settlement
Edited by Adeno Addis, Kebadu Mekonnen Gebremariam, Adem Kassie Abebe, and Abduletif Kedir Idris.

TSEHAI Publishers
www.tsehaipublishers.com
info@tsehaipublishers.com

Paperback ISBN: 978-1-59907-3378
Hardcover ISBN: 978-1-59907-3385
EBook ISBN: 978-1-59907-3392

First Edition 2025

Publisher: Elias Wondimu
Copy Editor: Jeff Nazarro
Cover Design and Typesetting: TSEHAI Design Lab.

A catalog record for this book is available from:
Wemezekir, Ethiopian National Library, Addis Ababa, Ethiopia.
U.S. Library of Congress, Washington, D.C., U.S.A.
British Library, London, U.K.

10 9 8 7 6 5 4 3 2 1

Printed in the United States of America

Dedicated to:

To the People of Ethiopia.

Contents

Part II:

National Citizenship in a Diverse Society

Part III:

Separation of Powers and Federalism

Notes on Contributors

Abduletif Kedir Idris is a student of interdisciplinary human rights, comparative constitutional and public law focusing on Ethiopia. He is currently a PhD candidate at the Max Planck Institute for Social Anthropology in Halle, Germany, and a Lecturer at the Center for Human Rights of Addis Ababa University, Ethiopia.

Adem Kassie Abebe (PhD) is Senior Advisor in the Constitutional Building Programme of the International Institute for Democracy and Electoral Assistance; Vice President of the African Network of Constitutional Lawyers; and Extraordinary Lecturer, at the Faculty of Law, Centre for Human Rights, University of Pretoria.

Adeno Addis holds the W.R. Irby Chair and is the W. Ray Forrester Professor of Public and Constitutional Law at Tulane University Law School. An internationally recognized expert in human rights, constitutional law, and political theory, his research focuses on dignity, belonging, statelessness, and constitutionalism in fractured societies, especially Ethiopia.

Alemayehu Fentaw Weldemariam, PhD Fellow at Indiana University Maurer School of Law's Center for Constitutional Democracy, specializes in comparative constitutionalism and democratic theory. He lectures at Mekelle University School of Law, has taught at various universities globally, and serves as Assistant Editor of the Blog of the International Association of Constitutional Law.

Asrar Adem Gebeyehu holds LLM from Pretoria University and LLB from Addis Ababa university. His research interests include disability rights, socio-economic rights, right to development and constitutional law. He has served as a lecturer of law at Bahir Dar university. Currently, he is working at the Ethiopian human rights commission.

Assefa Fiseha (Professor) is an expert in comparative federalism and devolution in Africa. His latest publication include, Federalism, Devolution and Cleavages in Africa (Palgrave, 2024).

Belachew Girma Degefie (LL.B., LL.M.) is a human rights and constitutional lawyer with experience in the academics, government office, practicing law, human rights advocacy and project management. His publications include constitutional adjudication and human rights.

Berihun Adugna Gebeye (PhD) is a Lecturer in the Faculty of Laws, University College London, and a Visiting Professor at the Central European University. He is the author of A Theory of African Constitutionalism (Oxford University Press 2021), and with Professor Richard Albert, he is editing The Oxford Handbook of African Constitutions (under contract with Oxford University Press).

Christophe Van der Beken (PhD, Ghent University, 2006) is Associate Professor at Addis Ababa University, College of Law and Governance Studies. His areas of expertise and research interests include public law, comparative constitutional law, federalism, human rights and minority rights, local government, and good governance.

Derese Getachew Kassa (Ph.D) is an Associate Professor of Sociology and Chairperson of the Department of Sociology and Criminal Justice at Iona University, New Rochelle, New York. He is also Director of the Iona Black Humanities Initiative (IBHI). His research explores the nexus between forced displacement, urbanization, and African states. He is author of the book, "Refugee Spaces and Urban Citizenship in Nairobi: Africa's Sanctuary City" (Lexington Books, MD, 2018).

Getachew Assefa Woldemariam (PhD) is Associate Professor of Law at Addis Ababa University. His academic and research interests include Ethiopian and Comparative constitutional law, federalism, human rights, constitutional adjudication, legal pluralism and law and religion. He has widely published in these areas.

Kebadu Mekonnen Gebremariam (PhD) is a Marie Sklodowska-Curie Postdoctoral Fellow at Leiden University and an associate member of the Hoover Chair in Social and Economic Ethics at UC Louvain. He was previously an Associate Professor of Philosophy at Addis Ababa University. His primary research interests lie in social and political philosophy, with a particular focus on justice, power, and the ethical foundations of political life in both contemporary and historical contexts.

Terefe Sahelu Gebreyesus (LLB, JD, PhD) is a teaching associate at the University of Queensland and a sessional academic at Griffith University, Australia. He researches comparative constitutional law, democratic transition and constitutional theory. Prior to commencing academia, he practiced as a federal prosecutor and a federal judge in Ethiopia.

Tsega Andualem Gelaye (SJD) is an Assistant Professor of Law at the Ethiopian Civil Service University, School of Law. He received his doctoral degree in Comparative Constitutional Law from Central European University. His area of research includes comparative constitutional law, human rights and criminal justice.

Yonatan Tesfaye Fessha is Professor of law and research chair in constitutional design and divided societies at the University of the Western Cape. He has published widely on matters pertaining to but not limited to federalism, constitutional design, autonomy, intergovernmental relations and politicized ethnicity

Zelalem Mogessie Teferra is Adjunct Assistant Professor of International Law at Addis Ababa University and a Senior Legal Adviser at the African Union. He holds a Ph.D. in International Law from the Geneva Graduate Institute and specializes in international human rights law, humanitarian law, counterterrorism, refugee law, migration, and peacebuilding.

Zelalem Shiferaw Woldemichael is a PhD candidate at the Melbourne Law School. Previously, Zelalem served as an Assistant Professor in law at the Law School of Jimma University, where he taught criminal procedure law and Ethiopian human rights systems. Zelalem's works cover constitutional protection of human rights, human trafficking, and the rights of vulnerable groups.

Zemelak Ayitenew Ayele (PhD) is a former director of, an associate professor at the Centre for Federal and Governance Studies of Addis Ababa University, and a research fellow at the Dullah Omar Institute of the University of the Western Cape. He is also co-convenor of the African School on Decentralisation (ASD)

Acknowledgments

A key factor that contributes to the success or failure of political reform, particularly in a divided society, is whether and how the reform process itself is seen as legitimate and also produces just and inclusive political and economic institutions. Shortly after it came to power in 2018, the current administration took significant, if brisk, strides towards political openness. Echoing historical precedents where shifts in political power have kindled a wave of optimism, the initial promise of democratic transformation stimulated several independent initiatives intent on informing political and institutional reforms. The idea of this book has its roots in one such high-level initiative to explore constitutional reform.

The initiative led to the establishment of two informal groupings of scholars interested in the constitutional dimension of the reforms, which morphed into some advocating conservation or minimal revision of the constitutional framework and others advocating for fundamental reform. Several rounds of intergroup discussions proved highly beneficial in clarifying the key issues of contention and in the identification of a list of issues that won the broad consensus of all as requiring further research and discussions. Subsequently, on each issue of central concern, a pair of experts with divergent perspectives was assigned to jointly undertake research in which they would clarify the underlying grounds of contest and offer a systematic audit of the key arguments, with a view to forging a list of agreed upon recommendations on the way forward. This approach was designed to foster mutual understanding and a step towards finding a suitable cure to what James Madison described in the Federalist No. 10 as "the mischiefs of faction." Moreover, participants to the deliberative meetings strove to address the question of constitutional reform from the vantagepoint of the grounds that underpin the enactment and adoption of a constitution in the first place—an approach that proved to be of great value for (re)imagining the Ethiopian constitution with fresh eyes. The last of these meetings took place in May 2021. The quality of presentations and conversations at that meeting was such that it inspired Melaku Geboye Desta to think about the possibility of producing this book, an idea we the editors inherited. We owe Melaku an immense debt of gratitude for this generous bequest as well as for his support and guidance throughout the process of producing this book. As conceived, the book's primary aim reads as follows:

> To contribute to scholarship relating to constitutionalism and constitution making in Ethiopia, generate potential input for ongoing constitutional reform debates, and provide an independent avenue for informed public discourse about the constitution. The project will do this primarily through independent scholarship on constitutionalism and the Ethiopian constitution, applying sound and rigorous methodology, subjecting each contribution to anonymous peer reviews where the quality of scholarship, rather than political and ideological preferences, are the only yardstick.

We strove to stay true to this original inspiration and mission, issued an open call for papers, assembled scholars with different perspectives and political persuasions, and produced a book that we believe will make a significant contribution to ongoing conversations on how best to organize the Ethiopian state and the structure of its basic institutions, both as a matter of process and substance. At least, that is our hope.

The editorial team would like to gratefully acknowledge the support that it has received along the way. First, we want to express our thanks to the Friedrich-Ebert-Stiftung for its financial support that enabled us to organize a highly successful conference in May 2023 in Addis Ababa, Ethiopia. The conference offered a platform for open, incisive, and stimulating discussions among the contributors to this project as well as other invited attendees. We would very much like to thank all who attended and made the conference a valuable forum for exchange of ideas about this "fractured country" of ours and what needs to be done to mend, both as a matter of process and substance, this fracture. Finally, we would be remiss if we did not publicly express our thanks to Elias Wondimu, the founding director of TSEHAI Publishers, not only for bringing this project to the public but for his extraordinary patience and encouragement throughout the process.

Introduction

Trust as a Constitutional and Social Good[1]: Institutionalizing Generalized Trust in a Fractured Country

Adeno Addis, Kebadu Mekonnen Gebremariam,
Adem Kassie Abebe, and Abduletif Kedir Idris

I. Introduction

One of the most important goods in social and political life is trust. The moral philosopher Bernard Williams once observed that "the first political question" is the Hobbesian one: how to secure, among other things, "trust and the conditions of cooperation."[2] The Hobbesian question invariably links the social good of trust with other goods and fundamental norms of political life, such as justice and fairness, as we shall show later in this introduction.[3]

No society or political community can function well and last long if there is no trust among members both as groups and as individuals (horizontal trust) and if members do not have a sufficient degree of trust towards the institutions within and through which public decisions are made and executed (vertical trust).[4] We might refer to the latter as institutional trust, by which we mean the circumstances where members of a political community as individuals and as groups (ethnic, linguistic, political, etc.) expect that political institutions[5] operate according to fair and agreed upon rules even in the absence of constant scrutiny. We substitute our lack of full information about governmental actions and activities with an assessment of the inclusiveness and trustworthiness of the institutions and the character of the people assigned to run them.

Why do certain societies in a post-conflict state succeed to cultivate the necessary level of trust among composite members (constituents) while others continue to register low level of trust, and even active mistrust, that appears to threaten their very ability to live together in one political community? The basic document of a political community, its constitution, which sets up the basic structure of society, plays an important role whether trust and the conditions of cooperation are cultivated and entrenched or, alternatively, undermined. A well-designed constitution will begin to foster and sustain trust both among members and towards public institutions. Members' trust in public institutions is vital if decisions and policies are to have legitimacy and if members are to see themselves as co-participants in a common project, rather than as strangers competing for domination in a zero-sum game. But trust is not only a function of the *substance* of the fundamental political frameworks/documents but also, and crucially, the *process* through which the framework is adopted and enforced. Put in another way, trust deficit can inhere in how the basic framework has organized the institutions that govern social and political life as well as in the manner in which the framework itself was constituted. This is especially the case in relation to frameworks that are meant to organize diverse societies, those that are already "fractured" or "divided."[6]

The focus of this book is on how best to organize (as a constitutional and institutional matter) the Ethiopian state and the structures of its basic institutions to ensure that trust among the composite members and towards public institutions are cultivated and entrenched. That there is currently a low level of horizontal trust, among the elites of the various ethnic groups, and, as significantly, a scarcity of trust towards the institutions of government is obvious. The current condition of the country attests to that fact.

Since its adoption in 1995, the Constitution of the Federal Democratic Republic of Ethiopia (Ethiopian Constitution) has been controversial. For some, the document laid the ground for a more sustainable and trusting relationship among what the Constitution calls "nations, nationalities and peoples."[7] Indeed, the preamble claims that the constitutional arrangement was meant to cultivate and promote trust and "shared interests" among the various ethnic and linguistic groups by "rectifying historically unjust relationships." Defenders of the Constitution argue that lodging sovereignty in the nations and giving those nations the right to self-determination up to and including the right to political divorce (secession) was meant to reassure the various groups that this association of political equals will endure. Otherwise, the argument goes, groups might not have had sufficient trust of fair treatment to join, much less to remain, in the compact.[8]

For others, including several contributors to this book project, the Constitution erected boundaries (conceptual, physical, and social) among ethnic/linguistic groups. The consequence of those boundaries has been that the historically soft and malleable parameters of ethnic and linguistic differences were transformed into the hard parameter of "nations," which often attempt to define and solidify their nationhood in opposition to and in contrast with other nations, evermore essentializing rather than softening differences. This act of essentializing and beholding of nations with a reductive gaze, the argument goes, has led to the widening rather than narrowing of the trust deficit among groups. Whether it is in relation to disputes about the territorial scope of each nation, or the issue of who properly belongs to that nation, or whether those who are not considered to be part of a nation have the same rights to participate fully in the institutions that govern their collective lives, the attitude of "us and them" has become worryingly widespread and entrenched, perhaps even broadly among ethnic groups themselves rather than just among the elites. The critique of the current Constitution has not only been that it has entrenched differences such that those differences are viewed not as contingent and malleable but as essential and primordial, but that some ethnic and linguistic groups have increasingly viewed each other as existential threats rather than as co-participants in a common project. Suspicion about, not trust of, nor respect for, the perceived "other" abounds. There is considerable scholarship that shows that often suspicion about and exclusion of the other go and in hand with this process of "people building."[9] Differences are often used politically or otherwise to consolidate and fundamentalize the peoplehood or nationhood of a particular group to make "identities which are always fluid, open and multilayered, seem closed, static and simple."[10] One contributor to this book argues that the notion of "ethnic self-determination" has in fact been a process of constructing the very self that is supposed to be self-determining.[11]

In addition, as several contributors note, the Constitution's recognition of the right of every nation to establish itself as a full-fledged country whenever that nation concludes that the political marriage is not working does not provide the necessary incentives for the constituent members to make the full commitment to make the political marriage work.[12] A fully ethnicized political and constitutional culture overlaid with a right to secession appears to lay the conditions for a dissociation order rather than one that builds trust and the conditions of cooperation.

So, why do certain diverse societies have difficulty building the necessary threshold of trust among constituent parts while others have done relatively better? The cause of distrust is not the existence and extent of diversity itself. Research has shown that distrust is not inherent in the mere existence of diversity[13] Rather, it is how that diversity is organized and marshaled as an institutional and political matter that determines whether diversity is turned into a source of conflict and tension or a source of opportunity and strength.[14] Barbara Walter makes this point directly and forcefully.[15]

Several of the contributors explore why and how the rich diversity of the country has become a source of an ongoing and destructive conflict and how, both as a matter of process and structure, best to fashion a constitutional and political arrangement to deal with the challenges of the scarcity of vertical and horizontal trust. Others explore one or another aspect of the current constitution to see whether it could (within its own terms) provide more space for democratic and equitable governance and less opportunity for exclusionary politics. In that regard, some authors argue for selective and perhaps strategic amendments of the current Constitution to start cultivating the necessary trust to build a fair, durable, and prosperous political community. Some of the areas of focus for amendment are the preambular narrative that sets the scene for the ethnic based constitutional framework, the secession article, the establishment of a constitutional court, and the like.

Other contributors indicate that a more fundamental rethinking of the constitutional arrangement, both as a matter of process and substance, is needed. However, there seems to be a consensus among the contributors that the current arrangement has fallen short of establishing trust and the conditions for cooperation both among groups and towards governmental institutions. Unsurprisingly, however, there is diversity in relation to the issue of how best to respond to these challenges so as to reclaim the missing virtue of trust and hence the conditions for cooperation.

The rest of this introduction proceeds as follows. First, it briefly explores the nature and importance of trust as an important social good for establishing and sustaining complex organizations such as a state or a political community. It examines how trust serves as a bridge in linking members of a complex organization as co-participants in a common project. As the introduction shows, as a general matter, trust is cultivated or undermined by institutions and social processes, by the *substance* of a basic framework and/or by the *processes* through which such a framework is adopted and *enforced*. Although none of the authors uses the word trust (at least not in a sustained way), we believe that their inquiries into both the substance of the current constitutional framework and the process through which the document was adopted speak to the issue of how "trust and the conditions of cooperation" have been affected significantly by how the basic document has organized social and political life and the process through which the document itself was adopted. Therefore, rather than summarizing the contents of each chapter, we thought it would be more helpful to the reader if we explored the arguments of the authors in the context of the theme of the social good of trust that we believe is central both to the process and substance of constitutional design for fractured societies.

II. The Nature of Trust

The observation that trust is central to human relations of various kinds is undeniably true.[16] Daniel Weinstock calls trust "the core constituent of social cement."[17] Trust allows friendships to flourish, groups and nations to emerge and develop precisely because members or parties rely on "the firm belief in the reliability"[18]and fairness of co-members and/or the institutions that link them. Members' "belief in the goodwill of the other"[19] is what sustains complex organizations. As the sociologist Georg Simmel put it long ago: "[w]ithout the general trust that people have in each other, society itself would disintegrate, for very few relationships are based entirely upon what is known with certainty" about other persons or groups or the functioning of institutions.[20] Trust is what makes it possible to have "imagined communities," to use a phrase Benedict Anderson coined and made popular.[21] In his address at his swearing-in ceremony, the new prime minister of Singapore, Lawrence Wong, observed that "the key" to the success of multilingual, multiracial and multireligious Singapore has been "our high level of trust in each other and our ability to work well together."[22]

Scholars often talk about two kinds (models) of trust: specific and general. Specific or particularized trust leads the truster to allegiances and ties within small groups and intimately familiar processes and institutions. It is in the context of interaction within a small group and a process familiar to members that specific or particularized trust emerges.

On the other hand, it is generalized trust[23] that enables large and complex organizations where there is no such intimate familiarity among members or with institutional processes--states, international organizations etc.—to function.[24] Generalized trust in both its social and political dimensions enables the emergence and sustenance of "imagined communities."

The difference between generalized and particularized trust can be analogized to Robert Putnam's distinction between bonding and bridging social capital.[25] We bond with our friends and people who are similar to us, but we form bridges with those "who are different from ourselves."[26] Generalized trust is the bridge that links members of a political community enabling them to see themselves (imagining themselves) as being engaged in a common enterprise. That can happen only when the institutions and processes that organize and govern their collective lives are seen as established in the best interest of all members of the community where members are treated (and feel that they are treated) fairly and justly and with "equal concern and respect," as Ronald Dworkin would put it.[27] T.M. Scanlon makes a similar argument about equality and equal treatment.[28] To discriminate against individuals just because they are members of an identity group is to treat them as less worth of concern and respect.

Research has shown that generalized trust is not just intrinsically good, but it is an important instrument for achieving other goods. It leads not only to stability and durability of political communities, but also to active engagement of members in those communities. That in turn produces more trust.[29] Generalized trusters are more tolerant of differing views, an important condition for establishing and sustaining a democratic culture. Even more importantly, research shows that a political community within which generalized trust reigns is one that will be conducive to distributive justice to narrow the gap of economic and other inequalities among members and across cleavages. Such gaps are of course sources of distrust among groups and towards institutions.[30]

To summarize, generalized trust is important for the cultivation and sustenance of large and complex entities such as a political community. However, generalized trust doesn't just emerge, it is created (or undermined) by institutions and their organizing ethos. As noted earlier, whether or not generalized trust is cultivated or undermined in a political community is significantly a function of the basic framework (notably the constitution, which embodies the social contract), how that document organizes the society and the machinery of government (the substance issue) and the process through which the document itself was adopted (the process issue). If the process is viewed as flawed, the substance of the document will have difficulty gaining acceptance even if, as an empirical matter, there is much to like in it. Of course, trust could also be undermined (or cultivated) by the manner in which the values, interests, and rights in the document are implemented (or not) (an issue of governance). *Process* and *substance* are two pressure points for exploring whether a basic document embodying the social contract has the capacity to cultivate vertical and horizontal trust sufficient to build a stable and durable political community, especially in a fractured society such as Ethiopia.

III. The Ethiopian Constitution's Impact on, and Contribution to, Generalized Trust

Many scholars, including some contributors to this book, have argued that the Ethiopian Constitution, both in the manner in which it was adopted (the process issue) and in the way that it has organized government and the larger society (the substance issue), has led to the widening of the trust gap, rather than progressively narrowing it or closing it.

In relation to the process of its adoption, the complaint has been that it was not inclusive enough of the wide spectrum of stakeholders when it was adopted. That is, it was not an outcome of genuine deliberation, understanding and compromise. In relation to the substance, the charge has been that the transformation of the country from a nation of citizens (even with all of its problems) to a nation of nations has tended to fundamentalize differences where the soft parameters of linguistic and ethnic diversity were turned into the hard parameter of deep and primordial differences. And some charge that the less than faithful implementation of aspects of the document has not only exacerbated the distrust towards governments and public institutions but it has also entrenched different classes of citizens and hence the prevalent attitude of "us and them."

A. The Impact of the Process of Constitution Making on Generalized Trust

1. The Constitution-Making Process

The cultivation of trust must begin at the process of consultation, deliberation and adoption, for mistrust of the process is likely to make it difficult to agree on the future dispensation and in fact might also lead to the distrust of the new dispensation as well, whatever its substantive quality.[31]

By "constitutional process," we mean to refer to "the manner in which a constitution is written…, from the instigation of a plan through to enactment and implementation."[32] A legitimate process is a crucial dimension of whether the resulting document manages to garner the legitimacy it needs to last.[33]

One of the reasons why constitutions in many countries, especially those that are described as fractured, have difficulty binding the community together is because the process through which they were adopted had either excluded a significant number of stakeholders from the process or those included as participants in the process were not viewed as genuine representatives of the relevant stakeholders. After studying closely eighteen national constitutions from sixteen different countries, Lorianne Toler concludes that "inclusion of all elites and factions appears key to constitutional success."[34]

One of the most persistent and trenchant criticisms of the Ethiopian Constitution since the very beginning has been that the process through which it was negotiated and adopted was flawed. A document that purported to be a document that manifests the interest of all "nations, nationalities and peoples" (NNPs) and a vindication of their sovereignty was in fact adopted without the full participation of several of those "nations".[35] Many groups denominated as NNPs did not have a meaningful say as to what the basic document should include and even whether they ought to be recognized and described as NNPs. Some contributors argue that the process was dominated by the Ethiopian Peoples' Revolutionary Democratic Front (EPRDF) which in turn was dominated by the Tigray People's Liberation Front (TPLF).[36] Critics observe that the process became not one of ascertaining the wishes of the various "nations," but rather the vindication of the wishes and ideological commitments of the elites of the liberation fronts. Berihun Adugna Gebeye, for example, argues that the EPRDF "reduced the Constitution to a mere tool of legitimation and justification of their politics by primarily considering it as 'legal account of the nation's history' rather than a fundamental legal document that binds and regulates actions of the state, its officials and citizens." Belachew Girma Degefie makes a similar point.

The legitimacy of the document was, therefore, contested from the very beginning, not only because the contents of the document were not viewed as sufficiently attentive to the rights and interests of the excluded, but also because of the perceived unfairness of the process itself. One contributor refers to the less than inclusive process as "the original sin."[37]

2. An Inclusive Process

We mentioned earlier the importance of an inclusive process in developing and crafting a basic document that will be endorsed by a sufficiently broad segment of the significant sectors of the political community. Inclusivity is notably relevant in relation to political elites, particularly in constitution making processes. While ordinary citizens are likely to focus on broader values and governance and service delivery issues, conversations over institutional issues, which are the bread and butter of constitutional deliberation, are often central to contestation among elites. Accordingly, while it is critical to ensure the participation of the broader public, it should not be seen as a substitute for or a justification to downplay or even bypass the need for elite deliberation and consensus.[38] There are several reasons why such a process is crucially important.

First, as we have seen in relation to the current document, a constitution that is crafted through a process that excluded (or was seen to have excluded) a significant segment of the society is unlikely to be viewed as legitimate.

Second, an inclusive process is more likely to lead to a substantively better document, for diverse views would have presented themselves and some might have been able to shape the document for the better. That is, such a process would have enhanced the common pool of reasoned arguments in the dialogue process. Even those who are considered extremists should perhaps not be excluded from the process. Fracture will not be mended only by those who occupied the imperial center (the moderates). A process that excludes groups or persons on the account that they are extremists or reactionary is likely to lead to a very truncated deliberative process and to outcomes that are likely to lead to continuing challenges. A "lasting stability will come about only as a result of moderation that is born of dialogue rather than one that is electorally engineered."[39]

Third, an inclusive process may in fact lead to a circumstance where participants who are required to listen to various points of view develop the important temperament that people in diverse societies should develop: the culture of tolerance, to hear and consider the views of others even, and especially, when the views expressed do not, as an initial matter, accord with one's own. Such a process will perhaps also provide the conditions for the interlocutors to develop empathetic sentiments towards one another. One value of a deliberative process where reasons are given about things and issues is that participants may get a better understanding of each other's interests and sympathies.[40] Studies have also shown how personal stories and testimonies from participants in deliberation across deeply divided societies often become triggers of empathy and were at times "transformative moments" in the dialogue process.[41] Conceived this way, deliberation provides a better way of achieving long-term stability in severely fractured societies, for it ensures, or at the minimum has the potential for, both inclusion and connection.[42]

Fourth, an inclusive process will be a crucially important first step in developing the social and political good of trust. The very nature of a deliberative process of justification assumes that participants in a collective decision making enter the dialogue with the view that "the reasons given, and the reasons responded to, have the capacity to change minds."[43]

The nature and level of inclusion that would be necessary to the cultivation of trust without undermining the possibility of consensus is not easily determined. However, what is certain is that a "consensus" that is reached after excluding persons with constituents from the deliberative process is not likely to last. If a process is to build a consensus that would last, it should err on the side of more inclusion. In this regard, there are several ideal types of constitution-making bodies.[44] Berihun Adugna Gebeye provides an account of one possible process that will be simultaneously inclusive and has the potential to lead to a durable elite and public consensus.

A deliberative body (instigating and drafting) could of course adopt rules to facilitate the deliberative process and a culture of trust so as to incline the process to lead to a consensus. The U.S. Constitutional Convention which drafted the current Constitution developed various rules that participants thought were likely to lead to a consensus document.[45] Whether or not any of these rules will be of any use to the Ethiopian circumstance is not the point. Rather, the point is that the rules governing the deliberative process will determine whether or not people deliberate in good faith and whether the process leads to a consensus document.

3. The Nature and Importance of Deliberative Consensus

By "consensus" we do not mean unanimity, which is hard to achieve in any process that involves large organizations, let alone fractured societies. Rather, the first element of a consensus is that the agreement is approved or adopted by, at a minimum, a significant majority of the critical stakeholders—negotiating and drafting groups as an initial matter and subsequently by the general populace, perhaps in a referendum.[46] Donald Horowitz make a similar point.[47]

The second element of a consensus agreement is that the agreement is not simply a result of bargains where individuals or groups come with set demands and then trade off on certain issues. The odds of such agreements lasting longer than the life of the negotiating group will likely be very low, as Donald Horowitz notes.[48] Rather, an enduring consensus will emerge from a process that requires participants in the relevant body to advance proposals and propositions with reasons that are acknowledged as such by and accessible to other participants.[49] The purpose is to try to persuade other participants that a particular position or proposition that they advocate is not only good for a sectional interest, but for the common good as well, and those who are properly motivated to live together could not reasonably reject.[50] So, the second element is that consensus requires a deliberative process where reason and persuasion are the paramount strategies. Persuasion will have a better chance if, and when, participants argue from a position that links the sectional interest to the common interest and broad values and principles. John Rawls makes a similar argument.[51] A document, which is a result of consensus in the way that we have described it, will have a much better chance of engendering trust and gaining legitimacy.

Third, a constitution is about looking forward, adopting a document for living together in politics. So, although a reflection on the history which got a particular political community where it finds itself is important and even necessary, the deliberative process must not be a prisoner of the past. There might not be a consensus on the history (and historians are better equipped to deal with that) and preoccupation with the nature of the past is likely to derail the deliberative process and the search for an arrangement that the overwhelming majority of participants will view as one for their common future.[52] In this regard, one contributor refers to the current Constitution as one that was adopted as a "legal account of the nation's history" rather than as a document for living together in politics.[53] Another reason why the constitutional framework ought not be a prisoner of the past is that such fixation stifles the evolution of society, in particular that of urban centers as cultural and ideological melting pots as well as sites of resistance against imposing doctrines. A recognition, through an inclusive process, of urban centers as sites of resistance restrains the constitutional framework from being overly prescriptive about acceptable modes of identity formation and expression. Deresse Kassa makes this claim.

Deliberation is of course much harder and takes more time than simple bargains, but a deliberative process where reasons are given creates a better condition for participants to get a better understanding of one another's interests and worries. Such a process offers better odds for achieving consensus. Consensus, in turn, will ensure the legitimacy and endurance of the document, for it would have contributed to the development and entrenchment of generalized trust.

A deliberative process may alter not only participants' view of their interest or their assessment of the common interest, but it may also alter people's perception of themselves. It is in the nature of a deliberative process that decisions will lead to further dialogue and revision, as participants take into account the preferences and views of others, and the process transforms their own views and preferences. John S. Dryzek refers to the open deliberative process as "social learning."[54] Understood this way, a deliberative process has the potential to contribute to the emergence of trust among participants. We must hasten to add here that although a deliberative process is about offering reasoned arguments for one's position, we do not mean to exclude other forms of intervention that may in fact advance that reasoned argument effectively. Research has shown that well-chosen personal testimonies, stories or even humor may be effective in inducing reflections and even being transformative.[55]

4. Commitment to a Process

It does not matter how inclusive or deliberative a process is if there is no full commitment from participants to that process. Often, there is the temptation that one will be committed to a process only to the extent that one perceives that one can dominate the process and as a result will win through the process. A different attitude is required for a deliberative process, especially for fractured societies. One will win only when other interlocutors also believe that they are winning, a win for all. This is consistent with a widely accepted view of a political community as a scheme of cooperation for mutual benefit, which is a conceptual and practical requisite for rendering any substantive account of how we ought to organize (a fractured) society receptive to standards of legitimacy and justice.[56]

A commitment to process has another dimension to it. It entails that participants will accept and respect the outcome of the process if the required threshold is achieved even if they as an initial matter were not in support of it. [57]

B. Designing Trust-Building Constitutions for Fractured Societies (The Substance of the Document)

Whatever system of government constitutions set up and however differently they may distribute institutional power, two common (and interlinking) purposes animate or should animate them. First, constitutions are designed to forge and develop a political community that enables members to see each other not as strangers engaged in an existential struggle against one another but as co-participants in a common project.[58] Second, the governmental structure the constitution sets up is checked within the institution itself (within the governmental structure) and is ultimately accountable to members of the political community. Accountability builds generalized trust.[59]

1. Boundaries or Bridges: Who is the Sovereign?

The Ethiopian Constitution is unique in that it lodges sovereignty, not in "We, the Ethiopian people," but rather in the "nations, nationalities and peoples" which ordained and established the Constitution for the country and in whom "all sovereign power resides." Indeed, the Constitution is said to be "an expression of their sovereignty."[60] The Constitution does not recognize the existence of an Ethiopian people as such, nor does it aspire as a normative matter to constitute such a people. Under this scheme, the Ethiopian people are not and cannot ever be sovereign as such. Only in their capacity as members of identified nations or peoples (i.e., ethnic groups) can citizens be considered to have sovereign authority. Ethiopian citizens are not linked directly, but through the mediative process of membership in the various "nations." The soft parameter of ethnic difference is now entrenched as a constitutionally relevant and politically salient hard parameter.

A great deal has been written on the impact of this institutional setup on the scope and reach of Ethiopian citizenship and the strength of the commitment to a durable political community.

Several contributors here explore in one way or another both the symbolic and institutional implications of how the Constitution defines the identity of the constitutional subject on whom it lodges ultimate sovereignty. Berihun Adugna Gebeye, for example, explores the impact of the way the constitutional subject is defined and sovereignty allocated on what he refers to as the *identity challenge*, both symbolically and substantively.[61] Terefe Sahelu Gebreyesus makes a similar argument.

Others explore the impact of the constitutional arrangement on the rights of ethnic and linguistic minorities living in the various ethnically diverse regional states.[62] They suggest ways to deal with such discrimination and to develop trust among members of various ethnic groups within the regional states and within the constitutional scheme.

Still others claim that the notion that the NNPs adopted the Constitution as an expression of their sovereignty is, as a matter of history and practice, a fiction. The story of NNPs' authorship was simply a means to give legitimacy to the political and social agenda of those who were in control of power. As part of his general inquiry into the notion of "constituent power" in the Ethiopian Constitution, Terefe Sahelu Gebreyesus advances the position and offers several reasons in support of it.

2. Boundaries or Bridges: Is the Right to Secession a Disincentive to a Full Commitment to the Political Marriage?

Article 47 of the Constitution establishes a federal system where the constituent units are organized primarily along ethnic/linguistic lines. At the time of the adoption of the Constitution there were nine such states. However, since Article 47 also provides for the right of NNPs within the existing regional states to demand that they be allowed to establish their own state if they so wished, four more states have been established. Many more NNPs have indicated that they seek to establish their own regional state.

While Article 47 declares that the Constitution is an "expression of [NNPs'] sovereignty" and a manifestation of their right to self-determination, Article 39 adds that self-determination includes the "unconditional" right to secede, to be a full-fledged country.

The Ethiopian Constitution is almost alone among national constitutions around the world in entrenching the right to secession. One can hardly create trust in a marriage (whether in relation to the union of individuals or political entities) by providing for a process of divorce at the time of the union. One contributor explores this issue as an important issue of *commitment*, or lack of it. He argues forcefully that the current federal structure that enshrines the right to secession "without even providing any justification or rationale" for the decision to exit makes the Ethiopian federation "a federation of convenience" rather than "a solemn commitment" for its continuity.[63]

There are several significant ways in which the right of secession manifests and entrenches the politics of difference that undermines the possibility of developing and entrenching generalized trust essential for building and sustaining a political community. First, as some scholars have argued, in a fully ethnicized political system and culture where identity becomes the primary lens (the prism) through which issues are seen and analyzed, the constitutional right of political divorce is likely to be deployed as a strategy for extorting power and resources—thus exacerbating rather than easing distrust among the various groups.[64] A federal structure with the right to secession to the constituent parts of the federation at any time for any reason arguably disincentivizes the cultivation of generalized trust which is essential for the process of open and sincere deliberation about fair terms of cooperation.[65] Genuine deliberation assumes not just equality of participants (each party is recognized by all others as an interlocutor) but the principle of reciprocity as well—participants are engaged in a common political enterprise. Strategic behavior is not conducive to a genuine deliberative process. As more NNPs demand and attain legal recognition as regional states, the occasions for more and more intensified politics of difference increase, and consequently the negative impact on generalized trust becomes highly consequential.

Second, it is not inconceivable that the constitutional right to secession will provide perverse incentives for strident ethnonationalists to engage directly or indirectly in the forcible displacement of residents from other ethnic or linguistic groups or to discourage such individuals from moving into the state. Given that secession requires that a majority of the state electorate vote affirmatively, it might be thought that the right of exit will be undermined (at least complicated) if there is a significant population from other ethnic or linguistic groups within the particular ethnostate.

Constitutionalizing secession can therefore have a corrosive effect on the national body politic to the extent that the inherent right to secede raises questions on the existence of full commitment to the political marriage. Several contributors make this point. No marriage, human or political, is likely to engender trust about the union and one another when dissolution or dissociation is a background principle accompanying the marriage vow.

One prominent area of dispute among the regional states which has probably been elevated to an existential conflict among the various "nations" by the constitutional entrenchment of the right to secession is the issue of boundary disputes. A border adjustment among states that might have been routinely normal if those states were administrative units becomes a serious existential issue when those adjustments are made in the context of a federation of "nations" where those nations have a constitutionally guaranteed right to leave the union. Who would cede a contested area to another "nation" which has the right to leave the union? This is not to say that there would not have been border conflicts if Article 39 had not existed. Organizing regional states as "nations," in the way that a "nation" is defined in the Constitution, was destined to push border disputes as existential conflicts. Rather, the argument is that the existence of Article 39 increased the intensity and anxiety of losing "one's territory" to a potentially foreign country.

3. Separation of Powers and the Cultivation of Generalized Trust

The notion of separation of powers—checks and balances within the governmental structure itself—is meant to ensure accountability of governmental entities and in the process instill confidence and trust in the governed that those who are entrusted with power exercise that authority according to law and within the constitutional scope of their authority. The belief that there is accountability within the governmental structure itself increases the level of vertical trust and, as importantly, horizontal trust as well, especially in a fractured society. This is to say that the principle of separation of powers is both about a mode of governance (political trust) and a mode of association (civic trust), the distinctive way in which members of the polity relate and recognize one another.

a. The Importance of an Independent Constitutional Review Body

An independent judiciary is part of that scheme of checks and balances. Under most national constitutions, the power to interpret the constitution and decide constitutional disputes is conferred upon an independent judiciary, whether that is a specialized constitutional court, such as what prevails in Germany and South Africa, or a court of general jurisdiction such as the Canadian and U.S supreme courts. However, as several of the contributors note, the Ethiopian Constitution does not vest the authority of constitutional interpretation in an independent judiciary. Rather, the power is vested in the second chamber of the parliament, the House of Federation (HoF). It is given the power "to interpret the Constitution" and to decide "[a]ll constitutional disputes." [66] Belachew Girma Degefie briefly explores why the HoF was chosen as the appropriate interpretive body[67] and then goes on to indicate some of the criticisms that have been made against that arrangement. Yonathan T. Fesseha also briefly touches on the reasons why the HoF was chosen as the appropriate organ for constitutional interpretation and for resolving constitutional disputes.

Without attributing all of them to Belachew Girma Degefie or Yonathan Fesseha, there could be several reasons why an independent judiciary rather than a political body should exercise that authority. First, vesting the power of constitutional interpretation in a political body such as the HoF will likely lead to many partisan political decisions. Such outcomes will not engender trust in governmental structures and institutions and respect for the basic document. Rather than fidelity to the Constitution, it is likely to be fidelity to the party (and the government of the day) that is likely to inform how a constitutional issue is analyzed and resolved or even entertained. That is likely not the best way to start cultivating trust and the rule of law in a fractured society.

Second, it is not just the likelihood that constitutional decisions of a political body will be partisan and political, but they are also unlikely to be consistent and systematic, as a matter of constitutional practice. This is partly because of the nature of political and partisan decisions, but it may also be because of the lack of competence and expertise of a political body, whose primary function is not constitutional interpretation, to develop and entrench a constitutional culture that vindicates the supremacy of the organic document. Yonathan Fesseha explains why the current arrangement leaves Ethiopia "without a competent, impartial, and suitable umpire that can police constitutional compliance and, broadly, constitutionalism." Such a process will not foster trust among those whose lives are to be governed by these decisions.

Third, judicial review of constitutional questions will not only be a more suitable process for developing and entrenching a robust, more coherent and stable constitutional culture and constitutionalism generally, but it may also be the appropriate process through which to fill perceived constitutional gaps. Because of interpretive expertise, independence, and focused attention, courts are likely to be in a better position to fashion a constitutional response to the "various crises of human affairs"[68] that require a constitutional response.

Another criticism of the current arrangement relates to the effective insulation of critical decisions of the House of Federation itself, which exercises formidable powers, such as the determination of the formula for the distribution of federal allocation of funding to the regions, from constitutional review. A good example is the constitutional case regarding the postponement of elections in 2020. While the focus was on the House of Peoples' Representatives, the House of Federation was also determining its own fate. The case involved the question of whether the House of Federation's term, alongside the first chamber and regional legislative councils, should be extended. In this case, the House was effectively serving as a judge in its own case.

Yonathan Fesseha notes that although the current constitution has been in force for almost three decades "Ethiopia has still to come up with a body of constitutional jurisprudence." The reason: "the unusual model of constitutional review" described above. So, what should replace the current arrangement? The widespread view is that there should be judicial review either by a specialized constitutional court or by courts of general jurisdiction. Alemayehu Fentaw Woldemariam would expand "the size and mandate of the CCI [Council of Constitutional Inquiry] and transform[] it into a full-fledged Constitutional Court." Yonathan Fesseha also argues that constitutional review could be performed by a reformed CCI which "can be the permanent organ that deals with constitutional disputes, not an advisory body that meets on a part-time basis." What is envisage here is a CCI that would "have the final and ultimate power on the interpretation of the Constitution, including the power of determining the constitutionality of legislation."

While there might be differences as to what should replace the current system—judicial review by a court of general jurisdiction, a specialized constitutional court, or a reformed CCI—what seems clear is that there is broad agreement that the current system of constitutional interpretation and resolution of constitutional disputes has not served well the vital purpose of entrenching a constitutional culture and constitutionalism generally.

b. Separation of Powers between the Executive and Legislative Branches

Zelalem Mogessie Teferra argues that the current parliamentary system "presents challenges when it comes to upholding the principle of separation of powers." He contends that, in the Ethiopian context, the nature of the parliamentary system (with a parliament dominated by one party with the prime minister at the head) is unlikely to position the parliament to provide meaningful checks on the executive branch. What is the Ethiopian context that he thinks will make it even less likely that the Parliament will exercise meaningful checks on the pronounced dominance of the executive branch? He refers to the culture and history of the country that he claims "is characterized by a centralized, authoritarian executive" as well as the state of the opposition currently: primarily organized along fractured and ethnic lines. He suggests as a potential solution the adoption of "a premier-presidential system" along the lines suggested by other scholars. A premier-presidential system "combines a popularly elected presidency with a prime minister who leads a cabinet, each having its well-defined substantial functions." He notes that to be effective this system will have to be supplemented with more institutional structures than are available in the current structure, and more robust mutual reciprocal supervisions between the two elected branches of government. The nature of those supplemental institutional structures is not teased out, but there are countries from which one could draw lessons.

Nigeria, Kenya, and Indonesia have presidential systems. The constitutions of these countries, each of which has a diverse population (ethnically, linguistically, and religiously diverse), attempt to incentivize presidential candidates to appeal to a wider segment of the fractured electorate rather than to rely on one or two identity groups sufficient to give them a majority of the total electorate. Thus, one requirement that has persisted in the various versions of the Nigerian Constitution is that the winning presidential candidate must not only get "the majority of the votes cast at the election" but also needs to have secured "not less than one-quarter of the votes cast at the election in each of at least two-thirds of the States".[69] The Kenyan Constitution has a similar provision. To be elected to the office, a presidential candidate needs to garner more than fifty percent of the popular vote and "at least twenty-five percent of the votes cast in each of more than half of the counties."[70] Indonesia's Constitution requires that any ticket for candidate for president and vice-president must secure more than 50 percent of the popular vote and in addition must secure "at least twenty percent of the votes in more than half of the total number of provinces in Indonesia."[71] A presidential system (in one of its various versions) may be one of the options that fractured Ethiopia needs to consider as an alternative for the current parliamentary system. If so, there are many countries under a presidential system of one or another kind which may shed light on the virtues and limitations of such a system to cultivate the social good of trust and the conditions of cooperation in a fractured political community.

4. The Role of Federalism in Fostering Trust

Federalism is both a theory of and advocacy for a system of government that splits sovereignty between a central government and constituent units (states, provinces, etc.). Certain powers are allocated to the central government (federal government) and others to the constituent units (states or provinces). Each is to be sovereign only over those issues and subject areas allocated to it. Many countries have adopted a federal system. Although the reasons for which federal systems are adopted are as diverse as the problems to which they are meant to respond, three common purposes emerge. First, federalism is thought to enhance the odds of protecting the liberty of citizens both by ensuring that there are power centers that check and make accountable the central government and by increasing the opportunities for citizens to participate in the decision-making process. Second, a federal arrangement is viewed as providing the best means for a diverse country to accommodate differences and cleavages—whatever the nature of the differences (regional, ethnic, etc.)—while building a common, democratic order. Third, federalism is premised on the proposition that such arrangement will likely facilitate the emergence of alternative solutions to similar problems, hence increasing the aggregate pool of solutions from which a central government may choose to draw and apply nationally.

Whether or not, as a conceptual and practical matter, the current ethnic federal arrangement has pursued, or is capable of pursuing, the above purposes is highly contested. Several contributors probe aspects of the current federal structure and conclude that the integrative structures and symbols are too weak to sustain a nation.[72] Some raise serious questions about the capacity of such an arrangement to cultivate trust and the conditions of cooperation while others suggest ways to improve the current arrangement by drawing from comparative studies.

Zelalem Shiferaw Woldemichael engages in a comparative study of India and Ethiopia on matters of federal intervention in the constituent units (states). After exploring the three different circumstances in which the national government could intervene in the affairs of constituent units, he concludes that the Ethiopian Constitution is not as protective of state autonomy as the Indian system. The Ethiopian Constitution is not "designed to allow adequate protection of state autonomy through the judiciary" and as a result there are very few real constraints on a federal government that wishes to intervene, especially in a parliamentary system where the parliament is likely to be dominated by the ruling party over which the Prime Minister is likely to have significant control.

Zemelak Ayitenew Ayele seeks to deepen federalism by pushing the constitutional structure to acknowledge and accommodate a constitutional status for local governments both to serve as a check on otherwise dominating state governments who attempt to exercise unconstrained power over local governments and to provide space for citizens to govern themselves at the local level. He cites several countries which provide constitutional status for local governments. After exploring various reasons which might have prevented the framers of the current Ethiopian Constitution from recognizing a constitutional status for local governments, one reason being the fear that the federal government will use those units as a backdoor way to weaken the state, he argues that the lack of recognized status has "diminished the political significance of local government." He recommends that "[a]t the minimum, the constitution should clearly and explicitly require the states to establish a democratically constituted local government" and guarantee "a system of local government by democratically elected local government councils." One effect of such an arrangement might be that territorially concentrated ethnic minorities would have the space to govern themselves. But that of course might also increase the trust gap between majorities and minorities.

5. The Scope of National Citizenship in a "Nation of Nations": A Community of Equals as a Source or Condition of Generalized Trust

As a normative matter, citizenship "is meant to guarantee full membership and equal standing to all members"[73] with that rank across the political community. Citizens are one another's equal "as participants in the affairs of the political community and as beneficiaries of the rights and privileges recognized and accorded to those holding that rank."[74] But it is also a rank that is meant to bind together all members of the political community to the extent that citizens (as a collective body) are both the originators and addressees of the laws that are meant to regulate their collective lives.[75] As a normative matter, citizenship therefore defines the relationship between the member and the state and the relationship among members themselves. Equality of membership promotes trust both towards government and across cleavages. As such, equality of membership (both substantively and symbolically) has, in the process of cultivating trust, an integrative function.

Citizenship is a primary social good.[76] It is, to quote the political theorist Hannah Arendt, "the right to have rights."[77] Under the current constitutional arrangement, Ethiopian national citizenship has not performed that function well. Ethiopian citizens are not treated as one another's equal in some of the regional states. Indeed, some regional states' constitutions distinguish between members of "their" ethno-nation and the rest, the former is regarded as a primary stakeholder (and "indigene") and the latter as mere residents. The political practice of exclusion and displacements of minority ethnic and linguistic groups in some of the regional states reinforce the distinction. Such exclusions and disenfranchisement have widened, rather than narrowed, the trust gap between those regarded as indigenes, part of the nation whose name the state carries and members of minority ethnic groups. In some cases, the fully sovereign indigenes are not even the majority in the particular state—the Benishangul-Gumuz and the Harari States are good examples.

As Christophe Van der Beken's contribution shows, as a practical matter Ethiopian citizenship has not shielded ethnic and linguistic minorities in some of the regional states from being discrimination against and from lack of full participation in the life of the relevant regional political community. As he put it, "[t]he lack of adequate constitutional protection for regional or intra-unit minorities (these are minorities at the level of the federated units) is of much more than mere academic importance, which is amply illustrated by the myriad of human rights violations and abuses targeting these groups."

Some may argue that the exclusionary practice is not just a matter of power holders not acting consistently with the national constitutional mandate, but rather an inherent feature of the constitutional arrangement. Whether it is a matter of poor political practice or a result of the structure itself, what remains clear is that many Ethiopian citizens are treated as second class citizens or, even worse, displaced from their homes on the account of their perceived membership to a different ethnic group. This is not a condition that will entrench trust among groups or towards governmental institutions. Van der Beken makes that point when he refers to the process of minority protection as having both intrinsic and instrumental values. He notes: "[e]nhanced legal protection is not only necessary to protect the rights and interests of regional minorities" and "to ensure citizens' substantive equality irrespective of their ethnic identity" but it is also "a tool to prevent tensions caused by discriminatory and exclusionary practices and, as such, to bring about improved societal harmony and stability." Van der Beken considers and recommends various arrangements for the protection of minorities in the various regional states both to protect their basic human rights and to ensure full participation in the social, cultural, and political life of their communities.

Another contributor, Asrar Adem, focuses on a different minority-- persons with disabilities. He argues that members of that group have been historically discriminated against and have not enjoyed the rights that attend to full citizenship. He argues for a constitutional entrenchment of the rights of that minority to ensure that people with disability can participate fully in the life of the nation.

Derese Kassa's contribution contrasts unfavorably the current constitutional arrangement that "privileged ethnic homelands" to what he calls "urban or metropolitan formations which are melting pots of various ethnicities, religions, and class formations" which will continue to "(re) imagine" the notion of citizenship. "When it comes to contesting the current ethno-federal design of Ethiopia and (re)imagining citizenship," Derese Kassa argues, "urban is indeed the future." Why does he think so? Because "the concept of citizenship itself and its various renditions…are articulated and debated in urban spaces." He claims that the truncated and ethnicized notion of citizenship "that privilege 'indigeneship' and ethnic identity" are being challenged "by millions of urbanites with mixed ethnic and religious heritage." Whether or not Derese Kassa is right as an empirical matter that urban Ethiopia is going in that direction might be contested.[78] What is, however, important is the suggestion that the citizenship that is going to entrench trust both among groups and towards institutions and thus keep the country together is one that over time softens the hard parameter of ethnic identity and treats citizens as a community of equals.

6. Managing Diversity Successfully: Is the Nation-State Model itself the Problem?

Here we have an indirect dialogue between two contributors: Getachew Assefa Woldemariam and Assefa Fiseha. Assefa Fiseha is not optimistic that the Western model of the nation-state will be able to deal successfully with identity-based cleavages so as to build a shared identity from competing and politically mobilized identities.[79] He indicates that the best model for having a relatively peaceful and stable Ethiopian state is a consociational parliamentary federation of "nations" that "would then deploy consensus-based decision making at the federal level on key political, diplomatic and economic issues that serve as trust-building scheme mitigating the potential for conflict." Thus, for Assefa Fiseha, the social good of trust in fractured Ethiopia will have a better chance of being entrenched if consociation (power sharing arrangement of some sort) is enshrined as a constitutional good. Indeed, he concludes that "[t]his is the best possible offer a country could provide (short of secession) as a means to ensure peace, unity, stability and a system of inclusive polity building." Assefa Fiseha is not entirely clear why the nation-state has had problem to manage diversity in Africa (especially Ethiopia) where it seems to have had better success in several Asian countries which are as diverse or even more diverse as any African country for which the nation-state is as foreign as it is to Africa. Indonesia and India come to mind. In this regard, it is worth observing that while Assefa Fiseha is suspicious of the nation-state's capacity to manage diversity, for he believes that it is unresponsively foreign to our conditions, he appears comfortable with the notion of "nations" (as ethnic groups) as a given Ethiopian condition.

Getachew Assefa Woldemariam, on the other hand, argues that the problem for the failure of many African states including Ethiopia to manage diversities successfully is not because the Western nation-state model is inherently unsuitable (incapable) of accommodating such diversities. Rather, a major factor for the problem of conflict and instability has been "state capture by the ruling political class, in most cases in the name of certain primordially corporatized ethnic groups," groups which are constructed, organized and marshalled by the political class itself. The violent competition among "the primordial bourgeoise classes" is assisted by the fact that the African bourgeoise is "resource-hungry" and seeks to use state power "as a means for resource control" and "the source of [its] economic gains." The primordial bourgeoise class manufactures ethnic cleavages, turning the soft parameter of linguistic differences into the hard parameters of nations with exclusive identities, so as to then exploit tensions and grievances for the purpose of acquiring and retaining power and to have access to state resources. Most of the conflicts and political violence that define fractured societies such as Ethiopia are fueled, he says, directly or indirectly "by the bourgeoisie classes of the primordial domain." For him, there is nothing primordial about ethnicity.[80] Ethnicity is as constructed and as foreign to Ethiopia as is the nation-state itself. He argues, successfully deconstructing the constructed ethnic partition and establishing "an accommodative state with attributes akin to the Western states can be made a reality in Africa."

IV. Amending the Constitution or Adopting a New One

As the introduction has indicated and as some of the contributions show, to deal with the scarcity of trust that has accompanied the current constitutional arrangement a new dispensation (constitution) might be the best course of action. The introduction has indicated what that could look like as a matter of process and substance. What would, however, need to be done if one were to work with the current constitution (amend it) to deal with the circumstances that undermine "trust and the conditions of cooperation"? Various contributors have suggested amendments from the very beginning (the preamble) to the end of the document (the amendment process), such as adding "We, the Ethiopian people" as a constituent power in the preamble, removing Article 39 (the right to secession), establishing a semi-presidential system of government, removing the power to interpret the Constitution from the House of Federation and investing it in an independent professional judicial body (such as a constitutional court) or a similar body, investing local governments with more robust authority, and amending the amendment process itself, especially the unanimity requirement of Article 105.

Three questions arise in relation to the issue of amending the Constitution. First is the question whether it is in fact possible to amend the Constitution, both as a political and procedural matter. The amendment processes are laid out in Articles 104 and 105. While the amendment process for most parts of the Constitution is similar to amendment processes found in other national constitutions, such as the U.S. Constitution, amending any provision in Chapter III of the Constitution, which happens to include Article 39, requires the unanimity of states. This is what constitutional scholars call "constructive unamendability" by which they mean that that the onerous formal amendment rules make the theoretically possible realistically unavailable.[81] Garnering the unanimous support of all states in any circumstance let alone in the current environment of mistrust would appear to be very challenging, especially when one may not be certain as to how the new amendment coheres with the rest of the constitutional arrangement. And theoretically a state with less than a million people could torpedo an amendment agreed to by the rest of the states.[82]

Second, those who advocate for amendments rather than an adoption of a new constitution will have to face the issue that is noted in the last paragraph.

That is, how coherent does the Constitution become with the new amendment, whatever the amendment is? Can one add the "Ethiopian people" as constituent power in the preamble without doing something about Articles 8 and 47? Grafting one or another amendment on the current Constitution without thinking through as to how things cohere might simply make the document a patchwork of ideas and commitments that might be in tension with one another or even contradict one another. The only thing that might be worse than a document that does not encourage and entrench trust, "unity and fraternity" in the words of the Constitution,[83] among its citizens, is one that is incoherent as to its objectives.

We make these observations simply to alert stakeholders to the challenges inherent in pursuing the amendment route. It could be the case that a deliberative body following the process we described in an earlier section arrives at a considered conclusion that such strategic amendments would enhance trust and the conditions of cooperation and the document that emerges from that process will also be a coherent whole. At any rate, to be legitimate such a process will have to be inclusive, deliberative and one that aims at a consensus document.

V. Trust and The Virtue of Incompletion: A Brief Observation

Drafters of modern constitutions, especially ones for societies described as fractured, often have the urge to be comprehensive and hence pursue a sense of completion. There is an attempt to deal with every conceivable issue as an issue of constitutional settlement, thus turning the basic document into a glorified statute.

Here we simply want to caution that although completion is a virtue in many areas of life, it might not be in the context of constitutional design, especially one meant to bind fractured societies. Indeed, in those circumstances incompletion is a virtue.[84] By incompletion or incompleteness we mean to suggest that not all controversial issues need to be settled by the basic document as an initial matter and some might actually be better left to the ordinary deliberative process for a later time when circumstances might become conducive for resolving them deliberatively and incrementally.[85] Ambiguity on some of the very divisive issues might not be a bad idea, at least as an initial matter. In the course of the continuing process of deliberation, a tradition, though not a text, may develop that becomes a focus of consensus.

Conclusion: Trust: The Missing Social Good

Trust, a "precious and fragile commodity" as the noted political theorist Phillip Pettit calls it[86], is essential to any society that seeks to have a higher level of social capital that is essential for the political viability and stability of a society. It is also crucial for democratic governance and economic development. As we have indicated in this introduction and as the various chapters show, the constitutional framework of a country plays a central role whether the necessary trust and conditions of cooperation are entrenched or undercut.

The contributions to this book project explore how, as a matter of both process and substance, the current Ethiopian Constitution has fallen short of cultivating that important condition of cooperation. There seems to be an agreement among contributors that it has not performed well. Unsurprisingly, however, contributors differ as to what process and institutional arrangements will better create the necessary conditions for a fair and durable political community. Some argue for changes in some aspects of the Constitution. Others call for a new process to adopt a new dispensation that garners the consent of both the elites and the public if that arrangement were to contribute to trust and the conditions for forging a lasting compact. As we noted earlier, research shows that the inclusion of "all elites and factions appears key to constitutional success." In fact, in many cases, "non-inclusiveness trumped all other positive elements of a process—public participation, transparency, and local expert involvement."[87]

We hope that the ideas raised and pursued in this book will contribute to the conversations among scholars, activists, government officials, political parties and the general public about fair and durable terms of cooperation. That there is a need for such reflection as an urgent matter is obvious, as the current state of the country amply illustrates.

Many had hoped that the establishment of the National Dialogue Commission (NDC) by the House of Peoples' Representatives[88] would start the first part of the dialogue, "[t]o see national consensus reached on the most fundamental issues of national significance"[89] and that the Constitution would be part of the conversation, but for various reasons that hope is yet to be realized. Our hope is that, whether in the ongoing national dialogue effort or in the future, the idea of trust will provide a framework in defining both the process of deliberation and negotiation of the constitutional dispensation, as well as the contents of the ultimate social, political and constitutional settlement.

Failing to grapple with the current constitutional arrangement and the trust-deficit that defines the political community both in the vertical and horizontal sense is to risk the very serious threat of fragmentation that the country is facing with the unimaginable consequences that would ensue. The likelihood of the country fragmenting into stable nation-states is minimal. Rather, if the country continues to follow the current course, something even worse is likely to happen: long, continuous, and mutually destructive civil conflicts which will turn the country back to a distant past.

In his essay *Defying Tribalism*, published in the *New York Review of Books*, the Irish author, Fintan O'Toole, tells what he refers to as a "local joke" in his home city of Dublin about the Northern Irish city of Belfast during the 30 years of sectarian conflict in Northern Ireland. "[W]hen planes landed at Belfast airport, the pilot announced, 'Welcome to Belfast. Put your watches back one hour and three hundred years.'"[90] We must do all we can to ensure that our country does not find itself where a similar advisory would need to be given, except here the advice might well be to turn watches to two hundred fifty-five years, to the start of the era of the princes.[91]

Notes

1 In his book *Constitutional Goods*, Alan Brunder explores in detail the notion of a social and constitutional good. Brunder, Alan. Brunder, *Constitutional Goods* (Oxford University press, 2004).

2 Bernard Williams, *In the Beginning was the Deed: Realism and Moralism in Political Argument* 3 edited by Geoffrey Hawthorn (Princeton University Press, 2005), 3. See also See also Thomas Hobbes, *Leviathan, or The Matter, Forme & Power of a Commonwealth, Ecclesiasticall and Civil* (C.J. Clay and Sons, 1904).

3 John Rawls, A Theory of Justice (Harvard University Press, 1971), 3. ("Justice is the first virtue of social institutions, as truth is of systems of thought.")

4 The distinction between vertical and horizontal trust is described by some scholars as the difference between political and social trust. See Bo Rothstein and Dietlend Stolle, "The State and Social Capital: An Institutional Theory of Generalized Trust," *Comparative Pol*itics 40, no. 4 (July 2008): 441-459. But we think that is not entirely accurate. Horizontal trust can be social or political (e.g. trust or lack of it among elites is both horizontal and political). We agree with those authors, however, to the extent that they observe that while political trust and social trust are different concepts, the level of social trust might correlate with the level of political trust.

5 For a helpful definition/description of what an institution is see Tommie Shelby, *Dark Ghettos: Injustices, Dissent, and Reform* (Harvard University Press, 2016), 25. (Institutions are "formal system[s] of roles and rules that enable and regulate sustained cooperative action for some specified purpose."). Cf. Abdalhadi. Alijla, *Trust in Divided Societies: State, Institutions and Governance in Lebanon, Syria and Palestine* (Bloomsbury Publishing Pic, 2021), 181. He defines "institutions" to include both formal and informal institutions.

6 Benjamin Reilly refers to fractured societies as those which are "ethnically diverse and where ethnicity is a politically salient cleavage around which interests are organized for political purposes such as elections." Benjamin Reilly, *Democracy in Divided Societies: Electoral Engineering for Conflict Management* (Cambridge University Press, 2000),.4. Under this definition, Ethiopia is clearly a fractured society: (a) it is ethnically/linguistically divided; (b) ethnicity frames the vast majority of political conflicts; (c) many regard divisions in the country as intractable and often present their demands as nonnegotiable; and (d) there is widespread identity-driven hostility and violence, creating an environment where citizens live under conditions of insecurity and unequal treatment. See also Adeno Addis, "Deliberative Democracy in Severely Fractured Societies," *Indiana Journal of Global Legal Studies* 16, no. 1 (Winter 2009): 63-65.

7 The various chapters in the book use "nations", "ethnic" or "linguistic" groups or NNPs as a shorthand.

8 Assefa. Fiseha, "Theory Versus Practice in the Implementation of Ethiopia's Ethnic Federalism," in *Ethnic Federalism: The Ethiopian Experience in Comparative Perspective*, edited by David Turner (James Curry, 2006), 135.

9 Matthew J. Gibney, "Statelessness and Citizenship in Ethical and Political Perspective," in *Nationality and Statelessness under International Law*, edited by Alice Edwards and Lura van Waas, (Cambridge University Press, 2014), 44-61. Neha Jain., "Manufacturing Statelessness," *American Journal of International Law* 116, no. 2 (2022): 237.

10 Fintan O'Toole, "Defying Tribalism." *New York Review of Books*, 70, no. 1 (2023): 18.

11 See Terefe Sahelu Gebreyesus. "Thus, ethnic self-determination has not been an end in itself, rather a means to construct ethnic identity." See also Getachew Assefa Woldemariam's chapter.

12 Berihun Adugna Gebeye makes this point. Several other contributors make the point in one way or another.

13 Alberto Alesina and Eliana LaFerrara. "Participation in Heterogeneous Communities," *Quarterly Journal of Economics* 115, no. 3 (2002): 847-904. Alberto Alesina and Eliana LaFerrara. "Who Trusts Others?," *Journal of Public Economics* 85 (2002): 207-234. Indonesia with "more than one thousand ethnic groups, who speak more than seven hundred languages" has managed to build a strong and relatively prosperous political community. Margaret. Scott, "Indonesia's Corrupt Democracy." *New York Review of Books* 71, no. 6 (April 2024): 40.

14 Eric Uslaner, "Does Diversity Drive Down Trust?," (2006) (SSRN) Does Diversity Drive Down Trust? by Eric M. Uslaner :: SSRN.: 21.

15 Barbara Walter, *How Civil Wars Start and How to Stop Them.* (Random House, 2022). Walter notes that two factors prove again and again as highly predictive of conflict and instability. One of those factors is whether a society has started to organize itself as primarily or exclusively around identity be it ethnic, linguistic or religious. "[E]very year those two factors continue, the risk increases," she observes in an interview with the Washington Post. See K.K. Ottesen, "'They are Part of War': An Expert in

Civil War Discusses Where Political Extremists are Taking the Country," *Washington Post*, March 8, 2022.

16 Russell Hardin, *Trust and Trustworthiness* (Russel Sage Foundation, 2002).

17 Daniel Weinstock, "Building Trust in Divided Societies," *Journal of Political Philosophy* 7, no. 3 (1999): 307.

18 Jacquelyn Schneider "A World Without Trust: The Insidious Cyberthreat," *Foreign Affairs* 101, no. 1 (January/February 2022): 24.; Rima Wildes and Carey Wu, "Ethnicity, Democracy, Trust," Social Forces 97 no. 1 (September 2018): 467.

19 Adam Seligman, *The Problem of Trust* (Princeton University Press, 1997), 43.

20 Georg Simmel, The Philosophy of Money (Routledge, 1978 [1900]), 179.

21 Benedict Anderson, *Imagining Communities: Reflection on the Origin and Spread of Nationalism*, (Verso, 1991).

22 Lawrence Wong's first speech as prime minister at swearing-in ceremony. In full: Lawrence Wong's first speech as Singapore's Prime Minister at swearing-in ceremony (youtube.com).

23 Eric Uslaner, *The Moral Foundation of Trust* (Cambridge University Press, 2002). Generalized trust is defined as trust in other people in general or trust in strangers. It is characterized by the absence of both a specified recipient of trust and a specific regard in which the recipient is trusted. Generalized trust is the perception that the people to whom trust is extended are part of one's moral community.

24 Niklas Luhmann. *Trust and Power* (Jonh Wiley and Sons, 1979), 4. The distinguished German sociologist (social theorist), Niklas Luhmann, was right when he observed that it was trust that reduces complexity in our social and political life and mitigate what would otherwise be "chaos and paralysing."

25 Robert Putnam. *Making Democracy Work* (Princeton University Press, 1993), 93. See also Uslaner, "Does Diversity Drive Down Trust?"

26 Uslaner, "Does Diversity Drive Down Trust?,"7.

27 Ronald Dworkin, *Taking Rights Seriously* (Harvard University Press, 1977), 180.

28 T.M. Scanlon, *What We Owe to Each Other* (Harvard University, 1998), 18-19.

29 Marc Hetherington, *Why Trust Matters: Declining Political Trust and the Demise of American Liberalism* (Princeton University Press, 2006).

30 Bo Rothstein and Dietlend Stolle. "The State and Capital: An Institutionalized Theory of General Trust," *Comparative Pol*itics 40, no. 4 (July 2008): 441.

31 One important reason why Chileans rejected a new proposed constitution by a significant majority, even when 80 percent of them had wanted a new constitution, was apparently because the process through which the document was adopted was viewed as less than inclusive.

32 Lorianne Toler. "Mapping the Constitutional Process," *Cambridge Journal of International and Comparative Law* 3, no. 4 (2014): 1262. See also Donald Horowitz, *Constitutional Process and Democratic Commitment* (New Haven, Yale University press, 2021)

33 Toler, Mapping," 3; see also Jon Elster, "Ways of Constitution Making" in *Democracy's Victory & Crisis*, edited by Axel Hadenius (Cambridge University Press, 1997), 137.

34 Toler, "Mapping," 1282.

35 Terefe Sahelu Gebreyesus makes this point.

36 See Alemayehu Fentaw Woldemariam; Terefe Sahelu Gebreyesus explores the drafting process of the Constitution and concludes that "The drafting process was highly dominated by the TPLF/EPRDF." Tsega Andualem Gelaye notes: "As many writers agree, the making of the FDRE constitution was dominated by ethnic based political organizations that defeated the Derg."

37 See Alemayehu Fentaw Woldemariam's chapter..

38 Alon Harel and Adam Shinar, "Two Concepts of Constitutional Legitimacy," *Global Constitutionalism* 12, no. 1 (October 2023): 80. Amal Sethi. *Looking Beyond the Constituent Power Theory: The Theory of Equitable Elite Bargaining* (Cambridge University, 2023).

39 Adeno Addis, "Deliberative Democracy in Severely Fractured Societies," *Indiana Journal of Global Legal Studies* 16, no. 1 (Winter 2009), 72.

40 Horowitz, *Constitutional Process*. Addis, "Deliberative Democracy".

41 Jürg Steiner, Maria Jaramillo, Rousiley Maia and Simona Mameli. *Deliberations Across Deeply Divided Societies* (Cambridge University Press, 2017).

42 This section tracks the arguments that were made in Addis, "Deliberative Democracy," 70-71.

43 Amy Guttman and Dennis Thompson, *Why Deliberative Democracy?* (Princeton University Press, 2004), 20.

44 Jonathan Wheatley and Fernando Mendez. *Patterns of Constitutional Design: The Role of Citizens and Elites in Constitution-Making* (Ashgate Publishing Limited, 2013). The constitution-making body could be directly elected (e.g. a constituent assembly) with or without a requirement that the constitution so adopted be subject to subsequent popular ratification. Or an elite body (selected rather than directly elected) drafts a constitution which is then subject to popular approval by referendum, etc. What is important is that the process gets right the tradeoffs between the mode of representation and the mode of legitimation.

45 The US Convention had several rules: secrecy, prohibition of the sharing of any details about the work of the convention, perfect attendance, prohibition on speaking a second time until all others had a chance to speak, etc.

46 Ronald Levy, Ian O'Flynn and Hoi L. Kong. *Deliberative Peace Referendums* (Oxford University Press, 2021).

47 Horowitz, *Constitutional Processes*, 92-123. Horowitz argues that "[a]t a minimum, a constitutional consensus should attempt to include those with the capacity for violent obstruction, but given the fragility of many severely divided societies, any consensus should, if possible, be greater than that. It should attempt to embrace all major segments of all significant groups or else risk later destabilization of the agreement." Id. 101.The South African constitutional negotiating process of the 1990s used the phrase "sufficient consensus" across parties and groups. See https://www.usip.org/sites/default/files/Framing%20the%20State/Chapter5_Framing.pdf.

48 Horowitz, *Constitutional Process*. But as Horowitz himself agrees, there might be time when consensus is impossible and negotiated compromise becomes a second-best method.

49 Addis, "Deliberative Democracy," 71.

50 Scanlon, *What We Owe*, 1-13, 189-247.

51 John Rawls, *Political Liberalism* (Columbia University Press, 2005), 133-172, 385-395.

52 Thus, for example, the Ethiopian Constitution asserts in its preamble that the NNPs were fully cognizant that their "common destiny can best be served by rectifying historically unjust relationships…" This observation is of course controversial. There is, as a historical matter, deep disagreement on whether there was in fact unjust relationships among ethnic groups themselves rather than successive regimes having exercised unjust and unconstrained power over "subjects." The issue of whether what existed was bad governance rather than governance on behalf of this or that ethnic group is a controversial issue that cannot be resolved in the context of drafting a constitution. Rather, it is likely to derail the process of adopting a document for their collective future.

53 See Berihun Adugna Gebeye's chapter.

54 John Dryzek, "Deliberative Democracy in Divided Societies: Alternatives to Agonism and Analgesia," *Political Theory* 33, no. 2 (April 2005): 222.

55 John Deyzek, "Democratization as Deliberative Capacity Building," *Comparative Political Studies* 42 (August 2009): 1379. Jane Mansbridge, "The Place of Self-Interest and the Role of Power in Deliberative Democracy," *Journal of Political Philosophy* 18 (March 2010): 67. Jürg Steiner, Maria Jaramillo, Rousiley Maia and Simona Mameli. *Deliberations Across Deeply Divided Societies* (Cambridge University Press, 2017), 110-111, 253-54.

56 Rawls, *Political Liberalism*, 15-22.

57 Adem Abebe, "Ethiopia Needs a Constitutional Convention to End Ethnic Divisions," *Foreign Policy* (April 2021).

58 Adeno Addis. "The Making of Strangers: Reflections on the Ethiopian Constitution," *Journal of Developing Societies* 38, no. 4 (December 2022): 421.

59 Soffie Marien and Marc Hooghe, "Does Political Trust Matter? An Empirical Investigation into the Relations between Political Trust and Support for Law Compliance," *European Journal of Political Research* 50, no. 2 (January 2011): 267.

60 Article 8.

61 Berihun Adugna Gebeye uses the preamble of the Swiss Constitution as an example of how the preamble of the Ethiopian constitution could be amended to deal with the identity challenge as s a symbolic matter.

62 See Christophe Van der Beken on minority rights: Terefe Sahelu Gebreyesus on constituent power.

63 Berihun Adugna Gebeye. In an earlier work, Kebadu Mekonnen makes a similar point See Kebadu Mekonnen Gebremariam, "Republican Renewal and Democratic Transition in Ethiopia: 'Medemer', A Lofty Mantra or a Laîcité for Contemporary Ethiopia?" In *Ethiopia: In the Wake of Political Reforms,* edited by in Melaku Desta et. al. (Tsehai publishers, 2020).

64 Cass Sunstein, "Constitutionalism and Secession," *University of Chicago Law Review* 58, no. 2 (1991): 633.

65 Addis, "The Making of Strangers," 430-32. Sunstein, "Constitutionalism and Secession," 634.

66 See Articles 62(1) and Article 83(1) respectively.

67 Belachew Girma Degefie reports that there were two major reasons why the framers

settled on the HoF as the appropriate interpretive body. First, the document was seen "as an embodiment of the political contract among the NNPs" and that such a document "should be interpreted by the signatories themselves, the NNPs through the HoF." Second, there was a belief that judges are not neutral and may therefore tilt their interpretation of the Constitution to respond to public opinion or to accommodate their own preferences, thereby distorting the Constitution and the rights of NNPs.

68 McCulloch v. Maryland, 17 U.S. 316, 4 Wheat. 316, 4 L. Ed. 579 (1819). In this famous case, Chief Justice John Marshall used a structural reading of the Constitution to conclude that the federal government had the power to establish a federal bank even though there was no specific mention of the power to establish a bank on the list of powers given to the Congress. Marshall argued that the fact that the Congress was given certain other specific powers (the power to regulate interstate commerce, the power to tax, etc.) that necessitate the existence of a bank to fully effectuate those powers, it follows that the power to establish a bank is impliedly given. This is what is referred to as a structural reading of the constitution made famous by Marshall both in this and other cases.

69 Nigeria Constitution 1999, Article 134(2).

70 Kenya Constitution 2010, Article 138(2).

71 Indonesia Constitution 2002, Article 6A(3).

72 Tsega Andualem Gelaye argues that "[C]ompared to India, the symbolic and instrumental integrative elements of the FDRE constitution are weak." He attributes this partly to the fact that the Constitution "contains a number of provisions starting from its preamble that militate against integration and national unity" and that in turn was a result of the fact that "the constitution-making process itself was not inclusive as it was dominated by ethnic-based political organizations" to the exclusion of parties "that were organized at the national level."

73 Adeno Addis "The Unbearable Thinness of National Citizenship in a Country Organized as a "Nation of Nations": The Case of Ethiopia"." In *Between Failure and Redemption: The Future of the Ethiopian Social Contract*, edited by Ibrahim, Abadir and Kokebe Wolde (2023) output.pdf (northwestern.pub), 192

74 Addis, "Unbearable Thinness," 199.

75 Jürgen Habermas, *Between Facts and Norms: Contributions to a Discourse Theory of Law and Democracy*. Translated by William Rehg (MIT Press,1996), 415.

76 Michale Walzer, *Spheres of Justice: A Defense of Pluralism and Equality* (Basic Books, 1983), 6-8.

77 Hannah Arendt, *The Origins of Totalitarianism* (Harcourt, Brace, 1951), 294.

78 Addis Ababa as an urban center and Wollo as a region were thought to resemble the future—melting pots where identities are ambiguated and then redefined. But some might argue that the current arrangement is attempting to transform both these places into spaces for ethnic contestation rather than the other way around.

79 See also Jonh Markakis, Günther Schlee, and John Young. *The Nation State: A Wrong Model for the Horn of Africa* (Max-Planck-Gesellschaft zur Förderung der Wissenschaften, 2021).

80 See also Kwame A. Appiah, *The Lies that Bind: Rethinking Identity* (Liveright, 2019).

81 Richard Albert, *Constitutional Amendments: Making, Breaking, and Changing Constitution* (Oxford University Press, 2019), 158-162.

82 A similar unanimity requirement per Article 13 of the U.S. Articles of Confederation (predecessor of the Constitution) was famously ignored by the Constitutional Convention that drafted the Constitution. And then in Article VII of the draft constitution, the framers of the new document simply declared that only "nine States shall be sufficient for the Establishment of this Constitution between States so ratifying of the Same." In addition, in countries with a Francophone political tradition, the idea of the "constituent power" has been invoked to justify the adoption of a new constitution outside of the parameters of the process of constitutional amendment. While these examples offer a potential way out of a legal paralysis, they also undermine legal certainty and continuity, regardless of the legitimacy of the extant constitutional framework. The issue should therefore be addressed with utmost care and based on broad political consensus.

83 Interestingly, under Article 88(2) the Constitution charges the government (indeed, imposes a duty on government), among other things, to strengthen "ties of equality, unity and fraternity" among the various constituent powers.

84 Adeno Addis, "Individualism, Communitarianism, and the Rights of Ethnic Minorities," *Notre Dame Law Review* 67, no. 3 (1992): 674-76. Addis, "Deliberative Democracy," 76-77.

85 Hanna Lerner, *Making Constitutions in Deeply Divided Societies* (Cambridge University Press, 2011), 110. Lerner explores the drafting and adoption of three national constitutions at the time of establishment of those countries—India, Ireland, and Israel. She argues that in one way or another all three avoided having to settle on some very divisive issues by adopting what she calls "constructive ambiguity." Take India, for example- India "adopted ambiguous provisions in order to avoid making difficult, unequivocal choices with respect to the most contested foundational issues." Id. at 110. Two disputes where such strategy was employed were in relation to "the uniform civil code and the national language." Id. The purpose of constructive ambiguity is to leave the issues to a later time when conditions are perhaps ripe. Lerner refers to the process as "constitutional incrementalism."

86 Phillip Pettit, "The Cunning of Trust," *Philosophy and Public Affairs* 24 (July 1995): 225.

87 Toler, "Mapping," 1282.

88 The Commission was established on December 29, 2021 by the House of Peoples' Representatives. See dialogue commission.pdf (lawethiopia.com). Proclamation No. 1265/2021.

89 See Commission website. Ethiopian National Dialogue Commission (ethiondc.org.et).

90 Fintan O'Toole, "Defying Tribalism." *New York Review of Books*, 70, no. 1 (November 2023): 18.

91 We are here of course thinking about the Era of the Princes. See Mordechai Abir, *Ethiopia in the Era of the Princes: The Challenge of Islam and the Re-unification of the Christian Empire (1769-1855)* (Tsehai Publishers, 2011).

Bibliography

Abebe, K. Adem. "Ethiopia Needs a Constitutional Convention to End Ethnic Divisions," *Foreign Policy* (April 2021).

Abir, Mordechai. *Ethiopia in the Era of the Princes: The Challenge of Islam and the Re-unification of the Christian Empire (1769-1855)*. Tsehai Publishers, 2011.

Addis, Adeno. "Individualism, Communitarianism, and the Rights of Ethnic Minorities." *Notre Dame Law Review* 67, no. 3 (1992): 615-676.

Addis, Adeno. "Deliberative Democracy in Severely Fractured Societies." *Indiana Journal of Global Legal Studies* 16, no. 1 (Winter 2009): 59-83.

Addis, Adeno. "The Making of Strangers: Reflections on the Ethiopian Constitution." *Journal of Developing Societies* 38, no. 4 (December 2022): 421-439.

Addis, Adeno. "The Unbearable Thinness of National Citizenship in a Country Organized as a "Nation of Nations": The Case of Ethiopia"." In *Between Failure and Redemption: The Future of the Ethiopian Social Contract*, edited by Abadir Ibrahim and Kokebe Wolde, 191-231. output.pdf (northwestern.pub)

Albert, Richard. *Constitutional Amendments: Making, Breaking, and Changing Constitutions*. Oxford University Press, 2019.

Alesina, Alberto and Eliana LaFerrara. "Participation in Heterogeneous Communities." *Quarterly Journal of Economics* 115, no. 3 (2002): 847-904.

Alesina, Alberto and Eliana LaFerrara. "Who Trusts Others?" *Journal of Public Economics* 85 (2002): 207-234.

Alijla, Abdalhadi. *Trust in Divided Societies: State, Institutions and Governance in Lebanon, Syria and Palestine*. Bloomsbury Publishing, 2021.

Anderson, Benedict. *Imagining Communities: Reflection on the Origin and Spread of Nationalism*. Verso, 1991.

Appiah, A. Kwame. *The Ethics of Identity*. Princeton University Press, 2005.

Appiah, A. Kwame, The Lies that Bind: Rethinking Identity. Liveright, 2019.

Arendt, Hannah, *The Origins of Totalitarianism*. Harcourt, Brace, 1951.

Brunder, Alan. *Constitutional Goods*. Oxford University press, 2004.

Constitution of the Federal Democratic Republic of Ethiopia, 1995.

Constitution of the Republic of Indonesia, 2002.

Constitution of Kenya, 2010.

Constitution of the Federal Republic of Nigeria, 1999.

Dryzek, John. "Deliberative Democracy in Divided Societies: Alternatives to Agonism and Analgesia." *Political Theory* 33, no. 2 (April 2005): 218-242.

Dryzek, John. "Democratization as Deliberative Capacity Building." *Comparative Political Studies* 42 (August 2009): 1379-1402.

Dworkin, Ronald. *Taking Rights Seriously*. Harvard University Press, 1978.

Elster, Jon. *The Cement of Society: A Study of Social Order*. Cambridge University Press, 1989.

Elster, Jon. "Ways of Constitution Making" in *Democracy's Victory & Crisis*, edited by Axel Hadenius. Cambridge University Press, 1997.

Fiseha, Assefa. "Theory Versus Practice in the Implementation of Ethiopia's Ethnic Federalism," in *Ethnic Federalism: The Ethiopian Experience in Comparative Perspective*, edited by David Turner, 131-164. James Curry, 2006.

Gebremariam, Kebadu Mekonnen. "Republican Renewal and Democratic Transition in Ethiopia: 'Medemer', A Lofty Mantra or a Laïcité for Contemporary Ethiopia?" In *Ethiopia: In the Wake of Political Reforms*, edited by Melaku Geboye Desta, Dereje F. Dori, and Mamo E. Mihretu, 85-122. Tsehay publishers, 2020.

Gibney, J. Matthew. "Statelessness and Citizenship in Ethical and Political Perspective" in *Nationality and Statelessness under International Law*, edited by Alice Edwards and Lura van Waas, 44-61. Cambridge University Press, 2014.

Guttman, Amy and Dennis Thompson. *Why Deliberative Democracy?* Princeton University Press, 2004.

Habermas, Jürgen. *Between Facts and Norms: Contributions to a Discourse Theory of Law and Democracy*. Translated by William Rehg. MIT Press,1996.

Hardin, Russell. *Trust and Trustworthiness*. Russel Sage Foundation, 2002.

Hardin, Russel. "Liberal Distrust." *European Review* 10, no. 1 (February 2002): 73-89.

Harel, Alon and Adam Shinar. "Two Concepts of Constitutional Legitimacy." *Global Constitutionalism* 12, no. 1 (October 2023): 80-105.

Hetherington, Marc. *Why Trust Matters: Declining Political Trust and the Demise of American Liberalism.* Princeton University Press, 2006.

Hobbes, *Thomas. Leviathan, or The Matter, Forme & Power of Commonwealth, Ecclesiastical and Civil.* Clay and Sons, 1904.

Horowitz, Donald. *Constitutional Processes and Democratic Commitment.* Yale University Press, 2021.

Jain, Neha. "Manufacturing Statelessness." *American Journal of International Law* 116, no. 2 (April 2022): 237-288.

Lerner, Hanna. *Making Constitutions in Deeply Divided Societies*. Cambridge University Press, 2011.

Levy, Ronald, Ian O'Flynn and Hoi L. Kong. *Deliberative Peace Referendums*. Oxford University Press, 2021.

Luhmann, Niklas. *Trust and Power*. John Wiley and Sons, 1978.

Marien, Soffie and Marc Hooghe. "Does Political Trust Matter? An Empirical Investigation into the Relations between Political Trust and Support for Law Compliance." *European Journal of Political Research* 50, no. 2 (January 2011): 267-291.

Markakis, John, Günther Schlee, and John Young. *The Nation State: A Wrong Model for the Horn of Africa*. Max-Planck-Gesellschaft zur Förderung der Wissenschaften, 2021.

McCulloch v. Maryland, 17 U.S. 316, 4 Wheat. 316, 4 L. Ed. 579 (1819).

Mistzal, Barbara. "The Notion of Trust in Social Theory." *Policy and Society* 5, no. 1 (Winter 1992): 6-15.

Mansbridge, Jane. "The Place of Self-Interest and the Role of Power in Deliberative Democracy." *Journal of Political Philosophy* 18 (March 2010): 67-100.

O'Toole, Fintan. "Defying Tribalism." *New York Review of Books*, 70, no. 1 (November 2023): 18-22.

Pettit, Phillip. "The Cunning of Trust." *Philosophy and Public Affairs* 24 (July 1995) 202-225.

Putnam, Robert. *Making Democracy Work*. Princeton University Press, 1993.

Rawls, John. *A Theory of Justice*. Harvard University Press, 1971.

Rawls, John. *Political Liberalism*. Columbia University Press, 2005.

Reilley, Benjamin. *Democracy in Divided Societies: Electoral Engineering for Conflict Management*. Cambridge University Press, 2001.

Rothstein, Bo and Dietlend Stolle. "The State and Capital: An Institutionalized Theory of General Trust." *Comparative Politics* 40, no. 4 (July 2008): 441-459.

Scanlon, T.M. *What We Owe to Each Other*. Harvard University Press, 1998.

Schneider, Jacquelyn. "A World Without Trust: The Insidious Cyberthreat." *Foreign Affairs* 101, no. 1 (January/February 2022): 22-31.

Scott, Margaret. "Indonesia's Corrupt Democracy." *New York Review of Books* 71, no. 6 (April 2024): 40-42.

Seligman, Adam. *The Problem of Trust*. Princeton University Press, 1997.

Sethi, Amal. *Looking Beyond the Constituent Power Theory: The Theory of Equitable Elite Bargaining*. Cambridge University Press, 2023.

Shelby, Tommie. *Dark Ghettos: Injustices, Dissent, and Reform*. Harvard University Press, 2016.

Simmel, Georg. *The Philosophy of Money*. Routledge (1978) ([1900].

Steiner, Jürg, Maria Jaramillo, Rousiley Maia and Simona Mameli. *Deliberations Across Deeply Divided Societies*. Cambridge University Press, 2017.

Sunstein, Cass. "Constitutionalism and Secession." *University of Chicago Law Review* 58, no. 2 (1991): 633-670.

Sunstein, Cass. *Designing Democracy: What Constitutions Do*. Oxford University Press, 2001.

Toler, Lorianne. "Mapping the Constitutional Process." *Cambridge Journal of International and Comparative Law* 3, no. 4 (2014): 1260-1286.

Uslaner, Eric. "Does Diversity Drive Down Trust?" (2006) (SSRN) Does Diversity Drive Down Trust? by Eric M. Uslaner :: SSRN

Uslaner, Eric. *The Moral Foundation of Trust*. Cambridge University Press, 2002.

Vitale, David. "Political Trust as the Basis for a Social Right Enforcement Framework." *Queens Law Journal* 44, no.1 (2018): 177-220.

Walter, Barbara. *How Civil Wars Start and How to Stop Them*. Random House, 2022.

Walzer, Michael. *Spheres of Justice: A Defense of Pluralism and Equality*. Basic Books, 1983.

Weinstock, Daniel. "Building Trust in Divided Societies." *Journal of Political Philosophy* 7, no. 3 (1999): 287-307.

Wheatley, Jonathan, and Fernando Mendez. *Patterns of Constitutional Design: The Role of Citizens and Elites in Constitution-Making*. Ashgate Publishing, 2013.

Williams, Bernard. *In the Beginning was the Deed: Realism and Moralism in Political Argument*. Edited by Geoffrey Hawthorn. Princeton University Press, 2005.

Wilkes, Rima, and Carey Wu. "Ethnicity, Democracy, Trust." Social Forces 97 no. 1 (September 2018): 465-494.

Part I

Constitutional Sovereignty in a Diverse Society: Process and Substance

Chapter 1

Towards a Constitution of Peace in Ethiopia: Issues of Process and Substance

Berihun Adugna Gebeye*

1. Introduction

It is highly unlikely for a civil war to occur in a functioning constitutional democracy. This is primarily because democracy creates the conditions for peaceful politics. Periodic elections regulate mass politics at the ballot box, parliaments facilitate and channel party politics, and courts judge disputes that might arise between and among different institutions, political parties, and citizens. All these would make and, indeed, have made civil war unnecessary in the democratic world.[1] The war in Northern Ethiopia and the widespread violence throughout the country signify the spectacular failure of the 1995 Constitution and its underlying political settlement. Precisely because there is a fundamental constitutional breakdown in the form of constitutional crisis and "constituticide," the 1995 Constitution, *regardless of our views on it*, could not return Ethiopia to peaceful politics. This, I argue, is and should be the starting point for thinking about returning Ethiopia to constitutional politics and consequently constituting peace in that land.

In this chapter, I identify and explain some issues of process and substance for the constitution of peace in Ethiopia. First, I explain both the road to Ethiopia's constitutional breakdown and the processes for Ethiopia's constitutional renewal. Second, I identify and examine what I think are some of Ethiopia's fundamental political problems, which stems from problems of transition from empire to republic. These problems of transition have brought about a crisis of statehood, a crisis of governance, and a crisis of citizenship, which, in turn, have brought about *commitment*, *governance*, and *identity challenges* in the federation, respectively. In this chapter, I show how the constitution of peace in Ethiopia largely depends on the process by which it comes into being and the extent to which it directly confronts the problems of Ethiopia's transition from empire to republic, namely the *commitment*, *governance*, and *identity challenges*.

2. Issues of Process: How Did We Get Here and How Do We Get Out of Here?

A. Ethiopia's State of Constitutional Affairs: Constitutional Crisis and "Constituticide"

Ethiopia is in a dual state of constitutional affairs: constitutional crisis and constituticide. The state of constitutional crisis is related to a situation where the constitution fails to keep political disagreements within the boundaries of constitutional law and politics. It is when the constitution is no longer able to resolve disputes among political actors. And when state institutions and their officials are unable and/or unwilling to perform their basic constitutional duties. And when force, or the threat of use of force, becomes the new dispute resolution mechanism. Constitutional crisis is the predominant state of constitutional affairs in Ethiopia today, except for Tigray.

The state of constituticide, on the other hand, is related not to the failure of the constitution but to its demise by the (violent) actions of competing political and government actors. It is a situation where the underlying political settlement that animates the normative, institutional, and symbolic force of the constitution collapses. In a state of constituticde, force or the threat of force cannot solve political disputes and contestations. Even more, it may further undermine the capacity to return to a new constitutional and political life. Constituticide captures and explains the state of constitutional affairs between Ethiopia and Tigray. With respect to Ethiopia and Tigray, the 1995 Constitution is no longer the supreme law as it used to be before the start of the war in November 2020. Despite its crisis, the Constitution is alive in the rest of the country because the members of the federation supported the federal government in its "rule of law operation" in Tigray. The fact that the war is called a "rule of law operation" and that members of the federation supported such an operation meant that they defended the Constitution. While constitutional crisis and constituticide are two distinct categories of constitutional affairs and, consequently, require different political and constitutional responses, they have been animated by and structured through some common sociopolitical and constitutional factors.

The state of constitutional crisis and constituticde did not happen overnight. At least constitutionally speaking, they brewed for over twenty-five years. The lack of original legitimacy in the making of the 1995 Constitution and the subsequent infidelity to and flagrant violation of this Constitution planted the seeds of these state of constitutional affairs.[2] The 1995 Constitution is a "victorious constitution" authored by the Ethiopian People's Revolutionary Democratic Front (EPRDF), a coalition of four ethnic-based parties that ruled Ethiopia from 1991–2018, excluding key political and demographic forces in the country.[3] From 1995–2018, the EPRDF reduced the Constitution to a mere tool of legitimation and justification of their politics by primarily considering it as a "legal account of the nation's history" rather than a fundamental legal document that binds and regulates the actions of the state, its officials, and its citizens.

The EPRDF instead had used revolutionary democracy as the "empirical constitution" of the country from which detailed legal and policy principles had developed for the past three decades.[4] Revolutionary democracy as applied by the EPRDF had several features, including democratic centralism, "one-to-five organization" of its members and the civil service, party evaluation, the developmental state model, and neopatrimonialism. Democratic centralism in the lexicon of revolutionary democracy, for example, refers to democratic deliberation and the unity of action within the EPRDF. Its democratic elements spring from its claim of "free deliberation," and its centralism is associated with the centrality of the decision-making processes within the party.

Under the constitution of revolutionary democracy, the Central Executive Committee of the EPRDF was the final decision-making body within the party and, by extension, in the country. The formal state institutions simply legitimized and legalized whatever was decided by the EPRDF Central Executive Committee. Moreover, as the Tigray People's Liberation Front (TPLF) was the dominant party within the EPRDF coalition, political and constitutional power and authority in the country had been in the hands of a Tigrayan elite and their close associates. TPLF/EPRDF's strong security and military power and structure had ensured the practice of revolutionary democracy for almost a quarter of a century, against the central tenets of the country's Constitution.

But the constitution of revolutionary democracy was challenged by a popular protest movement in the country's two largest regions—Oromia and Amhara, especially since 2015. This popular protest movement forced the EPRDF to elect Abiy Ahmed of the Oromo People's Democratic Organization

(OPDO) as its leader and later as prime minister in 2018. What initially appeared to be a personal and leadership change within the EPRDF planted the seeds of constitutional change within the party that has, in turn, activated the functioning of the 1995 Constitution differently.

This is primarily because Abiy Ahmed within a short period of time replaced revolutionary democracy with "Medemer" as the new political ideology of the EPRDF and, in 2019, transformed the coalition to a united party called the Prosperity Party (PP) that includes the ruling parties of all the regional states except Tigray (as the TPLF refused to join the new party). This political change within the party has introduced a new "empirical constitution" called Medemer, the key feature of which is the institutionalization of personal rule within the party and the country. One of the key differences between Medemer and revolutionary democracy is while the former bestows much political power to the party leader and combines it with some notions of majoritarian democracy, the latter concentrates power within a small group and combines it with some variants of consociational democracy.

As the transformation of the EPRDF to the PP made the TPLF an opposition political party, the first such party governing one of the regional states since the inauguration of the Ethiopian federation in 1995, the Constitution has become the primary frame of reference between these two parties and by extension between Ethiopia and Tigray. Particularly, the postponement of the sixth national election, which was scheduled for August 29, 2020, due to the COVID-19 pandemic, created a constitutional conundrum and political tension. The Constitution requires the conduct of a national election one month before the expiry of the five-year term of the previous government, in October 2020. In June 2020, in a contested constitutional interpretation, the House of Federation—the upper house of parliament with power to interpret the constitution—extended the term of office of Abiy Ahmed's government and the term of office of the regional governments until the next elections are held, COVID-19 permitting. The TPLF and other opposition political parties considered this decision to be an illegitimate extension of power against the Constitution and contended that the power of the incumbent would expire in October 2020.

The TPLF went even further. Despite the decision and repeated warnings of the House of Federation that a regional election would be null and void, the TPLF organized its own regional election in the state of Tigray on September 9, 2020. After winning 98.5 percent of the seats of the Tigray Regional Council, the TPLF declared the federal government to be illegitimate. The federal government in turn declared the Tigray state government illegitimate. This made intergovernmental relations between the two governments extremely difficult and, later, impossible. Because both the TPLF and the federal government justified their actions based on and in defense of the Constitution, the Constitution immediately lost its normative and institutional force between these actors. Put differently, they killed the Constitution, and this political and legal reality and the attendant war differentiates the constitutional situation in Tigray from the rest of the country.

The decision of the House of Federation and Tigray's regional election were constitutionally problematic. On the one hand, the right to self-determination including the right to secession is the founding block of the Constitution and permeates the resultant socio economic, cultural, political, and legal order of the country. This constitutional right cannot be limited or suspended even during a state of emergency such as the COVID-19 pandemic.[5] And electoral democracy is one of the mechanisms by which the constitutional right to self-determination could be exercised. This reading of the Constitution casts some doubts about whether Tigray's regional election was constitutionally permissible or not, although the management of elections throughout the country is a federal matter.[6] Additionally, and most importantly, in addition to issues of jurisdiction and prudence, the decision of the House of Federation violates one of the cardinal principles of natural justice and the rule of law: "No one should be a judge in their own cause."[7] In this decision, the House of Federation not only extended the terms of government and parliament but also its own. Even if this could be constitutionally permissible, it cannot be permissible under the principle of natural justice.

On the other hand, however, as the House of Federation is the final authority on constitutional interpretation, the TPLF had no option but to accept the decision of the House. But this did not happen. The decision of the House of Federation, along with the consequent actions of the federal government and the TPLF, have led to the state of constituticide.

As it stands, the Constitution has no normative and institutional force in Tigray and is in a very precarious condition throughout the country. It can neither arrest the ongoing war nor can it respond to the new political and military developments between Ethiopia and Tigray. While some of the constitutional values and principles could still be useful, a new political and constitutional settlement is required if the war in Northern Ethiopia is to stop.

However, a return to constitutional rule is possible (at least in principle) in the rest of the country if the federal government manages to reassert and reclaim its monopoly of violence. But this is difficult for two reasons. First, the constitutional crisis throughout the country is also linked with the state of constituticide in Tigray. Second, even if the federal government could eliminate or defeat the different rebel groups throughout the country, the restoration of the rule of law may require the production of consent. This ultimately requires addressing both the root causes of a rebel armed resistance to the Ethiopian state and governance and the sociocultural and political conditions that generate and structure such violent resistance. Precisely because of this state of constitutional affairs, the Constitution, whether we love it or hate it, cannot help us return Ethiopia to constitutional rule and constitutional politics. The restoration of peace in Ethiopia is highly tied to a new political and constitutional settlement.

B. Changing Ethiopia's State of Constitutional Affairs: Towards a Multistage Constitutional Reform Process

Because of the state of constituticide, there is no legal and constitutional solution to the war in Northern Ethiopia. Consequently, without a new political settlement between Tigray and Ethiopia, constitutional arguments and responses could be either simple impositions by a winning party on the battlefield or pointless in the sense of being unhelpful to address current political conditions. While it is difficult to anticipate the content of the political settlement that could arrest the war, it is plainly clear that such a settlement is a precondition for peace and the restoration of a new constitutional relationship between Ethiopia and Tigray. The Pretoria and Nairobi peace agreements between the TPLF and the federal government are simple testaments to the fact that the solution for our political condition lies in the domain of politics, not in the domain of constitutional law. The cessation of hostilities between the TPLF and the federal government and the consequent restoration of peace (at least for now) in Tigray is tied to the power of the political settlements they have had in Pretoria and Nairobi.

But the political settlement between Ethiopia and Tigray have also affected the political dynamics of the country, ushering in another war in the Amhara region between Amhara forces and the federal government. Like the war in Tigray, there is no legal or constitutional solution to the war in Amhara. As with the invisible war in Oromia. Especially since the start of the war in November 2020, the political (even social) conditions of the country have changed fundamentally. Only a political settlement can arrest such a situation. Such a move requires us to both depart from the constitutional discourse we have had for more than two decades and enter into the discourse of constitutional change.

If constitutional change is necessary, what processes should we follow? While there are numerous models of constitution making, we only have limited options due to the circumstances of the country.[8] The revolutionary-based model that helped to make a new constitution *ex nihilo* is not available and may not be available in the foreseeable future due to the particular social and political configurations of the country. We only have two possible options for constitutional change. The first is an internationally imposed constitution-making process because we failed to make constitutional changes by ourselves in due time, and the second is constitutional amendment and reform. The first option should be avoided in part because the country does not need any further conflict and war and in part because our constitutional choices would be greatly constrained by international actors.[9] The second option is the most suitable and immediately available option for constitutional change: constitutional amendment. The legal continuity inherent in constitutional amendment helps the country to govern itself according to the existing Constitution while undertaking important constitutional changes through Article 105, as I shall discuss below.

Constitutional amendment and reform offer a limited option for fundamental constitutional change.[10] But we can overcome some of the challenges that may arise from constitutional unamendability by combining the two pillars of constitutional change: legality and legitimacy.[11] Through legality, that is by following the existing rules of constitutional change, we can address any legal issues that may arise related to the proposed constitutional change. And through legitimacy, that is the social and political acceptability of the proposed change, we can reach out beyond momentary majorities and include the view of insular minorities. If the proposed constitutional change is both legal and legitimate, it could be helpful to constitute peace in the country. While the issue of legality is relatively straightforward, the issue of legitimacy is not. And I will start with legitimacy.

Legitimacy in our context requires the consideration of at least the following three main themes. The first is related to actors who should participate in the proposed constitutional change. We can identify two main actors: political elites and the public. Without elite consensus, it is extremely difficult to imagine a successful constitutional change. So, there should be a mechanism to include all competing elites and build consensus among them about the constitutional future of the country. The purpose of such elite consensus is to both create suitable conditions for constitution-making and constitutional practice and articulate and design constitutional institutions, principles, and values that can channel and sustain elite competition in the marketplace of ideas. But elite consensus is not enough. There should be public consensus about the constitutional future of the country. Several mechanisms can be devised to create and produce public consensus. And these mechanisms should aim at identifying, formulating, and articulating the ways in which the people could assert their rights and protect their interests against both the political elites and government. Beyond ceremonial spectacles of public participation in constitutional reform,[12] the point of this public consensus should be to generate constitutional ideas, norms, and institutions that could tame both political faction among the elites and prevent or at least minimize government dictatorship at all levels. To this end, like the elite consensus, the idea of such public consensus is to innovate constitutional institutions, principles, and values that prevent and push back against elite domination and government dictatorship at all levels. It is not necessary to put the nuts and bolts of this suggestion here. But we can adopt, for example, a dual theory of representation at both the regional and federal levels: one based on the democratic idea of one person, one vote; the other based on the notion of traditional representations rooted in the cultural traditions of the Nations, Nationalities, and Peoples of Ethiopia. The ultimate objective here is to build a mixed constitutional system that truly and genuinely represents the *powerful few* and *the many*.

The second is related to the translation of both elite and public consensuses to a single Constitutional Consensus Document containing the main constitutional principles, norms, and institutions that must be included in the proposed constitutional reform. This way we can judge if the proposed constitutional reform is based on the Constitutional Consensus Document. While this idea of a Constitutional Consensus Document is inspired by the South African constitution- making experience, it is different from the so-called "constitutional principles" included in their interim constitution in two major ways. Unlike the interim constitution of South Africa, this Constitutional Consensus Document will not be legally binding. It will only be politically binding. Additionally, unlike the interim constitution, which was an elite pact, the Constitutional Consensus Document will be a result of both elite and public consensuses. As a consequence, it could produce a much broader political legitimacy to the proposed constitutional reform.[13]

The third and final theme related to legitimacy is about insurance: how could actors ensure compliance with the Constitutional Consensus Document? Both elites and the public need some sort of insurance that what has been agreed will be implemented.[14] We can think of two major ways of ensuring compliance. The first is to include an institution, to be very specific, a constitutional court (whose members should have the support of both the competing elites and the public) in the Constitutional Consensus Document that certifies whether the proposed constitutional reform reflects this document. The second is to include referendum as another certification mechanism. Having a constitutional court and referendum as certification mechanisms could create more incentives for compliance with the Constitution Consensus Document and build legitimacy to the final constitution.

Once we address the issue of legitimacy through elite and public consensuses, adoption of a Constitutional Consensus Document, and putting in institutional mechanisms for its compliance, the next step is to activate the legal process for constitutional change. As we are undertaking a constitutional reform within the existing rules of constitutional change, an interim constitution or a transitional government is not required. To build more legitimacy to the process, however, it may be advisable to start this process after the next national election so that opposition political parties can freely compete for national, regional, and local elections.[15]

As legitimacy, legality in our context requires undertaking several initiatives, chief among them are the following. First, Parliament needs to establish a Constitutional Reform Commission which can produce a draft constitution based on the Constitutional Consensus Document and other relevant considerations. Second, the rules of constitutional amendment included in Article 105 of the 1995 Constitution need to be amended first following its procedure. Third, a substantive constitutional reform process should be initiated and undertaken following the new rules of constitutional amendment. Fourth, the draft constitution should be put for referendum. Fifth, the draft constitution should be sent to the constitutional court for certification, which heralds the adoption of the new constitution.

The processes I outline here are complex, difficult, time consuming, and, not least, expensive. But durable peace may require such processes. And I believe that these processes have the capacity to return Ethiopia to a new constitutional and political beginning. Yet these processes only can take us halfway to the constitution of peace. To travel the other half, we must confront and decide on some fundamental constitutional and political questions that have bedevilled the country and its people for so long, to which I now turn.

3. Issues of Substance: What Are Ethiopia's Fundamental Political Problems?

One of Ethiopia's fundamental political problems is the issue of "war and peace," which emanates from problems of transition from empire to republic. Such problems have brought about a crisis of statehood, a crisis of governance, and a crisis of citizenship.

First, the transformation from empire to republic involves the institutionalization of a permanent framework of government through a written constitution. In republics, the main subject of politics is the system of government, not the continuity or discontinuity of the state. As a matter of constitutional theory and constitutional law, a modern republican state proclaims its perpetual existence by establishing a permanent framework of government by providing the rules of constitutional change to adapt it with changing and new circumstances. But Ethiopia did not because it does not establish a permanent framework of government in its constitution. Consequently, both the state and government are the subject of ordinary politics, and much of the political problem and contestation arises from such kind of politics.

Second, the transformation of empire to a republic involves the change in the rules of succession. As there is no hereditary ruler in a republic, the only legitimate rule of succession is through democratic contestation. And democracy presupposes the equal dignity and worth of all citizens and their equal participation in public life. But Ethiopia has instituted ethnocracy, that is to say *rule by ethnos*, not democracy, that is *rule by the people*, as the rule of succession. Ethnocracy has brought about a crisis of governance at many levels.

Third, and finally, the transformation of empire to a republic heralds equal and universal citizenship to all the inhabitants of the republic. But this did not happen in Ethiopia. Because citizenship is conditional to prior membership in a political community called Nations, Nationalities, and Peoples. Such conditionality has created a crisis of citizenship and greatly affected horizontal solidarity among individuals and communities.

For the successful constitution of peace in Ethiopia, I argue, we must directly confront the crisis of statehood (that I characterized as the *commitment challenge*), the crisis of governance (the *governance challenge*), and the crisis of citizenship (the *identity challenge*). In the remainder of this chapter, I explain the commitment, governance, and identity challenges as they manifest under the 1995 Constitution and suggest how we may address them. But my primary aim in this discussion is to clearly show the constitutional foundation of these challenges and to encourage political elites and the public to think about them seriously.

A The Commitment Challenge: A Serious Federation or a Federation of Convenience?

The Ethiopian federation as it exists is a federation of convenience, which makes a serious federal political action and practice extremely volatile and indeterminate in time and place. One cannot establish a serious federal democratic republic with a federation of convenience. The question we should ask ourselves is whether we need a serious federation that can make a serious federal democratic republic or a federation of convenience that can make the viability of such a republic volatile. This is a choice that should be made by the people. But below I present why Ethiopian federalism is a federation of convenience.

Federalism is a covenant or pact among individuals and groups for mutual recognition and the promotion of unity among them within a polity.[16] Whether a federal system is adopted out of consideration for security, liberty, economic prosperity, freedom, and democracy—as in many Western federal democracies—or as an accommodation mechanism for ethnic, religious, and linguistic diversity—as in numerous post-Second World War examples such as Belgium, Nigeria, and India—federalism constitutionally commits itself to the continuity and indivisibility of the federal union.[17] Consider, for example, Nigeria and the United States: while the constitution of the former proclaims that Nigeria is "one indivisible and indissoluble sovereign nation," the constitution of the latter aspires to form "a more perfect union."[18] Federalism, then, is similar to a marriage vow, in that constituent units of the federation take each other "to have and to hold from this day forward ... until death do us part." Here the claim is not that the promise of indivisibility alone would bring a perpetual union.[19] Rather, as a matter of political theory and practice, democratic federations make a solemn commitment for their continuity during their founding moment. Whether such federations continue to exist is contingent upon several factors both within and beyond them. To use the marriage metaphor once again, we know that many marriages can end, and indeed do cease, in divorce, but the solemn vow to "take each other until death do us apart" is an essential part of the conclusion of marriage. It would be quite strange to both the spouses and the institution of marriage if the couple failed to take this solemn oath. Likewise, such a formal commitment to a federal union is also the case for the establishment of democratic federal systems. But Ethiopian federalism has no such commitment.

Ethiopian federalism was established based on the principle of the right to self-determination, including ethnic groups' right to secession. According to the Constitution, the various ethnic groups, using their right to self-determination, came together to form one political and economic community known as the Federal Democratic Republic of Ethiopia (FDRE) that would be based on the ideals of the rule of law, peace, and democracy.[20] The constitution also recognized that the ethnic groups have "an unconditional right to self-determination including the right to secession."[21] Unlike other polities, which built their federal systems on the notion of the *indivisibility of the state*, Ethiopia based its federalism on the notion of the *potential divisibility of the state* if it is ever needed.[22] Although the recognition of the right to secession is at odds with the very idea of federalism as a covenant towards "a more perfect union," as in the United States, Germany, Nigeria, and India, Ethiopia opted to construct its federal system based on this normative commitment.[23] From the perspective of the ethnic groups, then, Ethiopian federalism is a federation of convenience from which they can secede or break away at any time, without even providing any justification or rationale for doing so. As a matter of constitutional law, Ethiopian federalism has no solemn commitment to the continuity and territorial integrity of the Ethiopian state. To this extent, it is a federation of convenience in which the ethnic groups hold the sovereign power to make or unmake the Ethiopian state at any time, based on their own terms.

The reason as to why Ethiopia chose to build this federation based on convenience for ethnic groups has a long and complicated political and historical context that dates from the student movement of the 1960s and 1970s, which was related to the so-called "question of nationalities."[24] The question of nationalities concerned the nature of the Ethiopian state and the pre-existing ethnic relations in the country. A radical student movement group advanced the idea that Ethiopia was a "prison house of nationalities" like Tsarist Russia and that it marginalized many of its ethnic groups in its socioeconomic, cultural, and political makeup. These students claimed that Ethiopia only represented the culture, religion, and psychological makeup of the "Amhara-Tigre" (Ethiopia's two northern ethnic groups) while marginalizing other ethnolinguistic groups, of which there are more than eighty, in the national imagination. The solution to the question of nationalities, they proposed, was the recognition of the right to self-determination, including the concept that each nationality or ethnic group would have the right to secession.

The removal of the military regime that ruled Ethiopia from 1974–1991 by ethnonational armed groups such as the Eritrean People's Liberation Front (EPLF) and the TPLF, who shared similar views with the radical student movement in 1991, made possible the restructuring of the Ethiopian state based on the principle of the right to self-determination, including the right to secession.[25] In 1993, Eritrea voted on independence from Ethiopia and became an independent state. After two years of a highly controlled constitution-making process, the EPRDF—a coalition of four ethnic-based parties dominated by the TPLF that ruled Ethiopia from 1991–2018—restructured the Ethiopian state along the lines of ethnic federalism, guaranteeing each ethnic group the right to secession in a brand-new constitution.[26] As Alexander Hamilton noted in the *Federalist No. 1*, the Ethiopian choice for ethnic federalism was more a result of "accident and force" rather than the outcome of the people's "reflection and choice," as in the case of the constitution of socialist Ethiopia after the collapse of the monarchy in 1974 through revolution.[27]

Beyond this contested origin, the issue with this federation of convenience is not only that it is ethnic, but also that it has no constitutional commitment to the continuity of the Ethiopian state. Indeed, there are many studies that document the promises and pitfalls of ethnic federalism, and one prominent Ethiopian federalism scholar explains what he considers the "original sin of Ethiopian federalism."[28] However, the absence of a constitutional commitment to the federal union and its divisibility is problematic, whether the federal system is organized along ethnic or non-ethnic lines. The constitutional right of an ethnic group or a territorial unit to secession without any condition goes counter to the spirit of federalism, as it can make that federalism one of convenience, which could make a serious federal political action and practice extremely volatile and indeterminate in time and place.

There are at least two major problems associated with the constitutional recognition of secession in Ethiopian federalism. The first is that the constitutional design could create its own incentive structures for its enforcement and, in the case of the right to secession, this could challenge the stability and continuity of the federal constitutional order. This creates a collective action problem, which is the issue federalism primarily aims to address in the first place.[29] Consider, for example, that one of the ethnic groups, called X, wants to secede from Ethiopia. X thinks that it is in its best interest to form its own sovereign state as it has the population numbers, the economic resources, and the cultural attributes to be a viable and perhaps prosperous state. Another ethnic group, called Y, considers X's move towards secession very detrimental to its socio economic, cultural, and political well-being. However, a third ethnic group, Z, thinks that the secession of X is beneficial. Assume that the secession of X may also have some advantages for some ethnic groups and disadvantages for others (for example, the secession of Eritrea positioned the TPLF as the dominant actor in Ethiopian politics for three decades), regardless of how we define (dis)advantages. Within this scenario, X, following the constitutional procedure of Article 39 (4) (a), approves its demand for secession by a two-thirds majority in its legislative council and asks the federal government to organize a referendum as required by Article 39 (4) (b). If the federal government is loyal to the constitution, it has no alternative other than to organize a referendum that eventually will lead to the secession of X. The problem here is not primarily that X secedes, but that the federal government has no constitutional mechanism for resolving the disagreements between the other ethnic groups who support or oppose the secession.

Here the *Quebec Secession Reference* judgment is instructive in the exercise of the right to secession as an empirical matter.[30] As the Supreme Court of Canada noted in this judgment, while Quebec does not have a unilateral right of secession under the Canadian constitution or international law, the exercise of such a right imposes a "constitutional duty to negotiate" between Quebec, the federal government, and the provinces, considering the rights and interests of "all Canadians both within and outside of Quebec, and specifically the rights of minorities."[31] But the Ethiopian constitution does not even impose such a "constitutional duty to negotiate" in the exercise of the right to secession, as this right belongs to each ethnic group. Thus, the fact that secession is constitutionalized, which is predominantly an extra-constitutional, political, and international relations issue,[32] limits the capability of the federal government and the regional states to solve a fundamental collective action problem: an issue that no ethnic group or tier of government can resolve individually within the boundaries of constitutional law or politics.[33]

Second, if the constitutional design cannot be implemented in practice, this could raise serious issues about the enforceability of the constitution as a binding legal document that ultimately undermines the legitimacy of the constitution and the political order within which it operates.[34] In fact, there are some who argue that Article 39 was included as a token assurance for the various ethnonational forces during the making of the constitution,[35] and many others show how difficult it is to enforce this provision in part due to its complicated procedure, as well as the authoritarian political culture of the country.[36] The truth of the matter is that Article 39 is a binding law today, and if Ethiopia will have a democratic government that respects the constitution, some ethnic groups and political forces could resort to the peaceful option of using Article 39 for separation rather than raising arms. In this regard, for instance, the Oromo Liberation Front (OLF) and the Ogaden National Liberation Front (ONLF) fought against the EPRDF-led Ethiopian government for more than two decades for the liberation of their respective ethnic groups. With the coming to power of Abiy Ahmed in 2018 and the demise of the EPRDF, however, both the OLF and the ONLF have become opposition political parties who struggle for their cause through the ballot box. If they can manage to win the necessary votes and assume government power, it will be completely constitutional for them to initiate the secession process of Article 39 (4). If all the procedures of this article are met, the federal government has no option other than effectuating the secession process. Doing otherwise would be utterly unconstitutional and that may have a great potential to ignite conflict, chaos, or even civil war in the country. Viewed through these perspectives, the enforcement or nonenforcement of the constitutional right to secession will have an adverse impact on the constitutional order and the practice of federal democracy: doomed whether you do or do not.

The question both political elites and the public should think about during constitutional discussions and debates is this: whether we need a serious federation where we stay together in good or bad times as other federations do or a federation of convenience where serious federal political action and practice are extremely volatile and indeterminate in time and place, as we have seen since 2018. For any meaningful constitutional and political beginning, Ethiopians must confront their commitment issue with Ethiopia. This, I think, is a first-order question for the constitutional project we embark on to constitute peace in the country.

B. The Governance Challenge: Democracy or Ethnocracy?

Article 1 of the Ethiopian constitution provides that it has established a "Federal and Democratic State structure" and proclaims that Ethiopia shall be known as "The Federal Democratic Republic of Ethiopia." But a closer inspection of the *democratic nature* of the state shows otherwise. What the constitution constitutes is not a democracy but an ethnocracy. Democracy, *rule by demos*, is a system of government founded on the notion of equality of individuals, and this notion of equality permeates its institutional architecture. Unlike democracy, ethnocracy (*rule by ethnos*) rests not on the idea of equality of individuals but on their different treatment. It is a system of governance based on differentiation. Below I show how the governance system is ethnocratic and how this, in turn, has brought about several governance challenges from a democratic perspective.

According to Oren Yiftachel, who first developed the concept, ethnocracy means government by a particular ethnic group(s), *rule by ethnos*, in contrast with government by the people in general, *rule by demos*.[37] In ethnocratic states, the dominant ethnic group(s) "appropriates the state apparatus and attempts to structure the political system, public institutions, and state culture to further its control over the state and its territory."[38] The Ethiopian constitution largely sets out an ethnocratic system both at the national and subnational levels. This means that Ethiopian federalism does not genuinely and meaningfully address the demands of all ethnic groups for equal concern and treatment in the country. While it claims to address the "question of nationalities," it only considers the demands of some ethnic groups in some places, not those of all ethnic groups in all places.[39] Ethiopian federalism has created an ethnocratic system, rather than a democratic one.

The ethnocratic feature of the Ethiopian federation is more apparent at the subnational levels than at the national one in part due to constitutional nonenforcement (as revolutionary democracy was the "empirical constitution" of the country from 1995–2018) and in part due to a complicated constitutional architecture that hides such a feature. A good place to start decoding the ethnocratic feature of the federation at the national level is to investigate the institutional setup and composition of the federal government. The House of Peoples' Representatives (HPR) is the highest authority of the federal government and is responsible to the people as a whole.[40] The HPR is the sole legislative body of the federal government that makes laws on the twenty-one broad items assigned to the federal government. The HPR passes decisions by a majority vote.[41] As the Amhara and Oromo ethnic groups account for more than 64 percent of the Ethiopian population, according to the last 2007 national census, these two ethnic groups constitute more than half of the parliamentary seats, making all other ethnic groups perpetual minorities. Although members of the HPR, including Amhara and Oromo representatives, are governed by "the Constitution, the will of the people, and their conscience," given human nature they may also act in the interest of their own ethnic group, which may jeopardize the interests of the others.[42] One may also argue that members of the HPR are representatives of districts, not the entire ethnic group as such. But these districts are still ethnic districts located in different regional states structured along ethnic lines. Hence, the design of the HPR can make the Amhara and Oromo ethnic groups the main legislators of the federation.

Similarly, the House of Federation (HoF)—the upper house of parliament, tasked with constitutional interpretation—is also dominated by Amhara and Oromo representatives, as population number is a key consideration in its composition.[43] Like in the HPR, decisions of the HoF are passed through a majority vote.[44] Here members of the HoF, unlike the HPR, are guardians of ethnic interests and are expected to place the interest of their respective ethnic groups at the forefront of the decisions of the HoF. As in the legislative process, the Amhara and Oromo ethnic groups can dominate the constitutional interpretation process. For example, even if the HPR can pass legislation in the interest of the Ethiopian people as a whole, the HoF can still strike down such legislation if it thinks that it does not advance the interests of the two ethnic groups enough. In addition, if the HPR passes legislation that largely benefits the two big ethnic groups at the expense of the others, the HoF may find it constitutionally permissible. The crux of the argument here is that such an institutional arrangement of the law making and constitutional- interpretation bodies at the national level protects, or appears to safeguard, the interests of larger ethnic groups rather than smaller ones. Because of this, Article 8 of the constitution, which bestows sovereignty on all the ethnic groups, did not receive any meaningful expression in the architecture of the legislative and constitutional interpretation institutions. Against the central ethos of federalism, such an institutional arrangement can channel, and indeed has conveyed, as we shall see below, ethnic majority rule to both law making and constitutional interpretation in the federation.

Additionally, the parliamentary system can further advance and entrench ethnocracy. The essential feature of a parliamentary system is that the executive branch of government derives its power from and is accountable to the parliament.[45] The tenure of the prime minister and the cabinet depends upon the confidence of the parliament, as also reflected in the Ethiopian constitution.[46] In such systems, there is less of a separation of powers between the legislative and executive branches of government. The parliament and the political party system play a huge role in the operation of parliamentary governments.[47] Ultimately, the institutional design of parliament and the nature of the political party system drive the executive branch. As the Ethiopian Parliament is dominated by the Amhara and Oromo ethnic groups and the political party system operates within the orbit of ethnicity, these two ethnic groups can constitute and run the executive branch of government as they wish: they can hire or dismiss any government for the federation. Like parliament, the executive administration can be an apparatus of ethnocracy.

If this is what the constitution provides, one might ask why the Amhara and Oromo ethnic groups did not then play a major role at the national level for almost a quarter of a century, i.e., from 1995–2018. The answer is simple. The constitution was not practiced as it was designed.[48] This is primarily because, with a minority democratic base, the full implementation of the constitution would have displaced the TPLF at the national level immediately after the constitution came into force in 1995. The path the TPLF/EPRDF government chose was what the Kenyan legal scholar Okoth-Ogendo called "constitutions without constitutionalism."[49] In a system of constitutions without constitutionalism, the governing elite is committed to the idea of the constitution as a source of legitimacy for the state and its governance, but it also equally rejects the practice of constitutionalism, or the enforcement of constitutional rules and values in reality. The TPLF/EPRDF government, rather than considering the constitution as something to be implemented as a law, reduced it to a mere tool of legitimation and justification for its politics.[50]

The demise of the TPLF/EPRDF has shown how the constitution positions the two largest ethnic groups, Amhara and Oromo, as superpowers in the country, and it may be instructive as to what may come next. Although the TPLF/EPRDF regime stood on the tensions, historical disagreements, and rivalries between Amhara and Oromo political elites,[51] the ethnic constitutional and political party system has also made their cooperation possible. This is because, first, the alliance of these two ethnic groups, both at the level of political elites within the EPRDF and at the grassroots level in the popular protest movements, helped to displace the TPLF from its dominant position within the EPRDF. It is largely the alliance of these two ethnic groups, dubbed "Oro-Amhara," that brought Abiy Ahmed of the Oromo Democratic People's Organization (OPDO) to the premiership in April 2018. Second, it is the Oromo- and Amhara-dominated HoF that made the September 2020 Tigray regional election unconstitutional and void. Third and finally, it was predominantly the Oromo- and Amhara-led federal government that removed the TPLF from its home region of Tigray under a "rule of law operation," although later it regained control.[52] While we have to wait and see how the relationship between Oromo and Amhara political elites unfold in the future, the constitution gives them an enormous amount of power and authority at the national level that emanates from their huge population and vast territory, both of which are a creation of the constitution itself.

Intra-regional ethnic diversity in Ethiopia

Region	Ethnic groups						
Amhara	Amhara (91%), Agew (5%), Oromo (3%), Other (2%)						
Oromia	Oromo (87%), Amhara (7%), Gurage (1%), Somali (1%), Other (4%)						
Tigray	Tigrawi (96.55%), Kunama (0.7%), Irob/Saho (0.71%), Other (2.4%)						
SNNPR	Surma (0.17%)	Zeyise (0.10)	Gidecho 0.03%)	Arbore (0.04%)	Geleb	Kore (1.01%)	Gedeo (4.92%)
	Gurage (7.52%)	Hamer (0.31%)	Gewada (0.43%)	Basketo (0.52%)	Burji (0.37%)	Alba (1.35%)	Bena (0.17%)
	Kembata (3.81%)	Shinasha (0.01%)	Dawro (3%)	Bumi	Dime	Tembaro (0.64%)	Shekicho (0.44%)
	Kafficho (5.43%)	Wolaita (10.71%)	Gacho	Nao (0.05%)	Tsemay (0.13%)	Hadyia (8.02%)	Alba (1.35%)
	Qebena (0.29%)	Gamo (6.96%)	Derashe (0.19%)	Bench (2.33%)	Yem (0.5%)	Konta (0.54%)	Amhara (2.79%)
	Konso (1.46%)	Sidama (19%)	Me'enite (1%)	Mareko (0.38%)	Oida (0.05%)	Ari (1.89%)	
	Gofa (2.39%)	Oromo (1.57%)	Silte (5%)	Desenech (0.32%)	Surma (0.11%)		
Afar	Afar (90.3%), Amhara (5.22%), Argoba (1.5%), Other (2.98%)						
Gambella	Anyawaa (21.17%), Nuer (46.65%), Mejenger (4%), Amhara (8.42%), Oromo (4.33%), Other (18%)						
Benishangul-Gumuz	Berta (25.90%), Gumuz (21.11%), Shinasha (7.5%), Mao (2%), Koma (1%), Agew (5%), Amhara (21.25%), Oromo (13.32%), Other (2.92%)						
Harari	Harari (8.65%), Oromo (56%), Amhara (22%), Somali (3.87%), Gurage (4%), Other (2.92%)						

Source: FDRE Population Census Commission (2008).[53] *NB: This is the most recent official data available, as Ethiopia has not conducted a national census since 2008.*

Ethnocracy is more apparent and even practiced at the subnational levels. Although Ethiopia has more than eighty ethnolinguistic groups, they were originally supposed to live within nine regional states. This means that not every ethnic group has received its own regional state. Indeed, many of the ethnic groups (around fifty-six of them) were lumped together under the Southern Nations, Nationalities and Peoples Region (SNNPR), and other regional states also host many ethnic groups together.

The recent secession of the Sidama and the Southwest Ethiopian People's Regional State from the SNNPR increased the number of member states to eleven. In particular, seven of the regional states (Tigray, Afar, Amhara, Oromia, Somalia, Harari, and Sidama) out of eleven are named after a major ethnic group. The notable exception in this regard is the State of Harari, named after the minority Harari ethnic group, which constitutes one-seventh of the population of the Harari state. The constitutions of these regional states have created a socioeconomic, cultural, and political order for the ethnic group after which they are named, despite the presence of different ethnic groups in all these states, as the above table shows. In practice, in these states, the dominant ethnic group considers their respective states as their own "ethnic homeland" that primarily belongs to them and them alone. As the plethora of scholarship on this issue attests, minority ethnic groups in different regional states have been rendered "second-class citizens at best and unwelcome aliens at worst" and have been subjected to an ethnicized "local tyranny."[54] These regional ethnic minorities have become "foreigners" in their own country with almost no place in the socio economic, cultural, and political order of the states in which they reside: from exclusions and discriminations in political life and civil society, to severe restrictions in access to economic opportunities and social services, in addition to their forceful expulsion and the destruction of their properties, as well as their massacre and ethnic cleansing.[55] Here, almost every ethnic group is a victim if they live in a different region or do not have a region of their own, which is predominantly the case in the country.

The four remaining regional states that are not named after a single ethnic group are also ethnocratic. For example, the Benishangul-Gumuz regional state constitution identifies five ethnic groups as sole owners of the regional state, although there are many ethnic groups in large numbers, as can be seen from the above table, who live there.[56] Ethnic groups other than "the sole owners of the region" have been at the periphery in the socioeconomic and political life of the region at best and the subject of ethnic cleansing, displacement, and massacre at worst.[57] While the Southwestern Ethiopian People's Region and the SNNPR are multi-ethnic at the regional level, the various zones that constitute the regions each predominantly belong to one ethnic group, consequently excluding other ethnic groups from political life and civil society, as in other regional states.[58]

Therefore, the Ethiopian federation has established an ethnocratic system that serves or claims to serve the interests of some ethnic groups at both the national and subnational levels. As noted at the beginning, while ethnic federalism claims to address the "question of nationalities," it simply considers the demands of a few ethnic groups in some areas, not those of all ethnic groups in every place. Additionally, ethnic identity and geography determine what sorts of rights and duties one has as a citizen. For example, an Amhara, Oromo, or Somali can be a *citizen* in his/her own regional state, but a *subject* in a different one. The decentralized ethnocracy has created *ethnic groups that could be citizens* and *ethnic groups that could be subjects*, somehow akin to what Mahmood Mamdani called the "decentralized despotism" characterising the legacy of colonialism in much of Africa.[59]

The question both political elites and the public should think about during constitutional discussions and debates is this: whether we need a system of democracy where every individual is treated and valued equally or a system of ethnocracy where ethnicity and geography determine the equal concern and treatment of individuals. Like the commitment challenge, Ethiopians must confront their governance challenge directly and decisively. This is the second first-order question for the constitutional project we must embark on to constitute peace in the country.

C. The Identity Challenge: We the Nations, Nationalities, Peoples or We the Nations, Nationalities, Peoples, and Ethiopians?

Compared with the commitment and governance challenges, the identity challenge is relatively easy to solve. This is simply because the primary solution for questions of identity is recognition. It is a well-known fact that many can identify themselves with the constitutional notion of Nations, Nationalities, and Peoples. And these groups reject the notion of *We the People* that projects singular peoplehood. But it is also a well-known fact that many do not and, in some instances, cannot, as I explain below, identify themselves with the constitutional notion of Nations, Nationalities, and Peoples. These groups reject the constitutional notion of Nations, Nationalities, and Peoples that broadcast plural peoplehood. Here we have an impasse, an impasse primarily created by a lack of constitutional imagination, not only in the Ethiopian context but also more generally.

The idea of *We the People* is a global model for thinking about the notion of people in national constitutions. The Ethiopian constitution has introduced a new model, *We the Nations, Nationalities, and Peoples*, for thinking about peoplehood in national constitutions. We can reconcile the competing views of peoplehood by recognizing both, not choosing one over the other.[60] And we can do so by simply proclaiming and defining ourselves as "We the Nations, Nationalities, Peoples, and Ethiopians" in the preamble of the new constitution. In this regard, we can draw some lessons from countries such as Switzerland, where they define themselves in the preamble of their constitution as "the Swiss people and cantons," reflecting from their history and particular national circumstances. Regarding the identity challenge, let a thousand flowers bloom at the constitutional and extra-constitutional levels. But to let a thousand flowers bloom, we need to understand the identity challenge engineered by the notion of *We the Nations, Nationalities, and Peoples*. And that the new articulation of identity must animate and permeate the structural and normative frameworks of the new constitutional settlement from federalism to constitutional rights, from constitutional values to electoral systems.

The Ethiopian constitution has created two imagined political communities. The first includes the Nations, Nationalities and Peoples (NNPs), a collective name for ethnic groups, while the second is the Federal Democratic Republic of Ethiopia (FDRE). The constituent power that inaugurated the constitution did not rely on some reading of sovereignty or political authority which traditionally rests on the idea of the people in the singular.[61] Rather, it imagined a political community and claimed its constituent power as a derivative of that power through the right to self-determination.

The constituent power in the constitution derives its authority from the sovereign powers of the NNPs. It is important to reiterate the preamble of the constitution here: "We, the Nations, Nationalities and Peoples of Ethiopia ... Have therefore adopted ... this Constitution through representatives we have duly elected for this purpose as an instrument that binds us in a mutual commitment to fulfill the objectives and the principles set forth above." Questions like who the NNPs are, how they exist, and how they empower themselves to establish a constitution for Ethiopia necessarily require an Andersonian imagination.[62] Of course, what the NNPs represent are the events of the pre-constitutional period and evidence is not required to prove this. Nonetheless, the way the NNPs exist and ought to do so mandate an imagination without which the legitimacy of the constituent power would be questionable. Hence, the innovation of a prior imagined political community (the transformation of ethnic groups to political communities— NNPs) becomes necessary to conceive the constituted political community (FDRE). In this course, the right to self-determination offered the necessary foundational basis and frame of reference for the imagination.[63]

NNPs are imagined political communities because they are regarded as territorially limited, as sovereign, and as communities. They are territorially limited because NNPs are assumed to have a geographical base at either the regional state, zone (*liyu* zone), district (*liyu woreda*) or local (*liyu kebele*) levels.[64] They are perceived as sovereign states as they are bestowed with the right to self-determination up to secession.[65] They are viewed as communities because they are assumed, among other things, to share a common culture, language, identity, and psychological makeup.[66] As a matter of principle, the representatives of these NNPs can have the legitimate political authority and power to make a constitution for NNPs. Using their sovereign power, NNPs constituted the *nation states* of Tigray, Afar, Amhara, Oromia, Somalia, and Harari, and the *multination* state, which includes the Southern Nations, Nationalities, and Peoples, Benishangul/Gumuz and Gambella within the contours of another imagined political community called the FDRE.[67]

The other imagined political community is the FDRE. The FDRE is conceived as territorially limited as, for instance, it excludes Eritrea, unlike the pre-1991 era, and expressed through the territorial limits of its member states. In this regard, the constitution provides that: "...The territorial jurisdiction of Ethiopia shall comprise the territory of the members of the Federation and its boundaries shall be as determined by international agreements."[68] It is also envisaged as a sovereign state. Consider how the supremacy clause of the constitution articulated this sovereignty: "All sovereign power resides in the Nations, Nationalities and Peoples of Ethiopia; This Constitution is an expression of their sovereignty; [and] [t]heir sovereignty shall be expressed through their representatives elected in accordance with this Constitution and through their direct democratic participation."[69]

As is self-evident, its sovereign imagination is framed through NNPs. Furthermore, the FDRE is imagined as a community, to be precise, as a community of NNPs. The preamble of the constitution clearly spells out how the imagined community is a community of NNPs. For instance, the preamble reads,

> *Further convinced that by continuing to live with our rich and proud cultural legacies in territories we [NNPs] have long inhabited, have, through continuous interaction on various levels and forms of life, built up common interests and have also contributed to the emergence of a common outlook.... Fully cognizant that our common destiny can best be served by rectifying historically unjust relationships and by further promoting our shared interests.... Convinced that to live as one economic community is necessary in order to create sustainable and mutually supportive conditions for ensuring respect for our [NNPs] rights and freedoms and for the collective promotion of our interests.*

The phrase the "collective promotion of our interests" here in the preamble refers to the collective interests of NNPs, not those of individuals. Therefore, the FDRE is imagined as a political community in its territorial, sovereign, and community elements in the size, shape, and texture of NNPs.

Precisely because of the innovation of two imagined political communities in a single constitutional space, the constitution, as Fasil Nahum rightly observes, is a "constitution of a Nation of Nations."[70] To use Nahum's words, "his is not the constitution of the Ethiopian citizens simply lumped together as a people. [Instead], [t]he Ethiopian citizens are first categorized in their different ethnolinguistic groupings and then these groups come together as authors of, and beneficiaries from, the Constitution."[71] The result is that individual membership in the FDRE requires prior membership to NNPs. In other words, an individual's membership in the FDRE is no longer automatic but conditional. If we take the constitution seriously, one has to be, for instance, a Somali, Oromo, or Amhara first to be a member of the political community we call Ethiopia. Without a membership to or identification with one of the NNPs, it is impossible to be Ethiopian as a matter of constitutional design. Viewed through the prism of citizenship, the constitutional dispensation is more confederal than federal.[72] Like citizenship in a confederation, Ethiopian citizenship is conditional upon membership to one of the NNPs that established the federation. Even if Article 6 of the Constitution says, "any person of either sex shall be an Ethiopian national where both or either parent is Ethiopian," it does not say anything about how Ethiopian nationality is originally gained in the first place, i.e., how parents become Ethiopian nationals. As discussed above, being Ethiopian is essentially attached to and contingent upon being a member of one of the NNPs.

However, as a matter of practice, not everyone neatly belongs to one of the NNPs, nor are those who do not belong to or do not want to identify themselves with one of the NNPs foreign nationals. This simply means that there is a mismatch between constitutional design and Ethiopian reality as related to citizenship.

As it stands now, the constitutional design of two imagined political communities seems to gain even more traction as multiple ethnic nationalisms emerge.[73] As these ethnic nationalisms build their political activities and mobilizations within the constitutional prism of two imagined political communities, individuals are practically expected or coerced to identify themselves with one of the NNPs to belong to the FDRE. These individuals include those who do not want to identify with NNPs as part of their personal freedom of choice and those of mixed ethnic origin, who cover a larger segment of the Ethiopian population. Thus, due to the engineering of two imagined political communities in the federal constitutional dispensation, membership of one imagined political community is a condition that is a precedent for the other. The implication of confederal citizenship is not only that ethnicity becomes a primary site of citizenship for accessing the rights and opportunities available within the FDRE on an equal basis (which has created a favourable environment for multiple and competing ethnic nationalisms that have structured conflict throughout the country)[74] but also that federal democracy requires both the democratization of the primary political community—that is the NNPs—and of the second one—that is the FDRE. But this project of federal democracy is further complicated by the constitution's system of governance (ethnocracy) as discussed in the previous section.

The identity challenge also challenges the identity of the Ethiopian state: is it a federation, or is it a confederation? The state must choose its identity: it cannot be both a federation and confederation at the same time. But its citizens can have multiple identities. They can be Ethiopians without any conditionality. They can be Ethiopians and a member of one of the NNPs. And the idea of "We the Nations, Nationalities, Peoples, and Ethiopians" can solve the identity challenge for both citizens and the state.

Conclusion

As the Argentinian political philosopher and constitutional thinker Juan Bautista Alberdi notes, a good constitution should "identify and address the *main dramas* of its time, and at the same time provide *proper legal means* for tackling those problems."[75] The constitution of peace this chapter advances urges us to identify and address the main dramas of our time and directly tackle the fundamental political problems of Ethiopia through constitutional reform. Regardless of our views on the Ethiopian Constitution, it could not return the country to peaceful constitutional politics because it does not deal with the dramas of our time and does not offer a legal and constitutional solution to the fundamental problems confronting the country. The question is not whether constitutional change is necessary but when. It is advisable to initiate a constitutional reform process when this is possible, which is as soon as possible. If a constitutional reform process is pursued, such a process should be both legal and legitimate and must confront the *commitment*, *governance*, and *identity challenges* as outlined in this chapter. The constitution of peace in Ethiopia largely depends on the process by which it comes into being and the extent to which it directly confronts the fundamental political problems of the country, namely the crisis of statehood, the crisis of governance, and the crisis of citizenship, problems mainly associated with the transition from empire to republic.

Notes

1 *Lecturer in Law, Faculty of Laws, University College London and Visiting Professor, Department of Legal Studies, Central European University. Email: b.gebeye@ucl.ac.uk.

See Christopher Kutz, *On War and Democracy* (Princeton University Press, 2016).

2 See Gedion T Hessebon, "The Precarious Future of the Ethiopian Constitution" (2013). Journal of African Law 57, p. 215.

3 See Adem Kassie Abebe, "From the 'TPLF Constitution' to the 'Constitution of the People of Ethiopia': Constitutionalism and Proposals for Constitutional Reform." In: Constitutionalism and Democratic Governance in Africa: Contemporary Perspectives from Sub-Saharan Africa (PULP 2013). Morris Kiwinda Mbondenyi and Tom Ojienda, eds. .

4 See Jean-Nicolas Bach, "Abyotawi Democracy: Neither Revolutionary nor Democratic, a Critical Review of EPRDF's Conception of Revolutionary Democracy in Post-1991 Ethiopia" (2011). Journal of Eastern African Studies 5, p. 641.

5 See the Ethiopian Constitution, Article 93 (4) (c).

6 See the Ethiopian Constitution, Article 102.

7 About the essential elements of the rule of law see Tom Bingham, *The Rule of Law* (Penguin Books Limited 2011).

8 See Michel Rosenfeld, *The Identity of the Constitutional Subject: Selfhood, Citizenship, Culture, and Community* (1st edition, Routledge 2009), Chapter 6.

9 And not least because no internationally imposed constitution has worked well except for Germany and Japan following the end of the Second World War. The post-Cold War internationally imposed constitutions have been a disappointment, and the situation may not be any different for Ethiopia.

10 See Richard Albert, *Constitutional Amendments: Making, Breaking, and Changing Constitutions* (Oxford University Press 2019); Yaniv Roznai, *Unconstitutional Constitutional Amendments: The Limits of Amendment Powers* (Oxford University Press 2017).

11 See Richard H. Fallon, "Legitimacy and the Constitution" (2005). *Harvard Law Review* 118, p. 1787; Randy E. Barnett, "Constitutional Legitimacy" (2003. Columbia Law Review 103, pp. 111–48.

12 See Alexander Hudson, *The Veil of Participation: Citizens and Political Parties in Constitution-Making Processes* (Cambridge University Press 2021).

13 See Ran Hirschl, *Towards Juristocracy: The Origins and Consequences of the New Constitutionalism* (Harvard University Press 2007). Hirschl considers the South African constitution-making experience as one of hegemonic preservation.

14 See also Rosalind Dixon and Tom Ginsburg, "The Forms and Limits of Constitutions as Political Insurance" (2017). International Journal of Constitutional Law 15, p. 988.

15 In the meantime, we can work on the legitimacy aspect of the constitutional reform process: create elite and public consensus and produce a Constitutional Consensus Document.

16 Daniel J. Elazar, *Exploring Federalism* (1987, University of Alabama Press), p. 5.

17 Michael Burgess, *In Search of the Federal Spirit: New Comparative Empirical and Theoretical Perspectives* (2012, Oxford University Press).

18 See, for example, Herbert J. Storing and Murray Dry, "The Constitutional Convention: Toward a More Perfect Union." In: American Political Thought. J. Frisch Morton and G. Stevens Richard, eds., (2011, 3rd ed., Routledge).

19 See Sanford Levinson, "Perpetual Union, Free Love, and Secession: On the Limits to the Consent of the Governed" (2003). Tulsa Law Review 39, p. 457.

20 See the Constitution of Ethiopia 1995, Preamble and Article 1.

21 Id, Article 39.

22 See also John M. Cohen, "Ethnic Federalism in Ethiopia" (1995). *Northeast African Studies* 2, p. 157.

23 Alemante G. Selassie, "Ethnic Identity and Constitutional Design for Africa." Stanford Journal of International Law 29, pp. 47–49; Cass R. Sunstein, "Constitutionalism and Secession" (1991). The University of Chicago Law Review 58, p. 633.

24 Bahru Zewde, *The Quest for Socialist Utopia: The Ethiopian Student Movement, c. 1960-1974* (2014, James Currey), pp. 187–228; Merera Gudina, "Contradictory Interpretations of Ethiopian History: The Need for a New Consensus." I n: *Ethnic Federalism: The Ethiopian Experience in Comparative Perspective. David Turton, ed.* (2006, James Currey).

25 E. Centime Zeleke, *Ethiopia in Theory: Revolution and Knowledge Production, 1964–2016* (2019, Brill), pp. 143–45.

26 See Gedion T. Hessebon, "The Precarious Future of the Ethiopian Constitution" (2013). *Journal of African Law* 57, p. 215; Minasse Haile, "The New Ethiopian Constitution: Its Impact upon Unity, Human Rights and Development Lead Article" (1996). Suffolk Transnational Law Review 20, p. 1.

27 See Andargachew Tiruneh, *The Ethiopian Revolution 1974–1987: A Transformation from an Aristocratic to a Totalitarian Autocracy* (1993, Cambridge University Press).

28 Yonatan Tesfaye Fessha, "The Original Sin of Ethiopian Federalism" (2017). *Ethnopolitics* 16, p. 232.

29 See Robert D. Cooter and Neil S. Siegel, "Collective Action Federalism: A General Theory of Article I, Section 8." *Stanford Law Review* 63, p. 72.

30 See Peter Leslie, "Canada: The Supreme Court Sets Rules for the Secession of Quebec" (1999). *Publius Journal of Federalism* 29, p. 135.

31 *Reference Re Secession of Quebec*, [1998] 2 S.C.R. 217, para 92.

32 Nicolás Brando and Sergi Morales-Gálvez, "The Right to Secession: Remedial or Primary?" (2019). 18 *Ethnopolitics* 18, p. 107.

33 Aziz Huq, "Does the Logic of Collective Action Explain Federalism Doctrine?" (2013). *Sandford Law Review* 66, p. 1203.

34 Stephen Gardbaum, "The Place of Constitutional Law in the Legal System." In: *The Oxford Handbook of Comparative Constitutional Law, Michel Rosenfeld and András Sajó, eds.* (2012, Oxford University Press).

35 Alem Habtu, "Multiethnic Federalism in Ethiopia: A Study of the Secession Clause in the Constitution" (2005). *Publius* 35, pp. 326–327.

36 Daniel Abebe, "The Ethiopian Constitution and Ethnic Federalism." In: From Parchment to Practice. Tom Ginsburg and Aziz Z. Huq, eds. (2020, Cambridge University Press), p. 289.

37 Oren Yiftachel, *Ethnocracy: Land and Identity Politics in Israel/Palestine* (2006, University of Pennsylvania Press).

38 Ibid; Oren Yiftachel, "Ethnocracy and Its Discontents: Minorities, Protests, and the Israeli Polity" (2000). Critical Inquiry 26, p. 731.

39 See Yonatan Tesfaye Fessha, "The Original Sin of Ethiopian Federalism" (2017). *Ethnopolitics* 16, p. 232.

40 Ethiopian Constitution, Article 50 (3).

41 Id, Article 59.

42 Id, Article 54 (4).

43 Id, Article 61 (2).

44 Id, Article 64 (1).

45 Anthony W. Bradley and Cesare Pinelli, "Parliamentarism." In: *The Oxford Handbook of Comparative Constitutional Law. Michel Rosenfeld and András Sajó, eds.* (2012, Oxford University Press), p.652.

46 Ethiopian Constitution, Chapter 8.

47 Wolfgang C. Müller, "Political Parties in Parliamentary Democracies: Making Delegation and Accountability Work" (2000). *European Journal of Political Research* 37, p. 309.

48 Gedion T. Hessebon, "The Precarious Future of the Ethiopian Constitution" (2013). Journal of African Law 57, pp. 223–27.

49 HWO Okoth-Ogendo, "Constitutions without Constitutionalism: Reflections on an African Political Paradox." In: *Constitutionalism and Democracy: Transitions in the Contemporary World. Douglass Greenberg and others, eds.* (1993, Oxford University Press), pp.65–80.

50 See Abbink (n. 56); Abebe (n. 14); Gedamu (n. 63).

51 Merera Gudina, *Ethiopia: Competing Ethnic Nationalisms and the Quest for Democracy, 1960–2000* (Shaker 2003).

52 The immediate cause for the "rule of law operation" was the TPLF's preemptive attack on the Northern Command of the Ethiopian National Defense Force on 4 November 2020, the ultimate aim of which was either to remove Abiy Ahmed from power or to take the upper hand in the "national dialogue" this specific context would have brought about.

53 Zemelak Ayitenew Ayele, *Local Government in Ethiopia: Advancing Development and Accommodating Ethnic Minorities* (2014, Nomos), p. 122.

54 Solomon A. Dersso, *Taking Ethno-Cultural Diversity Seriously in Constitutional Design: A Theory of Minority Rights for Addressing Africa's Multi-Ethnic Challenge* (2012, Martinus Nijhoff Publishers), p. 215; Assefa Fiseha, "Theory versus Practice in the Implementation of Ethiopia's Ethnic Federalism." In: *Ethnic Federalism: The Ethiopian Experience in Comparative Perspective. David Turton, ed.* (2006, James Currey), p.136.

55 See Dersso (n. 93), p. 216; Takele Bulto, "Wolf in Sheep's Clothing? The Interpretation and Application of the Equality Guarantee under the Ethiopian Constitution" (2013). Afrika Focus 26, pp.11–35; Zemelak Ayitenew Ayele, *Local*

Government in Ethiopia: Advancing Development and Accommodating Ethnic Minorities (2014, Nomos).

56 Benishangul-Gumuz Constitution, 2003, Article 2.

57 See Aweke Amare Kenaw, "One Country – Two Citizenships: The Status of Settlers in Benishangul-Gumuz Regional State (BGRS) of Ethiopia" (2020). African Identities 0, p. 1. United Nations, "Ethiopia Humanitarian Country Team Visits Metekel Zone of Benishangul Region to See Humanitarian Situation, Response" (23 April 2022). < https://ethiopia.un.org/en/179072-ethiopia-humanitarian-country-team-visits-metekel-zone-benishangul-region-see-humanitarian> (accessed 5 June 2022).

58 Christophe Van der Beken, "Federalism in a Context of Extreme Ethnic Pluralism: The Case of Ethiopia's Southern Nations, Nationalities and Peoples Region" (2013). *VRÜ Verfassung und Recht in* Übersee 46, p. 3.

59 Mahmood Mamdani, *Citizen and Subject: Contemporary Africa and the Legacy of Late Colonialism* (1996, Princeton University Press).

60 On how we might reconcile the two conceptions of group rights with individual rights see Berihun Adugna Gebeye, "Toward Making a Proper Space for the Individual in the Ethiopian Constitution" (2017). *Human Rights Review* 18, p. 439.

61 See Joel Colon-Rios, *Constituent Power and the Law* (2020, Oxford University Press); Lucia Rubinelli, *Constituent Power: A History* (2020, Cambridge University Press).

62 Benedict Anderson, *Imagined Communities: Reflections on the Origin and Spread of Nationalism* (Revised edition, 2016, Verso), pp. 5–7.

63 Andreas Eshete, "The Protagonists in Constitution-Making in Ethiopia." In: *Constitution-Making and Democratization in Africa. Goran Hydén, ed,* (2001, Africa Institute of South Africa), p.69–78.

64 Ethiopian Constitution, Article 39 (5).

65 Id, Article 39 (1).

66 Id, Article 39 (5).

67 Id, Articles 1 and 47.

68 Id, Article 2.

69 Id, Article 8.

70 Fasil Nahum, *Constitution for a Nation of Nations: The Ethiopian Prospect* (1997, The Red Sea Press).

71 Id, 51.

72 See also John M. Cohen, "Ethnic Federalism in Ethiopia" (1995). *Northeast African Studies* 2, pp.157–58.

73 Tezera Tazebew, "Briefing: Amhara Nationalism: The Empire Strikes Back" (2021). *African Affairs* <https://doi.org/10.1093/afraf/adaa029>.

74 See Berihun Adugna Gebeye, "Citizenship and Human Rights in the Ethiopian Federal Republic." In: *Reimagining Ethiopian Federalism. Adem Kassie Abebe and Amen Taye, eds.* (*Ethiopian Constitutional and Public Law Series* 10, Addis Ababa University 2019).

75 Roberto Gargarella, "When Is a Constitution Doing Well? The Alberdian Test in the Americas." In: *Assessing Constitutional Performance, Tom Ginsburg and Aziz Huq, eds),.* (Cambridge University Press 2016) p. 102.

Bibliography

Abebe, Adem Kassie. "From the 'TPLF Constitution' to the 'Constitution of the people of Ethiopia': Constitutionalism and proposals for constitutional reform," in *Constitutionalism and Democratic Governance in Africa: Contemporary Perspectives from Sub-Saharan Africa*, edited by Morris Kiwinda Mbondenyi and Tom Ojienda (PULP, 2013).

Abebe, Daniel. "The Ethiopian Constitution and Ethnic Federalism' in *From Parchment to Practice: Implementing New Constitutions, edited by* Ginsburg, Tom and Huq, Aziz Z. Cambridge University Press, 2020.

Albert, Richard. *Constitutional Amendments: Making, Breaking, and Changing Constitutions.* Oxford University Press, 2019.

Anderson, Benedict. *Imagined Communities: Reflections on the Origin and Spread of Nationalism.* Verso, revised edition, 2016.

Ayele, Zemelak Ayitenew. *Local Government in Ethiopia: Advancing Development and Accommodating Ethnic Minorities*. Nomos, 2014.

Bach, Jean-Nicolas. "Abyotawi Democracy: Neither Revolutionary nor Democratic, a Critical Review of EPRDF's Conception of Revolutionary Democracy in Post-1991 Ethiopia." Journal of Eastern African Studies 5 (2011): 641.

Barnett, Randy E. "Constitutional Legitimacy." Colum. L. Rev. (2003): 1103."plainCitation":"Richard H Fallon, 'Legitimacy and the Constitution' (2005

Beken, Christophe Van der. "Federalism in a Context of Extreme Ethnic Pluralism: The Case of Ethiopia's Southern Nations, Nationalities and Peoples Region." VRÜ Verfassung und Recht in Übersee 46 (2013): 3.

Benishangul-Gumuz Constitution, 2003.

Bingham, Tom.*The Rule of Law.* Penguin Books Limited, 2011.

Bradley, Anthony W and Pinelli, Cesare. "Parliamentarism." in *The Oxford Handbook of Comparative Constitutional Law*, edited by Rosenfeld, Michel and Sajó, András. Oxford University Press, 2012.

Brando, Nicolás and Morales-Gálvez, Sergi. "The Right to Secession: Remedial or Primary?" Ethnopolitics 18 (2019): 107.

Bulto, Takele. "Wolf in sheep's clothing? The Interpretation and Application of the Equality Guarantee under the Ethiopian Constitution." Afrika Focus 26 (2013):1.

Burgess, Michael. *In Search of the Federal Spirit: New Comparative Empirical and Theoretical Perspectives*. Oxford University Press, 2012.

Cohen, John M. "Ethnic Federalism' in Ethiopia." Northeast African Studies 2(1995): 157.

Colon-Rios, Joel. *Constituent Power and the Law.* Oxford University Press, 2020.

Cooter, Robert D and Siegel, Neil S. "Collective Action Federalism: A General Theory of Article I, Section 8." Stanford Law Review 63 (2010): 72

Dersso, Solomon A. *Taking Ethno-Cultural Diversity Seriously in Constitutional Design: A Theory of Minority Rights for Addressing Africa's Multi-Ethnic Challenge*. Martinus Nijhoff Publishers, 2012.

Dixon, Rosalind and Ginsburg, Tom. "The Forms and Limits of Constitutions as Political Insurance." International Journal of Constitutional Law 15 (2017): 988.

Elazar, Daniel J. *Exploring Federalism*. University of Alabama Press, 1987.

Eshete, Andreas. "The Protagonists in Constitution Making in Ethiopia." in *Constitution-Making and Democratization in Africa,* edited by Hydén, Goran. Africa Institute of South Africa, 2001.

Ethiopian Constitution, 1995.

Fallon, Richard H. "Legitimacy and the Constitution." (2005) 118 Harvard Law Review 118 (2005): 1787.

Fessha, 'Yonatan Tesfaye. "The Original Sin of Ethiopian Federalism." Ethnopolitics 16 (2017): 232.

Fiseha, Assefa. 'Theory versus Practice in the Implementation of Ethiopia's Ethnic Federalism." in *Ethnic Federalism: The Ethiopian Experience in Comparative Perspective,* edited by Turton, David. James Currey 2006

Gardbaum, Stephen. "The Place of Constitutional Law in the Legal System." in, *The Oxford Handbook of Comparative Constitutional Law*, edited by Rosenfeld, Michel and Sajó, András. Oxford University Press, 2012.

Gebeye, 'Berihun Adugna. "Toward Making a Proper Space for the Individual in the Ethiopian Constitution." Human Rights Review 18 (2017): 439.

Gebeye, Berihun Adugna. "Citizenship and Human Rights in the Ethiopian Federal Republic." in *Reimagining Ethiopian Federalism*, edited by Abebe, Adem Kassie and Taye, Amen. Ethiopian Constitutional and Public Law Series 10 (2019).

Gudina, Merera. "Contradictory Interpretations of Ethiopian History: The Need for a New Consensus." in *Ethnic Federalism: The Ethiopian Experience in Comparative Perspective, edited by* Turton, David. James Currey, 2006

Gudina, Merera. *Ethiopia: Competing Ethnic Nationalisms and the Quest for Democracy, 1960 – 2000.* Shaker, 2003.

Habtu, 'Alem. "Multiethnic Federalism in Ethiopia: A Study of the Secession Clause in the Constitution." *Publius the Journal of Federalism* 35 (2005): 313.

Haile, Minasse. 'The New Ethiopian Constitution: Its Impact upon Unity, Human Rights and Development Lead Article." *Suffolk Transnational Law Review* 20 (1996): 1.

Hessebon, Gedion T. "The Precarious Future of the Ethiopian Constitution." *Journal of African Law* 57 (2013): 215.

Hirschl, Ran. *Towards Juristocracy The Origins and Consequences of the New Constitutionalism.* Harvard University Press, 2007.

Hudson, Alexander. *The Veil of Participation: Citizens and Political Parties in Constitution-Making Processes.* Cambridge University Press, 2021.

Huq, Aziz. "Does the Logic of Collective Action Explain Federalism Doctrine?" *Sandford Law Review* 66 (2013): 1203.

Kenaw, Aweke Amare. "One Country – Two Citizenships: The Status of Settlers in Benishangul-Gumuz Regional Sates (BGRS) of Ethiopia." *African Identities* 20(2022): 257.

Kutz, Christopher. *On War and Democracy*. Princeton University Press, 2016.

Leslie, 'Peter. "Canada: The Supreme Court Sets Rules for the Secession of Quebec." *Publius Journal of Federalism* 29 (1999): 135

Levinson, Sanford. "Perpetual Union, Free Love, and Secession: On the Limits to the Consent of the Governed." *Tusla Law Review* 39 (2003): 457.

Mamdani, Mahmood. *Citizen and Subject: Contemporary Africa and the Legacy of Late Colonialism*. Princeton University Press, 1996.

Müller, Wolfgang C. "Political Parties in Parliamentary Democracies: Making Delegation and Accountability Work." *European Journal of Political Research* 37 (2000): 309.

Nahum, Fasil. *Constitution for a Nation of Nations: The Ethiopian Prospect.* The Red Sea Press, 1997.

Okoth-Ogendo, HWO. "Constitutions without Constitutionalism: Reflections on an African Political Paradox." In *Constitutionalism and Democracy: Transitions in the Contemporary World, edited by* Greenberg, Douglass and others. Oxford University Press, 1993.

Reference Re Secession of Quebec, [1998] 2 S.C.R. 217.

Roberto Gargarella, Roberto. "When is a constitution doing well? The Alberdian test in the Americas." in *Assessing Constitutional Performance*, edited by Ginsburg, Tom and Huq, Aziz. Cambridge University Press, 2016.

Rosenfeld, Michel. *The Identity of the Constitutional Subject: Selfhood, Citizenship, Culture, and Community*. Routledge, 2009.

Roznai, Yaniv. *Unconstitutional Constitutional Amendments: The Limits of Amendment Powers*. Oxford University Press, 2017.

Rubinelli, Lucia. *Constituent Power: A History*. Cambridge University Press, 2020.

Selassie, Alemante G. "Ethnic Identity and Constitutional Design for Africa'." *Stanford Journal of International Law* 29 (1992): 1-56.

Storing, Herbert J and Dry, Murray. "The Constitutional Convention: Toward a More Perfect Union." in *American Political Thought*, edited by Morton, J. Frisch and Richard, G. Stevens. Routledge, 3rd ed, 2011.

Sunstein, Cass R. "Constitutionalism and Secession." *The University of Chicago Law Review* 58 (1991): 633

Tazebew, Tezera. "Briefing: Amhara Nationalism: The Empire Strikes Back." *African Affairs* 120 (2021): 297-313.

Tiruneh, Andargachew. *The Ethiopian Revolution 1974-1987: A Transformation from an Aristocratic to a Totalitarian Autocracy*. Cambridge University Press, 1993.

United Nations, 'Ethiopia Humanitarian Country Team Visits Metekel Zone of Benishangul Region to See Humanitarian Situation, Response' (23 April 2022) [https://ethiopia.un.org/en/179072-ethiopia-humanitarian-country-team-visits-metekel-zone-benishangul-region-see-humanitarian] accessed 5 June 2022.

Yiftachel, Oren. "'Ethnocracy' and Its Discontents: Minorities, Protests, and the Israeli Polity." *Critical Inquiry* 26(2000): 725.

Yiftachel, Oren. *Ethnocracy: Land and Identity Politics in Israel/Palestine.* University of Pennsylvania Press, 2006.

Zeleke, E Centime. *Ethiopia in Theory: Revolution and Knowledge Production, 1964-2016*. Brill, 2019.

Zewde, Bahru. *The Quest for Socialist Utopia: The Ethiopian Student Movement, c. 1960-1974.* James Currey, 2014.

Chapter 2

Nation (Polity) Building and Cleavages

Assefa Fiseha

1. Introduction

This chapter explores key and contested concepts such as nation building, state building and the nation-state in the context of deeply divided societies. It is partly a deconstruction of the nation-state, or at least the nation-state has to be problematized because the single nation assumed to exist in the nation-state is an anomaly when confronted by rival ethno-national and regional groups that assert self-government and recognition, key challenges in deeply divided societies. Yet before it is deconstructed it has to be explained.

In societies that are deeply divided, like Ethiopia, it is critical to understand the nation and nation building and explain how they are used or misused in the discourse. Their normative assumptions are also contested, and since the 1960's alternative theories have been on the rise. Part one discusses the nation-state, its origins, normative assumptions, and its limitations, while part two explores the concept of nation building and how it is understood across time. Part three provides the framework for polity building in divided societies. There is a rich separate literature on nation building and comparative federalism, but these two concepts are treated as distinct fields as if there is no link between them. Indeed, this is an important missing link that this chapter aims to address. This chapter creates a bridge between the two concepts and analyzes how federalism and devolution could be used for polity building in diverse societies. Polity building is all about designing an inclusive political system and nesting different identities by nurturing shared values, and thus there is a link between polity building and federalism. Federalism and devolution are ideally about designing a more inclusive political and economic system. If properly designed and implemented, federalism and devolution could be deployed for successful polity building in divided societies, and conflicts could be minimized or prevented. More importantly, this chapter provides the explanation for the distinct nature of federal and devolved systems in the Global South. Federal and devolved systems in Africa cannot be understood in isolation from the nature of state power on the continent. The nature of state power impacts federal and devolved systems in Africa in many more ways than one. The big man and hegemonic party system make institution building, division of power (hallmark of federations), substate autonomy and constitutionalism difficult, if not meaningless.

2. Nation State: Origin, Assumptions, and Implications

Experts make a useful distinction between the nation-state and nation building. Experts state, "Creating an independent nation-state with a flag, its government, territory, an army, an anthem, newly minted money, and freshly printed passports did not guarantee that citizens identified with the nation or that they accepted the authority of the state."[1] Creating a nation-state does not mean nation building is accomplished. They are two separate political processes. Once the nation-state is created, the state deploys enormous resources at its disposal to build the polity, that is, a massive work on the people to build a sense of shared and nested belongingness that prevails over and above other forms of manifestations of identity. The nation-state has an ideology that aims to turn "peasants to Frenchmen."[2] The Italian revolutionary Garibaldi is quoted to have said, "we have Italy, let us make the Italians."[3] He united southern and northern Italy in 1861, creating a country called Italy, but he knew this did not make the Italian nation. The idea of instilling in every Italian the sense of nationhood, shared identity, the *software* that unites all citizens of the country despite other differences (religion, region, or other manifestations of identity) is a much more complicated matter. The peasants do not automatically become French even if the French territory with its flag and government is created. The same applies to other states. Getting the right ideology, that is the framework for political integration, state building and public policy to establish shared social cohesion is a daunting task and a never-ending exercise. In this sense, polity building is not a new concept. It is an old one. There were many advocates of the nation-state (like John Stuart Mill), but the pioneer author is undoubtedly the

German philosopher Herder. He invoked the authority of God in his revelation that the "best political arrangements obtain when each nation forms a state of its own." He also described as "unnatural" states in which there is more than one nation: "they become oppressive and doomed to decay." He further stated that "only one language is implanted in an individual, only to one does he belong entirely, no matter how many he learns subsequently." Consequently, he drew the conclusion that '"a group which is a nation will cease to be one, if it is not constituted into a state."[4]

Nationalism is one of the contested concepts. In the most widely used notion, it is "in general a necessary condition of free institutions that the boundaries of government should coincide in the main with those of nationalities."[5] Ernst Gellner also wrote that nationalism is a "political principle, which holds that the political and the national unit should be congruent."[6] The process of establishing the nation-state has gone through several courses. The nation-state became prominent at the end of the eighteenth century and remained as a hegemonic framework until the 1960s.[7] The genesis of the "nation state" is widely associated with the rise of the European system of states, beginning with Westphalia in 1648 (no state shall interfere in the affairs of the other) and the next two centuries, particularly the eighteenth century with the emergence of popular sovereignty and self-determination (the French and American Revolutions[8]) giving birth to the nation-states.

Earlier on, empires, kingdoms, and caliphates dominated the world scene for centuries. In these forms of entities, the relationship between the ruler and ruled remained largely a relation of *master and servant* where the ruler could bring different entities together or break them apart without concern to the wishes of the people.[9] The treaty of Westphalia brought to an end the thirty years of civil wars in Europe and gave birth to the global order of nation-states along with sovereign statehood. Although presented as a religious war between Protestants and Catholics, the war was fought between emerging nation-states (France, the Netherlands, Sweden) on one hand and the German and Spanish armies on the other pushing for great empires, with the latter losing the war.[10] Indeed as Tilley wrote, "war and war settlements have been the great shapers of the European state system."[11] In addition to Westphalia, the Congress of Vienna (1815) that followed the defeat of Napoleon and reorganization of parts of Europe, the Treaty of Versailles (1919) that led to the collapse of Austro-Hungarian and Ottoman Empires[12] after WWI, the settlements that followed the Second World War,[13] the decolonization process after WWII, the end of the Cold War, and the disintegration of the Soviet Union and Yugoslavia resulted in the making and unmaking of states. World Wars I and II and the end of the Cold War in particular resulted in the defeat of several empires and the birth of new nation-states. The overall process resulted in a fourfold increase in the number of states (from 50 to 194), most of it related to collapse of empires or fragmentation of bigger states,[14] so much so that the saying goes that "nations are made by 'blood and iron.'"[15] Since its emergence in Europe, the nation-state has remained as the dominant framework not only in Europe where it was conceived but also elsewhere in the world.[16] The marriage between the nation and the state is reinforced by the ideology of nationalism, with its ideal of a culturally homogeneous society (core nation) reinforcing the state with legitimacy and loyalty. The nation-state as a homogenous unit faces different kinds of minorities (non-core groups) and as will be shown later initially insisted on assimilation, then on integration and slowly shifted to accommodation.

Alongside the making and unmaking of territorial boundaries, by the end of the eighteenth and early nineteenth centuries, new political and philosophical ideas emerged that shifted the *locus of power* from *divine right* to rule claimed by emperors and caliphates to the idea of *consent* of the governed: the principle that power/sovereignty comes from the people. Self-government and self-determination made the nation to have its own government. The people who declare themselves as a nation become a source of sovereignty and affirmatively identify themselves with it.[17] The nation state is about *identity*—collective self-identity and subjective self-identity that members of the nation think they share as a group.[18] As Connor stated, "The essence of the nation is not tangible. It is psychological, a matter of *attitude*, rather than of fact … nation is a self-differentiating group … with a popularly held *awareness or belief* that one's group is *distinct*"[19]from others. A further point that distinguishes it from an ethnic group is that the nation makes territorially based claims for self-government (often internal self-determination that if denied and depending on state response or lack thereof could evolve into secession) and thus has a political ambition.[20] It is not a mere anthropological fact. An ethnic group may share the same language and culture based on myth or reality but has no political ambition for self-government or a claim to a particular territory.[21] The relationship between groups and the boundary for differentiation could be based on language, as in Canada and Ethiopia or religion, as in Northern Ireland (Catholic vs. Protestant) and Sudan (South Sudan before 2011). As it is both self and others defined, interaction both vertical and horizontal (competition for power, resources and reaction to other groups and state policy) are a critical part of the definition of the nation. The interaction and reaction process results in reconstruction of the nation. Having functioning state institutions is vital but is not enough for polity building. Belgium, the UK, Canada, and Spain have those institutions but they have the Flanders, Scottish, Quebec, and Catalan problems that continue to threaten the core nation. There, the nation projected by the state collides with the nation projected by Flanders, Scottish,

Quebec, and Catalan respectively. Many have thought nationalism will wither away if political inclusion and access to economy are ensured, but that never happened, and Scottish, Quebec, and Catalan nationalism are living examples demonstrating that it goes beyond political and economic inclusion.[22] In fact, three of these subunits are economically rich regions, but that has not stopped them from asserting self-government and secession. Nationalism is dynamic and may take different forms across time.

In most developing countries, political and economic injustice caused by the state remains at the heart of identity-based mobilization (relative deprivation theory: systematic and identity-based deprivation of groups from power and resources/economy[23]) but the search for dignity, demand for recognition, collective security, and self-esteem are the core factors that flame and give it its emotive force. While the relative deprivation theory focuses on the power and resource element, the human needs theory[24] goes much further than that to include the need for collective security, right to exist as a group, and prevention from threats of genocide and ethnic cleansing—the passions and emotions go beyond the material interests of ethno-national minorities.[25] The gist, as argued by Connor, goes "Better a government run like hell by Filipinos than one run like heaven by Americans."[26] There is this pejorative that comes with the concept of a "minority" framed by the majority (when there is one) that the former want to end. It implies such a group has no voice or has only less voice. The response from the non-core group or the ethno-national minority is, Why become a mayor when one can be a president in a new nation-state? Why remain as a minority of, say, 20 percent when one can be a 100 percent majority in one's own new nation-state.

As indicated above, the nation-state *replaced* the different types of loose imperial and confederal political units that existed in Europe. It prescribes that the nation and its political boundaries should coincide so that states would be nation-states.[27] In its most extreme form, it required that every state contain within itself one and not more than one culturally homogenous nation, that every state should be a nation, and that every nation should be a state.[28] Two typical models of the nation-state were France (with its assimilation policy) and the United States as an integrationist state with its "melting pot" ideology rooted in individual rights. The US initially insisted on assimilation and realizing its failures shifted to soft multiculturalism, where it tolerated minority cultures in private while promoting one public identity. These were the two "nation-state" models that many aspired to replicate in their respective countries.[29]

The nation-state as a political framework (with a few exceptions) remained dominant across the globe until the 1960s. The nation began in France but was later adopted in Spain in the 1970s, Belgium (before it federalized in the 1990s), Portugal, Greece, Italy after unification, and many more countries in Europe and the rest of the world.[30] Westphalia focused on territory, interstate relations, and sovereignty but gave little attention to the aspirations of the people. The link between the nation and state through self-determination had to wait until the French Revolution. Yet even then this was not realized in East Europe and the Soviet Union; it came after the end of the Cold War.[31]

Yet the nation-state ignores the fact that it was historically created to satisfy the *particular historical needs of state formation* in Europe, where there existed shared history, culture, language, and affiliation with the state constructed by nationalism. In many cases a majority nation (core nation) existed that controlled the state, or else the state constructed them by force.[32] The process of establishing the nation-states was also coercive, although at later stages it was forced to open up space for sub-state entities. It promotes the values and interests of the core (titular) nation, as public institutions and policies are crafted to do exactly that. Will Kymlicka argued that the state as a possession of a dominant national group (titular nation) uses the nation-state and public policy instruments such as media, history, education, and language policy as a mask for the ruling elite to keep power and resources and nurture its privileged identity and status. The values and interests of the nation-state are thus rooted in the titular nation.[33] As will be shown later, this has implications for those left out from the nation-building process. The root causes of sub-state-based nationalism goes to this process.

Besides, the nation-state insisted on creating a homogenous society that pitted it with politically mobilized cleavages. As McGarry, Keating, and Moore argued, "The coercive policies to achieve linguistic and cultural homogeneity in France to create a single French nation attests to the fear and concern that cultural difference would translate into political difference and thus has to be eliminated."[34] Nation and state builders have always feared that "the failure to homogenize increased the likelihood that a state […] would fragment into its cultural subdivisions."[35]

The state deployed enormous resources and an ideology to "nationalize" non-core groups. Several theories were developed to serve this purpose. In the 1950s and 60s all schools of thought, such as Marxism, modernization, liberalism, and globalization, irrespective of their differences, predicted the demise of ethno-cultural diversity and the triumph of the nation-state. Marxists predicted that with the triumph of proletariat and universal socialism, nationalism would wither away. The proletariat is global and has no nationality, was their slogan. Liberalism assumed with respect and protection of individual rights that minorities would either assimilate or integrate into the dominant nation. Karl Deutsch, representing the dominant American modernist view, argued that modernization and increased social communication would erode differences (1953).[36] Eric Hobsbawm, as part of the left, argued that the new transnational order (post-nationalism) with its impact on nation-states, would put an end to all nationalisms, for example, through the European Union that gave birth to multiple identities.[37] Ethno-nationalism (tribalism being its pejorative name) is invariably cited as the source of political instability that has undermined modern government in Africa. As a result, almost all postcolonial African leaders employed several ideologies to ensure homogeneity in their respective countries.[38] Yet, in the former USSR and Yugoslavia, contrary to the predictions, it outlived socialism. Indeed, it was the cause for the demise of socialism. Even in the West, we are witnessing populist and identity-based movements gaining support more than mainstream political parties from the right and the left.[39]The European Union, a giant confederal regional institution meant to check the ugly consequences of the two nationalist-related World Wars, recently faced Brexit.[40]

The reality today is that most states are diverse, and experts have since the 1960s shifted their analyses from nation building, which forces non-core groups to assimilate, to managing diversity, which allows unity and yet has space for diversity. Those who were coerced to assimilate into the dominant nation would at a later stage resent the process and force the nation-state into a new social contract, most of it conducted in the 1960s and subsequent years in the name of minority rights, multiculturalism, indigenous people's rights, etc. Coercion worked only at the *formative* stage. Once the empire or the nation-state was created, there emerged the need to revisit the social contract to change the coercive process of nation building to a *democratic* one. Force cannot ensure the continuity of the state and its territory; consent of the governed could, if combined with other right political frameworks, institutions, and policies. Unhappy groups often want to break the chain imposed on them and are aware of the tension between those who want to keep the state as created by the coercive process and those who feel suffocated by it. Most European nation-states have democratized the state and since the 1960s have opened up, albeit painfully, the nation-state to allow sub units to enjoy political autonomy. Spain (Catalan), the UK (Scotland and Northern Ireland), Belgium (for the Flemish), and Canada (its French-speaking part) are prime examples of nation-states that amended their constitutions to accommodate those left out during the nation-building process. One needs to note that it is a two-step process. democratizing the nation-state by *revising the social contract* and detaching it from the coercive process of nation building, then granting autonomy to politically mobilized groups in the form of devolution, federation, or political autonomy with or without power sharing at the center.[41]

In Africa, the nation-state made its way because of colonialism, modernization, and globalization in different periods but was framed as a centralized integration scheme, even if the core nation was absent or a particular minority controlled power and pushed the agenda of nation building. Markakis, Young, and Schlee argue that the European model was "transposed to Africa, a vastly different world, without the slightest concession to its uniqueness, and the results have been tragic."[42]

Space will not allow diagnosing all sources of governance crisis in Africa. Yet two factors stand tall as major causes: the nature of state power (treated later) and managing cleavages. The African continent continues to defend artificial colonial borders and thus conflicts continue between subnational and regional groups that demand adjustment to colonial borders and leaders that prefer to keep the status quo. While the *Third Wave* democratization and liberalization were hoped to improve the state of affairs in Africa, the reality is grim.[43] An expert assessment shows that "by the end of 1998, only nineteen countries had stable political conditions; at least eleven countries were encountering political crisis and turbulence, and eighteen countries were engaged in armed conflict or civil strife. This means that toward the end of the 1990s, less than 40 percent of sub-Saharan African countries enjoyed relative political stability. Almost 25 percent faced serious political crisis, while a staggering 38 percent were wracked by violent conflicts."[44] A report issued by the

Peace and Security Council of the African Union as recently as February 2023 confirms there has been no progress since then. "As the analysis below reveals, the peace and security situation on the continent remains bleak, with the deteriorating security and humanitarian situation showing no sign of abating." The Ethiopian case remains the most outrageous, resulting in the death of millions of people in such a short period of time, demonstrating its highest level of brutality.[45] Sudan, Nigeria, Ethiopia, the Democratic Republic of Congo, Kenya, Mali and Niger (Tuareg), Morocco, Tanzania, Angola, Cameroon, Somalia, Senegal, Zambia, and Namibia (Lozi) faced tragic conflicts and have insurgents of one type or another, albeit to varying degrees of mobilization.[46]

As rightly depicted by Michael Keating, in divided societies there are "so many nations, but few states."[47] It is now clear that there exists "conspicuous discrepancy between the nation and the political borders of states in which there are close to two hundred states, all of whom together contain three thousand to five thousand nations in which there exist at least six hundred potential nation-states, a mismatch that at times leads to tension and conflicts between those who would like to exercise self-rule and those resisting it.[48] The Horn of Africa offers a prime example in which the contradiction between state-led and ethno-national/regional-based mobilization takes acute form. The conflicts in the Horn involve rival nation-state building projects fought in a zero-sum game, where one's gain is another's loss. The state becomes the center of conflict, with the centrist elites seeking to preserve and expand existing states, sub-state entities trying to secede and create their own states, irredentists fighting to secede from one state in order to join another, and others still vying to capture power within their own state. The nation-state, along with its centralizing feature in Africa, has been the source of state failure and neverending conflicts. Markakis aptly wrote:

> *"No state in this region (Horn of Africa) has been able to adequately perform the functions generally assumed of it: control its borders, exercise a monopoly on the means of force within its borders, enforce the law equitably throughout its domain, protect the life and property of its subjects, and administer justice impartially. The region holds several continental records for political unrest: five wars between states, two of the longest wars, two secessions from existing states, and one*

state collapse. Furthermore, almost every self-identifying ethno regional group has started at least one national liberation movement."49

To date the struggle to revise the map in this region has gone through two major phases. The first phase, typical of the African leaders in the 1960s, brought the consolidation of state units created by imperialism: Ethiopia, Sudan, and Somalia annexing territories (Eritrea, South Sudan, and Somaliland), while the second saw the reversal of the process of consolidation after the end of the Cold War. The first phase reduced the number of states in the Horn from seven to four after Eritrea, South Sudan, and Somaliland were annexed.

The second phase saw the fragmentation of Ethiopia, Sudan, and Somalia, with the secession of the three annexed units: Eritrea, South Sudan, and Somaliland *de facto,* increasing the number of states to seven. In the second phase, it was caused by insurgents (ethno-national and regional ones) challenging the state-led nationalism, the effect being the full restoration of the colonial map after decades of violent conflict took the lives of millions, dislocated the region's economy, and undermined its prospects for development. It also condemned its people to live under authoritarian rulers addicted to the use of force as the main instrument of government and polity building. The two phases demonstrate a head-on clash between state-led nationalism on one hand and ethno-nation or regional-based nationalism on the other, a clash of nationalisms so to speak. Unsurprisingly, since the state-led nationalism/nation building was chosen by the ruling elite, the projected nation's identity was to be the same as with the ruling elite's narrow identity. National integration, therefore, became a political imperative.[50] This required the dissolution of quasi-autonomous kingdoms and traditional systems of sociopolitical organization and of ethnic identities, as well as the effacement of ethnic languages and replacement by the identity, culture, tradition, and language of the nation-state builders. This was followed by national integration, that is the ruling elite's chosen identity being diffused throughout the state via a process of acculturation, assimilation, and, if need be, forced conversion.[51] The result, as indicated above, has been endless war and the making and unmaking of state boundaries, certainly at a heavy cost. None other than Basil Davidson (1992),[52] captures the problems of the nation-state in Africa. He concluded that the nation-state in Africa has been a "curse" and the "Black man's burden."[53]

This reminds us of the prominent article by Walker Connor, who a long time ago warned that "ation building could be nation destroying.[54] He argued, and this was at the time when nation building as a homogenizing concept was at its peak, that modernization, industrialization, and respect for individual rights do not necessarily minimize ethnic loyalty, and nation building may in the end be nation destroying in diverse societies. While demands of ethno-national minorities and the attendant theory of nationalism may have destructive implications when pushed to their extremes, as witnessed by the two World Wars, former Yugoslavia after the Cold War, and Rwanda (1994), the thinking that it will fade away seems far from reality. On the contrary, what we see is resurgence and hence the need for managing and accommodating it.[55]

Ethiopia is a textbook example of the contradictions between the nation-state as projected by the imperial ruling elite and its many rival politically mobilized cleavages. Despite centuries of non-centralized feudal structure in Ethiopia, the fact that Emperor Menelik II (1889–1913) created modern Ethiopia by liquidating and bringing all former quasi-autonomous kingdoms and emirates did not ensure all people in this territory to share the same common hood. Bringing different territories under one roof is one thing, creating institutional and policy systems to such communities and instilling a sense of common identity that cuts across sub-unit identities is a different matter. Many Ethiopian elites are unable to identify the difference between the two: creating the territory vs. polity building—the work that has to be done on the people to build a nested, shared, and cohesive society. One needs to have the right ideology, political framework, and public policy instruments to transform a conglomerate of identities into some sense of shared belongingness to the polity despite differences in language, culture, and religion. Some are stuck in the past hoping that the sub-units will dissolve one day and still envision a centralized nation-state that is Amharic-speaking and Ethiopian Christian or something close to it (geographic federalism and citizenship politics are the new versions of it). Identities do not wither away and are not transient, as the different schools of thought anticipated. We need to find ways to manage diversity, and there are by now many more advanced alternatives than the nation-state. Crafting the right policies and institutions that allow people to live together despite differences is now the new normal, not the nation-state.

In Ethiopia, the polity building was led by the centrist elites that had built the Ethiopian Empire.[56] The process of expanding and annexation of territories in the south, west, and east in the name of nation building was certainly brutal and coercive and had serious consequences on the local population that continue to be debated even today. The assimilation project was preceded by the liquidation of quasi-autonomous kingdoms, a project undertaken by Emperor Menelik II, ending what Clapham calls the era of "devolved autocracy."[57] The decentralized feudal state structure changed radically with the emergence of a strongly centralized unitary state toward the last quarter of the nineteenth century spearheaded by Emperor Menelik II that was further consolidated during the reign of Emperor Haile Selassie (1930–74),[58] an absolute monarch, followed by the military socialist regime (1974–91) that replaced it, giving rise to a protracted civil war and political instability for most of the last century.[59]

The process led to dispossession of land by the new elite that turned the local population to tenants (the *Gebar* system). With the central government expanding (others would say it reclaimed its previous territories) its control to the south and southwest along with the *Gebar* system (which provided land—a critical resource)to the imperial army in the conquered territories and left the local people landless and servants of the new lords.[60] With the emergence of the centralized unitary state, Showa, Menelik's home province, emerged as a hegemonic center of power and resources. According to Edmond Keller and Clapham, the 156 high-ranking officials recruited and appointed by the central government between 1944 and 1967 were predominantly from Showa, with only five coming from the peripheral areas. Nearly all provincial governors and cabinet members towards the end of 1960s came from Showa as well. Seventy percent of Ethiopian industrial activities were concentrated in Showa, the Awash Valley, and Asmara. Other sectors, such as education and health, also reflected massive imbalances between provinces, with Showa standing at the top.[61] Showa then emerged as the epicenter of power, resources, and a homogenizing centrist state, liquidating quasi-autonomous kingdoms.

Besides, in the imperial state, national integration was predicated on Christianity and the Amharic language and was aptly known as Amharization.[62] To do this, Tedla Hailu, a Belgium-trained centrist Ethiopian elitist and close family member of Emperor Haile Selassie, wrote, "Ethiopia has to adopt a policy of assimilation in which people will abandon their customs and social organization and adopt the language and religion of the Amhara."[63] This change of identity should be carried out, Tedla insisted, by the Oromos, who would thus become Amharas, rather than the other way around, because the Amharas alone possessed a written language, as well as what he termed superior customs and religion.[64] In a government-owned newspaper, it was written in 1926 (E.C.), that "the intention of the Ethiopian government (the then ruling elite) is clear. Every Ethiopian should learn and speak Amharic, it is key for national unity and integration."[65] This was reflected in the 1931 and 1955 constitutions and several other policies and remained the framework for centralized Ethiopia until 1991. Some experts, like Donald Levine,[66] even went to the extent of declaring "greater Ethiopia as a very successful nation built from within," focusing on the historical interactions and the Amhara- and Christian-based integration, only to be taken by surprise following the emergence of the Ethiopian Student Movement, the national liberation movements, and the post-1991 political developments. The loss of local autonomy following centralization, political and economic control by the ruling elite, the process of Amaharization, and the

Gebar system created a system of class and national oppression in most parts of Ethiopia, particularly in the south and southwest. The new ruling elite, distinct both in terms of class and identity, was to become a source of resentment and an incubator of ethno-nationalism, hence the articulation of these issues by the Ethiopian Student Movement, and their slogans "land to the tiller," "the nationality question," social justice, and religious equality became the main tools for mobilization leading to the 1974 revolution.[67]

The military junta made gestures to address the emerging demands from ethno-national groups when it came to power and toward the end of its era. It declared all nationalities to be equal but did not end the marginalization from power and resources and failed to ensure the right to self-rule. More importantly, its rigid insistence on military solutions to political issues blocked all hopes for peace. An obliterated form of regional self-rule was included in the 1987 constitution, but by then it was too little too late to attract already emboldened ethno-national groups.[68]

As it turned out, however, the promotion of dominant group nationalism was to be checkmated and confounded by the countervailing force of its opposite number, which was the emerging nationalism of ethno-national groups. Many resisted assimilation forcefully, ultimately making the task of the nation-state builder's mission impossible. The post-2018 centrist elites and Abiy had been trying it again (at least until mid-2022 in the official narrative) only to realize very soon that it had exploded in their face in Tigray following the November 2020 war.[69] Amharization and a relationship based on hierarchy created resentment within ethno-national groups, giving birth to the "nationality question" and the countless "national liberation fronts" that waged war against the center, the coalition of which brought the centralized nation-state to its knees in 1991. The centralized nation-building project was an incubator of sub-unit forces as a reaction to its political, economic, and identity-based suffocation. It was a lost century for the country.

Coming back to the nation-state, the above sections make it clear that the basic limitation of the nation-state is the fact that it is the antithesis to politically mobilized cleavages. Perhaps this is where one observes a head-on clash between state-led nationalism and subnational ethnonationalism or regionalism more visibly. Politically mobilized cleavages continue to threaten the nation-state. Following the end of the Cold War, such cleavages caused what Arend Lijphart dubs a "wave of ethnic conflicts"[70] instead of the promised "third wave of democracy."[71] Mobilized ethnonational minorities are "regionally concentrated ethnic groups who once enjoyed or aim to enjoy political autonomy and have become part of states in which they constitute an ethnic minority through conquest, annexation, colonization or incorporation during the coercive process of nation building."[72] They mobilize politically around assertions of national identity and self-determination. The goal of such mobilization is to recover the extensive self-government they claim to have enjoyed historically or they aspire to have now. The degree of self-government they seek ranges from autonomous, national self-government to independent statehood. Countries that have politically mobilized ethnonational groups cannot assume to have stable territory. The demands of such groups are framed and entrenched in relation to a particular territory over which they aim to exercise self-government and the very existence of *the unity and territorial integrity* of the state is put to the test.[73]We noted already how the map in the Horn has been made and unmade in the last decades, resulting in the emergence of new nation-states.

Ethno-national, or regional-based, mobilization is a very potent force that, if not managed carefully could result in fragmentation. It has resulted in the formation of some twenty-seven states that have joined the United Nations following the end of the Cold War.[74] As a result of cleavage, deeply divided countries continue to face the threat of fragmentation, albeit to varying degrees. Ethiopia lost Eritrea, and the threat of secession is still a problem as it harbors many national liberation movements, such as those of the Oromo, the Ogaden/Somali, and the Tigray, among others. Some ten ethno-national groups that used to administer themselves at the local government level in the south have followed the winds of change of 2018 and demanded a constituent unit status, and four new states have been established, increasing the number of states from nine to thirteen. The war between the federal government and Tigray, although it has multiple causes, is very much related to Tigray's age-old demand for genuine self-government[75] and fair representation in federal institutions. Ethno-national groups are thus demanding more, not less, even after two-and-a-half decades of federal practice.

Contrary to several predictions of its demise, it has survived and at times threatened nation-states. Experts have challenged the effort to eradicate sub-state nationalism as "post-national illusion"[76] and counseled actors to properly understand this force and to design appropriate institutions and policies to manage it. Territorially based and politically mobilized cleavages continue to challenge the process of nation building both in the developed (Canada, Spain, Belgium, the United Kingdom) and the developing worlds. Some African countries (Nigeria, Ethiopia, and Kenya), despite differences in the degree of mobilization, continue to face challenges related to group-based cleavages.

According to Horowitz, divided societies refer to cases in which identity-based politics have a high degree of salience, exceeding that accorded to alternative forms of political mobilization such as ideology, class, and gender, and the relationship between groups is affected by deep levels of mistrust and antagonism, making it less cooperative.[77] As argued by Sujit Choudhry, "A divided society is not merely a society which is ethnically, linguistically, religiously or culturally diverse .... It is hard to imagine a state today that is not diverse."[78] What makes a society divided is when the differences are politically salient and an identity-based distinct group uses it as the basis for political mobilization. As such, identity becomes the prime source of political mobilization around which political claims for recognition, resource control, accommodation, and self-government are framed, political parties are formed, elections contested and governments composed.[79] These forces affect the process of constitution making and constitutional design. A distinct identity-based political mobilization demands a more autonomous self-government. The nation is famously defined as a community that shares common identity and claims a particular territory, believes in *belonging together*,[80] and wants to determine its political destiny through a concerted political action directed at self-government and possibly statehood. The nation's main goal is self-government and statehood and that serves as the basis for *political action* linking the elite and the masses. Less mobilized groups and countries that are not deeply divided could be managed through integration and other softer options.[81]

The nation-state also faces the chronic problem of democratic deficit. Democracy within the African continent remains fragile (with a few exceptions). Within the federal and devolved systems, Nigeria and Kenya have made some progress in the last decade. They have seen peaceful transfers of power, albeit the elections were disputed. In both countries, the opposition has also been able to win at the subnational level, even though it lost at the national level. Yet the overall picture in Africa shows a focus on majoritarian democracy. Working majoritarian-based democracies in deeply divided societies could generate problems, necessitating the need for more inclusive options. Until deconstructed by Arend Lijphart (consociational democracy) and consistent with the concept of the nation-state, the dominant view simply reinforced majoritarian democracy anchored on the *core nation*: "The functioning of democracy requires linguistically unified *demos*. Significantly, this does not mean that all citizens must have the same first language to make democracy work, but merely that they generally have sufficient knowledge of one language in which communication can typically proceed with ease."[82] Joseph Lacey calls this the lingua franca thesis,[83] and it has also been advocated by Robert Dahl where he considered homogeneity as a precondition for a stable democracy.[84] Multilingualism is feared, as it may result in different public spheres and varying opinions and identity formations. This may lead to linguistically demarcated political mobilization and fragmentation. Theories on multinational democracy, however, see this argument with skepticism and counter it by demonstrating that majoritarian democracy is ill suited for deeply divided societies and thus suggests consociational democracy.

In many cases, as in Africa (for example, Ethiopia, Kenya, and Nigeria), the core nation *does not exist* and thus makes majoritarian democracy lack a *major foundation* for it to function. At an empirical level as well, Belgium, India, Switzerland, and Canada are democracies that counter the lingua franca thesis. Nor does homogeneity ensure stability and democracy, Somalia being a living example.

Ethiopia: ethnic group	%	Nigeria: Ethnic group	%	Kenya: ethnic group.	%
Oromo	34.4	Hausa-Fulani	29	Kikuyu	22
Amhara	27	Yoruba	21	Luhyia	14
Somali	6.2	Igbo	18	Luo	13
Tigray	6.1	Ijaw	10	Kalenjin	12
Sidama	4	Kanuri	4	Kambat	11
Guraghe	2.5	Ibibio	3.5		
Wolayta	2.3	Tiv	2.5		
Afar	1.7				

Note: None of the groups taken alone commands a 50 percent majority, and that brings a host of issues. In most of the countries where multiethnic, multinational federations are theorized (Canada, Spain, the UK—asymmetric decentralization), there is a core nation challenged by regional and ethno-national forces.

This is an area where institutional design for democracy matters a lot. How do we ensure a legitimate and inclusive government when different minority ethno-national groups compete for power? This is particularly acute and could lead to deadly conflicts as the drivers of the central government version of nationalism are not a majority. In many cases, as in the table shown above, there is no dominant ethno-national group that enjoys a demographic majority and could claim to have democratic majority to pursue its goals. It becomes a clash between a minority that has state resources at its disposal trying to impose its will on other minorities. Yet even if the central government's project of nationalism enjoys a majority, it pits a permanent majority against a permanent minority with no hope of becoming a majority. Arend Lijphart brought this tension to the fore in post-Saddam Iraq. Majoritarian democracy applied to Iraq would mean "a national government mainly or exclusively Shi'ite majority that excludes Sunnis and Kurds … and it will be naïve to expect such minorities condemned to permanent minority to remain loyal or constructive."[85] With it comes the issue of why ethno-national minorities under the perpetual rule of a majority could be expected to be loyal to such regimes and stay in the union. The general assumption of majoritarian democracy that the rulers alternate, such that today's political majority will become tomorrow's political minority, does not hold true in deeply divided societies. In this context, majoritarian institutions may suffer from a legitimacy crisis. The decisions of the majority are not accepted by the minority. The values of the centrist state such as the flag, the national anthem, public policy, the media, language, and cultural policies that are instruments of centralized nation building are deeply resented and rejected by ethno-national minorities. Thus, alternative theories such as consociational democracy have been recommended when the political system faces deeply divided cleavages. Instead of having winners and losers, consociational democracy brings major political actors either on an equal footing (as in Belgium) or through proportional arrangements to power and insists on consensus decision-making on fundamental issues. Joint- and consensus-based decision-making at the center could possibly reduce the tension between the different groups. Thus, those left in the majoritarian democracy become decision-makers through power sharing, reducing the potential for conflict. Distinct institutional arrangements thus matter in managing cleavages and reducing conflicts. Consensus-based decision-making at the federal level on key political, diplomatic, and economic issues serves as a trust-building scheme, mitigating the potential for conflict. In some countries, such power-sharing arrangements are combined with federalism that also ensures political autonomy at the constituent level. Such an arrangement builds a sense of belongingness to the overarching state and its institutions. Power-sharing arrangements could result in government crisis, as often seen in Belgium or Israel, and there is rich literature showing the risks; but the benefits outweigh its shortcomings when it comes to deeply divided societies. The choice for countries such as Ethiopia is between fragmentation and never-ending tension and war or possibly a durable, more inclusive and slow but consensus-based decision-making process. If securing durable peace and inclusion are identified as core goals, the benefits could outweigh its limitations.

3. Nation (Polity) Building

Nation building is one of the least understood, most confusing and abused concepts in the literature. There is little clarity on what it means, and authors continue to use it to mean different things. Some experts use it interchangeably with state building.[86] The two concepts are related but are not one and the same. State building as outlined by Weber refers to a state that has a monopoly over the legitimate use of force and that is able to deliver basic services such as security and crucial public goods.[87] It is about building tangible and functioning state institutions. This is normally assumed to exist in the West, but in many developing countries within the African continent, it is one of the daunting tasks, as the institutions continue to suffer under hegemonic one-party systems and big men. In most cases, the institutions also serve *factional* interests. Building functioning state institutions that are able to deliver basic services is on its own a significant progress but is not enough. The legitimacy of the institutions and how they are perceived by citizens remains critical.

Nation building, on the other hand, refers to sociopolitical cohesion and the legitimacy of institutions (more in later sections).[88] It is intangible *software* that we invest in the people with to build nested and shared belongingness to the polity cutting across divides. The distinction is important because when one writes about state failure, it is beyond the failure of state institutions.[89] It also implies that there is a crisis of legitimacy, and the social contract needs to be revisited because it is broken, betrayed, or is not enough. Most countries are inhabited by diverse societies, and tension often exists between national identity projected by the state and ethno-national, regional, religious identities pursued by sub-state entities. The center may pursue national integration while sub-units may push for accommodation and pluralism objecting to integration and the identity crafted by the state. Thus, integration and disintegration may happen at the same time unless one balances the divergent forces.[90] Nation building is thus a complex process that states and leaders invest in the people with to ensure sociopolitical cohesion by crafting the right ideology, designing appropriate institutions that address the legitimacy issue and promote shared values that cut across the different divides. It is not a top-down process but a *collective effort* at constructing common destiny built on shared and inclusive values.

Over the last three decades, several states collapsed, including Somalia, Yemen, Iraq, Libya, and Afghanistan. The international community invested a lot of resources and expertise to restore "law and order" in these countries, and most of it was done in the name of "nation building."[91] Yet, a careful reading of this approach does show that the effort is related to building state institutions to be able to ensure security and provide basic services. It is also more about democratization and the conduct of elections than nation building. Besides, the efforts were largely conducted in Western or other capitals detached from the very society meant to benefit from the process. In the case of South Sudan, both during the Comprehensive Peace Agreement (2005–11) and after independence, the focus was on peace and state building. With the exception of post-Second World War nation-building projects in Japan and Germany by the Allied Forces, it is rare to find successful state and nation building imposed from outside by a third party. Iraq was supposed to be a showcase for democracy in the Middle East before it faltered. The tragedy in Afghanistan and Libya is well known. The success in Japan and Germany was possible because both countries already had competent and *functioning state institutions* well before their destruction. Both countries had also the *core nation* missing in many deeply divided societies. The necessary human skill was already in place when the Allied Forces began the reconstruction.

In the past, "nation building" was used to mean the conscious creation of a homogenous society out of many diverse societies, often through coercion and assimilation.[92] In its most common form, the governing *core group* ("the nation") designs and pursues policies over the non-core group(s), constructing and promoting a particular narrative over any other. That becomes the sole and single public identity to which the non-core groups are required to assimilate or integrate. The goal, although it remained contested, was to ensure *integration* and individual loyalty to the nation-state. This is how the concept of nation building was used between the nineteenth and first half of the twentieth centuries until it was challenged by the human rights revolution and minority rights discourse in the 1960s.[93] The tools and instruments used vary but included assimilation (A plus B equals A or B, one group disappearing), fusion (A plus B equals C, an attempt to forge a new identity, as in Swahili in some East African countries), partition (as in India and Pakistan), segregation (South Africa and USA in the past), pan-Africanism, pan -Arabism, patriotism, and in the worst cases, ethnic cleansing and genocide.[94] Homogenizing the culture and language of the subjects to the core nation by promoting the language, culture, and religion of the chosen nation and standardization of education constituted a core part of the nation-building project. In an award-winning publication, Crawford Young (1976) and recently Will Kymlicka (2007) have attacked this model, and since then new approaches to nation building have been introduced.[95] Wimmer argued political equality between ethnic groups is a key defining element of nation building. Oppressing or even physically harming minorities shows that a nation-building project has failed.[96] As rightly argued by Connor, assimilation and marginalization of an ethno-national minority is not nation building but nation destroying.[97]

As part of his relational and exchange theory, Wimmer defines nation building as "extending networks of political and other forms of alliances, whatever their nature, across a territory between the state and society and *forge* political ties between citizen and state that reach across *ethnic divides* and *integrate* ethnic majorities and minorities in an *inclusive power arrangement* to imagine and then realize that they are nested together as a political community and feel *loyal* to co-nationals, above and *beyond* their attachment to an ethnic group, a tribe, a village community, or a religion."[98] He further argued nation building entails *national identification*: citizens begin to see themselves as members of a "national" community. Following the French Revolution, the nation determines and identifies itself with the state, the state is the creation of the nation and identification with it is assumed, not contested.[99] The nation then has an identity, and this very identity is what becomes contested, as will be elaborated later. Ethno-national and regional forces challenge that very identity as belonging to the core nation only and not to all. As a result of colonialism, open immigration policy, globalization, or other sociopolitical factors, the core nation may continue to face new diversity, but that does not make the nation-state obsolete, it makes polity building more problematic.[100] Two brief remarks here. Firstly, those who have written on nation building do rightly identify inclusion as key to the process of nation building, but the "how" issue is simply left as a side matter or is advocated to the limited transitional process of political settlement phase only. Yet, the "how" remains central to nation building, and it is here where non-centralized forms of governance come into the picture. Institutional design issues come here in many forms. Inclusion is also problematized from the perspective of the citizen and civil society (in the old liberal sense) and misses group- and regional-based politically mobilized cleavages, a major focus of this chapter.

Secondly, while Wimmer's conception of nation building is an advanced one, it suffers from some limitations. Identification with the state is contested in divided societies, as they could identify more with something else than the state. Nation building in the sense he adopted is a *deliberate* state act, and policy invested in the people living in a country to build the sense of *shared and nested belongingness* as a political community to the polity, beyond and above their bond to other forms of attachments such as language, ethnicity, region, religion, or other forms of diversity through inclusive power-sharing arrangements. With right and inclusive political ideology and functioning state institutions, it ensures that centrifugal forces remain loyal to the overarching state despite their sub-state national identities. One of the major limitations of Wimmer's concept of nation building is the fact that he refers to "identification with national identity" when that concept in itself is part of the controversy. There may or may not be a "national identity" in countries that are deeply divided. Possibly there is more than one national identity competing in the political space. He does not make a distinction between different categories of societies.

While analyzing nationality in divided societies, David Miller makes three useful classifications.[101] Rajeev Bhargava also adopts a similar notion to discuss India's complex diversity.[102] A typical nation-state is a political community bounded by a single culture (be it ethnic or religious) with its defined territory and having its own state and government. Some of the Western European nation-states are classic examples. Recent developments in India under Modi show there is shift from India as a multiethnic democracy to one based on militant Hindu nationalism, which some regret as an "ethnic democracy" that turns

Muslims and other minority groups to a secondary class.[103] Five decades of non-centralized and inclusive Indian multiethnic democracy is now being reshaped based on Hindu nationalism, which is a regression. Within the comparative federal studies, some federations are as well nation-state federations under the control of one core nation as in the United States, Germany, and Austria and have no aim of granting autonomy to a territorially based identity.

The second one is coalescent nationalism, also called multiethnic, where the constitution recognizes each separate culture and identity in the country, and, at times, each federal subunit is composed of a distinct society, yet each distinct society *sees itself as part of a larger* and overarching common identity. There may be one or more manifestations of local identity, but such groups also happily identify themselves with the overarching state. Some countries are diverse, but the diversity does not have any political meaning. As such it is not politically mobilized, and no particular region, subunit or political party pushes for territorial autonomy, self-government, or secession.[104] There is no prior history of discrimination and thus ordinary citizens live as happy ones despite differences in language or religion, identifying themselves with the overarching state and its institutions. Creating a common sense of belongingness that prevails over substate identity becomes not a difficult task.[105] At times this may include countries with politically conscious diversity but is not as such politically mobilized for self-determination. In the literature this is sometimes called a multiethnic society, and Switzerland, with the cantons cutting across linguistic and religious divides, is mentioned as a classic example.[106] As such, the different identities are nested to one another.[107]

The third category refers to countries that are not only diverse but in which the diversity is also *politically* mobilized. In the literature, these are also referred to as deeply divided societies, multination societies, pluri-national or countries with assertive and rival nationalism. Within this last category, Liam Anderson makes a further useful distinction between ethnic federations and ethno-territorial federations.[108] Ethnic federations are federations that explicitly provide *each* of the major ethno-national groups with their homeland, ensuring self-government and ethnicity is the defining feature of the system. It is also likely that as they often are inhabited by several rival groups, there is no one dominant core nation but several ethno-national groups, none of them constituting a majority. This raises chronic issues to both *democracy and federalism*. How we establish a legitimate and inclusive central government in this context, and how we accommodate the different groups both in the center and at the subunit level becomes very complicated because of the absence of the *core* nation.

Ethno-territorial federations, on the other hand, combine both the ethno-national and territorial features. "Ethno-territorial federations are those in which one or more territorially concentrated ethnic groups are accommodated via the provision of a subunit homeland, but *the numerically dominant ethnic group* (the core nation) is carved up (cracked) among multiple subunits. Examples include Canada (the English speaking part is divided into nine provinces), Spain (Castilian Spanish exist in fourteen autonomous communities, and India (Hindi speaking population are divided into nine provinces). Ethno-territorial federations fuse the logic of territorial and ethnic federalism to produce systems that are structurally and functionally distinguishable from both. In other words, they constitute a separate category of federal system."[109] Within these last sub-classifications one can also make a distinction between bi-communal federations such as Canada that are ethno-territorial, in which the English-speaking part is divided into several provinces while the French-speaking part is found in one province, and yet there is competition and rivalry between the two communities (English and French). There is a core nation (the English speaking part that is divided into several provinces) and an ethno-national minority. Ronald Watts argues bi-communal federations pose a peculiar challenge compared to those ethno-territorial federations that are home to many diverse groups. In the latter, possibility for shifting alliances among groups on issues makes political deadlock less likely while in the former it is a common challenge.[110] The above distinction is vital because the nature of the issues vary. In the ethno-territorial federations because of the existence of the core nation, it is only one of the members that is raising concerns. If we assume a family with many children, it is only one child in the family that feels mistreated and may think of staying in or has to leave. In the ethno-national federation that has no core nation, it is the entire family: parents and all the children that are not feeling well and that need serious treatment.

The above distinction on the nature of diversity and its level of political mobilization is useful because it affects institutional design. It is vital to note as well that the kind of *constitutional politics* in the third category is different from the former two groups. In the last category, a particular group or groups identify themselves with a particular nation that is different from the one projected by the state. Different identities are politically mobilized and often are found territorially making *claims* for political autonomy, self-determination, and possibly secession. Unlike normal constitutional politics that emerges in the previous two categories, here the claim by the ethno-national or regional group is for self-government, possibly with a sovereign state of its own. It is not simply a change of government within an existing state but change to the territorial and political system and assertion of self-government that may include a state of one's own.[111] The constitution and the values that it claims to promote are contested because it is perceived as promoting the *identity* of a single (core) nation; thus constitutional identity is part of the debate. Self-determination is thus a central and enduring element, and as a result the existence of the state itself is questioned, and if it should exist, the *terms* are debated. Political mistrust and rivalry between the different segments is integral to the political process: political power, the nature of democracy and federalism, institutional design, nature of political party, identity and public policy are often the areas of contestation. The "segmental identities" or the cleavages seek to enhance their political and territorial autonomy and mobilize resources and institutions at their disposal against the center, while the central government's focus is on the overarching identity, unity, and territorial integrity that may lead to deadly conflict. In short, as a result of the rival nationalism, one projected by the state and the other by segmental identities, the very existence of the state, its territory, and symbols are often contested.[112]

While in the two categories discussed above the nation and national integration concepts may make sense, in the third category, it is problematic. There is no one nation (*demos*) but many rival nations (*demoi*). The nature and type of political party configuration also differs. It is likely that there will be political parties whose sole purpose is articulating and defending the interests of the political community they claim to represent, and this is not without consequences unless serious effort is made to accommodate these forces. A study shows that the birth of a new nation-state from an existing multinational state is very high in particular if the ethno-national minority had already existing subunit institutions called "segmental institutions." Roeder wrote, "From 1901 to 2000, 177 new states were created and 153 of them (86%) had been segmental states prior to independence."[113] The logic is that political institutions have a significant effect in shaping and framing identities, as they provide a platform for national mobilization, and political ambitions for collective action and secession are as such an *upgrade* of the existing segmental institutions to a new nation-state. If rival nationalism exists, there is the possibility for the will and ambition to have one's own state or at least self-government. The fact that segmental institutions exist provides *capacity and resources* to substate elites to achieve what they plan to achieve. The opposite is also true. Society also shapes institutions, and indeed it is the major claim of this chapter that cleavages have an impact on the design of institutions. The making and unmaking of constituent unit boundaries and the principles and processes for doing so remain contested because they either aim to *frustrate* the ambition of segmental identity as they break a potential nation-state into pieces (Nigeria, Kenya, South Africa) often rejected by the ethno-national or regional elites as part of divide and conquer or promise to empower the segmental identity (Ethiopia—the promise was never implemented). This reality shapes constitutional politics and has an impact on constitutional design and can be managed before causing conflict and fragmentation.

Coming back to nation building, the question in the third category is how does one build a sense of shared and nested belongingness to the polity and instill it in the people so that they develop a shared vision that prevails over other forms of loyalties: ethnic, regional, religious, or otherwise? Is it even possible to build a shared and nested political community above and beyond ethnic or religious identity in those cases? And can the project be rightly called "nation building"? As mentioned briefly in this chapter, there is no one nation but two or more nations in a state, and each nation is perhaps in search of its own statehood. In other words, there are many nations without a state. Thus when one refers to national identity, the question comes: Which national identity? The one espoused by the state or by the ethno-nationalist/regional group? Because the project of nation building refers to both efforts: one led by the state and the other by the ethno-nationalist, often in reaction to repressive state policy and action. For purposes of avoiding such confusion, we have to find a more neutral concept that we can employ to the state-led effort in constructing the shared and nested belongingness to the overarching state. Polity building is a preferred concept in this respect. It is relational and part of exchange theory between the state and society and, as will be demonstrated shortly, it has several elements: among others, political integration, state and institution building, and public policy.

3.1 Instruments of Polity Building in Societies with Deep Divides

3.3.1 Political Integration and Representation

Andreas Wimmer asks, "Why did some countries fall apart, often along ethnic fault lines, while others held together over decades and centuries, despite hosting a diverse population?" in his fascinating book on nation building published in 2018.[114] One should add, why do some countries deliver public goods better than others? These are two major and separate but very much interlinked issues: one deals with what Wimmer calls nation building (referred here as polity building) and the other with state building.[115] State building refers to the building of institutions to enhance the ability of the state to deliver basic public goods such as security (army, police), services (bureaucracy), roads, education, and health. It is about building tangible and visible institutions of the state that continue to serve society regardless of changes in political parties as a result of elections.[116] State building is not the major focus of this chapter but is implied in several sections (delivery of public goods).

Yet we should note that state building is an integral part of polity building. There are many experts that analyze polity building from different aspects. Some focus on the *onset* and the *process*, while others focus on *outcome*.[117] Wimmer argues that polity building has several major components, and he analyzes the components within the framework of exchange relationship between state and society while focusing on political inclusion.[118]

For purposes of this chapter, we classify the components of polity building into the hardware and software of polity building. The terminology is carefully crafted to show the importance of both categories of instruments for polity building while conveying the message that the hardware is considered as *foundational* and the software as *catalyst*. In most cases they are not clearly stipulated as distinct concepts. Experts continue to ask why some people positively identify themselves with the state, its institutions, and symbols, while others do not or even identify more with their ethno-national, regional, or religious identity than with the overarching state. This is not an abstract and complex question, although that is how many prefer to stipulate it.

A fundamental element of the social contract between the state and society that impacts the process of polity building is whether the political and economic system of the polity is inclusive or not. Studies on minority rights, ethnic conflicts, and nation building have shown that *inclusive political systems and representation* of all sections of society in public institutions build the "we belong to the system" mentality and the corollary of positive identification of citizens with the overarching state above and beyond allegiances to ethno-national, regional, or religious identity.[119] Wimmer as well reinforces this finding and argues identification with the overarching state and its institutions and *success* in polity building is related to political representation and inclusion. He wrote that it is a matter of "power and politics, rather than the demographic makeup of the population."[120] This is fundamental because earlier studies have focused on the nature of society in the polity and whether it is heterogeneous or homogeneous, without linking to factors such as political mobilization and the role of the state. Depending on the nature of the cleavage and its level of mobilization, states need to design appropriate institutions and policies to accommodate and manage their diversity. The idea of political inclusion and representation is primarily about creating a *just* political and economic order in a polity, but it is also part of human psychology. Take print out of a group photo circulating among the group. There could be a few Marxists who argue, I see the photo as an entity (to mean people first), yet every member of the group instinctively looks at his/her own photo first and then sees it as an entity. It is part of human nature to see our own images in public institutions, the same way we prefer to see our own picture in the group photo. Public institutions in diverse societies need to reflect the diversity on the ground following the logic of the group photo. It impacts the *legitimacy* of the institutions and more importantly their *performance*. It is unrealistic to expect a public institution that suffers from a legitimacy crisis to deliver an effective service. So the inclusion and representation logic has direct relations with creating a just political and economic order. It has also *symbolic* importance in addition to the core aim of creating a just political and economic order.[121] It is for this reason that the political integration of a society through inclusion and representation, particularly in diverse societies, is considered as the foundation for polity building: it is the hardware of polity building. Yet it is vital to note at this stage that the inclusion and representation issue should be genuinely addressed. As often happens within the African context, central governments select *puppets* in the name of representation and inclusion, and the puppets neither deliver nor genuinely represent the very society meant to be represented. Such systems are exposed to a legitimacy crisis and in the end to violence. Ethiopia is a classic example, but it is also a concern in many other African countries.[122] In addition to the nature of state power on the continent, lack of inclusion and representation has been a major concern throughout postcolonial Africa leading to wars, conflicts, and at times secession.

Looked at from the above perspective, it is not difficult to locate where Africa stands. Since the 1960s, nation building and the nation-state have been put to the test, and alternative theories for polity building have been on the rise.[123] This is particularly relevant for Africa, where nation-building is linked with coercive and arbitrary processes, by which the same communities are subdivided into different countries by artificial colonial borders.[124]

In some African countries with deep cleavages, the state continues to suffer from structural problems where the central government is often accused of centralization of power under an imperial center (big man, hegemonic party), weak institutions, corruption, abuse of rights, and marginalization of the bulk of society. By the end of the 1980s, there was already a solid study showing the African state is weak and in crisis and needs overhauling, leading to the *Third Wave*[125] and other reforms, such as liberalization and decentralization.[126] Thus, claims for accommodation, ethnic conflicts, violence, civil war, threats of secession, and state fragmentation remain major challenges. Some postcolonial African countries attempted to address these challenges by resorting to some form of federation and autonomy, but with the exception of Nigeria, all such efforts collapsed within a decade of their establishment.[127] The failure of the federal experience resulted in centralized unitary governments, imperial presidents, and one-party rule.[128] The respective federations failed because they were confronted by strong, one-man leaders who thought federalism would lead to state fragmentation and were thus against their own vision of centralized nation building.[129] The political leaders of such a diverse continent thought federalism in the context of artificially drawn borders might lead to polarization and in the end put unity and territorial integrity at stake.[130]

Postcolonial African leaders thus resorted to integration, as the new leaders thought ethnic divisions would be obstacles to unity and national integration. Integration remained the dominant trend within the African continent, practiced in 80 percent of the countries.[131] Leaders thought the homogenization of the nation and its state came to be seen as an indispensable prerequisite for democracy, political stability, and modernization. The big men leaders of postcolonial Africa espousing nation building for the newly independent states aimed to construct a single national identity through centralized national institutions and policies. One-party state, dissolving federal, and quasi-federal arrangements (Ethiopia, Sudan, Cameroon, Kenya, Uganda, and several other federations in West and Central Africa), the banning of multiparty systems until the end of the Cold War, imposing national services such as sending high school and university students and peasants to places outside of their ethnic origin were part of the integration project and a common trend throughout the continent.[132] The motto was "kill the tribe to build the nation."[133] Some centrist nation builders like Siad Barre of Somalia even went so far as to kill a person that he thought symbolized clanism and buried him in public, signaling the end of clanism in Somalia, only to get life after his removal from power in 1991.[134] Kenneth Kaunda, former president of Zambia, is quoted to have said, "A multiparty system would bring chaos, bloodshed and death;" Cameroon's long-serving president, Paul Biya, defended the one-party system as follows: "A united Cameroon devoid of ethnic, linguistic and religious cleavages."[135] An expert observing this dominant trend wrote that integration is the existing framework in Africa that has to be pursued because departing from it will not be easy or power holders may react with violence.[136] Yet we know integration (a presidential unitary system that imposes one national identity) induced many of the civil wars and conflicts that engulfed African states in the 1980s. Integration and state-led nation building were associated with repression and marginalization, major causes of ethnic conflict. It often leads to an unstable political system because it promotes centralization, often in the hands of a president who represents only a fraction of society, combined with a winner-takes-all electoral system making elections *explosive*; it also promotes the marginalization of non-core groups and the construction of a single national identity, often through coercion, fueling conflicts.[137] Ethiopia, Sudan, Chad, Liberia, Somalia, Sierra Leone, and the Congo went, among other countries, through these failed integration projects in the 1980s. In many cases, the state is visible in the capital, but beyond that it does not have a monopoly over the legitimate use of violence—one of the pillars of a state. Control over territory is also contested, as it is possible that rebels and factional groups may control part of the state. The state is not able to deliver key services (absent state). In some countries, such as Ethiopia, some even questioned whether the assumption about the state as provider of security holds water within the African continent, as it became a source of abuse and insecurity. The state in Africa, owing to its brutality, is at times framed as a "criminal state."[138] That was how the countless national liberation fronts in Ethiopia were born and brought the regime to its knees in 1991 and wondered whether they should stay in the union or leave, leading to the (in)famous Article 39 on the right to self-determination and secession: let us see if it works, and we go if it fails. Thus, the nature of state power in Africa has to be problematized; it cannot be assumed, as is often the case in the West.

The concept of nation building and national integration came into attack by various groups, particularly in countries that were deeply divided in the 1960s. Instead of nation building, the new perspective became how to manage diversity and ensure unity while accommodating diversity. The literature on federalism and devolution in Africa and whether institutions matter took center stage, particularly after the end of the Cold War. What form the idea of inclusion and representation takes in federal and devolved systems is far from settled but surely there was a shift from integration and centralized nation building to more accommodative systems such as federalism, devolution, and power sharing. For now, it is enough to state that political inclusion and representation is a fundamental element of polity building and takes different forms. The most common manifestations include devolution, autonomy (federacy), federalism (many varieties), and power-sharing schemes. The compelling message is that the *political systems matter* most in polity building. It is a fundamental element of polity building. If this core issue is not addressed, all other relational and exchange theories between the state and society will not bear much fruit. It is also likely that if the political elite in power misses the political integration hardware, it will likely miss the software component of the polity building (see below). The political integration framework impacts all other subsidiary policies of polity building. In other words, if the political system is framed along centralization, it is likely that other supportive policies such as media, language, culture, education, and history will also be framed accordingly, impacting polity building negatively. If the political system is framed in an inclusive manner, the likelihood of having accommodative and supportive policies is also very high. The political framework defines public policies and remains decisive. It is for this reason that we argue there is a strong link between polity building and inclusive political systems. It is the *hardware* of polity building. At its core is the ideal of creating a just political and economic order in a society. A society living under a just political and economic order owns the thick social contract whose bond can rarely break. Thus, if we unmask all the pretensions, polity building is about having inclusive and representative institutions that have a goal of creating a just political and economic order in a polity. In those systems citizens in *return* support their government and happily identify themselves with the overarching state, its flag, the institutions, army, anthem, and other symbols of the state.

This is not about the framework alone but also about the *lived reality*. The experience of federalism and devolution on the African continent, including Ethiopia, is not a happy one, both in the past and the present. So, promise and design alone will not help; lived reality is what matters. Ethiopia promised autonomy to Eritrea following a UN Resolution (1952–62) and yet the center's grand agenda of a centralized Amharic-speaking nation building framed the federation as an obstacle to its absolute rule and dissolved it within a decade. What followed was not polity building but polity destroying: the secession of Eritrea. The *Derg* pursued a centralized political system by and large, and this was followed by a military solution to political issues. As a result, by 1991 Ethiopia was on the verge of collapse. The Ethiopian People's Revolutionary Democratic Front (EPRDF 1991–2018) promised a federal system and yet was very centralized, and its system of representation was party, not people, based. Representatives from Amhara or Oromia were perceived as *puppets* and party-handpicked cadres rather than genuine representatives of the people they claim to represent. Thus, despite the promise, both its operation and its system of representation failed and led to widespread protests in 2015. It got worse under Abiy, who assumed power in 2018 following the protests and resignation of Haile Mariam Desalegn (Ethiopia's prime minister 2012–18). Self-rule was fully obliterated and replaced by appointees from Addis in the name of a "command post," liquidation of the various coalition members of the party, and representation became a farce. The devastating war in Tigray was a living example and, as they say, the rest is history. Polity building ended up becoming polity destroying. The lesson is clear: if politics goes wrong, polity building also goes wrong and once again political integration of a society through inclusive institutions and policies (devolution, federalism, power sharing, and accommodative public policies) is the hardware of polity building. It is a fundamental element of the social contract that defines power relations between the state and society. It is the thick component of the social contract. All other elements of polity building we argue are supportive ones. The rest are the software of polity building. The software reinforces the hardware, and both combined could make polity building a possible success.

3.3.2 Delivery of Public Goods: Functioning State Institutions

The second component of polity building is the political economy aspect that refers to the resources that are traded between the state and society. These are the public goods provided by the government to society. The provision of impartial security to its citizens (competent army and police), roads, bridges, schools, and hospitals as tangible goods are part of the hardware (state building), while the *interconnected society* and the *bond* created as a result of the tangible goods is part of the software of polity building. Irrespective of whether the state is federal or unitary, democratic or authoritarian, there is a *tie* established through the provision of public goods. In return for the critical services and public goods provided by the state, citizens can support the government, offer military services, and pay taxes. This one may refer to the *thin* social contract between the state and society. Thin because the state could offer better than service delivery through respect for human rights and democratic elections that can better enhance the quality of the social contract. For now let us remain within the thin social contract based on the provision of public goods. A state that is able to deliver such crucial services on an equal basis and both in rural and urban areas has already created a *bond* with its citizens. It surely is not a strong bond but fair enough there is a tie created. This is one form of relational network or exchange network articulated by Wimmer. The state needs strong institutions (army, security, police, and bureaucracy) to deliver public goods and services to society on an equal basis. It is here that state and polity building overlap. State building through strong institutions enhances the sense of relationship between state and society. It builds the software, the invisible bond between state and society. As argued by Wimmer, "Nation building is easier in states capable of providing public goods."[139]

In most western states, capable state institutions were created way before the start of polity building and democratization during the nineteenth and early twentieth centuries. In most developing countries, institution building, democratization, and polity building is supposed to be done simultaneously, and this complicates the matter. The capacity of the state to collect revenue and mobilize resources to ensure basic services and bring economic growth alongside the private sector sounds simple but remains Africa's major challenge. Most states in Africa have little control over their territory, continue to face a legitimacy crisis, and do not deliver much outside of their capital. Capacity of the state to deliver (functioning state institutions), which is more about state building than polity building, makes a wealth of difference among states.

Provision of public goods and services "bridge divides, reduce the salience of ethnicity in politics, undermine support for separatism, make violent conflict and war less likely, and eventually lead citizens to identify with the overarching state and perceive it as a community of lived solidarity and shared political destiny despite diversity of one form or another."[140] Provision of public goods and services and the socioeconomic infrastructure is a *network* that connects citizens among themselves and with the state. It is a bridge that connects communities otherwise divided by language, ethnicity, region, or religion. They serve as bridges cutting across divides and walls. There is already well-established data that shows strongly connected communities or countries rarely go to conflict.[141]

They have a lot to lose. States that deliver public goods on an equal basis bind their people, irrespective of ethnic, religious, or other differences. If one gets the services right, one has less to complain about and more to identify with the overarching state; citizens know what it means to miss them. Efficient service delivery to citizens on an equal basis leaves little incentive for ethno-national mobilization. *Functioning state institutions* thus matter for polity building. If there is no ground for complaint, why mobilize in the first place? Functioning state institutions rob the many causes of mobilization.

3.3.3 State Power in Africa

This chapter does not aim to explain the nature of state power in Africa and how it impacts the delivery of services. A brief discussion is, however, relevant to hint at how it impacts governance, federalism, devolution, and constitutionalism. One of the most difficult issues in Africa is ensuring that power is exercised for *public purposes* and safeguarding constitutional governance that requires the *institutionalization of power*. That is ensuring that public institutions established by the constitution exercise their mandate as defined in the constitution, while respecting the limits of power expressed in the form of enforceable human rights, federalism, checks and balances, and the rule of law. One of the daunting tasks is to shift the exercise of power from personal rule/ party hegemony to institutions by enforcing the supreme law. Without shifting and institutionalizing power, separation of power, and rule of law, checks and balances make little sense because the locus of power is elsewhere. If it is the army (as is the case in Egypt, Zimbabwe, Sudan, and Nigeria in the past) or the party chair (Ethiopia and South Africa) behind the scene that is kingmaker, what purpose will introducing separation of powers or federalism serve? Power has to be first institutionalized before it can be separated or divided. While the link between constitutional adjudication and governance, and in particular the use and exercise of power, is a major issue generally; it brings distinct challenges in the African context.

Max Weber explained the nature of patrimonial regimes long before Europe shifted towards the modern state that respects rule of law and exercises checks and balances among the different branches of governments to ensure that power is used for public purposes.[142] The modern state is an impersonal *state* in which the relationship between ruler and citizen is not based on personal ties but on *merit* and technical knowledge.[143] The state emerges as a distinct entity with its autonomy and claims to serve everyone impartially and does not promote factional interests.[144] This is the general framework, although big companies and the economic class have over the years somehow compromised this basic foundation. In the patrimonial regimes, however, the polity remains the personal property of the ruler that could be an emperor, a big man, or one party.

According to Fukuyama, in this system "the state administration is essentially an extension of the ruler's household."[145] As such, there is little distinction between the private and public spheres. It lacks autonomy and is in the service of political elites and factional interests. In today's global world, most African states would not call themselves patrimonial, as there is a *formal pretension* in adopting a constitution with some element of separation of powers, democracy, and claim for the rule of law. Yet behind such crude formality the use of public power for private gains and its exercise based on personal, party, or ethnic ties is pervasive. Formal rules and institutions cannot stand in the way of the big man or the big party, and that is one of the reasons why institution building, federalism, and rule of law become difficult, because the powerful actors do not adhere to the formal rules.[146] This state of affairs has been brutally called by Bayart the "politics of the belly."[147] The merger between crude formality and patrimonial practice is referred to by some as a *neo-patrimonial* regime or extractive state.[148] The political elite in power continues to control (*capture*) state institutions, and through that the massive resources that it commands create patronage at different levels. In what Alex De Waal calls "political budget," the rulers spend a big part of the country's resources to pay for political loyalists, with little left for public goods, without accountability, as if it were a private resource.[149] Informal and personalized power, the conception of power, and the country's assets as if they were the ruler's private affair, the resources at its disposal creates a favorable condition for the incumbent to win elections.[150] Beneath the formal institutions, the ruling party (imperial president or big man) distributes the spoils of office to its supporters and punishes dissenters.[151] Despite constitutional principles, it also determines who may be engaged in politics and the space available for such engagement, the most often used tool being to divide and rule the opposition and weaken it. The informal networks weaken (or even override) formal institutions, undermining their ability to *deliver impersonal public* services.[152]

African leaders exhibit the above features, but some are more outrageous than others. Nigeria's oil wealth and the corruption associated with it are well known. Transparency international ranks Nigeria 154 out of 180 in the 2021 corruption index, in the high list.[153] Prime Minister Abiy boldly and arrogantly explained (*Chaka* Project) his new palace project, estimated to cost nearly equal to the country's annual budget, to members of parliament in 2022, briefing them that they can visit the project site but have no mandate to ask where the money comes from and how the project is being executed.[154] At a time where no less than twenty million people are in need of aid[155] and more than 5.1 million are internally displaced (one of the highest in the world)[156] due to drought, brutal civil war and conflicts, he is fascinated by a palace project and parks and tells parliament he is not going to be accountable to them. And the members listen and laugh!

To ensure that political power is used for public purposes, there is a need to shift the locus of power from the personal or party level to impersonal institutions and regulate it through the rule of law and a system of checks and balances. Meritocratic bureaucracies in the civil service, systems of checks and balances (both horizontal and vertical), and independent bodies such as a supreme court or constitutional court with a mandate to enforce the constitution (both to the ruler and ruled) are time-tested institutional safeguards against neo-patrimonial regimes. Without these reforms, it is hardly possible to speak and write about federalism (and the autonomy of sub-units) and constitutionalism, as they remain victims of the hegemonic center.

3.3.4 Public Policy

The third component of polity building relates to *public policy*. Here we include language, culture, media, anthem, flag, symbols and monuments, museums, legal and education systems, and not least, history. Each of them merits a book on their own, but the intention here is to show the link with polity building. Whoever thinks public policy is a neutral crafting of policy has to rethink his/her perspective seriously. These policies are the results of the political framework we identified already. Public policy is an instrument of a political project, and its link with polity building is direct. Gellner wrote that at the height of the centralized nation state, the centralized education system was the most important tool for nation building.[157] Public policy also demonstrates whose story is being *institutionalized* and narrated and which ones are thrown to the dustbin of history.[158] Those reflected in the policy remain in the institutional memory for generations; they are nurtured and promoted using state resources, while those not included are *erased* from history. That explains very well why issues related to identity and public policy such as language, symbols, culture, religion, and history remain emotionally provocative. They are strongly linked to identity and symbols. What do we want to achieve by using these policies? Are these policies instruments of a centralized political project or an accommodative policy that complements the political integration project? Public policy has both practical and symbolic importance. For example, the symbols that we put on currency and coins are sometimes carefully crafted to manifest diversity. If crafted carefully to be inclusive, citizens often identify themselves with the state, particularly if the political integration project is crafted right. It is also possible to have such symbols representing only a section of society. In Sudan, the tension between North and South Sudan before its secession was partly related to the symbols inserted on the flag, coins, and currency with the South Sudanese elite rejecting the symbols set by the North. The Northern elite identified itself as part of the Arab and Islamic world, while the Southerners' thought they were Africans. The policies that emanated from these two divergent political frameworks could not stand side by side, thus, combined with other factors, resulted in the secession of South Sudan in 2011.[159]

The same is true with history. Is the history written in a more balanced and inclusive way, or is it written to reflect the history of the state and its institutions alone, chronicling it, as it is often called, in a selective way? A brief reflection is in order here. While conducting my PhD thesis in Utrecht in the Netherlands (2001–5), writing the first chapter (the political and historical context that led to the federal system in Ethiopia) was the most difficult part. Here is the reason: I read several books on Ethiopia (history and politics). Teshale Tibebu,[160] Gebru Tarekegn,[161] Bahru Zewde,[162] Mohamed Hassen,[163] Richard Pankhurst,[164] and Harold Marcus.[165] The books are predominantly on modern Ethiopia covering more or less the same period. One can add to this list John Markakis's[166] anatomy of the political history of Ethiopia, a classic work published in 1974, and the careful analysis of history by Triulzi.[167] After reading these books, one cannot help but conclude that the books refer to the history of different countries, not the same country, Ethiopia. One narrates the history of the state and its institutions following the trend of chronicling the ruler's history: a very centrist approach. It leaves out the history of the periphery and the peasant struggle. The other narrates about the suffering of Ethiopian peasants an the hands of a brutal state. One narrates the life of the marginalized groups ("people without history") and one about the history of Oromo trying to find their place within Ethiopia or beyond. Triulzi carefully explains the paradox and makes some sense in linking the idea of history and how it relates to polity building and the political background of the authors. How do we reconcile the fundamental paradoxes? Ethiopia claims to be the only independent state in Africa, and that should imply the people who have inhabited the country have a long history not so much disturbed by colonial history. The role of the historian is to demonstrate the rich history of the people and how they have interacted (both in the negative and positive sense) with the state and its institutions linking the part and the whole through synthesis in an *inclusive and impartial way*. We know from practice that teaching history has become very controversial because some perceive it as not reflective of the whole, that it only tells part of the story, and thus is not inclusive. In some cases it could even be pejorative. It is as controversial as the country's political system. A more balanced, inclusive rewriting of history has an impact on the polity and kind of society we want to have. Exclusive and pejorative history and the chronicling of the history of the state and its centrist institutions is counterproductive for polity building and could indeed be a tool for "nation destroying." Those who think their history is not included, deliberately neglected,[168] or has been misrepresented will write (or rewrite) their history. The last five decades have been a period of the deconstruction of history. We will then have many histories, not one, and different imagined or real communities will follow. That is the foundation for further cracks in the system.

Culture, media, and language policies suffer from the same limitation. Indeed the controversy over history applies to these sectors as well. What is the language policy? Does it promote pluralism or force others to assimilate? Some talk even today of the need for a "national language." This is not only counterproductive but has been tried and failed. Haile Selassie and the Derg imposed Amharic as a national language, which besides the political crisis added fuel to the fire, ending in the failure of the project in 1991. Ethiopia, as the chapters in this book will show, is multinational, and one cannot impose one selected language to be "national" and then nurture and promote it at the expense of other languages and identities. It is also good to realize the fact that even if all Ethiopians were to speak one language, our problems will not go away. Somalia is a textbook example. It was considered in the 1960s the only blessed African nation-state with people speaking the same language and professing the same religion and having their own government. Speaking the same language and professing the same religion did not, however, save Somalia from collapse in 1991.

Whose culture is presented in public, in the media, and in formal events? Whose culture and language is nurtured and promoted and which ones are sidelined and why? Do we sense what the implications are? Is the cultural policy accommodative, or is it still a reflection of old Abyssinia? How does one create symbiosis between the individual cultures and the interactions among them and find a shared one? Symbols, museums, and monuments could be part of the problem or the solution as well. Who are our heroes and heroines? Do we have shared ones, or are we also divided on this? It seems someone's hero is the other's traitor. Emperor Menelik is portrayed as Ethiopia's symbol of unity on one side and a "colonizer and traitor" by the other. What is the role of the media in this regard? Is it promoting shared values, or is it a tool for centralized policy and propaganda? Is it promoting tolerance and mutual existence or hatred and animosity? What is the guiding policy, and is it inclusive or exclusive? Are we nesting or fragmenting society? The flag is even more controversial, and since the new government came to power in 2018, we do not even know which one is Ethiopia's flag. It is supposed to represent the people and the country, but as we know it, it remains the most divisive one. We are divided at the point where we were supposed to be united. So our athletes suffer because of our division when they are supposed to celebrate after winning a race. Some chose one type over the other: they cannot be immune from our divisions. At the moment, it is the author's view that we are a mess when it comes to public policies, the same way we are a mess at the political level. Public policies are truly part of the software of polity building. They are the results of deliberate political choice crafted to achieve certain goals. Carefully crafted and inclusive public policies including the flag have the potential to nest different identities, cutting across the divisions while the opposite happens when such policies are reflections of a narrow section of society. Inclusive public policies build the sense that we belong to the system, the same way as inclusive political systems. Exclusive and narrowly based public policies build the sense of isolation and ethno-nationalism and thus could facilitate state fragmentation.

Certainly quality of leadership remains critical for polity building. The differences between American founding father George Washington and Napoleon Bonaparte of France is visible, although both led major revolutions in their respective countries. The former served his country for eight years and despite popular calls for another term, he resisted and chose a democratic way, setting limited term for office and constitutionalism. The latter chose to be French emperor and military despot.[169] Selfless leaders like Nelson Mandela, former President of South Africa can unify a deeply divided country by race and inequality cutting across the divides. Divisive, corrupt and incompetent leaders could on the contrary fuel animosity and fragmentation in society. Often referred to as banal nationalism, with supportive political and public policy instruments (otherwise could also be divisive) sporting activities such as football and athletics play as well their role in unifying people, despite differences of one type or another.[170] Yet sport alone can do little; it can serve only as a supportive instrument to the hardware of polity building. Yascha Mounk, in an otherwise comprehensive work,[171] mentions *patriotism* (love and loyalty for one's country) as a unifying factor but does not explain how citizens and minorities treated as second-class citizens in their country would love their country and become patriots. In some cases, those citizens and minorities are victims of centuries of marginalization, and to expect these sections of society to fall into an abstract love for an otherwise brutal political system (criminal state) is more myth than reality. As mentioned already, ethno-national minorities resent such hierarchy and assert the right to self-government and even aim to secede if the social contract is not renegotiated. Patriotism comes only when there is an inclusive political and economic order; it does not come in the abstract.

Polity building is not a one-time exercise. It is also not a job for one generation only. So long as the society exists, polity building should exist in tandem with it. It is an incremental process where the new generation is supposed to build on it and hand it over to the next one. It is a never-ending process unless the polity ends by fragmentation, which on its own brings another issue of polity building in the new state.

Conclusion

Societies with deep divisions, as in Ethiopia, face enormous challenges related to politically mobilized identity-based cleavages that need distinct political, institutional, and policy arrangements. Nation building as understood in the traditional sense that insists on assimilation and integration can only fuel conflicts. Ethno-national/regional-based cleavage and political mobilization is often a reaction to the centrist elites' project and a search for finding a political and identity space. It is a sub-state nationalism framed in reaction to the central government's nationalism. There are competing nationalisms within the nation-state that if not addressed could lead to violence, civil war, and state fragmentation. Both are pursued in the name of nationalism and have the potential to fuel the passions and emotions from both sides of the political spectrum to cause political instability and state collapse. One is pursued by the central government in the name of nation building, patriotism, civic nationalism, unity, and ensuring territorial integrity and the other by the ethno-nationalist elite aiming for self-government, representation, and possibly secession. On the menu of options, theories such as consociational democracy have been recommended when the political system faces deeply divided cleavages. Instead of having winners and losers, consociational democracy brings major political actors either on an equal footing (as in Belgium) or through proportional arrangements to power and insists on consensus decision-making on fundamental issues. Thus those left out of the majoritarian democracy become decision-makers through power sharing, reducing the potential for conflict. Distinct institutional arrangements thus matter in managing cleavages and reducing conflicts. This usually is combined with federations that also adopt parliamentary systems. Consociational parliamentary federations would then deploy consensus-based decision-making at the federal level on key political, diplomatic, and economic issues that serve as trust-building schemes, mitigating the potential for conflict. In some countries, such power-sharing arrangements also ensure political autonomy at the constituent level. This is the best possible offer a country could provide (short of secession) as a means to ensure peace, unity, stability, and a system of inclusive polity building. This institutional arrangement builds the sense of belongingness and loyalty of different groups towards the overarching state above and beyond other manifestations of identity: a critical requirement for building the polity in societies with deep divisions.

One should, however, be cautious and face reality. Inclusive political systems of one type or another that have the potential for polity building are challenged by *ethnocracy* and a regime's determination and insistence to use violence to address political demands. This makes democratization and federalism mission impossible. Federalism, whatever form it may take, is inherently about a peaceful ongoing bargaining and negotiation between centripetal (unity) and centrifugal forces (diversity). Federalism takes a "system of negotiated political accommodation" as the *norm* and rules out violence.[172] Success in federalism implies an absence of war and violence. Threats of secession, as in Quebec and Scotland, do not wither away, but institutionalized federal bargaining provides an avenue for compromise. In many countries in Africa, including Ethiopia, negotiated political accommodation is replaced by violence. Federalism has not failed but has been *betrayed* both in the past and present from serving as a venue for intergovernmental bargain and negotiated reform.

While there has been a significant increase in the use of federalism and devolution in Africa since the end of the Cold War, they manifest centralizing features, as they are curtailed by the nature of state power on the continent. Whatever institutional designs are put in place, big men and hegemonic and dominant parties are the actual machines that operate the designs. The nature of power in Africa—an imperial center (regardless of whether the design in the constitution is presidential or parliamentary, integration or accommodation)—and the patron-client relations between the center and sub-units make stability imperative. The claim by the center to contain centrifugal forces also explains the unitary features of African federal and devolved systems. Within these broad observations, however, political pluralism and the progress towards democratization in Kenya and Nigeria has opened an opportunity for sub-state governors to assert and exercise some level of autonomy, as opposition parties have been able to win seats in several states, while in Ethiopia the hegemonic party has command and control over sub-units. Ethiopia is an extreme case of central political control and complete disregard of the constitution, with little or no progress towards democratization. This context explains the political implosion it continues to face. Donald Horowitz argues that the opening up of local political space (partly, as in Nigeria and Kenya, at least at the sub-unit level) averts the likelihood of ethnic separatism: losers at the federal level can still enjoy self-government at the sub-unit level. Politics is not anymore a zero-sum game, and this reduces the high stakes of power at the center. Marginalization at the federal level and denial of self-government at sub-unit levels reinforces alienation and separation.[173] This is what is happening in Ethiopia. It is a zero-sum game, and the stakes are high and risky at the center.

Notes

1 Andreas Wimmer, *Nation Building: Why Some Countries Come Together while Others Fall Apart* (Princeton University Press, 2018), p. 3.

2 In France, when various regional peasant populations who spoke Provencal, Aquitaine, Basque, and so on were assimilated into the French nation. See Eugen Weber, *Peasants into Frenchmen: The Modernisation of Rural France*, 1870–1914 (Chatto and Windus, 1979).

3 Denis Mack Smith, *Garibaldi: A Great Life in Brief* (Knopf, 1956).

4 Quoted in Elie Kedourie, *Nationalism* (Frederick A. Praeger, 1960).

5 John Stuart Mill, "Representative Government," in *Utilitarianism, on Liberty, and Considerations on Representative Government.* Geraint Williams, ed. (Everyman, 1993 [1861]), p. 394.

6 Ernest Gellner, *Nation and Nationalism* (Basil Blackwell, 1983) p. 1.

7 John Loughlin, "Reconfiguring the Nation State: Hybridity vs. Uniformity," In: *Routledge Handbook on Regionalism and Federalism. John Loughlin, John Kincaid, Wilfried Swenden, eds.* (Routledge, 2013) p. 2. Decentralization and demands for accommodation by territorially based cleavages forced many nation-states in Europe to open up space for self-government and political autonomy since the 1970s. Spain, Belgium, and the UK are examples. *p.* 12.

8 The French Revolution of 1789 brought the nation-state (Jacobin, centralized indivisible unitary state after annihilating those who proposed decentralization), while the American Revolution established a decade-old Confederation that later led to the US Federation of 1789. Switzerland, and to some extent the UK, remained an exception to the nation-state. Loughlin, *Reconfiguring the Nation state* , p. 7.

9 Rene Grotenhuis, *Nation Building as Necessary Effort in Fragile States* (Amsterdam: Amsterdam University Press, 2016), p. 19

10 See Yoram Hazony, *The Virtues of Nationalism* (Basic Books, 2018).

11 Charles Tilley, *The Formation of National States in Western Europe* (Princeton University Press, 1975), p. 75.

12 It ruled Turkey, Greece, Egypt, Bulgaria, Jordan, Lebanon, Romania, Palestine, and parts of North Africa for six hundred years.

13 Tilley *The Formation of Nation States* , p. 75.

14 Marc Sanjaume-Calvet, "Reconciling Liberal Democracy, Nationalism and Political Divorce." In: *Revisiting Unity and Diversity in Federal Countries: Changing Concepts, Reform Proposals and New Institutional Realities. Alain-G. Gagnon and Michael Burgess, eds.,* (Brill, Nijhoff, 2018) p. 375; see also Marina Ottaway, "Think Again: Nation Building." *Foreign Policy (2009).*

15 This is a speech made in 1862 by Otto von Bismarck, who played a role in unifying Germany. For details, see Tilly (n. 13), p. 75.

16 John Markakis, Gunther Schlee, and John Young, "Introduction." In: *The Nation State: A Wrong Model for the Horn of Africa. John Markakis, Gunther Schlee and John Young, eds.,* (Berlin: Max Planck: 2021), p. 10.

17 Grotenhuis *Nation Building* , p. 20.

18 Grotenhuis*Nation Building* , p. 28.

19 Walker Connor, "Nation-Building or Nation-Destroying?" World Politics 24, no. 3 (1972), p. 337.

20 Michael Keating, "So Many Nations, So Few States: Territory and Nationalism in the Global Era." In: *Multinational Democracies. Alain-G. Gagnon, James Tully, eds.* (Cambridge University Press, 2001), p. 44. Demand for self-government based on historical construction is not necessarily tied to secession, although that may come if the state denies or fails to respond after significant delay. In most cases, it can be accommodated using a variety of options: a decentralized unitary system, power sharing, federalism, autonomy, and asymmetry. Central governments can deploy a menu of options to address such demands.

21 David Miller, "Nationality in Divided Societies." In: *Multinational Democracies. Alain-G. Gagnon, James Tully, eds.* (Cambridge University Press, 2001), p. 302. If the ethnic group demands self-government or claims to a territory then it becomes a nation.

22 Gidon Gottlieb, *Nation Against State: A New Approach to Ethnic Conflicts and the Decline of Sovereignty* (New York: Council on Foreign Relations Press, 1993), pp. 25–26.

23 Ted Robert Gurr, *Minorities at Risk: A Global View of Ethnopolitical Conflict* (United States Institute of Peace Press, 1993), pp. 18–20; see also Sujit Choudhry and Nathan Hume, "Federalism, Devolution and Secession: From Classical to Post-Conflict Federalism." In: *Comparative Constitutional Law. Tom Ginsburg and Rosalind Dixon, eds.* (Cheltenham: Edward Elgar, 2011), p. 364.

24 See for details John Burton, *Violence Explained* (Manchester University Press, 1997), pp. 32–37

25 Dawn Walsh, *Territorial Self Government as Conflict Management Tool* (Palgrave Macmillan, 2018), pp. 4–5.

26 Connor, *Nation Building or Nation Destroying* , p. 343.

27 Genevieve Nootens, "Can Non-Territorial Autonomy Bring an Added Value to Theoretic and Policy-Oriented Analysis of Ethnic Politics?" In: *Minority Accommodation through Territorial and Non Territorial Autonomy. Malloy, Tove, and Francesco Palermo, eds..* (Oxford University Press, 2015), p. 38.

28 Alfred Stepan, Juan Linz, and Yogendra Yadiv, *Crafting State Nations: India and Other Multinational Democracies* (Johns Hopkins Press, 2011), p. 1.

29 See Will Kymlicka, *Multicultural Odysseys: Navigating the New International Politics of Diversity* (Oxford: Oxford University Press, 2007), p. 42.

30 Loughlin *Reconfiguring the Nation State*, pp. 7–8.

31 Gottlieb *Nation Against State*, pp. 24–25.

32 Ephraim Nimni, "Minority Accommodation through Territorial and Non-Territorial Autonomy" In: *Minorities and the Limits of Liberal Democracy: Democracy and Non-Territorial Autonomy. Tove Malloy and Francesco Palermo, eds.* (Oxford University Press, 2015), pp. 57–58.

33 Kymlicka, *Multicultural Odysseys* pp. 61–62.

34 John McGarry, Michael Keating, and Margaret Moore, "Introduction: European Integration and the nationalities question" In: *European Integration and the Nationality Question. John McGarry and Michael Keating eds.* (Routledge, 2006), pp. 1–2.

35 Charles Tilly, "Introduction" In: *The Formation of National States in Western Europe.* Charles Tilly, ed. (Princeton: Princeton University Press, 1975), p. 44.

36 Karl Deutsch, *Nationalism and Social Communication: An Inquiry into the Foundations of Nationalism* (Cambridge: Massachusetts, 1953). From the 1970s onward, modernization was subject to criticism from several angles, the most widely known being the attack from multiculturalism that accused both the nation-state and modernization for causing injustice to ethno-national minorities in the name of nation building. Kymlicka, *Multicultural Odysseys*, pp. 61–63.

37 See McGarry, Keating, and Moore, *Introduction*, p. 4.

38 John Markakis, "The Crisis of the State in the Horn of Africa." In: *The Nation State: A Wrong Model for the Horn of Africa. John Markakis, Gunther Schlee and John Young, eds.* (Max Planck: 2021), p. 13.

39 Ghia Nordia, "The End of the Postnational Illusion," (2017). *Journal of Democracy* 28, no. 2; Francis Fukuyama, *Identity: the Demand for Dignity and the Politics of Resentment* (Straus and Giroux, 2018); Amy Chua, *Political Tribes: Group Instinct and the Fate of Nations* (Penguin Press, 2018).

40 Grotenhuis *Nation Building*, p. 104.

41 Loughlin, Reconfiguring the Nation State.

42 John Markakis, Gunther Schlee, and John Young, Introduction, p. 13

43 See Catharine Newbury, "State at War: Confronting Conflicts in Africa" (2002). *African Studies Review* 45, no. 2, pp. 1–20.

44 Adebayo Adedeji. 1999a. "Comprehending African Conflicts." In: *Comprehending and Mastering African Conflicts: The Search for Sustainable Peace and Good Governance* (Zed Books, 1999), pp.4–5.

45 Olusegun Obasanjo, "Ethiopian Civil War: How We Brokered Peace." Available at https://dailytrust.com/ethiopia-civil-war-how-we-brokeredpeace-obasanjo/. See also report issued by the Peace and Security Council of the African Union by Amani Africa Media and Research Services, https://amaniafrica-et.org/the-peace-and-security-council-in-2022-the-year-in-review/ 23 February 2023.

46 *Secessionism in African Politics: Aspiration, Grievance, Performance, Disentrancement. In: Lotje De Vries, Pierre Englebert, and Mareike Schomerus, eds.* (Palgrave Macmillan, 2019).

47 Michael Keating, "So Many Nations, So Few States: Territory and Nationalism in the Global Era." *Multinational Democracies. Iin: Alain-G. Gagnon, James Tully, eds.* (Cambridge University Press, 2001), p. 39.

48 See Alesina, Alberto F. and Easterly, William and Devleeschauwer, Arnaud and Kurlat, Sergio and Wacziarg, Romain T., "Fractionalization" (June 2002). Available at SSRN: https://ssrn.com/abstract=319762 or http://dx.doi.org/10.2139/ssrn.319762; See also Ephraim Nimni, "Introduction: The National Cultural Autonomy Model Revisited." In: *National Cultural Autonomy and Its Contemporary Critics. Ephraim Nimni, ed.* (London: Rutledge, 2005), p. 1.

49 Markakis, *The Crisis of the State*, p. 20.

50 Markakis, *The Crisis of the State, p.* 21.

51 Markakis, *The Crisis of the State.*

52 Basil Davidson, *The Black Man's Burden: Africa and the Curse of the Nation State* (Time Books/ Random House, 1992).

53 Markakis, Schlee, and Young Introduction, p. 13.
54 Connor *Nation Building or Nation Destroying*, pp. 319–55.
55 See John McGarry, *et. al. Introduction*, p. 5.
56 See for details Edmond Keller, *Revolutionary Ethiopia: From Empire to People's Republic* (Indiana University Press, 1988).
57 Christopher Clapham, "The Ethiopian Experience of Devolved Government" (2013). Ethiopian Journal of Federal Studies 1, no. 1, p.18.
58 The 1955 Revised Constitution Article 4.
59 Gebru Tareke, *Ethiopia: Power and Protest: Peasant Revolts in the Twentieth Century* (Cambridge University Press 1991).
60 Christopher Clapham, *The Horn of Africa: State Formation and Decay* (Hurst and Co, 2017), p. 34.
61 Keller (n. 56), pp. 137–40; Christopher Clapham, "Centralization and Social Responses in Southern Ethiopia" (1975). 74 *African Affairs* 74, pp. 73–75.
62 Markakis The Crisis of the State, p. 25. The known provincial governor's name had to be changed as a result. Kumsa Bereda, the governor of Wollega, was baptized and given a Christian name, Gebre Egzabher. Ras Ali, king of Wollo, was renamed Ras Michael. The last ruler of Janjero, Abba Bagibo, was renamed Gebre Medhin. The last king of Limmu, Abba Gomboli, became Gebre Selassie.
63 See Richard Pankhurst, "Tedla Hailu and the Problem of Multiethnicity in Ethiopia" (1998). *North East African Studies* 5, no. 3, pp. 81–96.
64 Richard Pankhurst, *Tedla Hailu* p. 86.
65 Selam, *Gazetta Tahsas* 19, 1926 E.C.
66 Donald Levine, *Greater Ethiopia: The Evolution of a Multiethnic Society*, 2nd ed. (University of Chicago Press, 2000).
67 The 1955 Revised Constitution, Articles 125 and 126; 1987 Const., Article 116.
68 Andargachew Tiruneh, *The Ethiopian Revolution: 1974-1987* (Cambridge University Press, 1993).
69 Markakis, Schlee, and Young *Introduction*, p. 17.
70 Arend Lijphart, "The Wave of Power Sharing Democracy." In: *The Architecture of Democracy: Constitutional Design, Conflict Management and Democracy.* Andrew Reynolds, ed. (Oxford University Press, 2002), p. 37.
71 Samuel Huntington, *The Third Wave: Democratization in the Late 20th Century* (University of Oklahoma Press, 1991).
72 Ted Robert Gurr, *Minorities at Risk: A Global View of Ethnopolitical Conflict* (United States Institute of Peace Press, 1993), pp. 18–20.
73 George Anderson and Sujit Choudhry, "Territorial Cleavages and Constitutional Transitions: Political Mobilization, Constitution Making Processes and Constitutional Design." In: *Territory and Power in Constitutional Transitions. Anderson and Choudhry eds.* (Oxford University Press, 2019), p. 374.
74 See Stepan, Linz, and Yadiv Crafting State Nations, p. 14.
75 For details, see Assefa Fiseha, "Tigray: A Nation in Search of Statehood?" In: *International Journal of Minority and Group Rights* 30 no. 4 (2023).
76 Nordia, The End of the Postnational Illusion.

77 *See* Donald Horowitz, *Constitutional Design: Proposals, Process*, in *The Architecture of Democracy: Constitutional Design, Conflict Management and Democracy.* Andrew Reynolds, ed. (Oxford University Press, 2002).

78 Sujit Choudhry, "Bridging Comparative Politics and Comparative Constitutional Law: Constitutional Design in Divided Societies." In: *Constitutional Design for Divided Societies: Integration or Accommodation?* Sujit Choudhry, ed. (Oxford University Press, 2008), p. 5.

79 Anderson and Choudhry, Territorial Cleavages, p. 374.

80 See David Miller, *On Nationality* (Oxford: Clarendon Press, 1997), pp.17–18; Walker Connor, "A Nation Is a Nation, Is a State, Is an Ethnic Group, Is a…." *Nationalism. Iin: John Hutchinson and Anthony Smith eds.* (Oxford University Press, 1994), p. 36. There are objective and subjective elements of the definition, and both Miller and Connor focus on the subjective rather than the objective (common culture, language, religion, territory, or political institutions) elements. The nation exists in the hearts of the members and is manifested in the sense of *belonging together*.

81 Ronald Watts, *Comparing Federal Systems*, 3rd ed. (McGill, Queen's University Press, 2008), p. 84.

82 Joseph Lacey, *Centripetal Democracy* (Oxford University Press, 2017), p. 3; the idea originally belongs to Philippe Van Parijs, *Linguistic Justice for Europe and the World* (Oxford University Press, 2011), pp. 28–30.

83 Lacey, Centripetal Democracy, p. 5.

84 Robert Dahl, *Toward Democracy- A Journey, Reflections: 1940-1997* (Institute of Government Study Press, 1997).

85 Arend Lijphart, "Constitutional Design for Divided Societies. (2004). *Journal of Democracy* 15, no. 2: p. 98. The Shia are estimated to be 64 percent and the Sunni 34 percent. The Arab (65 percent) vs. Kurd (30 percent) divide is also an issue in Iraq.

86 Francis Fukuyama, *Nation Building Beyond Afghanistan and Iraq* (Johns Hopkins University Press 2006), p. 3.

87 Max Weber, *Essays in Sociology* (Routledge, 1957); see also, Daron Acemoğlu and James A. Robinson, *Why Nations Fail* (Crown Publisher, 2013).

88 For an insightful distinction between state and nation building see Nicolas Lemay-Hebert, "State Building without Nation Building? Legitimacy, State Failure and the Limits of the Institutional Approach," (2009). *Journal of Intervention and State Building* 3, no. 1, p.22.

89 Lemay-Hebert, *State Building*, p. 23.

90 Goran Hyden, *African Politics in Comparative Perspective,* 2nd ed. (Cambridge University Press, 2013), p. 54.

91 Fukuyama *Nation Building.*

92 The most classic work that advocated and predicted that minorities will assimilate and wither away with modernization and economic growth is Karl Deutsch (n. 36). See also, Harris Mylonas, *The Politics of Nation Building: Making Co-Nationals, Refugees and Minorities* (Cambridge University Press, 2012).

93 Kymlicka *Multicultural Odysseys*; Loughlin *Reconfiguring the Nation State* , pp. 7–8.

94 See Connor *Nation Building or Nation Destroying*, pp. 319–55.

95 Crawford Young, *The Politics of Cultural Pluralism* (The University of Wisconsin Press, 1976); Kymlicka (n. 29).

96 Wimmer Nation Building, p. 6.

97 Connor, *Nation Building or Nation Destroy*ing.

98 Wimmer *Nation Building*, p. 23; see also, Stepan, Linz and Yadiv Crafting State Nations, ; see also, Grotenhuis *Nation Building*, p. 30.

99 Grotenhuis, *Nation Building*, p. 20.

100 Grotenhuis, *Nation Building*, p. 30.

101 Miller *Nationality in Divided Societies*, pp. 300–2.

102 Rajeev Bhargava, "Should Indian Federalism Be Called Multinational?" *Multinational Federalism: Problems and Prospects. In: Michel Seymour and Alain-G. Gagnon, eds.* (Macmillan 2012), pp. 246–48.

103 Christophe Jaffrelot, *Modi's India: Hindu Nationalism and the Rise of Indian Democracy* (Westland Publications, 2021).

104 Alfred Stepan, "Towards a New Comparative Politics of Federalism, Multinationalism, and Democracy: Beyond Rikarian Federalism." In: Federalism and Democracy in Latin America. Edward L. Gibson, ed. (Johns Hopkins University Press, 2004).

105 Bhargava *Should Indian Federalism Be Called Multinational.*

106 Miller *Nationality in Divided Societies*; Stepan, Linz and Yadiv *Crafting State Nations*

107 Miller *Nationality in Divided Societies*, p. 305.

108 Liam Anderson, *Federal Solutions to Ethnic Problems: Accommodating Diversity* (Routledge, 2013), p. 7.

109 Anderson, *Federal Solutions.*

110 Watts *Comparing Federal Systems.*

111 Philip G. Roeder, *Where Nation-States Come From Institutional Change in the Age of Nationalism* (Princeton University Press, 2007), pp. 20–21.

112 Stepan, Linz, and Yadiv, Crafting State Nations, pp. 3–4; Anderson and Choudhry Territorial Cleavages, p. 374.

113 Roeder *Where Nation-States Come From,* pp. 18; 81-86. The relationship between the segmental state and the overarching state is, however, complex and not straightforward. As in Canada and the UK, it is possible to have a democratic overarching state that through an incremental political process accommodates demands from segmental identities that may in the process cause splits within the latter and moderation or an authoritarian overarching state, as in the former USSR, Yugoslavia, and currently Ethiopia that reinforces radical movements in the segmental state, leading to conflict and fragmentation. The nature of the segmental state elite has a similar impact as the overarching state. –

114 Wimmer *Nation Building.*

115 Two major works that explain why some states deliver better than others are Francis Fukuyama, *Political Order and Political Decay: From the Industrial Revolution to the Globalization of Democracy* (New York: Farrar, 2014); and Acemoglu and Robinson Why Nations Fail.

116 Grotenhuis Nation Building, p. 73.

117 See for details Mylonas *The Politics of Nation Building*. . . Those that focus on onset, like Anthony Smith, argue that nation building is impossible without *a core nation*. O'Leary also argued there must either be a core nation or alternatively an inclusive consociational political system. Anthony Smith, *Ethno-Symbolism and Nationalism: A Cultural Approach* (Routledge, 2009); Brendan O'Leary, "An Iron Law of Nationalism and Federation? A Neo-Diceyian Theory of the Necessity of a Federal Staatsvolk, and of Consociational Rescue (2001) *Nations and Nationalism* 7, NO. 3, P. 273. There are also those who focus on military and national services, as well as mass education, as a means to indoctrinate citizens about nation and nationalism. Others focus on processes like industrialization, modernization, and urbanization (Deutch, Gellner, and Anderson) that facilitate acculturation and integration. Both the onset- and process-based nation-building efforts did not succeed in societies with deep divisions, and Wimmer's approach to polity building on political inclusion that reaches out to all segments of society remains very powerful because it deals with the real issue, not the symptoms. Gellner *Nations and Nationalism*; Benedict Anderson, *Imagined Communities: Reflections on the Origin and Spread of Nationalism* (Verso, 1983); Deutsch *Nationalism and Social Communication*.

118 Wimmer Nation Building, pp. 2, 28.

119 Stepan, Linz, and Yadiv *Crafting State Nations*; Choudhry *Bridging Comparative Politics*; Lars-Erik Cederman, Andreas Wimmer, and Brian Min, "Why do Ethnic Groups Rebel? New Data and Analysis," (2010) *World Politics* 62, no. 1, p. 87.

120 Wimmer *Nation Building*, pp. 217, 227.

121 For details on this see Karlo Basta, *The Symbolic State: Minority Recognition, Majority Backlash and Secession in Multinational Countries* (McGill-Queen's University Press, 2021).

122 The author was presenting approaches to polity building in divided societies in the Summer Program of the Institute of Federalism, Fribourg, Switzerland, in August 2022, and when the issue of representation and the problem of puppets came in, participants from Asia and Africa were unanimous in pointing out how representation is misused in the gender- and minority-rights fields. They said *puppetism* is everywhere an issue.

123 Stepan, Linz, and Yadiv *Crafting State Nations(.*); Choudhry *Bridging Comparative Politics*, p. 4.

124 For the limitations of the nation-state, *see* Kymlicka Multicultural Odysseys, pp. 61–63.

125 Samuel Huntington, *The Third Wave.*

126 Hyden *African Politics*, p. 58.

127 Thomas Franck, "Why Federations Fail." In: *Why Federations Fail: An Inquiry into the Requisites for Successful Federalism.* Thomas Franck, ed. (New York University Press, 1968), pp. 167–200.

128 Ursula Hicks, *Federalism: Failure and Success, a Comparative Study* (The Macmillan Press, 1978), p. 4.

129 Daniel Elazar, *Exploring Federalism* (Tuscaloosa: University of Alabama Press, 1987), pp. 240–44; Hicks (n. 127), pp. 171–96.

130 Goran Hyden, "Electoral Systems and Political Reform." In: *Constitutionalism: Reflections and Recommendations, Proceedings of the Symposium on the Making of the New Ethiopian Constitution* (Inter Africa Group, 1993), p. 9.

131 Alan Kuperman, "Designing Constitutions to Reduce Domestic Conflict." In: *Constitutions and Conflict Management in Africa: Preventing Civil War through Institutional Design. Alan Kuperman, ed.* (Philadelphia: University of Pennsylvania Press, 2015), p. 21.

132 Crawford Young, "The End of the Post-Colonial State in Africa? Reflections on Changing African Political Dynamics. In: *The African Affairs Reader.* Nic Cheeseman, Lindsay Whitefield, and Carl Death, eds. (Oxford: Oxford University Press, 2012), p. 41; Hyden *African Politics*, p. 64.

133 A slogan of the Mozambique Liberation Front, quoted in Solomon Ayele Derso, *Taking Ethno Cultural Diversity*
Seriously in Constitutional Design: A Theory of Minority Rights for Addressing Africa's Multiethnic Challenge (Martinus Nijhoff Publishers, 2012), p.67.

134 Clapham *The Horn of Africa*, p. 56.

135 Both leaders quoted in Claude Ake, "What Is the Problem of Ethnicity in Africa?" *Transformation* 22 (1993), p. 7.

136 See Kuperman, *Designing Constitutions*.

137 Kuperman, while proposing integration over accommodation, admits this risk manifested in Kenya, Nigeria, Sudan, and Zimbabwe. See his chapter, Kuperman, Designing Constitutions p. 19. For a counterargument within the African continent, see Nic Cheeseman, "How Could We Design Democracy to Make it Work in the African Continent." In: *Democracy Elections and Constitutionalism in Africa.* Charles Fombad and Nico Steytler, eds. (Oxford University Press, 2021)

138 Grotenhuis, *Nation Building*, p. 42.

139 Wimmer, *Nation Building*, p. 28.

140 *Nation Building, p.* 1.

141 David Mitrany, *The Functional Theory of Politics* (St. Martin's Press, 1976); Ashutosh Varshney, *Ethnic Conflict and Civil Strife: Hindus and Muslims in India* (Yale University Press, 2002).

142 Max Weber, *Essays in Sociology* (Oxford University Press, 1957).

143 Some tend to understand this in the literal sense. In divided societies, the civil service as well should be inclusive, and merit is not necessarily in contradiction with representation. If one has to have a civil servant from the Somali or Afar region, it is possible to have a *competent* Somali or Afar. Merit and representation collide when the system shifts to *symbolic* instead of real and *merit*-based representation. The EPRDF's system of representation was nominal, not real representation. The OPDO and ANDM symbolically represented the Oromo and the Amhara but were never considered as real representatives of both groups, hence the 2015 protests. The same problem continued under the Prosperity Party.

144 Hyden, *African Politics*, p. 66.

145 Fukuyama *Political Order and Political Decay* ,

146 Hyden, *African Politics,* (n *pp.* 67–68. Botswana, Mauritius, and sometimes South Africa are considered as exceptions. South Africa seems to be slowly joining

the neo-patrimonial club. Despite a strong judiciary, scandal after scandal has been reported in the president's office and at the local government level, and the African National Congress (ANC) seems to be losing influence over its members.

147 Jean Francois Bayart, *The State in Africa: The Politics of the Belly* (Longman, 1993).

148 Acemoglu and Robinson *Why Nations Fail*

149 Alex De Waal, "When Kleptocracy becomes Insolvent: Brute Cause of the Civil War in South Sudan" (2014). *African Affairs* 113pp. 347–69.

150 Hyden, *African Politics*, p. 95.

151 Michael Bratton, "Vote Buying and Violence in Nigerian Election Campaigns" (2008). *Electoral Studies* 27, no. 4, pp. 621–32.

152 Patrick Chabal and Jean-Pascal Daloz, *Africa Works: Disorder as Political Instrument* (James Currey, 1999).

153 Ebenezer Obadare, 'Nigeria's All too Familiar Corruption Ranking Begs Broader Questions Around Normative Collapse' Council on Foreign Relations at https://www.cfr.org/article/nigerias-all-too-familiar-corruption-ranking-begs-broader-questions-around-normative

154 See his speech at https://www.youtube.com/watch?v=wTQCMjXth4I

155 See USAID update at https://www.usaid.gov/humanitarian-assistance/ethiopia

156 See report Internal Displacement Monitoring Report at https://www.internal-displacement.org/countries/ethiopia#:~:text=Disasters%2C%20mostly%20floods%20and%20drought,%2C%20Oromia%2C%20Somali%20and%20SNNP

157 Gellner, *Nations and Nationalism*.

158 Basta, *The Symbolic State*.

159 Omer Awadalla Ali Gasmelseid, *Federalism as Conflict Management Device for Multiethnic and Multicultural Societies: The case of Sudan* (Bale: Helbing &Lichtenhahn 2006). Certainly, the civil war in Sudan was not limited to symbols only but suffice to mention here symbols also played their role.

160 Teshale Tibebu, *The Making of Modern Ethiopia 1896-1974* (The Red Sea Press,1995).

161 Gebru Tareke, *Ethiopia: Power and Protest: Peasant Revolts in the Twentieth Century* (Cambridge University Press, 1991).

162 Bahru Zewde, *A History of Modern Ethiopia 1855-1974* (Ohio University Press, 1991).

163 Mohammed Hassen, *The Oromos of Ethiopia: A History 1570-1860* (Cambridge University Press, 1990).

164 Richard Pankhurst, *Social History of Ethiopia* (Red Sea Press, 1992).

165 Harold Marcus, *A History of Ethiopia* (University of California Press, 1994).

166 John Markakis, *Ethiopia: Anatomy of Traditional Polity* (Clarendon Press, 1974).

167 Alessandro, Triulzi, "Battling with the Past: New Frameworks for Ethiopian Historiography." In: *Remapping Ethiopia: Socialism and After.* Wendy James, Donald Donham, Eisei Kurimoto, and Alessandro Triulzi, eds. (James Currey, 2002), pp, 276–89.

168 In many writings and public displays in Addis Ababa, it is common to see photos of different rulers of modern Ethiopia, starting from Emperor Tewodros. Emperor Tekle Giorgis (short-lived emperor from Agaw) and Emperor Yohannes IV (Tigrayan) are deliberately left out of the narrative, as if they never existed. The new regime that assumed power in 2018 did all it could to undo Meles Zenawi's major

projects, including Africa's biggest dam, and has excluded him from the narrative. Alula—Africa's army general who defeated the Italians and the Egyptians in the nineteenth century—is nowhere in the narrative, despite Ethiopian's claim they are the only "non-colonized country" in Africa, which was mainly due to Alula's role. Ethiopia's paradoxes have no end!

169 See Mathew Flynn and Stephen Griffin, *Washington and Napoleon: Leadership in the Age of Revolution* (Potomac, 2012).

170 See Mylonas, *The Politics of Nation Building.*

171 Yascha Mounk, *The Great Experiment: Why Diverse Democracies Fall Apart and How They can Endure* (Penguin Press, 2022).

172 Thomas Hueglin and Alan Fenna, *Comparative Federalism: A Systematic Inquiry* (University of Toronto Press, 2015), p. 4.

173 Donald Horowitz, *A Democratic South Africa? Constitutional Engineering in a Divided Society* (University of California Press, 1991), p. 221–23.

References

Acemoğlu, Daron and James A. Robinson, *Why Nations fail.* Crown Publisher, 2013.

Adedeji, Adebayo. "Comprehending African Conflicts." In *Comprehending and Mastering African Conflicts: The Search for Sustainable Peace and Good Governance,* edited by Adedeji Adebayo. Zed Books, 1999.

Ake, Claude, "What is the Problem of Ethnicity in Africa?" *Transformation* 22(1993): 1-14.

Anderson, Benedict. *Imagined Communities: Reflections on the Origin and Spread of Nationalism.* Verso, 1983.

Anderson, George and Sujit Choudhry. "Territorial Cleavages and Constitutional Transitions: Political Mobilization, Constitution Making Processes and Constitutional Design." In *Territory and Power in Constitutional Transitions,* edited by George Anderson and Sujit Choudhry. Oxford University Press, 2019.

Anderson, Liam. *Federal Solutions to Ethnic Problems: Accommodating Diversity.* Routledge, 2013.

Awadalla Ali, Omer, Gasmelseid. *Federalism as Conflict Management Device for Multiethnic and Multicultural Societies: The case of Sudan.* Helbing &Lichtenhahn, 2006.

Zewde, Bahru. *A History of Modern Ethiopia 1855-1974.* Ohio University Press, 1991.

Basta, Karlo. *The Symbolic State Minority Recognition, Majority Backlash, and Secession in Multinational Countries.* McGill-Queen's University Press, 2021.

Bayrat, Jean Francois. *The State in Africa: The Politics of the Belly.* Longman, 1993.

Bhargava, Rajeev. "Should Indian Federalism Be Called Multinational?" In *Multinational Federalism: Problems and Prospects,* edited by Michel Seymour and Alain-G. Gagnon. Macmillan, 2012.

Bratton, Michael. "Vote Buying and Violence in Nigerian Election Campaigns." *Electoral Studies* 27 (2008): 621–32.

Burton, John. *Violence Explained.* Manchester University Press, 1997.

Cederman, Lars-Erik, Andreas Wimmer, and Brian Min. "Why do Ethnic Groups Rebel? New Data and Analysis." *World Politics* 62, 1 (2010):87-119.

Chabal, Patrick and Jean-Pascal Daloz. *Africa Works: Disorder as Political Instrument.* James Currey, 1999.

Cheeseman, Nic. "How could we Design Democracy to Make it Work in the African Continent." In *Democracy Elections and Constitutionalism in Africa,* edited by Charles Fombad and Nico Steytler. Oxford University Press, 2021.

Choudhry, Sujit, and Nathan Hume. "Federalism, Devolution and Secession: From Classical to Post-Conflict Federalism." In *Comparative Constitutional Law*, edited by Tom Ginsburg and Rosalind Dixon, 356-386. Edward Elgar, 2011.

Choudhry, Sujit. "Bridging Comparative Politics and Comparative Constitutional Law: Constitutional Design in Divided Societies." In *Constitutional Design for Divided Societies: Integration or Accommodation?*, edited by Sujit Choudhry. Oxford University Press, 2008.

Chua, Amy. *Political Tribes: Group Instinct and the Fate of Nations*. Penguin Press, 2018.

Clapham, Christopher. *The Horn of Africa: State Formation and Decay*. Hurst and Co, 2017.

Clapham, Christopher. "The Ethiopian Experience of Devolved Government," *Ethiopian Journal of Federal Studies* 1:1 (2013): 1-25.

Clapham, Christopher. "Centralization and Social Responses in Southern Ethiopia." *African Affairs* 74, 294 (1975): 73-75.

Connor, Walker. "Nation Building or Nation Destroying? *World Politics* 24, 3 (1972):319-355.

Dahl, Robert. *Toward Democracy- A Journey, Reflections: 1940-1997*. Institute of Government Study Press, 1997.

Davidson, Basil. *The Black Man's Burden: Africa and the Curse of the Nation State*. Time Books/ Random House, 1992.

De Vries, Lotje, Pierre Englebert, Mareike Schomerus eds. *Secessionism in African Politics: Aspiration, Grievance, Performance, Disentrancement.* Palgrave Macmillan, 2019.

De Waal, Alex. "When Kleptocracy becomes Insolvent: Brute Cause of the Civil War in South Sudan " *African Affairs* 113, 452 (2014): 347-369.

Deutsch, Karl. *Nationalism and Social Communication: An Inquiry into the Foundations of Nationalism*. Cambridge, MA, 1953.

Elazar, Daniel. *Exploring Federalism*. University of Alabama Press, 1987.

Fukuyama, Francis. *Identity: the Demand for Dignity and the Politics of Resentment*. Straus and Giroux, 2018.

Fukuyama, Francis. *Political Order and Political Decay: From the Industrial Revolution to the Globalization of Democracy*. Farrar, 2014.

Fukuyama, Francis. *Nation Building Beyond Afghanistan and Iraq*. Johns Hopkins University Press 2006.

Gebru Tareke. *Ethiopia: Power and Protest: Peasant Revolts in the Twentieth Century*. Cambridge University Press 1991.

Gellner, Ernest. *Nation and Nationalism*. Basil Blackwell, 1983.

Gottlieb, Gedon. *Nation Against State: New Approach to Ethnic Conflicts and the Decline of Sovereignty*. Council on Foreign Relations Press, 1993.

Grotenhuis, Rene. *Nation Building as Necessary Effort in Fragile States*. Amsterdam University Press, 2016.

Hazony, Yoran. *The Virtues of Nationalism*. Basic Books, 2018.

Hicks, Ursula. *Federalism: Failure and Success, a Comparative Study*. The Macmillan Press 1978.

Horowitz, Donald. "*Constitutional Design: Proposals, Process*." In *The Architecture of Democracy: Constitutional Design, Conflict Management and Democracy*, edited by Andrew Reynolds. Oxford University Press, 2002.

Horowitz, Donald, *A Democratic South Africa? Constitutional Engineering in a Divided Society*. University of California Press, 1991.

Hueglin, Thomas, and Alan Fenna. *Comparative Federalism: A Systematic Inquiry*. University of Toronto Press, 2015.

Huntington, Samuel. *The Third Wave: Democratization in the Late 20th Century*. University of Oklahoma Press, 1991.

Hyden, Goran. *African Politics in Comparative Perspective* 2nd edn. Cambridge University Press, 2013.

Hyden, Goran. "Electoral Systems and Political Reform." In *Constitutionalism: Reflections and Recommendations, Proceedings of the Symposium on the Making of the New Ethiopian Constitution*. Inter Africa Group, 1993.

Jaffrelot, Christophe. *Modi's India: Hindu Nationalism and the Rise of Indian Democracy*. Westland Publications, 2021.

Keating, Michael. "So Many Nations, So Few States: Territory and Nationalism in the Global Era." In *Multinational Democracies*, edited by Alain-G. Gagnon and James Tully. Cambridge University Press, 2001.

Kedourie, Elie. *Nationalism*. Frederick A. Praeger, 1960.

Keller, Edmond. *Revolutionary Ethiopia: From Empire to People's Republic*. Indiana University Press, 1988.

Kuperman, Alan. "Designing Constitutions to Reduce Domestic Conflict." In *Constitutions and Conflict Management in Africa: Preventing Civil War through Institutional Design*, edited by Alan Kuperman. University of Pennsylvania Press, 2015.

Pankhurst, Richard. *Social History of Ethiopia.* Red Sea Press, 1992.

Kymlicka, Will. *Multicultural Odysseys: Navigating the New International Politics of Diversity*. Oxford University Press, 2007.

Lacey, Joseph. *Centripetal Democracy*. Oxford University Press, 2017.

Lemay-Hebert, Nicolas. "State Building without Nation Building? Legitimacy, State Failure and the Limits of the Institutional Approach." *Journal of Intervention and State Building* 3, 1 (2009): 21-45.

Levine, Donald. *Greater Ethiopia: The Evolution of a Multiethnic Society*, 2nd edn. The University of Chicago Press, 2000.

Lijphart, Arend. "Constitutional Design for Divided Societies." *Journal of Democracy* 15, (2004): 96-109.

Lijpart, Arend. "The Wave of Power Sharing Democracy." In *The Architecture of Democracy: Constitutional Design, Conflict Management and Democracy*, edited by Andrew Reynolds. Oxford University Press, 2002.

Loughlin, John. "Reconfiguring the Nation State: Hybridity vs. Uniformity." In *Routledge Handbook on Regionalism and Federalism*, edited by John Loughlin, John Kincaid, Wilfried Swenden. Routledge, 2013.

Mack Smith. Denis, *Garibaldi: A Great Life in Brief.* Knopf, 1956.

Marcus, Harold. *A History of Ethiopia*. University of California Press, 1994.

Markakis, John, Gunther Schlee and John Young. "Introduction." In *The Nation State: A Wrong Model for the Horn of Africa*, edited by John Markakis, Gunther Schlee and John Young. Max Planck: 2021.

Markakis, John. "The Crisis of the State in the Horn of Africa." In *The Nation State: A Wrong Model for the Horn of Africa*, edited by John Markakis, Gunther Schlee and John Young. Max Planck: 2021.

McGarry, John, Michael Keating and Margaret Moore. "Introduction: European Integration and the nationalities question." In *European Integration and the Nationality Question*, edited by John McGarry and Michael Keating. Routledge, 2006.

Mill, John Stuart. "Representative Government." In *Utilitarianism, on Liberty, and Considerations on Representative Government*, edited by Geraint Williams. Everyman, 1993 [1861]).

Miller, David. "Nationality in Divided Societies." In. *Multinational Democracies*, edited by Alain-G. Gagnon, James Tull. Cambridge University Press, 2001.

Miller, David. *On Nationality*. Clarendon Press, 1997.

Mitrany, David. *The Functional Theory of Politics*. St. Martin's Press, 1976.

Mohammed Hassen. *The Oromos of Ethiopia: A History 1570-1860*. Cambridge University Press, 1990.

Mounk, Yascha. *The Great Experiment: Why Diverse Democracies Fall Apart and How They can Endure*. Penguin Press, 2022.

Mylonas, Harris. *The Politics of Nation Building: Making Co-Nationals, Refugees and Minorities*. Cambridge University Press, 2012.

Newbury, Catharine. "State at War: Confronting Conflicts in Africa" *African Studies Review* 45, 2 (2002): 1-20.

Nimni, Ephraim. "Minority Accommodation through Territorial and Non-Territorial Autonomy." In *Minorities and the Limits of Liberal Democracy: Democracy and Non-Territorial Autonomy*, edited by Tove Malloy and Francesco Palermo. Oxford University Press, 2015.

Nootens, Genevieve. "Can Non-Territorial Autonomy Bring an Added Value to Theoretic and Policy Oriented Analysis of Ethnic Politics?" In *Minority Accommodation through Territorial and Non Territorial Autonomy,* edited by Tove Malloy and Francesco Palermo. Oxford University Press, 2015.

Nordia, Ghia. "The End of the Postnational Illusion." *Journal of Democracy* 2 (2017): 5-19.

O'Leary, Brendan. "An Iron Law of Nationalism and Federation? A Neo-Diceyian Theory of the Necessity of a Federal Staatsvolk, and of Consociational Rescue." *Nations and Nationalism* 7, 3 (2001): 273-296.

Ottaway, Marina. "Nation Building." *Foreign Policy* (2002).

Robert Gurr, Ted. *Minorities at Risk: A Global View of Ethnopolitical Conflict.* United States Institute of Peace Press, 1993.

Roeder, Philip. *Where Nation-States Come From Institutional Change in the Age of Nationalism.* Princeton University Press, 2007.

Smith, Anthony. *Ethno-Symbolism and Nationalism: A Cultural Approach*. Routledge, 2009.

Sanjaume-Calvet, Marc. "Reconciling Liberal Democracy, Nationalism and Political Divorce." In *Revisiting Unity and Diversity in Federal Countries: Changing Concepts, Reform Proposals and New Institutional Realities,* edited by Alain-G. Gagnon and Michael Burgess. Brill, Nijhoff, 2018.

Solomon Ayele Derso. *Taking Ethno Cultural Diversity seriously in Constitutional Design: A Theory of Minority Rights for Addressing Africa's Multiethnic Challenge*. Martinus Nijhoff Publishers, 2012.

Stepan, Alfred, Juan Linz and Yogendra Yadiv. *Crafting State Nations: India and Other Multinational Democracies*. Johns Hopkins Press, 2011.

Stepan, Alfred Stepan. "Towards a New Comparative Politics of Federalism, Multinationalism and Democracy: Beyond Rikarian Federalism." In *Federalism and Democracy in Latin America,* edited by Edward L. Gibson. Johns Hopkins University Press, 2004.

Teshale Tibebu. *The Making of Modern Ethiopia 1896-1974*. The Red Sea Press, 1995.

Thomas, Franck. "Why Federations Fail?" In *Why Federations Fail: An Inquiry into the Requisites for Successful Federalism*, edited by Thomas Franck. New York University press, 1968.

Tilley, Charles. *The Formation of National States in Western Europe.* Princeton University Press, 1975.

Tilly, Charles. "Introduction." In *The Formation of National States in Western Europe*, edited by Charles Tilly. Princeton University Press 1975.

Triulzi, Alessandro. "Battling with the Past: New Frameworks for Ethiopian Historiography." In *Remapping Ethiopia: Socialism and After*, edited by Wendy James, Donald Donham, Eisei Kurimoto, and Alessandro Triulzi, 276-289. James Currey, 2002.

Tiruneh, Andargachew. *The Ethiopian Revolution: 1974-1987.* Cambridge University Press, 1993.

Van Parijs, Philippe. *Linguistic Justice for Europe and the World*. Oxford University Press, 2011.

Varshney, Ashutosh. *Ethnic Conflict and Civil Strife: Hindus and Muslims in India*. Yale University Press, 2002.

Walsh, Dawn. *Territorial Self Government as Conflict Management Tool.* Palgrave Macmillan, 2018.

Watts, Ronald. *Comparing Federal Systems*, 3rd edn. McGill, Queen's University Press, 2008.

Weber, Eugen. *Peasants into Frenchmen: The Modernisation of Rural France, 1870–1914*. Chatto and Windus, 1979.

Weber, Max. *Essays in Sociology*. Routledge, 1957.

Wimmer, Andreas. *Nation Building: Why Some Countries come Together while others Fall Apart?* Princeton University Press, 2018.

Young, Crawford. "The End of the Post-Colonial State in Africa? Reflections on Changing African Political Dynamics." In *The African Affairs Reader*, edited by Nic Cheeseman, Lindsay Whitefield, and Carl Death. Oxford University Press, 2012.

Young, Crawford. *The Politics of Cultural Pluralism*. The University of Wisconsin Press, 1976.

Chapter 3

Is the Nation-State Model Adopted by African States to Blame for Africa's Continuing Political Ills?

Getachew Assefa Woldemariam (PhD)

In a recent book,[1] the focus of which is the Horn of Africa, Markakis, Schlee, and Young argue that the wholesale importation of the Westphalian nation-state model adopted by African states as the governance structure is the main problem for the political crises in sub-Saharan Africa. According to the authors, the nation-state model had a natural moment of emergence on European soil accompanying the birth of capitalism—and the withering of feudalism—and its bourgeois structure.[2] "This model," the authors lament, "was transposed to Africa, a vastly different world, without the slightest concession to its uniqueness, and the results have been tragic."[3] In relation to the nation-building efforts of the postcolonial African states, the authors have the following to say:

> *Since most newly independent African states did not comprise homogeneous nations, homogeneity needed to be achieved by nation building, even by force if necessary. The forceful pursuit*

of nation building has been the cause of unending conflict in Africa, especially in the Horn, with ethnic cleansing, massive population displacement, successive waves of refugees, political instability and enormous human suffering.[4]

The authors further observe that the crisis resulted from the imposition in the mid-twentieth century of the Western state model across the region, "without preparation or adaptation to the continent" and from a "failure to consider material, social, cultural, and political contexts on a local level."[5] They argue that the phenomenon of imposing a model of political organization in an entirely alien setting created divisions "between tradition and modernization, nation and tribe, urban and rural society, the ruling elite and the rest of the population."[6] They conclude: "Much of sub-Saharan Africa's political turmoil is the result of this Procrustean experiment."[7]

It is important to note that the Western "nation-state" model under discussion by the authors is the typical Western European nation-state system such as that of the United Kingdom, Germany, and France, where the respective populations are supposed to belong to one nation, where the ethnicity, race, and language of the nondominant groups are not politically salient, and where assimilation and acculturation of smaller groups among the major nations is acceptable and pursued as a state policy. It is thence my understanding that state structures entrenching multiculturalism or linguistic/ethnic-based federalism or devolution of power are not "Western nation-state" models that are adjudged wrong for Africa by the authors. This line of thinking by the authors could be gleaned from Dr. Young's chapter in the book on the post-1991 state structure of Ethiopia.[8] My observations in this chapter are based on this understanding. My plan in this short piece is to try to show that a careful look at most of Africa's postcolonial political reality points more to a different set of problems than the model of state structure adopted by them.

The authors are led to the arguments they make in the book by looking at, among other things, the realities of seemingly endless conflicts and bad governance on the continent. Therefore, they say that the rampancy of costly conflicts on the continent in general and the Horn in particular, and the respective states' inability to manage them, should lead Africans to confront the question of whether the culprit is in fact the nation-state model copied from the West in the wake of colonialism, and if so, to "consider alternative methods of governance for the continent."[9]

As Markakis, Schlee, and Young have argued in the book, this fundamental question of the suitability of the Western state and institutional system to African societies has not been given sufficient attention. The authors state that one of the possible reasons for this lack of attention could be because the Western institutional framework has been unquestionably accepted by Western and non-Western scholars and political players. Objecting to this seemingly well-accepted notion would be sailing against the current.

It is true that the legal centralist position of the West has been meaningfully challenged by legal anthropologists and lawyers. The question in this case has been the appropriateness of the transplantation of Western laws and the institutional framework for bringing them into effect in Africa, with the intent of displacing (and ultimately extinguishing) African normative orderings and institutions. Many legal anthropologists and legal scholars have made a strong case against the attempt to totally replace African normative orderings and institutions with those imported from the West.[10] Opponents of this approach argue that, in Africa, there have always been robust customary laws and institutions that predate the emergence of the African states as we know them today.[11] The laws and institutions that are modeled on Western systems are recent additions that were largely brought to Africa with colonialism.

The policy of undermining the African normative orderings has been pursued more vigorously by the postcolonial rulers of the independent African states with the conviction that social and economic advancements were possible only with the adoption of laws and institutions modeled on the Western prototypes.[12] Undeniably, in most of post independence Africa, whatever is local or homegrown was declared "backward" and "primitive," while everything from the West was praised as "modern" and "civilized."

Most of the African revolutionaries who led the anti-colonial struggles were Western-educated personalities that were appreciative of the Western legal, social, and political systems. As Peter Ekeh observes, Africans who acquired Western education during the colonial era became the educated stratum of the society, becoming what he calls the "bourgeois class." The African bourgeoisie, in tandem with the colonial administrators, disparaged the African past—including some well-known civilizations in the continent—as backward and, on the contrary, praised the achievements obtained in the colonial territories under the colonial administration.[13] As Ekeh aptly observes, the African bourgeois class which had obtained Europeanized education accepted "the principles implicit in colonialism," but it rejected "the foreign personnel that ruled Africa." Members of this bourgeoisie class claimed to be as competent as the colonial personnel to rule their respective polities.[14] The anti-colonial struggle was waged by the African bourgeoisie against the colonial administrators in order to replace them as rulers but to continue to rule with the mindset bequeathed to them by the colonial rulers.

In this connection, Ekeh further notes that the Western-educated Africans developed ideologies first to overcome and replace the colonial rulers, and, once this was achieved, the second phase of their ideology was aimed at legitimating their position, vis-à-vis the relevant masses, as the rightful rulers.[15] "The fight for independence was thus a struggle for power between the two bourgeois classes [European and African] involved in the colonization of Africa. The intellectual poverty of the independence movement in Africa flows from this fact, that what was involved was not the issue of differences of ideas regarding moral principles but rather the issue of which bourgeois class should rule Africans."[16] Ekeh's unsympathetic observation may seem unfair to the leaders of anti-colonial movements, but what unfolded right after independence in most of the former colonies lends credence to his statement in the case of most of the former colonies.

The Western-educated African bourgeois class has been detached from the rest of African society. Because of its idolization of the Western educational, social, and governance systems, it did not have any pride in institutions and systems indigenous to Africa. It worked with the intention of uprooting the African traditional legal and institutional system. This created a divide between them and the African masses, including its traditional chiefs and institutions. At the same time, Western-educated Africans considered themselves the rightful rulers of their implicated societies, as they are the ones with Western educations and therefore have all it takes to lead their people to economic, political, and social advancement. As will be elaborated later, this put them on a collision course with their own societies and particularly with the traditional institutions.

As Peter Ekeh and others[17] observe, one of the deliberate actions of the colonial rulers, especially during the last few decades before their departure, was to create discord among the African bourgeois class and the traditional chiefs. The colonial rulers previously sought to replace the customary laws of the people and the traditional institutions with the laws and institutions of the colonizing powers. This was employed as a tactic to elongate the life of colonialism, which faced a serious challenge starting around the 1920s.[18] However, they dropped the idea of undermining customary institutions and started to recognize their powers over the local people and local matters. This led to a condition Mahmood Mamdani calls the "bifurcated state"[19] and Ekeh calls the "two publics"[20] in the African continent.[21]

According to Mamdani, the bifurcated state distinguished firstly between non-native colonial rulers and native majority populations on the basis of race and secondly among numerous tribal groupings within the native population, each to be ruled by their "traditional leaders" under "customary law." With "natives" in rural areas subordinated as the "subjects" of tribalized, and thereby fragmented, traditional customary regimes, urban areas emerged as the realm of primarily non-native "citizens" to be administered according to modern rule-of-law standards.[22] This bifurcated legal system came to pervade the entire colonial state.[23]

Ekeh developed the idea of the "two publics" in his 1975 seminal publication cited earlier in this chapter. He says that one of the two publics was a "civic" public while the second one is a "primordial" public. Put in a nutshell, the civic public is the one that was run directly by the colonial rulers (and their successors in post-colonial Africa) based on the Western legal and institutional standards, while the primordial public was the one that was by and large governed by the local (customary) laws and institutions. Ekeh rightly observed that "the structure of modern post-colonial politics in Africa owes a great deal to these two publics that exist side by side and that tend to grow together."[24]

Is the Nation-State Model the Main Problem?

Basil Davidson observes that when the United Kingdom briefly entertained the idea of leaving its West African colonies during the mid-nineteenth century, who could and should take over power when it did so and what kind of government structure would be appropriate were the thorny issues that were taken up by the Select Committee of Parliament. The committee took the position that power should be returned to the kings and chiefs—that were recognized by the colonial rulers—from whom it had been taken.[25] This issue of who the legitimate successors should be and the structure of government that was to be put in place was relevant to the rest of the colonies in Africa. The question remains relevant even today.

As Davidson and Ekeh have noted in their writings cited earlier, the Western-educated African elites (which Ekeh calls the "bourgeois class") insisted that they should be the rightful legatees of the departing colonial powers if Africa was to be delivered out of its backwardness and march on the road to development. Thus, the attempt by the departing colonial powers to promote the traditional chiefs and kings did not succeed.

Perhaps having seen the failure of their attempt to promote the traditional institutions as rightful occupants of the power vacuum they would leave behind in the face of the upcoming Western-educated bourgeois class, the departing colonial rulers suggested "a division within the bourgeois class along primordial ethnic lines" which, as Peter Ekeh aptly observes, "remains the red thread that runs through the whole of African politics."[26] The emergent African bourgeoisie took its partition along ethnic lines to an ideological level and defined its relation to power from an ethnic-domain perspective.[27] In post-colonial Africa, ethnicity started to obtain corporate existence in politics, which had not been the case in pre-colonial Africa. The agenda of "establishing" ethnic groups as identifiable corporate entities, predating the current African states, was developed hand in hand by the African bourgeois class and colonial rulers and historians.[28] In this connection, it is necessary to quote the relevant observation of Peter Ekeh in relation to Nigeria at some length here:

> *As we know them today, Nigerian ethnic groups developed their boundaries and even their character only within the context of Nigerian politics. But ideologies and myths do have reality creating functions, and the corporate character now attributed to various ethnic groups is the reality that flowed from the ideologies and myths invented by the bourgeoisie to consolidate their parcels of influence in the new Niger. No ethnic group existed before Nigeria as a corporate entity with the boundaries now claimed for them and the loyalties now directed at them. What existed before Nigeria were amorphous polities: many were organized around city-states, others in kingdoms and quasi-kingdoms, and yet others with the narrowness of villages with no conceptions of wider political entities within which they were implicated.*[29]

These valuable insights by Ekeh should show that political ethnicity in post-colonial Africa was a deliberate act of domain-creation efforts by the Western-educated African bourgeois class for purposes of legitimating their assumption of and hold on power. It is thus plausible to say that if colonialism had not happened in Africa, the kingdoms and various polities that existed in Africa could have followed their own paths of integration in ways completely different from the corporatization of ethnic groups, which we now know was deliberately created. These paths could have been the formation of institutions of governance like in the USA or the UK, France, Germany, or Switzerland. Or, the erstwhile polities could have developed their own autochthonous institutions of government owing to internal and external factors that would not make ethnicity a salient political issue. Even with the colonial experience, the same institutional development could have resulted if ethnic-domain creation were not undertaken by the Western-educated African bourgeois and the departing colonial rulers.

The first point I offer here to augment the arguments forwarded by Markakis, Schlee, and Young is that it would be helpful to take a step back and look at ethnic identity as a manufactured ideology of legitimation pursued religiously by the African bourgeois class.[30] This class uses its primordial domain as an instrument to fend off its opponents by presenting itself as the representative of the ethnic group to which it belongs. It is easy to see that most of the conflicts, coups, and other aspects of political violence are directly or indirectly related to grievances along ethnic lines, fueled by the bourgeois classes of the primordial domains.

In this sense, therefore, if we happen to be successful at deconstructing the constructed ethnic partition, an accommodative state with attributes akin to the Western states can be made a reality in Africa. As Professor Ekeh's findings cited earlier show, it is possible to argue that just like the Western nation-state model, ethnic identification was also alien to African societies. If the political elites and their auxiliary scholars are willing and committed to depoliticize ethnicity and instead focus on protecting the rights of all citizens—both as individuals and as members of cultural communities—of their respective countries, respecting the rule of law and institutionalizing democracy, the Western state structure—enriched by relevant indigenous values—can be used to organize the political life of the implicated African societies.

In my view, the political ills of the Horn of Africa (which is true for most of the rest of Africa as well) are more products of other factors than the adopted Western nation-state model. One such factor is state capture by the ruling political class, in most cases in the name of certain primordially corporatized ethnic groups. As Markakis, one of the authors of the book, notes, most of the violent conflicts by ethnic political actors claiming to represent ethno-national groups have come from the actors who feel denied of equal access to power and material resources and face social and cultural discrimination.[31] "These common denominators," Markakis says, "are the key ingredients in the chemistry of the conflict, whether it is fought in the name of nation, region, clan, or religion." He further notes, "The perennial crisis of the state in the Horn of Africa is variously attributed to ethnic strife, resource competition, weak political institutions, inappropriate policies, corrupt and authoritarian rulers."[32]

There is another important factor that serves as a catalyst for the violent competition among the primordial bourgeois classes. That is, the resource-hungry nature of the African bourgeois class. In the West, the political class does not enter politics for its riches. Due to the development of their economy, Western politicians come from self-sufficient economic statuses. But this is quite the opposite in the case of the African political class. State power in Africa is the means for resource control, which makes state power the source of their economic gains. Markakis, citing Frantz Fanon and Walter Rodney, observes:

> *The ruling bourgeois classes in the West had gained economic power before gaining state power, and thus could relinquish power through elections and be assured that their interests would be protected. In contrast, the petty bourgeois rulers in Africa had their*

> *origins in the state, had no independent economic basis, and clung to political power, which has regularly precipitated conflict.*[33]

This statement of fact gives rise to so many political problems. The primordial bourgeois class wants to hold on to state power until it is ousted by another primordial bourgeois class—through violence or other nondemocratic means. While it is in control of the state, it embezzles state resources, not only for the benefit of its extended family members but also, as much as possible, for other members of the primordial group perceived as the political and social basis of the class in power. This problem is compounded by the democratic irrelevance of the African electorate. That is, the absence of genuine, free, and fair elections means that a primordial bourgeois class in power cannot be removed from office through elections. It sustains itself through force and through foreign aid. In short, there is no democratic accountability to the masses in the name of whom they hold power.

The problems of the crises of states in Africa briefly outlined above, as Markakis understands it, should lead to an inquiry into how to resolve these issues. Unequal access to power and resources and other problems mentioned by Markakis should be addressed and resolved. If these problems occurred in the UK, France, or Spain, the affected political actors would no doubt engage in the same non-peaceful ways of rejecting their mistreatments, leading to ethnic or class or regional strife. The fact that the state is modeled on Western or Asian (like Japanese or South Korean) prototypes wouldn't make a difference. What matters is the existence of the exclusion and discrimination faced by the group(s) involved.

The difference between state structures in the UK or France on the one hand and those in the Horn of Africa on the other is that in the case of the latter state institutions that are the pillars for the proper operationalization of the state have never been allowed to develop. Constitutions and other fundamental laws that are meant to limit the powers of the government have never been respected. In effect, the Western nation-state model that is seemingly adopted has never been operationalized. It is rather instrumentalized by the political elites to clamp down on political opposition and the free media. These states of affairs normally exist in the context of massive violations of human rights and the rights of nondominant ethnic groups and the marginalization of the latter in the particular states. The Western state model in effect is instrumentalized by the bourgeois classes of the respective postcolonial states to hold on to power.

In fact, history is replete with examples of the instrumentalization of state institutions, even in the states that are found at the heart of Western Europe. The coming to power of Adolf Hitler's National Socialist German Workers'

Party was a case in point. Benito Mussolini's National Fascist Party was another case to remember. I do not think that we can blame these problems totally on the model of state adopted. In any case, these regrettable slippages of the Western societies have been pretty much quickly corrected by the development of civil society and institutions of government arranged to limit government power and hold it to account. Unfortunately, this has not been the case in most of Africa and more so in the Horn of Africa states.

The fact that the problem is not as such in the adoption of the Western state model by the African polities—at least so far as we can tell from past experience—can be seen from Ethiopia's experience. Ethiopian political history is a very complex one and cannot be recounted here. But for the purposes of this exercise, it would be necessary to make a few observations. Historical, social, and cultural evidence abounds for the existence of a continuous intermixture of various linguistic and cultural communities that inhabit present-day Ethiopia and Eritrea, starting from the prehistoric period onwards.[34] Levine observes that "far from the multiethnic Ethiopian state being the late-nineteenth century creation of an Amhara elite, as Prison House model proponents suggest, the Ethiopian state is of ancient origin and was multiethnic for most of its history."[35] As I have argued elsewhere, the position that there was an oppressor-oppressed relationship between the Amhara (Amhara-Tigre) and other ethnolinguistic communities belies the historical integration and intermixture among them.[36] Likewise, the position that the pre-1991 governments of Ethiopia were Amhara-dominated governments also is contrary to available evidence.

In any case, the controlling narrative since the 1960s has been that the Ethiopian state was dominated by the Amhara and that this domination led the various ethnolinguistic communities to wage struggle, including armed struggle, against the Amhara-dominated government, resulting in its final downfall in 1991. In this regard, John Young recounts in the book the EPRDF's explanation of the preceding decades-long war in northern Ethiopia as a product of an ethnically dominated state and that the EPRDF explicitly rejected the nation-state model that underpins Western states and was transplanted to Africa.[37] It needs to be pointed out here that Ethiopia had had a well-institutionalized monarchical system for more than two millennia. Hence, the idea of the transplantation of the Western state model does not quite apply to Ethiopia. In the twentieth century, when the transplantation into Africa of the Wesphalian state model took place, Ethiopia was under a monarchical system of government, which, from 1931 onwards, was designated by written constitutions. In 1974, when the last monarch was brought down by a military takeover, the military government subscribed to a socialist ideology that centralized all political decision-making power and outlawed a free press and political competition.

As Young has stated, the EPRDF rejected the nation-state model and opted for a state structure that made national/ethnic federalism its organizing principle. If there was national oppression in pre-1991 Ethiopia, that has now been broken, and the oppressed have been set free. If it were the Western nation-state model that was to blame, it has now been replaced by an ethnic/federal state structure. The question to consider then is this: Have the political problems been resolved in post-1991 Ethiopia? The answer is indisputably negative. Young himself admits that there is an "ongoing crisis" in Ethiopia.[38] It is a plain truth that there is not only an ongoing crisis but a worsening one. The point I am trying to make here is that the problem was not as such in the model of state structure adopted. In both pre- and post-1991 Ethiopia, state institutions such as the judiciary and the legislature have not been properly constituted and allowed to discharge their proper functions. Genuine elections have never taken place. The media was never free, except in the short windows during regime change or reform (as in 1974–75, 1991–92, and 2018–19). The executive—whether constituted as absolute monarch, president, or prime minister—wielded unchecked and unlimited powers. The state structures have changed, but this reality has not.

The same arguments can be made with regard to the other Horn of Africa states, such as Eritrea, Somalia, and South Sudan and indeed to other parts of Africa where the Western state model was transplanted only in name. The African bourgeois class in most of these states never attempted to operationalize the institutional requirements of the Western state model, such as the separation of powers, checks and balances, an independent judiciary, a free media, and genuine period elections. Of course, I am not saying that all is fine with the adoption of the Western state model in Africa and the resultant complete disregard of indigenous African institutional structures. My point here is that if the Western state model is genuinely operationalized in Africa, the political crises all around us may have significantly been reduced. After all, the Western state model operates on institutional pillars like independent judiciary, separation of powers and checks and balances, democratic elections, protection of rights and freedoms and free media. These are universal values that Africans also aspire to have, as do peoples elsewhere. Nonetheless, as alluded to above, the complete disregard of age-old African homegrown institutional structures should be pointed out as a mistake committed by the "modernizing" African political elites. I shall return to this point in the concluding section.

As my final point to challenge the argument that the nation-state model is the one to blame for the political problems of Africa, I mention the political success stories, or near-success stories, of some African states. Botswana, South Africa, Ghana, and Nigeria can be taken as good examples here. There is no question that these states follow state structures that mirror the typical Western nation-state model. Botswana held twelve consecutive free and fair elections, starting from 1965. Although the Botswana Democratic Party remained in power, over the years it has changed leaders peacefully, and the opposition party maintains a large number of seats (twenty out of fifty-seven elected seats in 2014) in the national assembly. The political story of South Africa since the defeat of Apartheid can be termed a success story, with its signature institutions like the Constitutional Court. Ghana[39] and Nigeria[40] are steadily making progress towards stable democratic systems.

To conclude this section, a closer look at the political ills of African states would reveal that the model of state structure adopted by them is not the real reason for the crises they face. The hollow transplantation of the Western state model without the necessary institutional pillars and principles that give effect to the model is rather the main reason for Africa's political pathology. Nonetheless, as I noted earlier, the complete disregard of the homegrown institutions of governance by the African political elites was a mistake that needed to be rectified.

What should be done to break free from the cycle of political ills?

I will not attempt to provide a complete package of solutions to the question posed above. This is not possible in such a short piece. My intention is rather to indicate a few points that I believe are worth taking into consideration when there is a deliberative process for constitutional reform with the aim of resolving the existing political problems at home or elsewhere in Africa, which is the main theme of this book. In fact, some of the suggestions that can be made are implicated in different ways in the arguments I made in the preceding section of this chapter.

As John Markakis has rightly argued (both in the book under consideration and his 1987 book[41]), "The state [which is 'the custodian of wealth and protector of privilege'] is both the goal of the contest [for power] and the principal means through which the contest is waged." In the Horn of Africa, the reason why the state is the centerpiece of political contestation, including through violent means, is because while it is such a valuable institution to control, it is not inclusive and democratic. Often a state in the Horn (and in fact most of Africa) is controlled by a ruling elite that is dominated by one or another ethnic group. In the absence of genuine periodic elections and the presence of other democratic institutions, the only means by which such a ruling class can be removed is through violence. Thus, we can break free from such cycles of violence only by making the state inclusive and democratic.

Basil Davidson, in his work cited earlier, suggested that one of the possible solutions to Africa's political and economic problems is to loosen up the commitment to state nationalism and instead embrace collective projects like regional economic communities that can progress into political communities, such as what the European Union has become.[42] This cannot be overemphasized. The creation of a wider regional framework makes absolute sense, especially in relation to the Horn states because of the many common linguistic communities all of the Horn states share. More integration is beneficial to the peoples concerned and the states, for it will contribute to peace and stability along the borders.

In addition to making the state inclusive and democratic, African states, including our own, should also rethink the place of indigenous institutions of governance and societal relations. That means the Western-modeled state institutions, in addition to being made effective, have to benefit from and be enriched by the social and moral values and norms of their African societies. One of the most befitting areas for consideration for enriching and complementing the institutional structures of the Western state model is the indigenous institutional arrangements for the settlement of disputes available in the various African societies.[43] The acceptable, and indeed workable, approach should be to move towards a cooperative existence of the formal state-sponsored laws and legal institutions and their customary counterparts.[44] Scholars in the field advise a pluralistic approach to laws and legal institutions whereby norms and institutions produced by different sources could be interwoven and relate with each other in a cooperative manner, with the goal of diversifying and increasing the avenues of justice for the members of the society. If properly empowered and allowed to function without the interference of the formal state machineries, the indigenous mechanisms for the settlement of disputes can play an indispensable role, especially in preventing and resolving conflicts, whether inter- or intra-ethnic conflicts.

The political elites and scholars should work on forging inter-ethnic and trans-ethnic solidarity among their peoples. The manufactured antagonism between ethnic groups since the 1960s should be countered by constructive narratives of harmony and coexistence that existed before the colonial experiences. As noted earlier, an inclusive policy, designed through an effective participation of the people, that addresses the cultural and linguistic as well as power and resource interests of the people in existing states could go a long way in rectifying the governance defects permeating them now. The African political elites have for decades tried in vain to produce solutions to the African problems based on their Western-influenced education and experience. It is time for them to "reestablish vital inner links"[45] with the grassroots people and incorporate the people's views and interests into their policies and decisions.

Notes

1 John Markakis, Günther Schlee and John Young, *The Nation State A Wrong Model for the Horn of Africa* (Max Planck Research Library for the History and Development of Knowledge, 2021).

2 Markakis, Schlee and Young, "Nation State," 12.

3 Markakis, Schlee and Young, "Nation State," 12.

4 Markakis, Schlee and Young, "Nation State," 13.

5 Markakis, Schlee and Young, "Nation State," 3.

6 Markakis, Schlee and Young, "Nation State," 54.

7 Markakis, Schlee and Youngl., "Nation State," 54.

8 See John Young, "Bolshevism and National Federalism in Ethiopia," in Markakis, Schlee and Young, "Nation State," 51.

9 Young, "Bolshevism," 10.

10 Many anthropologists, legal anthropologists and legal scholars interested in and advocating pluralist legal systems disagree with the notion of replacing one set of laws with another and argue that laws can be sourced from different sources and function in their own spheres or social fields, non-exclusively. See, e.g., John Griffiths, "What is legal pluralism?," *Journal of Legal Pluralism* 24 (1986): 1; Brian Z Tamanaha , "Understanding Legal Pluralism: Past to Present, Local to Global," *Sydney L Rev* 30 (2008): 375; Sally Falk Moore *Social Facts and Fabrications: 'Customary' Law on Kilimanjaro, 1880–1980*, (Cambridge, Cambridge University Press, 1986); Susanne Epple and Getachew Assefa (eds), *Legal Pluralism in Ethiopia: actors, challenges and solutions* (transcript Verlag, 2020); Olaf Zenker and Markus V. Hoehne, *The State and the Paradox of Customary Law in Africa* (Routledge, 2018); Mahmood Mamdani *Citizen and Subject: Contemporary Africa and the Legacy of Late Colonialism* (Princeton University Press, 1996).

11 See Zenker & Hoehne, "State and Customary Law".

12 In the case of Ethiopia, although there was no direct colonial rule by the Europeans, the imperial regimes, most clearly, Emperor Haile Selassie (r. 1930-1974) oversaw massive work of legal transplantation in the 1950s and 60s; See, Getachew A. Woldemariam, "Towards Widening the Constitutional Space for Customary Justice System in Ethiopia", in Susanne Epple & Getachew Assefa (eds), "Legal Pluralism," 43.

13 Peter Ekeh, "Colonialism and the Two Publics in Africa: A Theoretical Statement," *Comparative Studies in Society and History*, 17, no. 1 (1975): 91, 97. Frantz Fanon makes a similar and more powerful observation saying that colonialism resulted in the "death and burial" of the local cultural originality of the colonized people. He says: "The colonized is elevated above his jungle status in proportion to his adoption of the mother country's cultural standards. He becomes whiter as he renounces his blackness, his jungle"; Frantz Fanon, *Black Skin, White Mask*, new ed., trans. Charles Lam Markmann (Pluto Press, 2008): 9.

14 Fanon, "Blak Skin," 9.

15 Fanon, "Black Skin," 102.

16 Fanon, "Black Skin," 102.

17 Fanon, "Black Skin," 103; Mahmood Mamdani, *Define and Rule: Native as a political identity* (Harvard University Press, 2012): 49; Zenker & Hoehne, "State and Customary Law," 6-7.
18 Zenker & Hoehne, "State and Customary Law," 6-7.
19 See, Mamdani, "Define and Rule".
20 See, Ekeh, "the Two Publics".
21 See, Zenker & Hoehne, "State and Customary Law".
22 Cited in Zenker & Hoehne, "State and Customary Law," 10.
23 Zenker &Hoehne, "State and Customary Law," 10.
24 Ekeh, "the Two Publics," 106.
25 Basil Davidson, *The Black Man's Burden: Africa and the curse of the nation-state* (Times Books, 1992): 31-33.
26 Ekeh, "the Two Publics," 104.
27 Ekeh, "the Two Publics," 104.
28 Ekeh, "the Two Publics," 105.
29 Ekeh, "the Two Publics," 104.
30 The fact that ethnic groups are "social constructs" and that the notion was created in the colonial period has been stated by the authors as well; Markakis, Schlee and Young, "Nation State," 13.
31 John Markakis, "The Crisis of the State in the Horn of Africa" in Markakis Schlee and Young, "Nation State," 19
32 Markakis, "Crisis of the State," 19.
33 Markakis, Schlee and Young, "Nation State," 167.
34 See, e.g., Donald N. Levine, *Greater Ethiopia: The Evolution of a Multi-ethnic Society*, 2nd ed. (University of Chicago Press, 2000); Brian J. Yates, *The Other Abyssinians: The Northern Oromo and the Creation of Modern Ethiopia, 1855–1913* (University of Rochester Press, 2020).
35 Donald N. Levine, "A Revised Analytical Approach to the Evolution of Ethiopian Civilization" *International Journal of Ethiopian Studies* 6, no. 1/2 (2012): 29, 36.
36 See, Getachew A. Woldemariam, "The Continuing Quest for Inclusive Democratic Governance in Ethiopia", in Abadir Ibrahim and Kokebe Wolde (eds), *Between Failure and Redemption: The Future of the Ethiopian Social Contract* (Northwestern Roberta Buffett Institute for Global Affairs and Northwestern University Libraries, 2022): 355.
37 John Young (2021), "Bolshevism and National Federalism in Ethiopia" in Markakis, Schlee and Young, "Nation State," 55, 69.
38 Young, "Bolshevism," 57.
39 Ghana has for years been rated as "free" by the Freedom House, scoring 4 out of 4 in most of the criteria regarding political rights and freedoms; https://freedomhouse.org/country/ghana/freedom-world/2023.
40 See, for example, L. Hamalai et al., *Nigeria's 2015 General Elections: Continuity and Change in Electoral Democracy* (Springer, 2017).
41 See, John Markakis, *National and Class Conflict in the Horn of Africa.* (Cambridge University Press, 1987).
42 Davidson, "Black Man's Burden," 321-322.

43 On Ethiopia, see, e.g., Epple and Getachew, "Legal Pluralism"; Alula Pankhurst and Getachew Assefa (eds), *Grassroots Justice in Ethiopia: the Contribution of customary dispute resolution* (United printers Addis Ababa, 2008); Gebre Yntiso, Fekade Azeze and Assefa Fiseha (eds.), *Customary dispute resolution in Ethiopia* (The Ethiopian Arbitration and Conciliation, 2012).

44 Ekeh, "the Two Publics," 102.

45 Davidson, "Black Man's Burden," 291.

Bibliography

Davidson, Basil. The Black Man's Burden: Africa and the Curse of the Nation-State. Times Books, 1992.

Ekeh, Peter P. "Colonialism and the Two Publics in Africa: A Theoretical Statement." *Comparative Studies in Society and History* 17, no. 1 (1975): 91–112.

Epple, Susanne, and Getachew Assefa, eds. *Legal Pluralism in Ethiopia: Actors, Challenges and Solutions.* Transcript Verlag, 2020.

Fanon, Frantz. *Black Skin, White Masks.* New ed. Translated by Charles Lam Markmann. Pluto Press, 2008.

Freedom House. *Ghana: Freedom in the World 2023.* Accessed September 5, 2024. https://freedomhouse.org/country/ghana/freedom-world/2023

Griffiths, John. "What Is Legal Pluralism?" *Journal of Legal Pluralism* 24 (1986): 1–55.

Hamalai, L., et al. *Nigeria's 2015 General Elections: Continuity and Change in Electoral Democracy.* Springer, 2017.

Levine, Donald N. "A Revised Analytical Approach to the Evolution of Ethiopian Civilization." *International Journal of Ethiopian Studies* 6, no. 1/2 (2012): 29–36.

Levine, Donald N. *Greater Ethiopia: The Evolution of a Multi-Ethnic Society.* 2nd ed. University of Chicago Press, 2000.

Mamdani, Mahmood. *Citizen and Subject: Contemporary Africa and the Legacy of Late Colonialism.* Princeton University Press, 1996.

Mamdani, Mahmood. *Define and Rule: Native as a Political Identity.* Harvard University Press, 2012.

Markakis, John, Günther Schlee, and John Young. *The Nation State: A Wrong Model for the Horn of Africa.* Max Planck Research Library for the History and Development of Knowledge, 2021.

Markakis, John. "The Crisis of the State in the Horn of Africa." In *The Nation State: A Wrong Model for the Horn of Africa,* edited by John Markakis, Günther Schlee, and John Young, 19–40. Max Planck Research Library for the History and Development of Knowledge, 2021.

Markakis, John. *National and Class Conflict in the Horn of Africa.* Cambridge University Press, 1987.

Moore, Sally Falk. *Social Facts and Fabrications: 'Customary' Law on Kilimanjaro, 1880–1980.* Cambridge University Press, 1986.

Pankhurst, Alula, and Getachew Assefa, eds. *Grassroots Justice in Ethiopia: The Contribution of Customary Dispute Resolution.* United Printers, 2008.

Tamanaha, Brian Z. "Understanding Legal Pluralism: Past to Present, Local to Global." *Sydney Law Review* 30 (2008): 375–406.

Woldemariam, Getachew A. "The Continuing Quest for Inclusive Democratic Governance in Ethiopia." In *Between Failure and Redemption: The Future of the Ethiopian Social Contract,* edited by Abadir Ibrahim and Kokebe Wolde, 355–376. Northwestern Roberta Buffett Institute for Global Affairs and Northwestern University Libraries, 2022.

Woldemariam, Getachew A. "Towards Widening the Constitutional Space for Customary Justice System in Ethiopia." In *Legal Pluralism in Ethiopia: Actors, Challenges and Solutions,* edited by Susanne Epple and Getachew Assefa, 127–144. Transcript Verlag, 2020.

Yates, Brian J. *The Other Abyssinians: The Northern Oromo and the Creation of Modern Ethiopia, 1855–1913.* University of Rochester Press, 2020.

Yntiso, Gebre, Fekade Azeze, and Assefa Fiseha, eds. *Customary Dispute Resolution in Ethiopia.* The Ethiopian Arbitration and Conciliation, 2012.

Young, John. "Bolshevism and National Federalism in Ethiopia." In *The Nation State: A Wrong Model for the Horn of Africa,* edited by John Markakis, Günther Schlee, and John Young, 51–70. Max Planck Research Library for the History and Development of Knowledge, 2021.

Zenker, Olaf, and Markus V. Hoehne. *The State and the Paradox of Customary Law in Africa.* Routledge, 2018.

Chapter 4

Revisiting the Integrative Role of the FDRE Constitution: Lessons and way forward

Tsega Andualem Gelaye (SJD)

1. Introduction

Ethiopia is one of the oldest states in Africa, inhabited by diverse groups of people. The multinational character of the state has created unique challenges for managing diversity. When one looks at Ethiopian political and constitutional history, one can witness different approaches adopted by different regimes for this purpose. According to Aberra Degefa, the major strategy the monarchy that was in power until 1974 had relied on was assimilation.[1] As such, it attempted to foster unity in the country by using language and religion as an instrument (i.e., promoting one language and religion). In his view, what the monarchy tried to do was to create a nation-state out of a multinational state.[2] Also, if one looks at the 1931 and 1955 Constitutions, besides consolidating the powers of the central government and the emperor, they make no attempt to reflect the linguistic and religious diversity in the country. That contributed its part to the downfall of the regime in 1974.

A committee of military officers called the Derg assumed political power in 1974 by deposing Emperor Haile Selassie I. The Derg immediately abolished the 1955 Constitution and ruled the country for thirteen years without a formal constitution. The regime primarily subscribed to the socialist ideology popular in that period. This was also reflected in the Constitution of the People's Democratic Republic of Ethiopia (PDRE) that it adopted in 1987. Compared to its predecessors, the PDRE Constitution has gone one step ahead in terms of recognizing diversity. This fact is evident from its preamble, which characterizes the Ethiopian state as multinational. The substantive provisions of the Constitution also recognize the right of all nationalities to live in equality, as well as their right to promote their language on an equal basis.[3] Further, the Constitution also promises to ensure equitable development for all and promote regional autonomy.

Similarly, the PDRE Constitution contains many provisions that aim at preserving the unity of the country. In its preamble, for instance, in addition to acknowledging the existence of multiple nationalities, the Constitution claims that the continuous interactions among different nationalities has created togetherness as "one people" (the people of Ethiopia). It also acknowledges that the country was able to maintain its independence from colonialism due to the joint struggle of all nationalities (the Ethiopian people) and mentions the victory at Adwa in 1896 as a landmark achievement.[4] The substantive provisions of the Constitution further describe the unitary structure of the state and unequivocally state its indivisibility.

The preceding discussion may suggest that the PDRE Constitution has tried to recognize diversity and unity. Yet, some scholars take a critical view of the effort made by the PDRE Constitution in accommodating diversity. Their key argument is that the Derg regime basically strengthened the centralization process that began in the era of the monarchy and failed to implement meaningful regional autonomy.[5] They mention that most of the decisions were made centrally by the Working Party of Ethiopia and that the Constitution only paid lip service to promoting diversity of languages and cultures. This, in their view, is partly the reason why so many ethnic-based liberation organizations took up arms and fought the regime.[6] After many years of civil war, the Derg regime was overthrown in 1991. That paved the way for the adoption of the Federal Democratic Republic of Ethiopia (FDRE) Constitution.

As many writers agree, the making of the FDRE Constitution was dominated by ethnic-based political organizations that defeated the Derg.[7] Their main reason for fighting the Derg was to end the oppression of the nations, nationalities, and peoples of Ethiopia and ensure respect for their right to self-determination. These ideals were reflected in the FDRE Constitution from the start to the end.[8] The ethnic-based federal arrangement that the constitution prescribes could also be mentioned as one manifestation of this fact. Thus, in terms of acknowledging and accommodating the ethnic and linguistic diversity prevalent in the country, the FDRE Constitution is more progressive than its predecessors. Yet, the extent to which the Constitution attempted to balance diversity with the equally important goal of ensuring unity is controversial and under-explored in the existing literature. This contribution therefore seeks to fill that gap by critically evaluating the potential of the FDRE Constitution in promoting integration and creating national cohesion, while preserving diversity.

With this objective in mind, the next section tries to provide a general overview of the role constitutions play in promoting integration and social cohesion. It particularly investigates the reason why constitutions should play such a role in diverse societies. The experience of countries like India will be discussed here to give the reader a better insight as to how this is done in practice. This will be followed by the third section, which evaluates the integrative role of the FDRE Constitution by analyzing its preamble and substantive provisions. One thing worth noting here is that the makers of the FDRE Constitution do not seem to be alien to the idea of promoting unity while preserving diversity. Their assumption, however, is that if diversity is recognized robustly enough or without limitation, then unity or national cohesion will emerge naturally. The author takes issue with this assumption and seeks to show why their assumption is flawed in this part by highlighting concrete gaps in the Constitution. The final part will highlight the way forward for Ethiopia by taking lessons from India and from Ethiopia's past constitutions.

II. Integrative Functions of Constitutions: An Overview

Thoughts about constitutions often focus on their function in establishing various institutions of government and enabling and limiting their power through different mechanisms. Yet, constitutions also have an integrative function that is often overlooked. According to Dieter Grimm:

> *People expect the constitution to unify their society as a polity, thereby transcending the differences of opinion and conflicting interests that exist in all societies. The constitution is regarded as a guarantee of the fundamental consensus that is necessary for social cohesion. If a constitution is successful in this respect, it can even help shape a society's identity. The constitution then serves as a document in which society finds its basic convictions and aspirations expressed [emphasis added].*[9]

This function is particularly crucial in polities with diverse ethnic, cultural, and religious compositions, and in which the constitution could play a very important role in nation building. There is a widespread agreement among scholars that a constitution organizes a political community by outlining its shared values and commitments.[10] In so doing, it attempts to create a sense of solidarity and belongingness amongst compatriots. Furthermore, it conveys the message that the community is in a joint or common enterprise and that it is ready to utilize common opportunities and address challenges as one. Since the constitution is conceived as a manifestation of the will of the people, a supreme and founding document, it is a natural place to include elements that bind the society together. On the flip side, if a constitution fails in its basic mission of unifying the people, it may contribute to bringing about the disintegration/ dissolution of the political community by failing to coordinate them properly. That is because an absence of vision held commonly by members of a political community would make living as one "political community" a pointless exercise.

Some may, however, argue that integration is not something that can be achieved by a constitution. Rather, it is something that emerges naturally. To the best of the writer's knowledge, there is no literature that supports this assertion. The argument also seems to be illogical and something unproved in other jurisdictions. One thing worth noting here is that when an attempt is made by the constitution to recognize diversity, it may contribute towards unifying the society as the demand for recognition of different groups is fulfilled. Yet, this does not mean that this gesture is enough to bring about unity/national cohesion. As we can learn from the experience of many jurisdictions, achieving national cohesion is a herculean exercise that demands a conscious and exerted effort. This is why many constitutions take the issue of promoting national cohesion seriously and provide detailed provisions that aim at its concrete realization.[11]

The integrative function of a constitution mentioned above could be accomplished by using both instrumental and symbolic means. Among the instrumental tools of integration are the establishment of central legislative, executive, and judicial institutions, constituting a national army and utilizing a common currency.[12] Likewise, constitutions employ various means to foster symbolic integration. The most common means used by constitutions in this regard is the definition of the political community and setting the criteria for membership.[13] Regardless of the ethnic, linguistic, and religious diversity prevalent in a polity, most constitutions use the term "people" as a unified whole when they refer to the political community. They also make citizenship the primary criterion for membership in the political community and make popular sovereignty unified and indivisible.

This approach is justified because the term "We the people" refers to all individual citizens of the polity without exclusion. On the contrary, if membership in a certain political community is based on prior membership in another group defined along ethnic, linguistic, or religious lines, it would have excluded those who do not belong to those groups or who do not want to identify themselves with them. Further, making citizenship the basis of membership in a political community also aligns with the idea that sovereignty is indivisible and is something held by individual citizens collectively. The idea of constituting a political community based on membership in other groupings may divide sovereignty, which is indivisible and unified in its nature. As such, what constitutive units can have in a federation is autonomy not sovereignty.[14]

As such, besides constituting the political community on the basis of citizenship, constitutions also attempt to strengthen the bond between citizens by narrating and articulating their shared fundamental values and common achievements. The role fundamental-rights provisions of constitutions play in this regard is particularly crucial.[15] This is because the source and foundation of these rights is human dignity, which is a shared attribute of all human beings regardless of race, religion, language, and ethnicity. Furthermore, the ultimate end of fundamental constitutional rights is to preserve and protect human dignity, fundamental freedoms, and equality. These universal values, articulated in the form of fundamental rights, ought to be compelling to everyone and have the capacity to bind society together. The unifying force of these ideals lies in the interest of everyone to have them respected. This is particularly relevant in societies where other instruments of societal integration, such as common ethnicity, language, culture, religion, and history are missing.

Even when these characteristics are present they are not considered to be durable foundations for a multinational political community. This is because ethnic-based nationalism/togetherness is founded on an "us" versus "them" narrative, and it is inherently divisive.[16] There is also a tendency to portray one's own ethnic or religious group in a better light than others, which creates unnecessary competition among groups and may end in conflict. Further, however earnestly it is tried, it is difficult to build one political community based on nationalism because it is impossible to please everyone or meet every group's demand for equality and the terms of equality each group seeks to establish. This is why proponents of constitutional patriotism argue in favor of making universal values such as liberty, equality, and human dignity foundations for the political community.[17]

Here it is important to note that not all constitutions are equally effective in discharging their integrative role. History shows that some constitutions had their hand in the disintegration of the country rather than serving as forces of integration. The constitutions of the former Union of Soviet Socialist Republics (USSR) and Yugoslavia can be noted as paradigmatic examples of that.[18]

In contrast, the Constitution of India can be regarded as a good model for achieving national cohesion.[19] To understand this better, it is important to look at the political history of India. India gained its independence from Britain in 1947. Despite its multicultural diversity, British colonial rule did not give much place for recognizing diversity in India. Their rule rather focused on centralization. This created a feeling of resentment among many Indians. It also motivated political organizations during the anti-colonial struggle to use ethnolinguistic identity as a major tool for political mobilization.[20] When India became independent, a linguistic-based federal arrangement was adopted by the Indian Constitution to better manage ethnic, religious, cultural, and linguistic diversity.

In equal measure, makers of the Indian constitution have also underscored the importance of preserving the unity and territorial integrity of India. They particularly took a lesson from the separation of Pakistan from India and surmised that if ethnic- or religious-based autonomy is granted unconditionally, it may set the stage for the disintegration of the country.[21] In addition, the founders of the Constitution assumed that identity is socially constructed, layered, and flexible. As such, if primacy is given to ethnic or linguistic identity, it may have the effect of "freezing" it and may become an obstacle for the emergency of "more inclusive collective identity."[22] Thus, the design of the Indian federal setup was made to reflect not only language but also culture, geography, and economic development.

Accordingly, in the making of the Indian Constitution, the makers exerted serious effort to accommodate diversity and at the same time ensure the integrity of the state as well as the unity of the Indian people.[23] This is why some authors characterize the Indian model as a "state-nation" model of nation building.[24] This is different from the nation-state model, which seeks to create a single identity on the basis of ethnicity or language. It is also different from a pure multicultural approach, which gives unlimited autonomy to various ethnic/ linguistic groups.[25]

In contrast, the state-nation model gives recognition for multiple cultural identities within the Indian polity. This is also why Indian states are organized for the purpose of giving space to different cultural and linguistic communities to preserve their identity. However, this should in no way threaten or undermine the unity and integrity of India. This intention of the makers is clearly stipulated in the preamble, as it states the need to preserve the "unity of the Nation."[26] In addition, despite ethnic, linguistic, and religious diversity in India, the Constitution considers Indian people as one and refers to them as "the people of

India." The Constitution also clearly articulates the founding values of the state and the goals all Indian citizens wish to achieve, which include justice, liberty, equality, and fraternity.[27]

More importantly, unlike many other federations, the Indian Constitution gives the federal government significant powers aimed at ensuring better integration. That is why some characterize the Indian system as "unitary federalism" or quasi-federalism.[28] One manifestation of this is the supremacy of federal legislative and executive institutions over that of states. Also, when a constitution distributes power between the federal government and the states, most important powers and sources of revenue are reserved for the federal government.[29] In addition, the federal parliament was given the mandate to decide on the formation or reorganization of new states in India.[30] This has given the federal government the opportunity to form states in a manner that preserves the diversity and unity of India. Furthermore, the federal government is empowered to intervene in states when they engage in human rights violations or undertake discriminatory practices or when they violate the rights of minorities. The extensive power of adjudication of the federal Supreme Court of India, including enforcing human rights, is notable in this regard.[31] More importantly, the Indian Constitution does not recognize the right to secession, and in the event of an emergency, the central government is empowered to replace the federal structure with a unitary system.[32]

III. Evaluating the Integrative Role of the FDRE Constitution

The previous section highlighted how India uses its constitution for the purpose of integration and for creating social cohesion. Using that as a benchmark, this section evaluates the performance of the FDRE Constitution in achieving unity and cohesion in Ethiopia. One thing worth noting here is that when the FDRE Constitution was designed, the primary goal of the dominant actors in the drafting process (ethnic-based political organizations) was addressing the oppression of ethnic groups, or NNPs.[33] As such, maintaining the unity and integrity of the Ethiopian state was not their primary agenda. This does not, however, mean that the Constitution is devoid of any integrative elements. When we examine the preamble and other provisions, we see some symbolic and instrumental aspects of integration. Yet, they seem weak and incidental, as discussed below.

In the preamble it is mentioned that the nation, nationalities, and peoples of Ethiopia have committed themselves to creating one political and economic community for the purpose of achieving social and economic development. The inference one can draw from this statement is that the drafters did not accept the idea that a unified political community had existed in Ethiopia prior to the adoption of the Constitution. This contradicts the stipulation made in the same preamble of the PDRE Constitution, which claims that various communities in Ethiopia that had lived together for so long have created a common identity and could be regarded as "one people."[34] Moreover, what one can infer from the preamble of the FDRE Constitution is that the primary factor that motivated the various ethnic groups to live together under the umbrella of Ethiopia is to advance their economic interests. As discussed in previous sections, identifying shared interests is one means of symbolic integrations that constitutions employ. The only question here would be whether shared economic interest alone would be enough to ensure national cohesion and unity within a certain polity. The experience of other jurisdictions shows that economic factors are just one among many other factors that hold a society together.

The other point worth noting is the interaction among various nations, nationalities, and peoples in Ethiopia, which the preamble of the Constitution states. This statement acknowledges that the different ethnic groups in Ethiopia interacted for long and they are not alien to each other. It also claims that these interactions led to the creation of common interests and outlooks, though it fails to articulate what that means in precise terms. Common visions and goals are important means of integration, and what the constitution did here is worthy of appreciation. Yet, one can infer from the Constitution that the continuous interactions between various ethnic groups only led to the creation of a "common interest" and "common outlooks," not a shared identity.[35] The important question worth answering here is whether "common interest" is a sufficient foundation for a viable political community. I submit that a solid political community demands shared values and commitments in addition to having common interests. This means members of a political community need to have clear principles for articulating what they owe to one another, including how they ought to treat each other. Such commitments create a shared identity that transcends ethnicity, language, and religion. That could also play a crucial role in integrating the political community better.

That said, the preamble of the FDRE Constitution also talks about the importance of protecting fundamental rights, as they are a means for achieving economic and social development. What we see in other jurisdictions is the employment of fundamental rights as building blocks of the state and as the foundation for societal integration. This role of fundamental rights is limited in the FDRE Constitution as it reduces them to instruments of advancing the rule of law, peace, and economic development. Outside of the preamble, the provision of the Constitution dealing with the flag and national anthem could be considered symbolic means for advancing national unity. Yet, the lack of consensus on symbols, colors, and content of the flag and of the national anthem among Ethiopian society indicates the weak integrative role they have played.

Concerning instrumental means of integration, such as the establishment of centralized institutions of government and a common defense and currency, the FDRE constitution has some provisions worth noting. These include Articles 51 and 55, which list the powers of the federal government. Some of the important lawmaking powers reserved for the government include enacting laws on the utilization of resources, regulating interstate commerce, and enacting commercial and criminal codes. In addition, the federal government is granted the power to establish national defense, print money, and levy taxes on many areas. These powers are essential to facilitating economic integration, ensuring balanced growth among regions, and maintaining peace and security across the country.

However, compared to India, the symbolic and instrumental integrative elements of the FDRE Constitution are weak. In addition, the FDRE Constitution also contains a number of provisions starting from its preamble that militate against integration and national unity. This is partly because the constitution-making process itself was not inclusive, as it was dominated by ethnic-based political organizations.[36] Political parties that were organized at the national level were excluded from the process. In the absence of an inclusive constitution-making process, it is difficult to imagine a constitution that appeals to everyone and that unifies a nation. That aside, the way the FDRE Constitution defines the political community and the criteria for membership is equally problematic from an integrationist perspective.

Unlike many of its counterparts, the FDRE Constitution does not use the term "We the people" in reference to the Ethiopian political community. It rather employs the term "We the Nations, Nationalities and Peoples" of Ethiopia.[37] The definition given by the Constitution for this phrase refers to groups of people who have distinct languages, cultures, and identities. As such, the Constitution does not consider the Ethiopian people as unified or as people with common identity/shared values. This clearly undermines the integrative role of the Constitution, as it focuses on things that set different ethnic groups apart rather than on what unites them by articulating their shared values and interests. There are several questions that could be raised concerning the decision of the makers of the FDRE Constitution not to recognize Ethiopian peoples as one with a shared identity. One pertinent question is to ask how well this description is supported by the historical reality on the ground. As many scholars argue, the diverse ethnic and religious communities inhabiting Ethiopia have lived together for more than a century with very close trade and personal and communal interaction.[38] Intermarriage between different ethnic communities is also common in many parts of Ethiopia. One also can find many cultural similarities in different communities. Furthermore, even today a significant number of people from diverse ethnic and religious backgrounds perceive themselves simply as Ethiopians. In light of these facts, it is not clear why the drafters of the FDRE Constitution opted to deny the existence of a shared Ethiopian identity or are hesitant to portray the Ethiopian people as one.

Fasil Nahom, who took part in the drafting of the FDRE Constitution, claims that the choice for recognizing the nation, nationalities, and peoples instead of "Ethiopian People" was made to reflect the diversity prevalent in Ethiopia.[39] His reason is that the term "Ethiopian People" connotes homogeneity, a description inappropriate for the Ethiopian context. I believe this is a weak argument. One reason being that claiming that the various ethnic groups in Ethiopia could be considered as one Ethiopian people with shared identity in no way suggests a denial of cultural, religious, and linguistic diversity. When we see the constitutions of other multinational federations, they commonly use the phrase "We the people" to indicate the existence of a shared identity among various groups residing in their polity, which, I believe, is a critical foundation for any viable political community.

Were the drafters concerned about the "negative" connotation of the phrase "We the people," they could have explicitly recognized the diversity prevalent in the country as well as the rights of the nation, nationalities, and peoples, while acknowledging the existence of Ethiopian citizens (if not people) with shared identities. The basis of this identity could also be a commitment to universal values such as respect for human dignity, equality, freedom, and respect for diversity. However, such kinds of narratives would go against the ideology of ethnic-based political parties, which were dominant in the constitution-making process. In their view, the various ethnic communities in Ethiopia had existed independently and the Constitution was primarily designed to keep this state of affairs intact while ensuring some degree of cooperation between them. This is also the reason why some writers characterize the Ethiopian federal setup as a coming-together type.[40] Yet, it is not clear at what time in history were these groups independent entities and had independent sovereign existences.[41] The approach adopted by the FDRE Constitution would completely undermine its integrative and nation-building role, which is expected from any similar constitution.

In addition, the Constitution gives sovereign power to the Nations, Nationalities and Peoples rather than the Ethiopian people/citizens as a whole.[42] This goes against the fundamental principle that national sovereignty is indivisible. What is more, it also excludes a considerable number of people from its ambit. For instance, individuals with mixed identity (belonging to two or more ethnic groups) or individuals who do not want to associate with any of the ethnic groups will not be members of the political community because the constitution only recognizes Nations, Nationalities and Peoples. Similarly, millions of Ethiopians living in different urban centers may also find it difficult to fit into the NNP umbrella. A good example of this is the millions of people who reside in Addis Ababa. If one strictly applies the definition given to Nation, Nationalities or Peoples under the FDRE Constitution, many Addis Ababans may not neatly belong to any of them. This is also part of the reason why they do not have representation in the House of Federation. Thus, the criterion for becoming a member of the political community set under the FDRE Constitution needs to be revisited to make it more inclusive.

Following the logic of the FDRE Constitution, most state constitutions that were subsequently adopted empower certain ethnic groups in the region as sovereign.[43] This deprives other ethnic groups in the state, who are minorities, and in some cases considered "settlers," basic rights and relegate their status to second-class citizens. As highlighted above, other constitutions use citizenship as the primary criteria for defining membership in a political community and as the means for integration, as it signifies a common identity of the people of a certain polity in the public sphere while reserving a space for ethnolinguistic and religious identities in the private sphere. It also serves as the basis for enjoying rights on an equal basis. Contrary to this, the FDRE Constitution does not give a proper place for the notion of citizenship, as many rights are acquired on the basis of membership to a recognized ethnic community rather than being an Ethiopian citizen.[44] This has created a situation where individuals residing outside of their "home" state (the state where their ethnic group is based) are treated as outsider/aliens not entitled to important rights on an equal basis with the "natives." Such treatment in turn restricts the right to freedom of movement guaranteed for all Ethiopian citizens in the federal Constitution and weakens social integration.[45]

In addition, the way the FDRE Constitution recognizes the right to self-determination of the NNPs is also problematic when analyzed from the perspective of ensuring national unity and societal integration. This is because it grants the NNP's an unconditional right to self-determination, which includes secession.[46] Constitutions in most other jurisdictions either prohibit secession explicitly or keep quiet about the matter, considering it as belonging to an extra-constitutional sphere or as a matter to be resolved by adjudicatory bodies.[47] Under international law there is also no such thing as an unconditional right to secession.[48] It is only when internal aspects of the right to self-determination, such as the promotion of language and culture, are denied to a certain community and the government fails to address it that secession could be permitted exceptionally. This is intended to preserve the territorial integrity and unity of the state. Contrary to this, the FDRE Constitution allows secession in a manner that threatens the unity and integrity of the Ethiopian state.

Finally, as noted above, though the federal government is granted considerable powers by the FDRE Constitution, it still lacks key powers essential to bringing about greater integration. One example includes the supremacy clause of the US Constitution, under which federal law prevails over state laws.[49] This power is crucial for securing social and economic integration. The FDRE Constitution only talks about the supremacy of the federal Constitution and not about the supremacy of federal law. In addition, the Constitution empowers the House of Federation to empower the House of People's Representatives to make civil laws aimed at facilitating/creating one political and economic community.[50] Yet, it is difficult to imagine how the House of Federation, which represents the nations, nationalities, and peoples, would take measures that may effectively weaken the autonomy of ethnic groups with the aim of prompting greater integration. Also, in practice, the House of Federation appears to have limited engagement in this regard. Besides, the reference to civil laws may not cover other areas of law such as public law and human rights, which may touch upon matters reserved for states. These factors constrain the capacity of the federal government to enact laws that are aimed at better integration.

In addition, constitutions in other jurisdictions, such as the USA, empower the federal government to protect citizens from discrimination committed by the states.[51] This includes enacting anti discrimination laws and empowering federal courts to handle such cases. Such powers have not been specifically given to the Ethiopian federal government, and this has contributed to the impunity with which acts of discrimination are being committed by states in the area of employment, housing, property ownership, and movement. Here it may be argued that since it is the federal government that primarily assumes the international obligation to enforce human rights, it could enact laws dealing with human rights that could be applied to states without any explicit constitutional authorization. Yet, the constitutional practice in Ethiopia does not imply such an understanding. To illustrate, one could mention the reservation Ethiopia made on the Maputo Protocol concerning a minimum marriageable age.[52] The reservation was entered partly because many regional states in Ethiopia had family laws that set the minimum marriageable age below international standards. Since the Constitution reserves the right to enact family laws in states, the federal government found it difficult to comply with its international obligation or to enact a federal law that overrode the stipulations made in state laws.

Another important power with implications for integration is the extent of power given to the federal government in the formation of sub-units. As previously mentioned, the Constitution of India grants enormous power to the Indian federal government in the area of state formation.[53] In the Indian system, new states are created or reconstituted based on laws enacted by the federal government, taking into account several factors, including the unity of the Indian state, geography, economic development, and social cohesion. Such power is not conferred to the Ethiopian federal government, and this may be an obstacle to the implementation of measures aimed at ensuring greater national cohesion.

IV. Lessons Learned and the Way Forward

One of the lessons from the discussion so far is that constitutions play an important role in holding together and integrating diverse societies. This function of a constitution can only be achieved when the design process is participatory, inclusive, and has the aim of creating national cohesion by using the constitution as an instrument. In this regard, the FDRE Constitution has critical weaknesses. From the very start, the constitution-making process was not participatory and inclusive of all interests. As a result, the Constitution outlines the ideological inclinations of the then power holders, rather than serving as a compromise compact. This has significantly undermined its unifying force. As such, if the FDRE Constitution is going to be revised or amended or replaced, it is absolutely critical that it follows an inclusive process. In addition, when the FDRE Constitution was designed, national cohesion was not the main goal the makers aspired to achieve. This is also the reason why the Constitution has weak symbolic and instrumental integrative elements. Thus, future constitutional reform efforts should make national unity and societal integration core objectives of the Constitution.

In addition, the weak symbolic and integrative aspects of the Constitution need to be thoroughly addressed. This includes making the Ethiopian people as a whole sovereign and recognizing citizenship as the sole criteria for membership in the political community. Making such changes is absolutely critical because in the absence of a demos with shared interests, common goals, values, and aspirations, constituting a strong political community is impossible. It is also important to note that having a common language or culture is not imperative for the purpose of nation building. This is evidenced from the experiences of Switzerland, the USA, and India. In these jurisdictions, there is a great deal of linguistic, religious, and ethnic diversity. Yet, they chose to build a state on political values such as liberty, equality, freedom, fraternity, and respect for diversity.

In Ethiopia too there need not be a single language or culture or ethnic identity for Ethiopians to build a shared national identity. Focus should rather be on common values, achievements, and shared interests. For this we can use universal values such as respect for human dignity, equality, freedom, and diversity as things that can hold us together as one people while having different cultures and languages. There are also economic and security interests that all communities living under the umbrella of Ethiopia share. In addition, Ethiopian people have together achieved great things such as defeating colonizers and maintaining the independence of their country, a fact that has made Ethiopia a symbol of freedom and independence for many. Ethiopians can build on this notable achievement and strengthen their social bonds. The Ethiopian Constitution needs to reflect these and other common achievements that are sources of national pride and use them as bases for bringing the diverse people of Ethiopia together.

Further, the part of the Constitution that asserts the sovereignty of ethnic groups with an unconditional right to secession should be revised. As discussed above, most constitutions make sovereignty indivisible and do not recognize the right to secession as a premise for maintaining national unity. If the basic aspiration of the Ethiopian people is to live together within the umbrella of an Ethiopian state, sovereignty should belong to the Ethiopian people as a whole and not severally to ethnic groups. What the various nations, nationalities, and peoples will be entitled to instead should be the right to promote their language and culture. The current organization of states, which primarily takes into account ethnolinguistic factors, should be preserved to give space for communities to protect their identity. Changing this way of structuring the federal states from an ethnic-based arrangement to an arrangement based on geography may also invite vehement resistance and is not a feasible option. Yet, it may be possible to break bigger regions into smaller ones and create many states inhabited predominantly by a single ethnic community. As many scholars have argued, this may weaken regional loyalty and create interstate competition, which is good for the purpose of promoting integration.[54]

If designed this way, it would be possible to ensure the coexistence of ethnic identity with that of national or Ethiopian identity. It is also difficult to see why a person could not identify himself/herself with his/her ethnic group as well as with his/her own Ethiopian citizenship. One of the reasons why some individuals do not want to identify themselves with the Ethiopian state is the belief that Ethiopian identity is imposed on them against their will. This is understandable as the formation of the modern Ethiopian state was largely accomplished with the use of force rather than consent. Yet, it is possible to rectify this defect by founding a reconstituted Ethiopian political community on universal values that everyone accepts, such as respect for human dignity, freedom, equality, and diversity. The Constitution should explicitly recognize these values and associate what it means to be Ethiopian with them, among others.

Likewise, state constitutions that empower particular ethnic groups to be sovereigns within the states should also be amended to ensure societal integration. The rights different ethnic groups should have within the Ethiopian state are administrative autonomy and self-rule, not sovereignty. Until such amendments are done, the term "sovereign" in state constitutions should narrowly be construed to only recognize their right to protection from unjustified federal interference. The unconditional rights to secession stipulated in the FDRE Constitution should also be taken out, as it undermines national unity and encourages disintegration. Instead, the Constitution should clearly prohibit secession or make it conditional upon denial of the right to self-determination, as it is done in other constitutions.

Finally, additional powers ought to be granted to the federal government in regard to maintaining national unity and for ensuring the social and economic integration of the people. As we have seen in India and the USA, the federal government has been granted with substantial powers to maintain the unity of the state and protect the rights of citizens in all sub-units. Similarly, the FDRE Constitution should be revised in a manner that enables the federal government to take "all necessary and proper" measures capable of enhancing the integration of the people and deal with any threats that undermine it. These powers could be given to the federal legislative and executive branches, as well as judicial organs.

Notes

1 Aberra Degefa, "State building and issues of Legitimacy in Ethiopia: Chronicling Achievements, Failures and prospects" *Ethiopian Constitutional and Public Law Series, vol 8,* (2017): 5-28,
2 Degefa, *"State building"*, 5-28.
3 People's Democratic Republic of Ethiopia (PDRE) Constitution (1987) art 2(2-4)
4 PDRE Constitution , preamble
5 Assefa Fiseha, *Federalism and the Accommodation of Diversity in Ethiopia: A Comparative Study* (Wolf legal Publishers, 2006)
6 Fiseha, *"Federalism"*
7 Gedion T. Hessebon,"The Precarious Future of the Ethiopian Constitution". *Journal of African Law* 5, no. 2 (2013), 215–233,

8 Tsega A. Gelaye, "An Enduring Path for National Unity and Human Rights Protection in Ethiopia: A Case for Human Dignity Centered Constitutional Design and Interpretation", *Mizan Law Review* 15, (2021), 1-40,

9 Dieter Grimm, *Constitutionalism Past, Present, and Future* (Oxford University Press, 2016), 143-157.

10 Elliot Bulmer, "What is a Constitution? Principles and Concepts", (International IDEA Constitution-Building Primer 1, 2017), 6.

11 Constitution of Kenya (2010):Preamble, art: 27, 7, 19, 20, 22, 33, 40, 43, 48, 52 – 57. Kenya also adopted The National Cohesion and Integration Act (December, 2008) and established the National Cohesion and Integration Commission (NCIC) to consolidate National Cohesion and Unity.

12 Peter Van den Berg, "The Integrative Function of Constitutions: A Historical Perspective" in *The Constitutional Integrity of the European Union, ed.* F. Amtenbrink & Peter A.J. van den Berg (Asser Press 2010) ,13-53.

13 Van den Berg, *Integrative Function, 13-53.*

14 Erika Arban, "Sovereignty and Autonomy of Constituent Units in Federal and Regional Systems: A Case Study of Italy" in *Beyond Autonomy Practical and Theoretical Challenges to 21st Century Federalism, ed.* Tracy Fenwick and Andrew Banfield (BRILL 2021), 47.

15 Arban, "*Sovereignty and Autonomy*", 29.

16 Eline Kleppe, "The impacts of ethnic politics on conflicts in Ethiopia How the shaping of ethnic identity has challenged nation-building and a 'unified' Ethiopia" (Master's Thesis, University of South-Eastern Norway 2022), Jerry Muller, "Us and Them: The Enduring Power of Ethnic Nationalism" *Foreign Affairs* 87 , no.2 (2008),18-35.

17 Jan-Werner Müller & Kim Lane Scheppele, "Constitutional Patriotism: An introduction" *International Journal of Constitutional Law* 6, (2008), 67–71.

18 Alem Habtu, "Multi Ethnic Federalism in Ethiopia: A Study of the Secession Clause in the Constitution" *Publius* 35 no.2 (2005) ,313-335.

19 Rajeev Bhargava, "The Evolution and Distinctiveness of India's Linguistic Federalism", In *Ethnic Federalism the Ethiopian experience in a comparative perspective,* ed. David Turton (AAU Press 2006), 93-118.

20 Bhargava, "*India's Linguistic Federalism*", 93-118.

21 Bhargava, "*India's Linguistic Federalism*", 93-118.

22 Bhargava, "*India's Linguistic Federalism*", 93-118.

23 Domenico Amirante, "Nation Building Through Constitutionalism: Lessons from the Indian Experience" *HKLJ* 42 (2012), 23-42.

24 Alfred Stephan et al. *Crafting State-Nation India and other, Multinational Democracies*. (The Johns Hopkins University Press 2011), 2-8. 2 .

25 Stephan, *Crafting State-Nation* , 2-8.

26 The Constitution of India (1949), Preamble

27 Constitution of India,Preamble.

28 Amirante, *"Nation Building"*,23-42.

29 Bhargava, "*India's Linguistic Federalism*", 93-118.

30 Constitution of India ,art 3.

31 Amirante, *"Nation Building"*, 23-42.
32 Bhargava, "*India's Linguistic Federalism*", 93-118.
33 Tsegaye Regassa, "The making and legitimacy of the Ethiopian constitution: towards bridging the gap between constitutional design and constitutional practice. *Afrika focus* 23, (2010), 85-118.
34 PDRE Constitution, preamble
35 The Constitution of the Federal Democratic Republic of Ethiopia (1995) (FDRE Const), preamble
36 Hessebon, "Precarious Future",215–233.
37 FDRE Const, preamble
38 Legesse Mengie, "Federalism as an Instrument for Unity and the Protection of Minorities: A Comparative Overview: Ethiopia, India and the US" *Mizan Law Review* 10, no.2 (2016),265-295.
39 Fasil Nahom, *Constitution for Nation of Nations: The Ethiopian Prospect* (Red Sea Press 1997)
40 Andreas Eshete, "Ethnic federalism: New frontiers in Ethiopian politics, in First national conference of federalism, conflict and peace building" (Addis Ababa: United Printers 2003), 142-172.
41 Yonatan Fessha, *Ethnic Diversity and Federalism, Constitution making in South Africa and Ethiopia*, (Routledge 2010), 187-237.
42 FDRE Const. art 8
43 Christophe Van der Beken,*Completing the Constitutional Architecture: A Comparative Analysis of Sub-national Constitutions in Ethiopi*a (AAU Printing Press, 2017) 65, 74, 75.
44 Berihun Gebeye, "Toward Making a Proper Space for the Individual in the Ethiopian Constitution" *Human Rights* Review 18, no.4 (2017),439–458.
45 Yonas Adimassu, "Implication of Ethiopian Federalism on the Right to Freedom of Movement and Residence: Critical Analysis of the Law and the Practice", (LLM Thesis , Addis Ababa University College of Law and Governance, Addis Ababa, 2013).
46 FDRE Const. art 39.
47 Elisa Novic and Priya Urs, *Secession,* Max Planck Encyclopedia of Comparative Constitutional Law (2016)
48 Hurst Hannum, "The Right of Self-Determination in the Twenty-First Century', 55 *WASH. & LEE L. REV* 55, (1998), 773-780.
49 The Constitution of the United States of America (1789), Article VI, Paragraph 2
50 FDRE Const, arts 55(6) and 62(8)
51 Robert Kaczorowski, "Congress's Power to Enforce Fourteenth Amendment Rights: Lessons from Federal Remedies the Framers Enacted" *Harv. J. on Legis.* 42, (2005), 187.
52 Proclamation No.1082/2018, Proclamation to Ratify The Protocol to the African Charter On Human and Peoples Rights on The Rights of Women in Africa.
53 Constitution of India, art 3.
54 Yonatan Fesseha, "The Original Sin of Ethiopian Federalism", *Ethnopoltics* 17, no.3 (2017), 232-245.

Bibliography

Adimassu, Yonas. *Implication of Ethiopian Federalism on the Right to Freedom of Movement and Residence: Critical Analysis of the Law and the Practice.* LL.M. thesis, Addis Ababa University College of Law and Governance, 2013.

Amirante, Domenico. "Nation Building through Constitutionalism: Lessons from the Indian Experience." *Hong Kong Law Journal* 42 (2012): 23.

Arban, Erika. "Sovereignty and Autonomy of Constituent Units in Federal and Regional Systems: A Case Study of Italy." In *Beyond Autonomy: Practical and Theoretical Challenges to 21st Century Federalism*, edited by Tracy Fenwick and Andrew Banfield, 47. BRILL, 2021.

Bhargava, Rajeev. "The Evolution and Distinctiveness of India's Linguistic Federalism." In *Ethnic Federalism: The Ethiopian Experience in a Comparative Perspective*, edited by David Turton, 93–118. Addis Ababa University Press, 2006.

Bulmer, W. Elliot. *What Is a Constitution? Principles and Concepts.* Stockholm: International IDEA, 2014.

Constitution of Kenya (2010).

Degefa, Aberra. "State Building and Issues of Legitimacy in Ethiopia: Chronicling Achievements, Failures, and Prospects." *Ethiopian Constitutional and Public Law Series* 8 (2017): 5–28.

Eshete, Andreas. "Ethnic Federalism: New Frontiers in Ethiopian Politics." In *First National Conference of Federalism, Conflict and Peace Building*, 142–172. United Printers, 2003.

Fessha, Yonatan Tesfaye. "The Original Sin of Ethiopian Federalism." In *The Ethnopolitics of Ethnofederalism in Ethiopia*, 14–27. Routledge, 2017.

Fessha, Yonatan Tesfaye. *Ethnic Diversity and Federalism: Constitution Making in South Africa and Ethiopia.* Routledge, 2016.

Fiseha, Assefa. *Federalism and the Accommodation of Diversity in Ethiopia: A Comparative Study.* Wolf Legal Publishers, 2006.

Gebeye, Berihun Adugna. "Toward Making a Proper Space for the Individual in the Ethiopian Constitution." *Human Rights Review* 18, no. 4 (2017): 439–458.

Gelaye, Tsega A. "An Enduring Path for National Unity and Human Rights Protection in Ethiopia: A Case for Human Dignity-Centered Constitutional Design and Interpretation." *Mizan Law Review* 15 (2021): 1–40.

Grimm, Dieter. *Constitutionalism: Past, Present, and Future.* Oxford University Press, 2016.

Habtu, Alem. "Multi-Ethnic Federalism in Ethiopia: A Study of the Secession Clause in the Constitution." *Publius* 35, no. 2 (2005): 313–335.

Hannum, Hurst. "The Right of Self-Determination in the Twenty-First Century." *Washington and Lee Law Review* 55 (1998): 773.

Hessebon, Gedion T. "The Precarious Future of the Ethiopian Constitution." *Journal of African Law* 57, no. 2 (2013): 215–233.

Jan-Werner Müller and Kim Lane Scheppele. "Constitutional Patriotism: An Introduction." *International Journal of Constitutional Law* 6 (2008): 67–71.

Kaczorowski, Robert J. "Congress's Power to Enforce Fourteenth Amendment Rights: Lessons from Federal Remedies the Framers Enacted." *Harvard Journal on Legislation* 42 (2005): 187.

Kleppe, Eline. *The Impacts of Ethnic Politics on Conflicts in Ethiopia: How the Shaping of Ethnic Identity Has Challenged Nation-Building and a 'Unified' Ethiopia.* Master's thesis, University of South-Eastern Norway, 2022.

Mengie, Legesse. "Federalism as an Instrument for Unity and the Protection of Minorities: A Comparative Overview: Ethiopia, India and the US." *Mizan Law Review* 10, no. 2 (2016): 265–295.

Muller, Jerry. "Us and Them: The Enduring Power of Ethnic Nationalism." *Foreign Affairs* 87, no. 2 (2008): 18–35.

Nahom, Fasil. *Constitution for Nation of Nations. The Ethiopian Prospect.* Red Sea Press, 1997.

Novic, Elisa, and Priya Urs. "Secession." In *Max Planck Encyclopedia of Comparative Constitutional Law.* Oxford University Press, 2016.

People's Democratic Republic of Ethiopia (PDRE) Constitution (1987).

Proclamation No. 1082/2018. Proclamation to Ratify the Protocol to the African Charter on Human and Peoples' Rights on the Rights of Women in Africa.

Regassa, Tsegaye. "The Making and Legitimacy of the Ethiopian Constitution: Towards Bridging the Gap Between Constitutional Design and Constitutional Practice." *Afrika Focus* 23 (2010): 85–118.

Stephan, Alfred, Juan J. Linz, and Yogendra Yadav. *Crafting State-Nation: India and Other Multinational Democracies.* The Johns Hopkins University Press, 2011.

The Constitution of India (1949).

The Constitution of the Federal Democratic Republic of Ethiopia (1995).

The Constitution of the United States of America (1789).

Van den Berg, Peter. "The Integrative Function of Constitutions: A Historical Perspective." In *The Constitutional Integrity of the European Union*, edited by F. Amtenbrink and Peter A.J. van den Berg, 13–53. Asser Press, 2010.

Van der Beken, Christophe. *Completing the Constitutional Architecture: A Comparative Analysis of Sub-National Constitutions in Ethiopia.* Addis Ababa University Press, 2017.

Chapter 5

Constituent Power in the Ethiopian Constitution

Terefe Sahelu Gebreyesus

1. Introduction

Ethiopia is a multiethnic and multireligious country with a population of more than 120 million people. Its present boundaries and ethnic composition were established at the end of the nineteenth century. For most of its history, the country was governed by an emperor within a traditional feudal system. In the 1960s, university students started a movement that resulted in the overthrow of the feudal system, which led to the coming to power of a socialist military junta (the Derg) and a protracted civil war. One of the products of this movement, the Tigray People's Liberation Front (TPLF), was formed in the 1970s and started a successful guerilla war against the Derg. When the TPLF anticipated their victory and subsequent assumption of power in the capital, they created the Ethiopian Peoples' Revolutionary Democratic Front (EPRDF), a coalition party, with other parties of its own creation. In 1991, the TPLF/EPRDF established a transitional government. In 1994, through a constitutional a ssembly that it dominated, the TPLF/EPRDF adopted the country's fourth constitution, which established the "Federal Democratic Republic of Ethiopia."

In the Ethiopian Constitution, Nations, Nationalities and Peoples (NNP) are the constituent powers. The Constitution speaks in the name of "we the NNP of Ethiopia" (Ethiopian Constitution, Preamble). It states that the NNP of Ethiopia "adopted ... this constitution" and that "All sovereign power resides in the NNP of Ethiopia."[1] The Constitution recognizes that the "NNP" are the sovereign constituent powers of Ethiopia. Under the Ethiopian Constitution, there are multiple constituent powers. This language is very foreign both to the very limited constitutional history of the country and to the constitutional experience of many countries in the world.

The Constitution's attribution of constituent power to the NNP deviates radically from the approaches adopted by most other states in the world, including federations with similar ethnic, religious, and linguistic diversity. The constitutions of many countries with ethnic and religious diversities—such as India, Nigeria, and even the former Soviet Union (which inspired the EPRDF)—attribute constituent power to a single unified entity, "We, the people".[2] Other ethnically, linguistically, or religiously diverse countries, such as Switzerland, acknowledge the existence of two entities, a single unifying national identity and several subnational identities[3]. Ethiopia, however, adopted the highly unusual approach of locating sovereignty solely in its subnational identities.

The constitution provides that "NNP" constituted the political community called "Ethiopia." However, the status of this political entity and the people comprising it is unclear. According to the standard accounts of state formation, when individuals come together to create a new political entity, "Those who are associated in it take collectively the name of people, and severally citizens".[4] Most contemporary constitutions contain statements whereby the people are identified with the political community they have created. The people of India identify themselves as "we the people of India"; the people of Nigeria as "we the people of Nigeria." However, the Ethiopian constitution does not characterize the people in Ethiopia as an Ethiopian "people," and it is difficult to determine whether the "the nations, nationalities, and peoples" of Ethiopia are to be called "Ethiopians." Rather, it stipulates that the Constitution is an agreement among "sovereign" ethnic groups. Due to this peculiar nature of the Ethiopian Constitution, some scholars observe that the Ethiopian Constitution "is less that of a constitution [but rather] more like an international treaty among [sovereign] nations".[5]

Is the reference to the "NNP of Ethiopia" a normatively justified attribution of constituent power? This chapter investigates this question. The investigation starts with introducing the concept of constituent power. Then the inquiry addresses some conceptual and practical issues relating to constituent power in states in which the people are divided along ethnic, religious, or linguistic lines.

Constituent power in the Ethiopian Constitution will also be investigated in depth with justifications that the drafters of the constitution provided and other potential justifications. This chapter argues that theoretical claims and practical constitution making do not justify the attribution of constituent power to NNPs. Rather, constituent power should be attributed to a singular entity.

2. Constituent Power: Brief Introduction

a. General

The investigation of constituent power requires distinguishing among these three interrelated concepts: constitutions, constituent powers, and constituted powers. Constituted powers relate to powers and political arrangements created by constitutions. Constituent power is the power to create those powers and political arrangements in the first place—the power to make constitutions. Constituent power is a necessary precondition for constituted power. And constitutions are the instrument through which constituent power creates constituted power. The simple definition of constituent power is "the power to create constitutional orders". A historically informed definition of the concept of constituted power is "the power vested in the prince to rule," whereas constituent power is "the power through which the prince's power to rule was authorized"[6]. That is, constituent power is the source, and constituted power is the product. For Michael Hardt, "Constituted power is empty; it merely falls back on, contains, and recuperates the constituent forces."[7]. In this context, "A constitution is … [something] that flows from a constituent power … and posited by [its] will."[8]. In other words, a constitution is "an act of the constitution-maker"—a constituent power[9].

However, these definitions do not portray the full picture of the concept. One of the pictures that this definition fails to illuminate is the extent to which these definitions are descriptive or normative. Descriptively, any political entity, such as a military junta or a dictator, can establish some sort of constitutional order. Such an entity may be described as a constituent power[10]. The normative aspect of constituent power is the exercise of legitimate power. Some scholars give different names for the normative and descriptive aspects of constituent power. George Duke and Elisa Arcioni describe these two concepts as constituent power and constituent authority. For them, constituent power is a simple descriptive assessment of establishing political (constitutional) order without assessing its legitimacy.[11]

The origin of the concept of constituent power is the theological concept of creation *ex nihilo*.[12] In Christian theology, God is the ultimate constituent power creating the world order out of nothing and yet Him being part of the created world order. Transforming this concept to constitution making, it was argued that "the author of the constitution cannot become subject to it; he is the extra-constitutional origin of the constitution."[13] This notion of constituent power has been used to argue that a constituent power that gives rise to a legal order is not itself part of that order unless it loses its character.[14]. Starting from the eighteenth century, descriptions of the concept of constituent power began to adopt a secularized form. The notion that the people are the constituent power started to develop. In the American Declaration of Independence, it was written, "Whenever any form of government becomes destructive . . . it is the right of the people to alter or to abolish it and to institute new government".[15] Unlike the theological notion of the concept, the secularized form of constituent power accepted the idea that the "people" can be constituent power and obey the constituted power.

The concept was first articulated by Emmanuel Joseph Sieyes (also known as Abbé Sieyes) during the French Revolution.[16] In one of his speeches, he stated that "A constitution presupposes a constituent power".[17] He argued that for the [constitution] to be legitimate, it must be predicated on "the manifest will of he who has to obey".[18]. For him, *Pouvoir constituant* is the power to authorize the creation of political order.[19] Today, as many states are or claim to be democratic, and the constitutional drafting process is atributted to them, at least theoretically, "the people" of a political community is a constituent power. Historically, however, either the monarchs or the emperors were also thought to have constituent power.[20] Similar to the theological conception, scholars argue that the people's constituent power is unlimited. Sieyes argues that the nation is not, cannot, and should not be subject to a constitution that it makes.[21] On the contrary, Hannah Arendt insists that such unlimited constituent power is "a poisonous recipe for permanent revolution"[22].

b. Constituent Power in Divided Polities

Historically, the basic feature of constituent power is its singularity. Constitutions usually are made by people organized into a single political community—a state. The existence (the assumption) of political unity and social order in that state is a precondition for the validity of a constitution.[23] According to the standard account of state formation, when individuals come together to create a new political entity, those who are associated with it "collectively take the name of *people*; individually they are called *citizens*".[24] Abbe Sieyès argues that the people of the entire nation exercise the *pouvoir constituant* and that they do this by delegating the drafting of the constitution to representatives elected for that purpose. Sieyès insisted on the unitary nature of the body politic and that the nation must express its will through a singular legislative body.[25] He described this unified singular constituent power as a "nation."[26] However, his description of "nation" is different from a culturally or ethnically defined concept of a "nation." For him, a constituent power "nation" is "a body of associates living under a common law, represented by the same legislature".[27] Similarly, Martin Loughlin highlighted that "It is the government, not the nation that is constituted".[28] In the history of the concept, constituent power was understood as a singular entity, "the people" or "nation."

The singularity of constituent power is the generally accepted practice for attributing constituent power. All of the constitutions of states recognize a singular constituent power in one way or another. In some states, the people, at least the majority, are homogeneous in ethnic, religious, and/or linguistic identities. In such nations, there is both political and cultural oneness wherein identifying a unified, single "We" constituent power is not difficult. For instance, the constitutions of countries like Germany, South Korea, and Vietnam state "the German People," the Vietnamese People," and "the People of Kore," respectively.[29] In these states, the political unity was there before the constitutions were adopted. Accordingly, the constitutions merely recognized an existing political reality.

In other countries, the singularity of constituent power is created at the adoption of the constitution. For instance, the Australian constitution provides that "Whereas the People of New South Wales, Victoria, South Australia, Queensland, and Tasmania . . . have agreed to *unite in one indissoluble* federal Commonwealth under the Crown. . . ."[30] George Duke and Carlo Dellora argue that history and constitutional text support that "popular sovereignty is a normative foundation for the Commonwealth Constitution".[31] As Australia is identified as a coming-together federation, the peoples of the states do have political unity and existence. When they adopted the constitution, they created a political unity and a single constituent unit almost similar to "We the People of the Commonwealth of Australia." The oldest functioning constitution, the Constitution of the United States of America, states "We the People of the United States." It did not say "we the peoples" or "we the peoples of the states." By observing this, Justice Kennedy said . . . "It is well settled that the whole people of the United States asserted their political identity and unity of purpose when they created the federal system".[32] Even others who may disagree with this statement argue that "We the people" did indeed refer to a singular and national constituent people and also peoples of the states.[33]

In countries where ethnic, linguistic, and/or religious diversities are politically salient, their constitutions stress on the singularity of the constituent power. The Indian constitution states, "We the people of India". Similarly, the Nigerian constitution states, "We the people of the Federal Republic of Nigeria". The preamble of the 1977 Constitution of the Soviet Union, which is considered to have inspired drafters of the Ethiopian constitution regarding the accommodation of diversity, provides that "the Soviet People" enacted the constitution and that sovereign power belongs to "the people."

In regard to attributing constituent power to subunits, the Swiss constitution is the oldest and most peculiar example. It states, "The Swiss People and the Cantons." However, there are three essential differences in approaches between the Ethiopian and the Swiss constitutions. First, unlike the Ethiopian constitution, the Swi ss constitution recognizes a single constituent power—the "Swiss people." Second, arguably, the Swiss constitution does not attribute constituent power to some sort of ethnic identities. Rather, constituent power rests on substate political organs. In the Ethiopian context, however, it rests on ethnic groups that did not have their own political organ before the implementation of the constitution.

Bosnia and Herzegovina is another example with a similar constitutional setup. The constitution recognizes the Bosniacs, Croats, and Serbs as constituent peoples (along with other peoples) and constituent powers. However, it also recognizes that these distinct peoples form a single constituent power, "citizens of Bosnia and Herzegovina" (Preamble). Such a constitutional setup appears to have closer similarity to the Ethiopian design in recognizing pluralistic ethnic identities as constituent powers. The difference is that unlike Ethiopia, it recognizes the existence of one constituent power—citizens of Bosnia and Herzegovina.

In states with politically relevant ethnic, linguistic, and religious diversity, the correlation between the singularity of constituent power and diversities should be investigated. I argue that the singularity of constituent power does not necessarily require the formation of a single people in terms of culture, religion, or ethnic group. It is about creating a single political community. People of many ethnic, religious, racial, and linguistic identities can create a single political community. Of course, one can argue that ideally, societies come together to form a political community whenever they share some markers of identity. However, historically, many states were created by force either through expansion or colonialism. Therefore, the creation of a single political community was not a reflective and conscious decision. In these states, regardless of how they came about, and regardless of the diversities they are made of, as far as their making and adopting a constitution is concerned, they make and adopt as a single constituent power. That is, they have one unifying identity in common, that of citizenship. Stephen Tierney observes that the prevalent discussion about state and constituent power goes with the unity of the people.[34] This unity is quite often expressed in the form of "we the people."

Potentially, one can have two understandings of the concept "we the people." The first one is a sociological definition that gets close to "we the nation."

Even though there is disagreement about the exact sociological understanding of "nation," it relates to defining a group of people in terms of ethnic, cultural, or religious identities.[35] The other one is a definition that emanates from membership to a state. The first definition is more of an ascriptive definition, whereas the second is principally descriptive. Whatever our understanding of "we the people" is, the constituent power recognized in constitutions around the world is a single constituent power.

There is a debate as to whether this "the people" is a real association of individuals or a fictitious "perpetual constituent." The first line of argument is that ideally, since constituent power comes first before constituted power, the unified subject of the constitution—"we the people"—needs to be present before constitutions use this expression. The other argument is that in every constitution making, there is some act of inventing "the people".[36] This invention may mean that the act of constitution making itself determines who "the people" are.[37] Martin Loughlin thinks that the creation of political power needs the creation of "we the people".[38] However, this singularity of "we the people" mainly exists in the "realm of belief" that will take effect through some act, including "the use of force".[39] However, these inventions and imaginations have critical utility. Mark Tushnet points out the usefulness of this imaginative constituent power, arguing that the imaginative "we the people" is a *concept that helps explain the normative basis for a constitution's claim of authority. The claim . . . should be understood not as implicating something akin to sociological legitimacy, or the facts about whether or to what degree people actually believe themselves to be obliged to submit to authority, but rather in purely conceptual terms.*[40]

For divided states, another important purpose of using "we the people" is its unifying effect. First, this image-creating function of "we the people" helps people forge civic bonds and devotion across ethnic lines. It enables individuals to imagine and then discuss what unites them. Secondly, it gives the constituted power legitimacy to facilitate the creation and solidification of the people's unity in diversity.

A brief survey of constituent power reveals that, both conceptually and pragmatically, the recognition of a singular constituent power has been the norm. In almost all states, regardless of the presence of ethnic, linguistic, or religious diversity, constitutions claim to be enacted by a singular constituent power. Against the backdrop of this discovery, the following sections investigate constituent power in the Ethiopian Constitution.

III. Constituent Power in the Ethiopian Constitution

Ethiopia has had four constitutions: the 1931, 1955, 1987, and 1995 constitutions. In the first two constitutions, the constituent power was the monarchy. The preamble of the 1931 Constitution starts with "We, Haile Selassie I." Similarly, the 1955 Ethiopian Constitution also attributes constituent power to Emperor Haile Selassie. The third constitution, enacted by the military regime, was "the Constitution of the People's Democratic Republic of Ethiopia,." also known as the 1987 Constitution of Ethiopia. In this constitution, the constituent power is the "working people of Ethiopia" (Preamble). For the current constitution (the 1995 FDRE Constitution), however, the constituent powers are the "NNP." Except for the FDRE Constitution, in each of the earlier constitutions, the constituent power is a singular entity.

The FDRE Constitution defines "nation, nationality and people" as a "group of people who have or share large measure of a common culture or similar customs, mutual intelligibility of language, belief in a common or related identities, a common psychological make-up, and who inhibit an identifiable, predominantly contiguous territory"[41]. According to the Ethiopian constitution, the holders of the constituent power are not "ethnic groups" *per se.* Rather, ethnic groups with a recognizable homeland. This means that potentially, in the Ethiopian Constitution, there are more than eighty constituent powers.[42]

These constituent powers are "sovereign powers." The Constitution declares that "All sovereign power resides in the NNP of Ethiopia".[43] It further declares that "this Constitution is an expression of their sovereignty".[44] Furthermore, it provides that "their sovereignty shall be expressed through their representatives elected in accordance with this Constitution and through their direct democratic participation".[45]

These provisions invite us to make some preliminary observations. First, in the Ethiopian Constitution, "NNPs" are the sovereign constituent powers. Second, because these sovereign constituent powers exercise their sovereignty through regular elections, every election of representatives, whether it is for federal parliaments or sub-state (regional and local elections), is about electing individuals who represent ethnic groups. Therefore, theoretically, every election is an ethnic referendum. That is, when an electoral district elects its representatives to the House of People's Representatives, it is exercising its sovereign power as part of an NNP. Third, the Constitution replaced the idea of popular sovereignty with ethnic sovereignty. The simplest expression of popular sovereignty is "government of the people, by the people, for the people"[46]. At the outset, it seems that the Ethiopian Constitution replaced this notion with "government of ethnic groups in their homeland, by the ethnic groups in their homeland, for the ethnic groups in their homeland." What could have been the justifications for the constitutional drafters to adopt a plural constituent power and deny the existence of a singular constituent power? These potential justifications will be investigated in the following sections.

A. Justifications

1. Empirical (Reality)

One of the main justifications for attributing constituent power to NNPs is that it reflects the country's political realities. This argument relates to two issues. The first argument is that Ethiopian society is organized along ethnic lines and that constituent power should reflect this reality. Second, in the constitution-making process, these "NNPs" expressed their desire to be recognized as such and have exercised their constituent power.

i. Presence of NNPs and Absence of an Ethiopian Identity

The Constitution assumes that each "nation, nationality and people" has a fixed, homogenous, and primordial existence.[47] This itself is based on several assumptions. First, it assumes that each NNP has a fully constructed identity with clear ethnic demarcations and similar visions and interests. However, because of historical migration and intermarriage, ethnic boundaries are not as clear as the Constitution supposes.[48] Donald Levine observes that "the people of greater Ethiopia did not live as discrete isolated units. For the last two millennia, at least, they have been in more or less constant interactions through trade, warfare, religious activities, migration, intermarriage and exchange of special services . . . this relational network, now thick and now localized, now extensive and profound, but never absent."[49] Merera Gudina writes about a similar trend by using the Oromo as an example.[50] He observes that the Oromos had adopted some of the cultures and religions of other ethnic groups, and Oromos played an important role in the Amharan dynasties' political life.[51] As a result, each NNP has recognizable links or connections with its neighboring ethnic groups.

The second assumption is that each nation, nationality, or people has a clear and unified identity. Historically, the two largest ethnic groups, the Amhara and the Oromo, did not have a unified ethnic identity. Rather, they have had provincial identity.[52] Markakis argues that "the Amhara label has little meaning in the context of traditional provincialism, since the Amharignya-speaking population had been divided into clearly defined provincial units which served as the foci of provincial attachments and provide the framework for collective actions in defense of area of interests." The same can be said of the Oromo. Christopher Clapham argues that it was difficult to identify any politically coherent Oromo identity." Similarly, Merera asks, "Who is Oromo?" observing that the Oromo are mixed with other ethnic groups.[53] Maimire Mennasemay argues that Ethiopia "is a regionally rather than ethnically organized historical entity. Generally, a person was identified primarily by his or her region and only secondarily by his or her ethnic background."[54] In some situations, two or more "nations, nationalities or people" may have a very close cultural identity. One of them may be parent ethnicity to others.[55] In such scenarios, members of an ethnic group may disagree on what constitutes the ethnic group. In some ethnic groups, there is a lack of ethnic-identity consciousness. In others, there is disagreement on the boundaries and attributes of ethnic identities. Consequently, some ethnic nationalists are still trying to define and construct ethnic identities through ethnic nationalism. It can be argued that the federal arrangement along ethnic lines is one of the mechanisms by which this construction of ethnic nationalism is being achieved.

The third assumption is that each ethnic group occupies its own territory. However, none of the states that the Constitution created are homogeneous. Instead, even though there are majority ethnic groups, there are minorities from other ethnic groups.[56] The constitutional arrangement is that people who do not belong to the majority ethnic group in the state cannot participate in that state's "self-governance" because they are not part of the "self." If they want to exercise self-government, they must move to the state or territory where their ethnic fellows are a majority. For instance, if a group of ethnic Tigrayans reside in the state of Oromia, the Constitution does not guarantee their participation in the political life of the state. Regardless of the length they have lived in that state, they remain alien in the political life of the state. That is, constituent power is not invested on ethnic groups per se. It is on ethnic groups with their "own" territory. Members of an NNP do not have political power if they are not in their own territorial state. This seems to be the result of constitutional design. That is done firstly through the attribution of constituent power to ethnic groups and secondly by stating that the five big states are homelands of the respective ethnic group. According to the Constitution, the political life of the Regional State of Oromia belongs to the Oromos because political life is an act of self-determination and self-rule by the respective ethnic group. The political life of the Regional State of Tigray is for the Tigrayans in a similar way.[57]

The TPLF/EPRDF pursued a contradictory approach to the above assumptions. On the one hand, ethnicity is considered a primordial and an obvious fact, and political institutions cannot construct or deconstruct it. The definitions that the constitution provides go with this line of understanding of ethnicity. According to the Constitution, a "nation, nationality or people" is a group of people with a common culture, mutual language, belief in common or related identities, and a common psychological makeup.[58] This definition suggests that ethnic identities in Ethiopia are already constructed. It also means that when the TPLF/EPRDF created the ethnic federal system, it was merely meant to recognize an already constructed ethnic identity. On the other hand, the TPLF/EPRDF admitted that ethnic identity has not been constructed and activated well enough to use as a political instrument. Accordingly, ethnic nationalism should be constructed so that ethnicity and ethnic politics can be instruments for political mobilization that can "initiate the spirit of struggle".[59] Ethnic nationalism has the power to make individuals commit and sacrifice to an ethnic cause. Political elites can easily manipulate the masses and gain support through the emotional power that ethnic nationalism produces. For ethnicity to become an instrument of political mobilization, people's ethnic awareness should be activated.[60] In the Ethiopian context, ethnic nationalists activate ethnic identity through the use and abuse of history and the relationship that a given ethnic group has with others.[61] Similarly, for the EPRDF, ethnic identity is something that is constructed through political mobilization and ethnic-nationalistic indoctrination through use and abuse of history.[62] Thus, ethnic self-determination has not been an end in itself, rather a means to construct ethnic identity. If one observes the history of the EPRDF, it hugely mobilized the local people along ethnic lines.[63] It turned nonconscious peasants into ethnic nationalists who were ready to die for the political causes of the EPRDF[64]. In short, to some extent, the existence of an "NNP" with easily identifiable boundaries is at best contestable and at worst fictional.

The corollary to the above argument is that there is no preexisting "Ethiopian" identity in the country. That is, first, the Ethiopian identity is difficult to define, and even if it can be defined, no one wants to be identified with the Ethiopian identity. Thus, the argument goes, reality does not support the recognition of the Ethiopian people as a constituent power. However, many scholars argue that there is a strong Ethiopian identity[65]. For instance, Lovise argues that "the Ethiopians . . . have a stronger common identity, an idea of an overarching citizenship that transcends ethnic identities".[66] In addition, according to two surveys conducted in Ethiopia, consistently 96 percent of the population felt proud of their "Ethiopian" identity.[67] Therefore, the claim that the existence of these identities and the absence of a singular national identity justify attributing constituent power to "NNPs" has no foundation.

ii. Constitutional Making Process

The other justification for the adoption of "NNPs" as constituent powers is that indeed the constitution was adopted by them. This section explores this claim and concludes that it is theoretically incoherent and factually unsupported. First, this justification is incoherent because evaluating whether these ethnic groups adopted the Constitution assumes their existence as a defined, conscious, and distinct ethnic group with the will to politically and constitutionally act along their ethnic identities. As has been pointed out, it is difficult to definitively conclude that they in fact existed—as defined and conscious about their identity and with a single political objective and outlook—prior to the Constitution itself. It would then be difficult to argue that something that does not exist acted and adopted a constitution for itself. This tendency to assume the existence of ethnic groups "as if they were internally homogenous, externally bound groups, even unitary collective actors with common purposes" is prevalent in politics and scholarship.[68] Both conceptually and empirically, it is difficult to justify that internally homogenous, externally bounded, and unitary-collective-acting ethnic groups existed when the Constitution was adopted. For the sake of argument, let us assume that they existed and go on to explore the process by which they drafted and adopted the Constitution.

During the military government of Ethiopia, ethnic-based militias were formed to fight the military government. The oldest and most powerful of these fronts was the TPLF.[69] The TPLF waged a successful guerilla war against the military government of Ethiopia through the 1980s. Once political control was secured in Addis Ababa, the TPLF leadership recognized that it needed other parties to sustain and legitimize their rule over the whole country. For this reason, it worked towards the creation of the EPRDF.[70] The EPRDF was a coalition of four ethnic-based movements: the Tigray People's Liberation Front (TPLF), the Amhara National Democratic Movement (ANDM), the Oromo People's Democratic Organization (OPDO) and the Southern Ethiopia People's Democratic Movement (SEPDM).[71] Merara Gudina argues that the TPLF treated the three other member parties of the Front as its satellite parties.[72] It used them to "speak through the mouths of other ethnic groups, as well as allowing [the TPLF] to win elections more easily and to appear to rule the country in the name of "all the peoples of Ethiopia." As far as the power to make political decisions was concerned, the EPRDF was the TPLF. These parties claimed to represent the majority of Ethiopian ethnic groups. ANDM was intended to represent the Amhara ethnic group. The OPDO was intended to represent the Oromo ethnic group, and the SEPDM was intended to represent more than fifty ethnic groups in the southern part of the country.

After ousting the military government, the TPLF/EPRDF held a national conference to establish a transitional government. The established transitional government was dominated by the TPLF/EPRDF. There was almost no opposition in the transitional government for two reasons. First, the military government had ruled the country with an iron fist and without any opposition. Its collapse left "a perilous political vacuum in the center."[73] The potential opposition to the EPRDF would have been the political elites in the military government. However, having lost the civil war and been imprisoned for war crimes under the new order, they were excluded from the political process. Second, attendance to the conference was by invitation of the TPLF/EPRDF leadership."[74] Nonethnic and Ethiopian nationalist organizations were not invited and did not participate in the conference.[75] At the conference to adopt the transitional government charter, the TPLF/EPRDF dominated the discussion and overruled objections against some of the contents of the charter.[76]

The charter required the establishment of a transitional government consisting of a Council of Representatives (CR) and a Council of Ministers (Art. 7). The charter also mandated a process for the drafting and adoption of a permanent constitution consisting of three stages. The first stage was the establishment of a constitutional commission to draft a new constitution to be submitted to the CR (Charter, Art 10). The second stage involved popular discussion of the draft constitution. The final stage was the election of the Constituent Assembly to formally adopt the final draft of the Constitution.

The Constitutional Drafting Commission, composed of twenty-nine members, drafted the Constitution.[77] The CR assigned the members of the Constitutional Drafting Commission, the majority of whom were members of the council itself.[78] The majority of the commission were TPLF/EPRDF members. However, there were a few individuals representing many groups and interests.[79] These non-TPLF/EPRDF members were unable to have any substantial effect on the content of the Constitution because they were a tiny minority. In relation to controversial issues, the EPRDF always dominated the vote.[80] The commission was established to give the impression that the constitutional drafting process was participatory.

The drafting process was highly dominated by the TPLF/EPRDF. Theodore Vestalobserves that "the draft constitution embodies essentially what the EPRDF wishes the world and its own people to believe about the political order."[81] Similarly, Merera observes that "the Constitution was an attempt by the TPLF to canonize the remaking of Ethiopia according to its own image and ensure the permanency of its hegemonic position in the reordered state."[82] Meaza Ashenafi, who was part of the Constitutional Commission, observed that "the majority [the TPLF/EPRDF] at all stages knew that their position could not be seriously challenged".[83] The fundamental principles and structures of the Constitution, including placing the constituent power in the "NNPs" of Ethiopia were the policies of the TPLF since its founding.

The draft constitution was next sent to the CR, ostensibly to facilitate public discussion. However, the council members discussed the Constitution amongst themselves for a month, even though the charter did not mandate such discussion. The discussion was not intended to alter the content of the

Constitution but to develop a platform for educating the population about the content of the Constitution and thereby gain popular support for it.[84]

The draft was then presented to the people for discussion. Meetings were held for two days to discuss the content of the Constitution.[85] Popular interest and participation in the discussion was insignificant. Markakis observed that there was "little public interest in the matter."[86] Similarly, Vestal observed that the people who were present at the meetings "were compelled to go by threats to the recalcitrant of cessation of sales of sugar, edible oils, soaps, and salts at [local shops]—an especially effective inducement in the countryside."[87] Similarly, Markakis observes: "It is fair to say that not many Ethiopians who live in the countryside have a clear notion of what federalism means, or had the opportunity to express an opinion on its merits. There was simply no time to form a national consensus on the legitimacy of the new political system."[88]

Three reasons explain the absence of public interest in the discussion on the draft constitution. First, the TPLF/EPRDF was not a political organization that had secured widespread acceptance among the majority of Ethiopians.[89] Second, the opposition political parties did not take part in the process.[90] Many of the important political players who could have challenged the draft constitution were prevented from participating.[91] Third, the TPLF/EPRDF was not willing to change the content of the draft constitution that facilitated its firm grip on political power. James Paul observed that the public debate was meaningless.[92] These discussions did not change the content of the draft constitution.[93] The discussions that were conducted were not intended to affect the contents of the constitution; instead, they were "preaching sessions for the TPLF/EPRDF".[94]

In the adoption process, in 1994, a motion was conducted to elect Constitutional Assembly members to ratify the Constitution. The assembly consisted of 544 members. The EPRDF and its allies won 463 seats (85.1 percent) of the assembly.[95] Most of the remaining seats were filled by small parties from minority ethnic groups.[96] One of the main reasons why the TPLF/EPRDF "won" the election for the Constitutional Assembly was because it was ruling the country as a result of the 1992 election. The regional election was based on the mandates of the charter that decrees that elections for local and regional administrations should be conducted within three months of the establishment of the Transitional Government.[97] The TPLF/EPRDF won this election, enabling it to consolidate its total control over the political power of the whole country. The election was "premature, dubious and ill-conceived." (National 1992). One group of international observers of the election concluded that there was no competitive participation because opposing parties could not compete against "the EPRDF's local military and administrative power. This imbalance left opposition parties vulnerable to TPLF/EPRDF manipulation."[98]

Consequently, several opposition political parties withdrew from the election, believing that "it was better not to participate than to win a few seats here and there in an unfair competition".[99] During the election, "voters in several regions could only select individuals designated by the TPLF/EPRDF and its allies, rather than choose candidates from slates presented by competing parties."[100] The TPLF/EPRDF and its allies won the election by 96.6 percent.[101] As a result of this election, the TPLF/EPRDF was in total control of the political power of the country. Vestal thinks that this election taught the TPLF/EPRDF "how to run elections with effective opposition shut out and with a focus on the mechanics of voting, for the edification of astigmatic election observers."[102]

Once the TPLF/EPRDF assumed control of the country, it could channel any upcoming elections, including the election for the Constituent Assembly. The organized political parties that represented the many people in the Amhara and the Oromo regions did not participate in the elections as candidates for the Constituent Assembly.[103] Paul observes that "just as the EPRDF controlled the Constitutional Commission's work, so it controlled the election, and then the deliberations, of the Constitutional Assembly."[104]

Thus, the Constitution's claim that it was adopted by the "NNPs" through their representatives is unfounded for the following reasons. First, as pointed out earlier, political parties that made up the EPRDF, including those supposedly representing the biggest ethnic groups, the Amhara and the Oromo, were created by the TPLF to help it govern the whole country. Marina Ottaway observes that the "EPRDF was simply an instrument of the TPLF."[105] As the whole process was the result of military might, the ANDM and OPDO could not have the power to vigorously advocate the interests of the ethnic groups they claimed to represent. That is to say, they had no power to resist the TPLF's domination.

Second, the Ethiopian people were not given the opportunity to decide how they wanted to be represented. They were not given the opportunity to debate the possible use of ethnic identity in the political life of the state. Ethnic nationalism started in the 1960s with a small number of university students.[106] Even though the imperial and military regimes used the Amharic language as a nation-building instrument, these regimes were not ethnic.[107] The political and military elites were multiethnic.[108] Christopher Clapham argues that "Ethiopia is not, and as far as its long historical record reaches, has never been, an ethnic political community. It has consistently been comprised of different ethnic groups speaking different languages and practicing different religions."[109] Before the Ethiopian Student Movement of the 1960s, uprisings and discontent against the imperial regime occurred both in the north and south, among almost all the ethnic groups.[110] Until the emergence of the student movement, ethno-nationalism was not a significant factor either among the Oromos or Amharas.

The students who defined the relationship among ethnic groups as an ethnic oppression were not able to persuade the majority of peasants that that was in fact the case.[111] Thus, when the Constitution was adopted, ethnicity was not viewed as a politically relevant factor by most people in the country.

During the adoption of the Constitution, the two political parties that had some legitimacy among the small Oromo and Amhara nationalist elites were the Oromo Liberation Front (OLF) and All Amhara People's Organization (AAPO), respectively.[112] However, these political parties did not participate in the constitution-making process.[113] Both Ugo Mattei and Paul argue that the ethnic-based Constitution was supported only by the Tigray ethnic group, which is a small minority within Ethiopia.[114] However, this is based on the assumption that the TPLF was the legitimate representative of the Tigray people. However, the people from all ethnic groups were not given the chance to deliberate on the benefits and disadvantages of the political arrangement established by the draft constitution. Elections for the Constitutional Assembly and the 1992 elections were mere formal exercises without democratic deliberation and competent opponents.[115] The Constituent Assembly was the TPLF/EPRDF in disguise.

The constitution-making process of the Ethiopian Constitution was a flawed process without mature debate and inclusivity. Using this flawed constitution-making process, the TPLF/EPRDF adopted a constitution that granted constituent power to the NNPs. One of the explanations for this design was the desire to peacefully manage Ethiopia's ethnic diversity. However, among different constitutional approaches for placing constituent power in a divided nation, there was no sufficient justification for choosing such an extreme position. From the first peace conference to the adoption of the Constitution, "There was never any possibility that the" TPLF positions would not prevail.[116] Different Ethiopian communities have different visions as to who should hold constituent power. Vestal argues that the content of a constitution should be "basic legal conceptions of the community, their outlook on life, or *weltanschauung*, insofar as it can be embodied in general rules."[117] When a community lacks common basic legal conceptions and political outlook, negotiations, discussions, compromise, and constitutional imagining in the process of constitution making may pave the way for the creation of such conceptions and outlooks. The real motivation of the TPLF/EPRDF Constitution was to ensure that the TPLF maintained political power using the satellite ethnic political parties that constituted the EPRDF. As such, the constitution-making process shows that no genuine negotiation and discussion regarding this basic issue of attributing constituent power took place. Consequently, the constitution-making process shows that it was not the NNP who were sovereign, but rather it was the TPLF which became the sovereign constituent power.

2. Theoretical Justifications

Unlike many constitution-founding moments in the world, the Ethiopian constitution-founding process was devoid of philosophical debate and examination of the core fundamental ideals in it. Even the proponents of the Constitution, the TPLF/EPRDF, did not provide a sufficient theoretical and conceptual defense of the main organizing concepts of the constitution. This may be because they were more soldiers than political thinkers. In the following section, I will explore whatever supportive arguments can be gleaned from the constitutional text, the speeches, and a few writings of TPLF/EPRDF leaders, as well as their ideological sources.

i. Purposive justification

In addition to the realist justification that has been discussed for attributing constituent power to ethnic groups, the TPLF/EPRDF provided a purposive justification. In short, the purposive justification is that attributing constituent power to the "NNPs" is to facilitate and guarantee the protection of ethnic groups' rights. According to the TPLF/EPRDF, the purpose of the Constitution is to "rectify historically unjust relationships" and to promote "shared interests" (FDRE Constitution, Preamble). However, this is based on a misreading of Ethiopian political history as a history of relationships among ethnic groups. It is based on the assumption that the past regimes of the country were ethnic based, and the ruling ethnic group dominated and exploited other ethnic groups. The purpose of recognizing ethnic groups as sovereign constituent powers was, therefore, intended to secure interethnic equality.

The historical relationships between people from different ethnic and religious backgrounds of Ethiopia are complex. These complex relationships can be articulated by identifying three types of historical relationships: (1) the relationships between political elites and the people; (2) the relationships between people with different ethnic affiliations; and (3) the relationships of political elites with each other. To analyze (1), it is essential to look briefly at how the country was created. The country formed its present shape when Emperor Menelik II conducted extensive expansion from 1875 to 1889.[118] Before his expansion, traditional kings and chiefs, including Emperor Menelik II, administered small autonomous territories.[119] He accomplished his expansion through negotiation and coercion.[120] For the local leaders who submitted to his rule, Emperor Menelik II obtained their autonomy on the condition that they pay tribute to him and recognize his rule over them.

For those who resisted, he coerced them through military force, subsequently appointing his leaders and stationing his soldiers in their territories.[121] The self-governing arrangements were abolished by Emperor Haile Selassie and by the Italians during their brief occupation of the country, from 1935 to

1941.[122]. Up until 1974, the political system was a traditional feudal system that aimed at creating a nation-state around the Amharic language and Orthodox Christianity.[123]

Drawing from the historical relationships between the political elites and ethnic groups, three crucial points need consideration: most of the political elites of the country have been from the Shewa[124]-Amhara-Tigre north; in the process of expansion, these political elites resorted to force whenever locals resisted and attempted to build a nation-state based on the Amharic language and Orthodox Christianity.[125] However, these points do not give us a complete picture regarding the nature of these relationships. The following three points must be studied corollary to the observations made above. Firstly, the use of force to expand and dominate is not peculiar to the Amhara political elites. In the sixteenth century, the Oromo people carried out one of the greatest military expansions in the history of Africa.[126] The Oromo people forced others to vacate the area in which they eventually settled.[127] King Yohannes, from the Tigre ethnic group, attempted to build an empire and used force to subdue multiple autonomous regions.[128] That is to say, almost all the political elites from major ethnic groups in the country have used force against each other and everyone else. Secondly, the Ethiopian empire expanded through force, negotiation, compromise, and marriage between the ruling class. Many Oromo clans and other southern people did not resist the emperor's expansion. For those who yielded, the emperor appointed local leaders to administer their semiautonomous region under his rule.[129] In areas where the local people resisted, the emperor was merciless and brutal. Thirdly, he used force not only against the resisting south but against the north, including other Amhara local rulers.[130] One of the most formidable warriors who helped Menelik subdue Amhara rulers was Ras Gobena Dache, an Oromo.[131] Understanding this history, Merara Gudina argues that the Oromos were "part of the conquerors as well as the conquered; they produced Kings and queens.... Ethiopian Kings frequently married Oromos—Tewodros, Menelik and Haile Selassie.... The Oromo were able to become kings and queens of imperial Ethiopia—the best example being Iyyassu, Haile Sellassie, King Michael of Wollo and King Takle-Haymanot of Gojjam."[132] The use of force does not give moral justification for ethnic mobilization against other groups because the group that now considers itself a victim was once a perpetrator. If Ethiopian history and political practices are properly examined, one cannot justify ethnic nationalism and ethnic politics based on historical accounts. However, the use and abuse of historical interpretation is the main ideological justification for the development of ethnic nationalism and ethnic politics.

The social relationship between individuals of different ethnic groups has been relatively peaceful and integrative. Donald N. Levine describes the relationship between present-day Ethiopians as follows: "The people of greater Ethiopia did not live as discrete isolated units. For the last two millennia, at least, they have been in more or less constant interactions through trade, warfare, religious activities, migration, intermarriage and exchange of special services … this relational network, now thin and localized, now extensive and profound, but never absent."[133] People from many ethnic and religious backgrounds in Ethiopia have coexisted fairly peacefully.[134] And their relationships have not been exploitative. Overtime, multiple communities have been assimilated into other cultures in complex ways.

This complexity has enabled many scholars with political projects to make simplified and selective historical interpretations. At times, the historical interpretations and political visions tend to get closer to historical facts. At other times, historical interpretations are used and abused by political manipulators for political gain. The adoption of Marxist-Leninist political philosophy further necessitated the selective use of this history. Marxist-Leninist political elites defined ethnic groups as "nations and nationalities." They then characterized Ethiopian history as one of national operation, arguing that one ethnic group (nation) oppressed another.[135] After this characterization, they began constructing ethnic nationalism. This necessitated the use of selective historical interpretation to denote that each nation and nationality in Ethiopia was distinct. Again, history was used and abused to justify the right to self-determination and to claim that one "nation" was unfairly treated by another "nation," thus warranting secession. To use history to this end, they must disregard the integrative relationships that people of different ethnic groups have had. Christopher Clapham argues that history is used in Ethiopia as an instrument of intellectual and emotional justification for Marxist-Leninist political projects.[136] He finds that such an approach to historical selection is "crudely delineated … succumbing to the highly simplified narratives [that are politically] instrumental."[137] In short, selective and manipulative historical interpretations have contributed to the emergence of ethnic extremists in Ethiopia's political life. This practice coincides with similar nationalist movements in other parts of the world. Eric Hobsbawm argues that "nationalism requires too much belief in what is patently not much so".[138] Similarly, Snyder and Ballentine observe that "nationalist agitation and propaganda are always the necessary conditions to the development of a mass nationalist movement'.[139]

In short, the wider picture of Ethiopian politics and history does not justify characterizing the fundamental political problem of the country as an ethnic exploitation requiring unusual constitutional responses such as the recognition of plural constituent power. Even assuming that Ethiopian political history is in fact about ethnic inequalities, the adoption of plural constituent power is not necessary for achieving ethnic equality. As has been pointed out, many countries that attempt to attain ethnic and religious group equality do not adopt plural constituent power in their constitutions.

ii. Logical Coherence of attribution of constituent power

Another way of testing the legitimacy of the constituent power is to test its logical coherence. One way of testing this is by looking at whether the constitutional text provides mechanisms for the exercise of constituent power or not. That is, do the political institutions and the federal system reflect that the "NNPs" are in fact the holders of the constituent power?

The Constitution created a federal democratic state with a federal government and nine regions (states). Both the federal and state governments have legislative, executive, and judicial powers (FDRE Constitution, Art 50).[140] The states are created along ethnic lines identifying the state with the majority ethnic group in the territory. The prevailing idea is that each NNP will exercise the right to self-determination by governing itself using its own language and developing its culture. The Constitution defines "nation, nationality and people" as a "group of people who have or share large measure of a common culture or similar customs, mutual intelligibility of language, belief in a common or related identities, a common psychological makeup, and who inhibit an identifiable, predominantly contiguous territory".[141] However, when the states were created, the existence of these criteria was not thoroughly explored. The two easily visible criteria, territory and language, were used to create the states. Abbink thinks that the main elements of defining "nation, nationality, and people" and the main criteria in creating states were language and territory.[142]

The other question that goes with the sovereign constituent power of the "nation, nationalities, and peoples" is the structure and functioning of the government. In most other countries, the constitution is adopted by "the people" and the people exercise its constituent power through the elected members of the legislature. As a unified constituent power, "The people" is represented by the members of the legislature, any law or decision that the majority in the legislature adopts is considered to be "the people exercising its constituent power." In the Ethiopian case, however, there are multiple sovereign constituent powers. Logically, the law-making process seems to resemble the international law-making process where sovereign states make law. The question is how should a legislature representing many sovereign constituent powers make a law?

The House of Peoples' Representative (the parliament) makes laws and has the highest authority of the federal government.[143] The house is responsible to the people.[144] However, it is not clear to which people the constitution is referring. If this provision is taking the Ethiopian people as a whole, it does not align with the idea that each "nation, nationality and people" is a sovereign constituent power. One would also argue that since the House of Federation was established to reflect the notion that NNPs are sovereign constituent powers, it can be argued that this does not change the nature of the parliament. If the parliament represents "the whole people," then it may be considered that there is "the Ethiopian people" as a unified constituent power. However, such an interpretation contradicts the notion that the sovereignty of the "NNPs" is the fundamental constitutional principle.

Members of the parliament are chosen through a general election. Large ethnic groups will of course have many members in the parliament. Under the current rules of representation prepared by the National Electoral Board of Ethiopia, each state has a fixed number of seats.[145] Here is the current breakdown of membership: Tigray has 38; Afar 8; Amhara 138; Oromia 179; Somali 23; Benishangul Gumuz 9; Southern Nations, Nationalities, and Peoples 123; Gambella 3; Harari 2; Dire Dawa 2; and Addis Ababa 23.[146] These members and the constituents from which they get elected are organized ethnically.[147] Accordingly, they represent the "nations, nationalities and peoples" that elected them. The Constitution also provides that the parliament shall decide all issues by a majority vote (FDRE Constitution, Art 51). This means that theoretically the parliament may protect the interests of the major ethnic groups, and other ethnic groups are not sovereign because they are powerless. As we can see from the numbers, the Amhara and Oromia ethnic groups constitute a majority in the house accounting for 58 percent of the parliament. Let us assume that members of the parliament representing the sovereign constituent power of the Afar nation vehemently oppose a proposed law. Let us assume also that other sovereign constituent powers agree to the proposed bill. Since the parliament enacts laws based on a majority vote, the proposed bill will become the law. In such instances, the way the parliament is structured contradicts with the notion of multiple sovereign constituent power that was fundamental to the Constitution.

If negotiation is the main tool for making decisions in the parliament, the parliament may get close to ensuring the sovereignty of each nation, nationality and people. In the example above, the Afar nation, a sovereign constituent power, will have a chance to exercise its constituent power through negotiation. However, the Constitution does not provide for negotiated lawmaking. Had the constituent power rested on "the people of Ethiopia," it would have been constitutional for the parliament to act democratically and make laws based on a majority vote. These considerations may remain theoretical in the sense that the biggest ethnic groups may end up competing against each other rather than creating a working coalition. However, as a matter of constitutional design, the way the parliament was formed did not match the fundamental notion of the Constitution—sovereign constituent NNPs.

The Constitution also establishes the second chamber, namely the House of Federation (the house).[148] Members of the house represent the "NNPs".[149] Each "nation, nationality and people is represented by at least one member and an additional member for each million of its inhabitants".[150] Since many of the "nations, nationalities and peoples" are not populous, they are represented only by one member.[151] The biggest ethnic groups, the Oromo and the Amhara, were represented by 26 and 20 members, respectively.[152] Similar to the parliament, the house also decides by a majority vote.[153] Even though these numbers may not form a majority in the house, whose members are 135 (in the 2010–15 term), populous ethnic groups will have a big chance to secure their interest in the house. Members of the house are elected to the house either by state councils or the people of the several states.[154] The main functions of the house include constitutional adjudication and managing the relationship among states.[155] It does not have a role in the adoption of ordinary legislation. The theoretical justification behind creating the house is to have an organ that protects the rights and interests of the "NNPs" Once again, the members are meant to represent ethnic groups. However, it is the states that elect members. This arrangement is a mismatch in a federal system where each "nation, nationality and people" does not have its own state. This is because in states where there are many nationalities and peoples, the selection process is likely to be dominated by an ethnic group(s) with a relatively large population. And this results in the likelihood that minority ethnic groups may be dominated by majority ethnic groups that might not have the interest of the relevant minority ethnic group at heart.

The way the federal legislature is organized is not congenial for the exercise of the sovereign constituent power of each nation, nationality and people. In the ordinary legislation of the parliament and the functions of the House of Federation, the most populous ethnic groups are more sovereign than the smaller ethnic groups. The basic foundation of the constitution—the sovereign constituent power of each nation, nationality and people of Ethiopia—has not been properly translated into the structure and functioning of the federal legislature.

IV. The Paradox of Constituent Power in Constitutional Practice

Ideally, constitutional exercise of constituent power occurs when the body designated as the source of political power exercises its power according to the Constitution. The Ethiopian constitutional experiment is full of anomalies. The Constitution provides that the sovereign constituent powers are the "NNP." Yet, in practice, the TPLF/EPRDF governed the country as if the country was a unitary state.[156] The party controlled both the state and the federal governments. It controlled the legislature as well as the executives at all levels of government. Any policy decision was first decided by the party's central committee and then presented to the parliament or the house for affirmation. The EPRDF's political philosophy was the Leninist principle of "democratic centralism."[157] Its control was not established through free and fair elections but instead through electoral manipulation.

The main force behind this system of control was the TPLF. It not only created the other three parties in the EPRDF coalition, but it also used ideological tools that enabled it to control the political life of the country. It changed justifications and ideological tools wherever it thought that the existing tools were inadequate to maintain political power.[158] It used two related ideological tools for such control: Revolutionary democracy and democratic centralism. Revolutionary democracy, at least as the TPLF/EPRDF defines it, is not clear. It is not a well-articulated concept. The basic idea is that Ethiopian society needs economic, political, and sociological changes that are not incremental but revolutionary. However, the people were thought not to be ideologically conscious enough to be motivated to achieve revolutionary change. For this to happen, it was assumed, political elites should establish a "vanguard" party that could provide ideological guidance to the people.[159] Vestal observes that "at the heart of the concept of revolutionary democracy is the old communist idea that leaders of the Marxist-Leninist party should direct all aspects of society on the basis of a supposedly superior knowledge of the nature of social development".[160] The "democratic" component of the process is that this vanguard party should participate in the "nominal" elections that it would probably win. The TPLF/EPRDF stated that it is the only political party with the right policies to achieve these goals.[161]The TPLF/EPRDF appointed itself as the vanguard political party that knew the nature of Ethiopia's social development and had the capacity to lead Ethiopia's revolutionary change.

Democratic centralism is a process that Lenin devised for the party to make decisions. The democratic aspect of the process is that the members of the party can freely discuss the issues.[162] The "centralism" element of the process is that once the decision is made, the members are obligated to abide by that decision.[163] Democratic centralism was the main process that the TPLF/EPRDF used to govern the centralized federal system. The Central Committee of the TPLF/EPRDF made major decisions by a majority vote, and rank-and-file members of the party, as well as the whole population, abided by the decision. Leaders of the EPRDF decided on policy issues before those policies were to be presented for enactment into law. The members of the coalition then discussed the issues. The main purpose of the discussion was not so much to change the decision of the central committee. It was mainly to inform members of the party about these decisions. The decisions were then adopted as formal laws and implemented through the institutional apparatus of the state. This was done at the federal, state, and local levels. As a result of such a centralized party structure, federal, state, and local officials were accountable to the party leaders rather than to the "NNPs". Within democratic centralism, there is an evaluation process through which the members' performance, mainly their loyalty, is checked. This loyalty-checking mechanism helped TPLF leaders control the leaders of the various states.

Using such carefully designed control mechanisms, TPLF leaders controlled both the federal and regional state structures and processes. Gedion argues that "constitutional practice was controlled by the TPLF and that the constitutional practice of ethnic federalism was an elaborate scheme of indirect rule which also doubles as a strategy of divide and rule,".[164]

Since the adoption of the Constitution, Ethiopia has never had a democratic election.[165] Some observers characterize post-1991 Ethiopia as a blocked democracy.[166] Unfair and non-free elections were conducted usually under intimidation and threat of both the opposition political parties and the electorate.[167] In the majority of these elections, the TPLF/EPRDF won landslide victories.[168] From the very beginning, the TPLF/EPRDF's democracy "became a purely formal exercise."[169]

Over the last twenty-four years of constitutional practice, some policy decisions that may have enabled the "nation, nationalities, and peoples" to govern themselves have been implemented. However, these policies were not decided by the "NNPs" themselves in one form or another. Rather, they were decided by the central committee, the superior leaders of the political party, of the EPRDF.

V. Conclusion (Moving Forward)

The design of constituent power in the Ethiopian Constitution has two flaws. First is the adoption of many constituent powers and failing to recognize the singularity of constituent power. Second, the Constitution was not adopted by these claimed constituent powers. How do we understand the commonalities of groups in Ethiopia in terms of constituent power then? Lindhahl, relying on Schmitt, argues that "the first-person plural perspective of a collective as a unity in (constituent) action is *concrete*, in the sense that it involves a determination of what binds together the members of a community in mutuality and reciprocity."[170] Similarly, Carl Schmitt argues that "within each political unity there can only be one bearer of the constitution-making power."[171] Schmitt 1928). Lindhahl believes that "unless the multitude becomes a unity in action, unless it ceases to be a multitude and becomes a collective subject, it cannot constitute itself as a political community."[172] Normatively, the concept of constituent power is desirable, and in fact it makes sense when it contributes to the unity of and oneness of a political community.

In almost all countries, constitutions allow individuals to relate to each other as co-citizens striving to form a unity that they forged through symbolic acts of constituting a political order. In Ethiopia, however, when individuals relate to each other they must first discover the ethnic group to which they are supposed to belong and then communicate as members of ethnic groups. As this paper has tried to illuminate, there is descriptive and normative confusion to this. In moving forward, the Constitution needs to be founded on a singular constituent power of "we the people." As it currently stands, it is not even clear that there is a clearly defined notion of Ethiopian citizenship. Even if it were the case that there is such a status, it is a political identity with less entitlement than any other country in the world. Due to this peculiar circumstance, some scholars have argued that the Ethiopian Constitution "is less a constitution … and more like an international treaty."[173]

The power to determine constituent power in a constitution is a significant power. In the process of drafting the Ethiopian Constitution, the TPLF/EPRDF controlled the process and determined who had constituent power. It declared as a constitutional matter that the "NNPs" had the sovereign constituent powers.

The text of the Constitution and the constitutional practice show that the "NNPs" did not have constituent power. The constitutional design also seems to have a flaw in the way the parliament was designed. A parliament which functions on the basis of a majority decision-making process cannot be said to represent the "NNPs" as sovereign constituent powers. Theoretically, the Ethiopian parliament can be hugely influenced by the two biggest ethnic groups. However, in the last thirty years this has never been a problem because it was the TPLF/EPRDF that dictated the way in which the parliament functioned.

The constitutional practice has shown that the TPLF/EPRDF did not even live by the constitution it adopted. The "NNPs" did not exercise constituent power. The party controlled both the federal and state governments. Using ideological and operational tools, the TPLF dictated the functioning of both the state and federal governments. Even though the Constitution claims that the "NNPs" possess sovereign constituent power, in practice the TPLF had constituent power until it was ousted by the current regime. It is difficult to know who exercises constituent power in the current regime, as it is full of turbulence.

However, it can fairly be said that the NNPs do not exercise sovereignty because the political practice and decision-making process does not appear to be much different from that of the EPRDF regime.

Therefore, Ethiopian constitutional order should be founded on a single constituent power—*we the Ethiopian people* or *we the people of the Federal Democratic Republic of Ethiopia*. Admittedly, it might be hard to define who this *we the people* is as it has been difficult to definitively describe who "we the people" is in many constitutions in the world. In a political community in which a single national identity does not constitute a majority, this single constituent power may be "a bundle of groups."[174] However, as the practice in other countries shows, the inability to define the "we" should not hinder us from rational, normative, and pragmatic constitutional drafting and practice.

How would attributing constituent power to a single constituent power change the current constitution and its practice? This needs detailed exploration that should be done elsewhere. Nevertheless, I would like to provide a brief indication regarding what needs to change. First, the notion of sovereignty of the NNPs needs to be removed from the Constitution. This means that the author of the Constitution is "We the Ethiopian People." This singular "people" is plural in many ways, and it may be beneficial to acknowledge this plurality in the new constitution. In addition, adopting singular constituent power does not mean that people do not have the right to use their languages and politically govern themselves. However, substate formation and other structures of the Constitution that were predicated on the notion of sovereignty of the NNPs should also be reconsidered, reimagined, and redesigned. This rethinking should be done in a way that strengthens the political singularity of "the people" yet without restricting the people's right to use their language in political life and their right to self-government. One such option could be dividing the biggest ethnic groups into many states, as it is done in Nigeria.

Notes

1 Article 8(1), Constitution of the Federal Democratic Republic of Ethiopia.

2 The preamble of the constitution of the 1977 Constitution of the Soviet Union, which is considered to have inspired the Ethiopian constitutional drafters in issues relating ethnic diversity, provides that 'the Soviet People' enacted the constitution and that sovereign power belongs to 'the people'.

3 The Preamble of the Federal Constitution of the Swiss Confederation.

4 Jean-Jacques Rousseau, *The Social Contract*, trans. Donald A. Cress (Hackett Publishing Co., 1762) 39.

5 Paul H Brietzke, "Ethiopia's 'Leap in the Dark': Federalism and Self-Determination in the New Constitution," *Journal of African Law* 39, no 1: 33; Theodre Vestal, "An Analysis of the New Constitution of Ethiopia and the Process of its Adoption," *Northeast African Studies* 3, no. 2: 21-38. Duke and Arcioni 2022, 345.

6 Martin Loughlin, "On Constituent Power." In *Constitutionalism Beyond Liberalism*, eds. Michael Downdle and Michael Wilkinson (Cambridge University Press, 2017), 153.

7 Michal Hardt, "Forward: Three Keys to Understanding Constituent Power." In *Insurgencies: Constituent Power and the Modern State*, Antonio Negri (University of Minnesota Press, 1999), xi.

8 Hans Lindhahl, "Constituent Power and Reflexive Identity: Towards an Ontology of Collective Selfhood," In *The Paradox of Constitutionalism: Constituent Power and Constitutional Form*, eds. Martin Loughlin and Neil Walker (Oxford University Press, 2008), 12.

9 Carl Schmitt, *Constitutional Theory*, trans. Jeffrey Seitzer (Duke University Press, 2008). 75.

10 George Duke and Elisa Arcioni, "Between Constituent Power and Constituent Authority," *Oxford Journal of legal Studies* 42 no. 1 (2022): 345-8. doi:10.1093/ojls/gqab030.

11 Duke and Arcioni, "Between Constituent Power," 345-8.

12 Ulrich Preuss, "Constitutional Powermaking for the New Polity: Some Deliberations on the Relations Between Constituent Power and the Constitution," *Cardozo Law Review* 14, no. 3 (1993): 636.

13 Preuss, "Constitutional Powermaking," 640.

14 Lindhahl, "Connstituent Power," 17; Preuss, "Constitutional Powermaking," 640.

15 The Unanimous Declaration of The Thirteen States of America, July 4, 1776.

16 Lucia Rubinelli, "How to think beyond Sovereignty: on Sieyes and Constituent Power," European Journal of Political Theory 18 no. 1 (2019): 49; Yaviv Roznai, "We the People 'oui the people' and the Collected body: Perceptions on Constituent Power," In *Comparative Constitutional Theory*, eds. Garry Jacobsohn and Miguel Schor (Edward Elgar, 2018) 295.

17 Emmanuel Sieyes, "Reasoned Exposition of the Rigths of Man and Citizen", In *Emmanuel Joseph Sieyes: the essential political writings*, trans. and eds. Oliver W. Lembcke and Florian Weber (Brill, 2014) 172.

18 Sieyes, "Reasoned Exposition".

19 Rubinelli, "How to think"

20 R.M. Johnston, *The Corsican: A Diary of Napoleon's Life in His Own Words (*Houghton Mifflin, 1910) 182; Ethiopian Constitution of 1931.

21 Lucien Jaume, "Constituent Power in France: The Revolution and its Consequences in Selfhood," in *The Paradox of Constitutionalism: Constituent Power and Constitutional Form*, eds. Martin Loughlin and Neil Walker (Oxford University Press, 2008).

22 Hannah Arendt, *On Revolution* (Penguin, 1973)

23 Lindhahl, "Constituent Power," 13.

24 Jean-Jacques Rousseau, *The Social Contract*, trans. Donald Cress (Hackett Publishing, 1987), 12.

25 Lucia Rubinelli, *Constituent Power: History* (Cambridge University Press, 2020), 57-65.

26 Rubinelli, *Constituent Power*, 57-65.
27 Roznai, "We the People", 303.
28 Martin Loughlin, "The Concept of Constituent Power," European Journal of Political Theory 13 no. 1 (2014): 220.
29 German Constitution, Preamble; Vietnam Constitution, Preamble; Korean Constitution, Preamble.
30 The Constitution of the Commonwealth of Australia, Preamble.
31 George Duke and Carlo Dellora, "Constituent Power and the Commonwealth Constitution: A preliminary Investigation," *Sydney Law Review* 44 no. 2 (2022): 210.
32 *US Term Limits, Inc. V Thornton*, 115 S.Ct. 1972 (1995)
33 Justice Clarence Thomas, *Thornton.*
34 Stephen Tierney, "'We the Peoples': Constituent Power and Constitutionalism in Plurinational States," in *The Paradox of Constitutionalism: Constituent Power and Constitutional Form*, eds. Martin Loughlin and Neil Walker (Oxford University Press, 2008), 229-31.
35 Efraim Podoksik, "What is a Nation in Nationalism?," *Journal of Political Philosophy* 25, no. 3 (2017): 303.
36 Edmund Morgan, Inventing the People: *The Rise of Popular Sovereignty in England and America* (Norton, 1988)
37 Mark Tushnet, "Constitution-Making: An Introduction," *Texas Law Review* 91, no 7 (2013): 2983-2013.
38 Loughlin, "The Concept," 231.
39 Loughlin, "The Concept," 231.
40 Tushnet, "Constitution-Making," 1981.
41 Federal Democratic Republic of Ethiopia (FDRE) Constitution, Art 39.
42 Currently, seventy-five NNPs are recognized and represented in the House of Federation.
43 FDRE Constitution, Art 8(1).
44 FDRE Constitution, Art 8(2).
45 FDRE Constitution, Art 8(3).
46 Mark Blitz, "Conclusion: What is Popular Sovereignty?," in *People Power: Popular Sovereignty from Machiavelli to Modernity* eds. Christopher Barker and Robert Ingra (Manchester University Press, 2022) 255.
47 Lovise Aalen, *The Politics of Ethnicity in Ethiopia: Actors, Power and Mobilisation under Ethnic Federalism* (Brill, 2011), 38.
48 Donald Levine, Greater Ethiopia: The Evolution of a Multiethnic Society (University Press, 2000), 63.
49 Aalen, *The Politics,* 40
50 Merera Gudina, "Contradictory Interpretations of Ethiopian History: The Need for New Consensus," in *Ethnic Federalism: The Ethiopian Experience in Comparative Perspective* eds. David Turton (James Currey, 2006), 124-8.
51 Gudina, "Contradictory Interpretations" 124-8.
52 Yonatan Fessha, "The Original Sin of Ethiopian Federalism," *Ethnopolitics* 16, no 3. (2017): 237.
53 Gudina, "Contradictory Interpretations" 124-8.

54 Maimire Mennasemay, "Ethiopian History and Critical Theory: The Case of Adwa," in *The Battle of Adwa: Reflections on Ethiopia's Historic Victory against European Colonialism*, eds. Paulos Mikias and Getachew Metaferia (Algora, 2005), 281.

55 Beza Dessalegn and Niggussie Afesha, "The Quest for Identity and Self-Determination in the SNNP Region of Ethiopia," Mizan Law Review 13, no. 1 (2019): 68-74.

56 Yonatan Fessha and Biniyam Bezabih, "Federation Among Unequals: A Country Study of Constitutional Asymmetry in Ethiopia," in *Constitutional Asymmetry in Multinational Federalism: Managing Multinationalism in Multi-tiered Systems*, eds. Patricia Popelier and Maja Sahadzic (Palgrave Macmillan, 2019).

57 Some regional states may recognize other ethnic groups who could claim the state as their homeland.

58 FDRE Constitution, Art 39(5).

59 Aalen, *The Politics*, 37.

60 Joseph Marko, "What is Wrong with the Concept of Multinational Federalism? Some Thoughts about the Interrelationship between the Concepts of (Multi-) Nationalism, Federalism, Power Sharing and Conflict Resolution," *Ethnopolitcs* 19 no 4 (2020): 416-432; John McCauley and Daniel Posner, "The political Source of Religious Identification: Evidence from the Burkina Faso-Côte d'Ivoire Border," *British Journal of Political Science* 49 no 2 (2019): 421-441.

61 Christopher Clapham, "Rewriting Ethiopian History," *Annales d'Ethiopie* 18 no 1 (2002): 37-54.

62 Sara Vaughan and Kjetill Tronvoll, "The Culture of Power in Contemporary Ethiopian Political life," *SIDA Studies 10* (2003): 116-120.

63 John Young, *Peasant Revolution in Ethiopia: The Tigray People's Liberation Front, 1975-1991* (Cambridge University Press, 1997)

64 Young, Peasant Revolution,

65 Lovise Aalen, "Ethnic Federalism and Self-Determination for Nationalities in a Semi-Authoritarian State: The Case of Ethiopia," *International Journal on Minority and Group Rights* 13 no 2-3 (2006): 255-6.

66 Aalen, "Ethnic Federalism,"

67 World Value Survey, *Ethiopia* (Report 7, 2017), 84; World Value Survey, *Ethiopia* (Report 5, 2007): 74.

68 Roger Brubaker, Ethnicity without Groups (Cambridge University press, 2004) 8.

69 The Eritrean movements are the oldest of all. But for this article, our focus is on the Ethiopian ones.

70 Merera Gudina, "Elections and Democratization in Ethiopia, 1991-2000," Journal of African Studies 5 no. 4 (2011): 664-680.

71 Gudina, "Elections," 667.

72 Gudina, "Elections," 667.

73 John Markakis, *Ethiopia: The Last Two Frontiers* (James Currey, 2011) 230.

74 Gudina, "Elections," 667.

75 Markakis, *Ethiopia*, 232.

76 Markakis, *Ethiopia*, 232-3.

77 Theodre Vestal, "An Analysis of the New Constitution of Ethiopia and the Process of its Adoption," Northeastern African Studies 3 no 2 (1996): 23.
78 Vestal, "An Analysis," 23.
79 Meaza Ashenafi, "Ethiopia: process of Democratization and Development," in Human Rights under African Constitutions: Realizing the Promise for Ourselves, ed. Abdullahi An-Na'im (University of Pennsylvania Press, 2011) 28-51.
80 Ashenafi, "Ethiopia," 32.
81 Vestal, "An Analysis," 35.
82 Gudina, "Elections," 669.
83 Ashenafi, "Ethiopia," 33.
84 James Paul, "Ethnicity and the New Constitutional Orders of Ethiopia and Eritrea," in *Autonomy and Ethnicity: Negotiating Competing Claims*, ed. Yash Ghai (Cambridge University Press, 2000) 188-9.
85 Vestal, "An Analysis," 24.
86 Markakis, *Ethiopia*, 237.
87 Vestal, "An Analysis," 24.
88 Markakis, *Ethiopia*, 237
89 Markakis, *Ethiopia*, 237
90 Gedion Hassebon, "The Precarious Future of the Ethiopian Constitution," Journal of African Law 57 no 2(2013): 220.
91 Vestal, "An Analysis," 26.
92 Paul, "Ethnicity," 173.
93 Vestal, "An Analysis,"
94 Vestal, "An Analysis," 24-5.
95 Mechael Meier, "Ethiopia," in *Elections in Africa a Data Handbook*, eds. Dieter Nohlem, Michael Krennerich and Bernhard Thibaut (Oxford University Press, 1999) 382.
96 Hassebon, "The Precarious," 220.
97 The Transitional Period Charter of Ethiopia 1991, Article 13.
98 National Democratic Institute for International Affairs, "An Evaluation of the June 21, 1992 Elections in Ethiopia (1992): 3.
99 Lovise Aalen, "Ethnic Federalism in a Dominant Party State: The Ethiopian Experience 1991-2000," CMI Report (2002): 8
100 National Democratic Institute for International Affairs, "An Evaluation," 3.
101 National Democratic Institute for International Affairs, "An Evaluation," 3.
102 Vestal, "An Analysis," 25.
103 Paul, "Ethnicity," 189.
104 Paul, "Ethnicity," 189.
105 Marina Ottaway, "The Ethiopian Transition: Democratization or New Authoritarianism?", Northeast African Studies 2 no 3 (1995): 73.
106 Getachew Assefa, "The Constitutional Right to Self-determination as a Response to the 'Question of Nationalities' in Ethiopia," *International Journal on Minority and Group Rights* 25 no 1 (2018): 25-33.
107 Assefa, "The Constitutional," 25-33.
108 Gudina, "Contradictory Interpretations," 124-8.

109 Christopher Clapham, *Transformation and Continuity in Revolutionary Ethiopia* (Cambridge University Press, 1990) 28.
110 Assefa, "The Constitutional," 25-33.
111 Paul, "Ethnicity," 189.
112 Paul, "Ethnicity," 188.
113 Hassebon, "The Precarious," 220.
114 Paul, "Ethnicity," 189.
115 Vestal, "An Analysis,"; Gudina, "Elections".
116 Ottaway, "The Ethiopian," 71.
117 Vestal, "An Analysis," 25.
118 Bahru Zewde, The Quest for Socialist Utopia: The Ethiopian Student Movement c. 1960-1974. (James Currey, 2014), 188.
119 Markakis, *Ethiopia*, 89-95; Zewde, *The Quest*, 187-9.
120 Markakis, *Ethiopia*, 89-95; Zewde, *The Quest*, 187-9
121 Markakis, *Ethiopia*, 89-95; Zewde, *The Quest*, 187-9
122 Zewde, *The Quest*, 187-9
123 Markakis, *Ethiopia*, 89-108.
124 Shewa, sometimes spelled Showa or Shoa, is historically a territory in central Ethiopia. Historically, strong kingdoms rose from this territory. King Menelik was first a king in Shewa before expanding his dominion. For a brief Introduction see Encylopedia Britannica, "Shewa."
125 Markakis, *Ethiopia*, 89-108
126 Levine, *Greater Ethiopia*, 78-80.
127 Levine, *Greater Ethiopia*, 78-80.
128 Markakis, *Ethiopia.*
129 Levine, *Greater Ethiopia.*
130 Richard Pankhurst, The Ethiopians: A History (Blackwell Publishers, 2001), 177.
131 Pankhurst, The Ethiopians, 178
132 Gudina, "Contradictory Interpretations," 124-26.
133 Levine, *Greater Ethiopia*, 40.
134 There might be occasional conflicts based on economic resources such as grazing land. However, the communitiehave been solving these issues traditionally without engaging in violent conflict.
135 Gudina, "Contradictory Interpretations," 124-26.
136 Clapham, "Rewriting".
137 Clapham, "Rewriting".
138 Eric Hobsbawn, *Nations and Nationalism since 1780: Programme, Myth, Reality* (Cambridge University Press, 1992), 12.
139 Jack Synder and Karen Ballentine, "Nationalism and the Market Place of Ideas," International Security 21 no. 2 (1996): 10.
140 Currently, the number of regional states is 11.
141 (FDRE Constitution, Art 39).
142 Jon Abbink, "Ethnicity and Constitution in Contemporary Ethiopia," Journal of African Law 41 no 2 (1997): 159-174. Ethnicity, which is similar to "nation, nationality, and people," can be defined in many ways depending on a variety of

features such as language, history, common descent, religion, and so on. Similarly, constituent states of a federal country can be created based on a variety of factors.

143 FDRE Constitution, Art 50(3).

144 FDRE Constitution, Art 50(3).

145 Beza Dessalegn, "Challenges of Ethnic Representation in Ethiopia and the Need for Reform," Mizan Law Review 12 no 1 (2018): 9.

146 Dessalegn, "Challenges," 9.

147 Dessalegn, "Challenges," 9.

148 FDRE Constitution, Art 61.

149 FDRE Constitution, Art 61.

150 FDRE Constitution, Art 61.

151 Tesfa Bihonegn, "The House of Federation: The Practice and Limits of Federalism in the Ethiopia's Second Federal Chamber," Journal of Eastern African Studies 9 no 3 (2019): 401.

152 Bihonegn, "The House," 401.

153 FDRE Constitution, Art 61(1).

154 FDRE Constitution, Art 61(3).

155 FDRE Constitution, Art 62.

156 Paul, "Ethnicity"; Gudina, "Elections".

157 Gudina, "Elections," 665.

158 Tefera Negash Gebregziabher, "Ideology and Power in the TPLF's Ethiopia: A Historic Reversal in the Making?," Affrican Affairs 118 no 472 (2019).

159 Jean-Nicolas Bach, "Abiyotawi Democracy: Neither Revolutionary nor Democratic, a Critical Review of EPRDF's Conception of Revolutionary Democracy in Post-1991 Ethiopia," Journal of Eastern African Studies 5 no. 4 (2011) 641-663.

160 Theodore Vestal, *Ethiopia: A Post-Cold War African State*, (Praeger, 1999), 64.

161 Vestal, Ethiopia, 64.

162 Sarah Vaughan, "Revolutionary Democratic State-Building: Party, State and People in the EPRDF's Ethiopia," Journal of Eastern African Studies 5. No. 4 (2011): 636.

163 Vaughan, "Revolutionary," 636.

164 Hassebon, "The Precarious," 222.

165 Jon Abbink, "Ethnic-based Federalism and Ethnicity in Ethiopia: Reassessing the Experiment after 20 Years," Journal of Eastern African Studies 5 no 4 (2011): 596-618.

166 Jon Abbink, "The Ethiopian Second Republic and the Fragile 'Social Contract'," Africa Spectrum 44 no 2 (2009): 11.

167 Abbink, "The Ethiopian Second," 12.

168 Gudina, "Elections".

169 Ottaway, "The Ethiopian," 71.

170 Lindhahl, "Connstituent Power," 16.

171 Schmitt, *Constitutional Theory*, 105.

172 Lindhahl, "Connstituent Power," 18.

173 Paul Brietzke, "Ethiopia's 'Leap in the Dark': Federalism and Self-Determination in the New Constitution," Journal of African Law 39 no 1 (1995): 33.

174 Lindhahl, "Connstituent Power," 12.

Bibliogrphy

Aalen, Lovise. "Ethnic Federalism and Self-Determination for Nationalities in a Semi-Authoritarian State: The Case of Ethiopia". *International Journal on Minority and Group Rights* 13 no. 2-3 (2006): 243-261.

Aalen, Lovise. *Ethnic Federalism in a Dominant Party State: The Ethiopian Experience 1991-2000*. CMI Report, 2002.

Aalen, Lovise. *The Politics of Ethnicity in Ethiopia: Actors, Power and Mobilisation under Ethnic Federalism*. Leiden: BRILL, 2011.

Abbink, Jon. "Ethnic-based Federalism and Ethnicity in Ethiopia: Reassessing the Experiment after 20 Years". *Journal of Eastern African Studies* 5 no. 4 (2011): 596-618.

Abbink, Jon. "Ethnicity and Constitutionalism in Contemporary Ethiopia. *Journal of African Law* 41 no. 2 (1997): 159-174.

Abbink, Jon. "The Ethiopian Second Republic and the Fragile 'Social Contract'". *Africa Spectrum* 44 no. 2 (2009): 3-28.

Ardent, Hannah. *On Revolution*. Harmondsworth: Penguin, 1965.

Ashenafi. Meaza. "Ethiopia: Process of Democratization and Development" in *Human Rights under African Constitutions: Realizing the Promise for Ourselves* edited by Abdullahi An-Na'im, 28-51. University of Pensylvenia press, 2013.

Assefa, Getachew. "The Constitutional Right to Self-determination as a Response to the 'Question of Nationalities' in Ethiopia". *International Journal on Minority and Group Rights* 25 no. 1 (2018): 1-50.

Bach, Jean-Nicolas.. "Abyotawi Democracy: Neither Revolutionary nor Democratic, a Critical Review of EPRDF's Conception of Revolutionary Democracy in Post-1991 Ethiopia. *Journal of Eastern African Studies* 5 no. 4 (2011): 641-663.

Bihonegn, Tesfa. "The House of Federation: The Practice and Limits of Federalism in Ethiopia's Second Federal Chamber". *Journal of Easter African Studies* 9 no. 3 (2015): 394-411.

Blitz, Mark. "Conclusion: What is Popular Sovereignty?". *In People Power: Popular Sovereignty from Machiavelli to Modernity* edited by Christopher Barker and Robert Ingra, 255-267. Manchester University Press, 2022.

Brietzke, Paul H. "Ethiopia's 'Leap in the Dark': Federalism and Self-Determination in the New Constitution". *Journal of African Law* 39 no 1 (1995): 19-38.

Brubaker, Roger. *Ethnicity Without Groups*. Harvard University Press, 2006.

Clapham, Christopher. "Rewriting Ethiopian History". *Annales d'Ethiopie* 18 no 1(2002): 37-54.

Clapham, Christopher. *Transformation and Continuity in Revolutionary Ethiopia*. Cambridge University Press, 1990.

Constitution of Bosnia and Herzegovina.

Dessalegn, Beza and Afesha, Nigggussie. "The Quest for Identity and Self-Determination in the SNNP Region of Ethiopia". *Mizan Law Review* 13 no. 1(2019): 63-90.

Dessalegn, Beza. "Challenges of Ethnic Representation in Ethiopia and the Need for Reform". *Mizan Law Review* 12 no. 1 (2018): 1-28.

Duke, George and Arcioni, Elisa "Between Constituent Power and Constituent Authority," Oxford Journal of legal Studies 42 no. 1(2022): 345-365

Duke, George and Dellora, Carlo. "Constituent Power and the Commonwealth Constitution: A preliminary Investigation". *Sydney Law Review* 44 no. 2 (2022): 199-227.

Fesseha, Yonatan Tesfaye. "The Original Sin of Ethiopian Federalism". *Ethnopolitics* 16 no. 3 (2017): 232-245.

Fessha, Yonatan and Bezabih, Biniyam. "Federation Among unequals: A Country Study of Constitutional Asymmetry in Ethiopia". In *Constitutional Asymmetry in Multinational Federalism: Managing Multinationalism in Multi-tiered Systems* edited by patricia Popelier and Maja Sahadžić, 137-162. Palgrave Macmillan, 2019.

Gebregziabher, Tefera Negash. "Ideology and Power in the TPLF's Ethiopia: A Historic Reversal in the Making?". *African Affairs* 118 no. 472 (2018): 463-484.

Gudian, Merera. "Contradictory Interpretations of Ethiopian History: The Need for New Consensus'. In *Ethnic Federalism: The Ethiopian Experience in Comparative Perspective* edited by David Turton, 119-130. James Currey, 2006.

Gudina, merera. "Elections and Democratization in Ethiopia, 1991-2010". *Journal of African Studies* 5 no. 4 (2011): 664-680.

Hassebon, Gedion T. "The Precarious Future of the Ethiopian Constitution". *Journal of African Law* 57 no. 2 (2013): 215-233.

Jaume, Lucien. "Constituent power in France: the Revolution and its Consequences in Selfhood". In *the Paradox of Constitutionalism: Constituent Power and Constitutional Form* edited by Martin Loughlin and Neil Walker, 69-89. Oxford University Press, 2008.

Johnson, R.M. *The Corsican: A Diary of Napoleon's Life in His Own Words*. Houghton Mifflin Co, 1910.

Levine, Donald N. *Greater Ethiopia*. University of Chicago Press, 2000.

Lindhahl, Hans. "Constituent Power and Reflexive Identity: Towards an Ontology of Collective Selfhood". In *the Paradox of Constitutionalism: Constituent Power and Constitutional Form* edited by Martin Loughlin and Neil Walker, 9-24. Oxford University Press, 2008.

Loughlin, Martin, "The Concept of Constituent Power". *European Journal of Political Theory* 13 no. 1 (2014): 218-237.

Markakis, John. *Ethiopia: The Last Two Frontiers*. James Currey, 2011.

Marko, Joseph. "What is Wrong with the Concept of Multinational Federalism? Some Thoughts about the Interrelationship between the Concepts of (Multi-) Nationalism, Federalism, Power Sharing and Conflict Resolution". *Ethnopolitics* 19 no. 4 (2020): 416-432.

Mattei, Ugo. "The New Ethiopian Constitution: First Thoughts on ethnical Federalism and the Reception of Western Institutions", 1995.

McCauley, John F. and Posner, Daniel N. "The Political Sources of Religious Identification: Evidence from the Burkina Faso-Côte d'Ivoire Border". *British Journal of Political Science* 49 no. 2 (2019): 421-441.

Meier, Michael. "Ethiopia". In *Elections in Africa a Data Handbook* edited by Nohlen D. and Krennerich M, 373-386. Oxford Universiy Press, 1999.

Mennasemay, Maimire. "Ethiopian History and Critical Theory: The Case of Adwa". In *The Battle of Adwa: Reflections on Ethiopia's Historic Victory against European Colonialism* edited by Paulos Mikias and Getachew Metaferia, 255-300. Algora, 2005.

Morgan, Edmund S. *Inventing the People: The Rise of Popular Sovereignty in England and America*. Norton, 1988.

National Democratic Institute for International Affairs and African-American Institute. *An Evaluation of the June 21, 1992 Elections in Ethiopia*. 1992.

Ottaway, Marina. "The Ethiopian Transition: Democratization or New Authoritarianism?". *Northeast African Studies* 2 no. 3 (1995): 67-84.

Paul, James. "Ethnicity and the New Constitutional Orders of Ethiopia and Eritrea". In *Autonomy and Ethnicity: negotiating competing Claims* in Multi-ethnic States edited by Yash Ghai, 173-196. Cambridge University Press, 2000.

Podoksik, Efraim. "What is a Nation in Nationalism?". *Journal of Political Philosophy* 25 no. 3 (2017): 303-323

Preuss, Ulrich K. 1992. "Constitutional Powermaking for the New Polity: Some Deliberations on the Relations Between Constituent Power and the Constitution". *Cardozo Law Review 14* no. 3: 639-660

Rousseau, Jean-Jacques. *The Social Contract*. Translated by Donald A. Cress. Indianapolis: Hackett Publishing Co., 1762.

Roznai, Yaviv. "We the People, 'oui the people' and the Collected body: Perceptions onf Constituent Power". In *Comparative Constitutional Theory* edited by Gary Jacobsohn and Miguel Schor, 295-316. Edward Elgar, 2018.

Rubinelli, Lucia. "How to think beyond Sovereignty: on Sieyes and Constituent Power". *European Journal of Political Theory* 18 no. 1 (2019): 47-67.

Rubinelli, Lucia. *Constituent Power: A History*. Cambridge University Press, 2020.

Schmitt, Carl. *Constitutional Theory*. Translated by Jeffrey Seitzer. Duke University Press, 2008.

Sieyes, Emannuel, 'Reconnaisance et exposition raisonnee de Droit de L'Homme et du Cotoyen', 20 July 1879. In *Emmanuel Josheph Sieyès: The Essential Political Writings.* Translated by Oliver Lembcke and Florian Weber. BRILL, 2014.

The 1931 Constitution of Ethiopia

The 1995 Federal Democratic Republic of Ethiopia Constitution

The Commonwealth of Australia Constitution Act

The Constitution of India

The Constitution of the People's Democratic Republic of Ethiopia

The Constitution of the Republic of Korea

The Constitution of the Socialist Republic of Vietnam

The German Basic Law

The Nigeria's Constitution of 1999

The Transitional Period Charter of Ethiopia 1991

Tierney, Stephen. "'We the Peoples': Constituent Power and Constitutionalism in Plurinational States". In *the Paradox of Constitutionalism: Constituent Power and Constitutional Form,* edited by Martin Loughlin and Neil Walker, 229-245. Oxford University Press, 2008.

Tushnet, Mark. "Constitution-Making: An Introduction". *Texas Law Review* 91 no. 7 (2013): 2983-2013.

US Term Limits, Inc. V Thornton, 115 S.Ct. 1972 (1995).

Vaughan, Sara and Tronvoll, Kjetill. "The Culture of Power in Contemporary Ethiopian Political Life". *SIDA Studies 10*. Edita Severigie, 2003.

Vaughan, Sarah. "Revolutionary Democratic State-Building: Party, State and People in the EPRDF's Ethiopia." *Journal of Eastern African Studies* 5 no. 4 (2011): 619-640.

Vestal, Theodore M. *Ethiopia: A Post-Cold War African State*. Westport: Praeger, 1999.

Vestal, Theodre. "An Analysis of the New Constitution of Ethiopia and the Process of its Adoption". *Northeast African Studies* 3 no 2 (1996): 21-38.

World Value Survey Wave 5. 2007. *Ethiopia.*

World Value Survey Wave 7. 2017. *Ethiopia.*

Young, John. *Peasant Revolution in Ethiopia: The Tigray People's Liberation Front, 1975-1991*. Cambridge University Press, 1997.

Zewde, Bahru. *The Quest for Socialist Utopia: The Ethiopia Student Movement, c. 1960-1974*. James Currey, 2014.

Chapter 6

What Constitutions Do or Ought to Do: The Ethiopian Experience

Belachew Girma Degefie

Introduction

A constitution establishes a system of government, defines the powers and functions of its institutions, provides substantive limits on its operation, and regulates relations between institutions and the people.[1] In doing so, constitutions constrain government by generating a set of inviolable principles to which future lawmaking and government decisions must conform. But constitutions also enable government by empowering institutions and, in some cases, by requiring them to promote social welfare. Although the use of the term "constitution" in this way is relatively recent, the very idea of government has always included some notion, such as rules creating, empowering, and limiting government institutions.

The purpose of this chapter is to examine what constitutions do in comparative perspective and explore the Ethiopian experience in light of that perspective. It is important to note that the focus of the paper is not to examine the performance or efficacy of the FDRE Constitution.[2] The chapter specifically explores what the FDRE Constitution does in light of the functions of constitutions in other jurisdictions.

This chapter begins by highlighting the history of constitutions, with a particular focus on how they were conceived and how their purposes and functions were defined. The second section highlights the roles of constitutions in ensuring the rule of law in constitutional democracies. In the third section, the functions of constitutions in different types of regimes are discussed. The final section of the chapter is devoted to assessing what constitutions do in the Ethiopian context, specifically the FDRE Constitution.

1. A Brief History of Constitutions

The history of constitutions dates back to ancient times, where Aristotle described constitutions as "essential structures" of state organizations.[3] In the ancient Roman Empire, "contracts between the emperor and the imperial estates usurped the place of the *pactum ordinationis.*"[4] One may also mention some historical documents, such as the Magna Carta and others that had some of the functions of modern constitutions. In its modern iterations in European thought, "The idea of public law [including constitutions] evolved in the early modern period, flourished during the late-nineteenth and early-twentieth centuries, but has since waned."[5] Regardless of the differences with the modern concept of constitutions, it could be said that the history of constitutions may be traced back to the time when human beings started living as a society and the emergence of early forms of the state.

In its modern context, a constitution was perceived as *a limit to the powers of the government.* Thomas Paine, writing in the context of debates regarding the US Constitution, articulated that "the principal function of a constitution was to restrain government, and that any governmental act outside constitutional boundaries should be viewed as an expression of power without right."[6] There are, however, varying stages of development within Europe and the United States.

Carl Schmitt defined a constitution in its absolute and relative sense. In its absolute/normative sense, a constitution refers to the political unity of the people or a fundamental legal regulation.[7] Constitution in a relative/empirical sense means the individual constitutional law or the written constitution.[8] Accordingly, he distinguishes constitution and constitutional law, arguing as follows:

> *"A proper understanding requires that the meaning of the term "constitution" be limited to the constitution of the state, that is to say, the political unity of the people. In this limited meaning, 'constitution' can describe the state itself, and, indeed, an individual, concrete state*

> *as political unity or as a particular, concrete type and form of state existence. In this instance, it means the complete condition of political unity and order. Yet 'constitution' can also mean a closed system of norms and, then, in the same way, can designate a unity, however, not a concrete existing unity, but instead a reflective, ideal one. In both cases, the concept of the constitution is absolute because it expresses a (real or reflective) whole.*[9] *The theory was however criticized for narrowing down a constitution only for ethnos as opposed to demos."*[10]

The revolutions that occurred around the world in the seventeenth and eighteenth centuries significantly affected the older definitions.[11] "In the English-speaking world, a 'constitution' originally denotes a formally enacted law, but with the involvement of the Parliament in the legislative process."[12] "This understanding has, however, gradually been usurped by the word 'statute'."[13] In the seventeenth century power struggle, references were made to the "constitution" inconsistently.[14] Following the start of the civil war in England, the word "constitution" was often used in the plural to refer to "fundamental laws." In 1649, Charles I was accused of violating the "fundamental constitutions" of the kingdom. In 1688, James II was accused of seeking to "subvert the constitution of the kingdom."[15] The expression now always refers to the fundamental rules for the organization of the state. [16] The English modern constitution has been "transformed from being one of monarchical rule, subject to limited constraints imposed by law and by duties to consult and obtain consent of aristocracy and commons, to a system of representative parliamentary government."[17]

According to Dicey, a constitution consists of "all rules which directly or indirectly affect the distribution or the exercise of the sovereign power in the state," including "all rules which define the members of the sovereign power, all rules which regulate the relation of such members to each other, or which determine the mode in which the sovereign power, or the members thereof, exercise their authority."[18] For Cooley, a constitution is "the body of rules and maxims in accordance with which the powers of sovereignty are habitually exercised."[19]

In North America, a "constitution was understood as binding, written legal norms defining the powers and limits of local state power compiled in a formal document as opposed to its English counterpart."[20] Three important connotations could be drawn from here. Firstly, that "a constitution must be set down in writing, because 'a constitution … has not an ideal, but a real existence; and wherever it cannot be produced in a visible form, there is none.'"[21] "Secondly, the constitution must originate from the people and be beyond the reach of state power."[22] "A constitution is a thing antecedent to a government, and a government is only the creature of the constitution."[23] "The constitution of a country is not the act of its government, but of the people constituting a government."[24] Thirdly, "In light of the revolutionary experiences, the constitution exceeds a mere 'form of government' and must include material restraints on state power in the form of basic rights."[25] This understanding of a constitution has remained the dominant notion in modern constitutional law.

In the context of France, after the Revolution, as traditional state power was broken, the formalized and content-rich notion of the constitution took precedence.[26] Despite the influential works of Montesquieu and Rousseau predating the revolutionary period, the formal concept of a constitution was introduced later by writers such as Vattel. He argued that *"règlement fondamental qui détermine la manière dont l'autorité publique doit être exercée,"* adding that such a *"règlement"* can only originate with the nation but is not bound to any specific content or form.[27] Sieyès argued that "rule can only be legitimated as authority invested by the people and the mandatory relationship makes a constitution necessary."[28]

In Germany, "*Konstitution*" was understood to mean a law promulgated by the emperor, without reference to its significance or object. "Norms regulating the exercise of political rule are termed 'fundamental laws….' *Verfassung* is used in an empirical, and not in a normative sense and relates to the condition of a state."[29] Most authors define "constitution" as "the totality of all essential provisions … that relate to the organization of sovereignty by its necessary subject and the nature in which they are to possess such."[30] The constitution is then the political condition of the state as created by contract and determined by basic laws.[31]

Two powers within the state may distinguish the active supreme authority that is established by the basic constitution and the fundamental authority of the people as a whole.[32] This leads to the conclusion that there is no state without a constitution.

Despite the differences in the development of constitutions across jurisdictions, one can discern some common features of constitutions. The most evident distinction between a constitution and regular law is that the former is harder to change than the latter, being less likely to change and more challenging to modify. It is believed that constitutions are more deeply ingrained than regular legislation.[33] Another important common feature relates to the fact that the constitution, as a set of fundamental rules for the organization of a state, distributes the exercising of sovereign power in the state and hence limits the powers of the government. A constitution also serves to legitimize the authority vested by the people to governments. A constitution is also described as the political condition for the existence of a state. Even if there are agreements that constitutions should be made by the people, there are differing opinions as to their form.[34]

2. Constitutions and the Rule of Law

As has been discussed above, despite the differences in the contexts and developments across jurisdictions, constitutions in modern societies have emerged as limits to state power. Constitutions, as fundamental laws, lay ground rules to exercise political power along with limits, thereby introducing the rule of law. This section of the chapter discusses the nexus between constitutions and the rule of law.

Constitutions establish and "constrain the constrain a system of government, to create a stable set of rules for how the political game will be played."[35] The success of constitutions on whether they play these roles depends on the extent to which the major actors abide by these rules. "If powerful political actors felt free to change the game at any time by ignoring or revising any rules that they found disadvantageous, there would be no such thing as constitutionalism."[36]

The rule of law is a cornerstone of contemporary constitutional democracy, as has been underscored in different parts around the globe. In the broadest terms, "The rule of law requires that the state only subject the citizenry to publicly promulgated laws, that the state's legislative function be separate from the adjudicative function, and that no one within the polity be above the law."[37] Modern constitutional law is characterized by "limiting the powers of government, adherence to the rule of law, and protection of fundamental rights."[38] Constitutional democracy in the modern context is impossible without the rule of law.[39] In other words, constitutions lay the foundations for democracy by laying down the rules which shall be obeyed by all.

In the liberal world, constitutions establish a democracy where fundamental rights are protected and the rule of law prevails, making constitutions crucial in such polities. In the second half of the twentieth century, constitutional democracy became indispensable when contrasted with the totalitarian or authoritarian regimes.[40] This does not necessarily mean that constitutional democracy is always the best alternative. Rosenfeld provides an example where in a society that is homogeneous, deeply religious, and ruled by revered leaders, a theocracy would plainly seem more appropriate than a constitutional democracy—making instructions and directions imparted by the religious leaders would be paramount, leaving little, if any, room for the rule of law.[41] In contrast, Rosenfeld argues, as discussed later, that "constitutional democracy and adherence to the rule of law may well be indispensable to achieving political cohesion with minimum oppression in heterogeneous or pluralistic societies with various competing conceptions of the good."[42]

3. The Functions of Constitutions in Democracies and in Authoritarian Regimes: Comparisons with a Focus on Multiethnic Societies

As highlighted above, almost all countries in the world have constitutions, despite varying in forms and purposes. Mark Tushnet lists several reasons why a new state needs a constitution. Firstly, the international community considers a constitution to be a prerequisite for statehood, perhaps not as a matter of formal international law but as a matter of practical reality.[43] In other words, the contemporary world order considers having a constitution as a prerequisite for statehood. Secondly, domestic actors may treat the existence of a constitution as establishing or symbolizing the nation's existence as a state.[44] Thirdly, constitutions are convenient ways of laying out the formal contours of the mechanisms for exercising public power.[45] Finally, in nations with heterogeneous populations—an increasingly large proportion of the world's nations—"*a constitution can serve as an expression, perhaps the only one available, of national unity.*"[46] It's important to note that more than one of these several reasons may be relevant in a polity.

Relevant questions arise as to what valuable moral ends constitutions aspire to achieve, the design of constitutional arrangements and institutions, and how-to best approach constitutional interpretation. The works of varying scholars and pragmatic lessons across jurisdictions reveal that there may be a vast array of approaches to the above questions. "The focal case of a constitution comprised of fundamental rules, principles, and norms that aim to generate, sustain, and channel political authority and public power will involve channeling and enabling state power in a manner responsive to the good moral reasons we have for wanting authoritative political institutions."[47] A constitution and its constitutive rules, principles, and conventions should ultimately arrange institutions in such a way that they are apt to ensure the community is governed well and suited to the pursuit of the wide-ranging and complex conditions required for human flourishing. "If law's function is to settle what ought to be done through determinate rules, constitutional law's function is to settle the most basic matters regarding how we ought to organize society and government."[48] Looked at in terms of legal validity, constitutional law is the law that is highest in the validity chain.[49] Constitutions lay down the ground rules for governance as they "constitute" the government.[50]

When a constitution promulgates the structures, offices, and procedures for governance—the rules about how laws are to be made, how offices are to be filled, and which level of government and which officials within government are to have jurisdiction over which matters—the constitutional provisions in question are similar to assembly instructions that accompany gadgets or toys that we buy.[51]

In doing so, constitutions usually provide for bills of rights in different forms or models. There are three possibilities: First, the constitutional authors might be creating rights or making certain rights more determinate by means of rules granting various specific liberties and immunities. Second, the constitutional authors might not be creating or specifying rights through rules but might instead be incorporating real moral rights as they exist in the moral realm—that is, making certain real moral rights legally as well as morally binding on the government and enforceable by the judiciary. Third, the constitutional authors might be inventing or creating rights but without translating them into determinate rules.[52]

Even if constitutions play crucial roles in building polities, it does not mean that they can resolve all issues. Because a constitution can provide a "focal point for political cohesion"[53] of a nation or of a people, one might note here a tension between the idea that a constitution, written or not, is necessary for recognition of a state on the international scene and the idea that a constitution, again, written or not, constitutes a nation in the ethno-nationalist sense, a tension arising from the distinction between state and nation upon which ethno-nationalism rests.[54]

While the functions of a constitution discussed above are perceived to be applicable generally, they may have an additional and somewhat unique function in multiethnic or multinational societies. The roles that may be assumed by constitutionalism and constitutions in relation to the interplay between identity and diversity are complex and multifaceted.[55]

Furthermore, the relevant nexuses between identity and diversity are themselves numerous as well as fairly intricate. Strictly speaking, it is not a matter of any single identity emerging against a backdrop of multiple differences. Rather, issues concerning constitutionalism and constitutions arise in sociopolitical settings demarcated by clashes between competing identities. Among other identities, there are likely to be national, regional, linguistic, religious, ethnic, political, generational, class, and ideological identities. Moreover, it is far from obvious how these competing identities ought to be combined or divided to frame the kind of interplay between identity and diversity that is likely to conform with the fundamental tenets of constitutionalism.[56]

Pursuing the fundamental principles of constitutionalism is only logical in relation to sociopolitical contexts that can be understood as centered around the diametrically opposed poles of diversity and difference, as well as identity.[57] It is hard to see how one could defend the imposition of a constitutional order in the absence of a dominant identity, such as that of the sovereign nation or the constitutional self. In contrast, if a sociopolitical setting were so homogeneous as to lack differences susceptible to becoming implicated in political conflicts, there would appear to be no need for imposing the kind of constraints usually associated with constitutionalism."[5859] Rosenfeld strongly argues that all three features of modern constitutionalism are necessitated by diversity and difference.[60]

Constitutions, whether written or "unwritten," play irreplaceable functions in the legal systems of developed democracies in defining government structure to limit their power, entrench fundamental rights, and ultimately enable and strengthen the rule of law. A legal system is disrupted if constitutions are interpreted incorrectly in a legal system due to provisions that go against these goals.

In authoritarian regimes, constitutions serve a different role than in democratic systems. In such regimes, constitutions are enacted "consuming significant political energy and time.'"[61] Hence, there are reasons why such regimes enact a constitution. Ginsburg and Simpser argue that constitutions help authoritarian rulers to "coordinate multiple actors, control subordinates, and secure cooperation from subjects."[62] In other words, constitutions help authoritarian regimes perpetuate themselves, contrary to what they are supposed to do in democratic regimes.

Constitutions also serve as "operating manuals, blueprints, and window dressing."[63] By way of operating manuals, constitutions allocate powers to the government while actually being controlled by the party leaders who had control in their making.[64] Constitutions are also "advertisements" as policies of authoritarian leaders to either an outsider, usually the international community, or to the insider.[65]

The constitutions in multiethnic societies also have to "reconcile sameness and difference" by addressing identity politics. This objective implies that constitutions may receive the additional role of an instrument that can mediate identity conflicts, since major liberal virtues backing liberty and popular sovereignty—those of tolerance and trust, respectively—are not at hand.

4. What Does the Federal Democratic Republic of Ethiopia (FDRE) Constitution Do?

As discussed above, constitutions play key roles in democracies, such as establishing government entities, limiting government power, protecting fundamental rights, and enabling and promoting coexistence in diverse societies. In order to assess whether a constitution has played these roles, it is important to examine the various features of its design and practice. Another method may be to analyze the functions of the constitution in terms of representation, legislation, administration and adjudication.[66] There are also others who assess constitutional performance or efficacy by setting universal and context-specific criteria. Cognizant of these vast choices, this section examines the functions the FDRE Constitution played from the perspectives of limiting government powers, protecting human rights, and managing diversity.

Historically in Ethiopia, sources of legitimacy were derived from genealogical descendance and religion, the "Solomonic dynasty," and Orthodox Christianity. In ancient times, the "*Kebrenegest,*" and in the medieval period, the *Fethanegest* were also referred to to resolve disputes over monarchical rules. The 1931 Constitution, as the first written constitution for the country, had two purposes when enacted by Emperor Haile Sellasie I: to show to the Western powers that Ethiopia was a civilized nation and secondly to consolidate monarchical powers.[67] The Constitution was a grant of the emperor to his "subjects" and hence no conventional participatory constitution-making process was followed. This was because the imperial power derived its legitimacy from genealogy instead of the popular vote. Indeed, the process through which the 1931 Constitution was adopted as well as its content imply that the document had a different role than what constitutions are meant to do in liberal societies.

The 1955 Revised Constitution was again an imperial grant that was necessitated by the federation of Eritrea with Ethiopia in 1952 following the end of Italy's colonial rule over Eritrea. The Constitution included a list of human rights inspired by the Universal Declaration of Human Rights;[68] incorporated the notion of separation of powers despite the existence of the emperor's prerogatives;[69] established a two-chamber legislature, with the lower house to be directly elected by universal suffrage while the upper chamber was appointed by the emperor;[70] contemplated a ministerial government responsible to the monarch and parliament, etc. However, the regime instrumentalized the notion of having a "constitution" merely to consolidate and perhaps centralize political powers as it continued to reinforce the process of centralization.[71]

The 1987 Constitution was enacted by the *Derg* Regime after thirteen years of ruling the country without a constitution. There were, however, proclamations enacted during this period that played the functions of a constitution by establishing and structuring government bodies and defining their powers, the regime to operate. This Constitution was adopted amid civil war in different parts of the country. Even though the Constitution had attempted to address enduring contested issues such as the rights of "nations and nationalities" and autonomy, among others, the attempt was considered to be "too little, too late."[72] Many consider the Constitution a sham, a crude attempt to deal with the civil war.

The 1995 FDRE Constitution, the fourth written constitution for the country, was enacted following the transitional period, which ran for almost four years. The National Conference, held after the downfall of the *Derg* regime, among the ethno-national movements, resulted in the Transitional Charter, which actually served as a prelude to the Constitution. It introduced a predominantly ethnic-based federal system empowering ethno-linguistic groups to self-administration and a parliamentary form of government. Despite its recognition of fundamental rights, the FDRE Constitution is criticized for its risky focus on empowering "nations, nationalities and peoples" (NNPs) self-rule instead of fostering national unity, as well as for establishing a weak constitutional review mechanism,[73] loose control mechanisms on the executive, etc.

Despite the promises of the FDRE Constitution to "build a political community, in ensuring lasting peace, rule of law, guaranteeing democratic order, and advancing economic and social development,"[74] the past twenty-eight years have remained another challenging period for the country. In this section, a brief overview of the issues of design that may put the function of the constitution in jeopardy, as well as of practical experiences, are discussed.

It is important at this juncture to discuss why the functions of a constitution in liberal democracies is used as a yardstick to evaluate the FDRE Constitution. There are scholarly writings which argue that the Constitution is largely influenced by the communitarian ideology, instead of liberal thoughts, by citing the "socialist-ideology hangover" of the makers and the dominance of ethno-nationalist movements on the right to self-determination.[75] Added to this is the fact that "the individual is displaced and locked in the periphery as much of the socioeconomic and political ecology of the state is occupied by NNPs."[76] It is evident that the recognition of NNPs as political contractors and the "building bricks of the federation" shows that the Constitution does not take liberal thought for granted. The Constitution goes to the extent that the right to self-determination of the NNPs is the organizing principle of the constitutional system. "The constitutional framers' desire to uphold both the liberal and communitarian values in tandem, without priority or hierarchy, collapsed by tilting the balance in favor of the communitarian agenda at the expense of the liberal one."[77]

Nevertheless, a closer look at the Constitution's aspiration to uphold rule of law, as prescribed in the Preamble,[78] and the space devoted to fundamental rights under its Chapter Three, indicates that it incorporates liberal aspects. If the framers had a different conception of the rule of law than what is conventional in the liberal world, for instance, they would have defined it in the

Constitution. Hence, the liberal aspects reflected in the Constitution give us the impetus to apply the roles of constitutions in liberal systems to the Constitution. What constitutions in a specific jurisdiction are or appear to be may be discerned either from the designs in the constitutions or from practice or both. Hence, this section explores issues of design and practice to assess the experience of Ethiopia on what the Constitution has done and is doing.

1.1. Issues of Design: Features of the FDRE Constitution that Contradict the Roles of Constitutions Elsewhere

There has been a great deal of writing on the design of the FDRE Constitution from different perspectives, particularly on the process of its making, recognition of NNPs as sovereign, and a constitutional adjudication system. The legitimacy of the Constitution is contested on the ground that the process was not inclusive of significant political actors and was dominated by the TPLF-led EPRDF.[79] The flaws in the legitimacy are also attributed to the "subsequent serious lack of integrity and vitality in the constitutional system."[80] While there are writings that hail the constitutional recognition of the rights of NNPs to self-determination, it is argued that the arrangement "solved old problems of ethnic inequality and injustice, ethnic federalism has created new problems of ethnic tensions and conflict across Ethiopia."[81] It is also argued that "common citizenship is still underdeveloped, because it is not the basis of constitutional sovereignty and rights- as ethnicity is the prime basis of people's identity."[82] The following subsections attempt to highlight selected issues of design that imply basic functions of the constitution.

a. The Process of Making the FDRE Constitution and Its Contested Legitimacy

One of the distinct features of a constitution from other legal documents, which are reflections of the will of the majority, is that it is conceived to reflect the will of the people beyond the majority from which it derives its supremacy. In other words, the constitution derives its authority from the constituent power, which is the body of the people.[83] Hence, the process of making a constitution is crucial for its legitimacy, contextuality, and subsequent constitutional practice.[84] Constitution making commonly involves stages such as drafting, deliberation, ratification, and adoption. Inclusiveness in all these processes is desired.[85]

The process of making the FDRE Constitution has been criticized by many as involving "little meaningful public participatory debate, especially debate focused on devolution versus ethnic federalism."[86] Withdrawal of political parties from the transitional process, as well as from elections, left the Ethiopian Peoples' Revolutionary Democratic Front (EPRDF), and within it the Tigray

People's Liberation Front (TPLF), as a giant political actor dominating both the content and process of the constitution making.

The dominance of the EPRDF was reflected starting from the drafting stage, when the Constitutional Commission was established. Even if the commission was supposedly a technical body to draft the constitution, the members were appointed by the Council of Representatives, which was dominated, if not controlled, by the EPRDF. Most importantly, the constitution-adopting body, the Constituent Assembly, was jam-packed by the EPRDF.

The implications of such dominance by a single party is evident. In the process, the EPRDF constitutionalized the ethnic-based federal system based on the explanation that self-determination of ethnic groups would resolve recurrent conflicts in Ethiopia. The facts that the "nations, nationalities, and peoples" (NNP) are sovereign and bestowed with the right to self-determination including secession are described as the two salient and debated features of the Constitution.[87] An extension of this ethnocentric constitutional system is reflected in the constitutional adjudication system that empowers the House of Federation to interpret the constitution.

According to Ginsburg, that "where a single party believes it is likely to hold on to political power, it has little incentive to set up a neutral arbiter to resolve disputes about constitutional meaning ... [which] would rather retain the flexibility to dictate outcomes without constitutional constraint."[88] He argues that such tendencies are reflected by the absence of independent judicial review mechanisms under authoritarian constitutions.[89] Hence, had there been competing political forces, they would have pushed for a strong constitutional review mechanism as insurance to challenge government actions.[90] In light of this view, one could observe that the outcome of the EPRDF-dominated constitution-making process ended up choosing flexibility over strong review design.

One may recognize the sense of urgency in constitution making that "conduces to quick compromises without substantial attention being paid to how the constitution will operate once adopted."[91] However, a closer look at the context in which the FDRE Constitution was made shows that the sense of urgency or uncertainty was overshadowed by the dominance of the EPRDF both on the content and process, therefore leading to a document that does not reflect compromises on key aspects.[92]

In summary, the valid questions raised as to the inclusive nature of the making process of the FDRE Constitution implies that the Constitution was intended to play roles that are not intact in its very nature. In other words, the Constitution was made in a manner that goes against what a Constitution is meant to do in democracies by excluding significant political actors at the time and without meaningful popular participation.

b. Consideration of the Constitution as a "Political Contract between NNPs"

Looking back to the process of making the Constitution, the dominance of one party, the EPRDF, was evident in all stages—the drafting, deliberation, and adoption. The ethno-nationalist movements led by the TPLF and some others who accepted the call from the TPLF to join the National Conference adopted the Transitional Charter of Ethiopia in 1991. The charter introduced ethnic-based autonomy and self-determination as a solution for ending recurrent civil wars and bringing stability.[93] The charter was a precursor to what kind of constitutional system was established following the transitional period. In fact, the Constitutional Commission Proclamation No. 24/1992 tasked the commission with drafting a constitution "with the spirit of the Transitional Charter."[94]

With this background, the Constitution took "nations, nationalities, and peoples" as building bricks[95] of the federation, "author," and interpreter of the Constitution. It is therefore necessary to briefly examine how the framers perceived a constitution more generally in order to assess what functions the Constitution was intended to play by the framers.

There are several instances where the members of the Constituent Assembly that adopted the Constitution described what a constitution is supposed to do. In general, it could be discerned from the minutes of the Constituent Assembly that the framers acknowledged the constitutive, limiting roles of a constitution along with the need to recognize human rights in it.[96] However, the issue of whether the constitutional design was crafted to achieve these requires examination.

One clear indication is that the framers of the Constitution regarded it "as an embodiment of the political contract among the NNPs"[97] and not of the Ethiopian people (*demos*) as a whole. This notion of the Constitution results in the conclusion that the NNPs are the "body and soul" of the constitutional system, and its "constituent powers" as opposed to the *demos*. Accordingly, the consideration of the Constitution as a "political contract among NNPs" contradicts the dominant idea of modern constitutions as the will of the general public.

This notion has implications both in designing a constitution and implementing it. NNPs are considered "authors and interpreters of the Constitution"; sovereignty resides in them, and they have self-determination of all forms, including secession, etc.

This does not mean that the Constitution should disregard the ethnolinguistic diversity of the country. As discussed above, constitutions in diverse societies serve as expressions of national unity.[98] They may also be understood as "vehicles for the creation of a *demos.*"[99] A constitution, starting from the preamble, should adopt a design which duly recognizes heterogeneity with the ultimate goal of creating a polity. In this regard, the FDRE Constitution opens its Preamble with "Nations, Nationalities, Peoples" as opposed to the usual opening "We the People." As preambles and general principles can have legal force when they are embedded in constitutions, a more inclusive one should have been chosen instead.

As discussed in the previous sections, constitutions in liberal societies play the critical roles of constituting and constraining a government, ensuring prevalence of the rule of law and protection of fundamental rights. Despite the prevailing ideological foundations of the Constitution in entrenching the rights of NNPs, it does not reject these functions of constitutions. It instead aspires to build a "political community founded on the rule of law," extensively recognizes the fundamental rights devoting a chapter, sets rules of the game on how to assume political power, etc. The ideological basis has in fact blurred the very functions of constitutions to the extent of describing it as a "political contract among NNPs."

c. Weak Mechanism of Constitutional Review/Adjudication/Interpretation

Among the important issues of constitutional design today is that of the structures of constitutional review. Constitutional interpretation is a mechanism of ensuring the supremacy of the constitution by reviewing the constitutionality of laws, decisions, and practices of government entities. In other words, it checks whether the exercise of government powers is consistent with constitutional mandates or instructions. At times, this will be done in the context of interpreting constitutional provisions that are vague or ambiguous. It is also considered as a means of ensuring whether fundamental rights are duly protected. Hence, the practice of constitutional review can tell us whether the constitutional system has been taken seriously.

Given its importance, this power of constitutional review is commonly conferred upon either regular courts (decentralized) or specialized constitutional courts (centralized). The arrangement under the FDRE Constitution is unique in empowering a second chamber, the House of Federation, to interpret the Constitution.[100]

The rationale behind empowering the HoF relies on the argument that "the Constitution, as an embodiment of the political contract among the NNPs, should be interpreted by the signatories themselves, the NNPs through the HoF."[101] The rationale behind empowering the HoF relies on the argument that "the Constitution, as an embodiment of the political contract among the

NNPs, should be interpreted by the signatories themselves, the NNPs through the HoF."[102] The option of empowering courts was rejected on the ground that "judges are not neutral from the different public opinions and hence may tilt to the opinion they support and erode the rights of NNPs by interpreting the constitution in a distorted manner."[103] This arrangement has been criticized for being weak, lacking impartiality, and being unfit to interpret the Constitution.[104] It is also argued that the substantive argument of the framers is "deeply flawed."[105] Others also argue that "what motivated the constitution makers' preference for the HoF, as opposed to the courts, is not the democratic and contractual arguments they advanced but the fact that they fell into the trap of adopting a communitarian political viewpoint."[106]

1.2. Practical Realities: Did the Constitution Limit the Powers of the Government?

Examining the practical realities of what the FDRE Constitution has done and is doing requires an all-encompassing and multidisciplinary approach. This section, therefore, focuses on key functions of the FDRE Constitution as the guarantor of the rule of law, limiting the power of the government, and protecting fundamental rights. In light of this, it is important to highlight how governmental entities, particularly the law-making, executive, and adjudicatory bodies, have implemented the Constitution. Under this section, as reiterated above, the chapter does not aim to assess the constitutional efficacy or performance. It instead intends to showcase how the functions of a constitution are reflected in Ethiopia.

a. The House of Peoples Representatives (HPR)

Constitutions establish and structure governments and design procedures on how representative democracies function. In a parliamentary democracy, the parliament is the sovereign political body in charge of making laws and performing an oversight function for executive bodies. In the context of Ethiopia, the parliament "operated under the shadow of a one- or dominant-party system, neither of which is conducive to vibrant democratic governance, legislative process, or outcomes."[107] There were terms of office of the HPR where almost all seats were controlled by the ruling party. In the June 2021 election, the ruling Prosperity Party won in a landslide, taking 94 percent of the seats, indicating the continuity of one-party dominance in the HPR.

Regarding the issue of whether the HPR fostered democracy and the rule of law, empirical evidence reveals that the Ethiopian parliamentary system did not adequately consolidate democracy to discharge constitutionally bestowed duties and responsibilities.[108] The famous Anti-Corruption Special Procedure and Rules of Procedure (Amendment) Proclamation 239/2001, which denies bail rights to defendants suspected of crimes of corruption, is a good example. This law was enacted overnight to deny specific individuals the right to bail, indicating that the legislative process was subjected to the control of the executive. One may also mention the enactment by parliament of repressive laws repealed in the aftermath of the 2018 change of leadership that were used to stifle political dissent.[109] Its continuous rubber-stamping role to the executive implies that the politics instrumentalizes the law to achieve its ends.

b. The Council of Constitutional Inquiry/House of Federation

Constitutional interpretation is a mechanism for ensuring the supremacy of the constitution by reviewing the constitutionality of laws, decisions, and practices of government entities. Looking into the practice of constitutional review can show whether or not the constitutional system has been taken seriously.

In the context of Ethiopia, the power of constitutional interpretation is bestowed oddly on the House of Federation, assisted by the Council of Constitutional Inquiry.[110] The House of Federation is frequently criticized for being too political to impartially umpire constitutional disputes and unfit to interpret fundamental rights provisions of the Constitution.

There are cases where the constitution-interpreting body failed to genuinely examine the constitutionality of laws and the decisions of government organs over the past twenty-eight years. This does not mean that the HoF/CCI has not passed any decision that favors human rights or enabled the Constitution to play its role of limiting the powers of the government, constituting government, or strengthening unity, etc.

The case of the Constitutionality of the Anti-Corruption Proclamation, which denies bail to suspects, otherwise called the "Siye Abrha" case, could be mentioned.[111] The applicants were detained for an alleged crime of corruption by the Federal Police Commission and denied bail pursuant to the amended anti-corruption law. They argued that the right to bail is a constitutional right and hence, the legislators cannot deny the right apart from setting principles for the judiciary to decide on bail issues. The council looked into the case and decided that the legislation does not violate the constitutional rights of the applicants on the grounds that the HPR can restrict bail based on the types of crimes.

The *Coalition for Unity and Democracy v. Prime Minister Meles Zenawi Asres (Former)*[112] could also help discern how the constitutional-review mechanisms were instrumentalized for justifying political decisions instead of checking the powers of the executive. This case involved a decree of the then prime minister that banned demonstrations and assembly following the 2005 election. This decree was challenged by the Coalition for Unity and Democracy in court.

The Federal First Instance Court referred the case to the CCI for constitutional interpretation. The CCI looked into the case and inquired whether the decree issued by the prime minister violated the Constitution and whether there were sufficient conditions to issue the decree.[113] The CCI justified the prime minister's decree as constitutional, arguing that the prime minister, as the highest-ranking executive, has the power to assess the conditions on the ground for the decree. The detailed arguments of the CCI show the extent to which it went to justify the decree instead of assessing it from a human-rights perspective.

Another case where the regime was tested was Customs Regulation No. 155/2008, which allowed summary dismissal of employees at the absolute discretion of the director general of the Customs and Revenue Authority, without any review mechanism for the dismissed employees. This case was filed to the CCI twice: the first was submitted by former employees of the Authority dismissed by the director, and the second was submitted in 2016 by the Federal Civil Service Administration Tribunal.[114] While the same issue was presented to the same CCI, but in a *different political context*, the decisions were different. In the second case, the CCI found that the provision of the regulation that prohibits the review of decisions of the director by courts violates the right to access to justice of employees. Despite in fact reversing its earlier decision, neither the CCI nor the HoF mentioned the constitutional issue that was submitted and dismissed previously.

In the case of *Melaku Fenta et al* v. *Public Prosecutor of the Federal Anti-Corruption and Ethics Commission,*[115] the Federal High Court referred the case to the CCI to interpret whether Customs Proclamation No. 859/2014, which decriminalizes some acts with which the defendants were charged, could be applied. The acts that were decriminalized included abuse of power and misuse of duty-free privileges. As the defendants were charged with these acts, the court held that Article 182 of the proclamation provides that pending cases should continue with the previous law, the constitutionality of which should be reviewed in light of Article 22(2) of the FDRE Constitution and Article 5 of the Revised Criminal Code of Ethiopia. The CCI argued that Article 182 of Proclamation 859/2014 begins with the phrase "without prejudice to," and hence this same proclamation has excluded the defendants not benefit from its retrospective application.[116]" The CCI concluded that the phrase "without prejudice to" should be interpreted "in light of the aims of the law and other relevant laws on customs" and hence does not violate Article 22(2) of the Constitution.[117] The CCI's conclusion negates the very idea of entrenching fundamental rights in the Constitution by subjecting its arguments based on the aim of the law in question. However, the HoF reversed this decision of the CCI, arguing that

Article 182 of Proclamation No. 859/2014 should not be interpreted to deny the defendants their rights by the retrospective application of the law.

Other cases where the constitution interpreting bodies approached constitutional issues includes the constitutional complaints submitted by the individuals who were charged with the anti-terrorism law brought against journalists, religious leaders, and many others.[118] All these cases showed that the institutions empowered to interpret the Constitution tilted towards political interests of the incumbent than entertaining constitutional issues impartially. The partiality may relate to the very design of empowering a political body to interpret the constitution. Added to this, the absence of institutional independence of the CCI and the character of appointees within the CCI. This trend has affected the enforcement of human rights as well as the entrenchment of rule of law, functions that constitutions aspire to achieve in democratic societies.

c. The Federal Judiciary

One of the basic notions of the separation of powers is the fact that the judiciary has a crucial role in resolving disputes impartially, ensuring the rule of law, and in setting limits to power.[119] Commentators have repeatedly observed that the judiciary in Ethiopia never survives the regime that has established it, implying its partiality to the incumbent regimes.[120] Even if the constitution recognizes an independent and impartial judicial body, it has never been realized. Apart from this, it is evident to witness some laws that ousted courts from the ambit of their judicial function by restricting the laws' reviewability by ordinary courts. One could mention the famous Customs Regulation, which prohibited courts from reviewing the decision of the director of Customs Authority to fire an employee he/she suspects of corruption.[121]

The courts remained weak in checking the exercise of power by the judiciary. "The overall assessment is that the judiciary has not yet defined its role, has not properly interpreted the concept of separation of powers, and has not yet become a key organ for enforcing human rights."[122] There are legal and practical evidences that the judiciary has never been independent[123] as claimed by the regimes that established them.

2. Conclusion

In modern democracies, the conventional roles of constitutions include establishing and constituting governments, allocating powers among government entities, limiting such powers, and protecting fundamental rights. These roles, however, are different in authoritarian regimes, replacing them with functions of governing (coordinating multiple stakeholders, controlling subordinates, eliciting cooperation from subjects), and as "billboards, blue prints, window dressing."[124]

Therefore, the functions constitutions play may differ based on the motives of the makers (founders), which dictate what to use them for. In democratic regimes, constitutions set the order by which democratic values and fundamental rights are promoted and settled.

Constitutions play the additional roles of solidifying national unity in multiethnic societies. In light of this, the constitutions enacted in Ethiopia were instrumentalized by the respective regimes to establish their "legitimacy." The FDRE Constitution was considered by the framers as a political contract among NNPs, making it merely a political document recording the "negotiations among the NNPs." Even if the founders properly understood the functions of constitutions in democracies, they instrumentalized the Constitution to install their political ambitions regardless of whether that would inhibit the Constitution from serving those functions. It is evident in the making process that the dominance of the EPRDF severely affected the legitimacy of the Constitution as a non-inclusive and nonparticipatory process.

The practice since the enactment of the Constitution also proves that the FDRE Constitution did nothing more than perpetuate its founders' power. The enactment of repressive laws and their implementation, the weak constitutional review mechanism and weak judiciary indicate that the Constitution did not enable the rule of law and did not limit the powers of the government entities. The constitutional-review mechanism served the political interests of the incumbent instead of checking government powers in light of the Constitution.

Both the design and practical issues discussed in this paper indicate that the FDRE Constitution functioned in a manner akin to how a constitution in an authoritarian regime is utilized. The ruling parties use the constitution to advance their interests and justify political decisions. In the Ethiopian context, there is a need to reconsider and redefine the idea of a constitution so as to ensure that the document is able to perform the functions that constitutions are normally meant to perform: constrain power, protect fundamental rights, and provide space for a democratic governance.

Notes

1 Denis J. Galligan and Mila Versteeg, "Theoretical Perspectives on the Social and Political Foundations of Constitutions." In: *Social and Political Foundations of Constitutions. Denis J. Galligan and Mila Versteeg, eds.*(Cambridge University Press, 2013), 6.

2 Constitutional efficacy is defined as congruence between norm and behavior, be it that of politicians or ordinary citizens. Assessing constitutional efficacy

requires extensive empirical study. See, for instance, Andrea Pozas Loyo, "What Is 'Constitutional Efficacy?' Conceptual Obstacles for Research on the Effects of Constitutions" *Mexican Law Review* IX, No. 1. 23-44. https://andreapozas-loyo.com/wp-content/uploads/2022/11/2016-what-is-constitutional-efficacy.pdf; Tom Ginsburg and Aziz Z. Huq, eds. *Assessing Constitutional Performance* (Cambridge University Press, 2016).

3 Carl Schmitt, *Constitutional Theory.* Translated and edited by Jeffrey Seitzer (Durham: Duke University Press, 2008), 59.

4 Dieter Grimm, *Constitutionalism, Past, Present and Future.* (Oxford University Press, 2016), p. 90. The word "pactum" refers to "an informal agreement between two or more persons containing one or more promises and usually legally unenforceable even when supported by a sufficient consideration except for certain pacta declared enforceable by praetorian edicts and imperial constitutions if arising out of a lawful cause or inducement." https://www.merriam-webster.com/dictionary/pactum.

5 Martin Laughlin, *The Idea of Public Law* (Oxford University Press, 2003), 2.

6 Hanna Lerner, *Making Constitutions in Deeply Divided Societies* (Cambridge University Press, 2011). 16.

7 Schmitt, *Constitutional Theory.* 59.

8 Schmitt, *Constitutional Theory*, 59.

9 Schmitt, *Constitutional Theory*, 59

10 Martin Loughlin, "Against Constitutionalism" (Harvard University Press, 2022), Roberto Gargarella, "The Law as a Conversation Among Equals" (Cambridge University Press, 2022) review of Mark Tushnet, "Review Essay: For Constitutionalism," (September 4, 2022). *Harvard Public Law Working Paper No*. 23-47, https://ssrn.com/abstract=4209674 or http://dx.doi.org/10.2139/ssrn.4209674. Schmitt argues that democracy requires "first homogeneity and second—if the need arises—elimination or eradication of heterogeneity."

11 Grimm, *Constitutionalism*, 90.

12 Grimm, *Constitutionalism*, 91.

13 Grimm, *Constitutionalism*, 91.

14 Grimm, *Constitutionalism*, 91.

15 Grimm, *Constitutionalism*, 91.

16 Grimm, *Constitutionalism*, 91.

17 Denis Galligan and C. Palmer, "Patterns of Constitutional Thought from Fortescue to Bentham. In: *Constitutions and the Classics: Patterns of Constitutional Thought from Fortescue to Bentham.* Denis Galligan, ed. (Oxford University Press, 2015), 2.

18 Mark Tushnet, "Constitution." In: *Oxford Handbook of Constitutional Law. Michel Rosenfeld and Andras Sajo, eds.* (Oxford University Press, 2012), 226.

19 Tushnet, "Constitution", 226.

20 Grimm, *Constitutionalism,* 93.

21 Grimm, *Constitutionalism,* 93.

22 Grimm, *Constitutionalism,* 93.

23 Thomas Paine, *The Rights of Man* (1791). In: *Writings.* Moncure D. Conway,ed., vol. 2, 1902, reprint.

(1967), 309, as cited in Grimm, *Constitutionalism,* 93.

24 Grimm, *Constitutionalism,* 93.
25 Grimm, *Constitutionalism,* 93.
26 Grimm, *Constitutionalism,* 93.
27 Grimm, *Constitutionalism,* 94. The literal translation of "règlement fondamental qui détermine la manière dont l'autorité publique doit être exercée" is "basic regulation which determines the manner in which public authority is to be exercised."
28 Grimm, *Constitutionalism,* 94. In 1788, during the ensuing public controversy over the organization of the States General, Sieyès issued his pamphlet *Qu'est-ce que le tiers état?* (January 1789; "What Is the Third Estate?"), in which he identified the unprivileged Third Estate with the French nation and asserted that it alone had the right to draft a new constitution. For further discussion, *see https://www.britannica.com/biography/Emmanuel-Joseph-Sieyes, Accessed on December 28, 2022.*
29 Grimm, *Constitutionalism,* 94. The phrases with such connotations include "Grundgesetze," "leges fundamentales," and "Verfassung."
30 Grimm, *Constitutionalism,* 96.
31 Grimm, *Constitutionalism,* 93.
32 Grimm, *Constitutionalism,* 93.
33 Tushnet, "Constitution." 226.
34 Grimm, *Constitutionalism,* 98.
35 Daryl J. Levinson, "Parchment and Politics: The Positive Puzzle of Constitutional Commitment." *Harvard Law Review* 124, No. 3 (January 2011), 659.
36 Levinson, "Parchment", 659.
37 Michel Rosenfeld, "The Rule of Law and the Legitimacy of Constitutional Democracy." *Southern California Law Review* 74 (2001), 1307.
38 Rosenfeld, "Rule of Law", 1307.
39 Rosenfeld, "Rule of Law", 1307.
40 Rosenfeld, "Rule of Law", 1307.
41 Rosenfeld, "Rule of Law", 1307.
42 Rosenfeld, "Rule of Law", 1310. A society is "pluralistic-in-fact" if it is divided along ethnic, religious, linguistic, cultural, or ideological lines, or, in other words, if it is comprised of different groups who do not share the same values or conceptions of the good. Even a homogeneous society with an individualistic conception of the good, in which every person is viewed as entitled to pursue his or her own individual good, would qualify as being pluralistic-in-fact.
43 Mark Tushnet, *Advanced Introduction to Comparative Constitutional Law* (Edward Elgar Publishing Limited, 2014), 10.
44 Tushnet, *Comparative Constitutional Law,* 10.
45 Tushnet, *Comparative Constitutional Law,* 10.
46 Tushnet, *Comparative Constitutional Law,* 11. (emphasis added).
47 Conor Casey, "Constitutional Design and the Point of Constitutional Law." *The American Journal of Jurisprudence* 67, No. 2 (December 2022), 8. https://doi.org/10.1093/ajj/auac010.
48 Larry Alexander, "What Are Constitutions, and What Should (and Can) They Do?" In: *What Should Constitutions Do?* Ellen Frankel Paul, et. al., eds. (Cambridge University Press, 2011), 3.

49 Alexander, "What are Constitutions", 4.
50 Alexander, "What are Constitutions", 4.
51 Alexander, "What are Constitutions", 4.
52 Alexander, "What are Constitutions", 5.
53 Asem Khalil, "From Constitution to Constitutionalism in Arab States: Beyond Paradox to Opportunity."
1 *Transnational Legal Theory* 1 (2010), 421-423.
54 Tushnet, "Constitution.". 222.
55 Michel Rosenfeld, "Modern Constitutionalism as Interplay between Identity and Diversity." In: *Constitutionalism, Identity, Difference and Legitimacy*, Michel Rosenfeld, ed. (Duke University Press, 1994), 4.
56 Rosenfeld, "Modern Constitutionalism", 4.
57 Alexander, "What are Constitutions", 4.
58 Alexander, "What are Constitutions", 4.
59 Alexander, "What are Constitutions", 4–5.
60 Alexander, "What are Constitutions", 4-5.
61 Tom Ginsburg and Alberto Simpser, "Constitutions in Authoritarian Regimes: Introduction." In: *Constitutions in Authoritarian Regimes. Comparative Constitutional and Policy Series*. Tom Ginsburg and Alberto Simpser, eds. (Cambridge University Press 2014), 1.
62 Ginsburg and Simpser, "Constitutions in Authoritarian Regimes", 2.
63 Ginsburg and Simpser, "Constitutions in Authoritarian Regimes",6.
64 See Adam Przeworski, "Ruling against Rules." In: *Constitutions in Authoritarian Regimes.* Comparative Constitutional and Policy Series. Tom Ginsburg and Alberto Simpser, eds. (Cambridge University Press, 2014), 21–35.
65 Ginsburg and Simpser, "Constitutions in Authoritarian Regimes." 6.
66 William Wade, *Constitutional Fundamentals*, (Stevens and Suns Publishers, 1980),.1, https://socialsciences.exeter.ac.uk/media/universityofexeter/schoolofhumanitiesandsocialsciences/law/pdfs/Constitutional_Fundamentals.pdf. Wade identified these four aspects of the constitution to examine the causes of dissatisfaction with the constitution and provide reform areas.
67 Tsegaye Regassa, "Making Legal Sense of Human Rights: The Judicial Role in Protecting Human Rights in Ethiopia," *Mizan Law Review*, 3 no.2, (2009) 298.
68 Articles 37-65 of the 1955 Constitution.
69 Chapter 5 established the Ministerial Offices and Chapter 6 established the legislative chambers.
70 See Articles 93, 94, 101 of the 1955 Constitution.
71 Assefa Fiseha (PhD), *Federalism and the Accommodation of Diversity in Ethiopia: A Comparative Study*, (Wolf Legal Publishers, 2006), 45.
72 Assefa, *Federalism and Accommodation of Diversity*, 78.
73 See for instance, Chi Mgbako (et. al.), "Silencing the Ethiopian Courts: Non-Judicial Constitutional Review and its Impact on Human Rights." *Fordham International Law Journal* 32, No. 1 (2008), 259–97. Available on https://ir.lawnet.fordham.edu/ilj/vol32/iss1/15/. Last visited Dec. 07, 2023.
74 Paragraph 1 of the Preamble of the FDRE Constitution.

75 Gosaye Ayele, "Revisiting the Justifications for Vesting Constitutional Interpretation Authority in the House of Federation." *Ethiopian Journal of Federal Studies* 4, No. 1 *(2017)*, 58.

76 Berihun Adugna Gebeye, "Toward Making a Proper Space for the Individual in the Ethiopian Constitution." *Human Rights Review* 18, 439–58. Available on DOI 10.1007/s12142-017-0471-5. Last visited Nov. 20, 2023.

77 Gosaye Ayele, "Constitutional Interpretation". 59.

78 Paragraph One of the Preamble of the FDRE Constitution.

79 See, for instance, Tsegaye Regassa, "The Making and Legitimacy of the Ethiopian Constitution: Towards Bridging the Gap between Constitutional Design and Constitutional Practice." *Afrika Focus* 23, No. 1 (2010).

80 See Gedion T. Hessebon, "The Precarious Future of the Ethiopian Constitution." *Journal of African Law*

57, No. 2 (2013), 215–33. Available at https://www.jstor.org/stable/24734906.

81 Takele Bekele Bayu, "Is Federalism the Source of Ethnic Identity-Based Conflict in Ethiopia?" *Insight on Africa* 14, No. 1 (2022), 104. Available at https://doi.org/10.1177/09750878211057125.

82 John Abbink, "Ethnic-Based Federalism and Ethnicity in Ethiopia: Reassessing the Experiment after 20 years." *Journal of Eastern African Studies* 5, No. 4 (2011), p 612. Available at http://dx.doi.org/10.1080/17531055.2011.642516.

83 Damian Chalmers, "Constituent Power and the Pluralist Ethic.", In: *The Paradox of Constitutionalism: Constituent Power and Constitutional Form*, ed. Martin Laughlin & Neil Walker (Oxford University Press, 2007), 291

84 Tsegaye Regassa, "The Making and Legitimacy of the Ethiopian Constitution" 91-92.

85 Tsegaye Regassa, "The Making and Legitimacy of the Ethiopian Constitution" 91-92.

86 James C.N. Paul, "Ethnicity and the New Constitutional Orders of Ethiopia and Eritrea.", In: *Autonomy and Ethnicity: Negotiating Competing Claims in Multi-ethnic States*, ed. Yash Ghai, (Cambridge University Press, 2000)189.

87 Abbink, "Ethnic Based Federalism", 600.

88 Tom Ginsburg, *Judicial Review in New Democracies Constitutional Courts in Asian Cases*, (Cambridge University press, 2003), 24

89 Ginsburg, *Judicial Review*, 24.

90 Id. p. 25

91 Jon Elster, "Forces and Mechanisms in the Constitution-Making Process", *Duke Law Journal*, 45, (1995) 364-396.)

92 See further Tsegaye Regassa, "The Making and Legitimacy of the Ethiopian Constitution" 3.

93 This solution was propagated by the TPLF as an offspring of the Ethiopian Student Movement by defining the 'National Question' focused on the "operation of nationalities," that is, a ruling elite dominantly from one nationality controlling power, resources and narrowly defining the values and institutions of the state as a main cause. See Assefa Fisseha, *Federalism and Accommodation of Diversity*, 100.

94 Article 4 of Proclamation No. 24/1992, Constitutional Commission Establishment Proclamation.
95 Assefa Fisseha, *Federalism and Accommodation of Diversity*, 290.
96 See generally Minutes of the Constituent Assembly, Volume 02.
97 Minutes of the Constituent Assembly, Volume05, p. 04.
98 Tushnet, *Comparative Constitutional Law*, 10.
99 Tushnet, *Comparative Constitutional Law*, 14
100 See generally Belachew Girma Degefie, "Constitutional Adjudication by Parliaments: Lessons from Comparative Experience", *Mizan Law Review*, 12 no.1 (September 2018): http://dx.doi.org/10.4314/mlr.v12i1.2
101 Minutes of the Constituent Assembly, Volume 5, p. 04.
102 Minutes of the Constituent Assembly, Volume 5, p. 04.
103 Minutes of the Constituent Assembly, Volume 5, p. 04.
104 See for instance Chi Mgbako (*et al*), "Silencing the Ethiopian Courts" 84.
105 Gosaye Ayele, "Constitutional Interpretation" 40.
106 Gosaye Ayele, "Constitutional Interpretation" 40.
107 Kassahun Berhanu, "Parliament and Dominant Party System in Ethiopia.", In M. *African Parliaments: Between Governance and Government*, ed. A. Mohamed Salih. (Palgrave Macmillan, 2005) 162-182. See also Mercy Fekadu Mulugeta, *Parliament in Ethiopia: Participation, Representation and Resistance*, (Routledge, 2023): https://www.taylorfrancis.com/books/oa-mono/10.4324/9781003293163/parliament-ethiopia-mercy-fekadu-mulugeta.
108 See for instance, Solomon Tefera, "The Role of Parliament in Consolidating Democracy Under the Federal Democratic Republic of Ethiopia (FDRE) Constitution", *Research on Humanities and Social Sciences*, 11, no.9 (2021): https://www.iiste.org/Journals/index.php/RHSS/article/viewFile/56457/58297.
109 The Anti-terrorism Proclamation No. 652/2009, Civil Societies Proclamation No. 632/2009, Mass Media Proclamation could be mentioned as illustration.
110 Article 62 of the FDRE Constitution.
111 Constitutional Complaint submitted challenging the constitutionality of the Anti-Corruption Special Procedure and Rules of Procedure (Amendment) Proclamation 239/2001 article 51(2) that denies bail to defendants suspected of crime of corruption, CCI decision made December 11, 2003, (Unpublished).
112 *Coalition for Unity and Democracy v. Prime Minister Meles Zenawi Asres*, Fed. First Instance Ct., Lideta Div., File No. 54024 (Decision of 3 June 2005) (26 Ginbot 1997 E.C.)
113 For detailed analysis of the case, see Abdi Jibril Ali, "Distinguishing Limitation on Constitutional Rights from their Suspension: A Comment On The Cud Case", *Haramaya Law Review*, 1 no. 2 (2012): ,Https://Www.academia.edu/En/4086928/Distinguishing_limitation_on_constitutional_rights_from_their_suspension_a_comment_on_the_cud_case.
114 *The Federal Civil Service Administration Tribunal v. Federal Revenues and Customs Authority et al*, Council of Constitutional Inquiry File No. 2189/09 and House of Federation File No. 72/11, unpublished.
115 File No. 1421/07 Council of Constitutional Inquiry, unpublished.

116 Article 182 of Proclamation 859/2014 provides that 'cases pending before the effective date of the proclamation shall be disposed in accordance with the previous laws.
117 File No. 1421/07 Council of Constitutional Inquiry, unpublished.
118 See for instance CCI File No. 2356/2009, where the CCI upheld article 32(b) of the Anti- Terrorism Proclamation No. 652/2009 and article 4 of Witness Protection Proclamation No. 699/2010.
119 See Assefa Fiseha (PhD), "Separation of powers and its implications for the judiciary in Ethiopia", *Journal of Eastern African Studies*, 5 no. 4 (2011): https://doi.org/10.1080/17531055.2011.649576.
120 Assefa Fiseha (PhD), "Constitutional Adjudication in Ethiopia: Exploring the Experience of the House of Federation (HoF)", *Mizan Law Review*, 1 no. 1 (2007), 12: https://www.ajol.info/index.php/mlr/article/view/55611.
121 Customs and Revenues Regulation No. 155/2008.
122 Assefa Fiseha, "'Separation of Powers" 702
123 See for instance, Simeneh Kiros Assefa, "Conspicuous Absence of Independent Judiciary and 'Apolitical' Courts in Modern Ethiopia" *Mizan Law Review*, 15 no 2, (2021) 379-418, http://dx.doi.org/10.4314/mlr.v15i2.3 last visited May 05, 2023.
124 Ginsburg and Simpser, "Constitutions in Authoritarian Regimes", 2-5.

Bibliography

Books

Laughlin, Martin. *The Idea of Public Law.* (Oxford University Press, 2003).

Lerner, Hanna. *Making Constitutions in Deeply Divided Societies* (Cambridge University Press, 2011).

Ginsburg, Tom. *Judicial Review in New Democracies Constitutional Courts in Asian Cases*, (Cambridge University press, 2003).

Ginsburg, Tom and. Huq, Aziz Z. ,eds. *Assessing Constitutional Performance.* (Cambridge University Press, 2016).

Grimm, Dieter. *Constitutionalism, Past, Present and Future.* (Oxford University Press, 2016).

Fiseha, Assefa. *Federalism and the Accommodation of Diversity in Ethiopia: A Comparative Study*, (Wolf Legal Publishers, 2006).

Mulugeta, Mercy Fekadu. *Parliament in Ethiopia: Participation, Representation and Resistance.* (Routledge, 2023): https://www.taylorfrancis.com/books/oa-mono/10.4324/9781003293163/parliament-ethiopia-mercy-fekadu-mulugeta

Schmitt, Carl. *Constitutional Theory.* Translated and edited by Jeffrey Seitzer (Durham: Duke University Press, 2008).

Paine, Thomas. *The Rights of Man* (1791). In: *Writings.* Moncure D. Conway, ed., vol. 2, 1902, reprint. (1967).

Tushnet, Mark. *Advanced Introduction to Comparative Constitutional Law* (Edward Elgar Publishing Limited, 2014.

Wade, William. *Constitutional Fundamentals*, (Stevens and Suns Publishers, 1980). https://socialsciences.exeter.ac.uk/media/universityofexeter/schoolofhumanitiesandsocialsciences/law/pdfs/Constitutional_Fundamentals.pdf.

Book Chapters

Alexander, Larry. "What Are Constitutions, and What Should (and Can) They Do?" In: *What Should Constitutions Do?* Edited by Ellen Frankel Paul, *et. al.*, 1-24. Cambridge University Press, 2011.

Berhanu, Kassahun. "Parliament and Dominant Party System in Ethiopia." In: *African Parliaments: Between Governance and Government*, edited by A. Mohamed Salih, 162-182. Palgrave Macmillan, 2005.

Chalmers, Damian. "Constituent Power and the Pluralist Ethic.", In *The Paradox of Constitutionalism: Constituent Power and Constitutional Form*, edited by Martin Laughlin & Neil Walker, 291-314. Oxford University Press, 2007.

Galligan, Denis and Palmer, C. "Patterns of Constitutional Thought from Fortescue to Bentham. In: *Constitutions and the Classics: Patterns of Constitutional Thought from Fortescue to Bentham.* Edited by Denis Galligan. (Oxford University Press, 2015).

Ginsburg, Tom and Simpser, Alberto. "Constitutions in Authoritarian Regimes: Introduction." In: *Constitutions in Authoritarian Regimes. Comparative Constitutional and Policy Series*. Edited by Tom Ginsburg and Alberto Simpser, 1-20. Cambridge University Press 2014.

J. Galligan, Denis and Versteeg, Mila. "Theoretical Perspectives on the Social and Political Foundations of Constitutions." In: *Social and Political Foundations of Constitutions.* Edited by Denis J. Galligan and Mila Versteeg, 3-50. Cambridge University Press, 2013.

Przeworski, Adam. "Ruling against Rules." In: *Constitutions in Authoritarian Regimes. Comparative Constitutional and Policy Series*. Edited by Tom Ginsburg and Alberto Simpser, 21-35. Cambridge University Press, 2014.

Paul, James C.N. "Ethnicity and the New Constitutional Orders of Ethiopia and Eritrea." In *Autonomy and Ethnicity: Negotiating Competing Claims in Multi-ethnic States*, edited by Yash Ghai, 173-192. Cambridge University Press, 2000.

Rosenfeld, Michel. "Modern Constitutionalism as Interplay between Identity and Diversity." In: *Constitutionalism, Identity, Difference and Legitimacy.* Edited by Michel Rosenfeld, 3-38. Duke University Press, 1994.

Tushnet, Mark. "Constitution." In: *Oxford Handbook of Constitutional Law.* Edited by Michel Rosenfeld and Andras Sajo. (Oxford University Press, 2012).

Journal Articles

Abbink, John. "Ethnic-Based Federalism and Ethnicity in Ethiopia: Reassessing the Experiment after 20 years." *Journal of Eastern African Studies* 5, No. 4 (2011): 596–618. http://dx.doi.org/10.1080/17531055.2011.642516.

Ali, Abdi Jibril. "Distinguishing Limitation on Constitutional Rights from their Suspension: A Comment On The CUD Case", *Haramaya Law Review,* 1 no. 2 (2012): 1-28. https://www.academia.edu/en/4086928/distinguishing_limitation_on_constitutional_rights_from_their_suspension_a_comment_on_the_cud_case.

Assefa, Simeneh Kiros. "Conspicuous Absence of Independent Judiciary and 'Apolitical' Courts in Modern Ethiopia" *Mizan Law Review*, 15 no 2, (2021): 379-418, http://dx.doi.org/10.4314/mlr.v15i2.3

Ayele, Gosaye. "Revisiting the Justifications for Vesting Constitutional Interpretation Authority in the House of Federation." *Ethiopian Journal of Federal Studies* 4, No. 1 (2017): 37-61.

Bayu, Takele Bekele. "Is Federalism the Source of Ethnic Identity-Based Conflict in Ethiopia?" *Insight on Africa* 14, No. 1 (2022): 104–125. https://doi.org/10.1177/09750878211057125.

Casey, Conor. "Constitutional Design and the Point of Constitutional Law." *The American Journal of Jurisprudence* 67, No. 2 (December 2022): 173–197. https://doi.org/10.1093/ajj/auac010.

Daryl J. Levinson, "Parchment and Politics: The Positive Puzzle of Constitutional Commitment." *Harvard Law Review* 124, No. 3 (January 2011). 659-746. https://harvardlawreview.org/print/vol-124/parchment-and-politics-the-positive-puzzle-of-constitutional-commitment/

Degefie, Belachew Girma. "Constitutional Adjudication by Parliaments: Lessons from Comparative Experience", *Mizan Law Review*, 12 no.1 (September 2018): 30:70. http://dx.doi.org/10.4314/mlr.v12i1.2

Elster, Jon. "Forces and Mechanisms in the Constitution-Making Process", *Duke Law Journal,* 45, (1995) 364-396. https://scholarship.law.duke.edu/dlj/vol45/iss2/2

Fiseha, Assefa. "Separation of powers and its implications for the judiciary in Ethiopia", *Journal of Eastern African Studies*, 5 no. 4 (2011): 702–715. https://doi.org/10.1080/17531055.2011.649576

Fiseha, Assefa. "Constitutional Adjudication in Ethiopia: Exploring the Experience of the House of Federation (HoF)", *Mizan Law Review*, 1 no. 1 (2007): 1-32. DOI: https://doi.org/10.4314/mlr.v1i1.55611

Gebeye, Berihun Adugna. "Toward Making a Proper Space for the Individual in the Ethiopian Constitution." *Human Rights Review* 18, (2017): 439–58. DOI 10.1007/s12142-017-0471-5.

Hessebon, Gedion T. "The Precarious Future of the Ethiopian Constitution." *Journal of African Law;* 57, No. 2 (2013): 215–33. https://www.jstor.org/stable/24734906.

Khalil, Asem. "From Constitution to Constitutionalism in Arab States: Beyond Paradox to Opportunity." *Transnational Legal Theory* 1 No. 1 (2010). 421–451. https://fada.birzeit.edu/bitstream/20.500.11889/2108/1/04%20Khalil.pdf

Loyo, Andrea Pozas, "What Is 'Constitutional Efficacy?' Conceptual Obstacles for Research on the Effects of Constitutions." *Mexican Law Review* IX, No. 1. (2016): 23-44. https://andreapozas-loyo.com/wp-content/uploads/2022/11/2016-what-is-constitutional-efficacy.pdf

Mgbako, Chi (*et. al.*). "Silencing the Ethiopian Courts: Non-Judicial Constitutional Review and its Impact on Human Rights." *Fordham International Law Journal* 32, No. 1 (2008), 259–97. https://ir.lawnet.fordham.edu/ilj/vol32/iss1/15/.

Regassa, Tsegaye. "Making Legal Sense of Human Rights: The Judicial Role in Protecting Human Rights in Ethiopia." *Mizan Law Review*, 3 no.2, (2009): 288-330. https://doi.org/10.4314/mlr.v3i2.54014

Regassa, Tsegaye. "The Making and Legitimacy of the Ethiopian Constitution: Towards Bridging the Gap between Constitutional Design and Constitutional Practice." *Afrika Focus* 23, No. 1 (2010): 85-118. DOI: 10.21825/af.v23i1.5038.

Rosenfeld, Michel. "The Rule of Law and the Legitimacy of Constitutional Democracy." *Southern California Law Review* 74 (2001). 1307-1352. https://dl.icdst.org/pdfs/files/85d89797b7c0a4ac5322cfa68b2e6ad1.pdf

Tefera, Solomon. "The Role of Parliament in Consolidating Democracy Under the Federal Democratic Republic of Ethiopia (FDRE) Constitution", *Research on Humanities and Social Sciences*, 11, no.9 (2021): 31-36. https://www.iiste.org/Journals/index.php/RHSS/article/viewFile/56457/58297

Book Review

Loughlin, Martin. "Against Constitutionalism" (Harvard University Press, 2022), Gargarella, Roberto. "The Law as a Conversation Among Equals" (Cambridge University Press, 2022) Review of Mark Tushnet, "Review Essay: For Constitutionalism," (September 4, 2022). *Harvard Public Law Working Paper No.* 23-47. https://ssrn.com/abstract=4209674 or http://dx.doi.org/10.2139/ssrn.4209674.

Website Content

"What Is the Third Estate?" https://www.britannica.com/biography/Emmanuel-Joseph-Sieyes, Accessed December 2022.

Chapter 7

Constitutional Reform In Ethiopia: Opportunities & Obstacles[1]

Alemayehu Fentaw Weldemariam[2]

Prelude

A Tale of Three Preambles: The Evolution of Ethnic Federalism in Ethiopia

The history of modern Ethiopian constitutional development can be told as a tale of three radically different preambles, each reflecting the shifting locus of constituent power over time. This journey begins with the 1931 Constitution of Imperial Ethiopia. Before 1931, the Kibre Negest served as the "societal script" (Levine 2000, 100) of the Ethiopian Empire, functioning almost as a constitution. Often referred to as Ethiopia's "national epic" (Ibid), the Kibre Negest is a lengthy text redacted into Ge'ez around 1320 that chronicles the lineage of Ethiopian monarchs descending from King Solomon. Crafted in the fourteenth century, this narrative was designed to bolster the idea of a holy land and a divinely anointed sacred dynasty. It is "suffused with patriotic feelings and serves from first to last to glorify the land of Ethiopia and proclaim a proud Ethiopian identity" (Ibid, 101).

The Kibre Negest is a national epic in three key respects. First, it contains a myth of the founding of the Ethiopian nation, embodying crucial formative events in the national history, similar to how the Aeneid glorifies Rome's origins. Second, it expresses central psychological conflicts experienced during the evolution of a society. Third, it serves as a "literary expression of what Talcott Parsons calls a complex of constitutive symbolism," providing "cultural legitimation both for the societal enterprise as a whole and for privileged positions within the society" (Ibid).

The great significance accorded to the Kibre Negest by the Ethiopian people and their kings is evident from this communication. Emperor Yohannes IV's urgent request to Lord Granville underscores the Kibre Negest's vital role in Ethiopian governance and cultural identity. As Emperor Yohannes stated: "There is a book called 'Kivera Negust' [Kēbra Nagast], which contains the Law of the whole of Ethiopia, and the names of the Shums [Chiefs], Churches, and Provinces are in this book. I pray you find out who has got this book, and send it to me, for in my country my people will not obey my orders without it" (Budge 2004, xxvii). The return of one of the looted copies in 1872 further underscores its importance to nineteenth century Ethiopian society and authority.

In 1930, Tekle Hawariat Tekle Mariyam, an Ethiopian intellectual who spent his formative years in Russia under the mentorship of Count Nikolai Leontiev and as a cadet at prestigious Russian military academies, was commissioned to draft the maiden constitution. He modeled his draft on Japan's Meiji Constitution of 1889 (Zewde 2001, 110; Teklemariam 2006, 77-143; 400-402). On July 16, 1931, Emperor Haile Selassie declared the first constitution with these words: "...in order to enable Our State and Our people to obtain a high place in History, We have, after Our elevation to the Imperial Throne, and in the second year of Our Reign, in the Year of Grace 1923 (A.D. 1931), unasked and of Our own free will, decreed the present State Constitution." The emperor continued to extol his divine mission and plan for his empire in the preamble of Ethiopia's first Constitution, asserting his divine right and the nation's future prosperity through a centralized, absolute monarchy.

The 1931 Constitution established the legal framework for existing absolutism in Ethiopia. The debate preceding its promulgation highlighted the ongoing struggle between centralism and regionalism. The hereditary nobility, except for Ras Emeru Haile Selassie, advocated for retaining their regional prerogatives, while the new elite, composed of ministers and recently appointed nobles, argued for merit-based appointments. The compromise, influenced by the emperor, favored centralism, granting hereditary rights over tributary land to the nobility as a concession (Zewde 2001, 140).

Despite the constitutional attempts at reform, including the revised Constitution of 1955, the ageing Emperor Haile Selassie was unable to address the increasing demands for change. The Revised Constitution of 1955 included the most detailed succession plans any Ethiopian emperor had ever made. However, the 1974 revolution not only ended Haile Selassie's long reign but also the millennia old Solomonic dynasty. Ironically, Haile Selassie, who started his career fighting against conservatives, ended up as a symbol of resistance to change. His downfall highlighted the final crisis of Ethiopia's feudal system (Ibid, 209).

The nationalities question, heavily influenced by the Ethiopian Students Movement of the 1960s and 1970s, led to organized national liberation insurgencies against the military junta post-revolution. In response, the Derg introduced the 1976 National Democratic Revolution Program, aiming for equal recognition of all nationalities' rights, with an emphasis on cultural, linguistic, and religious autonomy. In March 1983, the Derg established the Institute for the Study of Ethiopian Nationalities, directed by Yayehirad Kitaw and staffed by academics from Addis Ababa University. The Institute's primary task was studying nationalities and drafting the PDRE constitution. The draft constitution followed a Leninist model, emphasizing Ethiopia's multi-national history and a state founded on workers' and peasants' alliance and democratic centralism (Clapham 1988, 93).

The 1987 Constitution restructured the state, granting autonomy to territories such as Eritrea, Assab, Tigray, Dire Dawa, and the Ogaden, while dividing the rest of the country into twenty-four administrative units based on the Institute's research (Constitution 1987, Chapter 8).

The preamble of the Constitution of the People's Democratic Republic of Ethiopia declared: "We, the Working People of Ethiopia, based on a centuries-old glorious history, are engaged in a great revolutionary struggle to extricate ourselves from our current state of backwardness, and to transform Ethiopia into a socialist society with a high level of development where justice, equality and social prosperity prevail..." (Constitution 1987, Preamble).

In 1991, the dictatorship of Colonel Mengistu Haile Mariam was toppled by the Ethiopian People's Revolutionary Democratic Front (EPRDF), led by the Tigray People's Liberation Front (TPLF). This marked the beginning of Ethiopia's federalization process, with the constituent units organized along ethnic lines. In 1995, the ethnic federal Constitution was adopted. This time, the preamble began not with "We, Emperor Haile Selassie," nor "We, the Working People," but with "We, the Nations, Nationalities and Peoples of Ethiopia."

> *We, the Nations, Nationalities and Peoples of Ethiopia: Strongly committed, in full and free exercise of our right to self-determination, to building a political community founded on the rule of law and capable of ensuring a lasting peace, guaranteeing a democratic order… [h]ave therefore adopted, on 8 December 1994, this Constitution. (Constitution 1995, Preamble).*

The 1995 Constitution established nine states and a self-administering Addis Ababa as members of the federation, alongside Dire Dawa, which has been self-administering de facto despite lacking a constitutional basis. The Constitution delineated powers both vertically and horizontally, enumerating the powers of the federal and state governments separately and reserving residual powers for the states. Sovereignty was vested in the Nations, Nationalities, and Peoples, granting them the right to self-determination, including secession (Article 39). This provision recognized the right to statehood for ethnic groups without established states, leading to the creation of additional states. Consequently, the total number of federation members increased to twelve with the dissolution of the Southern Nations, Nationalities, and Peoples Region, resulting in the formation of Sidama, Southwest Ethiopia, South Ethiopia, and Central Ethiopia Regional States.

The House of Federation holds the power to interpret the Constitution, organize referenda on statehood demands, and resolve inter-state boundary disputes. However, these boundaries remain major conflict fault-lines, with deadly conflicts occurring between regions such as Amhara and Tigray, Oromia and Somali, and Somali and Afar.

This complex historical backdrop sets the stage for my chapter, highlighting the evolving nature of Ethiopia's constitutional journey and tracing its origins to the advent of the politics of identity rooted in resentment. I want to close the prelude with a question implicated by the tale it told: is it high time for "We the People"?

Introduction

It must be stated at the very outset that Ethiopia is at a constitutional crossroads. The aim in this chapter is to make the case for constitutional reform and point out the challenges that constitutional reformers shall encounter if and when they embark on the path. Let me begin with a poignant quote from

Immanuel Kant, which was popularized by the eminent British political theorist and historian of ideas Isaiah Berlin: "Out of the crooked timber of humanity, no straight thing was ever made" (Berlin 2013, 446)." Berlin quotes Kant in adumbrating the eighteenth century advent of nationalism, which he says came to dominate much of Europe in the nineteenth century before anyone was able to foretell it. He writes:

> *There was one movement which dominated much of the nineteenth century in Europe and was so pervasive, so familiar, that it is only by a conscious effort of the imagination that one can conceive a world in which it played no part: it had its partisans and its enemies, its democratic, aristocratic and monarchist wings, it inspired men of action and artists, intellectual elites and the masses; but, oddly enough, no significant thinkers known to me predicted for it a future in which it would play an even more dominant role. Yet, it would, perhaps, be no overstatement to say that it is one of the most powerful, in some regions the most powerful, single movement at work in the world today; and that some of those who failed to foresee this development have paid for it with their liberty, indeed with their lives. This movement is nationalism (Ibid, 425).*

By nationalism, Berlin refers to "something more definite, ideologically important and dangerous" (Ibid, 431) For him, it is the conviction that individuals belong to a distinct human group with a unique way of life shaped by common elements. He sees society as an organic entity with common goals, asserting their supremacy in the face of conflicting values. Berlin emphasizes that these organic patterns cannot be artificially created and that the nation, not the individual, is the essential unit for human realization. Nationalists prioritize beliefs and actions based on the values of their group or nation, viewing them as the most compelling reasons for pursuing certain policies or ways of life. The separation from one's nation is seen as a loss of meaning and fulfillment, leading to a sense of aimlessness and nostalgia (Ibid).

Like Isaiah Berlin, Jill Lepore in *This America: The Case for the Nation* recognizes the dangers of nationalism by distinguishing between patriotism and nationalism, the latter being "less a love for your own country than a hatred of other countries and their people and a hatred of people within your own country who don't belong to an ethnic, racial, or religious majority" (Lepore 2019, 132). She writes that patriotism is not the same as nationalism: "Patriotism is animated by love, nationalism by hatred" (Ibid).

Steven Smith distinguishes patriotism from both nationalism and cosmopolitanism. Nationalism, according to Smith, has evolved into an ideology of grievance and resentment, often breeding contempt for those outside the dominant ethnic group. Patriotism, on the other hand, is rooted in loyalty and respect, akin to the love one has for family. It is about gratitude for one's birthplace and the traditions that shape one's identity. Cosmopolitanism, in contrast, emphasizes a global humanity and can lead to alienation from one's national culture (Smith 2021, 30-31). Smith argues that patriotism, nationalism, and cosmopolitanism can be understood along a continuum of excess and deficiency. Nationalism represents an excess of patriotism, manifesting as an unconditional attachment to one's country or cause, often leading to ideologies of resentment and exclusion. In contrast, cosmopolitanism exhibits a deficiency of patriotism, advocating for a global citizenship that can overlook or undermine national loyalties and traditions. Patriotism, positioned as a mean between these extremes, is characterized by a balanced love and loyalty to one's country, without exclusivity or alienation (Ibid, 106-109).

The kind of patriotism that I advocate for in this chapter is a robust form of "constitutional patriotism," a concept popularized by Jürgen Habermas. It centers on building collective identity through the principles of a liberal democratic constitution rather than national culture or global cosmopolitanism. Initially introduced by Dolf Sternberger in postwar West Germany, this idea gained traction through Habermas despite criticisms of its abstract nature and German-specific focus. Beyond its original context, constitutional patriotism holds promise for fostering political unity in multicultural societies and for guiding political integration in entities like the European Union. It is also seen as a potential source of cohesion in societies emerging from conflict or transitioning to democracy (Müller and Scheppele, 67–71).

Jan-Werner Müller traces the roots of constitutional patriotism, as later developed by Jürgen Habermas, to Karl Jaspers' post-war interventions. In *The Question of German Guilt,* Jaspers distinguished between criminal, moral, political, and metaphysical guilt, advocating for "collective responsibility" rather than "collective guilt." He believed democratic identity and social integration in Germany required acknowledging collective responsibility for past atrocities. Jaspers suggested that confronting a negative past could foster social cohesion and speculated on the future of German identity, contemplating a transition towards a cosmopolitan "world citizen" or a temporary "pariah" status. He emphasized that dealing with German guilt necessitated free public communication and the "solidarity of charitable struggle," ideas that influenced later thinkers like Sternberger and Habermas (Müller 2007, 16-18).

In a similar vein, Steven Smith argues that constitutional faith, as exemplified in the Federalist Papers, represents a new form of patriotism suitable for a modern representative republic. This patriotism is not solely about heroic self-sacrifice, as seen in the Declaration of Independence, but also involves the everyday maintenance of constitutional liberties such as the rule of law and due process. Constitutional faith is characterized by Americans' unique veneration for their Constitution. This faith stands in contrast to both nationalism, which breeds contempt for out-groups, and cosmopolitanism, which can lead to alienation from national culture. While constitutional faith involves reverence for the past, it also allows for constitutional change, albeit through an arduous process, to adapt to evolving social needs. Smith argues that protecting the Constitution from frequent changes fosters a sense of veneration that transcends partisanship and establishes the Constitution as the foundation of American national identity (Smith 2021, 99-105).

Smith argues that patriotism is a form of deep, affective loyalty, different from mere obligation or fidelity. It's not just loyalty to the people but also to the constitutional form of a nation, such as liberal democracy. He criticizes Habermas's idea of constitutional patriotism for lack of the emotional depth and cultural attachment that Smith believes are essential to true patriotism. Smith's ethos patriotism is rooted in a deep-seated commitment to the republic and a way of life, embodying both thought and feeling, and reflecting the character traits and habits that define a society's ethos (Ibid, 157-162).

In contrast, Habermas's constitutional patriotism emerged in postwar Germany as a response to hyper nationalism and the atrocities of the Third Reich. It seeks to base national identity on loyalty to the basic law of the country rather than on traditional notions of blood and soil, aiming to distance patriotism from the darker aspects of nationalism. However, Smith argues that this thin theory of legitimacy lacks the emotional and cultural elements that are crucial for a meaningful sense of patriotism (Ibid).

The foregoing paves the way for this exploratory chapter, laying out the opportunities and obstacles to constitutional reform in present-day Ethiopia. I fear that both ethnonationalism and Pan-Ethiopian nationalism have proved to be equally fatal. Ethiopia's experiment with ethnic federalism has demonstrated that ethnonationalism can be as potent and dangerous an ideology as Pan-Ethiopian nationalism, if not more so. By ethnonationalism, I mean the nationalisms of the diverse ethnic groups that make up a multinational state such as Ethiopia—for example, Amhara, Oromo, Tigrayan, etc. By nationalism, I mean one that relates to the nation-state, as in Pan-Ethiopian nationalism. So much blood has been spilled in the name of both types of nationalism.

The polarization of contemporary Ethiopian politics is rooted in part in the identity politics of the Ethiopian Student Movement of the late 1960s and early 1970s, which in turn is rooted in part in the competing historical narratives of Ethiopia that are reminiscent of what Friedrich Nietzsche calls "an excess of history" (Nietzsche 1997, 67). To blame for this state of affairs is our historians' failure to offer a new common history of Ethiopia, besides our politicians who borrowed the Stalinist ideology of national self-determination and misapplied it to the demand for recognition of the diverse ethnicities of the multiethnic state, rather than in a colonial context, without qualification. In examining the interplay between history and our well-being, Nietzsche underscores the pivotal role history plays in shaping individuals, societies, and cultures. He presents three distinct ways in which people relate to history: as active participants, as preservers and admirers, and as suffering individuals seeking emancipation. This trinity aligns with three methods of historical engagement: monumental, antiquarian, and critical (Ibid).

Nietzsche critiques the monumental method for its potential for deception and manipulation. He suggests that this approach, when wielded by the powerless, can incite chaos, instigate conflicts, and distort historical understanding. It becomes a tool for disguising resentment as admiration for past greatness. Antiquarians, by focusing solely on preserving the past, face the danger of becoming stagnant and losing interest in the future while critical history engages in the agony of the past to the exclusion of the glory. There isn't one right method; each approach has its place and can be used together under suitable conditions. Yet, if these methods are applied incorrectly, it may result in negative outcomes, comparable to the proliferation of "devastating weeds" (Nietzsche 1997, 72) that can plunge society into an abyss. Drawing on Nietzsche's insights, I argue that there's a monumental historical narrative that has dominated the Ethiopian intellectual landscape for so long, which retells the story of Ethiopia's past glory or greatness, animating chauvinistic Pan-Ethiopian nationalism. While the antiquarian narratives of the chroniclers of the kings of the past have made reforms unthinkable, the critical historical narratives have been feeding the jingoistic ethnonationalism of groups such as the TPLF and OLF, fueling up inter-ethnic conflicts and threatening to tear the integrity of the country at its seams, in its collision with chauvinistic Pan-Ethiopian nationalism.

Transitioning from the philosophy of history to political theory, it becomes clear that my defense of ethnic federalism is limited in scope, aligning with Professor Andreas Eshete's approach and interpreting it through the lens of John Rawls's nonideal theory (Eshete 2001, 78-79). Rawls, in his seminal work "A Theory of Justice," posits that a just society should be grounded on principles of liberty, equality, and fairness, which are collectively agreed upon through a hypothetical "original position" (Rawls 1971 [1999], 15-18; 102). In this thought experiment, individuals deliberate from behind a "veil of ignorance," (Ibid, 118-122) unaware of their own advantages or social positions. The outcome leads to principles that would be chosen by free, rational, and equal citizens.

However, Rawls also recognized that the real world lacks the ideal conditions of his theories. Therefore, in *The Law of Peoples* (1993) and *Justice as Fairness: A Restatement* (2001), Rawls addresses what he calls nonideal theory. This examines how societies that fall short of strict justice can still move in morally desirable directions under less-than-ideal circumstances. Nonideal theory deals with issues of partial compliance, burdened societies facing unfavorable conditions, and societies attempting to remedy historical injustices. It provides philosophical guidance on how to make progress towards more just institutions and social reforms within actual diverse societies facing deeply entrenched challenges (Rawls 1993; 2001).

It should now become evident that ethnic federalism lacks a defensible foundation under Rawls's ideal theory. In other words, it is not a political system universally applicable to all peoples and cultures across time and space, viewed from the eternal perspective "sub specie aeternitatis." There exists no ontological or metaphysical grounding for ethnic federalism as a political theory or practice, and I make no such claims. Instead, my defense of ethnic federalism stemmed from considering Ethiopia's conditions of diversity and the weight of its historical burdens (Eshete 2001, 78-79). It is not only that ethnic federalism is indefensible as a permanent feature of a stable liberal democratic state, but also that it is not my intention to do so.

The civil war that broke out in November 2020 has starkly revealed the limitations of ethnic federalism in Ethiopia. It is evident that we need to gradually move away from this system. One viable path forward is to embrace constitutional patriotism. Constitutional patriotism emerged in response to the atrocities of World War II and the culpability of German nationalism in those crimes. Similarly, Ethiopia must adopt this principle to prevent a relapse into an even more catastrophic humanitarian crisis. Constitutional patriotism can help us foster a shared national identity based on democratic values and the rule of law, rather than ethnic divisions, thereby promoting peace and stability in our country. It does so by transcending the dangers associated with the populist ethnonationalism of the diverse ethnic groups and the chauvinistic Pan-Ethiopian nationalism embraced by a section of society.

The chapter is organized in six interconnected sections, each contributing to a comprehensive exploration of the case for and challenges to constitutional reform in Ethiopia. The initial section provides a succinct historical account, paving the way for the subsequent analysis. It then transitions into two successive sections dedicated to illuminating the theoretical underpinnings of ethnic federalism. Drawing from John Rawls's political philosophy, it delves into the realms of non-ideal theory and modus vivendi, framing ethnic federalism as an institutional practice under unfavorable conditions. In the fourth section, attention turns to a critical examination of challenges confronted by constitutional reformers, offering insights into the intricate complexities inherent in this process. Following this, the fifth section proscribes the scope of the reform and introduces three specific areas of potential reform: Constitutional review, the right of secession, and the Constitutional amendment procedure. Finally, the chapter culminates in concluding remarks that succinctly encapsulate key findings and insights. This structured exploration aims to contribute meaningfully to the ongoing discourse on constitutional reform in Ethiopia, providing valuable insights for scholars, policymakers, and those actively engaged in Ethiopia's political development.

Ethiopia's Historical Context

To assess Ethiopia's experiment with ethnic federalism through the twin Rawlsian lenses of nonideal theory and modus vivendi, it is essential to understand the country's complex historical context of diversity, inequities, and conflict. Ethiopia, with a population of more than 115 million, is Africa's second most populous and diverse country, surpassed only by Nigeria. Throughout its history, Ethiopia has witnessed diverse forms of governance, transitioning from a devolved autocratic empire to a centralized state over the past century. Unfortunately, the absence of an inclusive governance system, a contentious constitutional design, and a disregard for constitutionalism have spawned civil conflicts and the emergence of politically mobilized ethno-national divisions. Some groups within Ethiopia advocate for political autonomy and, in extreme cases, secession. Regrettably, the prevailing authoritarian center has failed to adequately address these demands, leading to protracted conflicts (Weldemariam and Fiseha 2023, 140).

To comprehend the recent political developments, it is essential to briefly review Ethiopia's modern history. A critical lens to analyze Ethiopia's political history is the evolution of the center/periphery cleavage, which highlights the pivotal role of elites in the political development framework. The framework first developed by sociologist Edward Shils was adopted in comparative politics by Arend Lijphart, who contends that the center encompasses the authoritative part of society, while the periphery represents the hinterland subject to its authority (Shils 1982, 93-109). Lijphart argues that societies with deep cleavages like ethnicity are divided into a dominant center and a marginalized periphery, leading to power imbalances. For him, plural societies often experience political domination by a center (Lijphart 1977;1989, 33-48). The struggle between the center and periphery, and the centripetal and centrifugal forces, has defined Ethiopia's political trajectory since the end of the Era of Princes (1769-–1855) and the rise of Emperor Tewodros II. Subsequent rulers, Emperor Yohannes IV (who, despite his Tigrayan origin, made Amharic the court language), Emperor Menelik II, Emperor Haile Selassie, and President Mengistu Hailemariam, pursued Ethiopian unification, firmly shaping the country's political landscape.

As Donald Levine rightly observes in the Preface to the second edition of his classic study of Ethiopia, entitled Greater Ethiopia, "Throughout Ethiopia's history, there have been tensions between the national center and diverse regional and ethnic groups" (Levine 2000, xiv). The trajectory of the center-periphery cleavage, especially during Haile Selassie's reign, reveals the circumstances that led to the emergence of federalism in Ethiopia. Haile Selassie's reign was characterized by a persistent power struggle between the monarchy and the nobility. The introduction of the first constitution in 1931 aimed to assert the crown's absolute authority and resolve the center-periphery rivalry.

The constitution primarily regulated the relationship between the monarchy and the nobility, with a grudging inclusion of rights and duties for citizens. The parliament, consisting of a Senate and a Chamber of Deputies, reflected the belief that the public was not ready for active political participation. The Senate was composed of nobles chosen by the emperor, while the Chamber of Deputies was elected indirectly, with property qualifications excluding commoners (Zewde 2001,141).

The constitution solidified the emperor's absolute powers in appointments, justice, war declarations, and land grants. Nobles could no longer engage in treaties or receive foreign decorations without the emperor's permission. The signing ceremony for the constitution symbolized the nobility's diminished status, as loyalists of humble backgrounds presided over prominent nobles (Ibid, 143).

Ras Haylu of Gojjam resisted the constitution, but his political maneuvers and excessive taxation alienated his supporters, leading to his downfall. His involvement in a plot to free Iyyasu led to his imprisonment and wealth confiscation by Haile Selassie. By 1935, central control over the provinces was nearly complete, with progressive provincial administrations established in model provinces like Chercher. However, Tigray remained outside direct central control, ruled by Ras Seyoum Mengesha and Ras Gugsa Araya, despite attempts to integrate them through marriage alliances with the Shawan ruling house (Ibid, 143-146).

This centralization process reached its zenith after 1941, leading to unprecedented state power and unbridled autocracy (Zewde 1991, 201). Despite the 1955 Revised Constitution ostensibly granting basic freedoms, it primarily served to consolidate absolutism, emphasizing the emperor's sacred and indisputable powers. To make sense of this absolutist ambition of consolidation, one need not look further than Article 2 of the Revised Constitution, which stipulates that:

> *The imperial dignity shall remain perpetually attached to the line of Haile Selassie, whose line descends without interruption from the dynasty of Menelik First, son of the Queen of Sheba, and King Solomon of Jerusalem (Constitution 1955, Art. 2).*

Moreover, the Revised Constitution entrenched conservative positions, with Amharic designated as the sole official language and the Ethiopian Orthodox Church as the state religion. It was during the last years of the imperial era that the seeds of ethnonationalism -that later germinated during the Derg era were sown. After the monarchy's overthrow in 1974, ethnonationalist liberation movements, which had their roots in the Ethiopian Student Movement, came to replace the nobility as dominant regional forces. The irony is that ethnonationalism arose around the same time when many scholars declared that Ethiopia had achieved nationhood (Levine 1974; Wimmer 2013). This juxtaposition highlights the tension between the concept of a unified national identity and the emergence of strong ethnic identities seeking autonomy or recognition. This situation underscores the complexities of nation-building in a multi-ethnic state like Ethiopia, where the consolidation of a national identity can coexist with, or even provoke, the rise of ethnonationalist sentiments.

Successive regimes pursued autocratic systems and employed repressive measures to suppress opposition. The peak of this repression occurred during the Derg's rule from 1974 to 1991, marked by the crushing of dissent and the ruthless imprisonment or execution of hundreds of thousands of individuals. By the late 1980s, long-standing grievances culminated in ethnic insurgencies and civil unrest, further exacerbating the already intricate landscape of ethnic tensions, authoritarianism, and violence.

The demise of the Derg in 1991 led to the ascendance of ethno-nationalist liberation movements, assuming control of the center, at war's end. This historical cleavage gave rise to two models of state restructuring: the centralist-authoritarian approach and the federalist-democratic paradigm. However, a closer analysis reveals that the seemingly democratic federation relied more on repression than genuine persuasion.

This complex historical legacy forms the basis for understanding the essence of ethnic federalism in Ethiopia, as it represents a response to the multifaceted challenges posed by historical cleavages. A deep understanding of these historical underpinnings is crucial for forging a path towards a more inclusive and stable political landscape, promoting genuine democratic principles.

The center-periphery competition, a long -existing rivalry between the unitarist and the federalist, the Pan-Ethiopian nationalist, and the ethno-nationalist, explains the mechanics and dynamics of the regime change that took place in April 2018.

Ethnic Federalism as a Nonideal Solution

Ethnic federalism was not envisioned as the ideal political system for Ethiopia's multiethnic society; rather, it emerged from unfavorable political conditions. Andreas Eshete encapsulates this dilemma in his reflections at a 1997 international conference: "For a country that takes pride in its self-image as a nation-state, a self-image nourished for over a century in political life and for far longer in imaginary life, ethnic federalism was bound to be deeply unsettling. It is difficult to keep one's countenance before the threat that one's cherished self-image is on the verge of fading to nothing" (Eshete 2001, 72).

No attempt is made here to venerate this theoretical construct. Eminent thinkers from across the globe had gathered to discuss Ethiopia's predicament in the 1990s but mapping a country's future is not the work of theorists and purists. Instead, it is up to the political forces of the day to compromise and shape the proposed order to their interests and needs. It is almost inevitable that the result will be a fudge, and that is what our imperfect federation is.

The 1995 constitution addressed the demands of diverse nationalities for recognition, a rallying cry of the Marxist student movements of the 1960s and 70s, and of the ethnonational insurgencies rooted in those campaigns. Now, a quarter of a century later, we have almost come full circle. The origins and legitimacy of ethnic federalism are being contested by many, to the point of risking the disintegration of the state.

In 1993, the Inter Africa Group (IAG) convened a symposium in Addis Ababa on the making of the new Ethiopian Constitution, bringing together eminent figures such as Joshua Cohen, C. Edwin Baker, Elaine Scarry, Dean James Paul, and Mr. Paul Henze. This gathering included world-renowned lawyers, historians, political scientists, Ethiopianists, Africanists, and philosophers. Additionally, various foreign government agencies and non-profits were involved in consulting work for the Constitutional Commission, chaired by Kifle Wodajo. Notably, USAID as part of its Ethiopia Democracy/Governance Support Project commissioned a study by Harvard political scientist Samuel Huntington, whose contribution was particularly insightful regarding constitutional design (USAID Report 1994).

In his paper, Huntington observed: "Ethnicity is likely to be central to Ethiopian political parties, elections, and politics generally. Attempts to suppress ethnic identifications or to prevent ethnic political appeals are not likely to be successful" (Huntington 1993, 14). Despite recognizing the significance of ethnicity in Ethiopian politics, Huntington hesitated to endorse it as a primary organizing principle: "Drawing regional boundaries along ethnic lines… supplements what is unavoidable with what is undesirable…The combination of ethnic territorial units and ethnic parties…cumulates cleavages and can have a disastrous effect on national unity and political stability" (Ibid, 16).

Huntington noted a dilemma: while it was undesirable to exclude ethnic groups from government representation, banning their formation was equally problematic. He suggested that a dominant party capable of appealing across ethnic lines was essential for maintaining cohesion: "If a broad-based, ideological party exists which appeals across ethnic lines, then ethnic territorial lines can be tolerated" (Ibid, 16).

However, the ruling party, EPRDF, had been until it was dissolved and merged to form the Prosperity Party in November 2019, a broad-based coalition of four ethnic parties at the center, supported by satellite affiliated ethnic parties in the peripheries, in a federation whose constituent units were drawn along ethnic lines, combining the two undesirable elements that Huntington dreaded. For nearly three decades, EPRDF applied centripetal force to an ethnically demarcated federation, turning itself into a dominant party, maintaining relative stability and economic development despite increased repression and occasional challenges.

Huntington recommended a mixed electoral system, combining proportional representation with mechanisms like run-off elections, to encourage multiethnic cooperation while reflecting Ethiopia's diverse society. He suggested federalism or a highly decentralized unitary state to manage regional diversity and prevent any single group from monopolizing power. To avoid ethnic conflict and promote national unity, Huntington advised against formal ethnic representation in government, instead advocating for political and electoral systems that encourage multiethnic coalitions and appeals. This approach aimed to balance democratic values with the practicalities of governance in a diverse and developing country like Ethiopia (Ibid, 12-18).

The Constitution of the Federal Democratic Republic of Ethiopia (FDRE, 1995) established a federal and parliamentary government, granting sovereign power to the "Nations, Nationalities, and Peoples of Ethiopia" and declaring the Constitution as supreme, overriding any conflicting law.

Chapter Three of the Constitution outlines fundamental rights, including the right of self-determination for nations, nationalities, and peoples, including secession. However, the House of Federation (HoF), a political body representing ethnonational groups, is responsible for enforcing these rights and has become a critical platform in controlling the center and interpreting the Constitution.

The Constitution divides governmental power vertically and horizontally. Vertically, it divides power between the federal government and the regional state governments and horizontally among the three branches of government, namely the legislative, executive, and judiciary. However, the divisions are not neat as they fuse legislative and executive powers. As Andreas Eshete aptly observed, "The parliamentary system embraced in the new Constitution eliminates a clear separation of executive and legislative powers. The absence of a fully-fledged institution of judicial review renders the courts an uncertain source of remedy against executive and legislative abuse" (Eshete 2001, 81).

Ethiopia's experience with federalism can be divided into six phases. The first phase, 1991-–1994, is the transitional period, which marks the beginning of the federalization process. Following the fall of the Derg, the Ethiopian Peoples' Revolutionary Democratic Front (EPRDF) initiated the federalization of Ethiopia by setting up the Transitional Government of Ethiopia (TGE) in 1991.

The original sin that was committed in the course of the negotiations to set up the transitional government more than the power-sharing arrangement was the formula for the allocation of the seats in the Council. Commenting on this defect, Kifle Wodajo, Chairman of the Constitutional Drafting Commission, writes:

> *One issue that became particularly contentious was how and in what proportion the different forces opposed to the Derg would be represented in any transitional government. After all, there were some groups whose contribution to the struggle was very marginal, while others had been in the forefront of trying to topple the previous regime. The EPDRE came closest to offering a formula — although it was clear that the formula reflected its own role in the struggle —when it suggested that representation in the transitional government would be on the basis of the contribution that each opposition group had made to the Derg's downfall. The principal deviation from this formula*

> *was advanced by the OLF, which proposed that there should be a United Nations interim administration during the transition. This position may, at least in part, reflect the fact that fighting on the southern front, where the OLF was active, was not as intense as on the northern front, where it was clear that the final battles would be fought. Disagreement on this issue between the EPDRF and the OLF was the beginning of an acrimonious relationship that hampered the constitution-making process until the end (Wodajo 2001, 134-135).*

The first phase involved adopting the Transitional Charter that mandated ethnic federalization through devolution of the previously highly centralized unitary state, drafting a constitution, and decentralizing administrative and fiscal authority. Despite initial consideration of confederation, the TGE abandoned this approach, allowing Eritrea's secession in 1993. Recounting how the constitution-making process was affected by OLF's withdrawal, Kifle Wodajo, Chair of the Constitution Drafting Commission, writes, the "effort was tarnished by disagreements between the EPDRF and the OLF, which led to the latter boycotting the process. Nonetheless, the process helped produce a document that does not preclude a future reconciliation between these parties" (Wodajo 2001, 141). However, Kifle did not seem to see that the seeds of the future conflicts were sown by Proclamation No. 7, establishing ethnic-based sub-national governments. Andreas Eshete presciently argued:

> *A striking feature of the statute is that it defines regions almost exclusively by reference to ethnic identity. If the statute is upheld by the new constitution, Ethiopia will become a federation of self-governing ethnic communities. The strength of nationalist movements and their political entrenchment naturally arouses a fear that the citizenry and the political society will be fractured into separate ethnic communities. The cleavages and the fears they incite are susceptible to exploitation by elites intent on acquiring or preserving power and privilege. The danger, then, is that cultural divisions are liable to frustrate the realization of the rights of equal and free citizenship which a constitutional democracy promises (Eshete 1993, 10-11).*

The 1995 Constitution allowed states to establish their administrative hierarchy, and despite subsequent proclamations, misunderstandings persisted. The elections during this period faced challenges, marked by the EPRDF's dominance and key opposition parties' withdrawal. Disagreements over the future state's vision and ethnic autonomy led to boycotts. The Constituent Assembly election in 1994 saw the narrowing of the political space, complicating the top-down strategy of ethnic federalism. Despite debates, the Constituent Assembly ratified the Constitution in December 1994, establishing the FDRE. The 1995 elections, boycotted by major ethnic-based parties, intensified polarization and demands for secession by the OLF once again (Cohen 1995, 157-188).

The second phase, 1995-–2005, witnessed internal conflicts within the ruling coalition, particularly a split within the TPLF and the consolidation of TPLF dominance under Meles Zenawi's leadership. Notable changes included removing shadowy advisors from regional positions and revising the synoptic state constitutions en masse.

The third phase, 2005-2012, saw the re-opening of the political space, enabling anti-ethnic federalist parties to challenge the constitutional order. However, following the 2005 disputed elections, Meles focused on consolidating power by closing the political space and redirecting the EPRDF system towards national development. This approach, at times, led to tension with the Oromo population due to excessive emphasis on development over democratic principles. This period culminated in EPRDF's claim to total victory in the 2010 elections.

The fourth phase began in 2012 with the passing of Prime Minister Meles Zenawi, leading to a succession struggle within the EPRDF leadership, resulting in Hailemariam Desalegn's appointment as the new prime minister. For the first time, two more deputy prime ministers were appointed, which were later dropped quietly, and PM Desalegn saw himself surrounded by the old guard EPRDF heavyweights as advisors. These changes solidified the narrative of TPLF's dominance until April 2018.

The fifth phase involved three years of street protests, initially demanding Muslim religious freedom, which evolved into the Oromo First movement, supported by Amhara youth in Gondar, ultimately leading to Prime Minister Hailemariam Desalegn's resignation.

In the sixth phase, Abiy Ahmed emerged as a key figure within the EPRDF leadership in 2018, due to the anticipated successor, Lemma Megersa, lacking the required parliamentary seat. Abiy Ahmed promised extensive reforms, garnering broad domestic and international praise, but hegemonic political parties and centralized and increasingly personalized decision-making have limited the promise of self-government. Growing tensions between Abiy's government and the TPLF escalated into armed conflict following the replacement of the EPRDF with the Prosperity Party, removing the TPLF's influence. The conflict erupted in November 2020 due to severed relations, the TPLF's regional election assertion, and rejection of the federal government's legitimacy.

The trajectory of Prime Minister Abiy Ahmed offers a sobering case study on the challenges of managing identity politics rooted in resentment, nationalism turbocharged by populism, and illiberal democratic backsliding. Ethiopia under Meles Zenawi's leadership was previously cited as an illiberal democracy by Fareed Zakaria (1997, 22-43). Abiy's accession to power was initially lauded by Western leaders and journalists as a departure from illiberal democracy and ethnic-based politics. Journalists like Tom Gardner portrayed Abiy as a liberal democratic reformer for Ethiopia's fractured society (Gardner 2018). As political scientist Barbara F. Walter observed, "Abiy seemed to be a democrat's dream. He promised free and fair elections, instituted a more legitimate and inclusive political system, and invited long-exiled Oromos to return home. His reforms were, according to an American foreign service officer in Addis Ababa, 'beyond our wildest dreams'" (Walter 2022, 35).

However, subsequent developments in Ethiopia under Abiy's tenure have prompted a re-evaluation of his true ideology and impact. The devastating wars in Tigray, Amhara, and Oromia, potential state collapse, and the concentration of personalized power around Abiy have led figures like Gardner to reconsider their portrayal of the once-celebrated liberal democratic reformer as a nearly dictatorial figure undermining Ethiopia's democratic transition (Gardner 2024).

The Ethiopian experience serves as a stark reminder of the double-edged nature of identity politics—recognizing group identities while risking the exacerbation of inter-ethnic conflict and exclusionary nationalism. It highlights how democratically elected leaders buoyed by populist fervor can gradually erode pluralism and amass power in ways that betray their original democratic reformist platforms. The fragility of Ethiopia's transition reaffirms that populism, while channeling legitimate grievances, is an unstable foundation for lasting democratic progress when divorced from robust liberal values like minority rights, checks on power, and government accountability.

Given Ethiopia's challenges, comprehensive constitutional reform is vital to break the cycle of conflict. Drawing from successful federal models, Ethiopia should de-emphasize ethnicity, and strengthen separation of powers, checks and balances, and mechanisms for conflict prevention. Prioritizing national unity and inclusive governance is crucial for building a resilient nation celebrating diversity and fostering peace.

Rawls's nonideal theory underscores the need to reform unjust social systems to promote equity. In the case of Ethiopia, ethnic federalism represents an effort to address past injustices against marginalized groups. While it may not eradicate all injustices, proponents argue that ethnic federalism has moved

Ethiopia in a more just direction concerning the representation and rights of marginalized peoples.

From the perspective of nonideal theory, a crucial goal in divided societies is to reduce conflicts and promote peaceful coexistence among diverse communities. Ethiopia's ethnic federal system can potentially serve as an institutional mechanism to better manage tensions through self-rule provisions. Granting ethnic groups control over regional governance and local affairs can foster ethnic cooperation within the national framework, allowing groups to have a stake in the system while maintaining state integrity.

However, Ethiopia's ethnic federalism also faces significant criticisms and challenges. Decentralizing state power along ethnic lines may entrench divisive ethnic politics and identities, potentially undermining national integration and citizenship in favor of narrow ethnic affiliations. Moreover, decentralization has intensified competition between groups for regional control, resources, and contested borders. For example, Adeno Addis argues that the inclusion of the right of secession in Article 39 creates a constitutional framework that undermines the development of a stable and cohesive national identity. By allowing nations, nationalities, and peoples to exercise the right to secede, it becomes challenging to foster a sense of unity and collective identity among diverse groups. Furthermore, Addis suggests that the right of secession can be exploited by ethnonationalists- as a tool for strategic extortion, potentially leading to conflicts over resources and power allocation. The constitutional provision, in his view, provides a legal language that can be used by certain groups to advance their own interests and exert pressure on the central government. Another aspect of his critique is that the right of secession may lead to the displacement of residents belonging to other ethnic or linguistic groups. Adeno argues that ensuring a majority vote in favor of secession could incentivize ethnonationalists- to forcibly remove or discourage individuals from different ethnic backgrounds from residing within a particular state. This perpetuates a sense of exclusion and makes people feel like strangers in their own country. Overall, Adeno argues that the right of secession, as enshrined in the Ethiopian Constitution, has detrimental effects on the national body politic. He believes it intensifies divisions, hinders the development of a unified Ethiopian identity, and raises concerns about the potential misuse of the provision for personal or group interests (Addis 2020).

While the nonideal theory justification frames ethnic federalism as a pragmatic diversity -management political arrangement, it remains a subject of heated debate. Juggling the cultivation of ethnicity at the regional and local levels while fostering a shared national identity is an ongoing challenge for Ethiopia. Analyzing Ethiopia's complex ethnic federal system through Rawls's nonideal theory lens provides greater normative insight. The nonideal perspective recognizes ethnic federalism as an imperfect but pragmatic attempt to accommodate diversity, mitigate conflict, and remedy historical injustices against marginalized ethnic groups in deeply divided societies. Advocates view this as a means to empower marginalized groups and address past injustices through self-determination in their respective regions. However, critics rightly point out the risks of entrenching ethnic differences and undermining national integration. They argue that ethnic federalism has opened a Pandora's box of insecurity in the country, and for some, it is an enabler of systemic and widespread identity-based violence, even a ticking time bomb for the country's disintegration (Selassie 2003, 86).

Ethiopia's future trajectory depends on thoughtful institutional adaptation to balance providing meaningful ethnic inclusion and autonomy while fostering a unifying national identity and shared citizenship. The promises and pitfalls of ethnic federalism must continue to be rigorously debated as Ethiopia navigates its challenging transition. While far from an ideal system, proponents argue that ethnic federalism, at minimum, represents a constructive step towards justice under constrained nonideal conditions. Ensuring long-term stability, democracy, and national unity will require committed leadership and citizens working across ethnic lines to realize common interests.

Ethnic Federalism as Modus Vivendi

In the preceding sections, an attempt has been made to canvass that the FDRE Constitution, far from being the philosopher's ideal for a well-ordered society or universally acceptable to all reasonable persons across cultures and economic levels of development, is rather a modus vivendi. As such, it should not be seen as written in stone but as open to political negotiations and reevaluation over time.

Ethiopia is a country deeply fractured by ethnic and cultural diversity, leading to conflicts and tensions among its communities. In addressing the challenges of coexistence and national unity, the concept of "modus vivendi" emerges as a potential solution, particularly when contextualized within John Rawls's political philosophy.

Rawls focuses on establishing justice principles that can gain agreement among citizens in a democratic society. He distinguishes between "overlapping consensus" and "compromise" as methods of resolving disagreements. Compromise, akin to a "modus vivendi," entails parties accepting terms of political life without necessarily justifying their acceptance based on a specific type of reason (Rawls 2005, xxxixf, lviii, 146f).

In Ethiopia's context, ethnic federalism should not be seen little more than a modus vivendi for the accommodation of the diverse ethnic and religious communities while preserving their distinct identities within a unified multinational state. This approach acknowledges historical grievances and claims of various ethnicities, aiming to construct a pragmatic and inclusive framework for peaceful cohabitation. If viewed this way, reconfiguring the federation, which I believe must take place, or reforming the ethnic-federal arrangement itself, should not be kept out of reach of constitutional reformers when the system fails to function well, as it miserably does, and brings about undesired consequences.

Ethiopia's adoption of ethnic federalism exemplifies a paradigmatic case of compromise. Analogous to Rawls's example of the Edict of Nantes in France, Ethiopia's context involves ethnic groups with disparate historical and territorial claims. These groups have been engaged in conflicts, most recently some seeking to maintain or establish their identity and beliefs as the dominant force within the nation.

The original sin of the current ethnic federal system is that it was the handiwork of the victors of the civil war, who controlled the seats in the Constituent Assembly according to their contribution to the armed struggle to overthrow the military junta. This process excluded many other active political opposition groups, both inside and outside the country, as was later intimated by Chair Kifle Wodajo. Even worse, although it is hard to directly associate members of the Constitution Drafting Commission with the EPRDF, the draft Constitution was modeled upon the Transitional Charter, whose history is so sketchy. Therefore, the implementation of ethnic federalism in Ethiopia was not exclusively the outcome of peaceful democratic negotiations but rather imposed following an extended civil war. This raises concerns about the legitimacy of the compromise and the extent to which it genuinely represents the consent of all involved parties.

The architects devised a federal system that acknowledges the diverse ethnic identities and grants regional autonomy. The Constitution delineated administrative regions based on ethnicity, allowing each group to have its own cultural, linguistic, and political institutions. Adeno Addis emphasizes the significance of the right to use one's language in education and administration, particularly in multilingual states like Ethiopia. The ability for different groups to use their own language enhances their group identity and facilitates their participation in political and cultural life (Adeno 2001, 719-724; 780-783).

Adeno argues that language is important to cultural identity, meaning, and effective communication, providing a detailed discussion within the context of liberal cosmopolitanism (Ibid).

This arrangement embodies a compromise where groups conceded to avoid further violence and safeguard their fundamental interests. However, as Rawls underscores, a modus vivendi is not a comprehensive settlement of fundamental questions relating to justice underlying the basic structure of society. While ethnic federalism offers a pragmatic approach to coexistence, it may not fully align with principles of individual equality and liberty. The emphasis on ethnic identities in the federal system could inadvertently perpetuate divisive narratives and impede the recognition of individual rights beyond their ethnic affiliations.

In light of Rawls's insights, it becomes imperative to assess the limitations of a compromise-based modus vivendi. While it may serve as a steppingstone towards stability and peace, it may necessitate regular reexamination and refinement to ensure it fully upholds principles of justice, individual rights, and inclusivity.

Another defect of that arrangement has been its failure to recognize and protect the identities and rights of people of multi-ethnic or mixed heritage (Aalen 2006, 243, 261) and non-native settlers residing outside of their home states. Huntington highlighted this issue, stating that, "It also seems in appropriate in a country in which a substantial portion of the population are of mixed ethnic background or unsure as which ethnic group they belong to or wish to identify with" (Huntington 1993, 15). Furthermore, it has failed to build national unity around cross-cutting and overarching national symbols and a lingua franca. This systemic failure has been evident in various conflicts of varying intensities in the past three decades and was starkly confirmed during the outbreak of the war in Northern Ethiopia, exposing, among other things, Amharas, Gujjis, Qimants, and Tigrayans to displacements and ethnic cleansings.

In conclusion, Ethiopia's adoption of ethnic federalism embodies a modus vivendi aimed at addressing the country's profound divisions and promoting peaceful coexistence. While it reflects a pragmatic compromise among different ethnic groups, it may not entirely satisfy Rawlsian principles of justice and individual equality. As the nation struggles to strengthen its unity and stability, a critical examination and refinement of the modus vivendi approach becomes essential, ensuring its closer alignment with the ideals of a just and inclusive society. Balancing meaningful ethnic inclusion and autonomy while fostering a unifying national identity and shared citizenship remains a challenging yet crucial endeavor for Ethiopia's future progress.

An understanding of the Constitution as a modus vivendi entails a recognition of the troubles the country has faced in the past decades and exploring if and how the constitutional framework has contributed to the persistent political tension, conflict, patrimonialism, and authoritarianism. Because of the constitutional entrenchment of the nature of the socio-political system, such adaptation requires constitutional deliberation and, as needed, adaptation.

Challenges to Constitutional Reform

It is fascinating to analyze the Ethiopian constitutional system using architectural analogies from cloud computing. By comparing it to a monolithic architecture, we can gain valuable insights into the structure and vulnerabilities of the Ethiopian Constitution.

In cloud computing, a monolithic architecture refers to a design where all system components are tightly interconnected and dependent on one another, and therefore coherent (AWS 2024). Similarly, the Ethiopian constitutional system exhibits a monolithic architecture from its Preamble down to its Amendment Procedure, tightly binding all its elements together—such as the preamble, the sovereignty clause, the bill of rights, self-determination rights, the constitutional review mechanism, and amendment procedures—making piecemeal change difficult.

Ethnicity serves as the overarching organizing principle. Any attempt to de-ethnicize politics or reform a specific component of the Constitution can have unintended consequences, potentially leading to the dismemberment of the entire system rather than a seamless amendment.

To grasp the constitution's monolithic architecture, we must delve into its fundamental elements. The preamble plays a crucial role in establishing the constitution's identity and authorship, explicitly stating that the nations, nationalities, and peoples of Ethiopia are the architects. This declaration emphasizes the collective nature of the constitution's formation and underscores the inherent interconnectedness of its components.

Furthermore, Article 8 of the Ethiopian constitution bestows sovereignty upon the nations, nationalities, and peoples of Ethiopia. This provision solidifies the foundation of the constitutional order and emphasizes the self-governing authority of these entities. Consequently, any alteration or amendment to this sovereignty clause would have far-reaching implications throughout the entire system.

A significant aspect of the Ethiopian constitutional system is the recognition of self-determination rights, as enshrined in Article 39. This provision guarantees the right of each nation, nationality, and people within Ethiopia to exercise self-determination, including the option of secession. Such recognition of self-determination introduces a complex dynamic within the constitutional architecture, as it grants substantial autonomy to these entities while maintaining their connection to the overall system.

Moreover, Article 47 of the Constitution empowers nations, nationalities, and peoples without existing states with the right to demand statehood, further highlighting the intricate interplay between autonomy and unity within the constitutional structure. This provision acknowledges the diverse composition of Ethiopia and reflects the constitutional framework's attempt to address the aspirations and needs of various groups within the country. So far, the number of federated states has reached twelve, with the hatching of three more in the South since the coming to power of Prime Minister Abiy Ahmed, while the demands of many more are still pending.

The constitutional review mechanism, where the House of Federation, as the representative body of the nations, nationalities, and peoples, reviews the constitutionality of legislation or government action, further exemplifies the architectural design aspect of the Constitution.

To solidify the monolithic architecture, Articles 104 and 105 establish stringent requirements for amending the Constitution, particularly Chapter 3 and the amendment procedure itself. These provisions mandate unanimous consent from the state councils, effectively setting a high bar for any proposed alterations. By imposing such a rigorous process, the constitution ensures that any changes to its core elements require complete consensus and prevent hasty or ill-considered alterations. With the benefit of hindsight, it can now be safely concluded that the Constitution was designed with a one-party-dominated multinational state in mind for the long run. However, once the dominant position of the TPLF within the ruling coalition was called into question, the entire constitutional order was rendered unstable.

In conclusion, examining the Ethiopian constitutional system reveals its monolithic architecture. The interconnectedness of its components, the emphasis on collective authorship, the recognition of self-determination rights, and the super-stringent amendment requirements all contribute to its cohesive and resilient structure. Accordingly, it is crucial to acknowledge the inherent challenges in this architecture, as modifications to one component can potentially disrupt the entire system.

Scope of the Constitutional Reform and Proposed Areas of Reform

Richard Albert classifies constitutional reform procedures into three basic categories: the one-size-fits-all model (e.g., the German Basic Law), the dualist model (e.g., the Canadian Constitution), and the tripartite model (e.g., the Ecuadorian Constitution). Each model presents distinct strengths and weaknesses, with the tripartite model authorizing procedures for constitutional amendment, dismemberment, and replacement. Albert illustrates these models using examples like the failed Chilean Constitution, emphasizing the importance of codifying procedures to avoid controversies and political conflicts, as seen in the Kenyan Supreme Court's ruling on the Building Bridges Initiative Constitutional Amendment Bill. The Court declared it a constitutional dismemberment, highlighting the need for clear procedures in constitutional reforms (Albert 2022, 1586).

Albert distinguishes constitutional dismemberment from a constitutional amendment based on the scope of the reform. Constitutional dismemberment involves a fundamental transformation that exceeds the boundaries of the existing constitution, altering its core commitments. In contrast, a constitutional amendment maintains consistency with the constitution's design, framework, and presuppositions. Constitutional amendments serve purposes such as correction, elaboration, reformation, and restoration, each within the existing constitutional framework. The key distinction lies in the extent of change, with amendments preserving unity when the constitution is amended and avoiding transformative alterations (Albert 2018, 4).

Given the heightened risk, the form of constitutional reform proposed, even in ostensibly modest initiatives like the ones I shall suggest, for implementation in Ethiopia, seems to surpass the bounds of mere constitutional amendment. This situation notably aligns with Albert's conceptualization of "constitutional dismemberment" (Albert 2019, 61-92). Among the more audacious reform suggestions are the elimination of ethnicity as the organizing principle and the geographical restructuring of the federation. Importantly, these proposals inadequately acknowledge the rich historical ethnic diversity in the country and the deeply ingrained ethnic consciousness cultivated over the past three decades of Ethiopia's venture into ethnic federalism. While ethnicity may not have held a defining role in the country's history, its undeniable prominence and political significance today cannot be overlooked, as it has taken on a life of its own. Such radical reform propositions verge on constitutional replacement rather than amendment or dismemberment.

It would be salutary if the kind of constitutional dismemberment that the modest reform of Ethiopia's constitution would bring about would be the similar to what Richard Albert argues what the Reconstruction amendments brought about to the US Constitution in the form of dismemberment of the original constitution. Richard Albert argues that the paradigm case of constitutional dismemberment in the United States was the "Reconstruction Amendments" (Thirteenth, Fourteenth, and Fifteenth Amendments). Unlike typical constitutional amendments, these changes did not correct, elaborate, reform, or restore the original meaning of the constitution. Instead, they had a distinct effect, demolishing the infrastructure of slavery in the original constitution. While enacted through constitutional amendment procedures, Albert contends that these changes should have been enacted using procedures specifically designed for constitutional dismemberments, emphasizing the need to distinguish various categories of constitutional change based on their purposes and required thresholds (Ibid).

Ethiopian constitutional reformers are confronted with the uncertainty of whether the original constitution would endure potential dismemberment and what its repercussion on national peace and stability would be like, a political imponderable of highest degree. Advocating for a cautious approach, I propose modest reforms, especially in the aftermath of Ethiopia's descent into civil war. The consideration is that, after addressing the consequences of the conflict, constitutional reform can be pursued with due diligence.

Although the war with Tigray ended with the Permanent Cessation of Hostilities Agreement (PCoHA) signed in Pretoria, South Africa, in November 2022 between the federal government and the TPLF (Reuters 2022), another war has started with the Amhara on the heels of the PCoHA. No doubt, the PCoHA marked a significant political development that would have paved the way for national dialogue, which would have opened an opportunity for comprehensive constitutional reform. Nevertheless, it is not clear how the PCoHA dividend would positively impact constitutional reform dialogues that with the new war raging in Amhara and the counterinsurgency taking place in Oromia Regions. Indeed, it is encouraging to witness the disarmament, demobilization, and reintegration (DDR) efforts being undertaken by the TPLF, with heavy weaponry already handed over to the federal government (Al Jazeera 2023). An Interim Regional Administration has been established (Reuters 2023), and preparations were underway for a comprehensive national dialogue among political parties before the campaigns against the Fano in the Amhara Region were launched.

It is essential to recognize that the ongoing armed conflicts in Ethiopia, including the one concluded with Tigray, have constitutional roots. The first civil war ended in 1991 with the overthrow of the socialist military dictatorship, leading to the drafting and adoption of a federalist constitution that aimed to ensure self-government for diverse ethno-national groups. The second civil war ended in 2022 with the signing of the Pretoria peace accords, opening an opportunity for political dialogue and comprehensive constitutional reform, which is crucial for achieving lasting peace. However, instead of seizing on that opportunity, the federal government seems to have chosen to wage another war, on Amhara.

In conclusion, while the Pretoria peace accords represent a necessary step towards peace, lasting peace in Ethiopia can only be achieved through comprehensive constitutional reform. To emphasize the urgency of the situation, three key areas of reform are highlighted: constitutional review, amendment, and secession. Addressing these areas through a constitutional reform program is vital for Ethiopia's future stability and survival. These areas are chosen for their strategic significance. If constitutional reform in these areas is achieved, nothing else is impossible.

1. Constitutional Review

At the risk of oversimplification, there are two models of constitutional review: the American model and the Austrian model. In the American model, also known as judicial review, ordinary courts have the authority to review and invalidate legislation. On the other hand, the Austrian model of constitutional review operates differently, relying on a specialized court rather than ordinary courts to undertake the task of reviewing and invalidating legislation.

The American model owes its origins to Chief Justice John Marshall, who played a pivotal role in establishing the practice of judicial review through the landmark decision in Marbury v. Madison (1803) (5 U.S. 137). Through this case, Chief Justice Marshall asserted the power of the judiciary to declare legislative acts unconstitutional. This landmark decision laid the foundation for the American system of judicial review, in which ordinary courts possess the authority to assess the constitutionality of legislation. More recent constitutions specifically empower courts to review and invalidate legislation and executive decisions as unconstitutional.

In contrast, the Austrian model of constitutional review is credited to the influential legal theorist Hans Kelsen. During his time as a staff member of the constitution-drafting committee in Austria, Kelsen played a significant role in creating the institution of the constitutional court (Ferejohn 2002, 49-60). Under the Austrian model, this specialized court is entrusted with the responsibility of reviewing and invalidating legislation that is deemed to be inconsistent with the constitution.

While these models differ in the extent of judicial review entrusted to ordinary courts versus specialized constitutional courts, both systems aim to ensure that legislation is consistent with constitutional principles. Chief Justice John Marshall's contributions in establishing judicial review in the American model and Hans Kelsen's role in creating the institution of the constitutional court in the Austrian model have left indelible marks on the practice of constitutional review in their respective jurisdictions (Ibid).

Nevertheless, Ethiopia seems to have adopted a unique approach to constitutional review. It has neither vested the ordinary courts nor created a specialized constitutional court. Unlike the two models, Ethiopia has entrusted the upper chamber of its parliament, the House of Federation (HoF), with the authority to adjudicate constitutionality of legislation and action. The HoF is supported by the Council of Constitutional Inquiry (CCI), consisting of eleven members: the President of the Federal Supreme Court, who serves as its President; the Vice-President of the Federal Supreme Court, who acts as its Vice-President; six legal experts appointed by the President of the Republic based on recommendations from the House of Peoples' Representatives, all of whom must demonstrate professional competence and high moral standing; and three individuals chosen by the House of the Federation from among its members (See Fiseha 2017; Fisseha 2004; Abebe 2013).

However, the politicization of cases involving the separation of powers poses a significant challenge. The HoF, being a majoritarian political body controlled by the ruling party, is susceptible to political manipulation. As Assefa Fiseha presciently observed, "there has been one ruling party at federal and state levels and the HoF's impartiality has not been brought to test. With the emerging multiparty politics, however, it remains to be seen how far the HoF will serve as an impartial adjudicator on important intergovernmental conflicts (Fiseha 2007, 31; Abebe 2013, 68). And Adem underscores the heightened responsibility of Ethiopia's parliamentary system, emphasizing the need for careful consideration in assigning constitutional review power to the legislature to avoid an imbalance in the distribution of powers. He contends, "[g]iven the parliamentary form of government, confining constitutional adjudication to the legislative and political realm excessively empowers political actors, posing a threat to constitutionalism" (Abebe 2013, 83). The true test of the impartiality of the HoF had not arrived until the dispute between the National Election Board of Ethiopia (NEBE) and the House of Peoples' Representatives (HoPR) came to the fore in 2020. The NEBE announced the postponement of national and regional elections due to the COVID-19 pandemic, leading to a nationwide debate on how to resolve the election deadlock (Endeshaw 2020). Seeking constitutional advice, the HoPR turned to the CCI, which recommended extending the term of parliament and regional state councils until the elections could be held once the pandemic subsided.

Critics argued that the CCI's recommendations failed to place appropriate limits on the government' powers during the extension and granted it discretionary authority to determine the election date without a defined timeline (Sahlemariam and Geremew 2020). The HoF's decision to extend its own term revealed, if not confirmed, an existing defect in the design of the Constitution, allowing parliament to be the judge in its own case. Moreover, the HoF's endorsement of the CCI's recommendation showcased a disregard for the principles of federalism and constitutionalism (Weldemariam and Fiseha 2023, 142).

Tigray's strong objection to the HoF's decision escalated the conflict to an irreparable point and provided a catalyst for the subsequent civil war. The TPLF) argued that postponing the elections would be unconstitutional and lead to a power vacuum. It maintained that parliament's mandate would expire on October 10, 2020 and could not be extended under any circumstances. Furthermore, Tigray asserted its right to self-government by holding regional elections (Ibid).

Dismissing Tigray's claims, the HoF declared the Tigray state government's actions unconstitutional and nullified the regional election. Since Tigray lacked representation in the HoF, with Tigrayan representatives abandoning their seats in the House in protest, their argument regarding the right to self-government through regional elections was not given due consideration. This decision became the immediate trigger for the tragic civil war that followed. One more aspect of the HoF to consider here has to do with its composition. Even if Tigray had its representatives during the hearings on the postponement of the elections and voted against the proposal to postpone, the decision would not have been different, because Tigray would readily be outvoted and outnumbered. It's this majoritarian aspect of the upper chamber, which is an anomaly of Ethiopian federalism, that also needs to be reformed (Ibid).

The constitutional review mechanism provided by the FDRE Constitution has consistently proven ineffective. One significant issue, as highlighted by Takele Seboka Bulto, is the Council of Constitutional

Inquiry's (CCI) tendency to assume the powers of the House of Federation (HoF). Takele notes that the CCI often rejects cases by claiming they do not require constitutional interpretation, even though it is, in fact, interpreting the Constitution. This leads to a situation where the CCI equates the absence of a need for constitutional interpretation with a determination of no constitutional violation. Consequently, the CCI's findings of no need for constitutional interpretation do not have to be confirmed by the HoF, making the CCI's decisions final (Bulto 2011, 123). This problem is evident in the case of CUD v. PM Meles Zenawi Asres (2005), where a lower court referred the case to the CCI for constitutional interpretation. Takele writes:

> *the haste with which the case was referred to the CCI and the questions forwarded to the CCI/HoF borders on judicial abdication of the court's adjudicative powers over justiciable matters. The situation surrounding judicial referral of the CUD case goes some way to lending credence to the assertion that the courts usually seek an excuse for avoiding politically sensitive cases and take the first opportunity to relieve themselves of adjudicating controversies of the type involved in the CUD case. The consequence is judicial violation of the courts' constitutional mandate of adjudicating justiciable matters, and denial of judicial access to private parties (Ibid, .117-118).*

The CCI remanded the case back to the court, stating that it did not require interpretation. Subsequently, the court dismissed the challenge, finding no constitutional violation, despite the Constitution vesting emergency powers with the Council of Ministers rather than with the Prime Minister (Article 93).

This institutional arrangement has posed challenges to the enforcement of constitutional rights through judicial litigation. The first challenge is that courts, when faced with cases involving constitutional rights, tend to readily refer such cases to the CCI or HoF for constitutional interpretation, a phenomenon I call "judicial abdication" (Bulto 2011, 99-123). Since the new constitution came into effect, the judiciary has frequently referred cases involving constitutional claims to the CCI/HoF rather than adjudicating them, either due to fear of reprisal by the executive in high-stakes political cases or a belief that it lacks the competence to hear and decide such cases.

To date, there is a concerning trend of judicial abdication where regular courts readily refer constitutional issues to the HoF through the CCI, effectively surrendering their jurisdiction (Bulto 2011). This trend, exemplified by cases like Coalition for Unity and Democracy v. Prime Minister Meles Zenawi, indicates a reluctance by regular courts to interpret constitutional provisions directly. This reluctance is fueled by legal arguments arising from Article 83(1) of the Constitution, which some interpret as relieving courts of their duty to interpret and apply constitutional provisions (see Fisseha 2004; Fiseha 2017). Additionally, regular courts often avoid politically sensitive cases that may lead to constitutional disputes, further diminishing their role in constitutional interpretation. Meanwhile, the CCI and HoF have expanded their roles and powers in interpreting the constitution, potentially at the expense of the regular courts' jurisdiction. This dynamic has created jurisdictional dilemmas between the CCI/HoF and the regular courts (Bulto 2011, 100-101).

While the best institutional design for constitutional review in Ethiopia should ideally be determined through political or deliberative processes, I propose expanding the size and mandate of the CCI and transforming it into a full-fledged Constitutional Court. This would involve divesting the HoF of its constitutional review power and ensuring the Constitutional Court's independence from the legislative and executive branches of government (see Fisseha 2004).

2. Right To Secession

The secession clause in the Constitution of the Federal Democratic Republic of Ethiopia (FDRE) has been a contentious issue, inherited from the Transitional Charter. The Transitional Charter's preamble established the "self-determination of all peoples" as a governing principle, emphasizing the need to end ethnic conflicts, promote healing, and foster peace and stability.

The Charter recognized the right to self-determination of all "nations, nationalities, and peoples" (Article 2) and allowed for the creation of local and regional governments based on nationality (Article 13). Article 2 stated that each group had the right to preserve its identity, culture, and history, develop its language, and govern its own affairs in a defined territory. Additionally, it allowed for the right to self-determination of independence for any group whose rights were denied, abridged, or abrogated.

In 1994, Article 39 of the FDRE Constitution incorporated the secession clause of the Transitional Charter but omitted Article 2(c)'s substantive requirement, hence granting the unconditional right to self-determination, including secession.

In 1993, Samuel Assefa warned of the danger posed by the secession clause in a prescient paper delivered at the symposium on the making of the new Ethiopian constitution. Commenting on the secession clause, Samuel had this to say: "The attempt to combine these discrepant constitutional commitments —to vest all authority permanently in the center, on the one hand, and, on the other, to recognize the right of some or all local units to secession and independence

—would yield a most unwieldy hybrid, a genuinely neurotic constitution, one might say" (Assefa 1993, 113-125).

He further argued that what follows logically from a right of secession de jure is the de facto right of nullification of federal laws (Ibid). I should add to that absent a rule of the paramountcy of federal laws in the Constitution, a state's right of unilateral nullification of federal laws takes the force and effect of law and not of fact. This is what has transpired in the constitutional dispute between the federal government and the regional government of Tigray before the war. For instance, on January 26, 2019, the Tigray State Council passed a bill (Proclamation No. 3/2019) that nullified a federal proclamation providing for the establishment of the Identities and Boundaries Commission. The Tigray government also rejected the decision of the House of Federation on the postponement of the elections on grounds of the primacy of the right to self-determination.

The war has also exposed the imperfections of the constitutional right of secession. What good is a right that can't be invoked or exercised without waging a war? War negates the *ratio legis* of such a right, which was supposed to make exit out of the federation peaceful.

It is important to note that the secession clause has exacerbated existing mistrust and tensions between Amhara and Tigray over disputed territories of South and West Tigray, even at war's end. In an interview with Dawit Kebede of the Awramba Times, veteran TPLF leader Sebhat Nega said something to the effect that a declaration of the secession of Tigray by the TPLF is tantamount to a declaration of war with the federal and the Amhara Regional governments (Kebede 2020).

3. Constitutional Amendment Procedure

Discussing constitutional reform within the framework of an almost unamendable constitution presents an inherent contradiction. An unamendable constitution suggests that its fundamental principles and provisions are sacrosanct and cannot be altered. And if we do "not temper [our] doctrinaire logic with a little practical wisdom," to borrow an expression from Robert Jackson, "[t]here is danger that…[we] will convert the constitution … into a suicide pact"(Terminiello v. Chicago, 337 U.S. 1, 37 (1949). This, I hope, succinctly captures this notion, emphasizing the importance of upholding and protecting the constitution without jeopardizing the multinational state's survival or its core values.

It is noteworthy that even the United States Constitution of 1787, often hailed as a paragon of democracy, was made in blatant disregard of the amendment clause enshrined in the Articles of Confederation that it replaced. This highlights the recognition, even in the early stages of constitutional development, of the need for flexibility and adaptability. As stated by Laurence Tribe and Thomas Landry:

> *The American experience, interestingly, shows that textual amendments can be effected in ways that people come to accept as legitimate, in spite of a failure to meet the formal procedural requirements—the filing deadline, as it were. An illustration includes the powerful (and perhaps compelling) argument that the United States Constitution of 1787 was itself produced in violation of the agreed-upon procedures for amending the existing Articles of Confederation.... There is no doubt that if we seek to trace the legitimacy of the 1787 Constitution to some anterior document, we will hit a dead end (Tribe and Landry 1993, 627-646).*

However, it is crucial to acknowledge that the existence of an unamendable constitution does not necessarily preclude all forms of constitutional reform. Regarding the unamendability of the Articles of Confederation and its unavoidable replacement by the Constitution, Akhil Reed Amar writes:

> *The Articles of Confederation, framed by some of America's leading lights, had proved inadequate almost from the start. Could anyone absolutely guarantee that the Philadelphia Constitution itself would not suffer a similar fate? Hence the wisdom of leaving the door to future constitutional amendments wide-open. In one sense, the amendment issue defined the first and most fundamental item of business to be addressed at Philadelphia. State governments had sent their leading citizens to the city of brotherly love not to propose a new Constitution openly repudiating the Articles of Confederation, but rather to ponder possible amendments to the Confederation document rendering it adequate to its basic purpose. This charge presented a paradox, for it quickly became apparent to the delegates that the Confederation document's biggest—and indeed, fatal—flaw was its practical unamendability. According to the closing passage (Article XIII) of that document, any amendment to the Articles required the agreement of all thirteen state legislatures. Experience had shown that such unanimity was all but impossible to achieve. Repeatedly, the Confederation Congress in the early and mid-1780s had proposed amendments that would have enhanced the union's ability to perform its core functions; each time, one or more states had said no (Amar 2006, 285).*

Amar observes that given Rhode Island's resistance and the slim likelihood of unanimous state approval for proposed sweeping changes, the Constitutional Convention delegates recognized the need to deviate from their initial instructions. Instead of proposing amendments to the Articles of Confederation, they chose to create an entirely new constitution, eliminating the requirement for approval from each state legislature. The ironic transition from the Confederation's closing to Article VII of the Constitution marked a shift, enabling nine states to implement the new document among themselves. This change in amendment procedures, from the rigid unanimity requirement under the Confederation to the more flexible Article V in the Constitution, reflected the delegates' belief that an inflexible amendment process could render a governing document irrelevant. The new Constitution aimed for easier activation of its amendment procedures, rejecting the impractical demand for unanimous state consent and aligning with the vision of a more perfect union (Ibid).

While the sovereign powers are technically vested in the nations, nationalities, and peoples (NNPs) (Article 8), it appears that these powers are effectively relinquished to the states, as can be gathered from the amendment clause (Article 105). This presents a notable contradiction with the constituent power theory of the Constitution enshrined in the preamble and the sovereignty clause of the Constitution. One could argue that the NNPs lacking their own exclusive states have the right to demand the formation of one pursuant to Article 47. However, this poses a problem, since such NNPs are unable to participate in the amendment process until they have already established a state and a state council.

In summary, there exists a discrepancy between the theoretical allocation of sovereign powers and their practical implementation, as evidenced by the amendment clause. This inconsistency raises concerns regarding the adherence to both the spirit and the literal interpretation of the Constitution. Furthermore, the predicament faced by NNPs without their own exclusive states highlights the challenges they encounter in participating effectively in the amendment process. The proliferation of such demands for statehood by NNPs indicates that achieving consensus by the existing and future state councils for amending either the secession clause or the amendment clause itself is a virtual impossibility.

Amending the amendment clause will not only save the Constitution from facing the fate of the American Articles of Confederation, but it also saves the country from disintegration.

Conclusion

To recap, in November 2022, the Pretoria peace accords were signed between the Ethiopian government and the TPLF, ending a brutal two-year civil war triggered by postponed elections. Ethiopia's best chance for survival lies in seizing the opportunity presented by this agreement.

However, the popular demand for democratic reforms seems lost on the highest echelons of the parties to the Pretoria peace accords. Their aspiration appears to be a return to the antebellum status quo, ignoring the pro-democracy protests and calls for democratic reforms that were rife in the country and within the ruling party before Prime Minister Abiy Ahmed came to power.

To assume that the Pretoria accords alone would usher in peace in Ethiopia is unwise. Political and legal reforms are needed and necessary, if insufficient, to bring about lasting peace The Pretoria peace accords could lead to constitutional reform and a durable settlement if properly seized, or potential dismemberment like Yugoslavia if they falter and slide back to the brink of war. Indeed, the expanding problems in Amhara and Oromia do not bode well for a transition to national unity, peace, and democracy.

The federal government's ongoing counterinsurgencies, in Amhara against the Fano and in Oromia against the Oromo Liberation Army (OLA), underscore the necessity of further negotiations. Before an effective national dialogue and transitional justice can take place, the government must negotiate agreements with these groups. Achieving a sense of direction and diversity in unity requires closure and constitutional reform.

Defenders of Ethiopia's experiment with ethnic federalism used to complain about the impatience of its critics, claiming it had not been tested enough to pass judgment on its merits. But after more than a quarter of a century, the system failed, and Ethiopia descended into bloody ethnicized civil wars. Andreas Eshete, reflecting on the legacy of ethnic federalism, stated:

> *To say that ethnic federalism is an optimal path to democracy under unfavorable conditions is to admit that it is not settled whether or not it will endure as a constitutional value. With the creation of conditions more hospitable to democratic institutions, the importance of ethnic federalism in Ethiopia may fade.... If the federative arrangement succeeds in giving birth to these institutions, its value as an instrument of constitutional values may, over time, decline. In other words, it may be that federalism is a self-deflating instrument of constitutional democracy. The same point can be made in reference to the political agents empowered by the new Constitution. In ethnic federalism, Ethiopia and the new Ethiopian Constitution have found a novel answer to the question: who inherits Ethiopia? Its ethnic communities have now inherited Ethiopia. But as democracy*

> *flourishes, thanks to ethnic federalism, the legacy may either become less valuable, or it may be bequeathed to others (Eshete 2001, 83).*

I understand that the proposals for constitutional reform I have made are modest, and perhaps even difficult given the virtual unamendability of the constitution. However, given the enormity and gravity of the problems Ethiopia is facing, more radical reform must be considered. To foster constitutional patriotism in Ethiopia, it is essential to reconsider national symbols and holidays that currently exacerbate partisan and ethnic divisions. This includes reevaluating the May 28 celebrations of the Derg's downfall and revising the national flag's emblem. Furthermore, the Constitution should be revised to serve as a unifying instrument, eliminating references that perpetuate narratives of resentment and historical injustice. Instead, the state should promote the celebration of public holidays that rally Ethiopians around patriotic solidarity against foreign aggressions, such as the Victory at Adwa in the First Italo-Ethiopian War in 1896, the patriotic resistance movement against the Second Italo-Ethiopian War (1936-1941), and the liberation from Italian occupation in 1941, with official national ceremonies.

Our generation and those to come must continue to cultivate the patriotic solidarity that our forefathers displayed at Adwa, not only to confront external threats to our beloved country's territorial security but also to combat internal threats to our survival, such as poverty and underdevelopment, and to attain freedom from both fear and want. As G.W.F. Hegel put it: "Patriotism is often understood to mean only a readiness for exceptional sacrifices and actions. Essentially, however, it is the sentiment which, in the relationships of daily life and under ordinary conditions, habitually recognizes that the community is one's substantive groundwork and end" (Hegel 1967, 268).

Going forward, efforts must be made to reconfigure the political map by de-territorializing ethnicity to coincide with "historical divisions or major physical features" (Huntington 1993, 14) and breaking up the larger states into smaller and to an extent possible symmetrical units, thereby reducing the centrifugal political and financial incentives for political elites. By making these changes, Ethiopia can strengthen a sense of shared identity and commitment to the constitution.

In closing, I return to the question raised at the end of the prelude: is it high time that the "We the Nations, Nationalities, and Peoples of Ethiopia" give way to "We the People"? Democracy has not yet flourished. Rather, it seems we have gone back to square one. The Ethiopian experience underscores that sustainable progress requires patience, institutionalism, and a steadfast commitment to universal rights and representation for all groups.

Notes

1 This chapter arose from a paper delivered at the FES-Conference titled "Perspectives on a Fair and Durable Constitutional (Re)Settlement in Ethiopia," held on May 24-25, 2023, at the Inter Luxury Hotel in Addis Ababa, Ethiopia. I am deeply grateful to the editors of this volume, and I would like to extend my special thanks to Dr. Adem Abebe for his initial invitation to participate in the conference, for his thoughtful feedback, and patient collaboration throughout this process. I also wish to thank Professor Adeno Addis for his incisive comments, which significantly enhanced the quality of the chapter.

2 PhD Fellow, Center for Constitutional Democracy, Maurer School of Law, and Managing Editor, Africa Today, Indiana University, Bloomington

References

Aalen, Lovise. "Ethnic Federalism and Self-Determination for Nationalities in a Semi-Authoritarian State: The Case of Ethiopia." International Journal on Minority & Group Rights 13 (2006): 243-261.

Abebe, Adem Kassie. "Umpiring Federalism in Africa: Institutional Mosaic and Innovations." African Studies Quarterly 13, no. 4 (2013).

Abebe, Adem Kassie. "From the 'TPLF Constitution' to the 'Constitution of the People of Ethiopia': Constitutionalism and Proposals for Constitutional Reform." In Constitutionalism and Democratic Governance in Africa: Contemporary Perspectives from Sub-Saharan Africa, edited by Morris Kiwinda Mbondenyi and Tom Ojienda, 29-47. Pretoria: Pretoria University Law Press, 2013.

Addis, Adeno. "Cultural Integrity and Political Unity: The Politics of Language in Multilingual States." Arizona State Law Journal 33 (2001): 719-799.

Addis, Adeno. "The Making of Strangers: The Ethiopian Constitution as a Suicide Pact." Ethiopia Insight, September 18, 2020. https://www.ethiopia-insight.com/2020/09/18/the-making-of-strangers-the-ethiopian-constitution-as-a-suicide-pact/.

Albert, Richard. "Constitutional Dismemberment in Constitutional Design." Diritto pubblico comparato ed europeo 3 (2022): 1586-1604.

Albert, Richard. "Constitutional Amendment and Dismemberment." The Yale Journal of International Law 43, no. 1 (2018): 1-45.

Albert, Richard. Constitutional Amendments: Making, Breaking, and Changing Constitutions. New York: Oxford University Press, 2019.

Al Jazeera. "Ethiopia's Tigrayan Rebels Start Handing Over Heavy Weapons." Al Jazeera, January 11, 2023. https://www.aljazeera.com/

news/2023/1/11/ethiopias-tigray-rebels-start-handing-over-heavy-weapons.

Amar, Akhil Reed. America's Constitution: A Biography. New York: Random House, 2006.

Assefa, Samuel. "Of Federalism and Secession." In Constitutionalism: Reflections and Recommendations, Symposium on the Making of the New Ethiopian Constitution, 67-78. Addis Ababa: Center for Dialogue on Humanitarian Peace and Development Issues in the Horn of Africa, 1993.

AWS. "The Difference Between Monolithic and Microservices Architecture." https://aws.amazon.com/compare/the-difference-between-monolithic-and-microservices-architecture/.

Berlin, Isaiah. "Nationalism: Past Neglect and Present Power." In Against the Current: Essays in the History of Ideas, edited by Henry Hardy, 57-64. 2nd ed. Princeton: Princeton University Press, 2013.

Budge, E.A. Wallis. The Kebra Nagast. New York: Cosimo Classics, 2004.

Bulto, Takele Seboka. "Judicial Referral of Constitutional Disputes in Ethiopia: From Practice to Theory." African Journal of International and Comparative Law

Clapham, Christopher. Transformation and Continuity in Revolutionary Ethiopia. Cambridge: Cambridge University Press, 1988.

Cohen, John M. "Ethnic Federalism in Ethiopia." Northeast African Studies 2, no. 2 (1995): 157-188.

Donham, Donald and James, Wendy. The Southern Marches of Imperial Ethiopia. Eastern African Studies. Athens: Ohio University Press, second impression, 2002.

Endeshaw, Dawit. "Ethiopia Postpones August Election Due to Coronavirus." Reuters, April 1, 2020. https://www.reuters.com/article/us-ethiopia-election-idUSKBN21I2QU/.

Eshete, Andreas. "The Protagonists in the Constitution-Making in Ethiopia." In Constitution-Making and Democratization in Africa, edited by Goran Hyden and Denis Venter, 69-83. Pretoria: Africa Institute of South Africa, 2001.

Eshete, Andreas. "Implementing Human Rights and a Democratic Constitution in Ethiopia." Issue: A Journal of Opinion 21, no. 1/2 (1993): 8-13. Cambridge University Press.

Fentaw, Alemayehu and Fiseha, Assefa. "Ethiopia." In The 2022 Global Review of Constitutional Law. EUT Edizioni Università di Trieste, 2023.

Ferejohn, John E. "Constitutional Review in the Global Context." New York University Journal of Legislation and Public Policy 6, no. 1 (Fall 2002): 49-66.

Fessha, Yonatan Tesfaye. "Who Interprets the Constitution: A Descriptive and Normative Discourse on the Ethiopian Approach to Constitutional

Review." Unpublished LLM thesis, Faculty of Law, University of Western Cape, 2004.

Fiseha, Assefa. "Constitutional Adjudication through Second Chamber in Ethiopia." In The Ethnopolitics of Ethnofederalism in Ethiopia, Routledge, London, 2017.

Fiseha, Assefa. "Constitutional Adjudication in Ethiopia: Exploring the Experience of the House of Federation." Mizan Law Review 1, no. 1 (June 2007): 1-32.

Gardner, Tom. "Abiy Ahmed Is Not a Populist." *Foreign Policy*, December 5, 2018. https://foreignpolicy.com/2018/12/05/abiy-ahmed-is-not-a-populist-ethiopia-eprdf-tplf-modi-erdogan-populism/.

Gardner, Tom. *The Abiy Project: God, Power and War in the New Ethiopia*. London: Hurst Publishers, 2024.

G. Selassie, Alemante. "Ethnic Federalism: Its Promise and Pitfalls for Africa." Yale Journal of International Law 28 (2003): 51-86.

Hegel, G.W. Philosophy of Right. Translated by T.M. Knox. Oxford: Oxford University Press, 1967.

Huntington, Samuel P. "Political Development in Ethiopia: A Peasant-Based Dominant-Party Democracy?" Report prepared for USAID/Ethiopia, May 17, 1993.

Lepore, Jill. This America: The Case for the Nation. New York: Liveright, 2019

Levine, Donald. Greater Ethiopia: The Evolution of a Multiethnic Society. 2nd edition. Chicago: University of Chicago Press, 2000.

Lijphart, Arend. Democracy in Plural Societies: A Comparative Exploration. New Haven: Yale University Press, 1977.

Lijphart, Arend. "Democratic Political Systems." Journal of Theoretical Politics 1, no. 1 (1989): 33-52.

Marbury v. Madison, 5 U.S. 137 (1803).

Markakis, John. Ethiopia: The Last Two Frontiers. James Currey, 2011.

Müller, Jan-Werner. Constitutional Patriotism. Princeton: Princeton University Press, 2007.

Müller, Jan-Werner and Scheppele, Kim Lane. "Constitutional Patriotism: An Introduction." International Journal of Constitutional Law 6, no. 1 (January 2008): 67-71. https://doi.org/10.1093/icon/mom039.

Nietzsche, Friedrich. "On the Uses and Disadvantages of History for Life." In Nietzsche: Untimely Meditations, edited by Daniel Breazeale, 57-123. Cambridge Texts in the History of Philosophy. Cambridge: Cambridge University Press, 1997. https://search-ebscohost-com.proxyiub.uits.iu.edu/login.aspx?direct=true&db=nlebk&AN=55755&site=ehost-live&scope=site.

Rawls, John. A Theory of Justice. Revised edition. Cambridge, MA: Belknap Press of Harvard University Press, 1999.

Rawls, John. The Law of Peoples. Cambridge, MA: Harvard University Press, 2001.

Rawls, John. Justice as Fairness: A Restatement. Cambridge, MA: Harvard University Press, 2001.

Rawls, John. Political Liberalism. Expanded edition. New York: Columbia University Press, 2005.

Reuters. "Key Points in Ethiopia's Ceasefire Agreement." November 4, 2022. https://www.reuters.com/world/africa/key-points-ethiopias-ceasefire-agreement-2022-11-04/.

Reuters. "Ethiopia Establishes Tigray Interim Administration as Part of Peace Plan." March 23, 2023. https://www.reuters.com/world/africa/ethiopia-says-tigray-interim-administration-set-up-part-peace-plan-2023-03-23/.

Sahlemariam, Teklemichael Abebe and Geremew, Endalkachew. "Constitutional Inquiry Verdict: 'Because I Said So'." *Ethiopia Insight*, June 22, 2020. https://www.ethiopia-insight.com/2020/06/22/council-of-constitutional-inquiry-verdict-because-i-said-so/.

Shills, Edward. "Center and Periphery." In The Constitution of Society, edited by Morris Janowitz, 3-16. Chicago: University of Chicago Press, 1982.

Smith, Steven B. Reclaiming Patriotism in an Age of Extremes. New Haven: Yale University Press, 2021.

Tekle Mariyam, Tekle Hawariat. Autobiography, Addis Ababa University Press, 2006 (Amharic)

Tribe, Laurence H. and Landry, Thomas K. "Reflections on Constitution-Making." American University International Law Review 8, no. 2/3 (1993): 627-646.

The Constitution of the Empire of Ethiopia (1931)." In Public Administration in Ethiopia: A Study in Retrospect and Prospect, edited by Howard William E. H., 22-45. Groningen: J.B. Wolters, 1969

The Revised Constitution of Ethiopia: Proclamation No. 149 of 1955. Proclamation Promulgating the Revised Constitution of the Empire of Ethiopia. Nagārit gāzéṭā, vol. 15, no. 2 (November 4, 1955). Addis Ababa: Berhanena Selam Printing Press, 1955.

The Constitution of the People's Democratic Republic of Ethiopia: Proclamation No. I of 1987. Negarit Gazetta, vol. 47, no. 1 (September 12, 1987). Addis Ababa: Berhanena Selam Printing Press, 1987.

The Constitution of the Federal Democratic Republic of Ethiopia: Proclamation No. 1/1995. Federal Negarit Gazeta, 1st year, no. 1 (August 21, 1995). Addis Ababa: Berhanena Selam Printing Press, 1995.

The Inter-Africa Group. *Constitutionalism: Reflections and Recommendations - The Symposium on the Making of the New Ethiopian Constitution 17-21 May 1993*. Addis Ababa: Center for Dialogue on Humanitarian Peace and Development Issues in the Horn of Africa, May 1994.

United States Agency for International Development. *Evaluation Report: Ethiopia Democracy/Governance Support Project (633-0007)*. Draft Report Prepared for Ethiopia Mission. Addis Ababa, May 10, 1994. https://pdf.usaid.gov/pdf_docs/PDABK181.pdf.

Walter, Barbara F. How Civil Wars Start: And How to Stop Them. New York: Crown, 2022.

Wimmer, Andreas. Waves of War: Nationalism, State Formation, and Ethnic Exclusion in the Modern World. Cambridge Studies in Comparative Politics Series. Cambridge: Cambridge University Press, 2013.

Wodajo, Kifle. "The Making of the Ethiopian Constitution." In Constitution-Making and Democratization in Africa, edited by Goran Hyden and Denis Venter, 132-142. Pretoria: Africa Institute of South Africa, 2001.

Zakaria, Fareed. "The Rise of Illiberal Democracy." Foreign Affairs 76, no. 6 (November-December 1997): 22-43.

Zewde, Bahru. A History of Modern Ethiopia: 1855-1974. Addis Ababa: Addis Ababa University Press, 1991.

Part II

National Citizenship in a Diverse Society

Chapter 8

Urban Ethiopia and Ethnic Federalism: Resistance and (Re)imagining Citizenship.

Derese G Kassa

The Contours of Urban Citizenship

Part of Ethiopia's constitutional challenge is how to place the role of urbanites in the construction of national identity and citizenship. This issue deserves attention for several reasons. To begin with, the notion of citizenship itself emerged from the modern urban-based social revolutions of Europe and North America, where a nascent industrialist class flexed its muscle to claim not only the heights of capital but also government. Varasnyi remarks, "The etymology of the word citizenship reveals its urban origins: there is a clear connection, for instance, between the word citizen and the word that we now translate in English as a city-state." [1] The debate on the essence of citizenship, however, extends beyond the urban.

The most dominant strand is liberal social-contract theory, where citizens are depicted as members of a nation-state with a bundle of rights and obligations.

They are signatories of a social contract, a constitution, with a sovereign state whose powers are enumerated to secure and protect their security and freedoms. Prominent thinkers like T. H. Marshall[2] chronicled how the Westphalian state began to bestow certain civil (eighteenth century), political (nineteenth century) and social (twentieth century) rights to erstwhile subjects of monarchies. A critique of this liberal thesis often comes from communitarians, who harp on the notion of a "sacred" or a "cultural" "core" as the foundation on which the ethical and legal tenets of a modern republic ought to be built.

There is also a critique from civic republicans, not all of whom are communitarian, that a person should devote a significant amount of time and effort to building civic relations with other members and demonstrate both the moral and ethical responsibilities necessary to qualify as a citizen. In other words, paying taxes and voting are necessary but not sufficient requirements of citizenship. In fact, some criticize the city as one that erodes such a collective communitarian understanding of citizenship, where members barely know each other, let alone build enduring moral and ethical ties. Civic republicanism, therefore, stresses that "modern conceptions of citizenship are anchored in the world of the bounded community" and it "loses its precise meaning when divorced from territoriality, sovereignty, and shared nationality."[3] Nevertheless, both liberalism and civic republicanism privilege the notion that nationhood ought to be the outcome of the constitutional bonds the state provides and not just the mere cultural or linguistic allegiance or affinity people feel toward a given ethnic, religious, or caste community.

These arguments are interrogated by those who espouse the notion of a cosmopolitan citizenship. Cosmopolitan citizenship theory echoes classical Greek and Roman teachings of Stoicism, asserting all humans are "born into and hence a citizen of two res publicae: a particular city-state and the greater cosmopolis. In the event that such a situation should give rise to conflicting loyalties, a citizen's duties to the cosmopolis would always prevail."[4] Both civic republicans and liberals find such a formulation of citizenship unrealistic, since it does not consider the geographic and social distance among political communities and limitations to form moral and ethical bonds across the globe.

Nussbaum's[5] rejoinder to Hill's emphasis on the primacy of "national identity," "national pride," and "patriotism" is perhaps one of the most withering criticisms of both civic republican and liberal formulations of citizenship. She wrote,

Nationalism and ethnocentric particularism are not alien to one another, but akin—that to give support to nationalist sentiments subverts, ultimately, even the values that hold the nation together because it substitutes a colorful idol for the substantive universal values of justice and right. Once one said I am an Indian first, a citizen of the world second, once he or she made that morally questionable move of self-definition by a morally irrelevant characteristic then what indeed will stop that person from saying, ... I am Hindu first, and an Indian second, or I am an upper caste landlord first, and a Hindu second?

At heart is the question of qualifying and enumerating the bundle of ethical roles or responsibilities we owe to each other, mediated or obligated by the state. Whether the nation-state itself should be the sole or the primary domain to carry out these responsibilities or not is also a point of debate. Even here, whether our allegiance to the "national sentiment" should be anchored on some cultural core or only on the procedural virtues of democratic constitutionalism is not settled. This is, for instance, what is not clear about Jurgen Habermas's concept of "constitutional patriotism." Muller[6] asks,

> Who and how do we want to be, as far as political rule over ourselves is concerned? Do we see such rule centered on some kind of cultural essence that should be preserved over time? Or do we conceive of it as a project that sustains and, in turn, is enriched by a series of political conversations about the principles of justice that should govern political rule?

It also helps to remember that these geographic and social distances are incredibly reduced due to heightened globalization. At its latest stage, neo-liberalism has facilitated an unprecedented flow of capital, labor, technologies, and information. Post-Fordist methods of production and the digital age mean we have global supply chains and modes of production where products are processed and assembled worldwide. Political globalization means "reduction in the power of the nation state," where supranational ventures like the European Union now have prerogatives over the financial, transport, immigration, and education policies of member states. On the other hand, these states are met with subnational movements for more autonomy and devolution of power. The case of Scotland in the UK, Catalonia in Spain, and Quebec in Canada are cases in point where the nation-state has bequeathed powers and resources to provinces to tame ethno-nationalist and separatist tendencies.

The invention of the internet and the arrival of digital "commons" like YouTube means we are consuming or streaming cultural products of art, music, literature, and cinema worldwide, unbound by the limits of geography or time. Given all these, proponents of cosmopolitan citizenship remark that it is not futile or utopian to speak and write of us being "citizens of the world." Needless to mention that global emergencies such as climate change mean human beings need to act in concert, defying the limits of national "borders" and "sovereignties."

Most of these global flows of culture, commerce, technology, and power are directed, coordinated, and networked in cities. Globalization and planetary urbanization therefore mean that the notion of citizenship is being rescaled and discussed not just at the "national" but also the "urban" level. The literature on "urban citizenship" drew a lot from the works of the prominent French sociologist and geographer Henry Lefebvre. Lefebvre's classic work, entitled "Right to the City"[7] and his book "The Production of Space"[8] criticize the "traditional" modes of citizenship as confining. One becomes a citizen by "being born of the soil" ("jus soli") or claim it as a birth heritage from parents ("jus sanguinis"). In lieu of these, Lefebvre submits that urban citizenship needs to be based on the principle of "inhabitance," where *all* (despite ethnicity, race, creed, religion, or citizenship status, etc.) are welcome and endowed with "two principal rights," i.e. "the right to participation, and the right to appropriation."[9] The right to participation entails that "*citadins*[10] should play a central role in any decision that contributes to the production of urban space. The right to appropriation, on the other hand, implies the "right of inhabitants to physically access, occupy, and use urban space"[11]Lefebvre's formulation, therefore, localizes the scale of citizenship but universalizes the scope of what it should entail. One clearly hears echoes of those who spoke and wrote about cosmopolitan citizenship in Lefebvre's body of work but focused on the urban scale. These notions of urban citizenship are not idle speculations but are now informing the realm of policy mainly as "sanctuary city" or "solidarity city" practices. Several Western cities are now pushing for inclusive, pro-poor, and sustainable urban governance policies against the rising tide of exclusivist, hyper-nationalistic, anti-immigrant, and anti-labor policies of national governments.

Urban Ethiopia and the Ethno-Federal Design

A common refrain among urbanists is that Africa is the least urbanized continent of all, and the percentage of Ethiopians living in urban centers is extremely low, even by African standards. But if one sets aside the "demographic" optic, Ethiopia has pioneer urban settlements such as Axum (Circa, 100BC). Emperor Lalibela's rock-hewn churches during the Zagwe Dynasty (twelfth century AD) point at a flourishing settlement with cathedrals. Or one could speak of Debre Berhan, founded by Emperor Zara Yacob around 1456. Debre Berhan predates the city of Gondar, which rose to prominence from the early sixteenth century. Up until Gondar, the emperors in northern Ethiopia had roving capitals, building various centers of command, worship, and scholarship.

Addis Ababa emerged following Emperor Menelik II's consequential projects of southward conquest, centralization, and modernization during the late nineteenth century. These processes of centralization and modernization were accelerated during the long reign of Emperor Haile Sellasie I in the twentieth century, when Addis Ababa became the unrivaled capital city. A striking feature of Ethiopian urbanization is, therefore, the cardinal role the Ethiopian state has played as the primary agent of urbanization. This was also the case during the Derg era, where state led "socialist" projects of resettlement, villagization, and cooperativization led to the proliferation of various rural towns in central and southern Ethiopia. Across the country, the national government hired and deployed thousands of soldiers, teachers, and bureaucrats who became the street agents of Ethiopian nationalism and urbanism.

Up until 1991, therefore, the Ethiopian state oversaw the processes of urbanization and nation building concomitantly. This came to a grinding halt with the ascent of the Tigray People's Liberation Front (TPLF) led Ethiopian Peoples' Revolutionary Democratic Front (EPRDF) into power and the ratification of Ethiopia's latest constitution (1995). The new order fashioned the country into nine ethno-regional states, including, notably, Tigray, Amhara, and Oromia. Political membership in these provinces was primarily predicated on the individual claiming to be a member of one, and only one, ethnic community. This is the case for all regions except the Amhara regional constitution, which explicitly recognizes all the ethno-linguistic groups as constituent parts with recognizable territorial administrative rights. People of mixed ethnic heritage, the majority of whom lived in urban centers and identified themselves as "Ethiopian," became permanent minorities in most of these provinces. Louise Aalen [12] captures this in writing,

> As we have seen, the Constitution restricts the opportunities for Ethiopian citizens to register with mixed or pan-Ethiopian identity, and political practice shows that the most efficient way to be recognized and represented in local, regional, and national government is through ethnic groups and ethnically based parties. In the political order of ethnic federalism, it pays off to sharpen ethnic divides, and 'indigeneship' is thus becoming the favored way of identification and organization, at the expense of a common citizenship.

To sum up, the current constitution privileged ethnic homelands as opposed to urban or metropolitan formations, which are melting pots of various ethnicities, religions, and class formations.

From the outset, the TPLF/EPRDF era was beset with problems of constitutional design and a dispensational crisis. The drafting and promulgation of the 1995 Constitution happened in a post conflict political environment that solely reflected the ideological and political interests of the victor, i.e., the TPLF. The regime cherry-picked political parties that towed the ethno-nationalist line and, in some instances, went to manufacture or midwife various "ethnic" parties, the infamous Peoples' Democratic Organizations (PDOs). These makeshift parties later became "members" of the ruling EPRDF coalition, or "sister organizations," that oversaw regional states like Afar, Somali, Harari, Gambella, and Benishangul Gumuz. Even by ethnic standards, various communities were excluded from the process. The Amharas are a case in point here. There was no ethno-nationalist party, entity, or civil society organization present to articulate the various interests or preferences of the Amhara public then. In fact, one could argue that the Amhara regional state is a province created without any legitimate quest or struggle on the part of the Amharas to form one. In short, the process fell far short of being democratic.

There is debate as to whether the constitutional design was genuinely federal or merely structural (Keller,2003[13]; Aalen,2006;[14] and Semahagn, 2014[15]). Yes, various regional states were created and ethnic languages such as Tigrinya and Oromiyfaa became official languages of the regional states. The elite from various ethnic groups in these provinces managed to accede to power and privilege by holding administrative positions. But the prerogatives of the federal design were seriously undercut by party procedures and the decision-making of the vanguard front, the EPRDF, and its Leninist creed of "democratic centralism." All decisions flow from the central committee of the Front, which are dictated by the Politburo, which in turn is influenced by the Front leader. Even more, the design did not provide an effective system of judicial review or checks and balances. For instance, the final power to interpret the constitution and arbitrate and resolve constitutional disputes is given to the House of Federation, whose members are political appointees from the various councils of the regional states. They have so far all hailed from the incumbent Front. The design left little room for self-correction and amendment. And in so doing, the Constitution enabled a political order where the state effectively left its raison d'être at the mercy of a hegemonic party i.e., the TPLF/EPRDF.

These design flaws of the Constitution were apparent when it came to the status of the capital city, Addis Ababa. To begin with, the Constitution bestows the right to establish a "regional state" only on the "Nations, Nationalities and Peoples" of Ethiopia and not cities or urban residents (Article 47). Even so, two-thirds of the members of the already existing regional state council should endorse the request of the community before a referendum is held. This begs the question: What happens if the ethnic elite of the various regional states do not want to relinquish power to potential city-states such as Addis Ababa? Article 49 of the Constitution then outlines the status of Addis Ababa in ways that are vague and complicated. While sub-article 2 stipulates that the city of Addis Ababa will have the "full measure of self-government" sub-article 3 adds that the city administration shall be "responsible to the Federal government." It does not qualify what this "responsibility" entails. Sub-article 3 also stipulates that the "special interest of Oromia" regional state shall be respected on issues of natural resources management, special services, and joint administrative matters.

Not surprisingly, Addis Ababa's standing in the current ethno-federal design has become a cause of disagreement between residents of the city, the federal government and Oromia regional state officials. Since 1991, the EPRDF regime has appointed mayors from other regional states, mainly from Oromia,[16] to govern the capital city. This was met with resistance in 2005, when the EPRDF lost elections for Addis Ababa's entire city council to the opposition, the Coalition for Unity and Democracy (CUD). A decade later, Addis Ababa's growth and expansion to the outskirts of Oromia and the drafting of a new master plan became the lightning rods that sparked the "Qerro" resistance in many towns of Oromia. These protests in Oromia, coupled with resistance in the Amhara region, culminated in the selection of Abiy Ahmed, an ethnic Oromo, as the new prime minister of Ethiopia in April 2018. The process also ushered in the exit of the TPLF from prominence at the center and the subsequent reconstitution of the EPRDF as the Prosperity Party (PP) in December 2019.

The Urbanization of Resistance

I submit that urban communities of Ethiopia will remain at the forefront of contesting the design and dispensational forms of the current constitution. There are three major reasons why I think this will be the case. First, it has to do with the sheer demographic influx and bulge of Ethiopia's urban population. Consider the following statistics from the Word Bank.[17] Over the past two decades, Ethiopia's national population grew from an estimated 67 million in 2000 to 123 million in 2022 with an annual growth rate of 2.5 percent. At the same time, the urban population exploded from around 10.05 million in 2000 to an estimated total of 26.52 million in 2021. Percentage-wise, the urban population leaped to account for 23 percent of the total population in 2022, with an annual growth rate of 4.8 percent. It is important to underscore here that the urbanization rate is almost double the national population growth rate. The nation is rapidly urbanizing, and this will have far-reaching consequences in determining its political economy. Aside from the natural population increase, the excess of births over deaths, in Ethiopia's towns and rural-urban migration have also picked up momentum. If we only consider the number of people fleeing conflict areas in various parts of the country, the majority of the nation's IDP population resides in various towns of Ethiopia.

The second factor has to do with the economic allure of cities like Addis Ababa and their perils. Let us consider Addis Ababa's economy as a case in point. The major sector employing Addis Ababa's workforce is the service sector (51.5 percent) followed by trade (21.1 percent) and manufacturing (20.1 percent).[18] The city has many challenges. The latest Central Statistical Agency (CSA) figure for Addis Ababa's unemployment rate was at 20.2 percent.[19] In 2021, the average consumer in Addis saw a staggering 26.8 percent rise in food prices from 2020.[20] Housing supply, in general, and access to standard and habitable residential units with basic amenities is a major challenge. The World Bank estimates that 64 percent of the urban population in Ethiopia (most of whom reside in Addis Ababa) live in substandard, dilapidated slums. All these urban socioeconomic problems of unemployment, food poverty, hyperinflation, and the ever-rising cost of living and homelessness mean urban areas will be spaces of political resistance, agitation, and articulation in many ways.

For instance, the ruling Oromo Prosperity Party (OPP) elite has recently embarked on settlement, land, and condominium distribution projects for members, which many allege are aimed at altering the demographic and structural makeup of Addis Ababa. Furthermore, the "Sheger Town" project of enveloping Addis Ababa by incorporating a string of small towns in Oromia poses an attempt to frustrate Addis Ababa's outward expansion into the rural environs of Oromia. The intent of the policymakers aside, these measures are clear evidence of the nation's rapid urbanization and its collision course with the logic of ethnic federalism.

On the one hand, both measures attest to the active influx of capital and labor into the nation's capital- Addis Ababa- which has made real estate development, urban sprawl, and expansion into the adjacent Oromia kebeles a lucrative venture that benefits OPP cadres directly. But at the same time, the greater metropolitanization of Oromia with Addis Ababa at its core unsettles or destabilizes the claim of Oromo ethno-nationalists that Addis Ababa "belongs" to Oromia. This process is also at loggerheads with Ethiopia's constitutional design, which attempts to make land ownership and citizenship coterminous with ethnic identity. Sheger town, its demographic makeup, political economy, linkages with Addis Ababa proper, and prospects of consolidation into, or exclusion from, Addis will all be contested in the years to come.

The third major reason has to do with the pedigree that Addis Ababa has been the "command post" for political agitation, articulation, and regime change throughout twentieth and twenty-first century Ethiopia. Following Emperor Menelik's decree, the Shoan elite settled the dispute on succession in Addis by making Lij Iyassu heir to the throne, chaperoned by Ras Tessema Nadew as regent plenipotentiary. Lij Iyassu's brief reign (1910–16) ended with the coronation of Empress Zewditu and the appointment of Ras Teferi

Mekonnen as her prime minister. In addition to the landed aristocracy, a cadre of Western educated, urbane public servants backed Haile Sellasie's final ascent to power (1930). In fact, Haile Sellasie's image as a modernizer and reformer of the ancient regime helped him secure support from the country's youth, civil servants, intelligentsia, and the wider public for a prolonged period.

True, the agrarian question was the major issue that university students brought to the forefront on the eve of the Ethiopian Revolution (1974). But the revolution was thoroughly urban. Students held protests in the capital and other towns of the nation. Taxi drivers protested the rise in fuel prices. Trade unions demanded a significant increase in compensation and benefits for workers. Finally, commissioned officers from the army flocked to Addis Ababa to establish what soon became the "Derg," i.e., the provisional military administration committee that overthrew the monarchy. This is not to argue that Ethiopian peasants were passive or docile actors bent to shoulder feudal exploitation. There were also episodes of peasant revolt and rebellion, as was the case in Tigray, Gojjam, and Bale, etc. However, the social forces who articulated the conditions of the peasantry, mobilized the public, and forced the regime's demise were decidedly urban and modern actors, i.e., students, workers, civil servants, and soldiers.

It is easy to conclude that the overthrow of the Derg by the TPLF (1991) is another example of organized and armed peasant resistance against the center from Eritrea and Tigray. But, here again, such a reading downplays the level of dissatisfaction and resentment the urban public had against the violent excesses of the Derg, i.e., the death and terror it unleashed. In fact, the latter, coupled with the collapse of the Soviet Union (the major supplier of weapons and assistance to the Derg), meant the rebels managed to advance from the northernmost tip of the country with incredible speed and control the capital city without many major military showdowns. And as mentioned earlier, the Oromo Protests (2018) began by denouncing the expansion of Addis Ababa into adjacent Oromia provinces. But while the protests unfolded throughout Oromia, the political infighting between TPLF stalwarts and leaders of the then Oromo People's Democratic Organization (OPDO) was an urban affair. After a seventeen-day marathon meeting, the Central Committee of the EPRDF finally elected a successor to Prime Minister Haile Mariam Desalegn, who had resigned his post. All this attests to the fact that Ethiopia's urban polities and urban spaces have played a decisive role in organizing resistance and ushering regime changes for more than a century and two decades, and that is likely to remain the same, in the process challenging the formal political and constitutional dispensation exclusively founded on a singular ethnic identity.

Conclusion

Following his trip to St. Petersburg (then Petrograd) in the immediate aftermath of the Russian Revolution, Lincoln Steffen (1919) wrote to his friend, "I saw the future; and it works." When it comes to contesting the current ethno-federal design of Ethiopia and (re)imagining citizenship, urban is indeed the future. This is because the concept of citizenship itself and its various renditions—liberal, communitarian, civic republican, and cosmopolitan—are articulated and debated in urban spaces. In Ethiopia's case, the design flaws of the Constitution that privilege "indigeneship" and ethnic identity were and still are challenged by millions of urbanites with mixed ethnic and religious heritage. This chapter has fleshed out three major reasons why the urbanization of resistance is inevitable. The first has to do with the sheer demographic influx and bulge of Ethiopia's urban population. Secondly, the economic allure of cities like Addis Ababa means millions migrate from rural areas seeking greener pastures but are faced with intractable problems of urban unemployment, food poverty, hyperinflation, and the rising cost of living and homelessness. Finally, the article sketched out how Addis Ababa has long been the "command post" for political agitation, articulation, and regime change.

The avenues for urban (re)imagination may take any one of these forms or more. The abject material conditions of the urban populace could give rise to a politics of redistribution—one that demands gainful employment, affordable housing, or organizes against the excesses of development or conflict-induced displacements, gentrification, and ghettoization. The urban could also serve as a hub for a rainbow coalition of capital communities, trade unions, and civil society groups that cross cut ethnic boundaries and may check the ethno-nationalist excesses of the current dispensation. To that end, urban spaces have the benefit of housing global and national media outlets and policy platforms that frame and articulate subversive narratives. Most importantly, Ethiopia's urban spaces have the diversity and mobility of people, capital, technologies, and information, which may privilege them to produce "better" models of celebrating language and cultural rights within a liberal-democratic architecture. The future is urban; whether it works, and its exact implications for the political and constitutional framework of Ethiopia, remains to be seen.

Notes

1 Monica W. Varasnyi, "Interrogating "Urban Citizenship" vis-a`-vis Undocumented Migration", *Citizenship Studies*, Vol. 10, No. 2, (2006): 229.

2 TH Marshall, *Citizenship and Social Class*, (Cambridge University Press, 1950).

3 Andrew Linklater, "Cosmopolitan Citizenship" in *Citizenship Studies*, Vol.2, No. 1, (1999):23-41.

4 Hill. L., 'The two Republicae of the Roman Stoics: can a cosmopolite be a patriot?' in *Citizenship Studies*, 4(1) (2000) :65.

5 Nussbaum, M.C. 'Patriotism and cosmopolitanism'. in J. Cohen (Ed.), For Love of Country: Debating the Limits of Patriotism (Beacon Press, 1996):5.

6 Jan-Werner Muller, "A general theory of constitutional patriotism", in *I•CON*, Volume 6, Number 1, (2008):77.

7 Henry Lefebvre, *Le droit`a la ville (Right to the City)*, (Paris: Anthropos, 1968).

8 Henry Lefebvre, "The production of spaces", (1974), D. Nicholson-Smith, Trans., (Blackwell Publishers, 1991).

9 Mark Purcell, "Excavating Lefebvre: The right to the city and its urban politics of the inhabitant", in *GeoJournal*, Vol. 58, (2002):102.

10 Lefebvre fuses the words "citizen" and "denizen" and employs the term "citadin" in his works to emphasize his notion of "inhabitance."

11 Mark Purcell, "Excavating Lefebvre: The right to the city and its urban politics of the inhabitant", in *GeoJournal*, Vol. 58, (2002): 103.

12 Louise Aalen, "Ethnic Federalism and Self-Determination for Nationalities in a Semi-Authoritarian State: The Case of Ethiopia" in *International Journal on Minority and Group Rights*, 13(2), (2006): 261.

13 Edmond Keller, "Ethnic Federalism and Democratization in Ethiopia" in *Horn of Africa*, Vol. XXI, (2003), 30-43.

14 Lovise Aalen, "Ethnic Federalism and Self-Determination for Nationalities in a Semi-Authoritarian State: the Case of Ethiopia" in *International Journal on Minority and Group Rights*, Vol. 13, No 2/3, (2006), 243-261.

15 Semahagn Gashu, *The Last Post-Cold War Socialist Federation: Ethnicity, Ideology and Democracy in Ethiopia*, (Routledge, Taylor and Francis Group, 2014).

16 Since 1991, Addis Ababa had a total of nine mayors, six of whom came from Oromia. The remaining three were from Tigray, Amhara, and Southern regional states.

17 https://data.worldbank.org/country/ET

18 https://ethiopia.opendataforafrica.org/

19 https://ethiopia.opendataforafrica.org/

20 https://data.worldbank.org/country/ET

Bibliography

Aalen, Louise. "Ethnic Federalism and Self-Determination for Nationalities in a Semi-Authoritarian State: The Case of Ethiopia" in *International Journal on Minority and Group Rights*, 13(2), (2006):243-261

Hill. L., 'The two Republicae of the Roman Stoics: can a cosmopolite be a patriot?' in *Citizenship Studies*, 4(1) (2000): 65-79.

Keller, Edmond, "Ethnic Federalism and Democratization in Ethiopia" in *Horn of Africa*, Vol. XXI, (2003), 30-4

Lefebvre, Henry. *Le droit`a la ville, (Right to the City)*, (Paris: Anthropos, 1968).

Lefebvre, Henry. "The production of spaces", (1974), D. Nicholson-Smith, Trans., (Blackwell Publishers, 1991).

Linklater, Andrew. "Cosmopolitan Citizenship" in *Citizenship Studies*, Vol.2, No. 1, (1999):23-41.

Marshalls, T.H. *Citizenship and Social Class*, (Cambridge University Press, 1950).

Muller, Jan-Werner. "A general theory of constitutional patriotism", in *I•CON*, Volume 6, Number 1, (2008), 72–95.

Nussbaum, M.C. 'Patriotism and cosmopolitanism'. in J. Cohen (Ed.), For Love of Country: Debating the Limits of Patriotism (Beacon Press, 1996),3-17.

Purcell, Mark, "Excavating Lefebvre: The right to the city and its urban politics of the inhabitant", In *GeoJournal*, Vol. 58, (2002), 99-108.

Semahagn Gashu, *The Last Post-Cold War Socialist Federation: Ethnicity, Ideology and Democracy in Ethiopia*, (Routledge, Taylor and Francis Group, 2014).

Varasnyi, Monica W. "Interrogating "Urban Citizenship" vis-a`-vis Undocumented Migration", *Citizenship Studies*, Vol. 10, No. 2, (2006): 229–249.

Chapter 9

Towards a Comprehensive Protection of Minority Rights under Ethiopia's Constitutional Framework

Christophe Van der Beken

I. Introduction

Since the coming into effect of the Ethiopian Federal Constitution in 1995, its most controversial provision has without doubt been Article 39, which grants an identical right to self-determination to all of Ethiopia's nations, nationalities, and peoples (i.e., the constitutional vernacular for ethnic groups). The most notable component of the right to self-determination is its external dimension, which provides an unconditional right to secession, constitutionally warranting and even regulating the secession of all ethnic groups from the Ethiopian state. In the event that a constitutional reform process is initiated, it is highly likely that the right to secession will figure prominently on the reform agenda. Although this right is indeed, from a comparative constitutional law perspective, highly exceptional, it arguably has not had that much of an impact on Ethiopian sociopolitical and institutional dynamics. After an unsuccessful invocation of the right to secession by the Somali regional government in the early 1990s, the right came to assume a mainly academic importance. This was due to the hegemonic position and modus operandi of the ruling Ethiopian Peoples' Revolutionary Democratic Front (EPRDF), which effectively suppressed any secessionist tendency. The recent upsurge of Tigrayan nationalism, induced by political developments at the center and invigorated by a two-year armed conflict between the Ethiopian federal and Tigray regional governments (2020–22), has strengthened the practical relevance of the constitutional entrenchment of the right to secession.

Nevertheless, the other—internal—components of the right to self-determination, such as language and political representation rights (including the right to territorial self-governance short of secession), have played a much more prominent role in shaping sociopolitical and institutional dynamics in the country. For instance, the federal structure, which is enshrined in the Constitution, is founded on these internal components of the right to self-determination in that it aims to fulfill them. In other words, the twelve regional states that have hitherto been established aim to enable nations, nationalities, and peoples to exercise their right to self-determination. Firstly, Article 46(2) of the Constitution stipulates that regional states or regions "shall be delimited on the basis of the settlement patterns, language, identity, and consent of the peoples concerned," revealing that ethnic identity is a predominant criterion in the establishment of regional states. In other words, the regional states are established along ethnic lines, empowering specific ethnic groups through the grant of territorial autonomy. Second, in order to fulfill the ethnic groups' language rights, Article 5(3) of the Federal Constitution mandates the regional states to determine their own working language. The representation of nations, nationalities, and peoples in the federal government is, in turn, inter alia guaranteed through the House of Federation, in which each ethnic group is entitled to at least one representative, currently selected by regional state parliaments.

The connection between territory and ethnic empowerment, which is founded on the constitutional assumption and assertion that having a contiguous territory is one of the constituent characteristics of a nation, nationality, or people,[1] legitimizes the Ethiopian federation's designation as a multinational federation. Even so, one can easily infer from the fact that there are more than eighty formally recognized nations, nationalities, and peoples[2] that there is a far from perfect alignment between regional and ethnic territories.

This ethno-demographic reality amounts to the existence of a wide array of majority-minority relations at the level of the regional states. This reality is highly pertinent to any constitutional reform discussion since the current constitution does not anticipate it or, at least, does not provide adequate mechanisms to accommodate it. As said, the Constitution assumes that all ethnic groups have a contiguous territory so that their rights can best be realized within their own territory, in the form of a regional state. This constitutional assumption explains why Article 47(2) of the Constitution entitles all ethnic groups to establish a regional state of their own, creating the possibility for the establishment of more than eighty regional states in Ethiopia. The author of this chapter has argued before that such an ethnic-territorial strategy has obvious limitations, not only because it is administratively and financially unviable but also because it is practically impossible to gerrymander ethnically homogeneous units.[3] An ethnic-territorial strategy can, therefore, never comprehensively protect the rights and interests of ethnic minorities.

The lack of adequate constitutional protection for regional or intra-unit minorities (these are minorities at the level of the federated units) is of much more than mere academic importance, which is amply illustrated by the myriad of human rights violations and abuses targeting these groups. Grave human rights infringements disproportionately affecting intra-unit minorities have led and continue to lead to serious interethnic and interregional conflicts and constitute a considerable threat to Ethiopia's peace, stability, and socioeconomic development. All this is not to argue that constitutional and other public law reforms can by themselves solve the minority conundrum; for that to happen, much improved rule of law and a sociopolitical culture of respect for human rights are also necessary, but offering enhanced legal protection to regional or intra-unit minorities would at least provide them with better tools to assert and protect their rights and advance their interests.

Of course, one may also argue that rather than trying to fill legal lacunae in the current constitutional framework, one should advocate for an overhaul of the ethnic federal system, which is responsible for the creation of the regional majority-minority configurations in the first place. Although the reintroduction of a unitary system, considering its many historical pathologies in the Ethiopian context, does not look like a viable option, a convincing argument can be made for de-emphasizing the importance of ethnicity in delineating regional boundaries. This could, for instance, be done by carving up the existing large ethnic-based regions (such as the Amhara and Oromia regions) into multiple new ones.[4] Yet, even if such a system were to be introduced, there would still be a need to protect intra-regional minorities, as the examples of the Nigerian and Swiss federations exemplify. Furthermore, even unitary states are now under an international legal obligation not to engage in assimilation and instead to protect the linguistic, cultural, and public participation rights of ethnic minorities.[5]

Hence, the pertinence of ethnic minority protection is not limited to the current constitutional setup.

Providing enhanced legal protection to regional minorities constitutes the rationale for the chapter. Enhanced legal protection is not only necessary to protect the rights and interests of regional minorities—and, hence, to ensure citizens' substantive equality irrespective of their ethnic identity—it is simultaneously a tool to prevent tensions caused by discriminatory and exclusionary practices and, as such, to bring about improved societal harmony and stability. Minority protection, therefore, has both an intrinsic and instrumental value. On the other hand, one needs to be duly aware of the divisive potential of minority protection—it may further drive societal segmentation and, therefore, affect social cohesion. Such concern explains why this chapter strongly emphasizes the need for legal and policy mechanisms to enable and promote interethnic communication, learning, and reciprocal empathy. In other words, the chapter recommends the supplementation of accommodationist (or multicultural) mechanisms with integrationist (or intercultural) ones.[6]

The chapter argues that the regional minorities in Ethiopia are entitled to the protection international human rights law offers to national or ethnic minorities (the chapter uses both terms interchangeably). In the next section, the chapter makes the case for the recognition of regional minorities as minorities entitled to specific protection. The third section provides a succinct overview of the major international normative standards pertaining to ethnic minority rights. The fourth section discusses and analyzes the Ethiopian constitutional standards and institutional arrangements vis-à-vis international minority rights law and, by so doing, identifies the protective gaps in the former. Sections III and IV, respectively, serve as inspiration and a baseline for section V, which aims to make a number of recommendations towards more adequate and comprehensive minority protection in Ethiopia.

II. Regional Minorities as Minorities under International Law

One needs to acknowledge that the recognition of regional minorities as minorities entitled to specific protection is still contested. For instance, in *Balantyne et al. v. Canada*, the Human Rights Committee (HRC) argued that English-speaking Canadians did not constitute a minority group in the province of Québec, under the International Covenant on Civil and Political Rights.[7] Yet, this decision was contested, even by individual members of the HRC itself. In a similar vein, this chapter unequivocally argues that regional minorities in a multinational federation shall not be deprived of international minority rights protection. The establishment of ethnic-based units in a multinational federation basically replicates the nation-state model at the regional level, so that the justification for minority protection at the federal level—which includes the protection of minorities' rights and interests against majoritarian-based decision-making—equally applies at the subnational level.[8] Even ethnic groups that constitute a majority or that are dominant at the federal level may be in a minority position vis-à-vis regional government decisions.

The chapter's premise—the recognition of regional minorities as minorities deserving specific protection—has been corroborated by a number of UN Human Rights Treaty Bodies in their concluding observations on Ethiopia. For instance, whereas the HRC appreciated the "recognition of the rights of ethnic and linguistic communities to self-determination at the level of the regional state according to the ethnic federalism established by the Constitution," it simultaneously expressed its concern "about the lack of recognition and participation in public life of the ethnic and linguistic minorities living outside their designated ethnic regions." The HRC, therefore, recommended that "the state party should recognize the existence of the various ethnic and linguistic minorities in each regional state and ensure their adequate political representation and participation at regional, state and federal levels."[9] The Committee on the Elimination of Racial Discrimination (CERD), in its concluding observations on Ethiopia, noted as "positive aspects" the constitutional prohibition of racial discrimination and the language rights accorded to the nations, nationalities, and peoples. It also appreciated the guaranteed representation of minorities in parliament (as such referring to Article 54(3) of the Constitution; see section IV). On the other hand, it expressed its concern over "the absence of information on legislative and other measures taken by the state party to ensure the protection of the rights of racial and ethnic groups." CERD, therefore, recommended that Ethiopia "take all the necessary steps to ensure that all persons belonging to racial and ethnic groups are able to fully exercise their rights under the Convention. The Committee recommends that the State Party pay particular attention to the legislative, constitutional and other measures which must be taken at the level of the federal regions in order to give effect to the rights of these groups."[10] The latter challenge is taken up by this chapter.

III. International Standards on Minority Rights

Section III discusses both binding and nonbinding international standards on minority rights. In this regard, it focuses on the normative standards developed at the level of the United Nations (UN).

III.1. National Minorities: Conceptualization

Before delving into the issue, it is important to recall the fact that, until today, no universally agreed-upon definition of the "national minority" concept has been adopted. Even the 1992 UN Declaration on the Rights of Persons

Belonging to National or Ethnic, Religious and Linguistic Minorities (UN Minority Declaration) fails to include a definition of the concept. Nevertheless, the definition by Francesco Capotorti, who served as special rapporteur of the Sub-Commission on Prevention of Discrimination and Protection of Minorities, is used as a working definition in the chapter. The choice for Capotorti's definition is not only because of its wide acceptance but also because of its explanatory value in the Ethiopian context—as will be clarified in section IV. In his 1979 study, Capotorti defines an "ethnic, religious or linguistic minority", as such referring to the concepts mentioned in Article 27 of the International Covenant on Civil and Political Rights (ICCPR), as:

> *a group numerically inferior to the rest of a population of a State, in a non-dominant position, whose members—being nationals of the State—possess ethnic, religious or linguistic characteristics differing from those of the rest of the population and show, if only implicitly, a sense of solidarity, directed towards preserving their culture, traditions, religion or language.*[11]

In its General Comment 23 on Article 27, the HRC emphasizes that the absence of a legally binding definition does not mean that states can deny the presence of national minorities to the extent that the latter can be established by objective criteria.[12] For Ethiopia, this opinion of the HRC entails that even if regional constitutional documents do not recognize the presence of regional minorities, it does not absolve the federal government from the obligation to ensure that regional states respect, protect, and fulfill the rights of minorities that are objectively present—for instance, because they comply with the elements of Capotorti's definition.

The remainder of section III provides a succinct overview of the major UN normative standards (both binding and nonbinding ones) pertinent to the protection of the rights of national or ethnic minorities. The section adopts a thematic approach along the lines of the four different dimensions of minority protection. These dimensions are existence, nondiscrimination, identity, and participation.[13]

III.2. The Right to Existence

The right to existence of national or ethnic minorities is primarily guaranteed by the 1948 Genocide Convention.[14] Genocide, which the Convention proclaims a crime under international law, is defined as an act committed "with intent to destroy, in whole or in part, a national, ethnic, racial or religious group." Under the Convention, genocide does not only include killing members of the group, but also causing serious bodily or mental harm to the members of the group.[15] Ethnic-based violence is also prohibited by the International Convention on the Elimination of All Forms of Racial Discrimination (ICERD).[16] Article 5 of this convention grants, "without distinction as to race, color, or national or ethnic origin, (b) the right to security of person and protection by the State against violence or bodily harm." As such, the Convention offers an important protection to (members of) ethnic minority communities by protecting them from such violence as harassment and enforced displacement, which often disproportionately target members of minority communities.

III.3. Nondiscriminatory Enjoyment of Universal Human Rights

Before focusing on group-specific rights designed to protect (members of) national minorities, it is important to emphasize the importance of universal individual rights for the protection of national minorities. In fact, the thinking reflected in the Universal Declaration of Human Rights was that the rights of minorities could be adequately protected through the grant of universal individual rights to all human beings. It is obvious that such universal rights as the freedom of opinion and expression, the freedom of assembly and association, the right to equality and nondiscrimination, freedom of movement, the right to vote and be elected, and the right to own property are vital for the protection of (persons) belonging to minorities. Pursuant to Articles 1(1) and 5 of ICERD, these universal rights are equally guaranteed to both (members of) ethnic minority communities and others, implying that ethnic groups fall within the purview of the Racial Discrimination Convention.

The effective protection and enforcement of universal individual rights or citizenship rights could already go a long way in addressing minority grievances since one of the major problems affecting them is persistent and systematic discrimination.[17] Measures that could be taken by states in order to comply with these international legal obligations and to ensure substantive equality are, based on the ICERD, the enactment of hate speech and equality legislation and of affirmative action measures.[18] The abovementioned risk of social fragmentation inherent in minority protection is also acknowledged by ICERD, which mandates states to "encourage ... integrationist multiracial organisations and movements and other means of eliminating barriers between races."[19] In a similar vein, Article 7 of ICERD requires states parties to "adopt immediate and effective measures, particularly in the fields of teaching, education, culture and information, with a view to combating prejudices which lead to racial discrimination and to promoting understanding, tolerance and friendship among nations and racial or **ethnic groups**" (author's emphasis). Although universal individual rights are internationally recognized and, in Ethiopia, also constitutionally protected (see section IV), it is of course vital that there are effective enforcement mechanisms, notably through the agency of courts—an element also recognized by Article 6 of ICERD. Courts need to take effective action against crimes and human rights violations that disproportionately target minority communities. The chapter will point out in section IV that the lack of effective enforcement mechanisms significantly affects the enjoyment of universal rights by (persons belonging to) regional minorities in Ethiopia.

The foregoing demonstrates that, although ICERD does not include an explicit reference to minorities, it contains important minority guarantees.[20] This justifies the assertion by Keane and Castellino that minority rights find legally binding expression in ICERD.[21]

Although ICERD has thus offered tools to protect (members of) minorities since 1965, the core question, as aptly paraphrased by Henrard, was whether the prohibition of discrimination offered sufficient protection to members of minorities or whether additional protection in the form of group-specific or group rights was necessary.[22] The argument in favor of specific measures is that nondiscrimination, although essential, is not sufficient to achieve substantive equality. A state may claim to treat majority and minority members equally, but in practice majoritarian preferences and identities will prevail (for instance, in public decision-making, in the choice of the state's official language, or in the content of the educational curriculum).[23] International human rights law subscribed to the latter argument in 1966 with the adoption of the ICCPR.[24] Apart from repeating the general nondiscrimination principle in its Article 26, Article 27 of the Covenant contains an explicit reference to ethnic minorities:

> In those States in which ethnic, religious or linguistic minorities exist, persons belonging to such minorities shall not be denied the right, in community with the other members of their group, to enjoy their own culture, to profess and practice their own religion, or to use their own language.

With this, the ICCPR complemented the nondiscrimination principle with group-specific rights. The rights granted by Article 27 are still framed as individual rights, but they are not universal since they are specifically accorded to members of minority communities, hence their designation as group-specific. The group-specific rights in Article 27 refer to culture, religion, and language, or, in other words, to issues pertinent for the protection of minorities' distinct identities. These rights are the focus of section 3.4.

III.4. Identity Rights

Although the phrasing of Article 27, "shall not be denied the right", appears to indicate that states parties merely have negative obligations under this Article, the HRC, in its General Comment 23 on Article 27, pointed out that a state party also has a positive obligation "to ensure that the existence and the exercise of these rights are protected against their denial or violation."[25] This implies that the state party should not only refrain from violating the identity rights, but should also protect them against abuses by private actors.

Another UN convention explicitly recognizing the identity rights of minorities is the Convention on the Rights of the Child (CRC).[26] Article 30 of the CRC stipulates:

In those States in which ethnic, religious or linguistic minorities or persons of indigenous origin exist, a child belonging to such a minority or who is indigenous shall not be denied the right, in community with other members of his or her group, to enjoy his or her own culture, to profess and practise his or her own religion, or to use his or her own language.

Still another important provision that contains the cultural rights of ethnic minorities is Article 15(1a) of the International Covenant on Economic, Social and Cultural Rights (ICESCR),[27] which stipulates: "The States Parties to the present Covenant recognize the right of everyone: (a) To take part in cultural life." In its General Comment No. 21, the Committee on Economic, Social and Cultural Rights asserted that Article 15(1a) also includes "the right of minorities and of persons belonging to minorities to take part in the cultural life of society, and also to conserve, promote and develop their own culture." Minorities, according to the Committee, have the right "to their cultural diversity, traditions, customs, religion, forms of education, languages, communication media (press, radio, television, Internet) and other manifestations of their cultural identity and membership." With this, the Committee on Economic, Social and Cultural Rights recognized both the linguistic and cultural rights of minorities (implying the recognition of group rights proper) and of persons belonging to minorities. Both General Comment 23 of the HRC and General Comment 21 of the Committee on Economic, Social and Cultural Rights illustrate that the UN treaty monitoring bodies have contributed to the development of minority rights standards that are either explicit or implicitly enshrined in the respective covenants.[28]

Although several UN covenants contain identity rights for minorities, it was only in the early 1990s that a minority-specific document was adopted. At the beginning of the 1990s, increased attention to minority rights at the international level was spurred by a global rise of ethno-nationalism, as evidenced by the disintegration along ethnic lines of the communist multinational federations of Yugoslavia and the Soviet Union. This was the context in which the UN General Assembly adopted the UN Declaration on the Rights of Persons Belonging to National or Ethnic, Religious and Linguistic Minorities in 1992. Although the Declaration is not a legally binding document (until today, no convention on the rights of national minorities has been adopted), it has considerable moral authority.[29]

The UN Minority Declaration confirms the HRC's interpretation of Article 27 by proclaiming that states have positive obligations regarding the identity rights of minorities. More specifically, Article 1(1) of the Declaration stipulates: "states shall protect the existence and the national or ethnic, cultural, religious and linguistic identity of minorities within their respective territories and shall encourage conditions for the promotion of that identity." With regard to states' positive obligations in terms of language, Article 4(3) of the Declaration mandates states to "take appropriate measures" so that "persons belonging to minorities may have adequate opportunities to learn their mother tongue or to have instruction in their mother tongue." Regarding culture, states, according to Article 4(4), have the obligation to take measures in the field of education "in order to encourage knowledge of the history, traditions, language and culture of the minorities existing within their territory." An inclusive educational curriculum will enable children from minority communities to understand their culture while simultaneously stimulating interethnic understanding. The importance of interethnic understanding is stressed by Article 4(4)'s stipulation that "persons belonging to minorities should have adequate opportunities to gain knowledge of the society as a whole." The latter provision is another expression of the concern that minority protection should not lead to societal fragmentation and segmentation. Rather, the educational curriculum should contribute to a reciprocal understanding of the diverse cultures present in a society and, as such, serve the formation of an inclusive national identity or inclusive citizenship.[30] The role of education in promoting reciprocal understanding is also explicitly mentioned in Article 13(1) of the ICESCR, where it states that education shall promote "understanding, tolerance and friendship among all nations and all racial, ethnic or religious groups" (author's emphasis). Education will thus reduce the ability of "ethnic entrepreneurs" to propagate one-sided historical myths and exaggerations in pursuit of their short-term sociopolitical and economic objectives.[31] To achieve this, minorities who receive instruction in the minority language should also be given adequate opportunities to acquire sufficient knowledge of the majority language.[32] In fact, the ideal situation would be for students from both majority and minority communities to learn each other's languages. This would significantly facilitate their participation in the wider society. The issue of minorities' participation rights is discussed next.

III.5. Public Participation Rights

Apart from identity rights, international law grants minorities the right to participate in public decisions that affect them. Effective participation places minorities in a better position to protect their rights and interests through influencing laws and policies, and in this regard, it is argued that public participation is key to the enjoyment of all other rights.[33] Furthermore, public participation of minorities promotes their inclusion into the wider state and society. By doing so, it helps in the establishment and maintenance of social harmony, peace, and stability. Therefore, ensuring the public participation of minorities serves the interests of both the minorities and the state.[34] For this healthy effect to happen, representation of minorities should be guaranteed not only in political institutions such as the parliament and executive but also in the civil service, courts, public media, and law-enforcement agencies. The representation of minorities in law-enforcement agencies strengthens their societal legitimacy and, therefore, increases their effectiveness in guaranteeing peace and stability. The same applies for courts.

A right to participation can be inferred from Article 27 of the ICCPR. Although Article 27 does not explicitly mention the right to public representation and participation, General Comment 23, paragraph 7, of the HRC asserts that, regarding culture, states may need to take positive measures to ensure the effective participation of members of minority communities in decisions that affect them. Even if the Comment focuses on cultural rights, the argument could be used analogously for other rights—although this is not explicitly mentioned in the General Comment.[35] That the right to participation is not limited to cultural issues was confirmed by the UN Minority Declaration. First, in contrast with Article 27, Article 2(2) of the Declaration explicitly grants persons belonging to minorities the right to effectively participate in cultural, religious, social, economic, and public life. Next, Article 2(3) of the Declaration stipulates that "persons belonging to minorities have the right to participate effectively in decisions on the national and, where appropriate, regional level concerning the minority to which they belong or the regions in which they live, in a manner not incompatible with national legislation." Article 2(3) is also important for its grant of public participation rights at the regional level, corroborating this chapter's argument that minority protection should not only be guaranteed at the national level but at the regional level as well.

Based on the aforementioned UN normative framework, minorities (including, according to this chapter, regional minorities)—whose presence is determined on the basis of objective criteria—are entitled to equal protection of all universal rights, for which effective enforcement mechanisms (notably through the agency of courts) are paramount. Yet, in order to ensure the substantive equality of (persons belonging to) minorities, their identity rights (notably language and culture) and rights to public representation and participation are also guaranteed. Furthermore, in order to ensure that the protection of minority rights does not lead to segmented or even atomized groups, international human rights law emphasizes the importance of interethnic understanding to remove interethnic barriers. It strives to accomplish that through encouraging multiracial organizations and movements (ICERD) and inclusive educational curricula (the ICESCR and the Minority Declaration).

IV. Existing Protection of Minorities under the Ethiopian Constitutional Framework

This section discusses and analyzes the Ethiopian constitutional standards and institutional arrangements pertaining to minority rights from the perspective of international human rights law.

IV.1. Minorities at the Federal level

Although, as this chapter argues, the Ethiopian Federal Constitution contains provisions pertinent to the protection of ethnic minorities, there is only one place where the Constitution explicitly uses the term "minorities" and that is Article 54(3). This provision guarantees "Minority Nationalities and Peoples" at least twenty seats in the House of People's Representatives, the first directly elected chamber of the federal parliament. Yet, the Constitution does not specify or define who these "Minority Nationalities and Peoples" are. Article 13(1.d) of the Election Law[36] merely states that "minority nationalities which are deemed to require special representation shall be determined by the House of Federation based on clear criteria established in advance." In practice, "Minority Nationalities and Peoples" are nations, nationalities, and peoples that are too small to constitute the majority in an electoral district or constituency. The rationale for endowing these ethnic groups with guaranteed representation is that, in the context of a first-past-the-post electoral system with voting mainly taking place along ethnic lines, they would not get any representation in the House of People's Representatives without it. However, apart from their guaranteed representation in parliament, these minority nationalities and peoples are constitutionally treated in an identical manner as all other ethnic groups.

Nations, nationalities, and peoples have, according to Article 8(1) of the Constitution, all sovereign power and, pursuant to Article 39, an identical right to self-determination. Although the right to self-determination is allotted to nations, nationalities, and peoples, the author has argued in other publications that, in practice, it amounts to a right relevant to ethnic minorities.[37] This argument is substantiated by referring to Capotorti's definition of ethnic minorities, cited in section 3.1. According to this definition, in order to qualify as minorities, ethnic groups need to be both numerically inferior to the rest of the population of the state and in a nondominant position. As can be observed from the list included in the 2007 Ethiopian Population and Housing Census, the country's population is composed of more than eighty ethnic groups, or, to use the constitutional vernacular, "nations, nationalities and peoples."[38] Yet, even the numerically largest ethnic groups, the Oromo (34.5 percent of the total population) and the Amhara (26.9 percent), do not constitute an absolute majority, which means that, from a numerical perspective, all Ethiopia's ethnic groups find themselves in a minority position vis-à-vis the rest of the country's population. Even though, admittedly, it may conceal hidden power relations, neither the ethnic composition of both chambers of the federal parliament nor that of the federal cabinet demonstrate the dominance of one specific ethnic group, either. Hence, all Ethiopian ethnic groups comply with Capotorti's definition and can be qualified as ethnic minorities. Based on this premise, Article 39 grants extensive group rights to ethnic minorities, warranting the designation of the Ethiopian Federal Constitution as a minority-sensitive one. Yet, before taking a closer look at these group rights and comparing them with the international standards, it is important to point out that the Ethiopian Constitution also grants a number of other rights pertinent to the protection of ethnic minorities.

The existence of ethnic minorities is guaranteed by the prohibition of genocide, enshrined in Article 28 of the Constitution. Although the group rights enshrined in the Constitution have drawn most of the attention, it should be emphasized that Article 10 of the Constitution gives equal emphasis to citizenship rights. Indeed, the Constitution contains a wide range of universal rights that are guaranteed to all Ethiopian citizens, irrespective of their ethnic identity. As Yonatan rightly points out, the inclusion of expansive and extraordinary group rights has overshadowed these universal rights.[39] Nonetheless, many of the constitutionally entrenched human rights are highly pertinent to the protection of (persons belonging to) minorities, such as the freedom of opinion and expression, the freedom of assembly and association, due process of law, the right to equality and nondiscrimination, freedom of movement, the right to vote and be elected, and the right to own property. As pointed out in section 3.3, the effective protection and enforcement of universal individual rights or citizenship rights could already go a long way in addressing minority grievances, since one of the major problems affecting minorities is persistent and systematic discrimination. Of course, the effectiveness of these rights in offering robust protection to minorities depends on the existence of strong and capacitated enforcement institutions, a condition that is not fulfilled in the Ethiopian context—an issue that the chapter discusses below.

Returning to Article 39, it includes both identity rights (linguistic and cultural rights) and public representation rights. Furthermore, it also includes the right to territorial autonomy, which implies that all eighty-plus ethnic groups in the country are entitled to territorial self-governance. Whereas identity and public participation rights are currently granted to minorities by international law (see sections 3.4 and 3.5), international human rights law does not endow ethnic minorities with the right to territorial autonomy.[40] Territorial autonomy is so far only granted to indigenous peoples by Article 4 of the nonbinding UN Declaration on the Rights of Indigenous Peoples, adopted by the UN General Assembly in 2007. Article 39 even grants minorities, as the ultimate consequence of their sovereign power granted in Article 8, the right to secession. From a comparative constitutional law perspective, the constitutional entrenchment of a right to secession is rare, and the fact that it is allotted to all ethnic groups of the country is even more unique.[41] Article 39 of the Ethiopian Constitution, therefore, grants unparalleled minority rights to the ethnic minorities at the federal level. The Constitution doesn't leave it at that but also provides institutional mechanisms to fulfill minority rights through the federal structure it creates.

As mentioned in the introduction, Article 46(2) of the Constitution stipulates that the (regional) states of the federation "shall be delimited on the basis of the settlement patterns, language, identity, and consent of the peoples concerned," revealing that ethnic identity is a predominant criterion in the establishment of regional states. Article 47(1) of the Federal Constitution lists nine regional states: 1) the State of Tigray 2) the State of Afar 3) the State of Amhara 4) the State of Oromia 5) the State of Somali 6) the State of Benishangul/Gumuz 7) The state of the Southern Nations, Nationalities and Peoples 8) the State of the Gambella Peoples, and 9) the State of the Harari People. The ethnic basis of the regional states can be clearly inferred from the nomenclature of six states: Tigray, Afar, Amhara, Oromia, Somali, and Harar. These states are numerically and politically dominated (in the case of Harar, the Harari dominance is only political) by the eponymous ethnic groups. Since the country has eighty-plus ethnic groups that all hold an identical right to self-determination, Article 47(2) states that all other nations, nationalities, and peoples have the right to establish, at any time, their own states, and Article 47(3) outlines the procedure for that to happen. While this right has for a long time been merely theoretical, with the hegemonic EPRDF resisting and suppressing its invocation, the political dynamics of the past few years have given this right much more practical importance. For instance, using Article 47(2) and (3), two new regional states were established out of the Southern Nations, Nationalities, and Peoples Regional State (hereinafter the SNNPRS) in 2020 and 2021. The Sidama Regional State, numerically and politically dominated by its eponymous group, was established in June 2020, and one year later, in November 2021, the multiethnic South West Ethiopia Peoples' Regional State (hereafter the South West Regional State) became the eleventh regional state.42 A further disaggregation of the SNNPRS is envisaged. In July 2023, the House of Federation decided that six zones of the SNNPRS (the Konso,

Gedeo, Gamo, Gofa, South Omo, and Wolayita Zones) as well as five special woredas (Amaro, Ale, Basketo, Burji, and Derashe) would be reorganized into a new regional state entitled "South Ethiopia Regional State."43 What was left of the SNNPRS, i.e., Gurage, Silte, Kambata Tambaro, Halaba, Hadia Zones and Yem Special Woreda, are now organized as "Central Ethiopia Regional State" from late August 2023. Regional states thus constitute the forum where ethnic groups exercise territorial self-governance and are empowered to protect their identity rights, for instance through the selection of the group's language as the regional working language (Article 5.3 of the Constitution).

To ensure the exercise of minorities' public participation at the federal level, the federal Constitution contains only a few mechanisms. The chapter already mentioned Article 54(3), which guarantees the representation of all ethnic groups in the House of People's Representatives. All ethnic groups are also guaranteed representation in the House of Federation, the second federal chamber of the parliament. Article 61 of the Constitution stipulates that the House of Federation is composed of representatives of nations, nationalities, and peoples and that each of them shall have at least one representative in the House. Furthermore, each nation or nationality shall be represented by one additional representative for every million of its population.

Although all ethnic groups, therefore, have constitutionally guaranteed representation in the federal parliament, in practice there are a number of controversial issues pertaining to the equality and effectiveness of this representation. Regarding equality, although Article 13(1.b) of the Election Law states that electoral districts or constituencies for the House of People's Representatives shall be determined on the basis of population and that the number of people per constituency shall be comparable, this is obviously not the case. One can take the example of Somali representation to illustrate this. Currently, the Somali Regional State has twenty-three electoral districts and, since there is only one representative per district, 23 seats or representatives in the House. Based on the last official population data (released in 2007), the Somali regional population numbered 4,439,147. With this, they were slightly larger than the population of the Tigray Regional State, with 4,314,456. Nonetheless, the Tigray Regional State was allotted 38 seats in the House of People's Representatives. Also, in comparison with other regional states, such as Oromia and Amhara, the Somali Regional State is not proportionately represented. Based on a population size of 27,158,471, the Oromia Region was granted 178 seats, which is roughly 1 seat per 150,000 people. In the case of the Somali Region, there is only 1 seat per 190,000 people on average. This also contrasts with the Amhara Region (138 seats), which has 1 seat per 125,000 people. This means that the ethnic-based regional states do not equally empower the eponymous ethnic groups in the federal parliament. The same data also demonstrates that the Oromia and Amhara Regions together have 316 seats in the House of People's Representatives, which usually makes its decisions by a majority of the members present and voting.[44] In the absence of a minority veto, this implies that, theoretically, all decisions can be made by a coalition of Amhara and Oromo representatives, relegating all other ethnic communities to permanent minority status.

Furthermore, the Constitution does not guarantee the ethnic inclusiveness of the federal cabinet or of other federal government organs such as the courts, civil service, or security organs.[45] For instance, the Constitution does not require the prime minister to consider ethnicity while selecting candidates for federal cabinet positions or for other nominations. The only exception is Article 87(1) of the Federal Constitution, which stipulates that "the composition of the national armed forces shall reflect the equitable representation of the Nations, Nationalities and Peoples of Ethiopia." More solid and specific guarantees of ethnic inclusiveness can, for instance, be found in Kenya, where Article 7 of the National Cohesion and Integration Act of 2008 states that all public establishments shall seek to represent the diversity of the people of Kenya in the employment of staff. The law even adds that no public establishment shall have more than one-third of its staff from the same ethnic community.

While all of Ethiopia's ethnic groups are minorities at the federal level, at the level of the regional states, clear majority-minority configurations are observable. The next section presents these configurations and investigates whether, and if so in what form, the Ethiopian constitutional framework offers protection to the rights of these regional minorities.

IV.2. Minorities at the Regional Level

IV.2.1. Recognition of Minorities at the Regional Level

Section 4.1. pointed out that six of the nine constitutionally listed regional states are dominated by the eponymous groups. With the establishment of the Sidama Region in 2020, this number has now increased to seven. These groups, which constitute country-wide minorities, have, therefore, assumed majority status at the regional level.

However, since there are now seventy-six officially recognized ethnic groups in the country, this implies that most ethnic communities constitute a minority at the regional state level. Furthermore, not all persons belonging to the seven regional majority groups reside in "their" region. For instance, more than 4 million Amhara live outside the Amhara Region, and the same is true for more than 1.5 million Oromo.[46] Some of these minorities are recognized by the regional states. From the seven regional states that have empowered one specific ethnic community, four recognize the presence of regional minorities (although none of them uses the term "minorities" except the Amhara Regional Constitution, which, in a similar vein as the Federal Constitution, guarantees the representation of minority nationalities and peoples in the State Council). Article 39 of the Tigray Constitution recognizes, apart from the majority Tigray, the Irob and Kunama ethnic minorities in the state. Article 43(2) of the Afar Constitution recognizes the Argoba as an "indigenous" minority group in the state. The Harar Constitution explicitly mentions the Oromo as one of the other communities in the state (in fact, the Oromos constitute the absolute numerical majority of the Harar regional population).

Finally, Article 39(6) of the Amhara Constitution recognizes the Agew Himra, Awi, and Oromo as ethnic communities of the state. Furthermore, the Kemant and Argoba are recognized as regional minorities by Amhara ordinary laws. The remaining three states do not recognize specific ethnic groups other than the eponymous ones (these are the Oromo, Somali, and Sidama). The Oromia and Somali Constitutions recognize the ethnic diversity of their population[47] but fail to mention any specific group other than the Oromo and Somali. The Sidama Constitution is conspicuously silent about the presence of other ethnic communities in the state. Although recent data is not available, the 2007 population census indicated that more than 200,000 residents of the Sidama Zone (which transformed itself into a regional state) had a non-Sidama identity.[48] Five of the current twelve regional states (the Gambella, Benishangul-Gumuz, South Ethiopia, Central Ethiopia, and South West Regional States) are characterized by the lack of a dominant group; they can, therefore, be designated as minorities' regions. The constitutions of Benishangul-Gumuz and Gambella each recognize five ethnic groups/minorities (again, the term minorities is only used for the purpose of guaranteed representation in the State Council). Article 2 of the Benishangul-Gumuz Constitution lists the following five groups as "indigenous" communities of the state: the Berta (since 2022 officially called "Benishangul," pursuant to a decision of the State Council[49]), the Gumuz, the Shinasha, the Mao, and the Komo. Article 47(1) of the Gambella Constitution similarly mentions five ethnic groups as "founding members" of the regional state: the Anywaa, the Nuer, the Majang, the Opo, and the Komo. The SNNPRS and South West Regional Constitutions do not explicitly mention specific ethnic groups, but in both states, a large number of ethnic groups are recognized as indigenous.[50]

It should be pointed out at this juncture that the regional states are much more ethnically diverse than their regional constitutions and laws reveal. This means that only some ethnic minorities are recognized by the regional states. These minorities are either constitutionally or informally referred to as "indigenous" minorities, which implies that all the others are "nonindigenous" or "settlers."[51] There are major concerns regarding the rights and interests of the latter, but before delving into that, section 4.2.2. first provides an overview of the rights and institutional mechanisms afforded to indigenous minorities.

IV.2.2. Protection of "Indigenous" Minorities

The rights and institutional mechanisms designed to protect indigenous minorities are noticeably inspired by those included in the Federal Constitution. First of all, it goes without saying that persons belonging to indigenous minorities are Ethiopian citizens and, as such, are equally entitled to all citizenship rights included in both the federal and regional constitutions. The regional constitutions largely repeat the universal individual rights included in the Federal Constitution. Furthermore, the Federal Constitution is the supreme law of the land, which means that its human rights guarantees are binding on the regional states. This implies that although regional constitutional human rights guarantees can offer better protection, they cannot go below the standard set by the Federal Constitution.[52]

The regional constitutions also offer group rights in the form of the right to self-determination. In parallel with the Federal Constitution, the regional constitutions that recognize ethnic minorities endow the latter with a right to self-determination with identical components as those enshrined in Article 39 of the Federal Constitution.

The regions also provide institutional mechanisms to enable ethnic minorities to fulfill this right. The main mechanism is similar to the Federal Constitution: the establishment of ethnic-based sub-regional or local governments. Article 43(2) of the Afar Constitution recognizes the right of the Argoba people to have their own "special woreda" in the region, while the Irob administer their own woreda in the Tigray Regional State.[53] Article 73(1) of the Amhara Constitution establishes a Nationality Administration for the Oromo, Agew Himra, and Awi. Special woredas have furthermore been established for the Argoba and Kemant. In a similar vein, Article 74(1) of the Benishangul-Gumuz Constitution anticipates the establishment of "administrations of Nationalities," which are ethnic-based local governments for the five indigenous groups of the region. Ethnic-based nationality zones are also established for the Anywaa, Nuer, and Majang in the Gambella Region. According to Article 45(2) of the SNNPRS Constitution, all ethnic groups of the states—that is, the indigenous ones—have the right to establish a zone/special woreda. Similarly, Article 48(5) of the South West Constitution entitles all ethnic groups of the state to the establishment of their own zone or woreda. It goes beyond the scope of this chapter to provide an extensive overview of the institutional structure and competencies of these ethnic-based local governments. For the purpose of this chapter, it suffices to mention that the nationality administrations and nationality zones in the Amhara, Benishangul-Gumuz, Gambella, SNNPR, and South West states empower the concerned ethnic groups to protect their language (for instance, by using the ethnic language as the local working language) and culture. Although the Oromo do not have the right to set up an ethnic-based local government in Harar, their language rights are protected since Article 6 of the Harar Constitution designates Afaan Oromo as one of the two regional working languages (the other being Harari).

Another similarity with the Federal Constitution is that the regional constitutions only provide a few mechanisms to ensure the participation of the indigenous minorities in the regional government institutions. The constitutions of Amhara, Gambella, Benishangul-Gumuz, SNNPR, and South West Regional States guarantee the representation of "minority nationalities and peoples" in the State Council, the regional parliament. In the latter two regional states, the regional parliament is bicameral, with a Council of Nationalities that complements the State Council. In both regional states, all indigenous minorities are entitled to at least one (five in the South West) representative(s) in the Council of Nationalities and one additional (five in the South West) representative(s) for every million of their population.[54] By the same token, this also guarantees the representation of the indigenous minorities in regional constitutional interpretation, which is one of the mandates of the Councils of Nationalities. Similarly, representation of the indigenous minorities is also guaranteed in the Constitutional Interpretation Commissions (bodies of constitutional interpretation) of the Tigray, Afar, Amhara, Benishangul-Gumuz, and Gambella states.

In terms of guaranteeing the public representation of ethnic minorities in the regional cabinet or in other regional government organs such as the courts, civil service, or security organs, the regional constitutions are equally wanting as their federal counterpart. The only exception to this pattern is the new South West Constitution, which was adopted by the South West State Council in November 2021. Article 51 of this constitution contains a number of provisions ensuring ethnic pluralism in regional government institutions. Article 51(2) stipulates that the positions of speaker of the State Council, speaker of the Council of Nationalities, president and vice president of the Region, and president of the Supreme Court shall be held by persons with different ethnic identities. Article 51(4) adds that other government positions shall be "assumed equitably by the Nations, Nationalities and Peoples of the Region."

With the above, section 4.2.2. has demonstrated that the regional constitutions offer extensive protection to the recognized or "indigenous" minorities, a protection that is similar to and in some cases even goes beyond the protection offered by the Federal Constitution.

IV.2.3. Protection of "Nonindigenous" Minorities

While the regional constitutions explicitly grant "sovereign" power and the right to self-determination to the minorities designated or considered "indigenous," they have not enshrined minority-specific rights for the nonindigenous ones.[55] Nonetheless, the latter minorities are present in all regional states, and in some of them they constitute a considerable part of the regional population. For instance, according to the 2007 census data, the Amhara and Oromo constitute, respectively, 21.25 per cent and 13.32 per cent of the Benishangul-Gumuz regional population. The data for the Gambella State indicates that the Amhara constitute 8.42 per cent and the Oromo 4.83 per cent of the regional population.

Although the nonindigenous minorities cannot claim group-specific or group rights on the basis of the regional constitutions, it is undeniable that persons with nonindigenous identities are Ethiopian citizens and are, therefore, entitled to claim the citizenship rights included in both the federal and regional constitutions against regional government organs. Yet, a lack of capacity and neutrality among regional and local rule of law institutions (including security forces, prosecutorial bodies, and courts) has prevented the effectiveness of the constitutional individual rights guarantees. Rule of law institutions have failed to take effective actions against crimes and human rights violations, which disproportionately target minority communities. In the past couple of years, such abuses and violations have occurred with increased intensity in several states, such as the Amhara, Oromia, and Benishangul/Gumuz States.[56] It has forced persons belonging to nonindigenous ethnic groups to leave their place of residence and has led to a large number of internally displaced people. These dynamics have seriously affected social cohesion, peace, and stability in the Ethiopian polity. They have not only led to intra-regional conflict but also strained inter-regional relations with ethnic-based regional states acting or threatening to act on behalf of their ethnic kin.[57] Hence, a more effective and comprehensive protection of nonindigenous minorities would not only benefit minority rights and interests but also serve social harmony, peace, and stability in Ethiopia.

V. Towards a More Comprehensive Protection of Minority Rights

Section IV has unequivocally demonstrated that the major problem regarding minority protection in Ethiopia revolves around the "nonindigenous" regional minorities. Although they, based on Capotorti's definition, fully qualify to be considered as minorities, neither the federal nor the regional constitutions provide them with minority-specific rights. Even when it comes to universal individual rights, persons belonging to nonindigenous minorities are not equally treated. The chapter does not want to delve into the discussion of whether the regional distinction between indigenous and nonindigenous minorities is constitutional. It rather subscribes to the argument that even if such distinction were constitutional (emanating from the ethno-territorial approach prescribed by the Federal Constitution), it should not have discriminatory consequences for (persons belonging to) nonindigenous minorities. The chapter, therefore, aims to outline what a more comprehensive minority protection regime in Ethiopia could look like. The recommendations are inspired by the international and constitutional human rights obligations of Ethiopia, mentioned in previous sections. Pursuant to Article 9(4) of the Constitution, international conventions ratified by Ethiopia are part and parcel of the law of the land. Hence, the minority rights obligations included in the hard law instruments discussed in Section III are binding on Ethiopia. Furthermore, Article 10(2) of the Constitution requires respect for the human and democratic rights of citizens and peoples enshrined in the Constitution, which, according to Article 13(2), should be interpreted in line with Ethiopia's international human rights obligations.

The right of persons belonging to intra-unit minorities to enjoy, without any discrimination, all fundamental rights and freedoms protected in the Constitution and in international human rights law binding on Ethiopia can already be inferred from Article 25 of the Federal Constitution. Universal individual rights entrenched in the Federal Constitution are undeniably crucial for the protection of intra-unit minorities.[58] The Federal Constitution is the supreme law of the land (Article 9 of the Constitution), and its human rights provisions are, therefore, binding for the regional states. As such, the bill of rights included in the Federal Constitution offers a nationwide standard of protection. Yet, as mentioned at several junctures in this chapter, the institutional mechanisms to enforce these rights are not effective. Constitutional review power at the federal level is allotted to the House of Federation, a political institution with unequal representation of ethnic groups. The regional bodies mandated with constitutional review power (that is, the power to interpret the regional constitutions) are equally composed of political representatives and dominated by the indigenous communities.[59] The argument to reform the constitutional review mechanisms has been made repeatedly. It is, therefore, unfortunate that the drafters of the newest regional constitutions of Sidama and the South West Regions have not been bolder in the design of more effective (that is, human-rights-protecting) constitutional review mechanisms. On the other hand, an encouraging development is that Article 3 of the Federal Courts Proclamation of 2021 now explicitly mandates federal courts to enforce the human rights provisions of the Constitution as well as Ethiopia's international human rights obligations.[60]

Regarding identity rights, persons belonging to regional minorities should have the right to be educated in their language or at least learn their language and culture. Students who are educated in the minority language shall furthermore be enabled to learn the working language(s) of the federal government and of the respective ethnic-based regional or local government unit (such as nationality zones and special woredas) and gain knowledge of the society as a whole. On their part, students belonging to territorially empowered or indigenous communities shall be informed about the historical narratives, languages, and cultures of the regional minorities. The latter two recommendations emanate from the consideration that the educational curriculum should contribute to reciprocal understanding of the diverse cultures present in a society and, as such, serve social cohesion. The twofold objectives of protecting minorities' identity rights and strengthening social cohesion can also be served by the media. This is why regional minorities should have the right to broadcast time in their own language on public media owned by regional governments. This right should be subject to objective and empirically verifiable conditions, such as a minimum presence of minorities. The media should be used to protect, develop, and promote the minority language and culture as well as to inform the minority about the language and culture of the territorially empowered communities and about the activities of the government organs of the regional and local government units. Along the same lines, media can be used to promote values that support a cohesive and peaceful society, such as intercultural dialogue, understanding, tolerance, shared values, respect, and solidarity. With regard to the use of the minority language in the public service, subject to the fulfillment of such conditions as a minimum size of the minority and an explicit minority demand thereto, persons belonging to minorities should have the right to use and to be served in the minority language in their interactions with the public service.

The above recommendations emanate from the consideration that interethnic antagonisms are on the rise in Ethiopia and have now reached worrying levels. Measures to protect regional minorities' identity rights should, therefore, be accompanied by mechanisms focusing on intercultural dialogue, tolerance, and reciprocal integration. To put it differently, accommodationist measures of minority protection promoting "multiculturalism" should be accompanied by integrationist measures focusing on "interculturalism," an approach that recognizes social integration as the central concern in managing diversity.[61]

In order to ensure regional minorities public representation and effective participation, elements of consociationalism or power sharing should be considered.

For instance, one can recommend that regional minorities that constitute below 50 percent and above a minimum percentage of the total population of an ethnic-based regional or local government unit have guaranteed representation in the regional and local government councils. In order to ensure the minorities' effective participation, a minority veto could additionally be granted. For instance, one could legislate that a proposed council decision pertaining to issues of vital interest (i.e., issues directly impacting minority rights) to regional minorities shall not be adopted if the decision is opposed by a qualified majority vote of the intra-unit minority representatives. A useful example in this regard is the so-called alarm bell procedure entrenched in Article 54 of the Belgian constitution. In the case of a bill that requires a mere absolute majority, three-quarters of the members of one linguistic group can submit a motion declaring that the bill can gravely damage relations between the communities (in other words, the linguistic group rings the communitarian alarm bell). In this case, parliamentary procedure is suspended, and the motion is referred to the Council of Ministers, which needs to find a solution.

In regional or local government units where regional minorities have guaranteed representation in the elected councils, such representation should also be guaranteed in the units' executive organs. Useful inspiration can come from Kenya, where Article 35(1.a) of the County Governments Act 2012 requires the county governor to ensure that "to the fullest extent possible, the composition of the executive committee reflects the community and cultural diversity of the country." This requirement is backed up by the provision of Article 35(2), which mandates that the county assembly reject nominations to the executive committee that do not take this diversity into account. Although this is part of the nondiscrimination guarantee, it is good to mention here that persons belonging to regional minorities need to have equal opportunities to be employed in all other regional and local government institutions, such as the civil service, judiciary, security, and parastatals. Again, a reference to the Kenyan example is inspirational. With regard to the public service, Article 65 of the aforementioned County Governments Act stipulates that, in selecting candidates for appointment, the County Public Service Board needs to ensure that "at least 30 percent of the vacant posts at entry level are filled by candidates who are not from the dominant ethnic community in the county." Hence, no single ethnic group should get more than 70 percent of the posts at entry level.[62]

This chapter acknowledges the risk that consociational mechanisms may lead to "freezing" ethnic identities,[63] which may complicate interethnic cooperation and the achievement of sustainable social harmony. Yet, it argues that with the current degree of interethnic distrust and polarization characterizing the Ethiopian polity, it is necessary to offer the necessary institutional guarantees for descriptive or mirror ethnic representation through power-sharing mechanisms. While this would offer the necessary confidence to minority communities in the short run, the equal protection of individual rights and the aforementioned integrationist measures in the fields of language, education, and media would incrementally mitigate interethnic grievances and distrust.

Another consociational mechanism to ensure public participation is the granting of autonomy. As mentioned in section 4.1., international human rights law does not endow ethnic minorities with the right to territorial autonomy. Neither does this chapter recommend it for nonindigenous regional minorities. Territorially empowered communities are expected to be very reluctant to cede a degree of government power over "their" territory to nonindigenous minorities. Moreover, apart from the political, administrative, and financial costs it would engender, the creation of new ethnic-based local governments would create new majority-minority configurations and would not even empower all minority members, since many of them live scattered across the regions. This is why I have suggested in a number of publications the implementation of the non-territorial autonomy mechanism.[64] Non-territorial autonomy is an adequate device to enable ethnic minorities that are scattered over a territory to exercise their identity rights. The concept is based on a separation between autonomy and territory, so that autonomy is given to a certain ethnic group rather than linked to a particular territory. In the case of Ethiopia, this could mean that subnational minorities are given the right to have their own non-territorial council. This non-territorial council, composed exclusively of members of the concerned ethnic group, would be competent for identity-related matters such as culture, language, and education, and its authority would extend to all members of the concerned group regardless of where they live in the region.[65] Today, non-territorial autonomy arrangements are particularly popular in Central and Eastern European countries such as Estonia, Croatia, Hungary, Serbia, and Slovenia. Non-territorial administrations have very diverse institutional arrangements and competencies. While in some countries the system of cultural councils is established only at the national level, in others we find them at different administrative levels (where their establishment requires the fulfillment of numerical thresholds). In some countries, non-territorial autonomies have the right to consent to local and national decisions affecting minority rights, while in other jurisdictions, non-territorial councils are merely consultative and advisory bodies.[66]

It is important to conclude this section by pointing out that most of the aforementioned recommendations can be implemented without recourse to constitutional reform; they merely require the House of People's Representatives to enact a framework proclamation on the rights of national minorities. Apart from incorporating substantive provisions on minority rights, this law could also establish a council for minorities, which would be empowered to supervise and ensure the implementation of the framework proclamation. To this end, the council should serve as a center of expertise on minority rights and as a forum and channel for dialogue between governmental organs and intra-unit minorities.

VI. Conclusion

The multinational federal system created by the 1995 Ethiopian Federal Constitution is itself often criticized. In fact, it is the most prominent topic in constitutional reform discussions. This chapter does not delve into this discussion but starts from the observation that the existing constitutional arrangements created to achieve the constitutional unity in diversity objective are not adequate thereto. They do not offer comprehensive protection for diversity, nor do they include sufficient guarantees to achieve unity. To put it in more concrete terms, the current constitutional framework (including both the federal and twelve regional constitutions) does not offer sufficient and effective mechanisms to manage the ethnic diversity of the population of the regional states. While it offers expansive protection to territorially empowered ethnic communities, the non-empowered or "nonindigenous" ones are largely left to the mercy of the former. This assertion, empirically supported by a wide range of human rights violations and abuses affecting nonindigenous regional minorities, urgently calls for constitutional and other public law reforms. The chapter aims to support such reforms by offering a number of recommendations towards more effective and comprehensive protection for regional minorities. The chapter's premise is that regional minorities are minorities deserving specific protection under international human rights law. Although international human rights law has hitherto not developed a specific covenant on minority rights, several non-minority-specific human rights covenants offer important protection to minorities, ranging from nondiscriminatory enjoyment of universal rights to identity and public participation rights. These international law standards have induced and inspired the chapter's recommendations on how to better accommodate the rights and interests of regional minorities and, therefore, serve the constitutional diversity objective. Yet, although it is assumed to contribute to it, the mere protection of diversity does not automatically engender unity. There is a palpable risk that accommodationist approaches towards minorities may encourage ethnic fragmentation and segmentation, hardly conducive conditions for strengthening social cohesion in a highly polarized society such as Ethiopia. Such a risk is also duly acknowledged by the same international human rights documents that support minority rights protection. These documents, therefore, suggest supplementing minority protection with mechanisms focusing on intercultural communication, reciprocal learning, and understanding. In a similar vein, the chapter recommends the supplementation of accommodationist mechanisms of minority protection with integrationist ones such as nondiscriminatory protection of universal or citizenship rights and intercultural learning through education and media. The ambition is that such a hybrid approach will offer the necessary institutional guarantees to regional minorities while incrementally mitigating interethnic grievances and distrust in Ethiopia.

Notes

1 Article 39(5) of the Federal Constitution.

2 FDRE Population Census Commission, *Summary and Statistical Report of the 2007 Population and Housing Census* (United Nations Population Fund, 2008).

3 Christophe Van der Beken, "External and Internal Secession in Ethiopia's Multinational Federation," *International Journal on Minority and Group Rights* 28, no. 5 (2021): 944–71.

4 Yonatan Tesfaye Fessha, "The Original Sin of Ethiopian Federalism," *Ethnopolitics* 16, no. 3 (2017): 232–45.

5 CCPR General Comment No. 23: Article 27 (Rights of Minorities). Adopted at the Fiftieth Session of the Human Rights Committee, on 8 April 1994 CCPR/C/21/Rev.1/Add.5, para. 6.1.

6 This chapter interprets multicultural or accommodationist approaches towards ethnic diversity as approaches that emphasize the rights and interests of (persons belonging to) minorities. They focus on the institutional acknowledgement and expression of differences. Yet, the chapter agrees with Zapata-Barrero that this approach has failed to pay sufficient attention to the importance of interaction among different ethnic communities. As a supplementary mechanism, the intercultural or integrationist approach, therefore, focuses on interaction, community-building, and prejudice reduction. Ricardo Zapata-Barrero, "The Intercultural Turn in Europe: Process of Policy Paradigm Change and Formation," in *Interculturalism at the Crossroads – Comparative Perspectives on Concepts, Policies and Practices*, ed. Fethi Mansouri (UNESCO Publishing, 2017), 169–92. The chapter does not interpret integration as a unidirectional process but as an interactive and reciprocal one that requires that all members of a given society accept common

public institutions and have a shared sense of belonging to a common state and an inclusive society. OSCE, *The Ljubljana Guidelines on Integration of Diverse Societies & Explanatory Note* (OSCE High Commissioner on National Minorities, November 2012).

7 United Nations Human Rights Committee, Ballantyne, McIntyre v. Canada, Communications Nos 359/1989 and 385/1989, UN Doc. CCPR/C/47/D/359/1989/Rev. I (1993).

8 Christophe Van der Beken and Beza Dessalegn, "The Role of International and National Human Rights Systems in the Protection of Regional Minorities in Ethiopia," in *Alternative Approaches to Ethno-cultural Diversity Management at Sub-national levels: Ethiopia in Comparative Perspective*, eds. Christophe Van der Beken and Beza Dessalegn (Addis Ababa University, 2022), 19–70.

9 UN Human Rights Committee, Concluding Observations of the Human Rights Committee: Ethiopia, 19 August 2011, CCPR/C/ETH/CO/1.

10 Committee on the Elimination of Racial Discrimination, Consideration of Reports Submitted by States Parties under Article 9 of the Convention: Concluding Observations of the Committee on the Elimination of Racial Discrimination: Ethiopia, CERD/C/ETH/CO/7-16, 7 September 2009.

11 Francesco Capotorti, *Study on the Rights of Persons belonging to Ethnic, Religious and Linguistic Minorities* (UN, 1979).

12 CCPR General Comment No. 23: Article 27 (Rights of Minorities). Adopted at the Fiftieth Session of the Human Rights Committee, on 8 April 1994 CCPR/C/21/Rev.1/Add.5, para. 5.2.

13 Clive Baldwin, Chris Chapman, and Zoë Gray, *Minority Rights: The Key to Conflict Prevention* (Minority Rights Group International, 2007), 5.

14 Convention on the Prevention and Punishment of the Crime of Genocide, 9 December 1948 (ratified by Ethiopia on 1 July 1949).

15 Articles 1 and 2 of the Genocide Convention.

16 International Convention on the Elimination of All Forms of Racial Discrimination, 21 December 1965 (ratified by Ethiopia in 1976).

17 Baldwin, Chapman, and Gray, *Minority Rights: The Key to Conflict Prevention*, 5.

18 Joshua Castellino, "The Protection of Minorities and Indigenous Peoples," *International Journal on Minority and Group Rights* 17, no. 3 (2010): 420.

19 Article 2(1) ICERD.

20 Ivan Garvalov, "The United Nations International Convention on the Elimination of All Forms of Racial Discrimination," in *Synergies in Minority Protection: European and International Law Perspectives*, eds. Kristin Henrard and Robert Dunbar (Cambridge University Press, 2008), 277.

21 David Keane and Joshua Castellino, "Is the International Convention on the Elimination of All Forms of Racial Discrimination the De Facto Minority Rights Treaty?," in *Towards Convergence in International Human Rights Law*, eds. Carla M. Buckley, Alice Donald, and Philip Leach (Brill/Nijhoff, 2016), 275-95.

22 Kristin Henrard, *The Impact of International Non-discrimination Norms in Combination with General Human Rights for the Protection of National Minorities* (Council of Europe, 2006), accessed April 8, 2023, https://rm.coe.int/1680097f35 ().

23 Gaetano Pentassuglia, "Self-Determination, Human Rights, and the Nation-State: Revisiting Group Claims through a Complex Nexus in International Law," *International Community Law Review* 19, no. 4–5 (2017): 443–84.
24 International Covenant on Civil and Political Rights, 16 December 1966 (ratified by Ethiopia in 1993).
25 CCPR General Comment No. 23: Article 27 (Rights of Minorities). Adopted at the Fiftieth Session of the Human Rights Committee, on 8 April 1994 CCPR/C/21/Rev.1/Add.5, para. 6.1.
26 Convention on the Rights of the Child, 20 November 1989 (ratified by Ethiopia in 1991).
27 International Covenant on Economic, Social and Cultural Rights, 16 December 1966 (ratified by Ethiopia in 1993).
28 Keane and Castellino, "De Facto Minority Rights Treaty," 279.
29 Antonija Petricusic, "The Rights of Minorities in International Law: Tracing Developments in Normative Arrangements of International Organizations," *Croatian International Relations Review* 11, no. 38–39 (2005): 11.
30 Baldwin, Chapman, and Gray, *Minority Rights: The Key to Conflict Prevention*, 9.
31 Baldwin, Chapman, and Gray, *Minority Rights: The Key to Conflict Prevention*, 11.
32 Yousef T. Jabareen, "Towards Participatory Equality: Protecting Minority Rights under International Law," *Israel Law Review* 41, no. 3 (2008): 675.
33 Baldwin, Chapman, and Gray, *Minority Rights: The Key to Conflict Prevention*, 12.
34 Lamberto Zannier and Eleonora Lotti, "Integration of Diverse Societies as a Tool for Conflict Prevention – The Experience of the OSCE High Commissioner on National Minorities," in *OSCE Yearbook 2019* (2020), 235–45.
35 Annelies Verstichel, *Participation, Representation and Identity. The Right of Persons Belonging to Minorities to Effective Participation in Public Affairs: Content, Justification and Limits* (Intersentia, 2009), 169.
36 "Election Law, Proclamation No. 1162/2019", *Federal Negarit Gazette*, October 16, 2019.
37 See, inter alia: Christophe Van der Beken, "Minority Protection in Ethiopia: Unravelling and Improving Ethnic Federalism," *Recht in Afrika* (2010): 243–73; Christophe Van der Beken, "Balancing between Empowerment and Inclusion: Multinational Federalism and Citizenship Rights in Ethiopia," *African Journal of International and Comparative Law* 27, vol. 4 (2019): 588–608.
38 FDRE Population Census Commission, *Summary and Statistical Report of the 2007 Population and Housing Census* (United Nations Population Fund, 2008).
39 Yonatan Tesfaye Fessha, "In the Name of Diversity – The Disenfranchisement of Citizens in an African Federation," in *The Principle of Equality in Diverse States Reconciling Autonomy with Equal Rights and Opportunities*, eds. Eva Maria Belser, Thea Bächler, Sandra Egli, and Lawrence Zünd (Brill/Nijhoff, 2021), 398.
40 The conferral of territorial autonomy to national minorities has hitherto entirely depended on the constitutional practice of states: Francesco Palermo, "When the Lund Recommendations Are Ignored. Effective Participation of National Minorities through Territorial Autonomy," *International Journal on Minority and Group Rights* 16, no. 4 (2009): 657.

41 Van der Beken, "External and Internal Secession in Ethiopia's Multinational Federation."

42 Yared Tsegaye, "In Federal Ethiopia's Diverse South West, It's Time to Wake Up and Smell the Coffee," *Ethiopia Insight*, January 23, 2023, https://www.ethiopia-insight.com/2023/01/23/in-federal-ethiopias-diverse-south-west-its-time-to-wake-up-and-smell-the-coffee/

43 News: "Ethiopia House of Federation Officiates Creation of New State in Southern Ethiopia", *Addis Standard*, July 5, 2023, https://eng.addisstandard.com//news-ethiopia-house-of-federation-officiates-creation-of-new-state-in-southern-ethiopia/

44 Article 59(1) of the Ethiopian Federal Constitution.

45 Girma Belachew, "Consociation as a Guarantee for the Protection of Minority Rights in Ethiopia," *International Journal on Minority and Group Rights* 26, no. 3 (2019): 335–72.

46 Christophe Van der Beken, "Federalism, Local Government and Minority Protection in Ethiopia: Opportunities and Challenges," *Journal of African Law* 59, no. 1 (2015): 155.

47 Article 2 of the Oromia and Somali Constitutions.

48 The 2007 Population and Housing Census of Ethiopia: Statistical Report for Southern Nations, Nationalities and Peoples' Region.

49 ASDailyScoop, "Benishangul Gumuz State Council Approves Renaming of Berta Nation to Benishangul, Splits Assosa into Two Woredas," March 29, 2022, https://addisstandard.com/asdailyscoop-benishagul-gumuz-state-council-approves-renaming-of-berta-nation-to-benishangul/

50 Before the internal secession of the Sidama and South West Ethiopia Peoples' Regional States from the Southern Nations, Nationalities, and Peoples Regional State, fifty-six ethnic groups were formally recognized in the latter state. According to information provided by Southwest regional officials, thirteen of these fifty-six groups originated from the administrative areas that merged together to form the new South West Ethiopia Peoples' State. The Southwest Region thus recognizes thirteen ethnic groups as indigenous. The establishment of this state is the result of the amalgamation of five zones (Kaffa, Sheka, Bench Sheko, Dawro, West Omo) and the Konta Special Woreda (Article 47(1) of the South West Constitution).

51 Yonatan Tesfaye Fessha, "In the Name of Diversity," 397.

52 Christophe Van der Beken, *Completing the Constitutional Architecture: A Comparative Analysis of Sub-national Constitutions in Ethiopia* (Addis Ababa University Press, 2017), 78.

53 For a comprehensive overview of local governments in Ethiopia, see: Van der Beken, *Completing the Constitutional Architecture*; and Zemelak Ayitenew Ayele, *Local Government in Ethiopia: Advancing Development and Accommodation of Minorities* (Nomos, 2014).

54 Article 58(1–2) of the Constitution of the Southern Nations, Nationalities, and Peoples Region and Article 64(1–2) of the Constitution of the South West Ethiopia Peoples Region.

55 For an elaborate discussion of the differential treatment of nonindigenous minorities at the regional level, see Van der Beken, "Balancing between Empowerment and Inclusion," 588–608.

56 Assefa Fiseha, "Intra-Unit Minorities in the Context of Ethno-national Federation in Ethiopia," *Utrecht Law Review* 13, no. 1 (2017): 170–89; Semir Yusuf, *Drivers of Ethnic Conflict in Contemporary Ethiopia* (Institute for Security Studies, 2019), https://issafrica.org/research/monographs/drivers-of-ethnic-conflict-in-contemporary-ethiopia; Ethiopia Insight, "Minority Rights Dilemma Exemplifies Ethiopia's Brutal Identity Crisis," *Ethiopia Insight*, March 11, 2023, https://www.ethiopia-insight.com/2023/03/11/minority-rights-dilemma-exemplifies-ethiopias-brutal-identity-crisis/

57 Ethiopia Insight, "Minority Rights Dilemma."

58 Sumit Bisarya, *Protecting Ethnic Minorities within Minorities* (International Idea, Constitution Brief, March 2020), https://www.idea.int/publications/catalogue/protecting-ethnic-minorities-within-minorities

59 The regional constitutions, which have largely copied the universal human rights provisions of the Federal Constitution, could potentially offer an additional standard of protection to the regional minorities.

60 "Federal Courts Proclamation No. 1234/2021," *Federal Negarit Gazette*, April 26, 2021.

61 Avigail Eisenberg, "The Rights of National Majorities: Toxic Discourse or Democratic Catharsis," *Ethnicities* 20, no. 2 (2020): 320.

62 Institute of Economic Affairs, *Ethnicity and Ethnic Politics in Kenya* (Policy Brief, 2020), 11.

63 Baldwin, Chapman, and Gray, *Minority Rights: The Key to Conflict Prevention*, 16.

64 Van der Beken, "Federalism, Local Government and Minority Protection in Ethiopia," 150–77; Van der Beken, "Minority Protection in Ethiopia: Unravelling and Improving Ethnic Federalism,"243–73.

65 Van der Beken, "Federalism, Local Government and Minority Protection in Ethiopia", 172.

66 Balázs Vizi, "Non-territorial Autonomy as a Form of Minority Self-Government in Central Europe," in *Alternative Approaches to Ethno-cultural Diversity Management at Sub-national levels: Ethiopia in Comparative Perspective*, eds. Christophe Van der Beken and Beza Dessalegn (Addis Ababa University, 2022), 173–216; Balázs Dobos, "Autonomies in Their Name? National-Cultural Autonomies in Croatia and Estonia," in *Alternative Approaches to Ethno-cultural Diversity Management at Sub-national levels: Ethiopia in Comparative Perspective*, eds. Christophe Van der Beken and Beza Dessalegn (Addis Ababa University, 2022), 137–72.

Bibliography

Ayele, Zemelak Ayitenew. *Local Government in Ethiopia: Advancing Development and Accommodation of Minorities.* Nomos, 2014.

Baldwin, Clive, Chris Chapman, and Zoë Gray. *Minority Rights: The Key to Conflict Prevention*. Minority Rights Group International, 2007.

Bisarya, Sumit. *Protecting Ethnic Minorities within Minorities*. International Idea, March 2020, https://www.idea.int/publications/catalogue/protecting-ethnic-minorities-within-minorities.

Capotorti, Francesco. *Study on the Rights of Persons belonging to Ethnic, Religious and Linguistic Minorities*. UN, 1979.

Castellino, Joshua. "The Protection of Minorities and Indigenous Peoples." *International Journal on Minority and Group Rights* 17, no. 3 (2010): 393-422. DOI: 10.1163/157181110X512142.

Dobos, Balázs. "Autonomies in Their Name? National-Cultural Autonomies in Croatia and Estonia." In *Alternative Approaches to Ethno-cultural Diversity Management at Sub-national levels: Ethiopia in Comparative Perspective*, edited by Christophe Van der Beken and Beza Dessalegn, 137–72. Addis Ababa University, 2022.

Eisenberg, Avigail. "The Rights of National Majorities: Toxic Discourse or Democratic Catharsis." *Ethnicities* 20, no. 2 (2020): 312-30. https://doi.org/10.1177/1468796819866488.

Ethiopia Insight. "Minority Rights Dilemma Exemplifies Ethiopia's Brutal Identity Crisis." *Ethiopia Insight*, March 11, 2023. https://www.ethiopia-insight.com/2023/03/11/minority-rights-dilemma-exemplifies-ethiopias-brutal-identity-crisis/.

FDRE Population Census Commission. *Summary and Statistical Report of the 2007 Population and Housing Census*. United Nations Population Fund, 2008.

Fessha, Yonatan Tesfaye. "The Original Sin of Ethiopian Federalism." *Ethnopolitics* 16, no. 3 (2017): 232–45. https://doi.org/10.1080/17449057.2016.1254410.

-- "In the Name of Diversity – The Disenfranchisement of Citizens in an African Federation." In *The Principle of Equality in Diverse States Reconciling Autonomy with Equal Rights and Opportunities*, edited by Eva Maria Belser, Thea Bächler, Sandra Egli, and Lawrence Zünd, 394-414. Brill/Nijhoff, 2021.

Fiseha, Assefa. "Intra-Unit Minorities in the Context of Ethno-national Federation in Ethiopia." *Utrecht Law Review* 13, no. 1 (2017): 170–89. DOI: 10.18352/ulr.402.

Garvalov, Ivan. "The United Nations International Convention on the Elimination of All Forms of Racial Discrimination." In *Synergies in Minority Protection: European and International Law Perspectives*, edited by Kristin Henrard and Robert Dunbar, 249-77. Cambridge University Press, 2008.

Girma, Belachew. "Consociation as a Guarantee for the Protection of Minority Rights in Ethiopia." *International Journal on Minority and Group Rights* 26, no. 3 (2019): 335–72. https://www.jstor.org/stable/26776758.

Henrard, Kristin. *The Impact of International Non-discrimination Norms in Combination with General Human Rights for the Protection of National Minorities*. Council of Europe, 2006. https://rm.coe.int/1680097f35 ().

Institute of Economic Affairs. *Ethnicity and Ethnic Politics in Kenya.* Institute of Economic Affairs, 2020.

Jabareen, Yousef T. "Towards Participatory Equality: Protecting Minority Rights under International Law." *Israel Law Review* 41, no. 3 (2008): 635-76. https://doi.org/10.1017/S002122370000039X.

Keane, David, and Joshua Castellino. "Is the International Convention on the Elimination of All Forms of Racial Discrimination the De Facto Minority Rights Treaty?" In *Towards Convergence in International Human Rights Law*, edited by Carla M. Buckley, Alice Donald, and Philip Leach, 275-95. Brill/Nijhoff, 2016.

OSCE, *The Ljubljana Guidelines on Integration of Diverse Societies & Explanatory Note.* OSCE High Commissioner on National Minorities, November 2012.

Palermo, Francesco. "When the Lund Recommendations Are Ignored. Effective Participation of National Minorities through Territorial Autonomy." *International Journal on Minority and Group Rights* 16, no. 4 (2009): 653-63. https://doi.org/10.1163/15718115_016_04-12.

Pentassuglia, Gaetano. "Self-Determination, Human Rights, and the Nation-State: Revisiting Group Claims through a Complex Nexus in International Law." *International Community Law Review* 19, no. 4–5 (2017): 443–84. DOI: 10.1163/18719732-12340007.

Petricusic, Antonija. "The Rights of Minorities in International Law: Tracing Developments in Normative Arrangements of International Organizations." *Croatian International Relations Review* 11, no. 38–39 (2005): 1-23.

Tsegaye, Yared. "In Federal Ethiopia's Diverse South West, It's Time to Wake Up and Smell the Coffee." *Ethiopia Insight,* January 23, 2023, https://www.ethiopia-insight.com/2023/01/23/in-federal-ethiopias-diverse-south-west-its-time-to-wake-up-and-smell-the-coffee/.

Van der Beken, Christophe. "Minority Protection in Ethiopia: Unravelling and Improving Ethnic Federalism." *Recht in Afrika* (2010): 243–73.

____ "Federalism, Local Government and Minority Protection in Ethiopia: Opportunities and Challenges." *Journal of African Law* 59, no. 1 (2015): 150-77. doi:10.1017/S0021855314000205.

____ *Completing the Constitutional Architecture: A Comparative Analysis of Sub-national Constitutions in Ethiopia.* Addis Ababa University Press, 2017.

____ "Balancing between Empowerment and Inclusion: Multinational Federalism and Citizenship Rights in Ethiopia." *African Journal of International and Comparative Law* 27, vol. 4 (2019): 588–608.

____ "External and Internal Secession in Ethiopia's Multinational Federation." *International Journal on Minority and Group Rights* 28, no. 5 (2021): 944–71. https://doi.org/10.1163/15718115-bja10037.

Van der Beken, Christophe and Beza Dessalegn. "The Role of International and National Human Rights Systems in the Protection of Regional Minorities in Ethiopia." In *Alternative Approaches to Ethno-cultural Diversity Management at Sub-national levels: Ethiopia in Comparative Perspective*, edited by Christophe Van der Beken and Beza Dessalegn, 19-70. Addis Ababa University, 2022.

Verstichel, Annelies. *Participation, Representation and Identity. The Right of Persons Belonging to Minorities to Effective Participation in Public Affairs: Content, Justification and Limits*. Intersentia, 2009.

Vizi, Balázs. "Non-territorial Autonomy as a Form of Minority Self-Government in Central Europe." In *Alternative Approaches to Ethno-cultural Diversity Management at Sub-national levels: Ethiopia in Comparative Perspective*, edited by Christophe Van der Beken and Beza Dessalegn, 173–216. Addis Ababa University, 2022.

Yusuf, Semir. *Drivers of Ethnic Conflict in Contemporary Ethiopia*. Institute for Security Studies, 2019, https://issafrica org/research/monographs/drivers-of-ethnic-conflict-in-contemporary-ethiopia.

Zannier, Lamberto and Eleonora Lotti. "Integration of Diverse Societies as a Tool for Conflict Prevention – The Experience of the OSCE High Commissioner on National Minorities." In *OSCE Yearbook 2019*, edited by Institute for Peace Research and Security Policy at the University of Hamburg/IFSH, 235-45. Nomos, 2020.

Zapata-Barrero, Ricardo. "The Intercultural Turn in Europe: Process of Policy Paradigm Change and Formation." in *Interculturalism at the Crossroads – Comparative Perspectives on Concepts, Policies and Practices*, edited by Fethi Mansouri, 169-92. UNESCO Publishing, 2017.

Chapter 10

Constitutional Recognition of the Rights of Persons with Disabilities in Ethiopia

Asrar Adem

Introduction

PWDs are at the receiving end of marginalization and discrimination across the board due to their disability.[1] Although they are referred to as the world's largest minority, constituting more than one billion people, they are the most disadvantaged section of society.[2] The number of PWDs keep growing due to a variety of reasons, some of which are an increase in aging population and different diseases such as diabetes, blood pressure, and cancer.[3] However, despite the high prevalence of PWDs globally, they are excluded from the social, economic, and political spheres and deprived of their fundamental human rights.[4] They do not enjoy education, employment, and electoral rights on an equal basis with others.[5] A number of facilities such as "shops, public facilities and transport, and even information are largely out of reach" for PWDs.[6]

Similar to the global trend of PWDs highlighted above, studies conducted in connection with disability rights in Ethiopia reveal that PWDs face numerous barriers in exercising their fundamental human rights in the country.[7] Although it is challenging to find reliable and updated national data about the prevalence of PWDs, it is incontestable to conclude that a considerable amount of PWDs live in the country. PWDs comprise more than 17 percent of the population, according to the World Health Organization and the World Bank 2011 joint report.[8] As such, as is alluded to above, an enormous share of the Ethiopian population is not effectively enjoying their human rights on an equal basis with others, and the implication is multifold. Certainly, there is a need to have an appropriate legislative response to address the plight of these people. Particularly, Ethiopia needs to guarantee adequately the equal rights of PWDs in the supreme law of the polity, for there is a lack of a comprehensive human rights protection regime for them in the constitution. As it is stated above, different studies conducted in connection with PWDs have shown that they are highly vulnerable to discrimination and other forms of violence across the country due to their disability.[9] Legislations including constitutions, policies, and practices have contributed for the marginalization of PWDs in the economic, social, and political spheres of the country. This is clearly observed in the absence of sufficient constitutional guarantee for the human rights of PWDs. Hence, effective recognition of the rights of PWDs in the constitution will have a pivotal role in reducing those challenges and provide adequate remedy when rights violations occur. A clear constitutional statement of what it stands for in terms of disability rights and what it will not stand for in terms of exclusion and discrimination may form part of the nation's social contract, thereby contributing to the protection of PWDs. A meaningful inclusion of PWDs in the constitution is indispensable to ensuring equality and inclusion, among other things.

Ethiopia ratified the Convention for the Rights of Persons with Disabilities (CRPD) in 2010.[10] Although the CRPD imposes a general obligation on member states, including Ethiopia, to enact all necessary legislations that can facilitate the full enjoyment of the rights provided in the convention, its practical implementation by Ethiopia is underdeveloped.[11] Moreover, although the convention requires Ethiopia to modify or abolish existing discriminatory laws, regulations and practices against PWDs, in Ethiopia PWDs face barriers due to the presence of discriminatory laws and practices, including the constitution.[12] As a result, the involvement of the constitution of the country regarding the rights of PWDs is not satisfactory. Because it does not take into consideration the particular conditions and their vulnerability to various forms of discrimination. The CRPD requires member states such as Ethiopia to make legislations, including the constitution, in line with the convention.

As such, this book chapter is intended to examine how the human rights of PWDs are addressed in the constitutions of Ethiopia and how effective constitutional recognition of disability rights could enhance the human rights protection and promotion of PWDs. To this end, the book chapter comprises four sections. The first section deals with the general conceptual frameworks regarding PWDs and human rights. It will examine the definitions of disability and persons with disabilities. Furthermore, it will scrutinize how perspectives regarding disability evolved through time. In doing so, it will highlight approaches to disability and PWDs. Also, it will engage in a critical assessment of international human rights instruments and regional human rights documents in terms of the human rights of PWDs.

The second section attempts to highlight the fundamentals of constitutions and how these fundamentals of constitutions contribute for the protection of the rights of PWDs. It will attempt to shed light as to how the basic features of constitutions and how the symbolic or expressive functions of constitutions improve the protection and promotion of disability rights if the rights are properly included in constitutions.

The third section dwells on the recognition of the rights of PWDs in the past and present constitutions of Ethiopia. It tries to highlight how the previous constitutions of the country addressed the human rights of PWDs. It will also dissect the current FDRE constitution in relation to disability rights. This part, thus, intends to make a critical appraisal of the place accorded to disability rights in the constitution and the level of harmonization of the current Ethiopian constitution with the human rights of PWDs in the CRPD. Finally, part four sets out the way forward.

1. Persons with disabilities and human rights: conceptual framework

1.1 Delineating the meaning of the term disability

It is not easy to come up with a clear-cut definition for the term disability. The literature underscores the difficulty of ascribing a clear and precise definition for the concept of disability.[13] There is no universally agreed upon definition for the term disability. The notion of disability is "complex, dynamic, multidimensional and contested."[14] There are different viewpoints with respect to what disability is and consequently who should be identified as disabled, even among people with disabilities themselves. How society and the state should respond to disability is also a matter that is not definitively settled, as Emma Stone puts it:[15]

Conceptually, disability is broad and imprecise. Unless the context is circumscribed, and the criterion for determining disability is supplied, disability has the potential to include an extraordinarily wide range of people who at some stage in their life experience physical or mental restrictions that are regarded to be a departure from the norm or have the experience of being treated as such. Some restrictions may be permanent and others temporary. Some might be severe and others mild.[16]

When we look at the CRPD, it does not explicitly define disability. According to the CRPD, disability is an evolving notion, and it is a result of the "interaction between persons with impairments and attitudinal and environmental barriers that hinders their full and effective participation in society on an equal basis with others."[17] The convention further states that disability includes people with physical disabilities, sensory impairment such as visual impairment, hearing impairment, communication disabilities, intellectual disabilities, and psychosocial disabilities.[18] "Disfigurement, illness, disease, and the physical and mental limitations that are a natural consequence of aging can all be subsumed under disability, and so can people with latent conditions that do not cause any physical or mental restrictions."[19] The label of disability can arise from self-identification, or it might be assigned by other individuals, professionals and institutions.[20]

Thus, disability is a notion that is still evolving and not susceptible to a rigid, incontestable definition, and much depends on the context. "In the final analysis, disability is capable of a construction that is so fluid and so encompassing as to include virtually everyone at some stage in their lives."[21]

As it is highlighted above, the definition provided by the CRPD is not exhaustive. It only illustrates who PWDs include. Hence, we can see from this that there is no single definition of disability that has achieved international consensus as the notion of disability is changing. The notion has evolved from the initial charity or welfare perspective that viewed PWDs as objects of pity who required help; to the medical perspective that sought to treat the disability; to the current social and human rights perspective. Hereunder, an attempt will be made to highlight these perspectives to disability.

1.2 Perspectives to disability

A quick glance at the disability literature reveals that there are numerous perspectives to disability: "The medical model, the social model, the economic model, the minority group model, the universalist model, the Nordic relational model, the capabilities model and others."[22] This implies that there is a myriad of approaches that attempt to understand the issue of disability in different manners. However, in this chapter the main viewpoints of disability that will be highlighted and explored are the charity approach, the medical approach, the social approach, and the human rights approach.

1.2.1 The charity approach

The charity approach perceives PWDs as objects of pity that need to be supported through charity.[23] Thus, they are seen as objects to be protected or comforted. This approach is also described as the welfare approach to disabilities.[24] This perception of PWDs as objects and not subjects, and the tendency to react with pity rather than respect, has had implications for the operation of welfare systems. Welfare was generally used to support PWDs or to compensate them for their absence from the mainstream of society. This encouraged the creation of "specialized schemes within social welfare programs" in many industrialized countries.[25]

Thus, under this approach, PWDs are not empowered individuals and do not participate in any activities of society. PWDs are not rights holders. Rather they are helpless victims who cannot provide for themselves and hence "society provides for them."[26] According to the charity approach, PWDs are not in control of their lives.[27] As such, "charity houses, homes, foundations, churches, to which society delegates policies" on PWDs and responsibility towards persons with disabilities are established.[28]

Therefore, the charity approach perpetuates marginalization and discrimination of PWDs rather than promoting dignity and inclusion.

1.2.2 The medical approach

The medical approach portrays PWDs as ill persons who require medical treatment.[29] This approach also locates the problem of disability in the person. According to this approach, disability has to be fixed using medical treatment or therapy alone. Thus, it grants unlimited power to experts such as doctors, psychiatrists, and nurses over the lives of PWDs.[30]

The medical approach to disability has two assumptions that have negative consequences on PWDs.[31] The first one is that PWDs should be provided with shelter and welfare, and the second one is that disability results in legal incapacity.[32] The first attitude justifies isolated accommodations for PWDs such as "special schools, living institutions or sheltered workshops while the second one resulted in the creation of mental health and guardianship laws that take an incapacity approach to disability."[33] In sum, this approach, in its obsession with impairment as an innate characteristic of the individual, does not consider the environment or the social barrier as a disabling factor.

1.2.3 The social approach

The social approach to disability was advanced in 1981 by Mike Oliver, who is a person with disability himself.[34] The approach locates the challenges of disability on the shoulders of the state and society to remove structural, environmental, communication, legal, and attitudinal barriers that disable PWDs from interacting with society on an equal basis with others.[35] It puts emphasis on the disadvantage of restriction of activity caused by a social environment and society which takes no or little account of people who have impairments and thus excludes them from participation in the mainstream of social activities. "It is a deliberate attempt to shift attention away from the functional limitations of individuals with impairments onto the problems caused by disabling environments, barriers and cultures."[36]

According to the social approach to disability, for example, PWDs are limited and isolated from participating in the daily activities of society not just because of their disability but due to inaccessible justice systems and transportation, unsuitable buildings, rigid work environments, and lack of up to date aids and equipment.[37] They might have difficulties in accessing the work environment not because of their condition but because there are barriers, such as legal exclusions and inaccessible buses, buildings, information, and other barriers, that impede their access. A person with intellectual disability may face challenges in school due to the school community attitude, inappropriate curricula and learning materials. In a society where corrective lenses are available for a person with extreme myopia or shortsightedness, this person would not be considered as having a disability. But someone with the same condition where corrective lenses are absent would be considered as having a disability.[38]

The CRPD takes this approach a step further by upholding the human rights of all PWDs under international law and eventually develops a human-rights-based approach to disability.

1.2.4 The human rights approach

A human rights approach to disability states that PWDs are rights holders and that social structures and normative frameworks restricting or ignoring the rights of PWDS are discriminatory and result in exclusion.[39] This approach needs society, particularly states, to actively promote the necessary conditions for all individuals to fully realize their potential. According to the human rights approach, every person is considered to have immeasurable value and nobody is insignificant.[40] Individuals are to be valued not just because they are economically or otherwise useful but because of their innate self-worth.[41]

Under the human rights approach to disability, environmental or societal barriers are treated as discriminatory and provide safeguard mechanisms to prevent the violation of these rights. For instance, PWDs have the right to vote like anyone else in the society. However, if election materials are not in accessible format for PWDs, they cannot enjoy this right. A human rights approach to disability therefore considers the inaccessibility of the election system and the inability to fully participate in the system as discriminatory and places a responsibility on the state to ensure that such discriminatory barriers are removed.[42] This is one of the reasons why the duty of reasonable accommodation is guaranteed under the CRPD as a method of eliminating barriers. As such, the duty of reasonable accommodation goes along with the human rights approach to disability. Because society and the environment are not designed in a way that takes into consideration the particular needs of PWDs, there should be the duty to reasonably accommodate in order to enable PWDs to participate in the daily activities of society on an equal basis with others. For this reason, reasonable accommodation has been given due emphasis in the Convention. To this end, for effective realization of the rights of PWDs, it is imperative to properly include the duty of reasonable accommodation in the laws of a state, particularly in the constitution.

As it is stated above, the CRPD does not explicitly define disability. The preamble of the Convention affirms that "disability is an evolving concept and that disability results from the interaction between persons with impairments and attitudinal and environmental barriers that hinders full and effective participation in society on an equal basis with others."[43] As such, by virtue of the Convention, disability is not something that exists or resides in the individual. Disability is located in the community, and it is something that results between the individual and his/her interaction with the environment.[44] This is what we call the social model of disability coupled with the human rights approach to disability.

1.3 Putting disability rights in perspective within the general human rights framework

Human rights are those fundamental and universal norms that establish standards of behaviour that help protect every individual from social, economic and legal abuses.[45] As such, human rights pertain to all human beings at all times. They are claim rights that impose obligation primarily on the government. The main features of these rights as they are acknowledged by the 1993 Vienna declaration and program of action include universality, indivisibility, interdependence, and interrelatedness.[46] They are the universal rights of every human being that should be enjoyed without any discrimination on grounds such as race, religion, language, sex, gender, and disability. The UDHR states that human rights are rooted in the dignity and worth of human beings and in the requirements of domestic and international peace and security. These fundamental freedoms cannot be given away or be forfeited.[47] Human rights impose obligations on states and non-state actors. Thus, human rights principles are accepted by a number of international human rights instruments. Human rights are also grounded in the protection of personhood, which is seen in terms of the person's autonomy, the conception of a good life and being able to pursue it, and freedom from the interference of others.[48] Thus, human rights such as civil and political, social, economic, and cultural rights and other rights emanate from this idea of personhood.[49]

Disability rights emanate from this general idea of human rights. They are not a special or exceptional category of rights.[50] Disability rights reaffirm that PWDs are entitled to the respect of their inherent dignity and of all human rights and fundamental freedoms on an equal basis with others.[51] When conceived as human rights, which already inhere in individuals due to being human, disability rights become also moral rights and not merely legal claims or entitlements.[52]

To this end, disability rights are recognized by many international human rights instruments. For instance, we may consider the main international human rights instruments, such as the Universal Declaration of Human Rights (UDHR), the International Covenant on Civil and Political Rights (ICCPR), and the International Covenant on Economic, Social and Cultural Rights (ICESCR), collectively known as the International Bill of Rights. While they do not explicitly mention PWDs, there is an argument to be made that PWDs are covered by the provisions of these human rights documents.

For instance, the UDHR guarantees the enjoyment of all human rights by every human being without any distinction.[53] Although not specifically mentioned in any provision in a meaningful manner, PWDs are equally covered under the UDHR by its reference to "all human beings."[54] Likewise, although PWDs are not specifically mentioned in the ICCPR, it is agreed that they are guaranteed the same rights contained therein. The reading of the preamble of the ICCPR is indicative of this fact.[55] Moreover, the ICESCR committee, the body that monitors the implementation of economic, social and cultural rights in the ICESCR by state parties, in one of its general comments that deals with PWDs stated that disability is covered by the phrase "other status" in the ICESCR.[56] Thus, the ICCPR and ICESCR set forth numerous human rights that apply to everyone, including PWDs. The ICCPR safeguards a wide range of civil and political liberties, such as the right to life, liberty, and freedom of thought, privacy, and the right to take part in the conduct of public affairs.[57] The ICESCR protects the right to education, the right to participate in cultural life, and the right to enjoy the benefits of scientific progress and its applications, among other rights.[58] Apart from these instruments, other thematic human rights instruments such as the Convention on the Rights of the Child (CRC), African Charter on Human and Peoples' Rights (ACHPR) and African Charter on the Rights and Welfare of the Child (ACRWC(also speak about PWDs.

Many of these rights, and a number of other human rights, are also guaranteed in the Convention that is specific to PWDs, the CRPD. The CRPD was adopted after joint advocacy by PWDs and numerous civil society organizations over many years.[59] The Convention took five years of negotiations to achieve global recognition of disability as a human rights issue.[60] It is a paradigm shift in the conception of persons with disabilities from a medical or charity model to a human-rights-based model, recognizing that persons with disabilities have access and can participate in decisions that affect their lives and get remedies for violations of their rights [61] The CRPD comprises fifty articles, being one of the human-rights instruments addressing civil, political, economic, social, and cultural rights in the same document.[62]

Moreover, article 3 of the CRPD flesh out the principles of the Convention through which all the rights in the CRPD are considered. These principles include:

> *Respect for inherent dignity, individual autonomy including the freedom to make one's own choices and independence of persons;*
>
> *Non-discrimination;*
>
> *Full and effective participation and inclusion in society;*
>
> *Respect for difference and acceptance of persons with disabilities as part of human diversity and humanity;*
>
> *Equality of opportunity;*
>
> *Accessibility;*
>
> *Equality between men and women; and*
>
> *Respect for the evolving capacities of children with disabilities and respect for the right of children with disabilities to preserve their identities.*[63]

These general principles are supposed to guide everything regarding the rights of PWDs. They should also influence the development of laws and regulations and their interpretation. As a result, at this juncture, it must be underscored that these general principles should be reflected in the constitutional provisions of a state for effective realization of the rights of PWDs because constitutions can play a role in enforcing these broader principles.

On the contrary, in spite of ratification of this convention by Ethiopia, it is possible to contend that its provisions are not duly guaranteed in the fundamental law of the country. This lack of recognition of the human rights of PWDs in the constitution indicates the lack of serious commitment towards the rights of PWDs, and it would also lead to the violation of a number of human rights of PWDs. On the other hand, recognizing disability rights in the constitution fosters the protection and promotion of their human rights. This is because, as will be elaborated on later in this chapter, one of the functions of a constitution is ensuring protection and promotion of human rights and fundamental freedoms.[64] To this end, absence of constitutional recognition of the rights of PWDs will have a negative impact on effective realization of their human rights as provided in the CRPD.

Of course, some people might claim that constitutionalizing disability rights does not result in positive outcomes in practice. It is often noted that the constitutions of many states contain long lists of human rights provisions. It is not clear, however, that it has made much difference in terms of fulfilment of the rights.

However, this is a problem of constitutional implementation. The fact that the constitution might not be properly implemented by all states for some reasons is not an argument against the inclusion of disability rights in the constitutions of states that might honor their commitment at some point in time. Besides, courts across jurisdictions invoke constitutional provisions to uphold the rights of PWDs. For instance, the supreme court of Mexico "ordered damages" after a job vacancy posted by a private employer excluded PWDs from applying, "citing equal rights on the basis of disability in the constitution," while the supreme court of Brazil ruled that "a private school is not exempt from the constitution's commitment to inclusive education" and the courts of Canada and Iceland ordered that hospitals are required by the constitution to provide interpreters for people with hearing impairments.[65] This is not to claim that constitutionalizing disability rights is a panacea to the multifaceted challenges of PWDs. However, constitutional recognition may contribute to the realization of disability rights through different mechanisms, which will be elaborated further in this chapter.

2. Fundamentals of constitutions and their role for the protection of disability rights

2.1 The role of constitutions

A constitution is a legal, political, and social instrument.[66] Legally, it enshrines human rights and creates a predictable legal landscape.[67] As a supreme or higher law, its provisions provide a framework under which all regulations, legislation, institutions, and procedures operate.[68] It articulates the rights of citizens that institutions, procedures, or legislation must not infringe and which the state must strive to ensure.[69]

Countries across the board amend existing constitutions or design new constitutions for a variety of reasons. Of these, one of the major objectives is the need to entrench human rights and fundamental freedoms in constitutions.[70] A good constitution plays a vital role in the respect and protection of human rights, as well as serving as the foundation for democratic governance.[71] As a result, at the centre of current constitutions lie human rights.

Furthermore, constitutions regulate the relationship between individuals and the state.[72] Constitutions play a significant role in limiting the power of the government by providing different control mechanisms.[73] To this effect, disability rights need to be accorded adequate room in constitutions so as to benefit from the role modern constitutions play. This is because by entrenching fundamental rights constitutions express values and establish contracts between the state and its people to realize those values.[74] As will be elaborated on further in this section, through properly recognizing disability rights, a constitution can notably shape national discourse on PWDs to the right direction, thereby influencing social norms. By guaranteeing rights of PWDs such as equality, accessibility, and reasonable accommodation, a constitution can establish statements of value to guide its people. Similarly, if the rights of PWDs are not properly included in constitutions, it will contribute immensely to the challenges in the implementation of their human rights.

2.2 Functions of constitutions as protection from backsliding

Constitutions have numerous functions. Among others, constitutions can provide safeguards "against policy and legal changes that would undermine equal rights."[75] However, if constitutions do not explicitly recognize the rights of persons that are vulnerable to discrimination, the rights of these people "may face threats during political shifts or budgetary cutbacks."[76] For instance, the United States has protected the rights of PWDs, such as the right to education of children with disabilities and the right to work of PWDs, through legislation.[77] However, the equal rights of PWDs are not guaranteed in the US Constitution, and even though the laws recognizing the rights of PWDs are strong, it "would be far easier to dismantle or outright repeal than a constitutional protection against discrimination."[78] This has been observed "under the Donald Trump administration, which has targeted those laws."[79] Likewise, the same problem of regression might occur in the judiciary. If rights are not properly and clearly guaranteed in constitutions, courts might narrowly interpret rights and undermine equal treatment "especially as the courts' composition evolves."[80] Even if the judiciary decides in favour of equality, the lawmaking body may pass unfair legislation unless the constitution prevents them from doing so.[81]

As a result, it is possible to plausibly argue that the function of constitutions as guardians from backsliding necessitate robust recognition of disability rights so that they will be better protected. Constitutional recognition protects PWDs from things done by the government that might undermine their rights. They will also play an important role in protecting the rights of PWDs against violations by fellow citizens. As such, as stated above, although it might not be possible to claim that constitutional safeguards in itself provide complete security against human rights violation in general and disability rights violations in particular,[82] based on the forgoing discussion, it is possible to contend that constitutional recognition of the rights of PWDs will play a significant role in shifting norms towards equality as well as helping the judiciary provide effective remedies when rights violations occur.

2.3 The symbolic or expressive function of constitutions

Myriad people are concerned with the symbolic or expressive function of constitutions, with their role in describing a nation's goals and aspirations, as opposed to the instrumental effects of those constitutional provisions.83 This is because constitutions that recognize certain rights, such as nondiscrimination and accessibility, will eventually have a positive impact on the society's norms by providing guidance for public officials and the community at large. "This has been the case for the German constitution, and it has contributed to debates in Eastern Europe."84 Many people are concerned with the statement made by constitutional provisions quite apart from effects on social norms. "They may think that a role of the constitution is to reflect certain commitments and that this is important independently of consequences."85

As such, PWDs also stand to benefit from the symbolic or expressive function of constitutions if their rights are adequately guaranteed. The symbolic or expressive function of constitutions plays a significant role in the protection and promotion of disability rights. As highlighted above, some people appear to question the significance of constitutional recognition of disability rights because, according to them, even if disability rights are included in constitutions, they will not be a shield against their violation in practice. However, this argument appears to be indefensible. One of the reasons for legislation including the adoption of constitutions is their expressive function, as opposed to their instrumental functions.[86] As such, the statement made by constitutions about disability rights may be intended to impact social norms and eventually to affect both norms and behavior. Even if the recognition of disability rights in constitutions may not be a guarantee against the infringement of those rights, disability rights need to be given space in constitutions because of their effects on norms as a result of the statements made by them. Thus, PWDs might identify the norms to which they are committed and insist on their inclusion in constitutions even if the consequences of constitutional recognition are vague or unknown. It is, for example, necessary to insist on an antidiscrimination provision in the constitution for expressive reasons, even if it is not possible to know if the provision will actually be adhered to in practice. The point bears on the symbolic value of constitutions. When constitutions speak about certain issues such as disability rights, they are often taken to be speaking on behalf of the nation's basic principles and commitments.[87] This is a matter of importance quite apart from consequences.

2.3 Basic features of constitutions and their role for disability rights protection

There are benefits for disability rights protection and promotion that emanate from the basic features of constitutions, provided that the rights of PWDs are adequately included. These basic features of constitutions and their role for disability rights protection will be highlighted below.

2.3.1 Stability of constitutions

In principle, stability is one of the basic features of constitutions.[88] Stability of constitutions has a contribution for the protection of the human rights of PWDs. As is alluded to above, one of the vital roles played by constitutions is to guarantee human rights and fundamental freedoms. These rights and freedoms are not subject to frequent change due to steadiness of constitutions. Accordingly, since constitutions are not subject to recurrent variation, they will create stability for the rights of PWDs. The issues in constitutions including human rights are designed for an indefinite period of time.[89] This basic feature of constitutions has a positive impact for the rights of PWDs. For example, if the human rights of PWDs are explicitly recognized in constitutions, they will not be subject to frequent alteration, thereby making the human rights of PWDs durable and meaningful. This does not mean, however, that constitutions live forever. Constitutions also envisage reasonable circumstances that may require them to be flexible to reflect shifting social realities.[90]

In connection with the stability of constitutions, some might argue that recognizing disability rights in a constitution might make the constitution a constant focus of controversy for adding this or that right, this or that interest. This in turn impacts the effectiveness of the constitution and might undermine stability. However, seen in the light of the historical discrimination and marginalization some groups have faced, this claim might be objectionable. There is a problem of cultural values and traditional laws that perpetuates the inequality of some groups, including PWDs.[91] As a result, there is a need for constitutional provisions that protect and promote the equal rights of all people irrespective of any status and intervene to correct the legacy of inequalities which have discouraged groups for many years.[92]

For example, there has been a history of caste-based discrimination in India.[93] There has been a group of marginalized lower-caste people.[94] With the view of correcting historical discrimination against these groups, the constitution of India specifically set forth that "the State shall promote with special care the educational and economic interests of the weaker sections of the people, and, in particular, of the Scheduled Castes and the Scheduled Tribes, and shall protect them from social injustice and all forms of exploitation."[95] Similar circumstances might require constitutionalizing the rights of certain groups because such guarantees might be an indispensable way of expressing a commitment to overcome the legacy of marginalization.

Therefore, including disability rights in a constitution does not in any way affect constitutional stability. Because, as stated above, constitutions are not permanent or unalterable. Constitutions might reasonably change to reflect shifting social realities. For example, initially, human rights provisions were not included in the original US Constitution. However, many amendments later introduced enabled different groups to assert their human rights on the basis of the Constitution.[96]

2.3.2 Supremacy of constitutions

Supremacy of constitutions is another fundamental feature of constitutions.[97] This feature of constitutions accentuates that a constitution is the supreme law of the land and that all other legislation, practices, and decisions of government organs shall be made in line with constitutional provisions.[98] This principle requires all laws and other measures of any state to be attuned with the constitution.[99] If legislation or other legal measure adopted by the state does not conform with the constitution, then it should be declared null and void.[100]

From the above discussion, it is possible to conclude that the constitution, being the highest legal guarantee of people's well-being and interests, as well as a fundamental tool to shape the life of the society and to organize the state, will play a significant role in the protection and promotion of human rights in general and the rights of PWDs in particular. If the human rights of PWDs are clearly included in constitutions, by virtue of the supremacy of the constitution, the government is required to enact laws, regulations, directives, and other legal measures that are compatible with the disability rights provisions in the constitution.

2.3.3 Rigidity of constitutions

Rigidity as a basic feature of constitutions indicates that constitutions cannot be easily amended.[101] The main concept here is that the amendment process of constitutions is stringent and cumbersome compared to amendments to an ordinary law.[102] Thus, rigidity as a feature of constitutions needs more formal requirements to amend constitutions.

This stringent requirement for the amendment of constitutions again guards against the violation of the rights of PWDs because stringent amendment procedures help to make disability rights stable, reflecting constitutional commitment. For instance, when we look at the FDRE constitution, Article 105 has envisaged two categories of amendment processes. As a result, based on Article 105 (1), all rights and freedoms specified in Chapter Three of the constitution are subject to stringent amendment procedure.[103] Hence, if the human rights of PWDs are given a sufficient space in constitutions, they will not be arbitrarily disregarded and manipulated. In addition to that, the rigidity of constitutions plays a significant role in ensuring the protection and respect of disability rights, as the amendment process for human rights will be difficult.

3. Inclusion of disability rights under Ethiopian constitutions: past and present

The constitutional history of Ethiopia is composed of four constitutions.[104] These are the 1931 constitution, the 1955 constitution, the 1987 constitution and the 1995 FDRE constitution.[105] Below, an attempt will be made to examine the four Ethiopian constitutions in light of the room conferred to the rights of PWDs.

3.1 The 1931 constitution

One of the major purposes of designing the 1931 constitution was to consolidate the power of the monarchy and central government.[106] As a result, the constitution strengthened the power of the emperor. It was simply a mechanism fashioned to bestow unlimited power to the emperor.[107] To this end, the 1931 constitution listed the powers and prerogatives of Haile Selassie from Article 6 to Article 17.[108] A reading of Article 6 of the constitution reveals that the emperor is supreme.[109] Therefore, there was no constitutional supremacy.

When we examine the constitution with the view of the rights of PWDs, the constitution does not give recognition in the real sense to human rights in general and the rights of PWDs in particular. Generally, citizens were considered as subjects of the emperor.[110] As a result, the constitution did not contain meaningful provisions that give recognition to the fundamental human rights of individuals. For this reason, it is possible to conclude that persons with disabilities did not gain recognition in this constitution. Evidently, Articles 18–29 of the constitution provides the rights and duties of the subjects of the empire.[111] However, these provisions are very scant and do not address the human rights of citizens in a comprehensive manner. Additionally, the provisions do not make

Ethiopian citizens the subjects of rights; rather they were made the subjects of the emperor. Further, there was no independent judiciary to enforce the rights provided in the constitution.

In general, the 1931 constitution, rather than guaranteeing fundamental human rights of citizens and limiting the power of the government, consolidated and centralized it, thereby infringing on the rights of individuals.

3.2 The 1955 constitution

When we look at the 1955 revised constitution, comparatively speaking it has made an attempt to introduce some reforms at least on paper, such as expressly stipulating constitutional supremacy as opposed to supremacy of the emperor and introducing the concept of judicial independence.[112] However, it did not make a significant departure from its predecessor constitution in relation to human rights in general and the rights of PWDs in particular. The constitution, beginning from Article 37, provided for the fundamental human rights of individuals.[113] However, the human rights of citizens incorporated in the constitution were inadequate and insignificant. This is because the rights specified in the constitution did not effectively limit the power of the emperor.[114] Moreover, there was no institution established to construe and give effect to the constitution.[115] On top of that, a number of provisions in the constitution were designed with cloak clauses, such as in accordance with the law and in accordance with the conditions prescribed by law.[116] For example, Article 45 recognized the right to peaceful assembly of citizens without arms in accordance with the conditions prescribed by law.[117] Furthermore, although the constitution gave recognition to the principle of nondiscrimination in the exercise of civil rights under Article 38, it was not crafted in accordance with the UDHR. For example, the provision did not iron out lists of protected persons, which are a common feature of modern constitutions. Likewise, the article in question did not envisage nondiscrimination on the enjoyment of socioeconomic rights. In short, the 1955 constitution, apart from its failure regarding the general human-rights framework, does not address the issue of disability at all, thereby excluding PWDs from the constitution.

3.3 The 1987 constitution

After deposing the emperor and suspending the 1955 Revised Constitution, the Provisional Military Administrative Council, known as the Dergue, established itself as a provisional government and led the country for thirteen years without a constitution.[118] The Dergue then came up with a constitution in 1987. The PDRE Constitution was meant to build socialism.[119] Article 118 of the constitution provides for the supremacy of the constitution.[120] However, with respect to human rights, it does not recognize the rights of individuals in the real sense.[121] Attributable to the socialist influence, the constitution focuses on social, economic, and cultural rights.[122]

When we look at the constitution in light of disability rights, a clear mention of PWDs is provided under Article 22 of the constitution. The provision in question states that "the state and society shall provide special care for those disabled in the course of defending the sovereignty and territorial integrity of Ethiopia and safeguarding the revolution as well as the families of the martyrs."[123] However, the way the article was designed is problematic. This is because the provision is solely concerned about those PWDs who sustained injuries as a result of armed conflict. Also, the article in question is a reflection of the charity model of disability. On top of that, Article 50 of the same constitution contains a blanket prohibition of psychosocial disabilities from voting and being elected.[124] As a result, it is possible to claim that PWDs were not accorded meaningful space by the 1987 PDRE Constitution.

3.4 The 1995 FDRE Constitution

The 1995 FDRE Constitution has eleven chapters and 106 articles. It is a pact between the nations, nationalities and peoples of Ethiopia.[125] The preamble of the Constitution outlines its major aims and aspirations. One of its objectives is the commitment of the Constitution to human rights and fundamental freedoms.[126] The Constitution aspires to rectify historical wrongs.[127] Among other goals, it plans to achieve this by granting full respect to the fundamental rights and freedoms of individuals.

The 1995 FDRE Constitution has made a significant departure from the previous constitutions both in form and in content. Inter alia, the nature of the state it envisages and the government it establishes is different. As clearly indicated in the preamble of the constitution, one of the most important objectives of the constitution is to create one economic and political community based on good governance, respect for human rights, and democracy.[128]

The constitution comprises an extensive list of provisions on fundamental rights and freedoms, starting from Articles 13–44.[129] The chapter is classified into human rights (Arts. 14–28) and democratic rights (Arts. 29–44).[130] There is an argument that questions the validity of the classification.[131] It is difficult to understand how freedom of thought, women's rights and children's rights included under democratic rights differ from the rights included under human rights.

Article 13 of the Constitution determines the scope of application of provisions dealing with fundamental rights and freedoms. As such, it provides that all federal and state legislative, executive, and judicial organs at all levels shall have the responsibility and duty to respect and enforce the provisions of the chapter.[132] The fundamental rights and freedoms set forth in the chapter shall be interpreted in a manner conforming to the principles of the UDHR, International Covenants on Human Rights, and international instruments adopted by Ethiopia.[133]

The civil and political rights enshrined in the Constitution are a replica of the provisions of the UDHR. The list includes: the right to life, which outlaws the deprivation of life except as a punishment for a serious offense determined by law; the right to liberty, which prohibits arbitrary arrest and deprivation of liberty; and the right to protection against cruel, inhuman, or degrading treatment or punishment, including the banning of slavery and trafficking in human beings for whatever reason, and forced or compulsory labor.[134]

When we examine the constitution in light of disability rights, it is plausible to contend that persons with disabilities are left at the periphery of the Constitution. This is because the Constitution doesn't have provisions that sufficiently address the human rights of PWDs. To start with, the Constitution does not set a definition for the concept of disability. Ascribing a meaning for the term disability is essential to understanding the approach followed by the constitution and to confirm if it is compatible with the definition provided in the CRPD. Besides, defining disability in the Constitution is a *sine qua non* in order to guide other subsidiary laws and policies of Ethiopia towards the right direction. In fact, a constitutional misinterpretation as to what disability is and who persons with disabilities are will cause a negative repercussion on the rights of PWDs. As a result, it is important to delineate a meaning for the term disability in the Constitution.

As it stands now, the term disability in the Constitution can be located in Article 41(5), which reads, "the State shall, within available means, allocate resources to provide rehabilitation and assistance to the physically and mentally disabled, the aged, and children who are left without parents or guardians."[135] However, this provision is problematic in many respects. To begin with, it embodies an obsolete style in addressing the rights of PWDs. The expression "rehabilitation and assistance" denotes that the Constitution subscribes to the medical and charity models, which view PWDs as problems demanding them to be changed to fit the existing social system, which is different from the current human rights approach prescribed in the CRPD. Further, the fact that the models followed in the constitution are the charity and medical approaches to disability has profound consequences, since the policies and legislation on disability also emanate from the archaic understanding of disability, implying the need for systematic review.

Likewise, the way the provision is formulated is also problematic. The phrase "within available means" signifies a lack of commitment on the part of the government towards the rights of PWDs. Because the nature of the language employed does not impose strong obligations on the state. Pursuant to the wording of the article in question, the approach followed by the Constitution to the rights of PWDs is aspirational. Because the provision is not designed in an authoritative language and rights "considered aspirational when the enforcement of the right was stated as subject to the state's abilities or resources," among others.[136] This poor constitutional formulation of disability rights has resulted in absurd subsidiary legislations concerning PWDs. A good example in this regard is the Higher Education Proclamation No. 1152/2019. Article 41/1 and 2 of this proclamation read as follows:

> *41. Disabled students and Students with special talents*
>
> *1/ Institutions shall make, to the extent possible, their facilities and programs amicable to use with relative ease students with physical disabilities.*
>
> *2/ Institutions shall, to the extent that situations and resources permit, relocate classes, develop alternative testing procedures, and provide different educational auxiliary aids in the interest of students with physical disabilities and learning disabilities.*

Looking at the phrases used in this article, such as "to the extent possible" and "to the extent that situations and resources permit," reveals that the legislation is mimicking Article 41/5 of the Constitution, thereby making the duty of reasonable accommodation an aspirational right. This is because relocating classes, developing alternative testing procedures, and providing different educational auxiliary aids are part of reasonable accommodation measures that should be implemented in consultation with PWDs. This is a clear contradiction with the CRPD, which considers the duty of reasonable accommodation as a distinct and enforceable human right. Thus, from the reading of this provision, it is possible to observe that the article has not been drafted in a manner that imposes strong obligations on universities. This sort of poor formulation of the rights of PWDs by subsidiary legislation is a reflection of constitutional negligence to the rights of PWDs. There are also other laws that reflect the constitutional provision on disability and have a negative ramification on disability rights. However, it is beyond the scope of this chapter to engage in the discussion of these laws.

Adding insult to injury, PWDs are only mentioned in the part of the Constitution that talks about economic, social, and cultural rights. Consequently, the rights of PWDs in the sphere of civil and political rights are completely neglected by the Constitution. For this reason, the Constitution lacks comprehensiveness in addressing the fundamental rights of PWDs.

Additionally, under its nondiscrimination clause, the Constitution has prohibited all forms of discrimination "on grounds of race, nation, nationality, or other social origin, colour, sex, language, religion, political or other opinion, property, birth or other status" on the enjoyment of human rights.[137] Although it is possible to read disability within the phrase "other status," the absence of unequivocal reference to disability in the nondiscrimination provision could lead to violations of disability rights enumerated under the CRPD. A clear mention of disability as a prohibitive ground of discrimination is crucial in guarding against unfair and biased distinction and preference on the ground of disability. This is also aggravated due to the absence of separate equal rights legislation in the country, which is significant for the protection of the rights of PWDs. There is hope that a draft disability law that is currently under consideration will address disability rights in a comprehensive manner. However, at the time of writing this book chapter, the draft disability law is still being negotiated among different stakeholders and has not yet been endorsed.

4. The way forward and conclusion

4.1 The way forward

As discussed above, in order to effectively protect and promote disability rights in Ethiopia, there needs to be an adequate constitutional framework. As such, the FDRE Constitution needs to be revised and has to effectively address the fundamental rights of PWDs in the manner laid out below.

a. The equality and nondiscrimination provision needs to be revised

Equality and nondiscrimination are the keystones or touchstones of international human rights law. Because they are linked with human dignity, they are the cornerstones of all human rights.[138] The core international and regional human rights instruments clearly guarantee equality and nondiscrimination. For instance, the UDHR under Articles 1 and 2 states that all persons are equal in dignity and rights, and it prohibits discrimination on numerous grounds.[139] Similarly, the ICCPR and ICESCR recognize equality and nondiscrimination.[140] When we look at the CRPD, equality and nondiscrimination are recognized as principles and rights.[141] Article 3 recognizes them as principles, while Article 5 sees them as rights. They are mentioned "consistently throughout its substantive articles with the repeated use of the wording on an equal basis with others which links all substantive rights of the Convention to the non-discrimination principle."[142]

To this end, states are required to eliminate all forms of discrimination against PWDs. Under international human rights practice there are four forms of discrimination.[143] These are direct discrimination, indirect discrimination, denial of reasonable accommodation, and harassment.[144]

Direct discrimination is treating persons with disabilities in a manner that is less favorable than other persons in similar situations, owing to their disability.[145] Indirect discrimination, on the other hand, occurs when laws, policies, or practices that appear neutral at face value have adverse effects on PWDs.[146] Failure to reasonably accommodate PWDs is another form of discrimination against PWDs.[147] Finally, harassment constitutes discrimination when inappropriate conduct that infringes on the human dignity of PWDs occurs.[148] If the harassment is committed with the view of creating an environment that is intimidating, degrading, humiliating, offensive, or hostile to PWDs, it amounts to discrimination.[149]

As such, the constitution should unequivocally prohibit all forms of discrimination on the grounds of disability under its equality and nondiscrimination provisions. A comprehensive clause that prohibits discrimination in all its forms in a constitution plays a critical role in the protection of PWDs. As mentioned above, the absence of disability as a basis for discrimination could have negative repercussions on the rights of PWDs and may result in human rights violations. Consequently, a constitution should adopt a standalone antidiscrimination provision in order to prohibit discrimination on the basis of disability.

At this juncture, it is worth mentioning the 2010 constitution of Kenya. The 2010 constitution of Kenya includes persons with disabilities in a number of provisions. Among others, it explicitly prohibits discrimination on the grounds of disability under Article 27/4.[150] As such, direct or indirect discrimination against any person with disability on the basis of disability is forbidden. Hence, Ethiopia needs to take a lesson from the constitution of Kenya and include a provision that clearly prohibits discrimination on the grounds of disability.

b. The constitution should recognize the languages and cultures of PWDs

The FDRE constitution under Article 5 provides that all Ethiopian languages enjoy equal recognition.[151] However, the constitution fails to guarantee the peculiar languages and communication formats of PWDs, such as sign language and braille. Although Article 30 of the CRPD imposes a duty on Ethiopia to recognize and support the specific cultural and linguistic identity of PWDs, including sign languages and deaf culture, there is no mention of such rights in the constitution.[152]

The Kenyan constitution is much better in this regard. Article 54 of the constitution, which is a standalone provision regarding PWDs, entitles persons with disabilities to use sign language, braille, or other appropriate means of communication.[153] Additionally, article 7/3 of the Kenyan constitution affirms that Kenyan sign language would be used in official places together with English and Kiswahili.[154] Moreover, communication formats and technologies such as braille are also recognized in the same provision.[155] Accordingly, the Ethiopian constitution needs to draw inspiration from the constitution of Kenya and establish the full inclusion of PWDs by sufficiently addressing the human rights of PWDs, thereby making the constitution in line with CRPD.

c. The constitution should offer recognition for accessibility

Accessibility is provided under Article 3 as a guiding principle and Article 9 as a right to be enjoyed by PWDs in the CRPD.[156] It is considered a prerequisite to having effective and full participation in society on an equal basis with others.[157] As such, member states to the CRPD, including Ethiopia, have a duty to make available proper laws and policies to enhance accessibility for PWDs to the physical environment, transportation, information, and communications, including information and communication technologies and systems, and to other facilities and services open or provided to the public both in urban and rural areas.[158] However, PWDs in Ethiopia encounter scores of challenges in accessing the physical environment, transportation, information, and communications and other facilities and services. The right to accessibility of PWDs is not addressed in a comprehensive manner in Ethiopia.

Of course, with the view of addressing the barriers faced by PWDs in the built environment, the government adopted the building proclamation 624/2009. This proclamation provides for accessibility in the design and construction of any building to ensure suitability for persons with physical disability.[159] Article 36 of the building proclamation requires public buildings to have "a means of access suitable for use by physically impaired persons, including those who are obliged to use wheelchairs and those who are able to walk but unable to negotiate steps."[160] It also provides for any facilities in the building, like that of toilets, to be accessible to PWDs.

However, the proclamation fails to address the issue of accessibility in a comprehensive manner. It only targets public building accessibility, neglecting accessibility in a wide range of areas such as transportation, information, and communication. Additionally, the practical implementation of the proclamation is underdeveloped. PWDs in Ethiopia are still denied access to physical environment, transportation, information, and communication and other services and facilities open to the public. As a result, a clear and comprehensive provision on the right to accessibility of PWDs in the constitution will have a great value in rectifying the legal and practical setbacks by serving as a model. It is not uncommon for a constitution to include the right to accessibility of PWDs. The Kenyan constitution is a case in point. Under Article 54 the constitution stipulates that PWDs are entitled to reasonable access to all places, public transport, and information.[161]

D. The constitution needs to establish the right to legal capacity of PWDs

The right to legal capacity entails that the individual will be the subject of rights and duties and the ability to exercise those rights and obligations under the law.[162] In the past, PWDs have been denied the right to legal capacity.[163] This discrimination has been a result of unjustified conflation of the mental capacity and decision-making abilities of PWDs.[164] Particularly, persons with psychosocial disabilities are inexplicably affected by this.[165] Without legal capacity, it is not possible to enjoy the right to make decisions about one's own life.

To this end, Article 12 of the CRPD provides the right to legal capacity and supported decision-making for PWDs.[166] The convention prohibits legislation and practices that deny PWDs equal recognition before the law.[167] As such, it obligates Ethiopia as a state party to the CRPD to "take appropriate measures to provide access by persons with disabilities to the support they may require in exercising their legal capacity."[168] Hence, a state party to the convention is required to make sure that all legislation and practices have shifted from substituted decision making, such as a guardianship system, to that of supported decision-making.[169]

Nonetheless, PWDs in Ethiopia are deprived of their right to legal capacity. This is because there are discriminatory laws that restrict legal capacity in Ethiopia. Contrary to Article 12 of the CRPD, the Civil Code of Ethiopia lists the grounds of incapacity as notorious insanity, apparent infirmity, and judicial interdiction.[170] In its concluding observations on the initial report of Ethiopia, the Committee on the Rights of Persons with Disabilities expressed its concern that some provisions in the Civil Code are against the full legal capacity of PWDs.[171] According to this concluding observation, among the provisions that go against the legal capacity provision in the CRPD are Articles 339–88 of the Civil Code.[172] These provisions deal with judicial interdiction, insanity, and infirmity. As is pointed out above, the Civil Code of Ethiopia declares PWDs particularly persons with psychosocial disabilities to be legally incapable, that cannot take care of themselves and cannot administer their property.[173] In the view of the committee, these provisions restrict the rights of persons with psychosocial and intellectual disabilities to full enjoyment of their rights, in particular, the rights to marry, to act as a witness, to vote, and parental rights. As such, the committee recommended Ethiopia to repeal those provisions and secure the full legal capacity of PWDs.[174]

As a result, the FDRE Constitution needs to explicitly guarantee the right to the legal capacity of PWDs with the view of addressing the legal lacuna prevailing in the subsidiary laws of the country. It is the obligation of the government to make laws compatible with the CRPD.

E. The constitution should recognize the duty of reasonable accommodation

The CRPD for the first time under international law articulates the duty of reasonable accommodation as a distinct and enforceable human right. The duty of reasonable accommodation is a deeply entrenched concept in the CRPD.[175] It is unequivocally provided in the substantive articles of the right to liberty and security, education, the right to work, and the right of access to justice, among others.[176] Moreover, this duty is an inherent element of almost all of the substantive articles of the convention due to Articles 2 and 5 of the CRPD, which concern nondiscrimination and equality. Although it is specifically provided under the abovementioned substantive rights, the duty of reasonable accommodation falls within the articles of general application and therefore applies across all of the articles.[177]

The CRPD provides the definition of reasonable accommodation under Article 2. Thus, the duty of reasonable accommodation is defined in the CRPD in the following manner:

> Necessary and appropriate modification and adjustments not imposing a disproportionate or undue burden, where needed in a particular case, to ensure to persons with disabilities the enjoyment or exercise on an equal basis with others of all human rights and fundamental freedoms.[178]

By virtue of this definition, reasonable accommodation is concerned with the removal of barriers to which a PWD would otherwise be subjected to practices or systems that are not generally designed and developed to suit PWDs. Thus, the idea of reasonable accommodation is to eliminate challenges that PWDs encounter in exercising their fundamental rights. The duty of reasonable accommodation urges different treatment for people whose circumstances are appropriately different. This duty is concerned with achieving equality and avoiding discrimination.

Additionally, it needs change or modification in the ways activities are ordinarily done. This is because it would be very difficult or impossible for PWDs to participate unless these changes are made. Reasonable accommodation of PWDs is grounded on the idea that in some instances PWDs face barriers in their interaction with their physical or social environment that can result in the inability to perform a particular function, job, or activity in the conventional manner.[179]

However, although Ethiopia is duty bound to provide reasonable accommodation for PWDs by the CRPD, its implementation is only limited in the employment sector.[180] Other sectors envisaged by the convention are neglected with respect to reasonable accommodation. For this reason, in order to apply the principle of reasonable accommodation to a wide range of areas, the Constitution should adopt a comprehensive definition of reasonable accommodation that applies to all legislation. Thus, the Constitution should include the duty of reasonable accommodation as it is defined in the CRPD. Moreover, it should explicitly recognize that denial of reasonable accommodation as discrimination on the basis of disability.

F. The constitution needs to delineate a meaning for the term disability

As elaborated on above, providing a definition for the concept of disability in the Constitution will play a pivotal role in making sure that the Constitution is in conformity with the CRPD. Defining disability in the Constitution is quintessential in order to shape other subsidiary laws and policies of Ethiopia towards the right path. For instance, the 2010 constitution of Kenya serves as a model for other legislation and policies by defining the term "disability" under Article 260. As such, delineating a meaning for the term is necessary in the FDRE Constitution so that it will serve as a model for other laws and policies of the country.

G. The constitution needs to envisage a strong institution for the enforcement of disability rights

The FDRE Constitution needs to establish a national governmental organ with the responsibility of implementing the rights of PWDs. The former Ministry of Labour and Social Affairs (MOLSA) has been given the power to monitor enforcement of the CRPD at the federal level by the CRPD ratification proclamation.[181] MOLSA has also been entrusted to work in partnership with different stakeholders to enable PWDs to take part fully and effectively in their community.[182] Currently, the function of following up the implementation of the CRPD in the country has been transferred to the Ministry of Women and Social Affairs by virtue of Article 36/2 of proclamation No. 1263/2019. As such, the tasks entrusted to MOLSA are being performed by the Ministry of Women and Social Affairs. Besides, there are also other mechanisms that monitor the implementation of the CRPD in practice, such as national human rights institutions in the country. The Ethiopian Human Rights Commission (EHRC) and the Institution of Ombudsman have the mandate to follow up the promotion and protection of disability rights in Ethiopia.[183] In particular, the EHRC has a disability and older persons rights department that monitors and follows up the implementation of the CRPD and performs a number of related functions. Civil society organizations are also among the concerned bodies in following up on the implementation of disability rights in the country. However, the current institutional framework for the enforcement of disability rights is fragmented.[184] The institutional arrangement for monitoring the implementation of disability rights lacks uniformity throughout the country.[185]

As such, in order to create a robust enforcement mechanism, in addition to the above institutional frameworks, the FDRE Constitution needs to establish a national council for persons with disabilities. This institution should have the responsibility to protect and promote disability rights and mainstream disability issues into different walks of life in the country. This kind of institution is designed, for example, by the 2013 Persons with Disabilities Act of Kenya. This act empowered the national council for persons with disabilities, among others,

To formulate and develop measures and policies designed to achieve equal opportunities for persons with disabilities by ensuring to the maximum extent possible that they obtain education and employment, and participate fully in sporting, recreational and cultural activities and are afforded full access to community and social services; advise the Minister on the provisions of any international treaty or agreement relating to the welfare or rehabilitation of persons with disabilities and its benefits to the country; and encourage and secure the establishment of vocational rehabilitation centres and other institutions and other services for the welfare, rehabilitation and employment of persons with disabilities.[186]

As such, since Ethiopia has not yet approved a comprehensive disability law like that of its neighbouring country Kenya, the Constitution needs to include a similar institution with the view of rectifying the existing vacuum in the country.

4.2 Conclusion

This book chapter has made a case for the inclusion of PWDs in the FDRE Constitution of Ethiopia. To this effect, it has examined the past and present constitutions of Ethiopia. With the view of laying the foundation, the chapter first has outlined some of the basic conceptual issues with respect to disability. As such, issues like a definition of disability and different approaches to disability have been explored. Moreover, the chapter has placed disability rights in context within the general human rights framework. The book chapter has also highlighted how the fundamentals of a constitution play an important role in the protection and promotion of the human rights of PWDs if disability rights are adequately recognized in a constitution. Apart from this, the chapter has revealed that the present Constitution of Ethiopia does not offer sufficient recognition for the rights of PWDs. Although the Constitution has an extensive list of human rights in general, it neglects the fundamental human rights of PWDs. As a result, PWDs are left at the periphery in the current Constitution of Ethiopia. Additionally, it follows the medical and charity models of disability. It does not address the issue of disability-based discrimination. The Constitution does not say anything about the duty of reasonable accommodation. To this end, finally, the book chapter has made an attempt to offer recommendations for how to fill the constitutional vacuum with respect to disability rights.

Notes

1 Andrew Byrnes et al, From Exclusion to Equality: Realizing the Rights of Persons with Disabilities (United Nations Office of the High Commissioner for Human Rights, a handbook for parliamentarians on the rights of persons with disabilities and its optional protocol, 2007), 3.

2 World Bank and World Health Organization, "World Report on Disability", (2011), 11.

3 World Bank and World Health Organization, "World Report on Disability", 11.

4 Byrnes et al, From Exclusion to Equality: 3.

5 Byrnes et al, From Exclusion to Equality: 3.

6 Byrnes et al, From Exclusion to Equality: 3.

7 Sirak Akalu and Fiona Mckinnon, "Disability Rights Are Human Rights: Pushing Ethiopia towards a Rights-Based Movement," *Northwestern Journal of Human Rights* 19, no. 1 (2021), Muleta Hussein and Mohd Jameel, "Socio-economic Challenges of Persons with Disabilities: A Case Study of Ethiopia," *Global Journal of Human-Social Science: Sociology and Culture* 19, no. 1 (2019), Aschalew Ashagre, "Access to Justice for PWDs in Civil Proceedings before the Federal Courts of Ethiopia: The Law and Practice," *Mizan Law Review* 14, no. 1 (2020).

8 World Bank and World Health Organization, "World Report on Disability", 11.

9 Akalu and Mckinnon, "Disability Rights Are Human Rights:" 51-62, Hussein and Jameel, "Socio-economic Challenges of Persons with Disabilities:" 2-8.

10 FDRE Convention on the Rights of PWDs Ratification Proclamation, proclamation No. 676/2010, Fed. Neg. Gaz. Year 16, No. 32.

11 Convention on the Rights of Persons with Disabilities (CRPD), UN General Assembly, Treaty Series, Vol. 2515, (2006), Art. 4/1and 2 (

12 Id

13 Emma Stone, "Disability and Development: Learning from Action and Research on Disability in the Majority World," (Leeds: *The Disability Press* 1999), 3.

14 World Bank and World Health Organization, "World Report on Disability", 11.

15 Stone, "Disability and Development:" 3.

16 University of Pretoria, Changing the Landscape: Core Curriculum on Disability Rights for Undergraduate Law Students in Africa, (Pretoria University Law Press 2015), 14.

17 CRPD Preamble, Para. E.

18 Ibid

19 University of Pretoria, Changing the Landscape: 14.

20 University of Pretoria, Changing the Landscape: 14.

21 University of Pretoria, Changing the Landscape: 14.

22 Theresia Degener, "Disability in a Human Rights Context," laws, MDPI, 5, No. 3 (2016), 14.

23 Mariann Schulze, Understanding the UN Convention on the Rights of Persons with Disabilities, (*Handbook on the Human Rights of Persons with Disabilities* 2010), 10.

24 Schulze, Understanding the UN Convention on the Rights of Persons with Disabilities, 10.

25 Schulze, Understanding the UN Convention on the Rights of Persons with Disabilities, 10.

26 United Nations Office of the High Commissioner, "The Convention on the Rights of Persons with Disabilities: Training Guide." *Professional Training Series* No. 19 (2014), 16.

27 United Nations Office of the High Commissioner, The Convention on the Rights of Persons with Disabilities: 16.

28 United Nations Office of the High Commissioner, The Convention on the Rights of Persons with Disabilities: 16.

29 Arlene Kanter, The Development of Disability Rights under International Law: From Charity to Human Rights, (Routledge, 2015), 8.

30 Degener, "Disability in a Human Rights Context," 14.

31 Degener, "Disability in a Human Rights Context," 14.

32 Degener, "Disability in a Human Rights Context," 14.

33 Degener, "Disability in a Human Rights Context," 14.

34 Colin Barnes, "The Social Model of Disability: Valuable or Irrelevant," ed. Nick Watson et al, (*The Routledge Handbook of Disability Studies* 2012), 12–29.

35 Colin Barnes, "A Legacy of Oppression: A History of Disability in Western Culture," *Disability Studies: Past, Present and Future* ed. Len Barton and Mike Oliver, (the disability press, 1997), 9.

36 Barnes, "The Social Model of Disability:" 12–29.

37 Tom Shakespeare, "The Social Model of Disability," *The Disability Studies Reader,* (Routledge 2010), 2.

38 Degener, "Disability in a Human Rights Context," 14.

39 Degener, "Disability in a Human Rights Context," 14.

40 Theresia Degener, "A Human Rights Model of Disability," *Handbook of Disability Law and Human Rights,* (*Routledge* 2014), 6.

41 Degener, "A Human Rights Model of Disability," 6.

42 United Nations Office of the High Commissioner, "The Convention on the Rights of Persons with Disabilities:" 10.

43 CRPD preamble Para E.

44 Id

45 Magdalena Sepúlveda et al, Human Rights reference Handbook, (University for Peace, 2004), 6. Available at https://www.worldcat.org/title/human-rights-reference-handbook/oclc/58044058. Accessed on November 22, 2022.

46 Vienna Declaration and Program of Action, United Nation General Assembly (1993), Art. 5.
47 United Nations General Assembly, Universal Declaration for Human Rights (UDHR), (1948), art. 1.
48 Sepúlveda et al, Human Rights reference Handbook, 6.
49 Sepúlveda et al, Human Rights reference Handbook, 6.
50 University of Pretoria, Changing the Landscape: 8.
51 CRPD Art. 1.
52 University of Pretoria, Changing the Landscape: 6.
53 UDHR, Art. 1.
54 Id
55 International Covenant on Civil and Political Rights (ICCPR), (1966), *Treaty Series*, Vol. 999, p. 171 and Vol. 1057, adopted 1966 and entered into force 1976, Preamble.
56 United Nations, Committee on ICESCR, General Comment No. 5: "Persons with disabilities," (1994), para 5.
57 ICCPR arts 6, 9, 18, 17 and 25.
58 International Covenant on Economic, Social and Cultural Rights (ICESCR), United Nations, *Treaty Series*, Vol. 993, adopted 1966 and entered into force 1976, arts 13 and 15.
59 Kanter, The Development of Disability Rights under International Law: 21.
60 Office of United Nations High Commissioner for Human Rights, "Convention on the Rights of Persons with Disabilities: Advocacy Toolkit," In: *Professional Training Series No. 15* (2008), 1. https://www.ohchr.org/Documents/Publications/AdvocacyTool_en.pdf.
61 Office of United Nations High Commissioner for Human Rights, "Convention on the Rights of Persons with Disabilities:" 1.
62 Kanter, The Development of Disability Rights under International Law: 21.
63 CRPD, Art. 3.
64 United Nations Office of High Commissioner for Human Rights, "Human Rights and Constitution Making" (2018), 9.
65 World Policy Analysis Centre, "Constitutional Equal Rights of People with Disabilities," Fact Sheet 7 (2020). https://www.worldpolicycenter.org.
66 Elliot Bulmer, "What Is a Constitution? Principles and Concepts," International Idea, (Constitution Building Primer 1, 2017), 8.
67 Bulmer, "What Is a Constitution? Principles and Concepts," 8.
68 Bulmer, "What Is a Constitution? Principles and Concepts," 8.
69 Bulmer, "What Is a Constitution? Principles and Concepts," 8.
70 United Nations Office of High Commissioner for Human Rights. "Human Rights and Constitution Making," 9.
71 United Nations Office of High Commissioner for Human Rights. "Human Rights and Constitution Making," 9.
72 United Nations Office of High Commissioner for Human Rights. "Human Rights and Constitution Making," 9.
73 United Nations Office of High Commissioner for Human Rights. "Human Rights and Constitution Making," 9.

74 Jody Heymann et al, "Advancing Equality: How Constitutional Rights Can Make a Difference Worldwide," (University of California Press 2020), 27. https://doi.org/10.1525/ luminos.81
75 Heymann et al, "Advancing Equality:" 27.
76 Heymann et al, "Advancing Equality:" 27.
77 Heymann et al, "Advancing Equality:" 27.
78 Heymann et al, "Advancing Equality:" 27.
79 Heymann et al, "Advancing Equality:" 27.
80 Heymann et al, "Advancing Equality:" 27.
81 Heymann et al, "Advancing Equality:" 27.
82 Thomas Trier- Hansen et al, "The Constitutional Protection of Human Rights," (Danish Institute for Human Rights 2012), 7.
83 Cass R. Sunstein, "On the Expressive Function of Law," East European Constitutional Review 66 (Special Reports 1996), 3.
84 Sunstein, "On the Expressive Function of Law" 3.
85 Sunstein, "On the Expressive Function of Law" 3.
86 Sunstein, "On the Expressive Function of Law" 3.
87 Sunstein, "On the Expressive Function of Law" 3.
88 Getachew Assefa, Ethiopian Constitutional Law with Comparative Notes and Materials: a text book, (Getachew Assefa 2012), 25.
89 Assefa, Ethiopian Constitutional Law with Comparative Notes and Materials: 25.
90 Assefa, Ethiopian Constitutional Law with Comparative Notes and Materials: 25.
91 Muna Ndulo, "Constitutions and Constitutional Reforms in African Politics," Oxford Research Encyclopedias (2019), 11, https://doi.org/10.1093/acrefore/9780190228637.013.1324
92 Ndulo, "Constitutions and Constitutional Reforms in African Politics," 11.
93 Dawood Ahmed and Elliot Bulmer, "Social and Economic Rights," International Institute for Democracy and Electoral Assistance (International IDEA,2017), 16.
94 Ahmed and Bulmer, "Social and Economic Rights," 16.
95 Ahmed and Bulmer, "Social and Economic Rights," 16.
96 Young African Leaders Initiative (YALI). "Why Constitutions Need to Include Human Rights." https://yali.state.gov.
97 YALI "Why Constitutions Need to Include Human Rights"
98 The Constitution of the Federal Democratic Republic of Ethiopia (FDRE constitution), Proclamation No.1/1995, and Fed. Neg. Gaz, Art. 9(1)
99 United Nations Office of High Commissioner for Human Rights, "Human Rights and Constitution Making" 9.
100 Assefa, Ethiopian Constitutional Law with Comparative Notes and Materials: 25.
101 Kofa study, "Rigid and Flexible Constitution, Meaning, Merits and Demerits," https://www.kofastudy.com › constitution-week-3 › topic.
102 Kofa study, "Rigid and Flexible Constitution," Meaning, Merits and Demerits.
103 Assefa, Ethiopian Constitutional Law with Comparative Notes and Materials: 25.
104 Adem Kassie Abebe, "Human Rights under the Ethiopian Constitution: A Descriptive Overview," Mizan Law Review 5 no. 1, (2011), 1.
105 Abebe, "Human Rights under the Ethiopian Constitution:" 1.

106 Abebe, "Human Rights under the Ethiopian Constitution:" 1.
107 Tsegaye Regassa, "Making Legal Sense of Human Rights: The Judicial Role in Protecting Human Rights in Ethiopia." Mizan Law Review 3, no. 2, (2010), 10.
108 the 1931 Constitution of Ethiopia, Arts. 6–17
109 Id
110 Abebe, "Human Rights under the Ethiopian Constitution:" 1.
111 Regassa, "Making Legal Sense of Human Rights:" 10.
112 The 1955 revised constitution of Ethiopia, Arts. 122 and 110.
113 Id
114 Abebe, "Human Rights under the Ethiopian Constitution:" 1.
115 Abebe, "Human Rights under the Ethiopian Constitution:" 1.
116 Abebe, "Human Rights under the Ethiopian Constitution:" 1.
117 the 1931 Constitution of Ethiopia, Art 45.
118 Abebe, "Human Rights under the Ethiopian Constitution:" 11.
119 Abebe, "Human Rights under the Ethiopian Constitution:" 11.
120 The constitution of the people's democratic republic of Ethiopia (PDRE Constitution 1987), Art. 118.
121 Id
122 Id
123 Id Art. 22.
124 Id, Art. 50.
125 FDRE Constitution preamble, Para. 1.
126 Id
127 Id
128 Id
129 T.S. Twibell, "Ethiopian Constitutional Law: The Structure of the Ethiopian Government and the New Constitution's Ability to Overcome Ethiopia's Problems," Loyola of Los Angeles, international and comparative law review, 21 no. (199), 7.
130 Abebe, "Human Rights under the Ethiopian Constitution:" 11.
131 Abebe, "Human Rights under the Ethiopian Constitution:" 11.
132 FDRE Constitution, Art. 13/1.
133 Id, Art. 13/2.
134 Id, Arts. 14, 15, 17, and 18.
135 Id, Art. 41/5.
136 Amy Raub et al, "Constitutional Rights of Persons with Disabilities: An Analysis of 193 National Constitutions," 11, https://apps.hks.harvard.edu
137 FDRE Constitution, Art. 25.
138 UN Committee on the Rights of Persons with Disabilities (CRPD), "Equality and Non-discrimination." General Comment No. 6 (2018), Para 4.
139 UDHR Arts. 1 and 2.
140 ICCPR and ICESCR Art. 2.
141 CRPD Arts. 3 and 5.
142 UN Committee on the Rights of Persons with Disabilities, "Equality and Non-discrimination," Para. 7.

143 UN Committee on the Rights of Persons with Disabilities, "Equality and Non-discrimination," Para. 18.
144 UN Committee on the Rights of Persons with Disabilities, "Equality and Non-discrimination," Para. 18.
145 UN Committee on the Rights of Persons with Disabilities, "Equality and Non-discrimination," Para. 18(a).
146 UN Committee on the Rights of Persons with Disabilities, "Equality and Non-discrimination," Para. 18(b).
147 UN Committee on the Rights of Persons with Disabilities, "Equality and Non-discrimination," Para. 18(c).
148 UN Committee on the Rights of Persons with Disabilities, "Equality and Non-discrimination," Para. 18(d).
149 UN Committee on the Rights of Persons with Disabilities, "Equality and Non-discrimination," Para. 18(d).
150 The Constitution of Kenya (2010), Art. 27/4.
151 FDRE Constitution, Art. 5.
152 CRPD, Art. 30.
153 The constitution of Kenya, Art. 54.
154 Id, Art. 7/3.
155 Id
156 CRPD, Arts. 3 and 5.
157 UN Committee on the Rights of Persons with Disabilities (CRPD), "Accessibility." General Comment No. 2 (2014), Para. 1.
158 CRPD, Art. 9.
159 Federal Democratic Republic of Ethiopia building proclamation, proclamation No. 624/2009, Fed. Neg. Gaz., Year 15, No. 31, Art. 36.
160 Id
161 The Constitution of Kenya, art 54.
162 Kanter, The Development of Disability Rights under International Law: 235.
163 UN Committee on the Rights of Persons with Disabilities (CRPD), "Equal Recognition before the Law." General Comment No. 1 (2014), Para. 7.
164 Kanter, The Development of Disability Rights under International Law: 235.
165 Kanter, The Development of Disability Rights under International Law: 235.
166 CRPD, Art. 12.
167 Id
168 CRPD, Art. 12/3.
169 Kanter, The Development of Disability Rights under International Law: 235.
170 Federal Democratic Republic of Ethiopia civil code, proclamation No. 165 (1960), Fed. Neg. Gaz. Year, No. 2, Art. 192.
171 United Nations Committee on the Convention for Persons with Disabilities, "Concluding Observations on the Initial Report of Ethiopia," (2016), Para. 25.
172 United Nations Committee on the Convention for Persons with Disabilities, "Concluding Observations on the Initial Report of Ethiopia," Para. 25.
173 Civil Code, Arts. 339–88.

174 United Nations Committee on the Convention for Persons with Disabilities, "Concluding Observations on the Initial Report of Ethiopia," Para. 26.

175 Anna Lawson, Disability and Equality Law in Britain: The Role of Reasonable Adjustment, (Hart Publishing 2008), 12.

176 CRPD, Arts. 14(2), 24(2), 27, and 13(1).

177 Janet Lord and Rebecca Brown, "The Role of Reasonable Accommodation in Securing Substantive Equality for Persons with Disabilities: The UN Convention on the Rights of Persons with Disabilities," *Disability Law Journal* (2010), 7.

178 CRPD, Art. 2.

179 Lisa Waddington, "Reasonable Accommodation: Time to Extend the Duty to Accommodate Beyond Disability?" European Disability Law, (2011), 1.

180 United Nations Committee on the Convention for Persons with Disabilities, "Concluding Observations on the Initial Report of Ethiopia," Paras. 4 and 9.

181 Yonas Birmeta Adinew, "The Legal and Policy Framework for the Inclusion of Persons with Disabilities (PWDs) in Ethiopia," 27.

182 Adinew, "The Legal and Policy Framework for the Inclusion of Persons with Disabilities in Ethiopia" 27.

183 Adinew, "The Legal and Policy Framework for the Inclusion of Persons with Disabilities in Ethiopia" 27.

184 Ethiopian Human Rights Commission, "annual situation report on disability and older persons rights", (2023), 23.

185 Ethiopian Human Rights Commission, "annual situation report on disability and older persons rights", 23.

186 Kariuki Muigua, "securing the realization of environmental and social rights for persons with disabilities in Kenya", journal of conflict management and sustainable development, 2, no. 1 (2018), 45.

Bibliography

Abebe, Adem Kassie. "Human Rights under the Ethiopian Constitution: A Descriptive Overview," *Mizan Law Review* 5, no. 1 (2011).

Adinew, Yonas Birmeta. "The Legal and Policy Framework for the Inclusion of Persons with Disabilities (PWDs) in Ethiopia." Unpublished.

Ahmed, Dawood and Elliot Bulmer. *Social and Economic Rights*. International Institute for Democracy and Electoral Assistance (International IDEA), 2017.

Ashagre, Aschalew. "Access to Justice for PWDs in Civil Proceedings before the Federal Courts of Ethiopia: The Law and Practice." *Mizan Law Review* 14, no. 1 (2020).

Assefa, Getachew. *Ethiopian Constitutional Law with Comparative Notes and Materials: a textbook*. Getachew Assefa, 2012.

Barnes, Colin. "A Legacy of Oppression: A History of Disability in Western Culture." In *Disability Studies: Past, Present and Future,* edited by Len Barton and Mike Oliver, 3-24. The disability Press, 1997.

Barnes, Colin. "The Social Model of Disability: Valuable or Irrelevant." In *Routledge Handbook of Disability Studies*, edited by Nick Watson, Alan Roulstone, and Carol Thomas, 12-29. Routledge, 2012.

Bulmer, Elliot. "What Is a constitution? Principles and Concepts." International Idea, Constitution Building Primer 1, 2017.

Byrnes, Andrew et al. *From Exclusion to Equality: Realizing the Rights of Persons with Disabilities: handbook for parliamentarians on the rights of persons with disabilities and its optional protocol.* United Nations Office of the High Commissioner for Human Rights, 2007.

Degener, Theresia. "A Human Rights Model of Disability," In *Routledge Handbook of Disability Law and Human Rights*, edited by Peter Blanck and Eilionóir Flynn, 31-50. Routledge, 2014.

Degener, Theresia. "Disability in a Human Rights Context." *Laws* 5, no. 3 (2016): 35.

Ethiopian Human Rights Commission. "Annual Human Rights Situation Report on Disability Rights and Rights of Older Persons." *EHRC*, 2023.

Federal Democratic Republic of Ethiopia building proclamation, proclamation No. 624/2009, Fed. Neg. Gaz., Year 15, No. 31,

Federal Democratic Republic of Ethiopia civil code, proclamation No. 165 (1960), Fed. Neg. Gaz. Year, No. 2

Federal Democratic Republic of Ethiopia Convention on the Rights of PWDs Ratification Proclamation, proclamation No. 676/2010, Fed. Neg. Gaz. Year 16, No. 32.

Heymann, Jody, Aleta Sprague, and Amy Raub. *Advancing Equality: How Constitutional Rights Can Make a Difference Worldwide*. University of California Press, 2020.

Iyassu, Sirak Akalu and Fiona Mckinnon. "Disability Rights Are Human Rights: Pushing Ethiopia towards a Rights-Based Movement," *Northwestern Journal of Human Rights* 19, no. 1 (2021).

Kanter, Arlene S. *The Development of Disability Rights under International Law: From Charity to Human Rights*. Routledge, 2015.

Kofa Study. "Rigid and Flexible Constitution, Meaning, Merits and Demerits." https://www.kofastudy.com › constitution-week-3 › topic

Lawson, Anna. *Disability and Equality Law in Britain: The Role of Reasonable Adjustment*. Hart Publishing, 2008.

Lord, Janet E., and Rebecca Brown. "The Role of Reasonable Accommodation in Securing Substantive Equality for Persons with Disabilities: The UN Convention on the Rights of Persons with Disabilities." In *Critical Perspectives in Human Rights and Disability Law*, edited by Marcia H. Roue, Lee Ann Basser, and Melinda Jones, 273-307. Brill / Nijhoff, 2010.

Muigua, Kariuki. "Securing the Realization of Environmental and Social Rights for Persons with Disabilities in Kenya." *Journal of conflict management and sustainable development* 2, no. 1 (2018).

Ndulo, Muna. "Constitutions and Constitutional Reforms in African Politics." In *The Oxford Encyclopaedia of African Politics*, edited by Nic Cheeseman. Oxford University Press, 2020.

Office of the United Nations High Commissioner for Human Rights, "Convention on the Rights of Persons with Disabilities: Advocacy Toolkit," In: Professional Training Series No. 15 (2008).

Raub, Amy, Isabel Latz, Aleta Sprague, Michael Ashley Stein, and Jody Heymann. "Constitutional Rights of Persons with Disabilities: An Analysis of 193 National Constitutions." *Harvard Human Rights Journal* 29, no. 203 (2016).

Regassa, Tsegaye. "Making Legal Sense of Human Rights: The Judicial Role in Protecting Human Rights in Ethiopia." *Mizan Law Review* 3, no. 2 (2009).

Schulze, Marianne. *Understanding the UN Convention on the Rights of Persons with Disabilities: A Handbook on the Human Rights of Persons with Disabilities*. Handicap International, 2010.

Sedeto, Muleta Hussein, and Mohd Jameel Dar. "Socio-economic Challenges of Persons with Disabilities: A Case Study of Ethiopia," *Global Journal of Human-Social Science: Sociology and Culture* 19, no. 1 (2019).

Sepulveda, Magdalena, Theo van Banning, Gudrún D. Gudmundsdóttir, Christine Chamoun, and Willem van Genugten. *Human Rights reference Handbook*. University for Peace, 2004.

Shakespeare, Tom. "The Social Model of Disability." In *The Disability Studies Reader*, edited by Lennard J. Davis, 266-273. Routledge 2010.

Stone, Emma (ed.). *Disability and Development: Learning from Action and Research on Disability in the Majority World*. The Disability Press 1999.

Sunstein, Cass. "On the Expressive Function of Law." *University of Pennsylvania Law Review* 144, 2021 (1996).

The 1931 Constitution of Ethiopia.

The 1955 Revised Constitution of Ethiopia.

The Constitution of the Federal Democratic Republic of Ethiopia (FDRE constitution), Proclamation No.1/1995.

The Constitution of the People's Democratic Republic of Ethiopia (PDRE Constitution 1987).

Trier-Hansen, Thomas, Lisbeth A.N. Thonbo, et. al. *The Constitutional Protection of Human Rights*. Danish Institute for Human Rights, 2012.

Twibell, T. S. "Ethiopian Constitutional Law: The Structure of the Ethiopian Government and the New Constitution's Ability to Overcome Ethiopia's Problems," *Loyola of Los Angeles International and Comparative Law Review* 21, no. 399 (1999).

UN Committee on ICESCR, "Persons with disabilities," General Comment No. 5, (1994).

UN Committee on the Convention for Persons with Disabilities, "Concluding Observations on the Initial Report of Ethiopia," (2016).

UN Committee on the Rights of Persons with Disabilities (CRPD), "Accessibility." General Comment No. 2 (2014).

UN Committee on the Rights of Persons with Disabilities (CRPD), "Equality and Non-discrimination." General Comment No. 6 (2018).

UN Committee on the Rights of Persons with Disabilities (CRPD), "Equal Recognition before the Law." General Comment No. 1 (2014).

United Nations General Assembly, Convention on the Rights of Persons with Disabilities (CRPD), UN General Assembly, Treaty Series, Vol. 2515, (2006).

United Nations General Assembly, International Covenant on Civil and Political Rights (ICCPR), (1966), Treaty Series, Vol. 999, p. 171 and Vol. 1057, adopted 1966 and entered into force 1976.

United Nations General Assembly, International Covenant on Economic, Social and Cultural Rights (ICESCR), United Nations, Treaty Series, Vol. 993, adopted 1966 and entered into force 1976.

United Nations General Assembly, Universal Declaration for Human Rights (UDHR), (1948).

United Nations Office of High Commissioner for Human Rights, "Human Rights and Constitution Making" (2018).

United Nations Office of the High Commissioner, "The Convention on the Rights of Persons with Disabilities: Training Guide." Professional Training Series No. 19 (2014).

University of Pretoria. *Changing the Landscape: Core Curriculum on Disability Rights for Undergraduate Law Students in Africa*. Pretoria University Law Press, 2015.

Vienna Declaration and Program of Action, United Nation General Assembly (1993).

Waddington, Lisa. "Reasonable Accommodation: Time to Extend the Duty to Accommodate Beyond Disability?" *MTM*

NJCM- Bulletin 38, no. 2 (2011): 186-198.

World Bank and World Health Organization. "World Report on Disability." *WB and WHO*, 2011.

World Policy Analysis Centre, "Constitutional Equal Rights of People with Disabilities," Fact Sheet 7, (2020).

Young African Leaders Initiative (YALI). "More Than Just Words: Why Constitutions Need to Include Human Rights." YALI, 2016.

Part III

Separation of Powers and Federalism

Chapter 11

The Trinity of Government: The Theory and Practice of Separation of Powers in Ethiopia

Zelalem Mogessie Teferra

Introduction

In a live-streamed program, Abiy Ahmed, the current prime minister of Ethiopia, made two remarks that have caused significant shock and concern within the legal and larger communities in Ethiopia. The first remark pertains to the funding source for the government's "Chaka Project," the single-biggest project in Ethiopia's history, including the building of a palace and other luxurious amenities. When members of parliament inquired about the source and modalities of funding, the prime minister responded that the parliament did not have the authority to inquire about the source of the funding.[1] He further explained that he was not using the "government-approved" budget and instead relied on contributions from private entities or financial assistance from friendly foreign nations, often facilitated by his personal relationships with their leaders.

In a separate but equally noteworthy comment, prime minister Abiy addressed the escalating issue of corruption within the country, a concern also voiced by members of parliament. He described judges as "first-class thieves" in the nation[2], a controversial assertion made at a time when the judiciary was struggling to (re)gain public trust.

These statements raise questions about the role of parliament in overseeing government projects but also the extent to which the executive may engage in any actions or utter words that may have the potential to undermine the credibility and integrity of the judicial system. Most importantly, these statements coming from the prime minister only scratch the surface of the broader challenges facing Ethiopia in terms of maintaining a meaningful separation of powers in both theory and practice and establishing a democratic governance framework.

The foundation of a thriving democracy rests upon a strong judiciary, an independent legislature, and an executive branch that respects the inherent checks and balances within the system. However, Ethiopia's historical and current circumstances reveal a significant gap in achieving a genuine separation of powers. This chapter delves into the challenges that Ethiopia encounters in realizing separation of powers and seeks to suggest potential solutions for enhancing accountability and democratic governance. It begins by providing a brief overview of the origin, essence, and rationale behind the doctrine of separation of powers. Subsequently, it explores the historical evolution of this doctrine within the Ethiopian legal framework from 1931 to 1994. The third section focuses on the theory and practice of the separation of powers in the post-1994 era, with a particular focus on the triangular relationship among the executive, judiciary, and legislative branches. Finally, in conclusion, the chapter puts forth some concrete proposals, acknowledging that while some of them may not be entirely novel, they are critical for guiding future constitutional amendments. These recommendations are geared towards strengthening the implementation of the doctrine of separation of powers in Ethiopia, with a central focus on nurturing democratic accountability.

The Origin, Essence and Rationale of Separation of Powers

The doctrine of separation of powers has its origins in the writings of ancient Greek and Roman philosophers such as Plato, Aristotle, and Cicero.[3] However, the modern version of the doctrine was developed in the eighteenth century by the French philosopher Baron de Montesquieu. In his book *De l'esprit des loix* (*The Spirit of the Laws*),[4] Montesquieu asserted that political authority must be divided into the legislative, executive, and judiciary, and such powers should be conferred on different individuals or bodies, acting independently.[5] Montesquieu emphasized that this creates a balance of powers among the three branches and would prevent any one branch from becoming too powerful and a threat to people's liberty.

Montesquieu's notion of separation of powers later received currency among the framers of the United States Constitution, who formally adopted the doctrine in the US legal system by establishing three branches of government and giving each branch specific powers of making, interpreting, and implementing laws. The American Founding Fathers chose "a partial" version of separation of power by introducing a system of checks and balances among the legislature, the judiciary, and the executive.[6] The system of checks and balances refined the doctrine by instituting a scheme allowing a certain degree of mutual supervision among the three branches of government.[7] Currently, despite the "effusive praise and vitriolic opprobrium in equal measure"[8] that it has received, the doctrine of separation of power exists in almost all legal systems around the world in different forms and substance.

The essence of the doctrine of separation of powers lies in its proposal for a "division of labor" and its prohibition of concentration of power in one person or branch of government by creating a separation of institutions, functions, and personnel. As such, it has the dual objectives of defending liberty[9] and promoting efficiency.[10] The separation of power enables the allocation of specific powers and responsibilities to the different organs, and this allows for specialization, expertise, and focused decision-making within each branch, leading to more efficient and informed governance. It also serves as a safeguard against authoritarianism and despotism and any form of tyranny by preventing accumulation of excessive power in one branch or individual. Not only does this help in protecting human rights and fundamental freedoms but also establishes mechanisms for accountability and oversight.[11] Each branch can hold the others accountable for their actions, ensuring transparency, legality, and adherence to constitutional principles. This accountability prevents unchecked authority and fosters public trust in the government.

It is important to recognize that despite ongoing philosophical debates regarding the pure and partial theories of the separation of powers,[12] no country in the world has achieved an absolute separation of powers. Even in nations where this doctrine has a long-standing presence, there is no legislature, judiciary, or executive branch that possesses discrete and mutually exclusive functions. Instead, power is distributed among these three branches, interconnected by an interinstitutional thread of reciprocal oversight in the form of checks and balances.

Furthermore, the extent to which the separation of powers can be realized in a particular country depends on the nature of governmental, social, and economic realities and the overall prevailing political culture. For instance, it has been argued that achieving a genuine separation of powers is generally easier in a presidential system compared to a parliamentary system of government. This is due to the fact that in parliamentary systems, the legislature has the authority to select the political element of the executive, resulting in the two branches functioning "based on a fusion of powers"[13] rather than a strict separation. Based on this observation, some scholars, like Barber, even assert that the concept of separation of powers can only be fully applicable in presidential-style constitutional systems.[14]

However, it is not uncommon to find elements of both separation and supervision within even the most traditional parliamentary systems. In parliamentary systems, while the executive and legislative branches are not completely independent of each other, they still maintain a level of separation. The executive, typically headed by a prime minister or a similar position, derives its authority from the support of the legislative body. This relationship allows for a fusion of powers to some extent, but it also provides opportunities for checks and balances. The legislature can hold the executive accountable through mechanisms such as votes of no confidence or questioning sessions or inquiries or investigations into allegations of misconduct conducted by parliamentary committees. Moreover, parliamentary systems often have an independent judiciary that plays a crucial role in upholding the rule of law and ensuring the separation of powers. The judiciary acts as a check on both the executive and legislative branches, ensuring that their actions adhere to the constitution and are within the bounds of the law. Therefore, even in parliamentary systems, the principles of separation and supervision are typically present, although they may manifest differently compared to presidential systems. However, it is worth acknowledging that while both parliamentary and presidential systems embody these principles, presidential systems are generally characterized by a more explicit and pronounced separation of powers due to the distinct roles and functions of the executive and legislative branches.

The History of Separation of Powers in Ethiopia

The doctrine of separation of powers has a relatively short history in Ethiopia. It is only in the first half of the twentieth century that some formal elements of the doctrine were introduced into its legal system. Throughout much of its history, Ethiopia's political systems have been characterized by regimes that centralized power in the hands of a strong executive or leaders, resulting in limited checks and balances on their authority. This prevailing culture of strong executive authority has hindered the development of separation of powers, consequently limiting the independence and effectiveness of the judiciary and the legislature. While the change of regimes at various points in time has brought some positive impact on the recognition of the importance of separation of powers, the full application of this doctrine is yet to be achieved both in theory and practice.

In the following sections, the chapter delves into the historical journey of Ethiopia's separation of powers, highlighting the challenges faced and the progress achieved across three distinct temporal zones: the Imperial era (pre-1974 time), the Derg regime (1974), and the post-Derg era. Through this examination, the chapter aims at propounding a deeper understanding of Ethiopia's ongoing quest for a democratic system that embodies the essence and substance of a genuine separation of powers. By shedding light on the country's past, an attempt is made to highlight the country's unquenched trust for a democratic system of government and illuminate the path towards a future grounded in a robust and balanced governance structure.

i. Imperial Era (Pre-1974)

In Ethiopia's long history of state, the kings and queens wielded absolute authority over their subjects, exerting control over the executive, legislative, and judicial realms. This long-standing tradition persisted even during the reign of the last monarch, Emperor Haile Selassie. His rule, for the most part, exemplified the entrenched dominance of the executive branch, with limited checks and balances on the exercise of power. The source of his authority was claimed to mainly be divine power, and like his predecessors, he consistently asserted that he was "the elect of God" (*Siyume Egziabhere*). Although there were advisory councils and regional administrative bodies, they lacked substantial power and were largely dependent on the emperor's directives. At the lower echelons of government, local chiefs and provincial governors also often exercised both executive and judicial functions.[15]

However, in the first half of the twentieth century, Ethiopia embarked on a path of modernization and legal reform, driven by the necessity to adapt to an emerging complex public administration system and influential and changing global dynamics.[16] As part of this transformative process, the country began incorporating formal elements of separation of powers into its legal framework. A significant milestone in this journey was the adoption of the country's first written constitution in 1931[17] and its revised version in 1955, which established a constitutional monarchy.

a. The 1931 Constitution

The 1931 Constitution represented a watershed moment in Ethiopia's legal and political development, particularly in terms of embracing the concept of separation of powers.[18] It introduced a governmental structure inspired by the European model, with which the country was previously unfamiliar. The

Constitution established three distinct branches of government with legislative, judicial, and executive powers. However, the emperor dominated all the three branches. As the "sacred" figure whose "dignity is inviolable and power indisputable,"[19] he retained "the supreme power of the Ethiopian Empire"[20] over all affairs.[21]

In the 1931 Constitution, the legislative power was vested in a bicameral parliament consisting of the House of Senate (in Amharic, *Yehig Mewesegna Mikirbet*) and the House of Deputies (*Yehig Memria Mikerbet*).[22] Members of the Senate were appointed by his majesty, the emperor, from among dignitaries (*Mekuanent*) who had served the empire as princes, ministers, judges, or army leaders.[23] In contrast, members of the Chamber of Deputies would be chosen by dignitaries and local chiefs (*Shumoch*) until such time as "the people are capable of electing them themselves."[24] While the Constitution required that all laws be discussed by the chambers,[25] they could only come into effect upon receiving the emperor's confirmation.[26] In other words, the members had a sort of advisory role to the emperor, as their name in Amharic, *amakariwoch* (counselors) clearly suggested. Although the two chambers were entitled to express their opinions on legal and other matters, and their members enjoyed some immunity from prosecution,[27] these opinions would not be considered if the emperor did not accept them.[28] Additionally, the members of the Chamber of Deputies were legally obligated to receive and discuss proposals presented by the ministers of the various departments.[29] The emperor also held the right to initiate legislation, propose resolutions, and proclaim laws after their passage in parliament.[30]

The 1931 Constitution also established a judiciary and enshrined key principles governing the administration of justice, including regular and public sittings.[31] However, judges, selected from individuals with expertise in legal matters, were mandated to function and apply laws in the name of his majesty, the emperor.[32] The Constitution also recognized the existence of special courts with jurisdiction over administrative affairs.[33]

The Constitution entrusted executive power to the ministers of the empire, who were accountable to the emperor. Their main role was basically advisory, and when he asks for advice, they shall submit in writing their opinions to the emperor after deliberating on the matter.[34] Therefore, the emperor retained the absolute executive power for governing and administering the affairs of the nation.

Overall, the adoption of the 1931 Constitution, despite its ostensible introduction of the doctrine of separation of powers, served a dual purpose that ultimately reinforced the emperor's authority. On one hand, it aimed to project an image of modernity and governmental legitimacy, enhancing the emperor's standing.[35] On the other hand, it strategically enabled the emperor to exert control over regional power contenders, consolidating his power base. Hence, while the Constitution supposedly introduced the concept of separation of powers, its true effect was to serve as a double-edged sword, further strengthening the emperor's position domestically and preserving his international image as a progressive monarch.[36]

b. The Revised 1955 Constitution

In the years that transpired after the enactment of the 1931 Constitution, Ethiopia witnessed significant national and international developments. Notable among these were the second invasion by Italy in 1935, the upheaval of World War II and the subsequent adoption of the Universal Declaration of Human Rights (UDHR) in 1948, and the federation of Eritrea with Ethiopia in 1951.[37] These transformative events profoundly impacted the country, compelling the emperor to undertake various reforms, including a revision of the then constitutional framework. Consequently, the Revised Constitution was introduced in 1955,[38] incorporating some changes, such as the recognition and protection of human rights,[39] and a more detailed and refined separation of powers. It defined the roles and responsibilities of the executive, legislative, and judicial branches of government. However, power continued to remain heavily concentrated in the hands of the emperor. While the Revised Constitution introduced some reforms and expanded certain principles, the ultimate authority and decision-making power continued to be held by the emperor, and the Constitution primarily served as an instrument of "consolidation of absolutism."[40] The Revised Constitution proclaimed that the "Sovereignty of the Empire is vested in the Emperor and the supreme authority over all the affairs of the Empire is exercised by Him as the Head of the State."[41] The direct consequence of this was that all subjects owed loyalty to the emperor, and no one had "the right to bring suit against the Emperor."[42] The emperor had the exclusive power to determine the organization, powers, and duties of all ministries, executive departments, and the administration of the government and to appoint, promote, transfer, suspend, and dismiss the officials of the same.[43] He had also the right to convene the annual sessions of the legislative chambers, to initiate legislation and other resolutions, and to proclaim all laws[44] and even to dissolve the chambers.[45]

The Revised Constitution maintained the bicameral system of parliament that was established by the 1931 Constitution, with clearer mandates and procedures. It reaffirmed that members of the two houses had immunity from arrest and prosecution for words they spoke in discharge of their functions.[46] Departing from its predecessor, the Revised Constitution also introduced adult suffrage for the election of the Chamber of Deputies.[47] Worthy of note from the perspective of separation of powers is also that it further instituted a system of checks and balances between the parliament and the executive branch, exemplified by the Council of Ministers.[48] Under the Revised Constitution, ministers were granted the right to attend any sessions of the chambers, allowing them direct access to the parliamentary discussions. At the same time, ministers, including the prime minister, were obligated to respond to questions regarding legislation under consideration or any matters being discussed. They were required to do so in person or through their deputies when requested by a majority vote of the members of the parliament.[49]

The Revised Constitution further recognized the crucial principle of an independent judiciary, establishing that the judicial power would be vested in the courts as defined by law.[50] It emphasized the imperative for judges to maintain independence in their trial proceedings and rulings, being guided solely by the law submitting to no other authority.[51] However, it required that judges deliver justice acting in the name of the emperor. It also established the Supreme Imperial Court,[52] through which the emperor retained his traditional status as "the [highest] fountain of justice,"[53] which was presided over by the emperor, and exclusive authority to appoint judges resided with the emperor.[54] Consequently, it is hardly possible to say that judicial independence was guaranteed.[55]

Generally, the Revised Constitution introduced some reforms and expanded certain principles pertaining to democracy, the rule of law, and division of labor among the three organs of government, but power ultimately remained concentrated in the hands of the emperor. Despite efforts to establish a system of checks and balances and recognize the independence of the judiciary, the influence of the emperor and his control over all aspects of governance made the realization of true separation of powers impossible.

II. The Derg Era (1974–1991)

The adoption of the Revised Constitution in 1955 proved to be inadequate in addressing the profound changes and challenges that Ethiopia was facing, both domestically and globally. As the country grappled with rapid transformations, opposition to the imperial regime intensified from various segments of society, including students, farmers, security personnel, civil servants, and others. As historian Bahru Zewde noted, peasants rose up against increasing demands on their agricultural produce, ethnic groups demanded self-determination, and intellectuals advocated for a more just and equitable society. Even within the ruling class, there were those who believed that removing Haile Selassie was a necessary step to avert the complete collapse of the socioeconomic order.[56] The culmination of these diverse opposition movements set the stage for the 1974 Revolution, which witnessed the military seizing power in a coup against the emperor. This significant event reshaped

Ethiopia's political landscape, as the country entered a new era characterized by the rule of the military junta commonly known as the Derg.

True to its nature, the Derg regime disregarded the need for a formal constitution, and as a result, for the next thirteen years, Ethiopia was governed by the Provisional Military Administrative Council through a series of decrees and laws, relying on its control over the military and security apparatus. However, in 1987, the Derg promulgated the Constitution of the People's Democratic Republic of Ethiopia.[57] The Constitution created a unitary state where power was divided among the legislative, judiciary, and executive arms of the government.[58]

In a notable departure from the 1931 and 1955 Constitutions, the Derg Constitution established the National Shengo, a unicameral parliament, in a one-party system. This effectively moved the center of formal power from an entrenched absolute monarch to a sovereign parliament. The National Shengo was the supreme organ and possessed the power to decide on any national issue.[59] It was entitled to enact laws, establish administrative organs and regions, elect the president and vice president as well as the prime minister of the republic and appoint judges to the Supreme Court.[60] Despite this wide ranging set of powers, the National Shengo nonetheless could hold only one regular session per year, and any extraordinary session was to be held by the decision of the Council of State or the president of the republic.[61] During the intersession period, the Council of State, a standing body of the National Shengo, performed the functions of the Shengo.[62]

In the 1987 Constitution, judicial authority was vested in one Supreme Court—the highest judicial organ,[63] as well as in courts of administrative and autonomous regions and other courts established by law.[64] The Constitution enshrined the principle of judicial independence by prescribing that judges and people's assessors, who were elected among the people, by the National Shengo, shall exercise their judicial function in complete independence, guided by no authority but the law.[65] However, judges could be recalled by the Shengo anytime, and their tenure was limited to the term of the Shengo that elected them.[66]

Furthermore, the 1987 Constitution, like the 1955 Revised Constitution, entrusted executive power to the Council of Ministers as the highest executive and administrative organ of the state.[67] The Council of Ministers was composed of the prime minister, deputy prime ministers and other members, all elected by the National Shengo.[68] The Council was mandated to, inter alia, ensure the implementation of laws and decisions made by the Shengo.[69]

The 1987 Constitution, on the surface, appeared to uphold the principle of separation of powers by providing a clear structure and defined roles for the different branches of government. However, in theory as well as practice, the president of the republic held a position of immense authority as both the head of state and the commander-in-chief of the armed forces.[70] This allowed him, directly and indirectly through the Workers' Party, which controlled the National Shengo, to exert excessive influence over all institutions, including the Council of Ministers and the judiciary. Despite allocating substantial power to the National Shengo, the fact that it convened only once undermined its effectiveness, and the president arrogated to himself most of the powers granted to the Shengo. Consequently, the purported institutional, functional, and personal separations outlined in the Constitution were largely nominal, as the president's overwhelming power overshadowed any genuine separation of powers.

III. Post-Derg Era (1991-Present)

Following the downfall of the Derg in 1991, Ethiopia underwent a transitional period marked by efforts to establish a democratic system. The Ethiopian Peoples' Revolutionary Democratic Front (EPRDF) came to power and introduced a new constitution in 1995, the Constitution of the Federal Democratic Republic of Ethiopia (hereinafter "the FDRE Constitution").[71] During the preceding almost four years, the country was governed under a Transitional Charter, which only recognized transitional rudimentary executive and legislative bodies, with no mention of the judiciary.[72]

The adoption of the FDRE Constitution represented a momentous shift in Ethiopia's politics and governance. Setting it apart from previous constitutions, it introduced a federal system of government that placed significant emphasis on the rights of "nations, nationalities, and peoples" (ethnic groups), more particularly, the right to self-determination.[73] As evident in the preamble, the Constitution appears to take as its overarching goal and priority the crucial task of addressing the long-standing issue of nationality that has plagued the country's political landscape.[74] It is premised on claims of historical grievances and past injustices and unequal relationships among the different ethnic and religious groups, which supposedly needed to be addressed through a framework that promotes equality, inclusivity, and social cohesion.[75]

The FDRE Constitution establishes a parliamentary system of government and a two-tiered federal state structure consisting of federal and regional governments, each with its own executive, legislative, and judicial branches.[76] At the federal level, the executive branch, led by the prime minister, includes the president[77] and Council of Ministers, which is responsible for the day-to-day administration of the government. At regional levels, the state administration, which often is composed of a regional president, vice president(s) and heads of regional bureaus, constitutes the highest organ of executive power.[78]

The legislative framework creates, at the federal level, a bicameral parliament, albeit not a classical one, comprising the House of People's Representatives (HoPR) and the House of Federation (HoF), the latter having limited traditional legislative functions.[79] The HoPR, popularly elected every five years through universal suffrage,[80] is "the highest authority of the Federal Government"[81] and deals with matters falling under the jurisdiction of the federal government, including those related to national infrastructure, nationality, war, and federal statutes.[82] In contrast, members of the HoF are elected by regional state councils or directly by the people of the various regional states.[83] Some of its functions involve the interpretation of the Constitution and issues pertaining to rights, representation, and autonomy for the diverse "Nations, Nationalities, and Peoples."[84] Although it has limited formal legislative functions, its decision-making power in relation to the aforesaid matters and its interpretative power of the Constitution gives it a *sui generis* status as both a quasi-legislative organ and a quasi-judicial body.

At regional levels, states have their own legislative bodies called regional state councils, corresponding to the federal's HoPR. State councils perform legislative functions over matters falling within the competence of the regional state, including enacting laws and appointing and monitoring the executive. Most regional states also maintain a regional body corresponding to the HoF, whose principal function is the interpretation of the regional constitution.

The FDRE Constitution establishes an independent judiciary with the Federal Supreme Court as the supreme judicial authority. It guarantees the personal independence of judges by prohibiting interference in their function and providing them with tenure security.[85] The Constitution also safeguards the institutional independence of the judiciary by prohibiting the establishment of *ad hoc* tribunals that encroach upon the judicial powers of ordinary courts and allowing the judiciary to draw up its own operational budget.[86]

At first glance, the FDRE Constitution may suggest the existence of a national commitment to the principle of separation of powers. However, a more thorough analysis of its provisions, subsidiary laws, rules of procedure, and the intricate interplay between these branches unveils a contrasting reality. It becomes unmistakable that the executive branch occupies a position of pronounced dominance and exerts significant influence, in keeping with the traditional governance practices of the country. In fact, the practice is even worse, so much so that one could argue that genuine separation of powers is far from being achieved, even in its most rudimentary form. The subsequent sections substantiate this observation by examining the interplay among the executive, legislative, and judicial organs. Nevertheless, before proceeding, it is essential to provide some preliminary observations to shed light on the normative, structural, and temporal variables that have influenced the development of the doctrine, thereby setting the necessary context for a comprehensive exploration of the interrelationships among the executive, legislative, and judicial organs.

Normative, Structural and Temporal Variables

The first chapter of the FDRE Constitution is devoted to fundamental constitutional principles, which include popular sovereignty, supremacy of the Constitution, secularism, transparency, and accountability.[87] The Constitution does not specifically enumerate the principle of separation of powers as one of these fundamental tenets nor does it explicitly affirm the separation of the three branches of government. Instead, the Constitution establishes a division of labor among the executive, legislature, and judiciary by assigning distinct roles that align with their respective functions.

However, a detailed examination of the FDRE and regional constitutions along with the various other subsidiary laws, reveals a different picture. The practice is even worse, such that one can certainly say that Ethiopia is far from achieving proper and fully functional separation of powers. The *status quo* is generally characterized by the dominance of the executive, which exerts significant influence on the other two organs, the legislature and judiciary. This could be attributed to various factors, some of which are normative or structural and others contextual or temporal.

The normative or structural factors pertain to the system of government instituted by the FDRE Constitution. As noted earlier, the Constitution establishes a parliamentary form of government. The parliamentary nature of the system disfavors the achievement of genuine separation of powers given that the executive generally originates and draws its source of survival and legitimacy from the legislature.[88] In most cases, the chief executives (the prime minister and his cabinet) also maintain membership in and remain accountable to the legislative organ.[89] This offers the opportunity to play dual or overlapping executive and legislative roles—something that is clearly incongruent with the fundamental tenets of separation of powers.

Turning to the contextual/temporal factors, the level of influence exerted by the executive branch over the other two organs of government, namely the legislature and the party, has exhibited variations over time and in different contexts. From 1991 to 2012, during the tenure of the late Prime Minister Meles Zenawi, for example, the relationship between the executive and the legislature was characterized by a unique dynamic where the legislature not only functioned as an extension of the executive but also that of the ruling party, the EPRDF.[90] The HoPR, serving as the principal legislative organ, was perceived as subservient to the executive branch. It had a strongly dependent relationship, with the legislature relying entirely on the executive's guidance and directives.[91] Strict party discipline and democratic centralism were employed to ensure loyalty and control over the legislature, effectively reinforcing this hierarchical arrangement.[92]

Following the passing of Prime Minister Meles in 2012 and his replacement by a less powerful Hailemariam Desalegn, a shift in dynamics occurred, prompting the EPRDF to initiate reforms within the party. The reforms were forced by a confluence of factors, including leadership crisis, intraparty schisms, and increasing popular discontent and protests against the government. These internal party reforms had a notable impact on the legislature, leading to positive ripple effects. This period of transition provided a small window of opportunity for the legislature to engage in questioning and even openly criticizing the executive—an act that was previously considered taboo and grave misconduct. This was more prominent in some regional councils than the federal parliament, where the legislature started to exhibit greater assertiveness, and autonomy, and became more willing to challenge the executive's decisions and actions. The newfound ability to express dissent and hold the executive accountable marked a significant departure from the past.

After the resignation of Prime Minister Hailemariam Desalegn in 2018, Abiy Ahmed ascended to the premiership. This opened a new chapter of hope for a more discernible implementation of separation of powers. Indeed, some notable changes were introduced in this regard. One visible change was judicial reforms that allowed the courts to exercise independence and make decisions, some of which have been clearly unfavorable to the executive. The legislature, which has members from opposition parties, also continued to play its role of monitoring the executive, with members of the parliament and regional councils openly questioning ministers and heads of regional bureaus. However, as detailed below, such changes have not been incremental and consistent. There still appears to be a relapse to the EPRDF era in some respects while some positive reforms are partially maintained. Therefore, at this point, it suffices to say that the dynamic and evolving relationship among the three organs is generally a reflection of the changing political landscape and political context of the country. In view of this, the next sections explore the multidimensional institutional and operational relationships between the three organs, aiming to elucidate the actual state of separation of powers in the country.

I. Legislative-Executive Relations

Legislative-executive relations in Ethiopia are, normatively speaking, shaped by parliamentary sovereignty. The fusion of power existing between the two defines the interinstitutional, personal, and functional interactions between the two organs. While the Constitution permits the appointment of ministers who are not members of the parliament,[93] it is customary to select individuals who are also members affiliated with the ruling party.[94] This practice creates a dual role for them, as they simultaneously serve as members of the legislature and the executive. As pointed out earlier, the executive derives its authority from and is accountable to the legislature, but, interestingly, the executive also possesses the power to dissolve the legislature, even for what may sometimes be purely political reasons.[95]

The Constitution stipulates that members of parliament (MPs) should be loyal exclusively to the people, the constitution, and their conscience.[96] Nevertheless, the unfortunate reality is quite the opposite, as there is a situation of parliamentary dependency on the executive, with the latter exerting firm control over the parliament through various means.

The first tool that the executive uses is enforcing strict and excessive party discipline, which requires the MPs to unconditionally support government proposals and decisions in the parliament. This has made MPs primarily agents and representatives of the ruling party rather than that of the people who elected them. Most decisions are made at the party level and then often by the cabinet and then presented to the parliament merely for approval, resulting in a tendency to rubber-stamp them. The fact that the parliament is dominated by the ruling party has for the most part created an elective dictatorship. In recent years, the election of some opposition figures into the parliament has led to MPs demonstrating more assertiveness in scrutinizing executive decisions and proposals. However, this assertiveness does not necessarily translate into tangible outcomes during the final approval, given the ruling party's absolute majority and the persisting culture of party loyalty.

The executive's second method of controlling the legislature involves the appointment of speakers of parliament. As per the Constitution, the parliament possesses the authority to elect its speaker and deputy speaker.[97] Yet, in practice, the process of electing speakers is often conducted discreetly at the party level, primarily based on their political loyalty. The chosen candidates are then formally presented to the parliament for adoption, where nominations and voting occur to create the appearance of an election. Interestingly, this "election" usually takes place *on the first day* of the newly elected parliament's session, leaving MPs with limited opportunities to thoroughly assess the qualifications and capabilities of the nominated speakers.[98] As a result, the true power to choose the speakers lies within the ruling party, and MPs' ability to make independent and informed decisions on this critical position is limited.

Once elected, the speakers tend to maintain their party loyalty, and this allegiance plays a significant role in perpetuating the dependency of the parliament on the executive. As a result, the speakers wield considerable influence, and their roles become instrumental in aligning parliamentary proceedings with the interests of the ruling party. This, in turn, grants the executive a position of power and influence within the legislative body. This is more conspicuous when one examines the power of the House speakers. Article 9 of the HoPR's Rules of Procedure confers significant authority upon speakers, granting them the power to, *inter alia*, set agendas, oversee parliamentary discussions, and enforce discipline.[99] In theory, these powers highlight the importance of the speakers in ensuring the efficient and orderly operation of the House. Yet, in reality, rather than being employed to facilitate a productive legislative environment, these powers are harnessed to stifle voices that express critical perspectives. A notable example is speakers' tendency to deny speaking opportunities to MPs known for their government criticism, or more troublingly, to interrupt and silence critical voices in the name of upholding discipline and decorum. Furthermore, it is not uncommon for speakers in both federal and regional parliaments to decline proposed agendas for deliberations put forth by individual MPs, particularly when these agendas are seen as unfavorable to the government.[100] Compounding the situation, the MPs do not have avenues to challenge when the speakers abuse or misuse their power.[101]

The deficiency in accountability extends to the executive branch as well, a concern further exacerbated by its historical lack of substantial responsibility towards the legislature. Despite legal mandates stipulating its accountability to the legislative body and the legislature's authority to enact corrective measures, including through votes of no confidence,[102] a discernible trend of unaccountability persists. This trend seems to be rooted in the perception that the executive's duty is confined to reporting, while the legislature's function is merely to approve whatever is presented before it. It also finds manifestation in the actions of ministers, and most notably, former Prime Minister Meles Zenawi and current Prime Minister Abiy Ahmed. Repeatedly, these leaders have challenged the oversight and supervisory role of the legislative branch, implying that their function is limited to presenting reports rather than holding the executive accountable for its actions.[103] Clearly, the parliamentary nature of the government, coupled with the historical one-strong-man/one-party political culture of the country, amplifies the issue. Furthermore, the absence of an impartial judicial arbiter to resolve conflicts between the legislative and executive branches has blurred the lines of power division, making it challenging to ensure the proper balance of authority between the two. It implies that the mechanisms intended to maintain checks and balances are not functioning optimally, eroding the foundation of a transparent and accountable government. This not only hampers the legislature's ability to effectively fulfill its supervisory role but also leads to diminished public trust in the system as a whole.

II. Legislative-Judiciary

When examining the dynamics between the executive and legislative branches of government, it becomes evident that the relationship between the legislative and judicial branches at the federal level is relatively more balanced. Nonetheless, there are three critical issues that warrant consideration when discussing the separation of powers between these branches.

First and foremost, the legislative branch plays a significant role in the appointment and removal of judges. The Constitution bestows upon the HoPR the authority to appoint judges who have been nominated by the prime minister or remove them upon a recommendation by the Judicial Administration Council.[104] The House also approves the budget for the judiciary drawn up and submitted by the Federal Supreme Court.[105] Regrettably, there are instances where the legislature declines to endorse the proposed budget, leading to a situation where the judiciary is often understaffed and lacks the necessary resources to effectively dispense justice. [106]

The second crucial aspect to consider is that the HoF, which serves as the upper house of the legislative branch, has judicial authority to interpret the Constitution. While this authority is explicitly granted by the Constitution itself,[107] it raises concerns, as it encroaches upon a significant judicial role that traditionally, in comparative contexts, belongs to the judiciary—the interpretation of laws and resolution of disputes.[108] Additionally, there have been instances where the HoF reversed decisions of the Federal Supreme Court, particularly in its cassation division.[109] This practice can be viewed as a potential infringement on the judiciary's domain and undermines the essential element of separation of powers between these two branches of government.

The third critical concern pertains to the glaring absence of a well-defined system for reciprocal oversight between the legislative and judicial branches. While preserving the independence of these institutions is paramount, the current deficiency of effective mutual monitoring mechanisms, especially regarding the judiciary's ability to scrutinize legislative actions, significantly undermines the potential for checks and balances within the legislature. A practical hurdle in addressing this issue is the lack of clearly outlined procedures to hold the legislative body accountable when it oversteps its authority or engages in actions that are clearly unlawful. For instance, when the speakers of the parliament fail to execute their duties or unfairly restrict MPs from participating in deliberations, whether directly or indirectly, or disregard established procedural norms, there is no available avenue for the judiciary to intervene and rectify such situations. This is not a hypothetical scenario; rather, it is a pressing challenge frequently confronted by MPs at both the federal and state levels, where the issue of "speakers' dictatorship" is widely prevalent. [110]

III. Executive-Judiciary Relations

In January 2023, an unprecedented development unfolded in the realm of executive-judiciary relations when both the president and vice president of the Federal Supreme Court unexpectedly tendered their resignations. This surprising turn of events was followed by the parallel resignation of the president and vice president of the Federal High Court. The parliament subsequently appointed new presidents to fill these crucial positions. Notably, there was a conspicuous absence of an official explanation for this wave of resignations, giving rise to a plethora of speculations and questions. These resignations occurred against the backdrop of an increasingly strained relationship between the executive and the judiciary. Tensions had escalated when the prime minister publicly denigrated judges by labeling them as "first-class thieves." Furthermore, law enforcement agencies were also repeatedly disregarding court orders, undermining the authority and independence of the judiciary. Given this context, it is reasonable to infer that the resignations of the presidents might not have been entirely voluntary. The lack of transparency surrounding their unprecedented departures gives some credence to the existence of potential executive pressures or coercion, which may have played a role in their decisions. It is important to note that these events only added a layer of complexity to an already precarious state of executive-judiciary relations. The Constitution provides for an independent judiciary, but the executive still exerts so much influence over the judiciary in many ways, thereby eroding separation of powers.

As previously explained, the appointment of judges is a process carried out by the HoPR or the respective regional state councils, following nominations put forth by the prime minister or presidents of regional states. While the Judicial Administration Council plays a crucial role in screening and vetting potential judges,[111] the ultimate authority to present these nominees to the legislature resides with the executive branch.[112] Importantly, when it comes to the appointment of presidents and vice presidents of the Federal and regional Supreme Courts, the Judicial Administration Council's role is limited. In this specific context, the decision-making process primarily depends on the choices made by the prime minister or the presidents of the regional states. Accordingly, the executive branch has considerable influence over the selection of key leadership positions within the judiciary. [113]

The executive's influence over the judiciary extends to its control over budgetary allocations. Even though following recent reforms the judiciary is now responsible for formulating its budget and submitting it for approval to the legislature (rather than through the executive as it used to be), the executive has significant power in this process. This is primarily due to the executive's membership and dominant position within the legislative body, often leading to the restriction of the budget allocated to the judiciary. In essence, the executive indirectly dictates the approval of both capital and operational budgets for the judiciary, typically resulting in allocations that fall short of the judiciary's actual requirements and demands. In other words, the executive exerts financial pressure and maintains a tight grip on the independence and functioning of the judicial branch.

Another area of concern in the relationship between the executive and judiciary is judges' tenure security. While the Constitution affords judges tenure security, safeguarding them from dismissal or removal from office except in cases of misconduct, retirement, or gross incompetence or inefficiency,[114] the practical implementation of these protections often falls short of the constitutional intent. As mentioned above, the simultaneous and unexpected resignations of the presidents and vice presidents of both the Federal Supreme Court and the Federal High Court raise legitimate concerns. Such apparently coordinated "resignations," especially among high-ranking judicial officials, could indeed suggest the possibility of forced resignations rather than voluntary decisions. Furthermore, in recent years, there have also been reports of arrests and harassment of judges simply for carrying out their duties, making the situation even more deeply concerning.[115] Even when regular processes are followed to dismiss judges, the executive influence, including over the Judicial Administration Council and legislature, makes it a mere formality.

Finally, another troubling trend that has particularly become common in the last few years is the utter disregard of court orders or decisions by the police and other law enforcement agencies. One notable example is the famous opposition figure, Lidetu Ayalew's, case. Lidetu was arrested in July 2020 following the killing of the prominent singer Hachalu Hundessa, allegedly for organizing unrest in the town of Debre Zeit (Bishofto). Despite being granted bail by the courts and subsequently cleared of the initial charges, Lidetu was kept in detention on a separate charge of illegal firearm possession. The fact that multiple levels of Oromia regional courts granted him bail, only to have the police disregard these court orders for his release, was profoundly disconcerting. What makes this situation even more distressing was the pressing health issue Lidetu reportedly faced, requiring him to travel abroad for medical treatment related to a heart condition. This not only highlights the disregard for legal processes but also how lack of respect for the fundamental tenets of separation of powers could pose a serious risk to an individual's well-being. These incidents also erode public trust in the justice system and undermine the rule of law.

Consequences of Inadequate Separation of Powers

The preceding sections have demonstrated that despite the formal division of roles among the three branches of government, a genuine separation of powers still remains elusive in Ethiopia. In keeping with the country's tradition, the executive branch maintains a strong grip on the legislature and directly or indirectly influences the judiciary. This situation has effectively transformed the country into a system where the three branches of government operate like distinct hardware components, all running under the same governing software as a trinity. This prevailing reality is characterized by elements of party autocracy, cabinet and elective dictatorship, and speakers' authoritarianism, all of which stand in contrast to the ideals of parliamentary democracy and popular sovereignty.

As a result, there is a significant erosion of public trust in both the legislature and the judiciary, with many perceiving these branches as mere extensions of the executive and the ruling party. Despite the initial optimism and hope for a democratic transformation when Prime Minister Abiy assumed office in 2018, it now seems that these aspirations are too distant for many due to, among other things, the lack of clear demarcation and balance of power among the executive, judiciary, and legislature.

Indeed, the situation is further compounded by Ethiopia's persistent challenges, characterized by recurrent conflicts and various forms of violence. These issues are often rooted in the perception of inadequate representation and a lack of meaningful engagement with the legislature, difficulties in accessing justice through the judiciary, and a sense that human and democratic rights are not adequately respected by the executive branch. These challenges underscore the interconnectedness of governance issues and the importance of a well-functioning system with a proper separation of powers. When people feel unheard and disenfranchised, it leads to social unrest and conflicts of the kind we see in today's Ethiopia. The lack of trust in government institutions and the absence of clear mechanisms for addressing grievances exacerbate these issues. In such a context, achieving a more robust separation of powers and strengthening democratic institutions becomes even more imperative. A transparent and accountable system that ensures the representation of diverse voices and that provides avenues for addressing grievances can help mitigate conflicts, promote stability, and build a more inclusive and democratic society.

In conclusion, the failure to establish a genuine separation of powers has impacted governance in the country, hindering the realization of democratic ideals and impeding the country's progress towards stability and political maturity.

Moving Forward

Addressing the pressing issue of the inadequate separation of powers in Ethiopia and mitigating its far-reaching impact on governance, peace, and the overall stability of the nation calls for a comprehensive and multifaceted approach. This strategy should encompass a range of measures, from structural transformations through legal and institutional reforms to fostering a fundamental (and inevitably gradual) revolution in the political culture of the country. It is essential to recognize that this undertaking is something that should be considered an integral part of the perpetual project of Ethiopia's nation building.

Furthermore, there is no off-the-shelf solution readily available that we can bring from somewhere and apply. Ethiopia should carve out its own unique path and system of governance to address the distinctive challenges it confronts. To succeed in this endeavor, there must be a willingness and commitment to experiment with various governance models, continually adapting and evolving to establish a system that aligns with the country's unique characteristics and needs. Bearing this in mind, some proposed solutions are advanced hereunder with a view to enhancing the proper realization of separation of powers. These proposals mainly pertain to institutional (systemic) and/or legislative reforms.

I. Semi-Presidential System

As previously highlighted, the parliamentary system of government presents challenges when it comes to upholding the principle of separation of powers. This is particularly evident in countries like Ethiopia, where the political landscape and culture is characterized by a centralized, authoritarian executive, often led by a single individual or political party, along with a multitude of fragmented opposition groups primarily organized along ethnic lines. To deal with this, one potential solution worth considering is the adoption of a premier-presidential system in Ethiopia.[116]

A premier-presidential system combines a popularly elected presidency with a prime minister who leads a cabinet, each having its well-defined substantive functions.[117] Under premier-presidentialism, the prime minister and the cabinet ministers are selected by the president but they are only responsible and answerable to the legislature, even though they may not be MPs. In order to maintain checks and balances, the president's selection for the premiership must have majority support in the legislature, and once they are appointed, the prime minister and the ministers cannot be dismissed by the president from office unless the legislature passes a vote of no confidence.[118] In a divided and politically polarized society, this system may potentially create a dysfunctional and weak executive and paralyze government functions if, especially, the president and the prime minister come from different political parties or have divergent positions on policy issues.[119] However, in the Ethiopian context, this system is worth experimenting with for different reasons.

Firstly, the political landscape is not only polarized, there is also no structural incentive for cooperation across ideological and ethnic lines, partly because of the first-past-the-post electoral system of the country. Importantly, the entrenched political culture in the country has a historical tendency to concentrate power in one individual, political party, or the executive. The division of authority in a premier-presidential system could play a crucial role in addressing these issues. It not only promotes a balanced distribution of power among the three branches of government but also within the executive branch itself. This structural feature enhances chances for safeguards against the emergence of strongman rule, dominant political parties, or an overly powerful executive. The dual executive structure ensures that the president and the prime minister can act as checks on each other's powers, reducing the risk of authoritarianism or excessive concentration of authority, which has often had an overbearing effect on the judiciary and the legislature.

Secondly, in the current parliamentary system, neither the president nor the prime minister is directly elected by the people to assume his/her premier and presidency, respectively.[120] For this reason, their positions cannot claim direct popular legitimacy. However, a semi-presidential system with a president directly elected by a popular vote can provide a unifying figure for the nation, while the prime minister can represent the majority party in the legislature, allowing for broader representation in government.

In addition, given Ethiopia's diverse ethnic makeup, a semi-presidential system can facilitate trans-ethnic power-sharing arrangements among different ethnic and regional groups, promoting a more inclusive and equitable political landscape. A semi-presidential system encourages or even forces cooperation and coalition building, as the prime minister often needs the support of the legislature to govern effectively, and the president should collaborate with the prime minister if he/she wants to have a properly functioning government. This dynamic inherently necessitates inclusivity and cooperation among different ethnic and political factions. With power distributed between the premier and the presidency, the current exorbitant fixation on controlling the premiership is likely to diminish. Instead, both positions become attractive to political elites, potentially fostering a more balanced and cooperative political environment. Furthermore, term limits are more common in semi-presidential systems than parliamentary systems, and the adoption of such a system, alongside term limits, could enable a peaceful and predictable rotation of power (although term limits on a prime minister can technically be adopted even in parliamentary systems).

When contemplating the adoption of a semi-presidential system, it is imperative to recognize that such a transition brings forth a unique set of challenges.[121] This becomes even more significant within the intricate backdrop of Ethiopia's deeply ingrained political culture, characterized by a penchant for competition over collaboration, a zero-sum mentality prevailing over a win-win approach, and a tendency towards intransigence rather than compromise as the predominant *modus operandi.* Hence, it becomes necessary to introduce complementary legislative and institutional reforms alongside the implementation of the semi-presidential system to effectively address the potential challenges it might introduce. In this context, it is worth emphasizing two proposals that have consistently surfaced in Ethiopia's constitutional-reform discussions. These proposals have the potential to serve as crucial pillars in shaping a more balanced and inclusive governance structure for the country.

Firstly, the establishment of a constitutional court emerges as a crucial step. Such a court would specialize in interpreting the provisions of the constitution, which is particularly relevant within a semi-presidential system.[122] It can effectively handle and resolve potential disputes that may arise between the offices of the prime minister and the president, as well as issues involving the legislature. This court would serve as a vital mechanism to maintain the delicate balance of power inherent in a semi-presidential system.

Secondly, revisiting the existing first-past-the-post voting system and replacing it with a proportional representation electoral system is another proposal that merits serious consideration.[123] This transition not only empowers opposition parties but also ensures that the government reflects the diverse ethnic and political composition of the country. Moreover, it will play a supplementary role to foster a climate of cooperation among different political groups within both the legislature and the executive branch, promoting inclusivity and consensus building.[124]

II. A system of checks and balance between the legislative and the judiciary

An absolute and rigid institutional, functional, and personal separation of powers among and within the legislative, judiciary, and executive branches of government is both undesirable and impractical. Instead, a system of reciprocal checks and balances should be in place to deconcentrate power and prevent any one branch from monopolizing authority. In this vein, one serious challenge pointed out earlier is the absence of a system of mutual supervision between the legislature and judiciary in Ethiopia. Unless there is a case involving misconduct by an MP or judge leading to a criminal investigation or an instance of inefficiency, there exists limited interinstitutional monitoring between the legislative and judicial branches. This could be attributed to the legislature's status as the highest political authority, enjoying parliamentary privileges and immunities and representing the ultimate sovereign power of the nation, nationalities, and peoples of the country.[125] Similarly, the judiciary possesses its own privileges, such as independence and protection from interference or influence by any governmental entity, official, or external source. [126]

However, to achieve a proper separation of powers in Ethiopia, there should be a system that enables mutual reciprocal supervision between these two branches, extending beyond the existing framework. This becomes particularly crucial as the legislature is frequently hindered by partisan and "authoritarian" speakers, undermining the concept of popular sovereignty. In countries such as South Africa and India,[127] courts have engaged in judicial review of speakers' decisions, and a similar system of interlocking checks and balances could be established in Ethiopia through constitutional amendments to ensure a more pronounced separation of powers.

In addition to constitutional amendments, it is essential to undertake a comprehensive revision of the rules of procedure of the legislature at both the federal and state levels. Currently, the executive branch exerts its influence over the legislature through the speakers, using these procedural rules, which, at times, conflict with the letters and spirit of the Constitution and parliamentary democracy. While these rules were originally designed to govern procedural matters, they have been misused to curtail the substantive powers and functions of MPs. It is therefore important to carefully revise these rules to promote transparent and competitive elections of speakers, establish clear guidelines for agenda-setting, define session timelines, and regulate how deliberations are conducted.

Furthermore, the existing mechanism of vote of no confidence must be strengthened and further institutionalized, particularly in regional state councils, through clearer guidelines.[128] The rules of procedure must also provide for detailed reporting and accountability procedures of both the speakers and the executive. In the current practice, it is typically the executive that determines, through the speakers, when and how to report to the legislature, often forcing the legislature to adjust its timelines and accommodate the executive's convenience—as if it is the legislature which is answerable and accountable to the executive.

Conclusions

Ethiopia's journey toward a strong separation of powers has been a complex and evolving one. Despite historical aspirations for decentralized political authority, the nation has wrestled with a dominant executive branch that held concentrated power, a trend that dates back to the era of kings and queens. This trend has persisted to date. As a result, the country continues to grapple with the dominance of the executive branch, which wields substantial influence over both the legislative and judicial branches. The dominance of hegemonic parties has also undermined the role of the legislature as a platform for policy deliberation, with most decisions taken within party circles and the legislature largely stamping such decisions, giving the few opposition members and the broader public little space to understand and express opinions before the formal adoption of decisions.

The absence of a genuine separation of powers has hindered democratization efforts, nurturing a culture of repression. In practical terms, the legislature and judiciary are frequently seen as being aligned with or extensions of the ruling party or the executive, rather than serving as authentic representatives of the people and impartial arbiters of justice, respectively. The prevailing executive dominance can be attributed, in part, to the parliamentary nature of the system, which permits individuals to hold dual roles within the executive and the legislature.

Additionally, the historical governance patterns and the deeply entrenched political culture in the country, characterized by a history of power consolidation through coercive means, have substantially contributed to the development of executive dominance that traditionally exercised not only executive but also legislative and judicial functions. This situation raises an important question: What is the most suitable constitutional design for a country like Ethiopia, where a culture of strong executive influence over the judiciary and legislature persists? While there is no definitive answer, this paper proposes that Ethiopia should seriously contemplate experimenting with a premier-presidential system accompanied by a comprehensive set of legislative and institutional reforms. These reforms should encompass full institutionalization of votes of no confidence in the legislature, changing the electoral system, and the creation of a constitutional court. It is also crucial to strengthen existing democratic institutions such as the Ethiopian Human Rights Commission, National Election Board, and Ethics and Anti-Corruption Commission, enhance public awareness and engagement, and promote greater transparency and accountability. It will also require a sustained effort to build trust and cooperation among the various branches of government and civil society.

Finally, it is important to underscore that although a semi-presidential system could be a viable option for Ethiopia, its effectiveness would ultimately depend on the specific details of the constitution, evolution of the political culture, socioeconomic realities, and the commitment of political actors to democratic principles. As with any constitutional design, the legislative and institutional reforms should be undertaken through a transparent and inclusive process that takes into account the unique needs and aspirations of the Ethiopian people.

Notes

1 Oxford Analytica, "Abiy Seeks to Centralise Power in Ethiopia," *Expert Briefings* (2023), https://doi.org/10.1108/OXAN-DB278697, accessed November 24, 2023.

2 Sisay Sahlu, "PM's Comment on Judges Offends Association," *The Reporter*, June 18, 2022, https://www.thereporterethiopia.com/24384/, accessed November 25, 2023.

3 Iain Stewart, "Men of Class: Aristotle, Montesquieu and Dicey on 'Separation of Powers' and 'The Rule of Law,'" *Macquarie Law Journal* 4 (2004): 187–223. Eli Salzberger and Stefan Voigt, "Separation of Powers: New Perspectives and Empirical Findings—Introduction," *Constitutional Political Economy* 20 (2009): 197–201. Malcolm Schofield, *Cicero: Political Philosophy* (Oxford University Press, 2021), 29. John A. Fairlie, "The Separation of Powers," *Michigan Law Review* 21, no. 4 (1923): 394.

4 Baron de Montesquieu, *The Spirit of Laws*, trans. Thomas Nugent, 2 vols. (The Colonial Press, 1899).

5 Montesquieu, *The Spirit of Laws*, 151–16; see also J. Finnis, "Separation of Powers in the Australian Constitution: Some Preliminary Considerations," *Adelaide Law Review* 3 (1967): 159.

6 Barendt makes a distinction between "pure" and "partial" theories of separation of power. The pure version of separation of power requires a rigid delineation of power among the three branches, predicated on the premise that such division of power restrains the power of the state. On the other hand, the "partial" version posits that each branch is given some supervisory role on the other, and, accordingly, their functions are deliberately made to overlap to ensure checks and balances. This would allow some "interference by one branch into the functions and tasks of the other." For this reason, Marshall wondered whether the system of checks and balances is "part of, or a departure from, separation of powers theory." Eric Barendt, "Separation of Powers and Constitutional Government," *Public Law* (1995): 599–619; C. Munro, *Studies in Constitutional Law* (Oxford University Press, 2005), 307; Geoffrey Marshall, *Constitutional Theory* (Oxford: Clarendon

Press, 1971), 103; M. J. C. Vile, *Constitutionalism and the Separation of Powers* (Oxford University Press, 1967), 13.

7 Accordingly, in the US, the three branches of government can interact with each other and share power in some cases. For example, the president can veto laws passed by Congress, and the Supreme Court can strike down laws that it finds to be unconstitutional. Eoin Carolan, *The New Separation of Powers: A Theory of the Modern State* (Oxford University Press, 2009), 32.

8 Aileen Kavanagh, "The Constitutional Separation of Powers," in *Philosophical Foundations of Constitutional Law*, ed. David Dyzenhaus and Malcolm Thorburn (Oxford University Press, 2016), 223.

9 The prevention of autocracy and the protection of liberty were the primary considerations in Montesquieu's proposal of separation of power. In 1748, Montesquieu stated that "when the legislative and executive powers are united in the same person, or in the same body of magistrates, there can be no liberty ... there is no liberty if the power of judging is not separated from the legislative and executive ... there would be an end to everything, if the same man or the same body ... were to exercise those three powers." (See Charles de Secondat, Baron de Montesquieu, *The Spirit of Laws*, trans. Anne Cohler, Basia Miller, and Harold Stone (Cambridge University Press, 1989), 345.)). Barendt also subscribes to this view that the principal role of separation of power is the protection of freedom. See Barendt, "Separation of Powers and Constitutional Government," 599.

10 Barber asserts that the core of the doctrine is not liberty but efficiency, that is, separation of powers allows "matching of tasks to those bodies best suited to execute them".N. Barber, "Prelude to the Separation of Powers," *The Cambridge Law Journal* 60, no. 1 (2001): 59-88, 59. A. Kavanagh, "Separation of Powers," 229-33.

11 According to Vile, the division of power acts as a restraint on the power of the state and serves as a bulwark against autocracy. M. Vile, *Constitutionalism and the Separation of Powers*, (2nd ed. Indianapolis 1998), 14.

12 For a more detailed analysis of the debate, see Kavanagh, "The Constitutional Separation of Powers," 223–33.

13 W. Bagehot, *The English Constitution* (Watts & Co, 1964), cited in N. W. Barber, *The Principles of Constitutionalism* (Oxford University Press, 2018), 67.

14 Bagehot, *The English Constitution*, 68.

15 Assefa Fisseha, "Constitutional Adjudication in Ethiopia: Exploring the Experience of the House of Federation (Hof)," *Mizan Law Review* 1, no. 1 (2007): 12.

16 After World War I, the League of Nations was established, comprising "civilized nations." In 1923, Ethiopia became the first and only African country to be admitted to the League, a move met with controversy, as it did not fit the Eurocentric idea of civilization. Nevertheless, Ethiopia's unique history as an ancient Christian kingdom that had defeated a European colonial power in the previous century played a role in its successful bid for League membership. However, Western nations continued to pressure Ethiopia to modernize its governance and establish a rule-of-law-based political system. This pressure ultimately led to the emperor's introduction of the country's first written constitution in 1933, marking a significant

turning point in Ethiopia's history. See Antoinette Iadarola, "Ethiopia's Admission into the League of Nations: An Assessment of Motives," *The International Journal of African Historical Studies* 8, no. 4 (1975): 601–22.Megan Donaldson, "The League of Nations, Ethiopia and the Making of States," University of Cambridge Faculty of Law Research Paper No. 2/2019 (2019), available at SSRN: https://ssrn.com/abstract=3285894.

17 *Ethiopian Constitution of 1931*, established in the reign of His Majesty Haile Sellassie I, given at Addis Ababa, on the 9 Hamlie in the Year of Grace 1923 (16th July 1931) ("1931 Constitution").

18 According to Aberra Jembere, "This legal instrument marked the first step towards the use of formal law and legal science to develop the Ethiopian governmental structure and functions." Aberra Jembere, "Law and Judiciary," in *Encyclopaedia Aethiopica*, vol. 3, ed. Siegbert Uhlig (Wiesbaden: Harrassowitz, 2007), 507..

19 See Article 5, 1931 the Constitution.

20 Article 6, the 1931 Constitution

21 Awraris Kassaye, "Law making process from Menelik to Provisional Military Administrative council" (1987) (LLB Senior Essay, Faculty of Law, A.A.U.), pp. 22-27.

22 Articles 30 and 34, the 1931 Constitution.

23 Article 31, the 1931 Constitution.

24 Article 32, the 1931 Constitution.

25 This is with the exception of a decree that the emperor would promulgate "in case of necessity, in order to maintain order and avert public dangers" when parliament was not sitting (see Article 9). Article 10 also empowered the emperor to issue orders, ensure the execution of laws, maintain public order, ensure the execution of laws, maintain public order, and develop the prosperity of the nation.

26 Article 34, 1931 Constitution.

27 See Article 45, with respect to members of the Chamber of Deputies.

28 Article 36, the 1931 Constitution.

29 Article 35, the 1931 Constitution.

30 Article 35, the 1931 Constitution.

31 Article 50, the 1931 Constitution.

32 See also Article 51, the 1931 Constitution.

33 Article 54, the 1931 Constitution.

34 Article 49, the 1931 Constitution.

35 H. Scholler, "Ethiopian Constitutional Development," *Jahrbuch des öffentlichen Rechts der Gegenwart* 25 (1976): 499–585

36 Scholler, "Ethiopian Constitutional Development," 505.

37 On 2 December 1950, the United Nations decided that "Eritrea shall constitute an autonomous unit federated with Ethiopia" (see Ethiopia/Eritrea: UN General Assembly Resolution 390 A (V) of 2 December 1950). It is said that Eritrea at the time had a more modern political system, including a parliament whose members were directly elected by the people. In order to correct the mismatch between his archaic imperial rule with the more advanced system that had existed in Eritrea, the emperor initiated the revision of the 1931 Constitution. See Bahru Zewde,

A History of Modern Ethiopia, 1855–1974 (Addis Ababa University Press, 1995), 206–207.

38 *Proclamation Promulgating the Revised Constitution of Ethiopia*, Negarit Gazeta, Proc. No. 149 of 1955 ("the Revised Constitution of 1955").

39 The inclusion of human rights provisions in the Revised Constitution was evidently prompted by the Universal Declaration of Human Rights, which was a landmark international document adopted by the United Nations. It was a demonstration by the emperor, who was among the few leaders whose power survived the tumults of the previous decade, that Ethiopia remain part of the post-World-War-II global community committed to the principles of human rights. In fact, it is claimed that the Ethiopian Revised Constitution of 1955 was mainly based on the Constitution of the United States of America. Zuzanna Augustyniak, "The Genesis of the Contemporary Ethiopian Legal System" (2012), Department of African Languages and Cultures, University of Warsaw, *Studies of the Department of African Languages and Cultures*, 112.

40 Zewde, *A History of Modern Ethiopia*, 206.

41 Article 16, the Revised Constitution of 1955.

42 Articles 62, and 64, the Revised Constitution of 1955.

43 Article 27, the Revised Constitution of 1955.

44 Article 34, the Revised Constitution of 1955

45 Article 33, the Revised Constitution of 1955.

46 Articles 84-85, the Revised Constitution of 1955.

47 Articles 64, 93-95, the Revised Constitution of 1955. However, the emperor retained the power to appoint members of the Senate, including the president and vice presidents. See Articles 101 and 107.

48 Article 72, the Revised Constitution of 1955.

49 Articles 72-73, the Revised Constitution of 1955.

50 Article 108, the Revised Constitution of 1955.

51 Article 110, the Revised Constitution of 1955.

52 See also Article 3, Courts Proclamation No 195 of 1962 ('Proc No 195/1962'). The emperor, presiding over his *Zufan Chilot*, could review and even reverse the decision of the courts without any legal restrictions using his divine source of justice. (See William E. Howard, *Public Administration in Ethiopia: A Study in Retrospect and Prospect* (JB Wolters, 1955), 166). Sedler explains that "the *Chilot* represents the exercise of the sovereign's prerogative to do justice and has as its source the residuum of justice that it is submitted, remains in the sovereign notwithstanding the establishment of courts." Robert Allen Sedler, "The Chilot Jurisdiction of the Emperor of Ethiopia: A Legal Analysis in Historical and Comparative Perspective," *Journal of African Law* 8 (1964): 66.

53 Abera Jembere, *Legal History of Ethiopia, 1434-1974: Some Aspects of Substantive and Procedural Laws*, (Rotterdam: Erasmus University Press, 1998): 79. As Hambro rightly observed, "It is a thought dear to most Ethiopians that they can obtain justice from His Imperial Majesty even if the courts have failed them." E. Hambro, "The Rebellion Trials in Ethiopia," *Bulletin of the International Commission of Jurists* 12 (1961): 29–30.

54 Article 111, the Revised Constitution of 1955.

55 See Simeneh Kiros Assefa, "Conspicuous Absence of Independent Judiciary and 'Apolitical' Courts in Modern Ethiopia," *Mizan Law Review* 15, no. 2 (2021): 393–94.

56 *Zewde, A History of Modern Ethiopia, 209*; see also Andargachew Tiruneh, *The Ethiopian Revolution 1974–1987: A Transformation from an Aristocratic to a Totalitarian Autocracy* (Cambridge University Press, 1993), 38–39.

57 *Proclamation No.* 1 of 1987, Negarit Gazetta, vol. 47, No. 1 (12 September 1987).

58 Articles 2 and 59, *Proclamation No. 1 of 1987.*

59 Articles 29, 63, *Proclamation No. 1 of 1987.*

60 Articles 29,63, *Proclamation No. 1 of 1987.*

61 Article 67, *Proclamation No. 1 of 1987.*

62 The Council of State is established by the National Shengo, having its own president and vice president. See Article 63 (3) (a) and Article 81 (1) and (2), *Proclamation No. 1 of 1987.*

63 Article 103, *Proclamation No. 1 of 1987.*

64 Article 100, *Proclamation No. 1 of 1987.*

65 Articles 103 and 104, *Proclamation No. 1 of 1987.*

66 Article 101, *Proclamation No. 1 of 1987.*

67 Article 89, *Proclamation No. 1 of 1987.*

68 Article 89, *Proclamation No. 1 of 1987.*

69 Article 92, *Proclamation No. 1 of 1987.*

70 Articles 85-87, *Proclamation No. 1 of 1987.*

71 *The Constitution of the Federal Democratic Republic of Ethiopia*, Federal Negarit Gazeta, Proc. No. 1/1995, No. 1.

72 It established only the Council of Ministers and Council of Representatives. Articles 6–9, *the Transitional Period Charter of Ethiopia*, Negarit Gazeta, 50th Year, No. 1, 22 July 1991.

73 Preambular para. 5, FDRE Constitution.

74 Preambular para. 2. This also encompasses the right to secession. See article 39 (1) FDRE Constitution.

75 Articles 45 and 50, FDRE Constitution.

76 Article 73, FDRE Constitution.

77 Note that the Constitution establishes the Office of the President separately from the executive proper, which includes the Office of the Prime Minister and the Council of Ministers in which "the highest executive powers [are] vested." Despite this, the president's roles, however ceremonial they could be, are of an executive nature. See Chapters Seven and Eight of the FDRE Constitution.

78 Article 50 (6), FDRE Constitution.

79 Article 53, FDRE Constitution.

80 Article 54 (1), FDRE Constitution.

81 Articles 50 (3) and 54 (1), FDRE Constitution.

82 Articles 55, 58 (3), FDRE Constitution.

83 Article 61 (3), FDRE Constitution. In practice, members of the House of Federation are often members of the state council of the region they come from.

84 Article 60, FDRE Constitution.

85 Judges cannot be removed until retirement except on grounds of gross incompetence, illness, and approval by the HoP or Regional Council. See Article 79 (4), FDRE Constitution.

86 Article 78 (4) and Article 79 (6) (7), FDRE Constitution.

87 Articles 8–12, FDRE Constitution (1995).

88 See *supra* notes 11–12.

89 See Thomas O. Sargentich, "The Presidential and Parliamentary Models of National Government," *American University International Law Review* 8, no. 2/3 (1993): 579–92.

90 The absence of diversity of political parties in the parliament also contributed to the dominance of the executive and conflation of legislative-executive-party relations. In the May 2010 National Election, of the 547 seats, the EPRDF won 499 seats, and its allies, namely the Somali People's Democratic Party (SPDP), the Benishangul Gumuz People's Democratic Party (BGPDP), the Afar National Democratic Party (ANDP), the Gambela People's Unity Democratic Movement (GPUDM), the Harari National League, and the Argoba People's Democratic Organization (ADPO) won 46 seats. The opposition, the Ethiopian Federal Democratic Unity Forum (EFDUF)/Medrek won 1 seat, and an independent candidate won 1 seat.

91 Kassahun Berhanu, "Parliament and Dominant Party System," in *African Parliaments: Between Governance and Government*, ed. Mahmood Salih (London: Palgrave Macmillan, 2005), 162–82.

92 Assefa Fiseha, "Legislative–Executive Relations in the Ethiopian Parliamentary System: Towards Institutional and Legal Reform," in *Law and Constitution in Africa: Constitution-Building in Africa*, ed. Jaap de Visser, Nico Steytler, Derek Powell, and Ebenezer Durojaye (Nomos Verlagsgesellschaft, Baden-Baden, 2015), 248.

93 Article 74 (2) of the FDRE Constitution provides that the prime minister may submit for approval to the HoPR "nominees for ministerial posts from among members of the two Houses or from among *persons who are not members of either House and possess the required qualifications*" (emphasis added).

94 Following the 2021 national election, a noteworthy development occurred when the ruling party appointed MPs from the opposition to hold positions as minister of education and minister of science and technology, and a few others as deputy ministers. Such a move is uncommon in the country's political landscape.

95 Article 60 of the Constitution allows the prime minister to cause the dissolution of the House before the expiry of its term in order to hold new elections. Note that this does not compromise parliamentary sovereignty, as the prime minister can only do this with the consent of the parliament.

96 Article 54 (4), FDRE Constitution. A similar provision is also found in the constitutions of regional states. See for example, 48 (2) of the Revised Amhara National Regional Constitution approval proclamation No. 59/2001 (2001), Article 48 (3) of the Revised Oromia National Regional Constitution, Proclamation 46/2001 (2001).

97 See article 55 (19), FDRE Constitution.

98 See Article 8 (2), the Rules of Procedures of the House of Peoples' Representatives, Regulation No. 6// 2016

99 See also Article 30, Rules of Procedure of HoPR.

100 Article 32 (5) clearly provides that priority is *always* given to agendas proposed by the government over those proposed by individual MPs.

101 In principle, the House could remove the speakers at any time when it finds them incompetent or unable to discharge their responsibilities. However, in practice, this is nearly impossible, as the speakers themselves are the ones who set the agenda, and they would likely view any motions to remove them as disciplinary misconduct. More importantly, speakers enjoy strong support from the ruling party and the executive. When MPs do express concerns about their performance, they often employ party channels as shields to protect themselves.

102 See Articles 97 and 98 of the Rules of Procedure of the HoPR

103 In the famous Tamrat Layne case, for example, when Prime Minister Meles Zenawi announced his government's decision to dismiss the deputy prime minister at the time, Tamrat Layne, he seemed to suggest that his report to parliament was a mere formality, implying that he possessed the authority to remove ministers whom he had personally nominated (see Fiseha, "Legislative–Executive Relations," 245). Likewise, the present prime minister, Abiy Ahmed, has consistently argued that the parliament lacks the authority to investigate the funding sources of his "Chaka Project," contending that he is not utilizing a budget approved by the HoPR.

104 Article 80 (1) and (2), Article 79 (4) (c) FDRE Constitution.

105 For regional state courts, their budget is determined by the respective state councils. See Article 79 (6) and 95) of the FDRE Constitution.

106 For instance, in 2022, the Amhara Regional State Council rejected the president of the Amhara Regional State Supreme Court's proposal to allocate an annual budget equivalent to 5 percent of the region's overall annual budget to the courts. Despite the president's reference to established practices and critical budget shortfalls within the judiciary, the council refused to adopt the proposal.

107 Article 62 (1), and Article 83, FDRE Constitution.

108 Article 79 (1), FDRE Constitution.

109 As an example, the House of Federation (HoF) reversed the Supreme Court's verdict in the case of W/ro Sara v. W/ro Shewaye, File No. 20938 (2007), which pertained to divorce by disuse. Regardless of the merit of the HoF's decision, the fact that the House chose to revisit a matter that had already been definitively resolved by the Supreme Court raises significant concerns regarding the conclusiveness of judicial decisions. These concerns are further exacerbated when one observes the escalating number of cases that are "appealed" to the House of Federation after they have already been adjudicated by the Supreme Court in its cassation division (see Hirko Alemu, "The Binding Interpretation of the Federal Supreme Court Cassation Division: A Critical Analysis of its Novelty and Vulnerability," *Oromia Law Journal* 11, no. 1 (2022): 50).

110 Of course, MPs may initiate a vote of no confidence to remove the speakers, but that is a means within the legislature and is unlikely to result in success in view of the fact that speakers are highly supported by party and executive apparatuses.

111 See Article 81, FDRE Constitution.

112 It is worth noting that in some regional states, the ruling party maintains membership in the Judicial Administration Council. For example, in the Amhara region, the head of the branch office of the Prosperity Party, who was killed in 2023, was a member of the regional council, the executive, and the Judicial Administration Council.

113 A similar procedure is followed in the United States when it comes to the appointment of federal court judges, including Supreme Court justices. In this process, the president is responsible for nominating all judicial candidates. However, it's common for potential nominees to be recommended by senators or members of the House who belong to the president's political party. Following the nominations, the Senate Judiciary Committee conducts confirmation hearings for each nominee. In contrast, in Ethiopia, the procedure for appointing judges differs significantly. Once the judges are nominated by the prime minister, the legislative body has relatively little influence, and the customary practice is for members to raise their hands and approve the nominations without the extensive confirmation hearings that are common in the United States.

114 See Article 79 (4) of the FDRE Constitution.

115 "Outcry over Arrest of Three Oromia Supreme Court Judges after Allowing Bail to Jawar Mohammed's Security Detail," *Addis Standard*, November 5, 2022, https://addisstandard.com/news-outcry-over-arrest-of-three-oromia-supreme-court-judges-after-allowing-bail-to-jawar-mohammeds-security-detail/ accessed August 20, 2023.

116 This proposal was also put forward by Walle, who, after a thorough examination of the advantages and disadvantages of various governance models, arrived at the conclusion that a semi-presidential system is the more viable option for Ethiopia. (See Walle Engedayehu, "The Search for a Functioning Democracy in Ethiopia," *International Journal of Ethiopian Studies* 11, no. 1 & 2, Special Issue (2017): 139–68).Note that the country has experimented with imperial, presidential, and parliamentary systems of government, but none of them has delivered lasting solutions to the country's chronic political problems. Certainly, this cannot be solely attributed to the nature of the system, but it is also important to remain open to exploring different viable options, including the semi-presidential system.

117 According to Maurice Duverger, "A political regime is considered as semi-presidential if the constitution which established it combines three elements: (1) the president of the republic is elected by universal suffrage; (2) he possesses quite considerable powers; (3) he has opposite him, however, a prime minister and ministers who possess executive and governmental power and can stay in office only if the parliament does not show its opposition to them." Maurice Duverger, "A New Political System Model: Semi-Presidential Government," *European Journal of Political Research* 8 (1980): reprinted in *Parliamentary versus Presidential Government*, ed. Arend Lijphart (Oxford: Oxford University Press, 1992), 142.

118 Sujit Choudhry, Thomas Sedelius, and Julia Kyrychenko, *Semi-presidentialism and Inclusive Governance in Ukraine: Reflections for Constitutional Reform* (International IDEA,

2018); see also *Report on Semi-Presidentialism as Power-Sharing: Constitutional Reform after Arab Spring* (Center for Constitutional Transitions, International IDEA, 2016).

119 Roper argues that under cohabitation, a semi-presidential system may cause instability. Steven D. Roper, "Are All Semi-Presidential Regimes the Same? A Comparison of Premier-Presidential Regimes," *Comparative Politics* 34, no. 3 (2002): 253–72.

120 The prime minister secures a parliamentary seat through direct constituency elections, but his ascent to the position of prime minister hinges on garnering the backing of the parliamentary majority. As a result, the legitimacy of the premier role is not directly conferred by a popular vote.

121 Some authors argue that semi-presidential systems are more susceptible to democratic backsliding or decay compared to parliamentary systems (Connor McAfee, "Semi-Presidentialism: A Pathway to Democratic Backslide," *Penn State Journal of Law & International Affairs* 11 (2023): 184). However, it is crucial to acknowledge that every system of governance, whether parliamentary, presidential, or semi-presidential, comes with its own set of advantages and disadvantages. Assessing the merits and drawbacks of each system should be contextualized within the political culture of the country, and it should be accompanied by supplementary safeguards aimed at mitigating or rectifying the downsides inherent to the chosen system.

122 The composition of the constitutional court may not exclusively be lawyers. In order to allow legal and political considerations and flexibility, the constitutional court, as in other countries such as Benin, may be composed of lawyers and non-lawyers on the basis of well-defined and predetermined criteria. See Article 115, the Constitution of Republic of Benin (1990).

123 Getachew Assefa, Electoral System and Political Pluralism in Ethiopia: A Case for Reform, Ethiopian Constitutional Law Series (2015), 6–33, Adem Kassie Abebe, "The Winner Shall Not Take It All: Proposals for Electoral Reform to Ensure Inclusive Political Representation in Ethiopia," Constitutionnet, September 29, 2015, https://constitutionnet.org/news/winner-shall-not-take-it-all-proposals-electoral-reform-ensure-inclusive-political accessed October 26, 2023.

124 Needless to say, these initiatives will require a constitutional amendment, which itself requires creating consensus among the different political, ethnic, social, and religious groups of the country.

125 See Articles 8 (3) and 50 (3), FDRE Constitution.

126 See Articles 78 (1) and 79 (2), FDRE Constitution.

127 *United Democratic Movement v Speaker of the National Assembly*, Constitutional Court of South Africa, 2017 5 SA 300; see also Gurdeep Sappal, "How the Courts Played a Part in the Visible Curtailing of Speakers' Autonomy," *The Wire*, July 2022, https://thewire.in/law/speaker-supreme-court-maharashtra accessed August 20, 2023.

128 Many of the rules of procedure governing regional state councils do not envisage even the possibility in which MPs can initiate a motion of no confidence against either the executive or the speakers.

Bibliography

Books and Articles

Augustyniak, Zuzanna. "The Genesis of the Contemporary Ethiopian Legal System." Department of African Languages and Cultures University of Warsaw Studies of the Department of African Languages and Cultures, 2012.

Barendt, Eric. "Separation of Powers and Constitutional Government." Public Law (1995).

Barber, N. "Prelude to the Separation of Powers." The Cambridge Law Journal 60, no. 1 (2001).

Carolan, E. The New Separation of Powers: A Theory of the Modern State. Oxford University Press, 2009.

Choudhry, Sujit, Thomas Sedelius, and Julia Kyrychenko. Semi-Presidentialism and Inclusive Governance in Ukraine: Reflections for Constitutional Reform. International IDEA, 2018.

Donaldson, Megan. "The League of Nations, Ethiopia and the Making of States." University of Cambridge Faculty of Law Research Paper No. 2/2019. Available at SSRN: https://ssrn.com/abstract=3285894.

Duverger, Maurice. "A New Political System Model: Semi-Presidential Government." European Journal of Political Research 8 (1980). Reprinted in Parliamentary versus Presidential Government, edited by Arend Lijphart, Oxford University Press, 1992.

Engedayehu, Walle. "The Search for a Functioning Democracy in Ethiopia." International Journal of Ethiopian Studies 11, no. 1 & 2 (2017).

Fairlie, John A. "The Separation of Powers." Michigan Law Review 21, no. 4 (1923).

Fisseha, Assefa. "Constitutional Adjudication in Ethiopia: Exploring the Experience of the House of Federation (Hof)." Mizan Law Review 1, no. 1 (2007).

Fisseha, Assefa. "Legislative–Executive Relations in the Ethiopian Parliamentary System: Towards Institutional and Legal Reform." In Law and Constitution in Africa: Constitution-Building in Africa, edited by Jaap de Visser, Nico Steytler, Derek Powell, and Ebenezer Durojaye. Nomos Verlagsgesellschaft, Baden-Baden, 2015.

Howard, William E. Public Administration in Ethiopia: A Study in Retrospect and Prospect. JB Wolters, 1955.

Iadarola, Antoinette. "Ethiopia's Admission into the League of Nations: An Assessment of Motives." The International Journal of African Historical Studies 8, no. 4 (1975).

Jembere, Aberra. "Law and Judiciary." In Encyclopaedia Aethiopica, vol. 3, edited by Siegbert Uhlig. Wiesbaden: Harrassowitz, 2007.

Jembere, Aberra. Legal History of Ethiopia, 1434–1974: Some Aspects of Substantive and Procedural Laws. Rotterdam: Erasmus University Press, 1998.

Kavanagh, Aileen. "The Constitutional Separation of Powers." In Philosophical Foundations of Constitutional Law, edited by David Dyzenhaus and Malcolm Thorburn. Oxford University Press, 2016.

Kiros Assefa, Simeneh. "Conspicuous Absence of Independent Judiciary and 'Apolitical' Courts in Modern Ethiopia." Mizan Law Review 15, no. 2 (2021).

Marshall, Geoffrey. Constitutional Theory. Oxford: Clarendon Press, 1971.

McAfee, Connor. "Semi-Presidentialism: A Pathway to Democratic Backslide." Penn State Journal of Law & International Affairs 11 (2023).

Montesquieu, Charles de Secondat, Baron de. The Spirit of Laws. Translated by Thomas Nugent. 2 vols. The Colonial Press, 1899.

Montesquieu, Charles de Secondat, Baron de. The Spirit of Laws. Translated and edited by Anne Cohler, Basia Miller, and Harold Stone. New York: Cambridge University Press, 1989.

Munro, C. Studies in Constitutional Law. Oxford University Press, 2005.

Roper, Steven D. "Are All Semi-Presidential Regimes the Same? A Comparison of Premier-Presidential Regimes." Comparative Politics 34, no. 3 (2002).

Salzberger, Eli, and Stefan Voigt. "Separation of Powers: New Perspectives and Empirical Findings—Introduction." Constitutional Political Economy 20 (2009).

Sahlu, Sisay. "PM's Comment on Judges Offends Association." The Reporter, June 18, 2022. https://www.thereporterethiopia.com/24384/. Accessed November 25, 2023.

Schofield, Malcolm. Cicero: Political Philosophy. Oxford University Press, 2021.

Sedler, Robert Allen. "The Chilot Jurisdiction of the Emperor of Ethiopia: A Legal Analysis in Historical and Comparative Perspective." Journal of African Law 8, no. 1 (1964).

Sargentich, Thomas O. "The Presidential and Parliamentary Models of National Government." American University International Law Review 8, no. 2/3 (1993).

Scholler, H. "Ethiopian Constitutional Development." In Jahrbuch des öffentlichen Rechts der Gegenwart, vol. 25, 1976.

Stewart, Iain. "Men of Class: Aristotle, Montesquieu and Dicey on 'Separation of Powers' and 'The Rule of Law'." Macquarie Law Journal 4 (2004).

Tiruneh, Andargachew. The Ethiopian Revolution 1974–1987: A Transformation from an Aristocratic to a Totalitarian Autocracy. Cambridge University Press, 1993.

Vile, M. J. C. Constitutionalism and the Separation of Powers. 2nd ed. Indianapolis: Liberty Fund, 1998.

Walle Engedayehu. "The Search for a Functioning Democracy in Ethiopia." International Journal of Ethiopian Studies 11, no. 1 & 2 (2017).

Zewde, Bahru. A History of Modern Ethiopia, 1855–1974. Addis Ababa University Press, 1995.

Online Resources

Addis Standard. "Outcry over Arrest of Three Oromia Supreme Court Judges after Allowing Bail to Jawar Mohammed's Security Detail." November 5, 2022. https://addisstandard.com/news-outcry-over-arrest-of-three-oromia-supreme-court-judges-after-allowing-bail-to-jawar-mohammeds-security-detail/. Accessed August 20, 2023.

Oxford Analytica. "Abiy Seeks to Centralise Power in Ethiopia." 2023. Expert Briefings. https://doi.org/10.1108/OXAN-DB278697. Accessed November 24, 2023.

The Reporter. "PM's Comment on Judges Offends Association." June 18, 2022. https://www.thereporterethiopia.com/24384/. Accessed November 25, 2023.

Chapter 12

Brief Notes on the Unusual Model of Constitutional Review in Ethiopia

Yonatan T. Fessha

The Model

Under the Constitution, the courts are excluded from constitutional adjudication.[1] The power to adjudicate constitutional disputes is given to the House of Federation (House), the second chamber of the Ethiopian parliament.[2] This includes the power to interpret the Constitution, including determining the constitutionality of federal and state laws. The House is also entrusted with the power to decide on issues relating to the rights of ethnic communities to self-determination, including the right to secession[3] and the right of ethnic communities to establish their own state. An ethnic group "who believes that its self-identities are denied, its rights of self-administration are infringed, promotion of its culture, language and history are not respected, in general its rights enshrined in the Constitution are not respected or, violated for any reason"[4] can present its application to the House. The House has also the responsibility of seeking solutions to misunderstandings that may arise among states, including state border disputes, and has the duty to regulate federal interventions.[5]

In discharging its constitutional duty of adjudication, the House is assisted by the Council of Constitutional Inquiry (Council).[6] Headed by the chief justice of the Federal Supreme Court (FSC), its list of members includes the vice president of the FSC, six legal experts appointed by the president of the republic on recommendation by the lower house of the federal parliament, the House of Peoples' Representatives, and three other persons designated by the House from among its members.[7] Membership to the Council, thus, includes both legal experts and politicians. The Council is an advisory body whose main function is to examine constitutional issues and submit its findings to the House, where issues of constitutional interpretation arise. In relation to cases pending before courts, a constitutional matter is first referred to the Council by a court or an " interested party." The term "interested party" is taken to mean any person or body (i.e., an interested group, a human rights NGO, an association, a federal or regional agency) directly affected by the impugned legislation.[8]

Upon receiving the matter, the Council should deliberate upon it and submit its recommendations to the House if it believes that the matter raises an issue of constitutional interpretation. If the Council, on the other hand, believes that there is no need for constitutional interpretation, it may remand the case to the concerned court. In such a case, the petitioner for interpretation or the applicant can appeal to the House.[9] In this regard, the findings of the Council are mere recommendations. The House is at liberty to adopt or reject the recommendations. The Council is thus an institution with an advisory capacity. The House, on the other hand, is the body that is entrusted with the function of providing the ultimate and final decision both on constitutional interpretation and more specifically on the constitutionality of legislation. Indeed, on some important occasions, the House has either reversed the recommendations of the Council or confirmed the recommendations of the Council based on a different ground.[10]

Why is this an unusual model of constitutional review?

The choice of the constitutional review system was not a historical accident. It was instead a subject of serious contestations and therefore a deliberate outcome of the preferences, logic, and ideological orientation of the dominant political and intellectual forces at the time of the making of the Constitution.

Excluding the judiciary: The counter-majoritarian dilemma

According to the drafters of the Constitution, the judiciary is not the appropriate forum for constitutional interpretation.[11] They argued that unelected and virtually unaccountable judges should not be allowed to strike down statutes that are the "fruits of the majoritarian branches." The courts should not have the power to interpret a constitution made by the people. "How can a constitution that has been ratified by the people's assembly be allowed to be changed by professionals who have not been elected by the people," argued the secretary of the Constitutional Commission.[12]

It is not, however, clear whether the Constitution has successfully avoided the counter-majoritarian problem. This mainly has to do with the structure and composition of the House. The House, as mentioned earlier, is composed of representatives of ethnic groups. According to the Constitution, each ethnic group is represented by one additional representative for each one million of its population.[13] Members of the House are elected either directly or indirectly. The decision is left to the state councils.[14] Thus, a state council may decide to organize an election to have its members of the House elected directly by the people of the state, or the state council itself may elect the representatives. Adherence by all state councils to the first option, that is direct election by the people themselves, makes the House, in fact, a majoritarian body, directly elected by and accountable to the people. This would allow the Constitution to successfully avoid the counter-majoritarian problem. In practice, however, the first option has never been used.[15] No state council has ever held elections to have the members of the House directly elected by the state electorate. Rather, state councils themselves have elected representatives to the House. This indicates that the Ethiopian approach to constitutional review has not escaped from the same criticism to which judicial review has often been subjected. Its attempt to take the Constitution away from an "unelected and unaccountable body" is not successfully accomplished, as the Constitution has again found itself in the hands of a federal body composed of individuals who are not directly elected but rather appointed by the state councils.

One may argue that the state councils are themselves elected by the people, and their actions in this circumstance should be regarded as reflecting the wishes of the people who have elected them. Insofar as members of the House are not elected but appointed by the state councils, they are almost in the same position as judges of the Ethiopian courts. Presently all judges are appointed by the House of People's Representatives from a pool of nominees forwarded by the prime minister.[16] The prime minister, in turn, receives the names of candidates from the Federal Judicial Administration Council.[17] State Court judges are also appointed through a similar process. It is thus clear that judges survive the "majoritarian process of appointment and confirmation." Just like judges, members of the House are not elected and, thus, are not accountable to the people. The fact that they are appointed by the state councils does not make them any different from judges, as the latter are also appointed by the federal or state parliaments. This indicates that insofar as the members of the House are appointed by the state councils, the Ethiopian approach to constitutional review cannot escape the same criticisms that judicial review provokes.

Empowering the House: The Constitution as a political contract

The fact that the drafters of the Constitution regarded it as a "political contract" rather than a mere legal document also suggests that the interpretation of the Constitution was considered by them to be a political, rather than a judicial, function.[18] More directly, for the drafters of the Constitution, the document was a pact between ethnic groups, and the power of interpreting it should therefore belong to the body that is composed of their representatives. They, therefore, vested the power to interpret the Constitution in the House, which is a political body composed of ethnic representatives (the proclaimed authors of the Constitution).

A question, however, remains as to why they chose to entrust this task to the House while the House of People's Representatives is also composed of individuals directly elected by the people. This can be found, according to Andreas Eshete, in the Constitution, which vests all sovereign power in the Nations, Nationalities and Peoples of Ethiopia.[19] He makes reference to Articles 8 and 61 of the Constitution. Article 8 reads:

> *1. All sovereign power resides in the Nations, Nationalities and Peoples of Ethiopia.*
>
> *2. This constitution is an expression of their sovereignty.*

Thus, by linking Article 8 to Article 61, which states that the House is composed of representatives of the Nations, Nationalities and Peoples, he contends that the latter is the most legitimate body to interpret the Constitution as it, by implication, is the body in whom all sovereign powers reside, and the Constitution is but an expression of their sovereignty. Thus, according to Andreas Eshete, the drafters of the Constitution, by entrusting the task of interpreting the Constitution to the House, have given the Constitution back to the people, with whom all sovereign power resides.

A closer look at the organization of the House and the fact that it is assisted by a body that is composed of individuals representing different interests suggest that the Ethiopian approach may find its justification in a constitutional theory that considers a constitution not only as a legal document but also as a political pact. In contrast to the mainstream view that considers a constitution, regardless of its origin and the manner of its adoption, principally as higher law,[20] there are constitutional theorists who characterize a constitution as an instrument different in kind from ordinary law. For them, the "constitution, in addition to serving as a legal document, is also vital politically in the sense that it engineers the whole political order."[21] As a result, they regard the interpretation and enforcement of the constitution as an extraordinary political act.

Based on this understanding of a constitution, it is often suggested that issues involving constitutional interpretation should be investigated under a different sociopolitical context than the often legalistic environment under which ordinary law cases are examined. This means, among other things, that the organ that is entrusted to interpret a constitution should not merely be a collection of legal professionals. It must also have individuals who have substantial experience in the political arena. Some of the members must thus have a background in law, others in politics. The members must also be selected by a much more open and transparent political process than is the case with ordinary judges.[22]

The House is obviously a political body. Furthermore, the Council, which assists the House in interpreting the Constitution, is composed of individuals with both a legal and political background. In fact, three of the members of the Council are active members of the House representing their respective ethnic groups. As indicated earlier, the Council is composed of the president and vice president of the FSC, six legal experts appointed by the House of People's Representatives, and three other members designated from the House. The legal professionals are expected to provide the House with the necessary legal expertise, while the representatives from the political branch ensure that the findings of the Council do not "inject too many norms into the lawmaking process, supplanting legislative considerations of other arguably more important matters."[23] This, one may argue, makes the House a legitimate institution to interpret the Constitution and review legislation for constitutionality.

Is the Ethiopian Model of Constitutional Review Competent, Impartial, and Suitable?

The fact that the adopted system is consistent with some plausible principle of constitutional theory is of questionable value unless the system also embodies the necessary institutional structure and competence to carry out the task. The institution must also be well suited to discharge the function of interpreting the constitution and more specifically constitutional review. In other words, one also needs to consider if the House, as an institution for constitutional interpretation, is suited to discharge this responsibility and how well it has performed in that role thus far. This is about institutional competence and/or effectiveness to ensure the observance of constitutional norms. It is also about the impartiality of the House.

It is submitted that this unusual model of constitutional review leaves the country without a competent, impartial, and suitable umpire that can police constitutional compliance and, broadly, constitutionalism. To begin with, the House is composed of more than 120 members.[24] That, on its own, makes the House an inappropriate body to deal with constitutional disputes. Matters of constitutional disputes are better dealt with in a committee-format gathering. A large body such as the House is not the appropriate forum to reach a decision on the complex task of constitutional interpretation. Furthermore, the House, as an institution that is composed of representatives of ethnic communities, is a house that is composed of politicians. As a result, it does not have the necessary expertise to engage with the kind of analysis that constitutional adjudication requires. Constitutional disputes raise complex questions of law. As the profile of most members of the House reveals, most of them are either members of the executive branch of a state government or state council. The majority of them, however, do not have the necessary expertise (legal or otherwise) to engage in a detailed discussion of constitutionality. The problem is not only that there are not enough lawyers but also that those who are lawyers do not have the capacity to engage in detailed constitutional analysis. They hardly have the time to keep themselves up to date on recent legal developments. This is not, of course, unique to Ethiopian legislatures. Legislatures "are seldom competent to deconstruct the content and complications of complex constitutional rules."[25] According to Bickel, "Courts have certain capacities for dealing with matters of principle that legislatures and executives do not possess."[26]

The fact that the House is composed of members that are appointed by the state parliaments obviously begs the question of impartiality. If a complaint was submitted to the House against the actions or laws of the state government on grounds of unconstitutionality, members of the House, representing the state government whose actions or laws are challenged, would obviously have a direct stake in the outcome. Such an individual can hardly function as an independent member in discharging his or her function. This becomes a serious problem when one considers the fact that state councils often send their presidents to represent or lead the representation of their delegates. There is also no rule in the Constitution or the law that regulates the House, requiring members to recuse themselves from the adjudication of constitutional disputes. It suffices to point out that currently the House is exclusively composed of members of the ruling party. This makes it easy to see the House not as an impartial adjudicator on important intergovernmental disputes but as a House that is "inherently inclined to registering the preferences of the winning group."

Impact on the development of constitutional jurisprudence

Very few cases have made it to the House, as many petitions were dismissed by the Council based on procedural or technical grounds. [27] As noted by Adem Abebe, "Strategic constitutional rights litigation has been ignored by the Ethiopian CSOs."[28] Almost all of those that have made it to the House were referred by federal courts that had declined to adjudicate matters, owing to a lack of jurisdiction to deal with disputes requiring interpretation of the Constitution. The cases range from the application of Sharia law to the relevance of the language requirement to standing for election and the constitutionality of the emergency power declared by the prime minister in the aftermath of the highly contested 2005 election. A mere two dozen cases were submitted to the House; only a few of them received decisions, with most decided in favor of the government.

The dearth of cases decided on by the House has meant there is little or no meaningful interaction over questions about the meaning of the Constitution. There is no jurisprudence, for example, indicating how conflicts between federal and state laws can be resolved.[29] Of course, there have not been many major intergovernmental disputes that needed the attention of the House of Federation, as the federation operated under a dominant party state and such disputes are managed at the party level. But the absence of complex interaction over questions regarding the meaning of the provisions of the Constitution is not limited to its federal aspects. The same applies to the fundamental rights recognized by the Constitution. The scope of each of the rights guaranteed by the Constitution is still far from clear. There is no jurisprudence indicating what the right includes, who may exercise it, and in what manner. There are no indications as to the extent to which the government can limit the rights guaranteed by the Constitution. There are also no indications that help us determine whether any limitations imposed by the government are legitimate. These are all issues that could have been clarified by a body suited to discharge the task of constitutional interpretation. The lack or absence of such an institution has denied the country the opportunity to have institution(s) that explain constitutional values.

What is most concerning is that the nearly comprehensive Bill of Rights, which forms a big chunk of the Constitution, has rarely been applied by the courts or the House.[30] Considering the fact that the content of rights develops over time through an ongoing interpretation of their meaning in the context of concrete cases, the utter lack of interpretive and applicative precedent is and should be of serious concern. Such precedent has often proven to be a critical starting point to build a human rights jurisprudence that will help in the effective legitimation of the human rights standards. Unfortunately, however, very few court decisions could be identified that directly or indirectly apply or refer to human rights provisions incorporated in the Constitution. The same is also true with the House, which has decided very few cases in the last three decades.

The Constitution, unfortunately, has had little or no effect on cases litigated before the courts. The Constitution, as a result, has remained to be that "thin" document whose provisions contain principles stated in very general terms. The fact that the normative content of the rights recognized in the Constitution are less developed is a reflection of their exclusion from adjudication procedures. In other words, the absence of institutions that are suited to engage in complex interactions on the meaning of the provisions of the Constitution have made it impossible to develop a constitutional jurisprudence. Although almost three decades have passed since the Constitution came into force, Ethiopia has still to come up with a body of constitutional jurisprudence.

Concluding Remarks

The Ethiopian approach to constitutional review is problematic. The decision to totally exclude courts from the business of constitutional interpretation fails to consider the multitude of cases that are brought before courts that require the interpretation of the Constitution. The crafters of the Constitution failed to appreciate the fact that constitutions do not only deal with lofty ideals and principles but with mundane matters as well. As it currently stands, any matter that requires the final and authoritative interpretation of the Constitution has to be referred to the House through the Council. Not only does this pose a problem to the effective functioning of the courts, but it also unnecessarily elongates the process for claimants who require an immediate redress to their problem.

The responsibility of giving shape and texture to the Ethiopian Constitution is unusually left to the second chamber of the federal parliament. As an institution that is empowered to interpret the Constitution and, more importantly, resolve constitutional disputes, including, for example, intergovernmental disputes, the House is in a position to have a significant impact on the operation of the federation. It has the capacity to nudge the federation toward the centralizing or decentralizing end of the federal continuum. Yet it has not managed to have any meaningful effect. This is partly attributable to the dearth of cases that have come before it. In particular, not many cases involving federalism issues have been brought before the House, either by individuals or governmental actors.

The political developments that are currently unfolding in the country, including intergovernmental disputes, have, more than ever, brought to light the importance of a suitable, competent, and impartial umpire that can adjudicate constitutional disputes. It is clear that the unique model of Ethiopian constitutional review cannot play the important role of serving as the guardian of the constitution. This leads one to an unavoidable conclusion, namely that the present constitutional review system in Ethiopia should not be retained. The House should be deprived of the power to interpret the Constitution, including the power to annul legislation for unconstitutionality. What should, then, replace this unusual model of constitutional review?

Perhaps the standard response would be to resort to either the diffused system of constitutional review where all courts have the power to review the constitution or take the route of a concentrated system of constitutional review where the Supreme Court or a specialized court retains the power of constitutional review. Zemelak calls for the establishment of a specialized constitutional court.[31] But the task of constitutional review can also be discharged by an institution like the Council. The reformed Council can be the permanent organ that deals with constitutional disputes, not an advisory body that meets on a part-time basis. Under this proposal, the Council shall have the final and ultimate power on the interpretation of the Constitution, including the power of determining the constitutionality of legislation. As indicated earlier, the Council is composed of representatives from the two Houses, the judiciary, and other legal professionals. The composition of the Council, which more or less reflects the representation of different interests, makes it a good candidate for the task. The presence of elected representatives in the Council mitigates to a certain extent the potential contention that the Council is antidemocratic. The presence of legal professionals, on the other hand, provides the Council with the necessary legal expertise required to adequately enforce constitutional norms. Further, the composition of the Council must also reflect the diversity of the country in terms of ethnicity, gender, and religion.

As indicated earlier, denying courts any role in the interpretation of the Constitution is not advisable. The multitude of daily mundane cases that, however small, require the interpretation of the Constitution suggests that the courts must have some sort of adjudicating power on constitutional questions. Courts must, in other words, be given the power to interpret the provisions of the Constitution, though the power to determine the constitutionality of laws should be retained by the Council. The courts should refer matters that require a ruling on the constitutionality of any legislation to the Council.

Notes

1 Yonatan Tesfaye Fessha, "Whose power is it anyway? The courts and constitutional interpretation in Ethiopia," *Journal of Ethiopian Law,* (22, no. 1(2008): 12-144.

2 See Ethiopian Constitution, Articles 62(1) and 83(1).

3 See Ethiopian Constitution, Article 62(3).

4 Article 19(1) of Proclamation No.251/2001, Consolidation of the House of Federation and the Definition of its Powers and Responsibilities Proclamation, *Federal Negarit Gazeta*, 7th Year No. 41, Addis Ababa, 6 July 2001

5 See Ethiopian Constitution, Article 62(2) of the Constitution. The basic principle is that all state border disputes shall be settled by agreement of the concerned states. In the event where the disputing states fail to reach an agreement, the decision rests with the House which has to take into account 'the basis of settlement patterns and the wishes of the people concerned' in making the decision (See Ethiopian Constitution, Article 48).

6 See Ethiopian Constitution, Article 84(2), see also Art 3-5 of Proclamation 798/2013, A Proclamation To Re-enact For The Strengthening And Specifying The Powers and Duties of The Council of Constitutional Inquiry of the Federal Democratic Republic of Ethiopia, *Federal Negarit Gazetta*, 19th Year No. 65, August 2013

7 See Ethiopian Constitution, Article 82(2)

8 For further discussion see Abebe Mulatu, "Who is the Interested Party to initiate a challenge to the constitutionality of laws in Ethiopia," *The Law Student Bulletin*, no.1(1999): 9-12.

9 See Ethiopian Constitution, Article 84(3)

10 The House of the Federation of Federal Democratic Republic of Ethiopia, *Journal of Constitutional Decisions, 1, no. 1(2000)* :1-101.

11 Newsletter of the Constitution Commission No.3., See Minutes of the 94th Regular Session of the Council of Representatives of the Transitional Government of Ethiopia (unpublished) 213–17; See also Minutes of the Constitutional Assembly (unpublished), 5:4–19, 1994).

12 Newsletter of the Constitution Commission No.3., See Minutes of the 94th Regular Session of the Council of Representatives of the Transitional Government of Ethiopia (unpublished) 213–17; See also Minutes of the Constitutional Assembly (unpublished), 5:4–19, 1994).

13 See Ethiopian Constitution, Article 61

14 See Ethiopian Constitution, Art 61(3)

15 Yonatan Tesfaye Fessha, "Judicial Review and Democracy: A Normative Discourse on the (Novel) Ethiopian Approach to Constitutional Review," *African Journal of International and Comparative Law,* 14. no.53(2006): 72.

16 See Ethiopian Constitution, Article 81

17 The Federal Judicial Administration Council is responsible for the nomination of federal judges. It also determines matters of code of professional conduct and discipline as well as transfer of judges of any federal court. It is composed of

members of the Judiciary and the House of Peoples Representatives. See Ethiopian Constitution, Articles 78 and 81 of the Constitution.

18 Newsletter of the Constitution Commission No.3; See also Zemelak Ayele, "Ethiopia's 'unusual constitutional umpire: Revisiting the role of the House of Federation," (50 *Shades of Federalism*, 2020) Available at http://50shadesoffederalism.com/case-studies/ethiopias-unusual-constitutional-umpire-revisiting-the-role-of-the-house-of-federation/.

19 Comments by Andreas Eshete on the Draft Constitution (22 Nov 1994) p.5

20 Marbury v Madison 5 U.S 137 (1803); See also Sylvia Snowiss, Judicial Review and the Law of the Constitution (Yale University Press. 1990) 1

21 Walter F. Murphy, James E. Fleming, and Sotirios A. Barber. 1995. *American Constitutional Interpretation.* (The Foundation Press,1995)

22 Walter F Murphy, James E. Fleming, and Sotirios A. Barber, *American Constitutional Interpretation.*

23 Mark Tushnet, "Policy distortions and democratic debilitation: Comparative illumination of counter-majoritarian difficulty" *Michigan Law Review,* 94(1995): () 2-4.

24 Fessha, Yonatan Tesfaye. "Judicial Review and Democracy, 74.

25 Keith Whittington, "Legislative Sanctions and the Strategic Environment of Judicial Review". *International Journal of Constitutional Law* 3 (2003): 446- 452.

26 Alexander Bickel, *The Least Dangerous Branch: The Supreme Court at the Bar of Politics* (Yale University Press, 1986) 25

27 Yonatan Tesfaye Fessha. "A Federation Without Federal Credentials: The Story of Federalism in a Dominant Party State: in *Decentralization and constitutionalism in Africa,* eds. Steytler, Nicco and Fombad, Charles (Oxford University Press, 2019)

28 Adem Abebe Kassie, The potential role of constitutional review in the realisation of human rights in Ethiopia, http://hdl.handle.net/2263/23887. Accessed on January 10 2024, 205

29 Yonatan Tesfaye Fessha and Zemelak Ayele, "Giving shape and texture to a federal system? Ethiopia's courts and its unusual umpire" in *Federalism and courts in Africa: Design and impact in comparative perspective,* Yonatan Tesfaye and Karl Kossler eds. (Routledge 2020), 47 -67.; See also Gedion T Hessebon. and Abduletif K Idris, "The Supreme Court of Ethiopia: Federalism's Bystander," in *Courts in Federal Countries: Federalists or Unitarists?,* Aroney Nicolas and Kincaid eds., (University of Toronto Press, 2017) 185-186.

30 One important exception is the decision of the Cassation Division of the Federal Supreme Court that involved the interpretation and application of the provision of the Constitution that recognizes the best interest of the child (Tsedale Demissie v. Ato Kifle Demissie, Federal Supreme Court Cassation Division Cassation file no. 23632, 5 October 2007).

31 Ayele, Zemelak,'Ethiopia's 'unusual constitutional umpire

Bibliography

Abebe, Adem Kassie. "The potential role of constitutional review in the realisation of human rights in Ethiopia." http://hdl.handle.net/2263/23887. Accessed on January 10, 2024.

Ayele, Zemelak. "Ethiopia's 'unusual constitutional umpire: Revisiting the role of the House of Federation." 50 *Shades of Federalism*, 2020. Available at http://50shadesoffederalism.com/case-studies/ethiopias-unusual-constitutional-umpire-revisiting-the-role-of-the-house-of-federation/.

Bickel Alexander. *The Least Dangerous Branch: The Supreme Court at the Bar of Politics*. Yale University Press, 1986.

Fessha, Yonatan Tesfaye. "Whose power is it anyway? The courts and constitutional interpretation in Ethiopia." *Journal of Ethiopian Law*, 22, no. 1 (2008):12-144.

Fessha, Yonatan Tesfaye. "Judicial Review and Democracy: A Normative Discourse on the (Novel) Ethiopian Approach to Constitutional Review." *African Journal of International and Comparative Law*, 14, Issue 1 (2006):53-82.

Fessha, Yonatan Tesfaye. "A Federation Without Federal Credentials: The Story of Federalism in a Dominant Party State." In *Decentralization and constitutionalism in Africa*, edited by Steytler, Nicco and Fombad, Charles. Oxford University Press, 2019.

Fessha, Yonatan Tesfaye and Zemelak Ayele. "Giving shape and texture to a federal system? Ethiopia's courts and its unusual umpire." In *Federalism and courts in Africa: Design and impact in comparative perspective*, edited by Fessha Yonatan and Kossler Karl, 47 -67. Routledge, 2020.

Hessebon, Gedion T. and Abduletif K Idris. "The Supreme Court of Ethiopia: Federalism's Bystander," in *Courts in Federal Countries: Federalists or Unitarists?*, edited by Aroney Nicolas and Kincaid, 185-186. University of Toronto Press, 2017.

Mulatu, Abebe. "Who is the Interested Party to initiate a challenge to the constitutionality of laws in Ethiopia." *The Law Student Bulletin*, no.1(1999).

Murphy, Walter F, James E Fleming, and Sotirios A. Barber. *American Constitutional Interpretation.* The Foundation Press, 1995.

Snowiss, Sylvia. *Judicial Review and the Law of the Constitution*. Yale University Press, 1990.

Tushnet, Mark. "Policy distortions and democratic debilitation: Comparative illumination of counter-majoritarian difficulty." *Michigan Law Review*, 94(1995):

Whittington, Keith. "Legislative Sanctions and the Strategic Environment of Judicial Review." *International Journal of Constitutional Law* 3 (2003): 446-452.

_____ The House of the Federation of Federal Democratic Republic of Ethiopia. *Journal of Constitutional Decisions, 1, no. 1*(2000).

_____ Newsletter of the Constitution Commission No.3., Minutes of the 94th Regular Session of the Council of Representatives of the Transitional Government of Ethiopia (unpublished) 213–17.

_____ Minutes of the Constitutional Assembly (unpublished), 5:4–19, 1994).

Laws

Proclamation No. 1/1995, Proclamation of the Constitution of the Federal Democratic Republic of Ethiopia, Federal Negarit Gazeta, 1st Year No.1, Addis Ababa-21st August 1995, adopted on 8th of December 1994 and came into force 21st August 1995.

Proclamation No.251/2001, Consolidation of the House of Federation and the Definition of its Powers and Responsibilities Proclamation, *Federal Negarit Gazeta*, 7th Year No. 41, Addis Ababa, 6 July 2001.

Proclamation 798/2013, A Proclamation To Re-enact For The Strengthening And Specifying The Powers and Duties of The Council of Constitutional Inquiry of the Federal Democratic Republic of Ethiopia, *Federal Negarit Gazetta*, 19th Year No. 65, August 2013.

Cases

Marbury v Madison 5 U.S 137 (1803).

Tsedale Demissie v. Ato Kifle Demissie, Federal Supreme Court Cassation Division Cassation file no. 23632, 5 October 2007.

Chapter 13

Local Government in Ethiopia's Constitutional and Federal Matrix

Zemelak Ayitenew Ayele

Introduction

The World Bank's 1999/2000 World Development Report indicates that decentralization of powers, functions, and resources to local government would be one of the major global political trends of the twenty-first century.[1] Decentralization to local government is taking place or at least being discussed across "developed countries, developing countries, transitional countries, federal countries, and unitary countries".[2] This is mainly because there is a growing call for involving the public in decision-making and that local government is considered to be best situated for the purpose. The rising role of local government, especially cities, in the national and global economy also entails the need to elevate their political status.

As part of this trend, there is a growing call for the constitutional recognition of local government as an autonomous order of government. Several regional and global charters have been adopted that require states to accord local governments constitutional status. The 1985 European

Charter on Local Self-Government requires European states, whenever practicable, to recognise "the principle of local self-government" in their national constitutions.[3] The Common Wealth Principles on Good Practice for Local Democracy and Good Governance require the constitutional recognition of local government so that local democracy has institutional security.[4] At the African level, the African Union has adopted a charter that encourages its member states to elevate the political status of local government, though not necessarily through a constitutional method.[5] Local Government Associations (LGAs) have been established at the continental and global levels and are lobbying for the constitutional entrenchment of local government.

In view of these international and continental developments, and ongoing debates on the organization of the Ethiopian state, this brief note interrogates the constitutional status of local government in Ethiopia. How does its constitutional status (or lack thereof) impact the institutional security and democratic pedigree of local government, and therefore their value and effectiveness?

Local government in federations

It is ideal for local governments in federations to have a constitutional status, since a federal system is a political system based on a written constitution. On the flip side, constituent units of federations tend to resist the constitutional entrenchment of local government since they view that as a "zero-sum game" that would mean reduced power and resources for them.[6] In general, there are three approaches that federations adopt regarding the place of local government in their federal and constitutional matrix.[7] The first approach is a complete silence of some federal constitutions on the place and status of local government in their federal design. This is especially the approach that classic federations such as the US, Australia, and Canada have adopted. This is mainly because of how these federations came to be. These federations are what Alfred Stepan calls "coming together federations", where subnational units predate the federation in existence.[8] As former independent states, the subnational units joined these federations with their own state and sub-state structures and institutions, including local government, which remained more or less intact. Local government in these federations is hence an exclusively state matter and is not even mentioned explicitly or otherwise in the federal constitutions.

Some federal constitutions recognise the existence of and give constitutional protection to local government without considering it as a third level of government. Local government is considered to be within the exclusive competencies of the states under this approach. The states are, as a rule, entitled to define the institutional organization, functions, and powers of local government. Their power in this respect is not, however, unrestricted. The federal constitutions require local government to be a democratically constituted government, as opposed to an administrative level, with a certain degree of autonomy. Federations that follow this approach include Argentina, Germany, Switzerland, Pakistan, Nigeria, and India.[9] The Basic Law of Germany, for instance, provides that counties and municipalities have councils in which the people are represented through elections. It further adds "municipalities must be guaranteed" a degree of autonomy "within the limits prescribed by [state] law."[10] The constitutions of federations such as Russia and Malaysia, while making local government within the functional competencies of the states, still provide extensive legislative power to the federal government concerning local government.

There are multilevel federations in which local government is recognized as one of and coequal with federal and state levels of government, including Nepal, Brazil, and South Africa.[11] For instance, Article 18 of the Brazilian constitution states that "the political and administrative organization of the Federative Republic of Brazil comprises the Union, the states, the Federal District and the municipalities, all of them autonomous, as this Constitution provides." Local government is thus mentioned as one of the autonomous levels of government that make up the federal system of the country. Likewise, the South African constitution provides that "in the Republic, government is constituted as national, provincial, and local spheres of government which are distinctive, interdependent and interrelated," making local government, at least in principle, a coequal of provincial and national levels of government.[12]

Local government in the FDRE Constitution

The 1995 Ethiopian Constitution does not appear to follow either of the three approaches mentioned above. It is not completely silent on the issue of local government. Nor does it explicitly recognize local government as an autonomous order of government. It does not also explicitly enjoin the states to establish a democratically constituted autonomous local government. It simply implies the existence of local government. Under Article 39(3) it implies that there would be ethnically organized sub-state level governments which would be established for geographically concentrated ethnic communities that do not have their own state and are found in multi-ethnic states such as the former Southern Nations Nationalities and Peoples Region, Amhara, Benishangul-Gumuz, Tigray, and Gambella states.[13] Article 50(4) authorizes states to establish a sub-state "administrative level" that they "deem necessary" and to devolve "adequate power to it." Article 50(4) is a rather vague provision that could be interpreted to mean that states are at liberty to create a sub-state administrative structure that serves as their own agent instead of a politically autonomous and democratically constituted local government.[14] Indeed, that was precisely the kind of administrative structure the states created in the immediate aftermath of the adoption of the 1995 Constitution. Despite having local councils, local governments could not decide on their budget and plans, which needed the approval of the state governments. This changed only in the 2000s when the federal government launched a plan on district level decentralisation Plan.[15] Nevertheless, even today, states largely run local government as an administrative structure rather than as an autonomous level of government. The Oromia state, for instance, passed a law that centralizes the appointment of mayors in the office of the state president, which is against the notion of an autonomous local government.[16]

Why did the framers of the FDRE Constitution leave local government without explicit recognition as an autonomous and democratic level of government? In fact, the drafters of the Constitution debated the issue of whether local government should be constitutionally entrenched. Some were of the view that it was necessary to explicitly recognize local government as an autonomous order of government that is not simply an agent of the states. Others opposed this for two reasons: first, it was deemed that to recognize local government as autonomous would contradict the right to self-determination of ethnic communities, which is the foundational principle of the constitutional and federal system of the country. Ethnic communities, as part of the exercise of self-determination, should be allowed to decide how to structure sub-state levels of government.[17] Second, there was a fear that the federal government would use local government as a back door to intervene in the states and undermine their autonomy.[18] The fear in this respect almost came true when, after the Tigray state organized in September 2020 what the federal government considered "unconstitutional state elections." The House of Federation, having ordered the federal government to suspend transferring funds to the Tigray state, instructed the federal government to directly interact with woreda, urban, and kebele governments in order to ensure the continued provision of basic public services.[19] The federal government could not have direct interactions with local authorities in Tigray since the local authorities were more loyal to their state authorities than to the federal government. However, the attempt of the federal government to do so shows that the fear of the states was not totally unfounded.[20]

The implications of the ambiguous constitutional status of local government in Ethiopia

The lack of an explicit recognition to local government has several implications:

1. The existence of the local government, as a level of government and each unit of local government, lacks institutional security. The existence of local government, to the extent it does exist, is more a result of a political preference than a commitment to a constitutional principle requiring the establishment of an autonomous order of government. This preference may change, and the existence of local government may come to an end. The various units of local government also lack institutional security. A case in point is the top-down decision to reorganize zonal boundaries in Oromia, disregarding communal preferences and historical factors, which led to violent conflicts in East and West Guji and other zones.[21]
2. The lack of explicit recognition to local government has diminished the political significance of local government. This is clear from the fact that opposition parties have not taken part in local elections since 1995. Granted, participating in local elections is much more difficult than participating in general elections. However, the difficulty was not the only, even the major, factor behind their decision to boycott local elections. Opposition parties do not deem that local government is worth the fight. They boycotted all five local elections that have been held since the adoption of the 1995 constitution.
3. It has been over ten years since the last local elections were held. The sixth local election was indefinitely postponed in 2013. Such indefinite postponement of local elections has not, however, raised eyebrows among the political actors of the country. This can be contrasted with the uproar caused by the postponement, just for one year, of the sixth general elections in 2020.

Conclusion

As the above discussion clearly shows, local government does not have a clear constitutional status under the FDRE Constitution, and that has detrimental effects on local democracy. This needs to change. The democratization of local government is especially important since citizens of the country experience the authoritarian character of the regime in power most directly at the local level.

Local authorities serve as means of control and as gatekeepers for the party in power at the federal level. Indeed, the recognition of local government as the third order of government, as is the case in Brazil and South Africa, is not an option in Ethiopia. This would contradict the foundational principle of the Ethiopian federal system: the right to self-determination of the ethnic communities. Deciding on the organization of sub-state structures is an aspect of the right to self-determination. The ethnic communities would have a reduced right to self-determination if local government is not constitutionally established as the third tier of government. The constitutional entrenchment of local government may also deny the necessary flexibility in terms of designing local government based on the geographic, social, and economic context of each state. Besides, the federal government is likely to be tempted to use local government as a back door to intervene in and undermine the autonomy of the states. Indeed, a constitutionally entrenched local government, which is established based on a logic other than ethnic self-determination, may ameliorate the problems that are associated with the singular focus on ethnic accommodation in determining state boundaries, which Yonatan Fessha (2017) calls "the original sin of the Ethiopian federal system." This is indeed a debate that should be had. At the minimum, the constitution should clearly and explicitly require the states to establish a democratically constituted local government. It should guarantee, in line with the approach adopted by the Nigerian constitution, a system of local government by democratically elected local government councils with clearly defined functional competencies and sources of revenue, including entitlement to financial transfers from senior levels of government.

Notes

1 World Bank, *World Development Report 1999/2000: Entering the 21st Century* (Oxford University Press, 1999), 108.

2 Richard M. Bird & Robert D. Ebel, "Fiscal Federalism and National Unity," in *Handbook of Fiscal Federalism, ed.* Ehtisham Ahmad and Giorgio Brosio (Edward Elgar Publishing, 2006).

3 Congress of Local and Regional Authorities of the Council of Europe, *The European Charter of Local Self-Government Strasbourg*, 15.X, 1985.

4 Commonwealth Local Government Forum *Aberdeen Agenda: Commonwealth Principles on Good Practice for Local Democracy and Good Governance*, 2005.

5 African Union, African Charter on the Values and Principles of Decentralisation, Local Governance and Local Development (2014).

6 Nico Steytler, 'Introduction' in *The Place and Role of Local Government in Federal Systems*, ed. Nico Steytler, (Konard-Adenaur-Stiftung occasional papers) 1-9.

7 Nico Steytler (2009) 'Comparative Conclusion' in *A Global Dialogue on Federalism: Local Government and Metropolitan Regions in Federal Systems, ed.* Nico Steytler (McGill-Queen's University Press, 2009) 393-441

8 AC Stepan, "Federalism and Democracy: Beyond the U.S. Model," *Journal of Democracy* 10, no 4 (1999): 19-34

9 Steytler, "Comparative Conclusion".

10 The Basic Law for Federal Republic of Germany (1945).

11 Steytler, "Comparative Conclusion".

12 The Constitution of the Republic of South Africa (1996), Section 40(1).

13 Federal Democratic Republic Ethiopia Constitution (1995).

14 Zemelak Ayele and Yonatan Fessha, "The Constitutional Status of Local Government in Federal Systems: The Case of Ethiopia", *Africa Today 50, no 4 (2012):* 89-109.

15 Samson Mesfin and Tegegne Teka, "The Practice of Fiscal Decentralization at Local Level in Ethiopia: Evidence from Oromia and Afar Regional States", *Cogent Social Sciences 9, no* 2 (2023): 2.

16 Magalata Oromia: A Proclamation to Amend Proclamation No 65 (2003) The Urban Local Government of Oromia National Regional State Proclamation No. 116 (2006).

17 Ayele and Fessha, "The place"; Assefa Fiseha, *Federalism and the Accommodation of Diversity in Ethiopia: A Comparative Study* (Wolf Legal Publishers, 2007).

18 Ayele and Fessha "The Place".

19 Fana Broadcasting Corporation "Federal Government Severs Relations with Tigray Regional State", 07 October 2020. https://www.fanabc.com/english/federal-govt-severs-relationship-with-tigray-regional-state/.

20 Zemelak Ayele, "Far-sighted Federal Solidarity, not Power Politics and Legalism, Is Needed to Solve Tigray Dispute," *Ethiopia Insight*, October 9, 2020, https://www.ethiopia-insight.com/2020/10/09/far-sighted-federal-solidarity-not-power-politics-and-legalism-is-needed-to-solve-tigray-dispute/.

21 Nagessa Dube, "New Zone in Ethiopia's Oromia Region Triggers More Unrest," Ethiopia Insight September 23, 2023, https://www.ethiopia-insight.com/2023/09/23/new-zone-in-ethiopias-oromia-region-triggers-more-unrest/.

Bibliography

African Union, African Charter on the Values and Principles of Decentralisation, Local Governance and Local Development. https://au.int/sites/default/files/treaties/36387-treaty-0049_african_charter_on_the_values_and_principles_of_decentralisation_local_governance_and_local_development_e.pdf (last accessed on 18 July 2023).

Ayele, Zemelak. "Far-sighted Federal Solidarity, not Power Politics and Legalism, Is Needed to Solve Tigray Dispute." *Ethiopia Insight*, 9 October 2020.

https://www.ethiopia-insight.com/2020/10/09/far-sighted-federal-solidarity-not-power-politics-and-legalism-is-needed-to-solve-tigray-dispute/.

Ayele, Zemelak and Yonatan Fessha. "The Constitutional Status of Local Government in Federal Systems: The Case of Ethiopia." *Africa Today* 50, no 4 (2012): 89–109.

Bird, Richard, and Robert D. Ebel. "Fiscal Federalism and National Unity." In: *Handbook of Fiscal Federalism*, edited by Ehtisham Ahmad and Giorgio Brosiok. Edward Elgar Publishing, 2006.

Commonwealth Local Government Forum *Aberdeen Agenda: Commonwealth Principles on Good Practice for Local Democracy and Good Governance*, 2005" http://www.clgf.org.uk/userfiles/1/file/AberdeenAgendaleaflet8pp.pdf (last accessed on 17 May 2012).

Congress of Local and Regional Authorities of the Council of Europe, *The European Charter of Local Self-Government Strasbourg*, 15.X, 1985. http://conventions.coe.int/Treaty/en/Treaties/html/122.htm.

Dube, Nagessa. "New Zone in Ethiopia's Oromia Region Triggers More Unrest." *Ethiopia Insight*, 23 September 2023. https://www.ethiopia-insight.com/2023/09/23/new-zone-in-ethiopias-oromia-region-triggers-more-unrest/.

Fana Broadcasting Corporation. "Federal Government Severs Relations with Tigray Regional State." 07 October 2020. https://www.fanabc.com/english/federal-govt-severs-relationship-with-tigray-regional-state/.

Fiseha, Assefa. *Federalism and the Accommodation of Diversity in Ethiopia: A Comparative Study*. Wolf Legal Publishers, 2007.

Magalata Oromia: A Proclamation to Amend Proclamation No 65 (2003) The Urban Local Government of Oromia National Regional State Proclamation No. 116 (2006).

Mesfin, Samson and Tegegne Teka, "The Practice of Fiscal Decentralization at Local Level in Ethiopia: Evidence from Oromia and Afar Regional States," *Cogent Social Sciences 9, no* 2 (2023).

Stepan, Alfred. "Federalism and Democracy: Beyond the U.S. Model." *Journal of Democracy* 10, no 4 (1999): 19–34.

Steytler, Nico. "Comparative Conclusion." In: *Local Government and Metropolitan Regions in Federal Systems: A Global Dialogue on Federalism,* edited by Nico Steytler, 393–441. McGill-Queen's University Press, 2009.

Steytler, Nico. "Introduction." In: *The Place and Role of Local Government in Federal Systems,* edited by Nico Steytler, 1–9. Konard-Adenaur-Stiftung, 2005.

World Bank. *World Development Report 1999/2000: Entering the 21st Century.* Oxford University Press, 1999.

Chapter 14

Federal Intervention vis-à-vis State Autonomy: Comparing the Case of Ethiopia with India

Zelalem Shiferaw Woldemichael*

1. Introduction

The entry into force of the Constitution of the Federal Democratic Republic of Ethiopia (FDRE Constitution or the Constitution) marked a turning point in the history of the Ethiopian constitutional system, as it for the first time formally introduced a federal system in the country, ending the historical centralized system of administration. The Constitution establishes two levels of government: the federal government and the states. The states are delimited based on settlement patterns, language, identity, and consent of the people concerned.[1] Based on the said criteria, the Constitution created nine states, namely: the State of Tigray, the State of Afar, the State of Amhara, the State of Oromia, the State of Somalia, the State of Benishangul/Gumuz, the State of the Southern Nations, Nationalities, and Peoples (SNNP), the State of the Gambela Peoples, and the State of the Harari People.[2] With the creation of four new states out of the former SNNP, namely the States of Sidama, South West, South Ethiopia, and

Central Ethiopia Regions, the number of federating units has now reached thirteen.[3] Two administrative regions are accountable to the federal government: Addis Ababa, which is the capital city of the federation, and the Dire Dawa city administration—the latter's status is defined in legislation (not the constitution) due to disputes over its control between Oromia and Somalia regional states.

The federal government and states have constitutional responsibilities to respect and prevent human rights violations and maintain law and order, among others. These may be drawn from Articles 51(1) and 52(2)(a), which require the federal government and states, respectively, to protect and defend the FDRE Constitution, including its human rights provisions.[4] Besides, Article 13(1) enjoins the legislative, executive, and judicial organs of governments to respect and ensure human rights inscribed under Chapter 3 of the Constitution.[5] The levels of government are also responsible for maintaining law and order.[6] The state's obligations on the above matters are limited at the state level.[7] The federal government's obligation, nonetheless, may transcend beyond the administrative regions under its direct responsibility —Addis Ababa and Dire Dawa—and cover a particular state or the entire country in some extraordinary circumstances. These cases are outlined in Articles 51(14), 55(16), 62(9), and 93 of the FDRE Constitution, which authorize the federal government to intervene in states in the event of a deteriorating security situation, human rights violations, acts of states that endanger the constitutional order, and states of emergency, respectively.

The federal government is bound to respect the powers of states[8] and must exercise its powers with strict adherence to and respect for the constitutional provisions. It cannot step into state matters under the guise of upholding law and order or preventing human rights violations that otherwise would lead to an encroachment on state autonomy. Given this, the FDRE Constitution contains mechanisms to constrain the federal government's power of intervention and safeguard state autonomy. This includes the procedures set out in the emergency provisions, which require the state of emergency decree issued by the Council of Ministers to be subject to approval by the House of Peoples' Representatives (parliament) within forty-eight hours if parliament is in session and within fifteen days if it is not in session.[9] The federal government's intervention in case of human rights violations is also based on the joint decision of the two houses of the federal parliament. The federal government has so far invoked the intervention clauses on very limited occasions. The party line has been the most prominent (extra-constitutional) mechanism the federal government has used to settle security matters in states.[10] The constitutional compatibility of the rarely used cases of interventions with the right to autonomy of states is questionable.[11]

This chapter assesses whether the FDRE Constitution has established adequate safeguards for state autonomy during federal intervention in states. This is done by comparing the provisions of the FDRE Constitution that allow the federal government to intervene in states in extraordinary situations with their counterparts in the Indian Constitution. India is chosen as a comparator state considering that the drafters of the FDRE Constitution drew inspiration from the Indian Constitution when crafting the provisions on federal intervention in extraordinary situations.[12] This helps to understand the contexts in which the emergency provisions were designed to operate and broadly analyze their implications for state autonomy.

The following section explores the key aspects of the Ethiopian and Indian federal systems. Next, the constitutional recognition of state autonomy in Ethiopia and India is examined. Then, the chapter discusses the grounds for federal intervention in the two countries in national emergencies and other extraordinary situations. Following this, the chapter conducts a comparative analysis of the safeguards for state autonomy during federal intervention into states in the two federal systems. The final section wraps up the discussions.

2. Overview of the federal systems of Ethiopia and India

The architects of the Ethiopian federal system are proclaimed to be the nations, nationalities, and peoples (ethnic groups). This is reflected in the preamble, which begins with the phrase "we, the nations, nationalities, and peoples of Ethiopia," to imply, as some have commented, that the Constitution is a social contract amongst ethnic groups.[13] Ethnic groups, as Article 8 declares, are holders of sovereign powers, and the Constitution is an expression of their sovereignty. The states are also demarcated taking largely ethnic identity into account. These led many scholars to refer to the Ethiopian federal arrangement as "ethnic-based federalism."[14] The Constitution's significant focus on ethnic identity is not unexpected, since its drafting was heavily influenced by the Ethiopian Peoples' Revolutionary Democratic Front (EPRDF), a coalition of ethnically affiliated parties.[15] The EPRDF, notably the dominant Tigray People's Liberation Front (TPLF), fought the prior regime to reconfigure the Ethiopian polity in a way that advances ethnic groups' rights to self-determination.[16]

The pattern of distribution of powers in the FDRE Constitution is such that those powers that are not given expressly to the federal government alone or concurrently to the federal government and the states are reserved to the states. The expressly listed powers of the federal government include: protecting and defending the FDRE Constitution, foreign investment, establishing and administering national defense, formulating and implementing foreign policy, and negotiating and ratifying international treaties.[17] The enumerated powers of states are very scanty and include the power to establish a state administration, to protect and defend the FDRE Constitution, and to enact and execute the state constitution and other laws.[18] Concurrent powers exist mainly concerning taxation. It includes the power of the governments to jointly levy and collect profits, sales, excise, and personal income taxes on enterprises they jointly establish.[19]

At the federal level, a bicameral parliament has been established, comprising the House of Peoples' Representatives (HPR), the lower house, which consists of members elected from constituencies, and the House of the Federation (HoF), the upper house comprising members that represent ethnic groups inhabiting constituent units.[20] The HPR has legislative powers over all matters assigned to the federal government. It also has non-legislative functions, such as approving the appointment of federal judges and members of the council of ministers and dealing with human rights violations in states.[21] Members of the HPR are elected for a five-year term.[22] The HoF does not take part in the ordinary lawmaking process.[23] Yet it has the power, among other things, to participate in the constitutional amendment process, strive to find solutions to disputes or misunderstandings between states, and finally and authoritatively interpret the Constitution.[24]

The Ethiopian federal system comprises a parliamentary system of government. The prime minister is selected by and from the HPR. Along with the council of ministers (which consists of the prime minister, the deputy prime minister, ministers, and other members), the prime minister wields the highest executive powers of the federal government.[25] In the government structure of the states, as described in Article 50(6) of the FDRE Constitution, the highest executive power is vested in the state administrations.

Judicial function both at the federal and state level is bestowed upon the judiciary. The Constitution establishes three tiers of courts both at the federal and state level: Supreme, High, and First Instance Courts.[26] Unlike the case in many federal states, the courts in Ethiopia lack the power of constitutional interpretation, which is exercised by the HoF.

The Indian federation comprises the central government (the union) and states. At the time the Constitution took effect in 1950, India had fourteen states and six union territories.[27] The federation now consists of twenty-eight states and seven union territories after undergoing several reorganizations of its states.[28] The union government has the authority to administer the union territories. For historical reasons, the Constitution has granted greater autonomy to Jammu and Kashmir than to other states.[29] Since 2019, the special status granted to the territories by the Constitution has been revoked by the government.[30] The tiers of government have legislative, executive, and judicial organs.

The constitutional distribution of power has three lists of legislative competencies: the union list, the state list, and the concurrent list. Items listed under the union list include defense, foreign affairs, banking, and intellectual properties.[31]State powers include public order, public health and sanitation, agriculture, and fisheries.[32] Concurrent powers comprise items concerning which both the union government and states exercise legislative powers. Union legislation, however, prevails when conflict between the two laws on the concurrent list arises. The items on the concurrent list include criminal law and procedure, preventive detention, marriage and divorce, and registration of deeds and documents.[33]

The Parliament of the Union consists of the president and two houses: the Lok Sabha (House of the People) and the Rajya Sabha (Council of States) as the lower and upper houses, respectively.[34] The Lok Sabha is the assembly of representatives of the people, comprising members chosen from territorial constituencies in the states and union territories.[35] The Rajya Sabha consists of representatives of the states and the union territories, as well as members nominated by the president with special knowledge or practical experience in respect of literature, science, and social service.[36] The president is the head of state and is elected for a five-year term by an electoral college consisting of the members of the two houses of the union legislature and the legislative assemblies of the states.[37] The president, who holds a ceremonial position, discharges the constitutionally assigned responsibilities with the aid and advice of the prime minister and the Council of Ministers.[38]

The Indian Constitution has established a parliamentary form of government inspired by the United Kingdom: government power is exercised by a party securing a majority of seats in the lower house.[39] The prime minister, the head of the government, is elected by the president out of the majority political party in the lower house.[40] Although the Constitution bestows executive power in the hands of the president, the actual executive power is exercised by the prime minister and the Council of Ministers, which aid and advise the president.

Unlike in Ethiopia and most other federal systems, the Constitution of India does not provide for a dual system of courts. It establishes a single, integrated system of courts for the union and the states, which administer the laws of all levels of government.[41] The Supreme Court is at the apex of the hierarchy of courts, below which stand the High Courts of the different states.[42] Under the High Court lies a hierarchy of other courts.[43] The Supreme Court is not only the highest court that wields the power to interpret the Constitution; it also exercises the highest appellate jurisdiction over civil and criminal cases.[44]

3. The Constitutional Recognition of State Autonomy

Federalism entails the division of governing authority between the central government and two or more constituent units, with the latter enjoying significant constitutionally derived autonomy over their competencies.[45] In Daniel J. Elazar's view, the recognition of self-rule and shared rule are the hallmarks of federalism.[46] Shared rule occurs when constituent units are represented and participate in the decisions of the central legislature that concern the whole political community.[47] Self-rule, also known as "autonomy" in the literature, refers to the degree to which constituent units (states in the Ethiopian context) are free to decide, finance, and implement their policies.[48] The degree of autonomy of states, in the opinion of Elazar, can be determined by looking into the scope of policy for which they are responsible, the extent to which they control their financial sources, and the extent to which the constituent units are provided with representative institutions.[49] Practice reveals that the degree of autonomy enjoyed by the constituent units varies considerably. Some federations are highly centralized, with the central government wielding concentrated power. Others, on the contrary, uphold a decentralized system, investing the constituent units with extensive levels of autonomy and discretion.[50]

In the Ethiopian federal system, the state's right to autonomy is derived from an ethnic group's right to self-government. Under Article 39(3), ethnic groups are guaranteed the right to a full measure of self-government, including the right to establish government institutions in the territory they inhabit and to equitable representation in states and the federal government.[51] The right to self-determination goes to the extent of allowing ethnic groups to establish a new state. Article 47 of the Constitution provides that ethnic groups within states may, at any time, establish their own state.

Furthermore, each ethnic group is guaranteed the right to secede from the federation unconditionally.[52] The details on how secession takes effect are laid out in Article 39(4). What is striking about the procedures is that secession, a rather rare concept in world constitutionalism,[53] can be realized with the decision solely of the legislative councils of the concerned ethnic groups but without the involvement of the HoF, the upper house that comprises members who represent ethnic groups inhabiting the constituent units. Ethnic groups that had a say in the determination of the structure of the federal system are, in effect, denied taking part in the process that entails its modification.[54]

The right to self-government of ethnic groups cannot be easily modified or abolished by the federal government unilaterally. It can only be modified or repealed through the amendment procedures outlined in the FDRE Constitution. The Constitution has placed more stringent amendment procedures for human rights, which include the right to self-government of ethnic groups, and Article 105 (which deals with constitutional amendment) than other provisions. The amendment of human rights and Article 105 can only occur when the proposal for their amendment is approved by a two-thirds majority in both houses of the federal parliament and by a majority in all state councils.[55] For other provisions of the Constitution, amendments can take place if the proposed amendment is approved by a two-thirds majority vote in the joint session of the federal houses and by a majority vote in two-thirds of state councils.[56]

The federal government cannot alter or change the boundaries of states or interfere in their internal administration except in some cases that the next section examines. The levels of government, in exercising their powers, are required to respect the powers of each other.[57] This is subject to the cases of federal intervention in states that the next sections of the chapter analyze.

In the Indian federal system, the Government of India Act of 1935 was instrumental in laying the foundation for state autonomy. Under the act, the provinces (now states) and the central government were assigned distinct legislative competencies, and the former were recognized as independent and autonomous administrative units.[58] Though the constitution adopted after independence granted states more elaborated competencies, reinforcing their autonomy, it also has aspects that, according to some commentators, have tended to centralize state power and erode the autonomy of states. Among such aspects is the power of the Union Parliament under Article 3 to create a new state(s), change the areas, boundaries, or names of states, and even abolish a state by an ordinary legislative procedure.[59] This power may be exercised by the parliament without ascertaining the views of the state legislature.[60]

The powers of the president over state governments are also strongly criticized for diminishing the federal character of the form of government. As appointees of the president, state governors act as agents of the union government, send periodic reports to the president, and reserve state bills to be considered by the president.[61] According to Article 200, the president, in the latter case, has the power to either give his assent to the reserved bills or exercise his veto power over them. The constitutional provisions outlining the residual powers of the Union Parliament and the legislative powers of the union government over state matters, Articles 248 and 249, respectively, are also perceived as non-federal aspects.[62]

The Union Parliament under Article 249 passes legislation on matters on state lists if the Council of States (the second federal legislative chamber) by a two-thirds majority vote has declared by a resolution that a given matter in the list is necessary or expedient in the national interest. This power of the Union Parliament, in the opinion of H. M. Rajashekara, would entail big intrusion into state legislative powers because the two-thirds majority vote given may not necessarily reflect the interest of most of the states, among others.[63]

The other contested provisions of the Indian Constitution considered to impact the state's autonomy are the emergency provisions that allow Union intervention into state jurisdiction—Articles 352 (National Emergency), 356 (Failure of Constitutional Machinery), and 360 (Financial Emergency).[64] The next section compares the grounds for federal intervention provided in these provisions with those provided in the intervention clauses of the FDRE Constitution.

4. The Grounds for Federal Intervention in States in Extraordinary Cases

At the earlier stages of the drafting of the FDRE Constitution, the need for drawing lessons from the experience of foreign states, such as India, to deal with emergent situations was emphasized. A member of the Constitutional Commission, the organ that prepared the first draft of the FDRE Constitution, commenting on the proposed provisions of the Constitution for emergencies, for example, noted, "As the trend in India suggests, the federal government may use coercive measures to arrest human rights violations in states committed in defiance of the decisions of the High Court. The experience of other states also demonstrates that the federal government may declare a state of emergency to contain internal disturbances arising in the sub-units where the legislative authorities of the sub-units are involved and ignore federal orders to arrest the situation" (translation mine).[65] Implicit in the member's explanation is that the federal government should use a state of emergency decree to arrest internal disturbances in states that are caused by state authorities. This did not, however, turn out in the final version of the emergency provisions of the FDRE Constitution.

The federal government has the power to declare a state of emergency when "an external invasion, a breakdown of law and order that endangers the constitutional order and cannot be controlled by the regular law enforcement agencies and personnel, a natural disaster, or an epidemic occur."[66] Contrary to the suggestion by a member of the Constitutional Commission noted above, security problems caused by state authorities do not fall within the ambit of a state of emergency. This may be inferred from the clause "… cannot be controlled by the regular law enforcement agencies and personnel." The provision explains situations that go beyond the capacity of state authorities despite their utmost effort, instead of emergent situations not arrested by state authorities because of their involvement in the problem. When the risk to the constitutional order is brought by the state, Article 62(9), which the chapter shortly considers, will be put into operation. A state of emergency decree authorizes the federal government to intervene in the concerned states to maintain public security, law, and order—a task that, in times of normalcy, is to be carried out by states.[67]

The power to decree a state of emergency is not exclusive to the federal government. State executives may also proclaim a statewide state of emergency when a natural disaster or epidemic occurs.[68] As a result, the federal government and states may concurrently proclaim a state of emergency in response to a natural disaster or epidemic that erupted in the state. The conflict between the laws of the levels of government that may arise due to the overlap in legislative power is difficult to resolve, given that neither law is superior to the other. Following the outbreak of COVID-19, for instance, both the federal government and the State of Tigray passed a state of emergency decree that prohibited the shaking of hands, gathering of people, sporting activities, cinemas, and the like.[69] The governments could not resolve the challenge through consultation and cooperation, owing to the antagonism between the parties ruling the federal government and the State of Tigray, which later escalated into a military conflict.

The FDRE Constitution also allows the federal government to intervene in states in extraordinary cases other than the emergencies discussed above. These are provided in Articles 51(14), 55(16), and 62(9) of the FDRE Constitution. The federal government has passed Proclamation No. 359/2003 ("the Proclamation" hereafter) to elaborate on these instances.[70]

In the first case, the federal government intervenes in states to arrest a deteriorating security situation. Article 51(14) provides, "It [the federal government] shall deploy, at the request of a state administration, federal defense forces to arrest a deteriorating security situation within the requesting state when its authorities are unable to control it." Deterioration of security, as the Proclamation defines it, is an activity that disturbs the peace and safety of the public and that the law enforcement agency and judiciary of the state are unable to arrest by the law.[71]

Federal intervention in the second case occurs when there is a human rights violation in a state that the state is unable to arrest. Article 55(16) of the FDRE Constitution reads:

> *It [the lower House] shall, on its own initiative, request a joint session of the House of the Federation and of the House of Peoples' Representatives to take appropriate measures when State authorities are unable to arrest violations of human rights within their jurisdiction. It shall, on the basis of the joint decision of the House, give directives to the concerned State authorities.*

The phrase "unable to arrest" in the above provision's language suggests that the article applies to instances of human rights violations that happen without the state's intentional involvement. It does not cover acts of human rights violations in a state that are carried out with the participation or consent of the state. This position is also espoused by the Proclamation. According to Article 8 of the Proclamation, the House of People's Representatives may, when it receives reports of human rights violations in a state, send a team to the state that investigates the alleged violations of human rights. As Article 9 puts forth, the team must report "efforts made and measures taken by the state" to arrest such violations of human rights. The Proclamation refers to a state that has not participated in or consented to human rights violations committed within its boundary since such a state will not presumably make any efforts to stop or address them.

The type and extent of human rights violations that trigger federal intervention are defined neither in the FDRE Constitution nor in the Proclamation. The Proclamation replicates the wording of the constitution without clarifying what constitutes human rights violations. It defined human rights violations as acts committed in a state that violate the provisions of the human rights stipulated in the Constitution and laws promulgated in pursuance of the Constitution and that the state's law enforcement agency and the judiciary are unable to arrest.[72] When taken together, the provisions imply that the important factor is the existence of human rights violations that a state's law enforcement and judiciary organs are unable to arrest.

In the final case, federal intervention occurs when any state endangers the constitutional order.[73] The Proclamation has listed acts that endanger the constitutional order. These include armed uprisings, resolving conflicts between states or ethnic groups through non-peaceful means, disturbing the peace and security of the federal government, and violating directives given to a state by the federal parliament following the above second case of intervention.[74] If a state is involved in any of these acts, the federal government will get the authority to intervene in the state when the HoF orders it.

The above three cases are instances of federal intervention into state jurisdiction since the matters that the federal government deals with upon intervention—maintaining security (Article 51(14)), arresting human rights violations (Article 55(16)), and maintaining the constitutional order (Article 62(9))—are state matters, according to the constitutional division of power.[75]

In the Indian Constitution, extraordinary situations that warrant federal intervention in states are dealt with in its emergency provisions (Articles 352-360). Three types of emergencies are provided in the Constitution: (i) A national emergency,[76] (ii) A failure of constitutional machinery in a state,[77] and (iii) a financial emergency.[78]

The president has the power to proclaim a national emergency when the security of India or any part of the territory thereof is threatened, whether by war, external aggression, or armed rebellion. As opposed to the case in many countries, including Ethiopia, the president may adopt the proclamation before the actual occurrence of the exigencies, such as when external aggression is apprehended.[79] During an emergency period, the executive powers of the union extend to the giving of directives to any state as to how the executive power thereof is to be exercised.[80] The proclamation of emergency also authorizes the union to exercise legislative power over state matters concurrently with the concerned states.[81]

A proclamation of failure of constitutional machinery, also commonly referred to as "president's rule" or "state emergency," is issued when the president, after assessing the report received from the governor, is satisfied that the government of the state cannot be carried on by the Constitution.[82] The president assesses the report of the governor and decides based on the advice and aid of the Council of Ministers and the prime minister.[83] As some have commented, the article was established to enable the president to deal with a political breakdown in any of the states of the federation by, inter alia, preventing factional strife from paralyzing the governmental machinery.[84]

Furthermore, failure by the state to comply with any of the union's directions also serves as a ground for the president to intervene in the state, proclaiming the failure of constitutional machinery.[85] The federal government gives directions to states when exercising the power entrusted to it by Articles 256, 257, and 339 of the Constitution to control the state's executive power. Article 256 prescribes that when exercising their executive authority, states must comply with the laws made by parliament and any existing laws that apply within their jurisdiction. Article 257 obliges states to refrain from impeding or prejudicing the exercise of the executive powers of the union government when exercising their executive powers. The union government may give directions to states that guide them to comply with these requirements. The union government has, in addition, the power to give directions to states as to the construction and maintenance of means of communication having military or national importance and the protection of railways within a state.[86] Article 339 describes the union's powers to give directions to states regarding the administration of the "scheduled areas" and the welfare of "scheduled tribes" in the states.[87]

A financial emergency may be adopted as per Article 360 if the president is satisfied that a situation has arisen whereby the financial stability or credit of India or any part of the territory thereof is threatened. The president's decision is not based on his satisfaction; it must be supplemented by the recommendations of the Council of Ministers headed by the prime minister.[88] The emergency proclamation empowers the executive authority of the union to give directions to any state to observe such canons of financial propriety as may be specified in the directions and to give such other directions as the president may deem necessary and adequate for the purpose.[89]

From the above, it is possible to analyze the influence that the Indian experience had on the approach that Ethiopia followed to contain extraordinary circumstances. As with the case in India, the FDRE Constitution allows the federal government to intervene in states and deal with extraordinary situations with or without an emergency proclamation, depending on the nature of the situations encountered. In both cases, for example, a war or external invasion serves as a ground for the adoption of an emergency proclamation by the federal government. Besides, the grounds that allow the federal government to intervene in states without declaring a state of emergency, most importantly Article 62(9) of the FDRE Constitution, exhibit close similarities with Article 356 of the Indian Constitution. Endangering the constitutional order referred to in Article 62(9) of the FDRE Constitution, it can be argued, includes the situation covered by Article 356 of the Indian Constitution, i.e., the creation of an environment where the government of the state cannot be carried on according to the constitution.

Distinctions between the two systems abound. To mention but a few, the Ethiopian state of emergency regime does not include financial emergencies and is not tailored to counter emergencies that are about to materialize, as opposed to the counterpart provisions of the Indian Constitution (Article 352). The union government of India resorts to national emergencies to contain armed rebellions in a state. Under the Ethiopian federal system, the federal government may invoke either state of emergency provisions or Article 62(9) to respond to the armed rebellion based on the involvement of the concerned state in the problem. As already remarked earlier, it will use the first option if the armed rebellion that endangers the constitutional order is beyond the capacity of regular law enforcement and the second option if the state is the cause of the problem. The two systems also differ in how they safeguard state autonomy during federal intervention in extraordinary circumstances, as analyzed below.

5. Federal Intervention Powers and the Constitutional Safeguards for State Autonomy

Federal constitutions must strike a balance between the need for state autonomy and the need for unity, efficient administration, and the sharing of resources that are necessary in extraordinary situations.[90] The optimal balance between the above interests is subject to change, with different priorities prevailing at different times and in different circumstances. Many constitutions, including the constitutions of Ethiopia and India discussed above, confer greater power to the federal government (such as the power to intervene in the constituent units) in extraordinary circumstances, overriding the constitutional provisions that protect state autonomy. However, the powers of the federal government may be subject to abuse, entailing unnecessary encroachment on state autonomy. Given this, most federal constitutions have devised techniques for constraining the use of such powers.[91] The techniques involve the legislative branch, whose consent is often necessary for the approval, renewal, and termination of the emergency decree, and the judiciary, which assesses its constitutionality.[92] The following section compares the techniques available in the FDRE Constitution and the Constitution of India to safeguard state autonomy during federal intervention in extraordinary circumstances.

5.1. Constraints on the Executive's Power to Intervene: The Role of the Legislative Branch

As is the case in many parliamentary systems, the cabinets and prime ministers play a prominent role in the declaration of a state of emergency in Ethiopia and India. A state of emergency in Ethiopia is declared based on the decision of the Council of Ministers, chaired by the prime minister.[93] The Council of Ministers makes its decision after assessing the security situation in a particular part of the country. The decree may also be proclaimed when the federal government is requested as such by a state where an emergent situation has arisen. The Council of Ministers, for example, passed a state of emergency after receiving a request from the State of Amhara on August 3, 2023, to take appropriate measures in response to the armed struggle between local militiamen ("fano") and the government's security forces.[94]

The federal government is seized with the security situation of the concerned state soon after a state of emergency decree is proclaimed. Yet the decree must be submitted to the lower house of the federal parliament for approval. The approval should be made by a two-thirds majority vote of the members of the house. The nonfulfillment of the required supermajority votes will entail the lapse of the decree.[95] The procedure hardly serves as an appropriate safeguard against encroachment into state autonomy, as the decree takes effect without states consenting to it. The problem will not be rectified, even with the requirement for the consent of the second chamber being set as a requirement, since it does not technically comprise representatives of states (instead representing ethnic groups).

The impact of the parliamentary nature of government on the effectiveness of legislative oversight of executive functions should also not be overlooked. As the Council of Ministers, including its chair, the prime minister, are parliamentarians, it is very difficult to expect the parliament to revoke a state of emergency prioritizing state autonomy. The problem is also exacerbated by the long-standing party discipline in Ethiopia, where parliamentarians of the ruling party are required to support bills of the executive without much scrutiny or debate.[96]

The approved state of emergency decree can remain in force for up to six months.[97] The parliament has the power to renew the emergency decree by a two-thirds majority vote every four months from the date the decree is proclaimed.[98] To this end, the parliament solicits the views of the State of Emergency Enquiry Board, which it organizes when approving the decree.[99] Renewal decisions may either approve the continuous application of the decree without any change or vary its provisions and duration of application. The Constitution has not set a limit on the number of renewals of the decree, which implies that it can be renewed for an indefinite period so long as the parliament is convinced of its importance.

The Constitution is silent on how the decree may be terminated. But it is implied in the above that it may terminate when the fixed period expires, and the parliament does not renew it. The parliament may, when reviewing the decree, also decide to terminate it ahead of its expiration when it believes that the grounds that caused the decree are no longer a threat to the country. This occurred in February 2022, when the parliament ended the sixth-month state of emergency decree passed in November 2021, set to remain in force until May 2022, to repel rebel Tigrayan forces who were fighting government and allied forces.[100] The decision followed the retreat of Tigrayan forces to their home state, the State of Tigray.[101]

The federal parliament is involved when interventions happen in non-emergency cases. The directive given to a state when human rights violations occur in that state (Article 55(16) of the FDRE Constitution), as noted above, is issued by a joint decision of the two houses of parliament. Intervention under Article 62(9) takes place through the order of the upper house when a state endangers the constitutional order. The executive branch does not require the approval of parliament when it intervenes in states invoking Article 51(14). What it needs is a request by the concerned state to arrest a deteriorating security situation that goes beyond its control.

The Ethiopian parliament's role in constraining the use of intervention power by the executive in extraordinary cases discussed above has notable distinctions from its counterpart in India. To begin with the state of emergency, the composition of the legislative branch that scrutinizes the emergency law in the two systems varies. In the Ethiopian federal system, the lower house that approves the decree is composed of the representatives of Ethiopia as a whole. And only one of the two houses of parliament is involved in the approval process. In the Indian federal system, on the other hand, the approval of the emergency law proclaimed by the president under Article 352 involves not only the lower house but also the upper house, which comprises representatives of the states and the union territories.[102] States in Ethiopia are not offered this opportunity since the upper house, as noted above, is not composed of state representatives in the first place.

Besides, the period in which a state of emergency declared by the executive applies without the approval of the parliament is shorter in Ethiopia than in India. According to Article 352(4) of the Indian Constitution, a proclamation of emergency will cease to function if the houses of parliament do not approve it by resolution within one month of its issue. The parliament must approve it within the specified time, whether it is in session or not. The FDRE Constitution has fixed forty-eight hours for a decree to apply without the parliament's approval if the parliament is in session and a maximum of fifteen days if the parliament is not in session.[103] The time frames set in the two constitutions reveal that the FDRE Constitution has adopted a mechanism that ensures quicker scrutiny of the executive's potential intrusion into state autonomy than the Indian Constitution.

A question arises as to the fate of a state of emergency that the Council of Ministers of Ethiopia issues when the parliament that has yet to approve it is dissolved before or after the expiration of its term limits. The parliament may be dissolved before the end of its term limits when the prime minister proposes and the members of the parliament consent.[104] In such cases, a new election to reconstitute the parliament will be held within six months of the dissolution.[105] The issue that needs an answer is whether the state of emergency decree will continue to apply without legislative approval until parliament is reconstituted following a new election. If the answer is in the affirmative, when will the parliament approve the decree after it is reconstituted? The FDRE Constitution does not address these issues. Even though the situation has not so far occurred in practice, it is essential to deal with the constitutional silence, as it could risk state autonomy by entailing a prolonged application of a decree not reviewed by parliament.

The Indian Constitution has proactively dealt with the complications that may arise when the proclamation of emergency is issued when the parliament has been dissolved, or the parliament is dissolved within one month after the proclamation was issued without approving the proclamation. It has provided that the proclamation of emergency in both scenarios will apply until one month since the House of the People first sits after its reconstitution, provided that the Council of States has passed a resolution approving the proclamation.[106] The proclamation may continue to apply if the house, before the expiration of the said period, passes a resolution approving the proclamation.[107]

The Ethiopian Parliament will also be dissolved when its five-year term fixed by the FDRE Constitution expires. To fill the power vacuum that may be created until the parliament is reconstituted after its dissolution, the FDRE Constitution has required elections to be conducted one month before the expiration of the house's term limit.[108] The HoF, in its recent decision on the COVID-19-related case, has addressed an extreme scenario that may occur when the national election is postponed due to emergencies. In the said case, the House elaborated that the parliament's term limit will be extended until the House is reconstituted following a national election that will be held after the situation is controlled.[109]

And lastly, the procedure involved in discontinuing an emergency law is different in the two countries. In India, the House of the People may at any time pass a resolution to determine the continuity of the proclamation of emergency after notifying the president or the speaker of the House in writing, signed by at least one-tenth of the total members. The president will revoke the proclamation when the House, by a simple majority vote, objects to its continuance.[110] No similar procedure exists in Ethiopia for terminating an emergency law. As considered above, the state of emergency will be discontinued if it is not renewed with the support of a two-thirds majority vote in parliament.

As regards other extraordinary situations as well, the roles that the parliaments of the two systems play in checking the executive's emergency power vary. The Indian Constitution subjects the president's power to intervene in states on the grounds of a failure of constitutional machinery (Article 356) to the approval of the parliament. Once the proclamation is approved, the president may take any of the measures laid down in Article 356(1), which include assuming to himself all or any of the functions of the government of the state and all or any of the powers vested in or exercisable by the governor and suspending the operation of any authority in the state.

When it comes to Ethiopia, the FDRE Constitution does not explain the powers that the executive branch exercises when the lower and upper houses of parliament issue directives to the states following human rights violations in a state and order federal intervention at a time a state endangers the constitutional order, respectively.[111] The mentioned issues are fleshed out in the proclamation. Arguably, the directive the parliament issues to the state during human rights violations must, at the very least, enjoin the concerned state to address human rights violations. Considering this, the proclamation appears to be consistent with the Constitution when it explains that the directive may require the state to arrest acts of violation of human rights and bring the perpetrators to justice.[112]

An order for federal intervention under Article 62(9) of the FDRE Constitution, as explained in the proclamation, empowers the federal government to set up a provisional administration that is accountable to the federal government by suspending the state council and the highest executive organs of the state aside from deploying the federal police, federal defense force, or both.[113] It is questionable whether the possibility of suspending the state administration was envisaged by the Constitution, given its serious impact on state autonomy. The matter was not given much concern at the time of the drafting of the Constitution. It was, however, somehow discussed at the deliberations of the parliament when it enacted the proclamation referred to above. The issue debated was whether the federal government's power under the above constitutional provision includes suspending state governments when doing so becomes necessary under the circumstances. An official of the now defunct Ministry of Federal Affairs at the time opined that while the federal government's power in extraordinary times, such as the case covered by Article 62(9), permits the suspension of state organs, it does not include such power during a state of emergency.[114] It is not clear how the official arrived at this conclusion since the FDRE Constitution does not prohibit the suspension of the right to state autonomy during a state of emergency. The right of ethnic groups to self-government, the basis of state autonomy, is a right that can be limited during a state of emergency.[115] The federal government may suspend the state administration if it finds that doing so is necessary to repel the danger.

In addition to emergency cases, the right to self-government may also be subject to restriction in other extraordinary circumstances, such as crises that endanger the constitutional order in a state. As it is not an absolute right, the federal parliament may pass a law that restricts the right under certain circumstances, as it does for other rights guaranteed by the FDRE Constitution. The restriction, however, must be justified by the pursuance of a legitimate aim and proportional—it must be appropriate to pursue the objective, and it may not go beyond what is required to effectively achieve that aim as the widely accepted rule of restriction of rights prescribes.[116] Accordingly, the intervention measures to be taken when applying Article 62(9) of the FDRE Constitution, which includes suspending the concerned state's councils and the highest executive organs of the state, must be necessary to arrest the situation that endangered the constitutional order.[117] The measures must also be proportional to the needs of the case.[118]

A proclamation under Article 356 of the Indian Constitution, when the parliament approves it, may last up to six months. The parliament may extend the proclamation to three years if there is a national security emergency and difficulties in holding elections arise.[119] The FDRE Constitution does not provide for how long federal intervention under Article 62(9) lasts. The proclamation elaborates that the provisional administration that the federal government organizes upon intervention may stay in the state for a period not exceeding two years.[120] Where necessary, the HoF may extend the above time to a period not exceeding six months.[121]

5.2. Judicial Control of Federal Interventions

Until recently, the Ethiopian federal government rarely expressly invoked the constitutional provisions that provide for a state of emergency and authorize federal intervention in states. This is despite the frequent public protests that often erupt in the country in the aftermath of national elections, as well as armed resistance, notably in the Oromia and Somali regions. The federal government effectively silenced dissent and suppressed public protests without declaring a state of emergency or undertaking massive military intervention in states. The situation, however, significantly changed when it began confronting heightened and widespread public protest, beginning in 2014, across the country, most notably in the States of Oromia and Amhara, which culminated in a reshuffle within the EPRDF and the control of government power, with the dethroning of the TPLF as the dominant coalition member in 2018. The federal government increasingly invoked the above constitutional provisions to quell the public protests and the crises in some states, such as the States of Tigray and Somali, which were discontented with the new political dynamics.[122] Yet, the constitutionality of the federal government's measures remained a subject of controversy.

For example, in justifying the military measures it took in the State of Tigray in 2020, which it designated as "law enforcement," the federal government reasoned that the intervention was justified under Article 62(9) of the FDRE Constitution, since the TPLF endangered the constitutional order by attacking the National Defense Forces, among other things.[123] The TPLF leaders, on the other hand, rejected the claim, arguing that they did not initiate the attack.[124] The issue was not settled through constitutional means. Instead, it escalated into a civil war. Some commentators also questioned the compatibility of the federal government's military intervention in the State of Somali in August 2018, which followed the tragic human rights violations in the state, with state autonomy.[125]

The de jure and de facto states of emergency were not challenged in the judiciary. Nevertheless, controversies abound. A controversy arose about the state of emergency declared in March 2018 because the speaker of the parliament declared the approval of the declaration without the fulfillment of the two-thirds majority vote set in the Constitution.[126] The number of members of parliament at the time, as the speaker disclosed, was 539.[127] The decree needed at least two-thirds of 539 (359 or more) to be approved. But the speaker, after counting the votes given, announced that the decree was approved with 346 members voting in favor of it, 88 objecting to it, and 7 abstaining.[128] Later, the speaker appeared on state-owned television and apologized that there was a mathematical error committed during the process. [129]According to the speaker, the number of votes cast in favor of the decree was communicated mistakenly as 346, due to the erroneous calculation of votes, when it was 395.[130] The decree entered into force without the confusion being clarified by an impartial arbiter. A question may arise as to whether it is possible to contest the constitutional validity of federal actions of this type in the first place.

In the Indian federal system, the Forty-Fourth Amendment Act passed in 1978 allowed judicial review of a proclamation of emergency under Article 352.[131] The judicial review covers assessing (i) the requirement of satisfaction of the president in deciding to proclaim the emergency; and (ii) the measures taken by the president in exercising the emergency powers.[132] The president's rule under Article 356 is also subject to judicial review. This was elaborated in *Bommai's case*, where the Supreme Court ruled that courts have the power to review (i) whether the proclamation was issued based on any material, (ii) whether the material was relevant, and (iii) whether the proclamation was used mala fide.[133]

The constitutional system of Ethiopia is not designed to allow adequate protection of state autonomy through the judiciary. The Constitution assigns the power of constitutional interpretation neither to the Supreme Court, as is the case in India and many other federal states, nor to a special constitutional court, as is the case in states such as Germany and South Africa. It instead conferred such power on a nonjudicial body, the HoF, which comprises representatives of ethnic groups, appointed by states, and in practice, including regional presidents. The House decides cases based on the recommendation of the Council of Constitutional Inquiry (CCI)—an organ established by the Constitution composed of eleven members, the majority of whom are legal professionals.[134] This unique approach, as its legislative history suggests, was chosen by the drafters to mainly deal with the counter-majoritarian problem.[135] The Constituent Assembly, an organ that approved the final draft of the Constitution, held the position that the power to interpret the Constitution must be entrusted to an entity that consists of elected representatives of ethnic groups who authored the Constitution, rather than unelected judges.[136] According to the Assembly, judges are not suited to such a task, as they may reflect their assumptions or the ideologies of the ruling government when interpreting the Constitution, rather than the wishes of its authors.[137]

As it stands now, the judiciary's role in constitutional interpretation is far from clear, leading to contrasting viewpoints on the matter. The Constitution unequivocally vests the power to decide *all constitutional disputes* in the HoF.[138] It further provides that the House will make a final decision on the recommendations referred to it by the CCI on applications that challenge the constitutionality of laws passed by the legislative branches of the federal government or states.[139]

Some scholars, including Takele Soboka Bulto, have argued that the above do not mean that courts are stripped of the power to interpret the Constitution. Bulto contended that courts should refer cases to the House for constitutional interpretation only when they find it impossible to apply an ordinary law without an authoritative interpretation of the Constitution.[140] In Adem Kassie Abebe's observation, the process of determining whether there is a constitutional issue in a case leads courts to carry out a preliminary constitutional interpretation. The courts will declare a law constitutional and proceed to apply it after ascertaining, through interpreting the Constitution, that there is no doubt that the law could be unconstitutional.[141] Other Ethiopian scholars, on the contrary, held the view that courts are excluded from getting involved in the task of constitutional interpretation. Getachew Assefa Woldemariam, espousing this position, has, for example, argued that courts are not allowed to deal with constitutional interpretation; they are bound to refer any questions of constitutionality, whether simple or complex, to the HoF.[142]

The latter position appears to be in line with the drafter's understanding of constitutional interpretation. It was indicated in the discussions of the Constituent Assembly that the judicial branch's inherent power to interpret laws does not include the power to interpret the Constitution. Mr. Hassen Ali, chairperson of the committee that drafted the provisions on constitutional interpretation at the time of deliberations, said, "The judiciary's ordinary task is interpreting laws. Yet, the issue now is whether this includes the power to interpret the Constitution. The constitution, a political contract concluded by ethnic groups, must be interpreted by the contracting parties themselves" (translation mine).[143] As is evident, the drafters wanted the judiciary to stick to its ordinary task of interpreting laws without including the FDRE Constitution. This arguably manifests the drafter's intention to reserve any task that involves constitutional interpretation, such as determining the constitutionality of laws and the meaning, content, and scope of constitutional provisions, exclusively to the House.

The exercise of power over *all constitutional disputes* by the HoF means that the House will not only deal with the determination of the constitutionality of federal or state laws but also with the decisions of government organs. This has been explained in the laws detailing the powers and functions of the House and its advisory body, the CCI. According to these laws, the House has the power to review the constitutionality of federal or state laws, as well as any decision made by a government organ.[144] Hence, the House has the competence to decide cases that question, for instance, the compatibility of the state of emergency decree passed by the executive branch either before or after it has been approved by parliament with state autonomy. It also has the power to determine the constitutionality of directives that the federal parliament issues to the state under Article 55(16) or orders for federal intervention into states under Article 62(9).

To date, the HoF has not decided any case that contests the conformity of an emergency decree or federal intervention with the constitutionally protected state autonomy. This may in part be due to the problems related to *locus standi* to bring applications to challenge the constitutionality of federal laws and decisions and the very unlikely situation that the one-party dominance both before and after the 2018 political reform created for such applications to come up.

The *locus standi* to move the House on the above grounds, in the current arrangement, is not available for all persons. The laws that define the powers and functions of the House and the CCI allow only individuals whose rights are violated by the laws or decisions of governments or persons who have vested interests in the case to petition the House.[145] These preclude abstract constitutional questions that do not involve disputing parties or proving vested interest in the outcome of the case.

The state legislative or executive branches may petition the House for a constitutional interpretation of a nonjusticiable matter, such as to ascertain the constitutionality of federal emergency laws or decisions, provided the request is supported by one-third or more members of the respective branches.[146] Fulfilling the stated condition was nearly impossible before the political reform, due to the one-party dominance (the EPRDF ruling) at the federal and state levels. The situation has also continued after the political reform, with the only change being the replacement of the EPRDF with the Prosperity Party. In such an environment, states tend to relinquish their power, let alone contest the laws and decisions of the federal government on constitutional grounds. The

State of Tigray, ruled by a party, the TPLF, which refused to join the Prosperity Party, was, for example, the only state that issued a state of emergency decree to contain the outbreak of COVID-19 in 2020.[147] The rest of the states relied on the federal state of emergency decree to deal with the pandemic, even though they could also issue state-level decrees tailored to their specific situations.[148]

The HoF is not constituted to serve as an umpire that safeguards state autonomy through constitutional adjudication, though its members, as noted above, are, in practice, representatives of state governments. As an ethnic group in a state is represented by at least one member in the House, in theory, it can be assumed that its decisions will be highly influenced by states with diverse ethnic groups, such as the central Ethiopia region and the south Ethiopia region.

Besides, the House's loyalty to the ruling government may also hinder its ability to defend state autonomy. The CCI hardly mitigates the deficiency, as some of its decisions, though not directly related to issues of state autonomy, manifest this reality. A case in point is the decision it passed on the Coalition for Unity and Democracy (CUD) vs. the late Prime Minister Meles Zenawi in 2005.[149] In this case, the CUD, an opposition political party, initially requested the federal First Instance Court to annul the prime minister's decree that banned assembly and demonstration in Addis Ababa and its vicinity. The court referred the case to the CCI, considering that the matter needed constitutional interpretation. Inexplicably, the CCI decided that the case does not require constitutional interpretation, without explaining how the prime minister's decree, passed without following the procedures laid down in the emergency provisions of the Constitution, could be constitutional.[150] The CCI simply reasoned that the prime minister could pass such a decree as he wields wide constitutional power.[151] But it never explicitly pinpointed which constitutional provisions justified the prime minister's act.

The HoF is also not suited to assess the constitutionality of federal interventions in cases of human rights violations in a state or when a state endangers the constitutional order. As discussed above, federal intervention in both cases occurs with the involvement of the House. Requiring the House to rule on the constitutionality of the interventions would, as a result, amount to requesting it to be a judge in its case.

Concluding Remarks

State autonomy in the Ethiopian federal system is derived from the ethnic group's right to self-government. Under the FDRE Constitution, ethnic groups are entitled to administer their affairs in the territory that they inhabit and to equitable representation in the state and the federal government. The Constitution has adopted more stringent amendment procedures for the rights of ethnic groups to self-government and other human rights than for the rest of the constitutional provisions. Even more, it has extended the right of ethnic groups to self-government to include the possibility of leaving the federation whenever they wish to, unconditionally.

But as the comparison of the constitutional provisions on federal intervention into states in Ethiopia and India reveals, the FDRE Constitution has not offered adequate protection to state autonomy as it appears to be. Although the Constitution's drafters drew lessons from India when crafting the provisions on federal intervention, they have failed to incorporate essential aspects of the Indian system that have profound significance in safeguarding state autonomy during federal intervention into states. The study arrived at this conclusion by comparing the roles of the legislative branch and the judiciary of the two systems in constraining and controlling the intervention powers of the executive in extraordinary cases. In so doing, the emergency provisions and those that allow federal intervention in non-emergency situations (Articles 51(14), 55(16), and 62(9)) of the FDRE Constitution) were compared against the constitutional provisions of India on national emergency (Article 352) and President's Rule (Article 356), respectively.

The Ethiopian parliament is not constituted in a way that makes it as sensitive as the Indian parliament for state autonomy since its upper house, unlike the case in India, does not comprise representatives of states. Although the house members in Ethiopia are drawn from state executives in practice, they lack an explicit mandate to represent the states, as they are representatives of ethnic groups. The potential consequence is that the impact of the state of emergency decree issued by the executive on state autonomy will not be adequately assessed, at least as is the case in India during the approval process. Besides, the sham national elections conducted so far have led the parliament at the federal and state levels to be dominated by a single party. This, coupled with the control of the legislative and executive branches by the ruling party caused by the parliamentary nature of the parliament and the party discipline in the ruling party that requires the party members to support bills in all cases, has entailed the automatic approval of the state of emergency decrees issued by the executive, so far without significant scrutiny as to their impact on state autonomy. The problem could be ameliorated by revising the FDRE Constitution to make the approval process more stringent. To this end, requiring the approval process to involve each house of parliament, like in India, may help, although the upper house in Ethiopia does not have state representatives.

Related to this, the chapter also observed that the FDRE Constitution has not specified how a state of emergency decree could be approved by the parliament if the latter is dissolved by the prime minister before the expiry of its term limits, either at the time or after the decree was issued. One may consider this a rare scenario considering that the parliament has a shorter time to approve the decree (whenever compared with, for example, India) and that the prime minister may not consider it appropriate to dissolve the parliament within such a time. But there is no guarantee that the situation will not arise, as the prime minister is not prohibited from doing so. Filling the gap is essential, as it may entail a prolonged application of a state of emergency without the approval of parliament. Lessons could be learned from India to fix a time frame within which the parliament must approve after its reconstitution.

The chapter observed that the judiciary in Ethiopia has a diminished role in safeguarding state autonomy. The power to interpret the constitution, as opposed to the case in India, is entrusted to a nonjudicial body, the HoF, consisting of representatives of ethnic groups. As each ethnic group in a state is represented in the House (though in practice, they are drawn from state executives), the House's impartiality in its decisions is questionable, given that it may be influenced by states with diverse ethnic groups. In practice, the impartiality of the House's decision is heavily impacted by its loyalty to the ruling government.

The House is also not technically competent to pass an impartial decision on cases that contest the constitutionality of federal interventions that occur when there are human rights violations in a state (Article 55(16)) and the states endanger the constitutional order (Article 62(9)). This is because the decisions for federal intervention in the mentioned cases are made with the House's involvement. It is hardly possible to ensure adequate protection of state autonomy without assigning the power to interpret the Constitution to an impartial umpire. The widely used mechanisms for constitutional interpretation—the use of a constitutional court or regular courts—should be thoroughly investigated and assessed to this end.

Notes

* This chapter is a modified version of the paper I presented at the conference on "Perspectives on a Fair and Durable Constitutional (Re)Settlement in Ethiopia," held on May 24 and 25, 2023, in Addis Ababa. I would like to express my gratitude to the conference organizers for inviting me to present my work and covering

my lodging expenses, and to Melbourne Law School for covering my round-trip transportation costs from Melbourne to Ethiopia. I would like to thank the conference participants and reviewers of the initial versions of this work, whose questions and critical comments, respectively, have immensely helped enrich this work. I am also grateful to my supervisors, Professor Cheryl Saunders and Professor Michael Crommelin, as well as my fellow PhD candidate, John Sebastian, for their critical and insightful comments on the earlier version of this work.

1 Proclamation of the Constitution of the Federal Democratic Republic of Ethiopia, Proclamation No.1/1995 Art.46(2) ('FDRE Constitution').

2 FDRE Constitution, Art.47(1).

3 "Ethiopia's Two New Regional States Formed: Central Ethiopia, South Ethiopia," *Borkena Ethiopian News* (20 August 2023) <https://borkena.com/2023/08/19/ethiopias-two-new-regional-states-formed-central-ethiopia-south-ethiopia/> ('Ethiopia's Two New Regional States Formed').

4 The FDRE Constitution has dedicated close to one-third of its provisions to human rights. The rights guaranteed include the right to life, liberty, and security (Article 15), the right to privacy (Article 26), and the right to thought, opinion, and expression (Article 29)

5 Article 13(2) allows reference to international human rights treaties ratified by Ethiopia to get clarity around the meanings of the provisions of the human rights chapter. Accordingly, the obligation to ensure human rights in the above constitutional provision can be determined by looking at the elaborations of, for example, the Human Rights Committee, an organ established to monitor the implementation of the International Covenant on Civil and Political Rights by state parties. The Human Rights Committee has commented that ensuring human rights includes the duty to prevent human rights violations, in addition to investigating, prosecuting, and punishing violations of human rights (Human Rights Committee. "General Comment No. 31 [80] The Nature of the General Legal Obligation Imposed on States Parties to the Covenant," para 8.)

6 FDRE Constitution, Articles 51(7) and 52(2)(g).

7 FDRE Constitution, Art. 52(a)(g).

8 FDRE Constitution, Art. 50(8).

9 FDRE Constitution, Art. 93(2).

10 Fiseha Haftetsion, "The State of Vertical Division of Political Power in the Ethiopian Federation" (PhD diss, Addis Ababa University, 2017) 162–163

11 Seife Hailu Gebreslassie, "Ethiopian Federalism: Philosophical and Institutional Design Limitations and a Case for Loose Federalism" International Journal on Minority and Group Rights 28.no.5(2021):894,917 https://brill.com/view/journals/ijgr/28/5/article-p894_894.xml, Endalkachew Geremew, "Concerns Surrounding Federal Intervention" The Reporter, September 8,2018, https://www.thereporterethiopia.com/6358/

12 "Minutes of the Constitutional Commission of Ethiopia," Vol.2 (February 26/1993-October 27/1993), 169.

13 Adem Kassie Abebe, "The Federal Democratic Republic of Ethiopia: Introductory Note" *Oxford University Press* (2011):29.

14 Jon Abbink, "Ethnic-Based Federalism and Ethnicity in Ethiopia: Reassessing the Experiment after 20 Years" *Journal of Eastern African Studies* 5 no.4 (2011):596, 596; Alem Habtu, 'Ethnic Federalism in Ethiopia: Background, Present Conditions and Future Prospects' *The Second EAF International Symposium on Contemporary Development Issues in Ethiopia, July 11-12, 2003, Addis Ababa Ethiopia.*

15 Out of the 547 seats in the Constituent Assembly that approved the final draft constitution, for example, 408 were controlled by the EPRDF and its allies. Read, Theodor Vestal, "The Lost Opportunity for Ethiopia: The Failure to Move toward Democratic Governance" (2013) 1 25.

16 A Berhe, "The Origins of the Tigray People's Liberation Front" *African Affairs* 103, no.413 (October 2004): 569 <https://academic.oup.com/afraf/article-lookup/doi/10.1093/afraf/adh024>.

17 FDRE Constitution, Art.51.

18 FDRE Constitution, Art.52(1).

19 FDRE Constitution, Art. 98(1).

20 FDRE Constitution, Articles 53, 54(1), and 61.

21 FDRE Constitution, Articles 55(13) and 55(16).

22 FDRE Constitution, Art. 58(3).

23 FDRE Constitution, Look at Articles 61–64.

24 FDRE Constitution, Art. 62.

25 FDRE Constitution, Articles 72 and 76.

26 FDRE Constitution, Art. 78.

27 George Mathew, "Republic of India" in Akhtar Majeed, Ronald L Watts and Douglas M Brown (eds), *Distribution of Powers and Responsibilities in Federal Countries* (McGill-Queen's Univ. Press, 2006) 156.

28 Mathew,156

29 Cheryl Saunders, "Options for Decentralizing Power: Federalism to Decentralization" 21. Accordingly, the present work does not cover the application of the constitutional rules of India in these states.

30 'Article 370: What Happened with Kashmir and Why It Matters', *BBC News* (online, 5 August 2019) <https://www.bbc.com/news/world-asia-india-49234708> ('Article 370').

31 The Constitution of India [As of May 2022] 2022] 2022, Seventh Schedule, List I-Union List.

32 The Constitution of India, Seventh Schedule, List II—State List.

33 The Constitution of India, Seventh Schedule, List III—Concurrent List.

34 The Constitution of India, Art.79.

35 The Constitution of India, Art.81.

36 The Constitution of India, Art.80(3).

37 The Constitution of India, Articles 54 and 56.

38 The Constitution of India, Articles 74 and 78.

39 Benegal Narsing Rau, "The Parliamentary System of Government in India" Washington Law Review 24 no.1(January 1949): 91.

40 The Constitution of India, Art.53.

41 Durga Das Basu, *Introduction to the Constitution of India* (2011) 299.

42 Basu, Introduction,299.
43 The Constitution of India, Articles 233-237.
44 Basu, Introduction,305.
45 Cheryl Saunders, Options for Decentralizing Power; 'Elliot Bulmer, Bicameralism, International IDEA Constitution-Building Premier' <https://www.idea.int/sites/default/files/publications/bicameralism-primer.pdf> accessed 16 December 2022; George Anderson, *Federalism: An Introduction*, (Oxford University Press, 2008) pp 1-5.
46 Daniel J Elazar, *Exploring Federalism* (University of Alabama Press, 1987) 5.
47 Thibaut Noel, *Second Chambers in Federal Systems* (IDEA, 2022) 1; Sean Mueller, "Self-Rule and Shared Rule", *50 Shades of Federalism* (25 October 2017) <http://50shadesoffederalism.com/theory/self-rule-shared-rule/>.
48 Mueller, Self-Rule and Shared Rule.
49 Daniel J. Elazar, *Federal Systems of the World: A Handbook of Federal, Confederal and Autonomy Arrangements*; cited in Gary Marks, Liesbet Hooghe and Arjan H Schakel, "Patterns of Regional Authority" *Regional & Federal* Studies18 no (2-3) (2008):167, 4.
50 Anderson, Federalism, 2.
51 FDRE Constitution, Art.8.
52 FDRE Constitution, Art.39(1).
53 Adeno Addis, "From A Nation of Citizens to A "Nation of Nations" National Citizenship Without Depth" *International Journal of Ethiopian Studies* 14 No.1/2 (2020) 148
54 The House of the Federation is established to represent the ethnic groups who are the authors of the FDRE Constitution and bearers of sovereign power (read Article 8(1) of the FDRE Constitution).
55 FDRE Constitution, Art.105(1).
56 FDRE Constitution, Art.105(2).
57 FDRE Constitution, Art.50(8).
58 Waseem Ahmad Sofi, *Autonomy of a State in a Federation: A Special Case Study of Jammu and Kashmir* (Springer Singapore, 2021) 38.
59 Sofi, Autonomy of a State in a Federation, 47.
60 H. M. Rajashekara, "The Nature of Indian Federalism: A Critique" *Asian Survey*,37 No.3 (March 1997):247.
61 Rajashekara, The Nature of Indian Federalism, 247.
62 Rajashekara, The Nature of Indian Federalism, 248.
63 Rajashekara, The Nature of Indian Federalism,248.
64 Sofi, Autonomy of a State in a Federation, 47.
65 "Minutes of the Constitutional Commission of Ethiopia," Vol.2,169.
66 FDRE Constitution, Art. 93(1)(a).
67 FDRE Constitution, Art. 52(2)(g).
68 FDRE Constitution, Art. 93(1)(b).
69 Zemelak Ayele and Yonatan Tesfaye Fessha, "Controlling Public Health Emergencies in Federal Systems: The Case of Ethiopia" in Nico Steytler (ed), *Comparative Federalism and Covid-19: Combating the Pandemic* (Routledge, 1st ed, 2021) 325–328 <https://www.taylorfrancis.com/books/9781003166771>.

70 *System for the Intervention of the Federal Government in the Regions Proclamation No. 359/2003* ('*Proclamation No. 359/2003*').

71 Proclamation No. 359/2003, Art. 3(1).

72 Proclamation No. 359/2003, Art. 7.

73 FDRE Constitution, Art. 62(9).

74 Proclamation No. 359/2003, Art. 12.

75 FDRE Constitution, Articles 52(2)(g),13(1), and 52(1).

76 The Constitution of India, Art.352.

77 The Constitution of India, Art.356.

78 The Constitution of India, Art.360.

79 Basu, Introduction,357.

80 The Constitution of India, Art.353(a).

81 Basu, Introduction, 363.

82 The Constitution of India, Art.356.

83 The Constitution of India, Art.74(1).

84 Basu, Introduction,364.

85 The Constitution of India, Art. 365.

86 The Constitution of India, Art. 57(2) and (3).

87 "Scheduled areas" are places in the states and union territories other than Assam, Meghalaya, Tripura, and Mizoram that are inhabited by "scheduled tribes." The "scheduled tribes," on the other hand, are certain communities in India to whom the framers of the Constitution determined to ensure special consideration for safeguarding their interests due to the extreme social, educational, and economic backwardness they suffered (https://www.clearias.com/scheduled-areas-and-tribal-areas/).

88 Vidushi Sanghadia, "Justiciability of a Presidential Proclamation of Emergency Under Article 352(1) of the Constitution" *NALSAR Student Law Review* 12 No.73(2017):2.

89 The Constitution of India, Art. 360(3).

90 Elliot Bulmer, *Emergency Powers: International IDEA Constitution-Building Primer 18* (IDEA, 2018) 8 <https://www.idea.int/publications/catalogue/emergency-powers>.

91 Anderson, Federalism,57–58.

92 Anderson, Federalism, 57.

93 FDRE Constitution, Art.93(1).

94 "Ethiopia's Amhara Region Requests Federal Help over Militia Unrest", Reuters' <https://www.reuters.com/world/africa/mobile-internet-outages-ethiopias-amhara-amid-fighting-residents-say-2023-08-03/>; Dawit Endeshaw, "Ethiopia Declares Six-Month State of Emergency in Amhara after Clashes" *Reuters* (4 August 2023) <https://www.reuters.com/world/africa/ethiopia-declares-state-emergency-following-militia-clashes-2023-08-04/>.

95 FDRE Constitution, Art.93(2)(a).

96 Kassahun Berhanu, "Parliament and Dominant Party System in Ethiopia" in MA Mohamed Salih (ed), *African Parliaments* (Palgrave Macmillan US, 2005) 162, 177 <http://link.springer.com/10.1057/9781403979308_9>.

97 FDRE Constitution, Art.93(3).

98 FDRE Constitution, Art 93(3).

99 FDRE Constitution, Art. 93(6)(e).

100 "Ethiopia Parliament Votes to Lift State of Emergency Early" <https://www.aljazeera.com/news/2022/2/15/ethiopia-parliament-votes-to-lift-state-of-emergency>.

101 Ethiopia Parliament Votes to Lift State of Emergency Early.

102 The Constitution of India, Art.352(4).

103 The annual session of the House of People's Representatives, as stipulated in Article 58(2) of the FDRE Constitution, begins on Monday of the final week of the Ethiopian Meskerem (September) and ends on the thirtieth day of the Ethiopian month of Sene (June). During such a session, the house adjourns for one month of recess.

104 FDRE Constitution, Art.60(1).

105 FDRE Constitution, Art. 60(3).

106 The Constitution of India, Art. 352(4).

107 The Constitution of India, Art. 352.

108 FDRE Constitution, Art. 58(3).

109 Council of Constitutional Inquiry of the FDRE, "Recommendation on the Request of the FDRE House of Peoples' Representatives for Constitutional Interpretation Submitted to the Council of Constitutional Inquiry Regarding the Impact of the COVID-19 Pandemic on the 6th General National Election" Paragraphs 43–53 https://www.cci.gov.et/wp-content/uploads/2020/11/CCI-English-version.pdf.

110 The Constitution of India, Art. 352(7).

111 As I discussed earlier, federal intervention under Article 51(14) occurs at the request of a state where there is a deteriorating security situation that the state is unable to control without the consent of parliament.

112 Proclamation No. 359/2003, Art. 11.

113 Proclamation No. 359/2003, Art.14.

114 Geremew, Concerns Surrounding Federal Intervention.

115 FDRE Constitution, Art.93(4)(c).

116 Olivier De Schutter, *International Human Rights Law Cases, Materials, Commentary* (Cambridge University Press,2010), 288.

117 Proclamation No. 359/2003, Art.14.

118 Proclamation No. 359/2003, Art.14(5).

119 The Constitution of India, Art.356(4); Rahul Sagar, "Emergency Powers" in Sujit Choudhry, Madhav Khosla, and Pratap Bhanu Mehta (eds), *The Oxford Handbook of the Indian Constitution* (Oxford University Press 2016),215.

120 Proclamation No. 359/2003, Art.15(3).

121 Proclamation No. 359/2003, Art.15(3).

122 In February 2016, the federal government declared a six-month state of emergency to control the widespread public protests in the States of Oromia and Amhara. In 2018, a state of emergency was declared following the sudden resignation of Prime Minister Hailemariam Desalegn to stem a wave of anti-government protests.

Ethiopia also passed through a state of emergency in 2021, which the federal government issued to repel Tigrayan forces, and in 2023, mainly covering the Amhara region. See US Department of State, "2016 Country Reports on Human Rights Practices: Ethiopia"; "2018 Country Reports on Human Rights Practices: Ethiopia" (2018).

123 'The Ongoing Law Enforcement Operations in Tigray: Causes and Objectives' (14 November 2020) <https://www.fanabc.com/english/the-ongoing-law-enforcement-operations-in-tigray-causes-and-objectives/> ('The Ongoing Law Enforcement Operations in Tigray').

124 'Inside a Military Base in Ethiopia's Tigray: Soldiers Decry Betrayal by Former Comrades', *Reuters* (online, 17 December 2020) <https://www.reuters.com/article/us-ethiopia-conflict-attack-idUSKBN28R1IE> ('Inside a Military Base in Ethiopia's Tigray').

125 Gebreslassie, Ethiopian Federalism, 917; Geremew, Concerns Surrounding Federal Intervention.

126 Etenesh Abera, "News: House speaker Abadula Gemeda Apologizes for Erring Vote Counting on State of Emergency as Decision Sparks Fresh Protests." Addis Standard, March 4,2018

127 Tewelde Aregawi, News

128 Abera, News.

129 Abera, News.

130 Abera, News.

131 Sanghadia, Justiciability,4.

132 Sanghadia, Justiciability,4.

133 Basu, Introduction, 362.

134 FDRE Constitution, Art 82(2).

135 'Minute of the Constituent Assembly of Ethiopia, Vol 5(November 1994)' 6; Yonatan Tesfaye Fessha, "Judicial Review and Democracy: A Normative Discourse on the (Novel) Ethiopian Approach to Constitutional Review" *African Journal of International and Comparative Law* 14 no.1 (2006)53, 54.

136 'Minute of the Constituent Assembly of Ethiopia, Vol 5,6.

137 Minute of the Constituent Assembly of Ethiopia, Vol 5, 6.

138 FDRE Constitution, Art.83(1).

139 FDRE Constitution, Art.84(2).

140 Takele Soboka Bulto, "Judicial Referral of Constitutional Disputes in Ethiopia: From Practice to Theory" African *Journal of International and Comparative Law* 19 no.1, (2011),118.

141 Adem Kassie Abebe, "The Potential Role of Constitutional Review in the Realization of Human Rights in Ethiopia" (Thesis LLD, University of Pretoria, 2012) 172.

142 Getachew Assefa, "All about Words: Discovering the Intention of the Makers of the Ethiopian Constitution on the Scope and Meaning of Constitutional Interpretation," *Journal of Ethiopian Law* 24 no.2(December 2010),165.

143 Minute of the Constituent Assembly of Ethiopia, Vol 5, 9.

144 *A Proclamation to Define the Powers and Functions of the House of Federation, Proclamation*

No.1261/2021 5(2); *Council of Constitutional Inquiry Proclamation No.798/2013* Art.3(1) ('*Proclamation No.798/2013*').

145 Proclamation No.1261/2021, Art.9; Proclamation No.798/2013, Articles 4 and 5.

146 Proclamation No.798/2013, Art.3(2)(c).

147 Tewelde Aregawi, "News Alert: Tigray Region Declares State of Emergency to Prevent Spread of #COVID19" (26 March 2020) *Addis Standard* <https://addisstandard.com/news-alert-tigray-region-declares-state-of-emergency-to-prevent-spread-of-covid19/> ('News Alert').

148 *Proclamation 3/2020 A State of Emergency Proclamation Enacted to Counter and Control the Spread of COVID-19 and Mitigate Its Impact.*

149 Abdi Jibril Ali, "Distinguishing Limitation on Constitutional Rights from their Suspension: A Comment on the CUD Case," *SSRN Scholarly Paper No 2297370* (2012) 3 <https://papers.ssrn.com/abstract=2297370> ('Distinguishing Limitation on Constitutional Rights from Their Suspension').

150 Ali, A Comment on the CUD Case, 5.

151 Ali, A Comment on the CUD Case,5.

Bibliography

Abbink, Jon. "Ethnic-Based Federalism and Ethnicity in Ethiopia: Reassessing the Experiment after 20 Years," Journal of Eastern African Studies 5, no. 4 (2011)

Addis, Adeno. 'From a Nation of Citizens to a "Nation of Nations" National Citizenship without Depth'. International Journal of Ethiopian Studies, 14, No. 1 (2020)

Abebe, Adem Kassie. "The Federal Democratic Republic of Ethiopia: Introductory Note", Oxford University Press, 2011.

Abebe, Adem Kassie. "The Potential Role of Constitutional Review in the Realization of Human Rights in Ethiopia" (LLD Thesis, University of Pretoria, 2012)

Ali, Abdi Jibril. "Distinguishing Limitation on Constitutional Rights from Their Suspension: A Comment on the CUD Case," Haramaya Law Review, 2 No 1, (2013).

Anderson, George. *Federalism: An Introduction.* Toronto; New York: Oxford University Press, 2008.

Aregawi, Tewelde. "News Alert: Tigray Region Declares State of Emergency to Prevent Spread of COVID19". *Addis Standard*, 26 March 2020. https://addisstandard.com/news-alert-tigray-region-declares-state-of-emergency-to-prevent-spread-of-covid19/.

Abera, Etenesh. "News: House Speaker Abadula Gemeda Apologizes for Erring Vote Counting on State of Emergency as Decision Sparks Fresh Protests". *Addis Standard* (blog), 4 March 2018. https://addisstandard.com/news-house-speaker-abadula-gemeda-apologizes-erring-vote-counting-state-emergency-decision-sparks-fresh-protests/.

Assefa, Getachew. "All about Words: Discovering the Intention of the Makers of the Ethiopian Constitution on the Scope and Meaning of Constitutional Interpretation," Journal of Ethiopian Law 24, No.2 (2010)

Ayele, Zemelak and Fessha, Yonatan Tesfaye. "Controlling Public Health Emergencies in Federal Systems: The Case of Ethiopia." In *Comparative Federalism and Covid-19: Combating the Pandemic*, edited by Nico Steytler, 1st ed. London: Routledge, 2021.

BBC News. "Article 370: What Happened with Kashmir and Why It Matters." 5 August 2019, sec. India. https://www.bbc.com/news/world-asia-india-49234708.

Berhanu, Kassahun. "Parliament and Dominant Party System in Ethiopia," In *African Parliaments*, edited by M. A. Mohamed Salih, 162–82. New York: Palgrave Macmillan US, 2005.

Berhe, A. "The Origins of the Tigray People's Liberation Front", African Affairs 103, no. 413 (2004)

Bulmer, Elliot. *Emergency Powers: International IDEA Constitution-Building Primer 18*. IDEA, 2018. https://doi.org/10.31752/idea.2018.29.

Bulmer, Elliot. *Bicameralism*, International IDEA Constitution-Building Premier, 2017. https://www.idea.int/sites/default/files/publications/bicameralism-primer.pdf.

Bulto, Takele Soboka. "Judicial Referral of Constitutional Disputes in Ethiopia: From Practice to Theory," *African Journal of International and Comparative Law* 19, no. 1 (2011)

Council of Constitutional Inquiry of the FDRE. "Recommendation on the Request of the FDRE House of Peoples' Representatives for Constitutional Interpretation Submitted to the Council of Constitutional Inquiry Regarding the Impact of the COVID-19 Pandemic on the 6thGeneral National Election," https://www.cci.gov.et/wp-content/uploads/2020/11/CCI-English-version.pdf.

Das Basu, Durga. *Introduction to the Constitution of India*, S.C. Sarkar Publishers, 1966.

De Schutter, Olivier. *International Human Rights Law Cases, Materials, Commentary*, Cambridge University Press, 2010

Elazar, Daniel J. *Exploring Federalism*, University of Alabama Press, 1987

Elazar, Daniel J. *Federal Systems of the World: A Handbook of Federal, Confederal and Autonomy Arrangements*, Longman Current Affairs, 1991

Endeshaw, Dawit. "Ethiopia Declares Six-Month State of Emergency in Amhara after Clashes," *Reuters*, 4 August 2023, https://www.reuters.com/world/africa/ethiopia-declares-state-emergency-following-militia-clashes-2023-08-04/.

'Ethiopia's Two New Regional States Formed: Central Ethiopia, South Ethiopia'. *Borkena Ethiopian News* (blog), 20 August 2023. https://borkena.com/2023/08/19/ethiopias-two-new-regional-states-formed-central-ethiopia-south-ethiopia/.

'Ethiopia Parliament Votes to Lift State of Emergency Early'. Accessed 11 September 2023. https://www.aljazeera.com/news/2022/2/15/ethiopia-parliament-votes-to-lift-state-of-emergency.

'Ethiopia's Amhara Region Requests Federal Help over Militia Unrest | Reuters', 9 September 2023. https://www.reuters.com/world/africa/mobile-internet-outages-ethiopias-amhara-amid-fighting-residents-say-2023-08-03/.

Fessha, Yonatan Tesfaye. "Judicial Review and Democracy: A Normative Discourse on the (Novel) Ethiopian Approach to Constitutional Review," African Journal of International and Comparative Law 14, no. 1 (2006): 53–82.

Gebreslassie, Seife Hailu. "Ethiopian Federalism: Philosophical and Institutional Design Limitations and a Case for Loose Federalism", International Journal on Minority and Group Rights 28, no. 5 (28 October 2021): 894–926.

Geremew, Endalkachew. "Concerns Surrounding Federal Intervention", 8 September 2018. https://www.thereporterethiopia.com/6358/

Habtu, Alem. "Ethnic Federalism in Ethiopia: Background, Present Conditions and Future Prospects,"1–33. *International Conference on African Development Archives*, Western Michigan University (2003). https://scholarworks.wmich.edu/cgi/viewcontent.cgi?article=1078&context=africancenter_icad_archive

Haftetsion, Fiseha. "The State of Vertical Division of Political Power in the Ethiopian Federation," (PhD Thesis, Addis Ababa University, 2017) http://etd.aau.edu.et/handle/123456789/27477.

Marks, Gary. Hooghe, Liesbet. and Schakel, Arjan H. "Patterns of Regional Authority," Regional & Federal Studies 18, no. 2–3 (2008)

Mathew, George. "Republic of India". In *Distribution of Powers and Responsibilities in Federal Countries*, edited by Akhtar Majeed, Ronald L Watts, and Douglas M. Brown. A Global Dialogue on Federalism Book Series 2, Montréal: McGill-Queen's University Press, 2006

Minute of the Constitutional Commission of Ethiopia, Vol.2 (February 26/1993-October 27/1993).

Minute of the Constituent Assembly of Ethiopia, Vol 5 (November 1994)

Mueller, Sean. "Self-Rule and Shared Rule," *50 Shades of Federalism* (blog), 25 October 2017. http://50shadesoffederalism.com/theory/self-rule-shared-rule/.

Noel, Thibaut. *Second Chambers in Federal Systems*, (International IDEA, 2022).

Rajashekara, H.M. "The Nature of Indian Federalism: A Critique," Asian Survey, 37, No.3 (1997).

Rau, Benegal Narsing. "The Parliamentary System of Government in India'. *W*ashington Law Review 24, No. 1 (1949).

Reuters. "Inside a Military Base in Ethiopia's Tigray: Soldiers Decry Betrayal by Former Comrades," 17 December 2020, https://www.reuters.com/article/us-ethiopia-conflict-attack-idUSKBN28R1IE.

Sagar, Rahul. "Emergency Powers". In *The Oxford Handbook of the Indian Constitution*, edited by Sujit Choudhry, Madhav Khosla, and Pratap Bhanu Mehta, Oxford University Press, 2016

Sanghadia, Vidushi. "Justiciability of a Presidential Proclamation of Emergency Under Article 352(1) of the Constitution" NALSAR Student Law Review 12, No.73 (2017)

Saunders, Cheryl. "Options for Decentralizing Power: Federalism to Decentralization", https://comparativeconstitutionsproject.org/files/federalism.pdf

Sofi, Waseem Ahmad. *Autonomy of a State in a Federation: A Special Case Study of Jammu and Kashmir*, Palgrave Macmillan, 2021

'The Ongoing Law Enforcement Operations in Tigray: Causes and Objectives', FANA, 14 November 2020, https://www.fanabc.com/english/the-ongoing-law-enforcement-operations-in-tigray-causes-and-objectives/.

U.S Department of State. "2016 Country Reports on Human Rights Practices: Ethiopia."

Vestal, Theodor. "The Lost Opportunity for Ethiopia: The Failure to Move toward Democratic Governance" International Journal of African Development, 1, no. 1 (2013).

Index

www.ingramcontent.com/pod-product-compliance
Ingram Content Group UK Ltd.
Pitfield, Milton Keynes, MK11 3LW, UK
UKHW040233290926
15471UKWH00002B/176

9 781599 073378